Microsoft Excel VBA and Macros: Your guide to efficient automation

Tracy Syrstad
Bill Jelen

Microsoft Excel VBA and Macros: Your guide to efficient automation

Published with the authorization of Microsoft Corporation by:

Pearson Education, Inc.

Copyright © 2026 by Pearson Education, Inc.

Hoboken, New Jersey

ISBN-13: 978-0-13-541023-3

ISBN-10: 0-13-541023-1

Library of Congress Control Number: 2025943857

1 2025

Trademarks

Warning and Disclaimer

EXECUTIVE EDITOR
Loretta Yates

ACQUISITIONS EDITOR
Shourav Bose

DEVELOPMENT EDITOR
Rick Kughen

MANAGING EDITOR
Sandra Schroeder

SENIOR PROJECT EDITOR
Tracey Croom

COPY EDITOR
Rick Kughen

INDEXER
Rachel Kuhn

PROOFREADER
Donna E. Mulder

TECHNICAL EDITOR
Bob Umlas

COVER DESIGNER
Twist Creative, Seattle

COMPOSITOR
codeMantra

COVER ILLUSTRATION
ImageFlow/Shutterstock

Dedication

*For Tracy Syrstad. Thanks for being a great coauthor for
20 years!*

—Bill Jelen

*To the clients who made this book possible—Marlee Jo J., Dale
W., Eddie G., and all the others over the years—thank you for the
challenging projects, sharp questions, and unexpected curveballs.
You didn't just keep me on my toes—you made me better.*

—Tracy Syrstad

Contents at a Glance

Contents

Chapter 25 **Customizing the ribbon to run macros**   **573**

Acknowledgments

They say it takes an army to get a celebrity ready for the red carpet—stylists, coaches, and a whole lot of behind-the-scenes magic. Writing this book wasn't so different. I had my own team making sure the seams didn't show.

To Loretta: The calm in the storm, the keeper of continuity, and the person who managed to steer this whole thing without ever once raising her voice—at least not where I could hear it.

To Bill Jelen: Thank you for opening the door, showing me the path, and walking it with me. You've made this journey possible.

To Robert L., for keeping me fueled with cookies; to Chris H., for giving me the stage to share my VBA bag of tricks; to Geoff W., for tossing me puzzles that demanded real out-of-the-box thinking; and to Ash—technically, a client but really a collaborator—for helping me think in versions, not just answers. Your clarity cut through my fog every time. Consulting has introduced me to people across every kind of industry, and it's the variety—the weird bugs, the clever fixes, the unexpected questions—that make this work so much fun.

To Icarus, MeltedCake, and Chilly: You reminded me that "It wasn't a phase, Mom" can be a way of life. Thanks for the chaos, the loyalty, and the perfectly timed distractions.

To Jareth, Luna, Sam, and Anita: Your daily antics are worth the 2 a.m. feedings and zoomies.

And to John: Thank you for being my steady in the storm, from the moment I left the corporate grind and started building this strange, wonderful path of my own.

—*Tracy*

At Pearson, Loretta Yates is an excellent executive editor. Thanks to Rick Kughen for guiding this book through production.

Along the way, I've learned a lot about VBA programming from the awesome community at the MrExcel.com message board. VoG, Richard Schollar, and Jon von der Heyden all stand out as having contributed posts that led to ideas in this book. Thanks to Pam Gensel for Excel macro lesson #1. Mala Singh taught me about creating charts in VBA. Suat Özgür keeps me current on new VBA trends and contributed many ideas to Chapter 18.

My family was incredibly supportive during this time. Thanks to Mary Ellen Jelen.

—*Bill*

About the Authors

Tracy Syrstad is the author of 11 Excel books and a veteran Excel developer with decades of experience building custom Excel solutions for businesses and individuals. Since 1997, she's helped clients streamline workflows, automate reporting, and tame messy data using the full power of Excel and VBA. Her writing reflects the same approach she brings to her consulting—clear, practical, and focused on helping real people solve real problems.

Bill Jelen, Excel MVP and the host of MrExcel.com, has been using spreadsheets since 1985, and he launched the MrExcel.com website in 1998. Bill was a regular guest on *Call for Help* with Leo Laporte and has produced more than 2,500 episodes of his video podcast, *Learn Excel from MrExcel*. He is the author of 71 books about Microsoft Excel and writes the monthly Excel column for *Strategic Finance* magazine. Before founding MrExcel.com, Bill spent 12 years in the trenches—working as a financial analyst for finance, marketing, accounting, and operations departments of a $500 million public company. He lives in Merritt Island, Florida, with his wife, Mary Ellen.

Introduction

In this Introduction, you will:

- Find out what is in this book.

- Have a peek at the future of VBA and Windows versions of Excel.

- Learn about special elements and typographical conventions in this book.

- Learn where to find the code files for this book.

As corporate IT departments have found themselves with long backlogs of requests, Excel users have discovered that they can produce the reports needed to run their businesses themselves using the macro language *Visual Basic for Applications* (VBA). VBA enables you to achieve tremendous efficiencies in your day-to-day use of Excel. VBA helps you figure out how to import data and produce reports in Excel so that you don't have to wait for the IT department to help you.

Is TypeScript a threat to VBA?

Your first questions are likely: "Should I invest time in learning VBA? How long will Microsoft support VBA? Will the TypeScript language released for Excel Online replace VBA?"

Your investments in VBA will serve you well until at least 2049. The last macro language change—from XLM to VBA—happened in 1993. XLM is still supported in Excel to this day. That was a case where VBA was better than XLM, but XLM is still supported 28 years later. Microsoft introduced TypeScript for Excel Online in February 2020. I expect that they will continue to support VBA in the Windows and Mac versions of Excel for the next 28 years.

In the Excel universe today, there are versions of Excel running in Windows, in macOS, on mobile phones powered by Android and iOS, and in modern browsers using Excel Online. In my world, I use Excel 99% of the time on a Windows computer. There's perhaps 1% of the time I use Excel Online. But if you are in a mobile environment where you are using Excel in a browser, then the TypeScript UDFs might be appropriate for you.

For an introduction to TypeScript UDFs in Excel, read Suat M. Özgür's *Excel Custom Functions Straight to the Point* (ISBN 978-1-61547-259-8).

However, TypeScript performance is still horrible. If you don't need your macros to run in Excel Online, the VBA version of your macro will run eight times more quickly than the TypeScript version. For people who plan to run Excel only on the Mac or Windows platforms, VBA will be your go-to macro language for another decade.

The threat to Excel VBA is the new Excel Power Query tools found in the Get & Transform group of the Data tab in Excel for Windows. If you are writing macros to clean imported data, you should consider cleaning the data once with Power Query and then refreshing the query each day. Bill has a lot of Power Query workflows set up that would have previously required VBA. For a primer on Power Query, check out *Master Your Data with Excel and Power BI: Leveraging Power Query to Get & Transform Your Task Flow* by Ken Puls and Miguel Escobar (ISBN 978-1-61547-058-7).

Is Python a threat to VBA?

Python in Excel is not made to automate chores like VBA. It doesn't control the workbook, respond to events, or handle formatting and file tasks. Instead, it's a powerful alternative to analyzing worksheet data—ideal for advanced calculations, reshaping data with pandas, or creating custom visuals. Think of it as a next-gen formula engine, not a macro tool.

Python runs in Excel as a special formula type using the =PY() function. You write Python code directly in a cell, and Excel sends that code to a sandbox-secure cloud environment to execute. The result is returned to the worksheet.

The function supports libraries like pandas, matplotlib, NumPy, and seaborn. This makes it a great option for complex analysis, but Python can't modify the workbook or sheet structure or trigger actions. For now, that means VBA is still your go-to for automating tasks, controlling Excel behavior, and building interactive tools.

What is in this book?

You have taken the right step by purchasing this book. We can help you reduce the learning curve so that you can write your own VBA macros and put an end to the burden of generating reports manually.

Reducing the learning curve

This Introduction provides a case study about the power of macros. Chapter 1, "Unleashing the power of Excel with VBA," introduces the tools and confirms what you probably already know: The macro recorder does not work reliably. Chapter 2, "This sounds like BASIC, so why doesn't it look familiar?" helps you understand the crazy syntax of VBA. Chapter 3, "Referring to ranges, names, and tables," cracks the code on how to work efficiently with ranges, cells, defined names, and tables.

Chapter 4, "Laying the groundwork with variables and structures," lays the groundwork for writing flexible, maintainable VBA code by introducing key concepts like procedures, variables, object references, and code structure tools such as With blocks and compiler directives. These building blocks will help you understand—and eventually master—the code you'll encounter throughout the book.

Chapter 5, "Looping and flow control," covers the power of looping using VBA. The case study in this chapter demonstrates creating a program to produce a department report and then wrapping that report routine in a loop to produce 46 reports.

Chapter 6, "R1C1 style formulas," covers, obviously, R1C1 style formulas. Chapter 7, "Event programming," shows how user interaction and automatic Excel functionality, such as calculations, can be used to trigger procedures. Chapter 8, "Arrays," covers arrays. Chapter 9, "Creating custom objects and collections," covers creating custom objects and collections, great tools for organizing data. Chapter 10, "Userforms: An introduction," introduces custom dialog boxes that you can use to collect information from a human using Excel.

Excel VBA power

Chapters 11, "Data mining with Advanced Filter," and 12, "Using VBA to create pivot tables," provide an in-depth look at Filter, Advanced Filter, and pivot tables. Report automation tools rely heavily on these concepts. Chapters 13, "Excel power," and 14, "Sample user-defined functions," include dozens of code samples designed to exhibit the power of Excel VBA and custom functions. Chapter 13 includes the section, "Leveling up: Real project issues, real solutions," which features various project issues I run into and how I resolve them.

Chapters 15, "Creating charts," through 20, "Automating Word," handle charting, data visualizations, web queries, sparklines, and automating Word.

Techie stuff needed to produce applications

Chapter 21, "Using Access as a back end to enhance multiuser access to data," handles reading and writing to Access databases and SQL Server. The techniques for using Access databases enable you to build an application with the multiuser features of Access while keeping the friendly front end of Excel.

Chapter 22, "Advanced userform techniques," shows you how to go further with userforms. Chapter 23, "The Windows Application Programming Interface (API)," teaches some tricky ways to achieve tasks using the Windows API. Chapters 24, "Handling errors," through 26, "Creating Excel add-ins," deal with error handling, custom menus, and add-ins. Chapter 27, "An introduction to creating Office Add-ins," provides a brief introduction to building your own Office Script application within Excel.

Does this book teach Excel?

Not exactly. We assume you already use Excel and are ready to go further with VBA. While we don't walk through every feature, we do point out powerful tools, such as pivot tables and Power Query, when they matter to the code. If you haven't used them before, you'll know what to explore.

Bill regularly presents a Power Excel seminar for accountants—people who use Excel 30 to 40 hours a week. Yet two things happen at every seminar. First, half the room gasps when they see how fast a feature like automatic subtotals or pivot tables can be. Second, someone always trumps Bill. He'll answer a question, and someone in the second row chimes in with a better solution.

The point? Both the authors and readers of this book know Excel—but we still assume that in any given chapter, many readers haven't used pivot tables, and even fewer have tried features like the Top 10 Filter. So, before we automate something in VBA, we'll briefly show how to do it manually in Excel. This isn't a how-to on pivot tables, but it will let you know when it's time to look one up.

Case study: Monthly accounting reports

This is a true story. Valerie is a business analyst in the accounting department of a medium-sized corporation. Her company recently installed an overbudget $16 million enterprise resource planning (ERP) system. As the project ground to a close, there were no resources left in the IT budget to produce the monthly report that this corporation used to summarize each department.

However, Valerie had been close enough to the implementation to think of a way to produce the report herself. She understood that she could export general ledger data from the ERP system to a text file with comma-separated values. Using Excel, Valerie was able to import the general ledger data from the ERP system into Excel.

Creating the report was not easy. As in many other companies, there were exceptions in the data. Valerie knew that certain accounts in one particular cost center needed to be reclassified as expenses. She knew that other accounts needed to be excluded from the report entirely. Working carefully in Excel, Valerie made these adjustments. She created one pivot table to produce the first summary section of the report. She cut the pivot table results and pasted them into a blank worksheet. Then she created a new pivot table report for the second section of the summary. After about three hours, she had imported the data, produced five pivot tables, arranged them in a summary, and neatly formatted the report in color.

Becoming the hero

Valerie handed the report to her manager. The manager had just heard from the IT department that it would be months before they could get around to producing "that convoluted report." When Valerie created the Excel report, she became the instant hero of the day. In three hours, Valerie had managed to do the impossible. Valerie was on cloud nine after some well-deserved recognition.

More cheers

The next day, Valerie's manager attended the monthly department meeting. When the department managers started complaining that they could not get the report from the ERP system, this manager pulled out his department's report and placed it on the table. The other managers were amazed. How was he able to produce this report? Everyone was relieved to hear that someone had cracked the code. The company president asked Valerie's manager if he could have the report produced for each department.

Cheers turn to dread

You can probably see what's coming. This particular company had 46 departments. That means 46 one-page summaries had to be produced once a month. Each report required importing data from the ERP system, backing out certain accounts, producing five pivot tables, and then formatting the reports in color. It had taken Valerie three hours to produce the first report, but after she got into the swing of things, she could produce the 46 reports in 40 hours. Even after she reduced her time per report, though, this is horrible. Valerie had a job to do before she became responsible for spending 40 hours a month producing these reports in Excel.

VBA to the rescue

Valerie found Bill's company, MrExcel Consulting, and explained her situation. In the course of about a week, Bill was able to produce a series of macros in Visual Basic that did all the mundane tasks. For example, the macros imported the data, backed out certain accounts, made five pivot tables, and applied the color formatting. From start to finish, the entire 40-hour manual process was reduced to two button clicks and about 4 minutes.

Right now, either you or someone in your company is probably stuck doing manual tasks in Excel that can be automated with VBA. We are confident that we can walk into any company that has 20 or more Excel users and find a case just as amazing as Valerie's.

Versions of Excel

This eighth edition of *VBA and Macros* is designed to work with Microsoft 365 features released up through July 2025. The previous editions of this book covered code for Excel 97 through Excel 365 (2021). In 80 percent of the chapters, the code today is identical to the code in previous versions.

Differences for Mac users

Although Excel for Windows and Excel for the Mac are similar in terms of user interface, there are a number of differences when you compare the VBA environment. Certainly, nothing in Chapter 23 that uses the Windows API will work on the Mac. That said, the overall concepts discussed in this book apply to the Mac. You can find a general list of differences as they apply to the Mac at *http://www.mrexcel.com/macvba.html*. The VBA Editor for the Mac does not let you design UserForms (Chapter 10). It also has a bug that makes it difficult to create event handler macros (Chapter 7). Excel throws an error when you try to select from the drop-downs at the top of the Code window. You have to first copy and paste an empty event procedure; then the drop-downs will work.

Special elements and typographical conventions

The following typographical conventions are used in this book:

- *Italic*—Indicates new terms when they are defined, special emphasis, non-English words or phrases, and letters or words used as words.

- `Monospace`—Indicates parts of VBA code, such as object or method names.

- **Bold**—Indicates user input.

In addition to these typographical conventions, there are several special elements. Many chapters have at least one case study that presents a real-world solution to common problems. The case study also demonstrates practical applications of the topics discussed in the chapter.

In addition to the case studies, you will see Level Up, Note, Tip, and Caution sidebars.

Level Up!

Level Up sidebars offer deeper insights or clever techniques that go beyond the basics. They're optional side explorations—perfect if you're ready to stretch your skills a bit further than what the current section assumes.

Note   Notes provide additional information outside the main thread of the chapter discussion that might be useful for you to know.

Tip   Tips provide quick workarounds and time-saving techniques to help you work more efficiently.

Caution   Cautions warn about potential pitfalls you might encounter. Pay attention to the Cautions; they alert you to problems that might otherwise cause you hours of frustration.

About the companion content

As a thank-you for buying this book, we have put together a set of 50 Excel workbooks that demonstrate the concepts included in this book. This set of files includes all the code from the book, sample data, and additional notes from the authors.

To download the code files, visit this book's webpage at *MicrosoftPressStore.com/XLVBAAuto/downloads*.

Errata, updates, and book support

We've made every effort to ensure the accuracy of this book and its companion content. Any errors that have been reported since this book was published are listed at

MicrosoftPressStore.com/XLVBAAuto/errata.

If you find an error that is not already listed, you can report it to us through the same page.

For additional book support and information, please visit *MicrosoftPressStore.com/Support*.

Please note that product support for Microsoft software and hardware is not offered through the previous addresses. For help with Microsoft software or hardware, go to *support.microsoft.com*.

Stay in touch

Let's keep the conversation going! We're on X:

x.com/MicrosoftPress

x.com/MrExcel

bsky.app/profile/tsyrstad.bsky.social

CHAPTER 1

Unleashing the power of Excel with VBA

In this chapter, you will:

- Understand the power of Excel

- Understand the two main barriers to learning VBA

- Get to know your tools: The Developer tab

- Understand which file types allow macros

- Be introduced to macro security

- Get an overview of recording, storing, and running a macro

- Understand the VB Editor

- Understand the shortcomings of the macro recorder

Visual Basic for Applications (VBA) combined with Microsoft Excel is probably the most powerful tool available to you. VBA is sitting on the desktops of 850 million users of Microsoft Office, and most have never figured out how to harness the power of VBA in Excel. Using VBA, you can speed up the production of any task in Excel. If you regularly use Excel to produce a series of monthly charts, for example, you can have VBA do that task for you in a matter of seconds.

Barriers to entry

There are two barriers to learning successful VBA programming. First, Excel's macro recorder is flawed and does not produce workable code for you to use as a model. Second, for many who learned a programming language such as BASIC, the syntax of VBA is horribly frustrating.

The macro recorder doesn't work!

Microsoft began to dominate the spreadsheet market in the mid-1990s. Although it was wildly successful in building a powerful spreadsheet program to which any Lotus 1-2-3 user could easily transition, the macro language was just too different. Anyone proficient in recording Lotus 1-2-3 macros who tried recording a few macros in Excel most likely failed. Although the Microsoft VBA programming language is much more powerful than the Lotus 1-2-3 macro language, the fundamental flaw is that the macro recorder does not work when you use the default settings.

With Lotus 1-2-3, you could record a macro today and play it back tomorrow, and it would faithfully work. When you attempt the same feat in Microsoft Excel, the macro might work today but not tomorrow. In 1995, when I tried to record my first Excel macro, I was horribly frustrated by this. In this book, I teach you the three rules for getting the most out of the macro recorder.

No one person on the Excel team is focused on the macro recorder

As Microsoft adds new features to Excel, the individual project manager for a feature makes sure that the macro recorder will record something when you execute the command. In the past decade, the recorded code might work in some situations, but it often does not work in all situations. If Microsoft had someone who was focused on creating a useful macro recorder, the recorded code could often be a lot more general than it currently is.

It used to be that you could record a command in any of five ways, and the recorded code would work. Unfortunately, today, if you want to use the macro recorder, you often have to try recording the macro several different ways to find a set of steps that records code that reliably works.

Visual Basic is not like BASIC

When I first saw the code generated by the macro recorder, I didn't know what to make of it. It said this was "Visual Basic" (VB). I'd worked with a few different programming languages over the years; this bizarre-looking language was horribly unintuitive and did not resemble the BASIC language I had learned in high school.

For Bill, who'd had even more experience with programming languages than me, things became more difficult. In 1995, he was the spreadsheet expert in his office. His company had forced everyone to convert from Lotus 1-2-3 to Excel, which meant he was faced with a macro recorder that didn't work and a language that he couldn't understand. This was not a good combination of events.

My assumption in writing this book is that you are pretty talented with a spreadsheet. You probably know more than 90 percent of the people in your office. I also assume that even though you are not a programmer, you might have taken a class in BASIC at some point. However, knowing BASIC is not a requirement—it's actually a barrier to entry into the ranks of being a successful VBA programmer. There is a good chance that you have recorded a macro in Excel, and there's a similar chance that you were not happy with the results.

> **Note** If you're already familiar with programming concepts—or even an experienced VBA user—don't let the early chapters fool you. While we start with the fundamentals, this book quickly moves into more advanced territory: cleaner code, smarter structures, and solutions designed for real-world use. Whether you're self-taught or coming from another language, there's plenty here to expand your skills and streamline your work.

Good news: Climbing the learning curve is easy

Even if you've been frustrated with the macro recorder, it is really just a small speed bump on your road to writing powerful programs in Excel. This book teaches you not only why the macro recorder fails but also how to change the recorded code into something useful.

Great news: Excel with VBA is worth the effort

Although you probably have been frustrated with Microsoft over the inability to record macros in Excel, the great news is that Excel VBA is powerful. Almost anything you can do in the Excel interface can be duplicated with stunning speed in Excel VBA. The exceptions, such as including a description for a LAMBDA function, are rare. If you find yourself routinely creating the same reports manually day after day or week after week, Excel VBA will greatly streamline those tasks.

The authors of this book have provided Excel consulting for over 20 years. We have automated reports for hundreds of clients. The stories are often similar: The IT department has a several-month backlog of requests. Someone in accounting or engineering discovers that they can import some data into Excel and get the reports necessary to run the business. This is a liberating event: You no longer need to wait months for the IT department to write a program. However, the problem is that after you import the data into Excel and win accolades from your manager for producing the report, you will likely be asked to produce the same report every month or every week. This becomes very tedious.

Again, the great news is that with a few hours of VBA programming, you can automate the reporting process and turn it into a few button clicks. The reward is great. So, hang with me as we cover a few of the basics.

This chapter exposes why the macro recorder does not work. It also walks through an example of recorded code and demonstrates why it works today but will fail tomorrow. I realize that the code you see in this chapter might not be familiar to you, but that's okay. The point of this chapter is to demonstrate the fundamental problem with the macro recorder. This chapter also explains the fundamentals of the Visual Basic environment.

Knowing your tools: The Developer tab

Let's start with a basic overview of the tools needed to use VBA. By default, Microsoft hides the VBA tools. You need to complete the following steps to change a setting to access the Developer tab:

1. Right-click the ribbon and choose Customize The Ribbon.

2. In the right list box, select the Developer checkbox.

3. Click OK to return to Excel.

Excel displays the Developer tab, as shown in Figure 1-1.

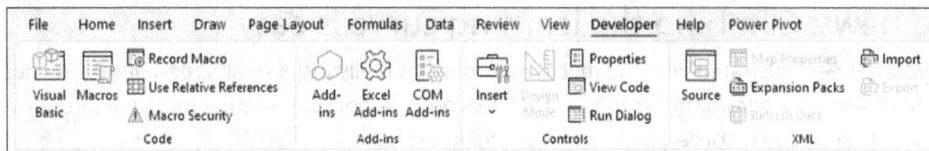

FIGURE 1-1 The Developer tab provides an interface for running and recording macros.

The Code group on the Developer tab contains the icons used for recording and playing back VBA macros, as listed here:

- **Visual Basic**—Opens the Visual Basic Editor.

- **Macros**—Displays the Macro dialog, where you can choose to run or edit a macro from the list of macros.

- **Record Macro**—Begins the process of recording a macro.

- **Use Relative References**—Toggles between using relative or absolute recording. With relative recording, Excel records that you move down three cells. With absolute recording, Excel records that you selected cell A4.

- **Macro Security**—Accesses the Trust Center, where you can choose to allow or disallow macros to run on this computer.

The Add-ins group provides icons for managing Office add-ins, regular add-ins, and COM add-ins.

The Controls group of the Developer tab contains an Insert menu where you can access a variety of programming controls that can be placed on the worksheet. See "Other ways to run a macro," in Chapter 25, "Customizing the ribbon to run macros." Other icons in this group enable you to work with the on-sheet controls.

> **Note** The Run Dialog button is a legacy feature with no practical use in modern versions of Excel. It was originally tied to custom dialogs or legacy form behavior but has since become largely obsolete. Most users can ignore it entirely.

The XML group of the Developer tab contains tools for importing and exporting XML documents.

Understanding which file types allow macros

Excel supports four primary workbook formats for saving files. These file types are listed here:

- **Excel Workbook (.xlsx)**—Files are stored as a series of XML objects and then zipped into a single file. This creates significantly smaller file sizes. It also allows other applications (even Notepad!) to edit or create Excel workbooks. Unfortunately, macros cannot be stored in files with an .xlsx extension.

- **Excel Macro-Enabled Workbook (.xlsm)**—This is similar to the default .xlsx format, except macros are allowed. The basic concept is that if someone has an .xlsx file, they will not need to worry about malicious macros. However, if they see an .xlsm file, they should be concerned that there might be macros attached.

- **Excel Binary Workbook (.xlsb)**—This is a binary format designed to handle the larger 1-million-row grid size introduced in Excel 2007. Legacy versions of Excel stored their files in a proprietary binary format. Although binary formats might load more quickly, they are more prone to corruption, and a few lost bits can destroy a whole file. Macros are allowed in this format.

- **Excel 97-2003 Workbook (.xls)**—This format produces files that can be read by anyone using legacy versions of Excel. Macros are allowed in this binary format; however, when you save in this format, you lose access to any cells outside A1:IV65536. In addition, if someone opens the file in Excel 2003, they lose access to anything that used features introduced in Excel 2007 or later.

To avoid having to choose a macro-enabled workbook as your file type every time you save a new macro workbook, customize your copy of Excel to always save new files in the .xlsm format by following these steps:

1. Click the File menu and select Options.

2. In the Excel Options dialog, select the Save category from the left navigation pane.

3. From the Save Files In This Format dropdown, select Excel Macro-Enabled Workbook (*.xlsm). Click OK.

> **Note** Although you and I are not afraid to use macros, some users are cautious about the .xlsm file type. The format can raise red flags for users in more locked-down or security-conscious environments.
>
> If you encounter someone who seems to have a fear of the .xlsm file type, remind them of these points:
>
> - Every workbook created in the past 30 years could have had macros, but in fact, most did not.
>
> - If someone is trying to avoid macros, they should use the security settings to prevent macros from running anyway. They can still open the .xlsm file to get the data in the spreadsheet.
>
> With these arguments, I hope you can overcome any fears of the .xlsm file type so that it can be your default file type.

Macro security

After a Word VBA macro was used as the delivery method for the Melissa virus, Microsoft changed the default security settings to prevent macros from running. Therefore, before we can begin discussing the recording of a macro, it's important to look at how to adjust the default settings.

In Excel, you can either globally adjust the security settings or control macro settings for certain workbooks by saving the workbooks in a trusted location. Any workbook stored in a folder that is marked as a trusted location automatically has its macros enabled.

You can find the macro security settings under the Macro Security icon on the Developer tab. When you click this icon, the Macro Settings category of the Trust Center is displayed. You can use the left navigation bar in the dialog to access the Trusted Locations list.

Adding a trusted location

You can choose to store your macro workbooks in a folder that is marked as a trusted location. Any workbook stored in a trusted folder will have its macros enabled. Microsoft suggests that a trusted location should be on your hard drive. The default setting is that you cannot trust a location on a network drive.

To specify a trusted location, follow these steps:

1. Click Macro Security in the Developer tab.

2. Click Trusted Locations in the left navigation pane of the Trust Center.

3. If you want to trust a location on a network drive, select Allow Trusted Locations On My Network.

4. Click the Add New Location button. Excel displays the Microsoft Office Trusted Location dialog (see Figure 1-2).

5. Click the Browse button. Excel displays the Browse dialog.

6. Browse to the parent folder of the folder you want to be a trusted location. Click the trusted folder. Click OK. The folder path will appear in the Path text box.

7. If you want to trust subfolders of the selected folder, select Subfolders Of This Location Are Also Trusted.

8. Click OK to add the folder to the Trusted Locations list.

> **Caution** Use care when selecting a trusted location. When you double-click an Excel attachment in an email message, Outlook stores the file in a temporary folder on your C: drive. You will not want to add the C drive globally and all subfolders to the Trusted Locations list.

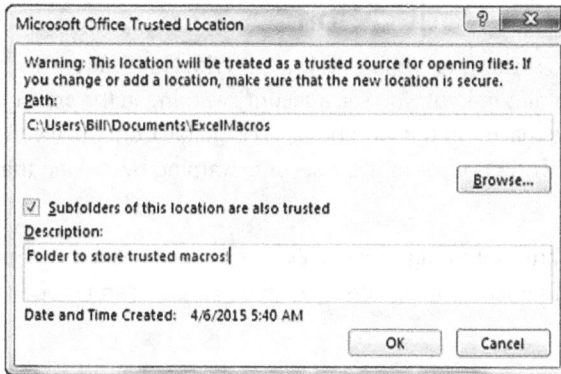

FIGURE 1-2 Trusted folders are managed in the Trusted Locations category of the Trust Center.

Using macro settings to enable macros in workbooks outside trusted locations

For all macros not stored in a trusted location, Excel relies on the macro settings. To access these settings, click Macro Security in the Developer tab. Excel displays the Macro Settings category of the Trust Center dialog. Select the second option, Disable All Macros With Notification. A description of each option follows:

- **Disable VBA Macros Without Notification**—This setting prevents all macros from running. This setting is for people who never intend to run macros. Because you are currently holding a book that teaches you how to use macros, it is assumed that this setting is not for you. With this setting, only macros in the Trusted Locations folders can run.

- **Disable VBA Macros With Notification**—The operative words in this setting are "With Notification." This means that you see a notification when you open a file with macros, and you can choose to enable the content. If you ignore the notification, the macros remain disabled. This setting is the recommended setting. In Excel, a message is displayed in the Message area, indicating that macros have been disabled. You can choose to enable the content by clicking that option, as shown in Figure 1-3.

- **Disable VBA Macros Except Digitally Signed Macros**—This setting requires you to obtain a digital signing tool from Verisign or another provider. This might be appropriate if you are going to be selling add-ins to others, but it's a bit of a hassle if you just want to write macros for your own use.

- **Enable VBA Macros (Not Recommended: Potentially Dangerous Code Can Run)**—This setting allows all macros to run. Although it requires the least amount of hassle, it also opens your computer to attacks from malicious Melissa-like viruses. Microsoft suggests that you not use this setting.

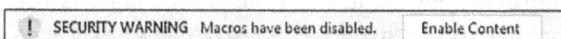

FIGURE 1-3 The Enable Content button appears when you choose Disable All Macros With Notification.

Using Disable All Macros With Notification

It is recommended that you set your macro settings to Disable All Macros With Notification. If you use this setting and open a workbook that contains macros, you see a security warning in the area just above the formula bar. If you are expecting macros in this workbook, click Enable Content. If you do not want to enable macros for the current workbook, dismiss the security warning by clicking the X at the far right of the message bar.

If you forget to enable the macros and attempt to run a macro, Excel indicates that you cannot run the macro because all macros have been disabled. If this occurs, close the workbook and reopen it to access the message bar again.

> **Caution**   If you download a macro-enabled workbook from the web or receive it via email, Excel might block the file and disable macros without warning. To prevent this, right-click the downloaded file, choose Properties, check the Unblock box (if present), and click OK.

Overview of recording, storing, and running a macro

Recording a macro is useful when you do not have experience writing lines of code in a macro. As you gain more knowledge and experience, you will record macros less frequently.

To begin recording a macro, select Record Macro from the Developer tab. Before recording begins, Excel displays the Record Macro dialog, as shown in Figure 1-4.

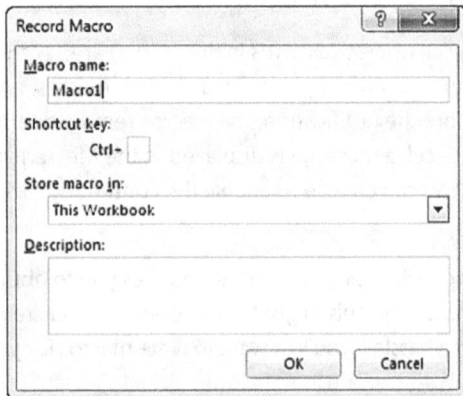

FIGURE 1-4 Use the Record Macro dialog to assign a Macro Name and Shortcut Key to the macro being recorded.

Filling out the Record Macro dialog

In the Macro Name field, type a name for the macro. Be sure to type continuous characters. For example, type **Macro1** (without a space), not **Macro 1** (with a space). A macro name can include letters, numbers, and the underscore character. The name cannot start with a number. Assuming that you will soon be creating many macros, use a meaningful name for the macro. A name such as FormatReport is more useful than one like Macro1.

The second field in the Record Macro dialog is a shortcut key. If you type a lowercase j in this field and later press Ctrl+J, this macro runs. Be careful, however, because Ctrl+A through Ctrl+Z (except Ctrl+J and Ctrl+M) are all already assigned to other tasks in Excel. If you assign a macro to Ctrl+B, you won't be able to use Ctrl+B for bold anymore. One alternative is to assign the macros to Ctrl+Shift+A through Ctrl+Shift+Z. To assign a macro to Ctrl+Shift+A, you type an uppercase A in the shortcut key box. The fact that you have to use the shift key to get an uppercase A makes it part of the shortcut.

> **Caution**   You can reuse a shortcut key for a macro. For example, if you assign a macro to Ctrl+C, Excel runs your macro instead of doing the normal copy action.

> **Note**   Refer to "Other ways to run a macro" in Chapter 25, "Customizing the ribbon to run macros," for other ways you can run macros, such as from hyperlinks, buttons, or shapes.

In the Record Macro dialog, choose where you want to save a macro when it is recorded: Personal Macro Workbook, New Workbook, or This Workbook. My recommendation is that you store macros related to a particular workbook in This Workbook.

The Personal Macro Workbook (Personal.xlsb) is not visible; it is created if you choose to save the recording in the Personal Macro Workbook. This workbook is used to save a macro in a workbook that opens automatically when you start Excel, thereby enabling you to use the macro. After Excel is started, the workbook is hidden. If you want to display it, select Unhide from the View tab.

> **Tip**   I do not recommend that you use the personal workbook for every macro you save. Save only those macros that assist you in general tasks—not in tasks that are performed in a specific sheet or workbook.

The fourth box in the Record Macro dialog is for a description. This description is added as a comment to the beginning of your macro.

After you select the location where you want to store the macro, click OK. Record your macro. For this example, type **Hello World** in the active cell and press Ctrl+Enter to accept the entry and stay in the same cell. When you are finished recording the macro, click the Stop Recording icon in the Developer tab.

> **Tip**   You also can access a Stop Recording icon in the lower-left corner of the Excel window. Look for a small white square to the right of the word Ready in the status bar. Using this Stop button might be more convenient than returning to the Developer tab. After you record your first macro, this area usually has a Record Macro icon, which is a small dot on an Excel worksheet.

Running a macro

If you have assigned a shortcut key to your macro, you can run it by pressing the key combination. You also can assign macros to a button on the ribbon or the Quick Access Toolbar, form controls, or drawing objects, or you can run them from the Macro dialog. Refer to "Other ways to run a macro" in Chapter 25, "Customizing the ribbon to run macros."

Understanding the VB Editor

If you want to edit a recorded macro, you do it in the VB Editor. Press Alt+F11 or use the Visual Basic icon in the Developer tab.

Figure 1-5 shows an example of a typical VB Editor screen. You can see three windows: the Project Explorer, the Properties window, and the Programming window. Don't worry if your window doesn't look exactly like this because you will see how to display the windows you need in this review of the Editor.

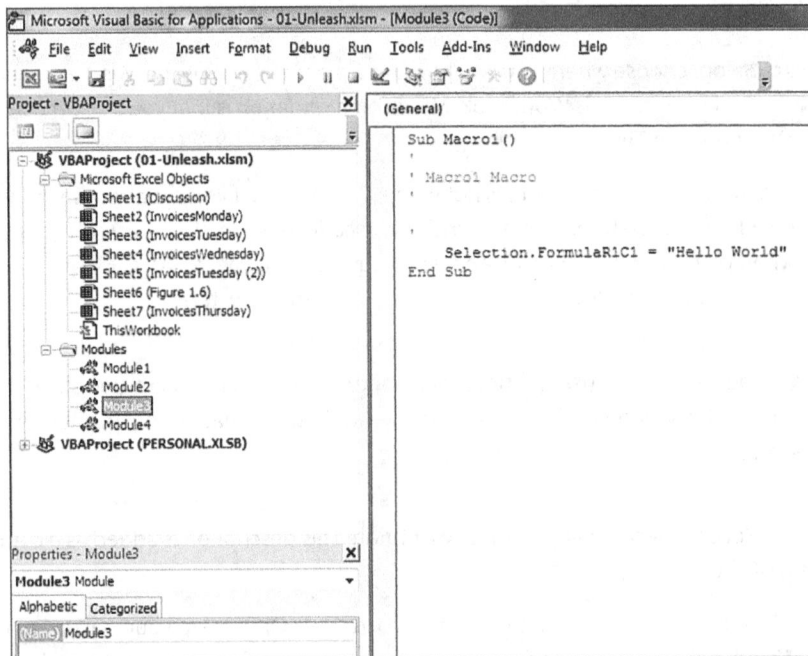

FIGURE 1-5 The VB Editor window.

VB Editor settings

Several settings in the VB Editor enable you to customize this editor and assist you in writing your macros.

Under Tools | Options | Editor, you will find several useful settings. All settings except for one are set correctly by default. The remaining setting— Require Variable Declaration—requires some consideration on your part. By default, Excel does not require you to declare variables. My coauthor prefers disabling this setting because it can save time when creating a program. I prefer to change this setting to require variable declaration. This change forces the compiler to stop if it finds a variable that it does not recognize, which reduces misspelled variable names. Declaring variables with certain data types is important to catch data type-related errors. Whether you turn this setting on or keep it off is a matter of your personal preference.

The Project Explorer

The Project Explorer lists any open workbooks and add-ins that are loaded. If you click the + icon next to the VBA Project, you see that there is a folder containing Microsoft Excel objects. There can also be folders for forms, class modules, and standard modules. Each folder includes one or more individual components.

Right-clicking a component and selecting View Code or just double-clicking the components brings up any code in the Programming window. The exception is userforms, where double-clicking displays the userform in the Design view.

To display the Project Explorer window, select View | Project Explorer from the menu or press Ctrl+R or locate the bizarre Project Explorer icon just below the Tools menu, sandwiched between Design Mode and Properties Window.

To insert a module, right-click your project, select Insert, and then choose the type of module you want. The available modules are as follows:

- **Microsoft Excel objects**—By default, a project consists of sheet modules for each sheet in the workbook and a single ThisWorkbook module. Code specific to a sheet, such as controls or sheet events, is placed on the corresponding sheet. Workbook events are placed in the ThisWorkbook module. You read more about events in Chapter 7, "Event programming."

- **Forms**—Excel enables you to design your own forms to interact with the user. You read more about these forms in Chapter 10, "Userforms: An Introduction."

- **Modules**—When you record a macro, Excel automatically creates a module in which to place the code. Most of your code resides in these types of modules.

- **Class modules**—Class modules are Excel's way of letting you create your own objects. They also allow pieces of code to be shared among programmers without the programmer needing to understand how it works. You read more about class modules in Chapter 9, "Creating custom objects and collections."

The Properties window

The Properties window enables you to edit the properties of various components such as sheets, workbooks, modules, and form controls. The properties list varies according to what component is selected. To display this window, select View, Properties Window from the menu, press F4, or click the Project Properties icon on the toolbar.

Understanding the shortcomings of the macro recorder

Suppose you work in an accounting department. Each day, you receive a text file from the company system showing all the invoices produced the prior day. This text file has commas separating the fields. The columns in the file are Invoice Date, Invoice Number, Sales Rep Number, Customer Number, Product Revenue, Service Revenue, and Product Cost (see Figure 1-6).

```
invoice.txt - Notepad
File  Edit  Format  View  Help
InvDate,InvNbr,RepNbr,CustNbr,ProdRevenue,ServRevenue,ProdCost
6/05/2021,123813,S82,C8754,716100,12000,423986
6/05/2021,123814,,C4894,224200,0,131243
6/05/2021,123815,S43,C7278,277000,0,139208
6/05/2021,123816,S54,C6425,746100,15000,350683
6/05/2021,123817,S43,C6291,928300,0,488988
6/05/2021,123818,S43,C1000,723200,0,383069
6/05/2021,123819,S82,C6025,982600,0,544025
6/05/2021,123820,S17,C8026,490100,45000,243808
6/05/2021,123821,S43,C4244,615800,0,300579
```

FIGURE 1-6 The Invoice.txt file has seven columns separated by commas.

Each morning, you manually import this file into Excel. You add a total row to the data, bold the headings, and then print the report for distribution to a few managers.

This seems like a simple process that would be ideally suited to using the macro recorder. However, due to some problems with the macro recorder, your first few attempts might not be successful. The following example explains how to overcome these problems.

Case study: Preparing to record a macro

The task mentioned in the preceding section is perfect for a macro. However, before you record a macro, think about the steps you will use. In this case, the steps are as follows:

1. Click the File menu and select Open.

2. Navigate to the folder where Invoice.txt is stored.

3. Select All Files (*.*) from the Files Of Type dropdown.

4. Select Invoice.txt.

5. Click Open.

6. In the Text Import Wizard—Step 1 Of 3 dialog, select Delimited from the Original Data Type section.

7. Click Next.

8. In the Text Import Wizard—Step 2 Of 3 dialog, clear the Tab key and select Comma in the Delimiters section.

9. Click Next.

10. In the Text Import Wizard—Step 3 Of 3 dialog, select General in the Column Data Format section and change it to Date: MDY.

11. Click Finish to import the file.

12. Press the Ctrl key and the down arrow key to move to the last row of data.

13. Release the Ctrl key, and then press the down arrow one more time to move to the total row.

14. Type the word Total.

15. Press the right arrow key four times to move to column E of the total row.

16. Click the AutoSum button and press Ctrl+Enter to add a total to the Product Revenue column while remaining in that cell.

17. Click the AutoFill handle and drag it from column E to column G to copy the total formula to columns F and G.

18. Highlight row 1 and click the Bold icon on the Home tab to set the headings in bold.

19. Highlight the total row and click the Bold icon on the Home tab to set the totals in bold.

20. Press Ctrl+* to select the current region.

21. From the Home tab, select Format, AutoFit Column Width.

After you have rehearsed these steps in your head, you are ready to record your first macro. Open a blank workbook and save it with a name such as MacroToImportInvoices. xlsm. Click the Record Macro button on the Developer tab.

In the Record Macro dialog, the default macro name is Macro1. Change this to something descriptive like ImportInvoice. Make sure that the macros will be stored in This Workbook. You might want an easy way to run this macro later, so type the letter **i** in the Shortcut Key field. In the Description field, add a little descriptive text to tell what the macro is doing (see Figure 1-7). Click OK when you are ready.

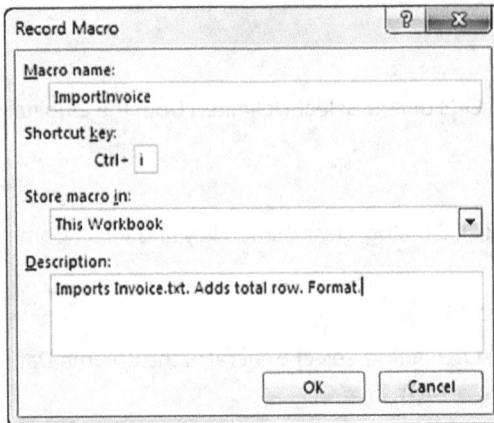

FIGURE 1-7 Before recording the macro, you need to complete the Record Macro dialog.

Recording the macro

The macro recorder is now recording your every move. For this reason, perform your steps in the exact order without extraneous actions. If you accidentally move to column F, type a value, clear the value, and then move back to column E to enter the first total, the recorded macro will blindly make that same mistake day after day after day. Recorded macros move fast, but there is nothing like watching the macro recorder play out your mistakes repeatedly.

Carefully execute all the actions necessary to produce the report. After you have performed the final step, click the Stop Recording button in the Developer tab of the ribbon.

Examining code in the Programming window

Let's look at the code you just recorded in the "Preparing to record a macro" section. Don't worry if it doesn't make sense yet.

To open the VB Editor, press Alt+F11. In your VBA project (MacroToImportInvoices.xlsm), find and right-click the Module1 component, and select View Code. Notice that some lines start with an apostrophe; these are comments and are ignored by the program. The macro recorder starts your macros with a few comments using the description you entered in the Record Macro dialog. The comment for the keyboard shortcut is there to remind you of the shortcut.

> **Note** The comment does not assign the shortcut. If you change the comment to Ctrl+J, it does not change the shortcut. You must change the setting in the Macro dialog in Excel or run this line of code:
>
> ```
> Application.MacroOptions Macro:="ImportInvoice", _
>  Description:="", ShortcutKey:="j"
> ```

Recorded macro code is usually pretty tidy (see Figure 1-8). Each line of code that is not a comment is indented four characters. If a line is longer than 100 characters, the recorder breaks it into multiple lines and indents the continued lines an additional four characters. To continue a line of code, type a space and an underscore at the end of the first line and then continue the code on the next line. Don't forget the space before the underscore. Using an underscore without the preceding space causes an error.

> **Note** The physical limitations of this book do not allow 100 characters on a single line. Therefore, the lines are broken at 80 characters so that they fit on a page. For this reason, your recorded macro might look slightly different from the ones that appear in this book.

```
Sub ImportInvoice()
'
' ImportInvoice Macro
' Import Invoice.txt. Add Total Row. Format.
'
' Keyboard Shortcut: Ctrl+i
'
    Workbooks.OpenText Filename:="G:\2016VBA\SampleFiles\invoice.txt", Origin:= _
        437, StartRow:=1, DataType:=xlDelimited, TextQualifier:=xlDoubleQuote, _
        ConsecutiveDelimiter:=False, Tab:=False, Semicolon:=False, Comma:=True _
        , Space:=False, Other:=False, FieldInfo:=Array(Array(1, 3), Array(2, 1), _
        Array(3, 1), Array(4, 1), Array(5, 1), Array(6, 1), Array(7, 1)), TrailingMinusNumbers _
        :=True
    Selection.End(xlDown).Select
    Range("A11").Select
    ActiveCell.FormulaR1C1 = "Total"
    Range("E11").Select
    Selection.FormulaR1C1 = "=SUM(R[-9]C:R[-1]C)"
    Selection.AutoFill Destination:=Range("E11:G11"), Type:=xlFillDefault
    Range("E11:G11").Select
    Rows("1:1").Select
    Selection.Font.Bold = True
    Rows("11:11").Select
    Selection.Font.Bold = True
    Selection.CurrentRegion.Select
    Selection.Columns.AutoFit
End Sub
```

FIGURE 1-8 The recorded macro is neat-looking and nicely indented.

Consider that the following six lines of recorded code are actually only one line of code that has been broken into six lines for readability:

```
Workbooks.OpenText Filename:=ThisPath & "invoice.txt", Origin:=437, _
    StartRow:=1, DataType:=xlDelimited, TextQualifier:=xlDoubleQuote, _
    ConsecutiveDelimiter:=False, Tab:=False, Semicolon:=False, Comma:=True, _
    Space:=False, Other:=False, FieldInfo:=Array(Array(1, 3), Array(2, 1), _
    Array(3, 1), Array(4, 1), Array(5, 1), Array(6, 1), Array(7, 1)), _
    TrailingMinusNumbers:=True
```

Counting this as one line, the macro recorder was able to record the 21-step process in 14 lines of code, which is pretty impressive.

> **Note** Each action you perform in the Excel user interface might equate to one or more lines of recorded code. Some actions might generate a dozen lines of code.

Test each macro

It is always a good idea to test macros. To test your new macro, return to the regular Excel interface by pressing Alt+F11 or Alt+Q. Close Invoice.txt without saving any changes. MacroToImportInvoices.xlsm is still open.

Press Ctrl+I to run the recorded macro. It should work well if you have completed the steps correctly. The data is imported, totals are added, bold formatting is applied, and the columns have been made wider. This seems like a perfect solution (see Figure 1-9).

	A	B	C	D	E	F	G	H
1	InvDate	InvNbr	RepNbr	CustNbr	ProdRevenue	ServRevenue	ProdCost	
2	6/5/2025	123813	S82	C8754	716100	12000	423986	
3	6/5/2025	123814		C4894	224200	0	131243	
4	6/5/2025	123815	S43	C7278	277000	0	139208	
5	6/5/2025	123816	S54	C6425	746100	15000	350683	
6	6/5/2025	123817	S43	C6291	928300	0	488988	
7	6/5/2025	123818	S43	C1000	723200	0	383069	
8	6/5/2025	123819	S82	C6025	982600	0	544025	
9	6/5/2025	123820	S17	C8026	490100	45000	243808	
10	6/5/2025	123821	S43	C4244	615800	0	300579	
11	Total				5703400	72000	3005589	
12								

FIGURE 1-9 The macro formats the data in the sheet.

Running the macro on another day produces undesired results

After testing the macro, be sure to save your macro file to use on another day. But suppose that the next day, after receiving a new Invoice.txt file from the system, you open the macro and press Ctrl+I to run it, and disaster strikes. The data for June 5 happened to have 9 invoices, but the data for June 6 now has 17 invoices. The recorded macro blindly added the totals in Row 11 because this was where you put the totals when the macro was recorded (see Figure 1-10).

For those of you working along using the sample files in this book, follow these steps to try importing data for another day:

1. Close Invoice.txt in Excel.

2. In Windows Explorer, rename Invoice.txt as **Invoice1.txt**.

3. In Windows Explorer, rename Invoice2.txt as **Invoice.txt**.

4. Return to Excel and the MacroToImportInvoices.xlsm workbook.

5. Press Ctrl+I to run the macro with the larger data set.

This problem arises because the macro recorder is recording all your actions in Absolute mode by default. As an alternative to using the default state of the macro recorder, the next section discusses relative recording and how it might get you closer to the desired solution.

	A	B	C	D	E	F	G	H
1	**InvDate**	**InvNbr**	**RepNbr**	**CustNbr**	**ProdRevenue**	**ServRevenue**	**ProdCost**	
2	6/6/2025	123829	S21	C8754	21000	0	9875	
3	6/6/2025	123830	S45	C3390	188100	0	85083	
4	6/6/2025	123831	S54	C2523	510600	0	281158	
5	6/6/2025	123832	S21	C5519	86200	0	49967	
6	6/6/2025	123833	S45	C3245	800100	0	388277	
7	6/6/2025	123834	S54	C7796	339000	0	195298	
8	6/6/2025	123835	S21	C1654	161000	0	90761	
9	6/6/2025	123836	S45	C6460	275500	10000	146341	
10	6/6/2025	123837	S54	C5143	925400	0	473515	
11	**Total**	**123838**	**S21**	**C7868**	**3306900**	**10000**	**1720275**	
12	6/6/2025	123839	S45	C3310	890200	0	468333	
13	6/6/2025	123840	S54	C2959	986000	0	528980	
14	6/6/2025	123841	S21	C8361	94400	0	53180	
15	6/6/2025	123842	S45	C1842	36500	55000	20696	
16	6/6/2025	123843	S54	C4107	599700	0	276718	
17	6/6/2025	123844	S21	C5205	244900	0	143393	
18	6/6/2025	123845	S45	C7745	63000	0	35102	
19	6/6/2025	123846	S54	C1730	212600	0	117787	
20	6/6/2025	123847	S21	C6292	974700	0	478731	
21	6/6/2025	123848	S45	C2008	327700	0	170968	
22	6/6/2025	123849	S54	C4096	30700	0	18056	

FIGURE 1-10 The intent of the recorded macro was to add a total at the end of the data, but the recorder made a macro that always adds totals at row 11.

Possible solution: Use relative references when recording

By default, the macro recorder records all actions as *absolute* actions. If you navigate to row 11 when you record the macro, the macro will always go to row 11 when the macro is run. This is rarely appropriate when dealing with variable numbers of rows of data. The better option is to use relative references when recording.

Macros recorded with absolute references note the actual address of the cell pointer, such as A11. Macros recorded with relative references note that the cell pointer should move a certain number of rows and columns from its current position. For example, if the cell pointer starts in cell A1, the code `ActiveCell.Offset(16, 1).Select` would move the cell pointer to B17, which is the cell 16 rows down and 1 column to the right.

Although relative recording is appropriate in most situations, there are times when you need to do something absolute while recording a macro. Here's a great example: After adding the totals to a data set, you need to return to row 1. If you simply click row 1 while in Relative mode, Excel records that you want to select the row 10 rows above the current row. This works with the first invoice file but not with longer or shorter invoice files. Here are two workarounds:

- Toggle relative recording off, click row 1, and then toggle relative recording back on.
- Keep relative recording turned on. Display the Go To dialog by pressing F5. Type **A1** and click OK. The Go To dialog is recorded as always, going to the absolute address you typed, even if relative recording is enabled. A variation of this method is used in the following example.

The next example shows the same task as before but uses relative references this time. The solution will be much closer to working correctly.

Case study: Recording a macro with relative references

Let's try to record the macro again, this time using relative references.

> **Note**   If you are following along with the sample files, complete these steps first:
>
> 1. Close Invoice.txt in Excel.
> 2. Rename Invoice.txt as **Invoice2.txt**.
> 3. Rename Invoice1.txt as **Invoice.txt**.
> 4. Return to the MacroToImportInvoices.xlsm workbook.

In the Developer tab, choose Use Relative References to toggle on relative recording. This setting persists until you turn it off or until you close Excel.

In the workbook MacroToImportInvoices.xlsm, record a new macro by selecting Record Macro from the Developer tab. Rename the macro **ImportInvoicesRelative** and assign a different shortcut key, such as Ctrl+J.

Repeat steps 1 through 11 from the "Preparing to record a macro" section to import the file, and then follow these steps:

1. Press Ctrl+down arrow to move to the last row of data.
2. Press the down arrow key one more time to move to the total row.
3. Type the word **Total**.
4. Press the right arrow key four times to move to column E of the total row.
5. Hold the Shift key while pressing the right arrow key twice to select E11:G11.
6. Click the AutoSum button.
7. Press Shift+spacebar to select the entire row. Type Ctrl+B to apply bold formatting.
8. Press F5 to display the Go To dialog.
9. In the Go To dialog, type **A1:G1** and click OK. Even though relative recording is enabled, any navigation through the Go To dialog is recorded as an absolute reference.

10. Click the Bold icon to set the headings in bold.

11. Press Ctrl+* to select all data in the current region.

12. From the Home tab, select Format | AutoFit Column Width.

13. Stop recording.

Press Alt+F11 to go to the VB Editor to review your code. The new macro appears in Module1 below the previous macro.

If you close Excel between recording the first and second macros, Excel inserts a new module called Module2 for the newly recorded macro:

```
Sub ImportInvoicesRelative()
'ImportInvoicesRelative Macro
'Import. Total Row. Format.
'Keyboard Shortcut: Ctrl+j
Workbooks.OpenText Filename:="C:\data\invoice.txt", _
  Origin:= 437, StartRow:=1, DataType:=xlDelimited, _
  TextQualifier:=xlDoubleQuote, ConsecutiveDelimiter:=False, _
  Tab:=False, Semicolon:=False, Comma:=True, Space:=False, _
  Other:=False, FieldInfo:=Array(Array(1, 3), Array(2, 1), _
  Array(3, 1), Array(4, 1), Array(5, 1), Array(6, 1), _
  Array(7, 1)), TrailingMinusNumbers:=True
Selection.End(xlDown).Select
ActiveCell.Offset(1, 0).Range("A1").Select
ActiveCell.FormulaR1C1 = "Total"
ActiveCell.Offset(0, 4).Range("A1:C1").Select
Selection.FormulaR1C1 = "=SUM(R[-9]C:R[-1]C)"
ActiveCell.Rows("1:1").EntireRow.Select
ActiveCell.Activate
Selection.Font.Bold = True
Application.Goto Reference:="R1C1:R1C7"
Selection.Font.Bold = True
Selection.CurrentRegion.Select
Selection.Columns.AutoFit
End Sub
```

To test the macro, close Invoice.txt without saving and then run the macro with Ctrl+J. Everything should look good, and you should get the same results as with the macro you created with the macro recorder.

The next test is to see whether the program works on the next day when you might have more rows. If you are working along with the sample files, close Invoice.txt in Excel. Rename Invoice.txt to Invoice1.txt. Rename Invoice2.txt to Invoice.txt.

Open MacroToImportInvoices.xlsm and run the new macro with Ctrl+J. This time, everything should look good, with the totals in the correct places. Look at Figure 1-11. Do you see anything out of the ordinary?

If you aren't careful, you might print these reports for your manager. If you did, you would be in trouble. When you look at cell E23, you can see that Excel has inserted a green triangle to tell you to look at the cell.

When you move the cell pointer to E23, an alert indicator pops up near the cell. This indicator tells you that the formula fails to include adjacent cells. If you look in the formula bar, you see that the macro totaled only from row 14 to row 22. Neither the relative recording nor the nonrelative recording is smart enough to replicate the logic of the AutoSum button.

Imagine that you had fewer invoice records on this particular day. Excel would have rewarded you with the illogical formula =SUM(E6:E1048574), as shown in Figure 1-12. Because this formula would be in E7, circular reference warnings would appear in the status bar.

> **Note** To try this yourself, close Invoice.txt in Excel. Rename Invoice.txt to **Invoice2.txt**. Rename Invoice4.txt to **Invoice.txt**.

	A	B	C	D	E	F	G	H
1	InvDate	InvNbr	RepNbr	CustNbr	ProdRevenue	ServRevenue	ProdCost	
2	6/6/2025	123829	S21	C8754	21000	0	9875	
3	6/6/2025	123830	S45	C3390	188100	0	85083	
4	6/6/2025	123831	S54	C2523	510600	0	281158	
5	6/6/2025	123832	S21	C5519	86200	0	49967	
6	6/6/2025	123833	S45	C3245	800100	0	388277	
7	6/6/2025	123834	S54	C7796	339000	0	195298	
8	6/6/2025	123835	S21	C1654	161000	0	90761	
9	6/6/2025	123836	S45	C6460	275500	10000	146341	
10	6/6/2025	123837	S54	C5143	925400	0	473515	
11	6/6/2025	123838	S21	C7868	148200	0	75700	
12	6/6/2025	123839	S45	C3310	890200	0	468333	
13	6/6/2025	123840	S54	C2959	986000	0	528980	
14	6/6/2025	123841	S21	C8361	94400	0	53180	
15	6/6/2025	123842	S45	C1842	36500	55000	20696	
16	6/6/2025	123843	S54	C4107	599700	0	276718	
17	6/6/2025	123844	S21	C5205	244900	0	143393	
18	6/6/2025	123845	S45	C7745	63000	0	35102	
19	6/6/2025	123846	S54	C1730	212600	0	117787	
20	6/6/2025	123847	S21	C6292	974700	0	478731	
21	6/6/2025	123848	S45	C2008	327700	0	170968	
22	6/6/2025	123849	S54	C4096	30700	0	18056	
23	Total				2584200	55000	1314631	

FIGURE 1-11 After running the Relative macro, the totals appear in the correct row.

	E7				f_x	=SUM(E6:E1048574)			
	A	B	C	D	E	F	G	H
1	InvDate	InvNbr	RepNbr	CustNbr	ProdRevenue	ServRevenue	ProdCost	
2	6/7/2025	123850		C1654	161000	0	90761	
3	6/7/2025	123851		C6460	275500	10000	146341	
4	6/7/2025	123852		C5143	925400	0	473515	
5	6/7/2025	123853		C7868	148200	0	75700	
6	6/7/2025	123854		C3310	890200	0	468333	
7	Total				0	0	0	

FIGURE 1-12 An incorrect formula appears when you run the relative macro with fewer invoice records.

If you have tried using the macro recorder, most likely you have run into problems similar to the ones produced in this section. Although this is frustrating, you should be happy to know that the macro recorder actually gets you 95 percent of the way to a useful macro.

Your job is to recognize where the macro recorder is likely to fail and then be able to dive into the VBA code to fix the one or two lines that require adjusting to have a perfect macro. With some added human intelligence, you can produce awesome macros to speed up your daily work.

Never use AutoSum or Quick Analysis while recording a macro

There actually is a macro recorder solution to the current problem with recording an AutoSum. It is important to recognize that the macro recorder will never correctly record the intent of the AutoSum button.

If you are in cell E99 and click the AutoSum button, Excel starts scanning from cell E98 upward until it locates a text cell, a blank cell, or a formula. It then proposes a formula that sums everything between the current cell and the found cell.

However, the macro recorder records the particular result of that search on the day that the macro was recorded. Rather than record something along the lines of "do the normal AutoSum logic," the macro recorder inserts a single line of code to add up the previous 98 cells.

And then there's the Quick Analysis feature:

1. Select E2:G99.

2. Click the Quick Analysis icon that appears below and to the right of a rectangular selection.

3. Choose Totals | Sum at Bottom. The correct totals now appear in row 100. The macro recorder hard-codes the formulas to always appear in row 100 and to always total row 2 through row 99.

The somewhat bizarre workaround is to type a SUM function that uses a mix of relative and absolute row references. If you type **=SUM(E$2:E10)** while the macro recorder is running, Excel correctly adds code that always sums from a fixed row two down to the relative reference that is just above the current cell.

Here is the resulting code, with a few comments:

```
Sub FormatInvoice3()
'FormatInvoice3 Macro
'Import. Total. Format.
'Keyboard Shortcut: Ctrl+k
Workbooks.OpenText Filename:="C:\Data\invoice.txt", _
    Origin:=437, StartRow:=1, DataType:=xlDelimited, _
    TextQualifier:=xlDoubleQuote, ConsecutiveDelimiter:=False, _
    Tab:=False, Semicolon:=False, Comma:=True, Space:=False, _
    Other:=False, FieldInfo:=Array(Array(1, 3), Array(2, 1), _
    Array(3, 1), Array(4, 1), Array(5, 1), Array(6, 1), _
    Array(7, 1)), TrailingMinusNumbers:=True
Selection.End(xlDown).Select
ActiveCell.Offset(1, 0).Range("A1").Select
ActiveCell.FormulaR1C1 = "Total"
ActiveCell.Offset(0, 4).Range("A1").Select
Selection.FormulaR1C1 = "=SUM(R2C:R[-1]C)"
Selection.AutoFill Destination:=ActiveCell.Range("A1:C1"), _
    Type:=xlFillDefault
ActiveCell.Range("A1:C1").Select
ActiveCell.Rows("1:1").EntireRow.Select
ActiveCell.Activate
Selection.Font.Bold = True
Application.Goto Reference:="R1C1:R1C7"
Selection.Font.Bold = True
Selection.CurrentRegion.Select
Selection.Columns.AutoFit
End Sub
```

This third macro consistently works with a data set of any size.

Four tips for using the macro recorder

You will rarely be able to record 100 percent of your macros and have them work. However, you will get much closer by using the following four tips.

Tip 1: Turn on the Use Relative References setting

Microsoft should have made this setting the default. Turn on the setting and leave it on while recording your macros.

Tip 2: Use special navigation keys to move to the bottom of a data set

If you are at the top of a data set and need to move to the last cell that contains data, you can press Ctrl+down arrow or press the End key and then the down arrow key.

Similarly, to move to the last column in the current row of the data set, press Ctrl+right arrow or press End and then press the right arrow key.

By using these navigation keys, you can jump to the end of the data set, no matter how many rows or columns you have today.

Use Ctrl+* to select the current region around the active cell. Provided that you have no blank rows or blank columns in your data, this key combination selects the entire data set.

Tip 3: Never touch the AutoSum icon while recording a macro

The macro recorder does not record the "essence" of the AutoSum button. Instead, it hard codes the formula that resulted from pressing the AutoSum button. This formula does not work any time you have more or fewer records in the data set.

Instead, type a formula with a single dollar sign, such as =SUM(E$2:E10). When this is done, the macro recorder records the first E$2 as a fixed reference and starts the SUM range directly below the row 1 headings. Provided that the active cell is E11, the macro recorder recognizes E10 as a relative reference pointing directly above the current cell.

Tip 4: Try recording different methods if one method does not work

There are often many ways to perform tasks in Excel. If you encounter buggy code from one method, try another method. With 16 different project managers on the Excel team, a different group likely programmed each method. In one of the case studies in this chapter, one task involved applying AutoFit Column Width to all cells. Some people might press Ctrl+A to select all cells. Others might press Ctrl+*. Since Excel 2007, the code generated by Ctrl+A does not work. The Ctrl+* shortcut is very old and continues to work in all cases.

Next steps

In this chapter, you learned how to record a macro and run it to automate basic tasks in Excel. While the macro recorder is a helpful starting point, it often produces inefficient or confusing code.

Chapter 2, "This sounds like BASIC, so why doesn't it look familiar?" examines the three macros you recorded in this chapter to make more sense of them. When you know how to decode the VBA code, it will feel natural to either correct the recorded code or simply write code from scratch. Hang on through one more chapter. You'll soon learn that VBA is the solution, and you'll be writing useful code that works consistently.

CHAPTER 2

This sounds like BASIC, so why doesn't it look familiar?

In this chapter, you will:

- Find out how VBA is different from BASIC
- Understand the parts of VBA "speech"
- Find out that learning VBA is not really hard
- Examine recorded macro code using the VB Editor and Help
- Use debugging tools to figure out recorded code
- Get to know the Object Browser
- Learn seven tips for cleaning up recorded code

As mentioned in Chapter 1, "Unleashing the power of Excel with VBA," if you have taken a class in a procedural language such as BASIC or COBOL, you might be confused when you look at VBA code. Even though VBA stands for *Visual Basic for Applications*, it is an *object-oriented* version of BASIC. Here is a bit of recorded VBA code:

```
Selection.End(xlDown).Select
Range("A11").Select
ActiveCell.FormulaR1C1 = "Total"
Range("E11").Select
Selection.FormulaR1C1 = _
  "=SUM(R[-9]C:R[-1]C)"
Selection.AutoFill _
  Destination:=Range("E11:G11"), _
  Type:=xlFillDefault
```

This code likely makes no sense to anyone who knows only procedural languages. Unfortunately, your first introduction to programming in school (assuming that you are more than 40 years old) would have been a procedural language.

Here is a section of code written in the BASIC language:

```
For x = 0 to 9
  Print Rpt$(" ",x)
  Print "*"
Next x
```

If you run this code, you get a pyramid of asterisks on your screen:

```
*
 *
  *
   *
    *
     *
      *
       *
        *
         *
```

If you have ever been in a procedural programming class, you can probably look at the code and figure out what is going on because procedural languages are more English-like than object-oriented languages. The statement `Print "Hello World"` follows the verb–object format, which is how you would generally talk. Let's step away from programming for a second and look at a concrete example.

Understanding the parts of VBA "speech"

If you were going to write code for instructions to play soccer using BASIC, the instruction to kick a ball would look something like this:

```
"Kick the Ball"
```

Hey, this is how you talk! It makes sense. You have a verb (*kick*) and then a noun (*ball*). The BASIC code in the preceding section has a verb (`Print`) and a noun (the asterisk, `*`). Life is good.

Here is the problem: VBA doesn't work like this. In fact, no object-oriented language works like this. In an object-oriented language, the objects (nouns) are most important, hence the name, "object-oriented." If you were going to write code for instructions to play soccer with VBA, the basic structure would be as follows:

```
Ball.Kick
```

You have a noun (`Ball`), which comes first. In VBA, this is an *object*. Then, you have the verb (`Kick`), which comes next. In VBA, this is a *method*.

The basic structure of VBA is a bunch of lines of code with this syntax:

```
Object.Method
```

Needless to say, this is not English. If you took a romance language in high school, you will remember that those languages use a "noun–adjective" construct. However, no one uses "noun–verb" to tell someone to do something:

```
Water.Drink
Food.Eat
Girl.Kiss
```

That is why VBA is confusing to someone who previously took a procedural programming class.

Let's carry the analogy a bit further. Imagine that you walk onto a grassy field, and there are five balls in front of you: a soccer ball, basketball, baseball, bowling ball, and tennis ball. You want to instruct a kid on your soccer team to "kick the soccer ball."

If you tell them to kick the ball (or Ball.Kick), you really aren't sure which one of the five balls they will kick. Maybe they will kick the one closest to them, which could be a problem if they are standing in front of the bowling ball.

For almost any noun or object in VBA, there is a collection of that object. Think about Excel. If you can have one row, you can have a bunch of rows. If you can have one cell, you can have a bunch of cells. If you can have one worksheet, you can have a bunch of worksheets. The only difference between an object and a collection is that you add an *s* to the name of the object:

Row becomes Rows.

Cell becomes Cells.

Ball becomes Balls.

When you refer to something that is a collection, you have to tell the programming language to which item you are referring. There are a couple of ways to do this. You can refer to an item by using a number. For example, if the soccer ball is the second ball, you might say this:

```
Balls(2).Kick
```

This works fine, but it could be a dangerous way to program. For example, it might work on Tuesday. However, if you get to the field on Wednesday and someone has rearranged the balls, Balls(2).Kick might be a painful exercise.

A much safer way to go is to use a name for the object in a collection. You can say the following:

```
Balls("Soccer").Kick
```

With this method, you always know that it will be the soccer ball that is being kicked.

So far, so good. You know that a ball will be kicked, and you know that it will be a soccer ball. For most of the verbs or methods in Excel VBA, there are *parameters* that tell *how* to do the action. These parameters act as adverbs. You might want the soccer ball to be kicked to the left and with a hard force.

In this case, the method would have a number of parameters that tell how the program should perform the method:

```
Balls("Soccer").Kick Direction:=Left, Force:=Hard
```

When you are looking at VBA code, the colon–equal sign combination (:=) indicates that you are looking at the parameters of how the verb should be performed.

Sometimes, a method will have a list of 10 parameters, some of which are optional. For example, if the Kick method has an Elevation parameter, you would have this line of code:

```
Balls("Soccer").Kick Direction:=Left, Force:=Hard, Elevation:=High
```

Here is the confusing part: Every method has a default order for its parameters. If you are not a conscientious programmer and happen to know the order of the parameters, you can leave off the parameter names. The following code is equivalent to the previous line of code:

```
Balls("Soccer").Kick Left, Hard, High
```

This throws a monkey wrench into our understanding. Without :=, it is not obvious that you have parameters. Unless you know the parameter order, you might not understand what is being said. It is pretty easy with Left, Hard, and High, but when you have parameters like the following:

```
ActiveSheet.Shapes.AddShape Type:=1, Left:=10, Top:=20, Width:=100, Height:=200
```

It gets confusing if you instead have this:

```
ActiveSheet.Shapes.AddShape 1, 10, 20, 100, 200
```

The preceding line is valid code. However, unless you know that the default order of the parameters for this Add method is Type, Left, Top, Width, Height, this code does not make sense. The default order for any particular method is the order of the parameters, as shown in the Help topic for that method.

To make life more confusing, you are allowed to start specifying parameters in their default order without naming them, and then you can switch to naming parameters when you hit one that does not match the default order. If you want to kick the ball to the left and high but do not care about the force (that is, you are willing to accept the default force), the following two statements are equivalent:

```
Balls("Soccer").Kick Direction:=Left, Elevation:=High
Balls("Soccer").Kick Left, Elevation:=High
```

However, keep in mind that as soon as you start naming parameters, they have to be named for the remainder of that line of code.

Some methods simply act on their own. To simulate pressing the F9 key, you use this code:

```
Application.Calculate
```

Other methods perform an action and create something. For example, you can add a worksheet by using the following:

```
Worksheets.Add Before:=Worksheets(1)
```

However, because `Worksheets.Add` creates a new object, you can assign the results of this method to a variable. In this case, you must surround the parameters with parentheses:

```
Set MyWorksheet = Worksheets.Add(Before:=Worksheets(1))
```

> **Note** Don't worry if the use of `Set` isn't clear yet. This command and other foundational concepts are covered in more detail in Chapter 4, "Laying the groundwork with variables and structures."

One final bit of grammar is necessary: adjectives. Just as adjectives describe a noun, *properties* describe an object. Because you are an Excel fan, let's switch from the soccer analogy to an Excel analogy. There is an object to describe the active cell. Fortunately, it has a very intuitive name:

```
ActiveCell
```

Suppose you want to change the color of the active cell to red. There is a property called `Interior.Color` for a cell that uses a complex series of codes. However, you can turn a cell to red by using this code:

```
ActiveCell.Interior.Color = 255
```

You can see how this can be confusing. Again, there is the *noun-dot-something* construct, but this time, it is `Object.Property` rather than `Object.Method`. How you tell them apart is quite subtle: There is no colon before the equal sign. A property is almost always set equal to something, or perhaps the value of a property is assigned to something else.

To make this cell color the same as cell A1, you might say this:

```
ActiveCell.Interior.Color = Range("A1").Interior.Color
```

`Interior.Color` is a property. Actually, `Interior` is a property of the `Range` object, and `Color` is a property of the `Interior` property. By changing the value of a property, you can make things look different. It is kind of bizarre: Change an adjective, and you are actually doing something to the cell. Humans would say, "Color the cell red," whereas VBA says this:

```
ActiveCell.Interior.Color = 255
```

Table 2-1 summarizes the VBA "parts of speech."

TABLE 2-1 Parts of the VBA programming language

VBA Component	Analogous To	Notes
Object	Noun	Examples include cell or sheet.
Collection	Plural noun	Usually specifies which object: `Worksheets(1)`.
Method	Verb	Appears as `Object.Method`.
Parameter	Adverb	Lists parameters after the method. Separate the parameter name from its value with :=.
Property	Adjective	You can set a property (for example, `ActiveCell.Height=10`) or store the value of a property (for example, `x = ActiveCell.Height`).

VBA is not really hard

Knowing whether you are dealing with properties or methods helps you set up the correct syntax for your code. Don't worry if it all seems confusing right now. When you are writing VBA code from scratch, it is tough to know whether the process of changing a cell to yellow requires a verb or an adjective. Is it a method or a property?

This is where the macro recorder is especially helpful. When you don't know how to code something, you record a short little macro, look at the recorded code, and figure out what is going on.

VBA Help files: Using F1 to find anything

Excel VBA Help is an amazing feature, provided that you are connected to the Internet. If you are going to write VBA macros, you absolutely *must* have access to the VBA Help topics installed. Follow these steps to see how easy it is to get help in VBA:

1. Open Excel and switch to the VB Editor by pressing Alt+F11. From the Insert menu, select Module.

2. Type these three lines of code:

```
Sub Test()
   MsgBox "Hello World!"
End Sub
```

3. Click inside the word MsgBox.

4. With the cursor in the word MsgBox, press F1. If you can reach the Internet, you will see the Help topic for the MsgBox function.

Using Help topics

If you request help on a function or method, the Help topic walks you through the various available arguments. If you browse to the bottom of a Help topic, you can see a great resource: code samples under the Example heading (see Figure 2-1).

It is possible to select the code, copy it to the Clipboard by clicking the Copy shortcut in the top-right corner of the code box, and then paste it into a module by pressing Ctrl+V.

After you record a macro, if there are objects or methods about which you are unsure, you can get help by inserting the cursor in any keyword and pressing F1.

Example

This example uses the **MsgBox** function to display a critical-error message in a dialog box with **Yes** and **No** buttons. The **No** button is specified as the default response. The value returned by the **MsgBox** function depends on the button chosen by the user. This example assumes that DEMO.HLP is a Help file that contains a topic with a Help context number equal to 1000.

VB   ⎘ Copy

```vb
Dim Msg, Style, Title, Help, Ctxt, Response, MyString
Msg = "Do you want to continue ?"    ' Define message.
Style = vbYesNo Or vbCritical Or vbDefaultButton2    ' Define buttons.
Title = "MsgBox Demonstration"    ' Define title.
Help = "DEMO.HLP"    ' Define Help file.
Ctxt = 1000    ' Define topic context.
        ' Display message.
Response = MsgBox(Msg, Style, Title, Help, Ctxt)
If Response = vbYes Then    ' User chose Yes.
    MyString = "Yes"    ' Perform some action.
Else    ' User chose No.
    MyString = "No"    ' Perform some action.
End If
```

FIGURE 2-1 Most Help topics include code samples.

Examining recorded macro code: Using the VB Editor and Help

Let's take a look at the code you recorded in Chapter 1 to see whether it makes more sense now that you know about objects, properties, and methods. You can also see whether it's possible to correct the errors created by the macro recorder.

Figure 2-2 shows the first code that Excel recorded in the example from Chapter 1.

Now that you understand the concept of Noun.Verb or Object.Method, consider the first line of code that reads Workbooks.OpenText. In this case, Workbooks is a collection object, and OpenText is a method. Click the word OpenText and press F1 for an explanation of the OpenText method (see Figure 2-3).

The Help file confirms that OpenText is a method, or an action word. The default order for all the arguments that can be used with OpenText appears in a Parameters table. Notice that only one argument is required: Filename. All the other arguments are listed as optional.

```
(General)                                                                        ▼

  Sub ImportInvoice()
  '
  ' ImportInvoice Macro
  ' Import Invoice.txt. Add Total Row. Format.
  '
  ' Keyboard Shortcut: Ctrl+i

      Workbooks.OpenText Filename:="G:\2016VBA\SampleFiles\invoice.txt", Origin:= _
          437, StartRow:=1, DataType:=xlDelimited, TextQualifier:=xlDoubleQuote, _
          ConsecutiveDelimiter:=False, Tab:=False, Semicolon:=False, Comma:=True _
          , Space:=False, Other:=False, FieldInfo:=Array(Array(1, 3), Array(2, 1), _
          Array(3, 1), Array(4, 1), Array(5, 1), Array(6, 1), Array(7, 1)), TrailingMinusNumbers _
          :=True
      Selection.End(xlDown).Select
      Range("A11").Select
      ActiveCell.FormulaR1C1 = "Total"
      Range("E11").Select
      Selection.FormulaR1C1 = "=SUM(R[-9]C:R[-1]C)"
      Selection.AutoFill Destination:=Range("E11:G11"), Type:=xlFillDefault
      Range("E11:G11").Select
      Rows("1:1").Select
      Selection.Font.Bold = True
      Rows("11:11").Select
      Selection.Font.Bold = True
      Selection.CurrentRegion.Select
      Selection.Columns.AutoFit
  End Sub
```

FIGURE 2-2 Here is the recorded code from the example in Chapter 1.

Parameters			
Filename	Required	**String**	Specifies the file name of the text file to be opened and parsed.
Origin	Optional	**Variant**	Specifies the origin of the text file. Can be one of the following **XlPlatform** constants: **xlMacintosh**, **xlWindows**, or **xlMSDOS**. Additionally, this could be an integer representing the code page number of the desired code page. For example, "1256" would specify that the encoding of the source text file is Arabic (Windows). If this argument is omitted, the method uses the current setting of the **File Origin** option in the **Text Import Wizard**.
StartRow	Optional	**Variant**	The row number at which to start parsing text. The default value is 1.
DataType	Optional	**Variant**	Specifies the column format of the data in the file. Can be one of the following XlTextParsingType constants: **xlDelimited** or **xlFixedWidth**. If this argument is not specified, Microsoft Excel attempts to determine the column format when it opens the file.
TextQualifier	Optional	XlTextQualifier	Specifies the text qualifier.
ConsecutiveDelimiter	Optional	**Variant**	**True** to have consecutive delimiters considered one delimiter. The default is **False**.

FIGURE 2-3 This shows part of the Help topic for the OpenText method.

Optional parameters

The Help file can tell you what happens if you skip an optional parameter. For StartRow, the Help file indicates that the default value is 1. If you leave out the StartRow parameter, Excel starts importing at row 1. This is fairly safe.

Now look at the Help file note about `Origin`. If this argument is omitted, you inherit whatever value was used for `Origin` the last time someone used this feature in Excel on this computer. That is a recipe for disaster. For example, your code might work 98 percent of the time. However, immediately after someone imports an Arabic file, Excel remembers the setting for Arabic and thereafter assumes that this is what your macro wants if you don't explicitly code this parameter.

Defined constants

Look at the Help file entry for `DataType` in Figure 2-3, which says it can be one of these constants: `xlDelimited` or `xlFixedWidth`. The Help file says these are the valid `xlTextParsingType` constants that are predefined in Excel VBA. In the VB Editor, press Ctrl+G to bring up the Immediate window. In the Immediate window, type this line and press Enter:

```
Print xlFixedWidth
```

The answer appears in the Immediate window. `xlFixedWidth` is the equivalent of saying 2 (see Figure 2-4). In the Immediate window, type **Print xlDelimited**, which is really the same as typing **1**. Microsoft correctly assumes that it is easier for someone to read code that uses the somewhat English-like `xlDelimited` term than to read 1.

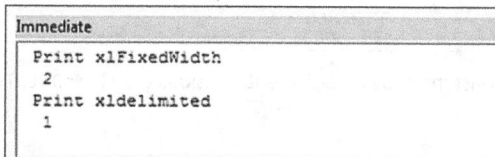

```
Immediate
  Print xlFixedWidth
   2
  Print xldelimited
   1
```

FIGURE 2-4 In the Immediate window of the VB Editor, you can query to see the true value of constants such as `xlFixedWidth`.

If you were an evil programmer, you could certainly memorize all these constants and write code using the numeric equivalents of the constants. However, the programming gods (and the next person who has to look at your code) will curse you for doing so.

In most cases, the Help file either specifically calls out the valid values of the constants or offers a hyperlink that opens the Help topic, showing the complete enumeration and the valid values for the constants (see Figure 2-5).

If you read the Help topic on `OpenText`, you can surmise that it is basically the equivalent of opening a file using the Text Import Wizard. In step 1 of the wizard, you normally choose either Delimited or Fixed Width. You also specify the file origin and at which row to start. This first step of the wizard is handled by these parameters of the `OpenText` method:

```
Origin:=437
StartRow:=1
DataType:=xlDelimited
```

XlColumnDataType enumeration (Excel)

06/08/2017 · 2 minutes to read · 🔲 🔲 🌐 👤

Specifies how a column is to be parsed.

Name	Value	Description
xlDMYFormat	4	DMY date format.
xlDYMFormat	7	DYM date format.
xlEMDFormat	10	EMD date format.
xlGeneralFormat	1	General.
xlMDYFormat	3	MDY date format.
xlMYDFormat	6	MYD date format.
xlSkipColumn	9	Column is not parsed.
xlTextFormat	2	Text.
xlYDMFormat	8	YDM date format.
xlYMDFormat	5	YMD date format.

FIGURE 2-5 Click the hyperlink to see all the possible constant values. Here, the 10 possible `xlColumnDataType` constants are revealed in a new Help topic.

Step 2 of the Text Import Wizard enables you to specify that your fields be delimited by commas. Because you do not want to treat two commas as a single comma, the Treat Consecutive Delimiters As One checkbox should not be selected. Sometimes, a field may contain a comma, such as "XYZ, Inc." In this case, the field should have quotes around the value, as specified in the Text Qualifier box. This second step of the wizard is handled by the following parameters of the OpenText method:

```
TextQualifier:=xlDoubleQuote
ConsecutiveDelimiter:=False
Tab:=False
Semicolon:=False
Comma:=True
Space:=False
Other:=False
```

Step 3 of the wizard is where you actually identify the field types. In this case, you leave all fields as General except for the first field, which is marked as a date in MDY (Month, Day, Year) format. This is represented in code by the `FieldInfo` parameter.

The third step of the Text Import Wizard is fairly complex. The entire `FieldInfo` parameter of the `OpenText` method duplicates the choices made in this step of the wizard. If you happen to click the Advanced button on the third step of the wizard, you have an opportunity to specify something other than the default decimal and thousands separators, as well as the setting Trailing Minus For Negative Numbers.

> **Note** Note that the macro recorder does not write code for `DecimalSeparator` or `ThousandsSeparator` unless you change these from the defaults. The macro recorder does, however, always record the `TrailingMinusNumbers` parameter.

Remember that every action you perform in Excel while recording a macro gets translated to VBA code. In the case of many dialogs, the settings you do not change are often recorded along with the items you do change. When you click OK to close the dialog, the macro recorder often records all the current settings from the dialog in the macro.

Here is another example. The next line of code in the macro is this:

```
Selection.End(xlDown).Select
```

You can click to get help for three topics in this line of code: `Selection`, `End`, and `Select`. Assuming that `Selection` and `Select` are somewhat self-explanatory, click in the word `End` and press F1 for Help.

This Help topic says that `End` is a property. It returns a `Range` object that is equivalent to pressing End+up arrow or End+down arrow in the Excel interface (see Figure 2-6). If you click the blue hyperlink for `xlDirection`, you see the valid parameters that can be passed to the `End` function.

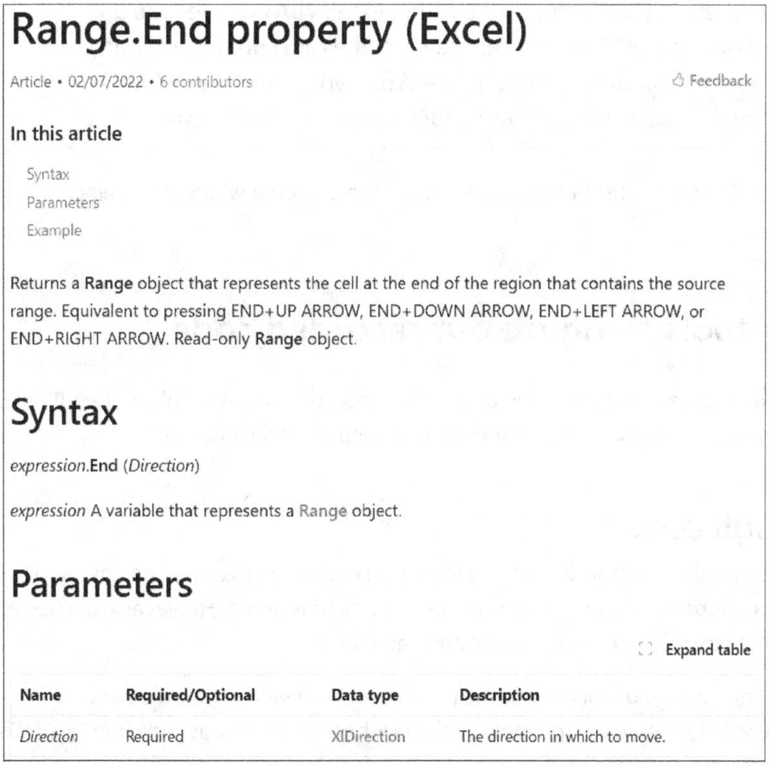

Range.End property (Excel)

Article • 02/07/2022 • 6 contributors Feedback

In this article

Syntax
Parameters
Example

Returns a **Range** object that represents the cell at the end of the region that contains the source range. Equivalent to pressing END+UP ARROW, END+DOWN ARROW, END+LEFT ARROW, or END+RIGHT ARROW. Read-only **Range** object.

Syntax

expression.**End** (*Direction*)

expression A variable that represents a Range object.

Parameters

Expand table

Name	Required/Optional	Data type	Description
Direction	Required	XlDirection	The direction in which to move.

FIGURE 2-6 The correct Help topic for the End property.

Properties can return objects

In VBA, some properties give you simple values—like a number, a string, or True/False. But other properties give you something more powerful—another object. This is called *returning an object*. For example, the End(xlDown) property doesn't just give you a value—it gives you a Range object that represents a specific cell. Once you have that object, you can do things with it, like select it, read its contents, or format it.

Consider the line of code currently under examination:

```
Selection.End(xlDown).Select
```

The End keyword is a property, but from the Help file, you see that it returns a Range object. You then call Select on that returned object. In the end, you're calling a method (Select) on the result of a property (End). You'll do this often in VBA when a property gives you an object you can immediately act on.

Selection **is actually a property of** Application

Selection might look like an object, but if you bring up the help topic for Selection, you'll see that it is actually a property. In reality, the proper code would be Application.Selection. However, when you are writing code within Excel, VBA assumes you are referring to the Excel object model, so you can leave off the Application prefix. If you were to automate Excel from another program, like Word, you'd need to include an object reference before the Selection property, such as ExcelApp.Selection.

Selection can return different types of objects. It returns the object of whatever is selected, such as cells, charts, etc.

Using debugging tools to figure out recorded code

The following sections introduce some awesome debugging tools that are available in the VB Editor. These tools are excellent for helping you see what a recorded macro code is doing.

Stepping through code

Generally, a macro runs quickly: You start it, and less than a second later, it's done. If something goes wrong, you don't have an opportunity to figure out what the macro is doing. However, using Excel's Step Into feature makes it possible to run one line of code at a time.

To use this feature, make sure your cursor is in the procedure you want to run, such as the ImportInvoice procedure, and then from the menu, select Debug | Step Into, as shown in Figure 2-7. Alternatively, you can press F8.

The VB Editor is now in Break mode. The line about to be executed is highlighted in yellow, with a yellow arrow in the margin before the code (see Figure 2-8).

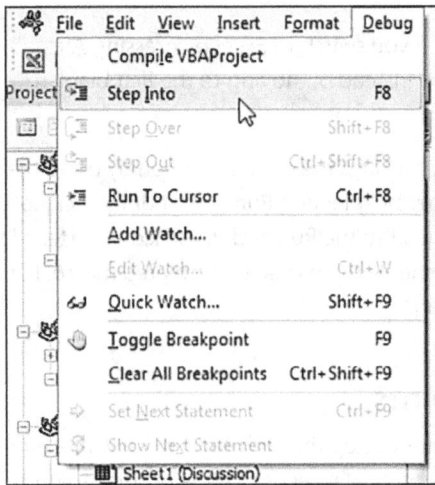

FIGURE 2-7 You can use the Step Into feature to run a single line of code at a time.

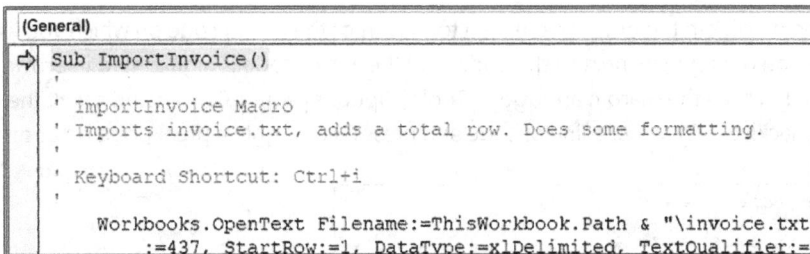

FIGURE 2-8 The first line of the macro is about to run.

In this case, the next line to be executed is the Sub ImportInvoice() line. This basically says, "You are about to start running this procedure." Press the F8 key to execute the line in yellow and move to the next line of code. The long code for OpenText is then highlighted. Press F8 to run this line of code. When you see that Selection.End(xlDown).Select is highlighted, you know that Visual Basic has finished running the OpenText command. At this point, you can press Alt+Tab to switch to Excel and see that the Invoice.txt file has been parsed into Excel. Note that A1 is selected.

> **Tip** If you have a wide monitor, you can use the Restore Down icon at the top right of the VBA window to arrange the window so that you can see both the VBA window and the Excel window. (Restore Down is the two-tiled window icon between the Minimize "dash" and the Close Window *X* icon at the top of every maximized window).
>
> This is also a great trick to use while recording new code. You can actually watch the code appear as you do things in Excel.

Switch back to the VB Editor by pressing Alt+Tab. The next line about to be executed is `Selection.End(xlDown).Select`. Press F8 to run this code. Switch to Excel to see that the last cell in your data set is selected.

Press F8 again to run the `Range("A11").Select` line. If you switch to Excel by pressing Alt+Tab, you see that this is where the macro starts to have problems. Instead of moving to the first blank row, the program moves to the wrong row.

Now that you have identified the problem area, you can stop the code execution by using the Reset command. You can start the Reset command either by selecting Run | Reset or by clicking the Reset button on the toolbar (the small blue square next to the Run and Pause icons). After clicking Reset, you should return to Excel and undo anything done by the partially completed macro. In this case, you need to close the Invoice.txt file without saving.

More debugging options: Breakpoints

If you have hundreds of lines of code, you might not want to step through each line one at a time. If you have a general idea that a problem is happening in one particular section of the program, you can set a breakpoint. You can then have the code start to run, but the macro pauses just before it executes the breakpoint line of code.

To set a breakpoint, click in the gray margin area to the left of the line of code on which you want to break. A large maroon dot appears next to this code, and the line of code is highlighted in brown (see Figure 2-9). (If you don't see the margin area, go to Tools | Options | Editor Format and select the Margin Indicator Bar checkbox.) Or select a line of code and press F9 to toggle a breakpoint on or off.

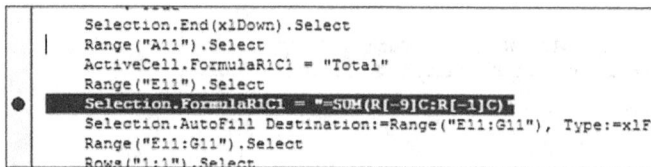

```
    Selection.End(xlDown).Select
    Range("A11").Select
    ActiveCell.FormulaR1C1 = "Total"
    Range("E11").Select
    Selection.FormulaR1C1 = "=SUM(R[-9]C:R[-1]C)"
    Selection.AutoFill Destination:=Range("E11:G11"), Type:=xlFi
    Range("E11:G11").Select
    Rows("1:1").Select
```

FIGURE 2-9   The large maroon dot signifies a breakpoint.

Next, from the Visual Basic menu, select Run | Run Sub/UserForm or press F5. The program executes but stops just before running the line in the breakpoint. The VB Editor shows the breakpoint line highlighted in yellow. You can now press F8 to begin stepping through the code.

After you have finished debugging your code, remove the breakpoints by clicking the dark brown dot in the margin next to each breakpoint to toggle it off. Alternatively, you can select Debug | Clear All Breakpoints or press Ctrl+Shift+F9 to clear all breakpoints that you set in the project.

Backing up or moving forward in code

When you are stepping through code, you might want to jump over some lines of code, or you might have corrected some lines of code that you want to run again. This is easy to do when you are working in Break mode. One favorite method is to use the mouse to grab the yellow arrow. The cursor changes to a three-arrow icon, which enables you to move the next line up or down. Drag the yellow line to whichever line you want to execute next. The other option is to right-click the line to which you want to jump and then select Set Next Statement.

Not stepping through each line of code

When you are stepping through code, you might want to run a section of code without stepping through each line, such as when you get to a loop. You might want VBA to run through the loop 100 times so you can step through the lines after the loop. It is particularly monotonous to press the F8 key hundreds of times to step through a loop. Instead, click the cursor on the line you want to step to and then press Ctrl+F8 or select Debug | Run To Cursor. This command is also available in the right-click menu.

Querying anything while stepping through code

Even though variables have not yet been discussed, you can query the value of anything while in Break mode. However, keep in mind that the macro recorder never records a variable.

Using the Immediate window

Press Ctrl+G to display the Immediate window in the VB Editor. While the macro is in Break mode, you can ask the VB Editor to tell you the currently selected cell, the name of the active sheet, or the value of any variable. Figure 2-10 shows several examples of queries typed into the Immediate window.

```
Immediate
Print Selection.address
$A$6
Print Selection.Value
6/8/2017
Print ActiveSheet.Name
invoice
```

FIGURE 2-10 Queries that can be typed into the Immediate window while a macro is in Break mode, shown along with their answers.

> **Tip** Instead of typing `Print`, you can type a question mark: `? Selection.Address`. Read the question mark as, "What is."

When invoked with Ctrl+G, the Immediate window usually appears at the bottom of the code window. You can use the resize handle, which is located above the Immediate title bar, to make the window larger or smaller.

There is a scrollbar on the side of the Immediate window that you can use to scroll backward or forward through past entries.

It is not necessary to run queries only at the bottom of the Immediate window. For example, if you have just run a line of code, type ?Selection.Address in the Immediate window to ensure that this line of code worked.

Next, press the F8 key to run the next line of code. Instead of retyping the same query, in the Immediate window, click anywhere in the line that contains the last query and press Enter. The Immediate window runs this query again, displays the results on the next line, and pushes the old results farther down the window.

You also can use this method to change the query by clicking to the right of the word Address in the Immediate window. Press the Backspace key to erase the word Address and instead type Columns.Count. Press Enter, and the Immediate window shows the number of columns in the selection.

This is an excellent technique to use when you are trying to figure out a sticky bit of code. For example, you can query the name of the active sheet (?ActiveSheet.Name), the selection (?Selection. Address), the active cell (?ActiveCell.Address), the formula in the active cell (?ActiveCell.Formula), the value of the active cell (?ActiveCell.Value or ?ActiveCell because Value is the default property of a cell), and so on.

To dismiss the Immediate window, click the X in its upper-right corner.

> **Note** Ctrl+G does not toggle the window off. Use the X at the top right of the Immediate window to close it.

> **Tip** The Immediate window is a very useful tool, and I always have it and the Watches window open. If your monitor is big enough, I highly recommend this setup. If you have multiple monitors, you can move these windows to another monitor.

Querying by hovering

In many instances, you can hover the cursor over an expression in code and then wait a second for a tooltip to show the current value of the expression. This is incredibly helpful when you get to looping in Chapter 5, "Looping and flow control." It also comes in handy with recorded code. Note that the expression that you hover over does not have to be in the line of code just executed. In Figure 2-11, Visual Basic just selected E11, making E11 the active cell. If you hover the cursor over ActiveCell.FormulaR1C1, you see a tooltip showing that the formula in the active cell is "=SUM(R[-9]C:R[-1]C)".

```
        Range("A11").Select
        ActiveCell.FormulaR1C1 = "Total"
ActiveCell.FormulaR1C1 = "=SUM(R[-9]C:R[-1]C)"
        Selection.FormulaR1C1 = "=SUM(R[-9]C:R[-1]C)"
        Selection.AutoFill Destination:=Range("E11:G11"), Type:=xlFillDefault
        Range("E11:G11").Select
```

FIGURE 2-11 Hover the mouse cursor over any expression for a few seconds, and a tooltip shows the current value of the expression.

Sometimes, the VBA window seems to not respond to hovering. Because some expressions are not supposed to show values, it is difficult to tell whether VBA is not displaying a value on purpose or whether you are in the buggy "not responding" mode. Try hovering over something that you know should respond, such as a variable. If you get no response, hover, click into the variable, and continue to hover. This tends to wake Excel from its stupor, and hovering works again.

Are you impressed yet? This chapter started with a complaint that VBA doesn't seem much like BASIC. However, by now, you have to admit that the Visual Basic environment is great to work in and that the debugging tools are excellent.

Querying by using a Watches window

In Visual Basic, a watch is not something you wear on your wrist; instead, it allows you to watch the value of any expression while you step through code. Let's say that in the current example, you want to watch to see what is selected as the code runs. You can do this by setting up a watch for Selection.Address.

From the Debug menu, select Add Watch. In the Add Watch dialog, enter **Selection.Address** in the Expression text box and click OK (see Figure 2-12).

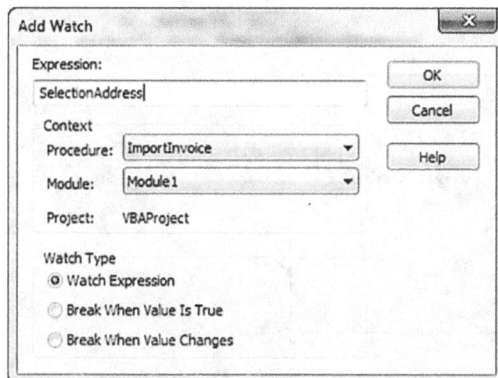

FIGURE 2-12 Setting up a watch to see the address of the current selection.

A Watches window is added to the busy Visual Basic window, usually at the bottom of the code window. When you start stepping through the code, it imports the file and then selects the last row with data. The Watches window confirms that Selection.Address is $A$18 (see Figure 2-13).

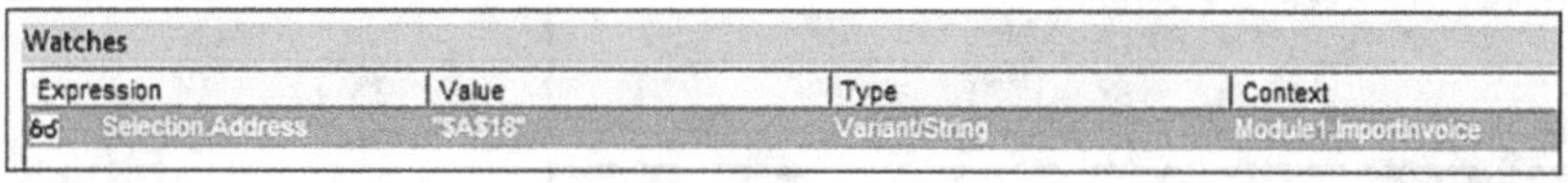

FIGURE 2-13 Without having to hover or type in the Immediate window, you can always see the value of watched expressions.

Press the F8 key to run the code to the line after Rows("1:1").Select. The Watches window is updated to show that the current address of the Selection is now $1:$1.

In the Watches window, the value column is read/write (where possible)! You can type a new value here and see it change on the worksheet. For example, if your watch expression is `Selection.Value`, you can click on the value and enter a new one.

Using a watch to set a breakpoint

Right-click the `Selection.Address` expression in the Watches window and select Edit Watch. In the Watch Type section of the Edit Watch dialog, select Break When Value Changes. Click OK.

The glasses icon to the left of the expression changes to a hand with a triangle icon. You can now press F5 to run the code. The macro starts running lines of code until something new is selected. This is very powerful. Instead of having to step through each line of code, you can now conveniently have the macro stop only when something important has happened. You also can set up a watch to stop when the value of a particular variable changes.

Using a watch on an object

In the preceding example, you watched a specific property: `Selection.Address`. It is also possible to watch an object such as `Selection`. In Figure 2-14, when a watch has been set up on `Selection`, you get the glasses icon and a + icon.

```
        Selection.End(xlDown).Select
⇨       Range("A11").Select
        ActiveCell.FormulaR1C1 = "Total"
        Range("E11").Select
        Selection.FormulaR1C1 = "=SUM(R[-9]C:R[-1]C)"
        Selection.AutoFill Destination:=Range("E11:G11"), Type:=xlFillDefault
        Range("E11:G11").Select
        Rows("1:1").Select
        Selection.Font.Bold = True
        Rows("11:11").Select
        Selection.Font.Bold = True
        Selection.CurrentRegion.Select
        Selection.Columns.AutoFit
    End Sub
    Sub ImportInvoicesRelative()
    '
    ' ImportInvoicesRelative Macro
    ' Import Invoice.txt, Total Row. Format.
    '
    ' Keyboard Shortcut: Ctrl+j
    '
        Workbooks.OpenText Filename:="G:\2016VBA\SampleFiles\invoice.txt", Origin
            437, StartRow:=1, DataType:=xlDelimited, TextQualifier:=xlDoubleQuote
            ConsecutiveDelimiter:=False, Tab:=False, Semicolon:=False, Comma:=Tru
            , Space:=False, Other:=False, FieldInfo:=Array(Array(1, 3), Array(2,
            Array(3, 1), Array(4, 1), Array(5, 1), Array(6, 1), Array(7, 1)), Tra
            :=True
        Selection.End(xlDown).Select
        ActiveCell.Offset(1, 0).Range("A1").Select
```

Expression	Value	Type	Context
⊞ Selection	6/5/2017	Object/Range	Module1.ImportInvoice
Selection.Address	"$A$18"	Variant/String	Module1.ImportInvoice

FIGURE 2-14 Setting a watch on an object gives you a + icon next to the glasses.

By clicking the + icon, you can see all the properties associated with `Selection`. When you look at Figure 2-15, you can see more than you ever wanted to know about `Selection`! There are properties you probably never realized are available. You can see that the AddIndent property is set to False, and the AllowEdit property is set to True. There are useful properties further down in the list, such as the Formula of the selection.

In this Watches window, some entries can be expanded. For example, the Borders collection has a + next to it, which means you can click any + icon to see more details.

Expression	Value	Type
Selection	6/5/2017	Object/Range
AddIndent	False	Variant/Boolean
AllowEdit	True	Boolean
Application		Application/Application
Areas		Areas/Areas
Borders		Borders/Borders
Cells		Range/Range
Column	1	Long
ColumnWidth	8.43	Variant/Double
Comment	Nothing	Comment
Count	1	Long
CountLarge	1^	Variant/LongLong
Creator	xlCreatorCode	XlCreator
CurrentArray	<No cells were found.>	Range
CurrentRegion		Range/Range
Dependents	<No cells were found.>	Range
DirectDependents	<No cells were found.>	Range

FIGURE 2-15 Clicking the + icon shows a plethora of properties and their current values.

Object Browser: The ultimate reference

In the VB Editor, press F2 to open the Object Browser, which lets you browse and search the entire Excel object library. The built-in Object Browser is always available; you simply press the F2 key. The next few pages show you how to use it.

By default, the Object Browser opens where the code window normally appears. However, you can resize the window and reposition it anywhere you like, including on another monitor.

The topmost dropdown currently shows <All Libraries>. There are entries in this dropdown for Excel, Office, VBA, and each workbook that you have open, plus additional entries for anything you check in Tools | References. For now, go to the dropdown and select Excel.

In the bottom-left window of the Object Browser is a list of all classes available for Excel (see Figure 2-16). Click the Application class in the left window. The right window adjusts to show all properties and methods that apply to the Application object. Click something in the right window, such as ActiveCell. The bottom window of the Object Browser tells you that ActiveCell is a property that returns a range. It also tells you that ActiveCell is read-only (an alert that you cannot assign an address to ActiveCell to move the cell pointer).

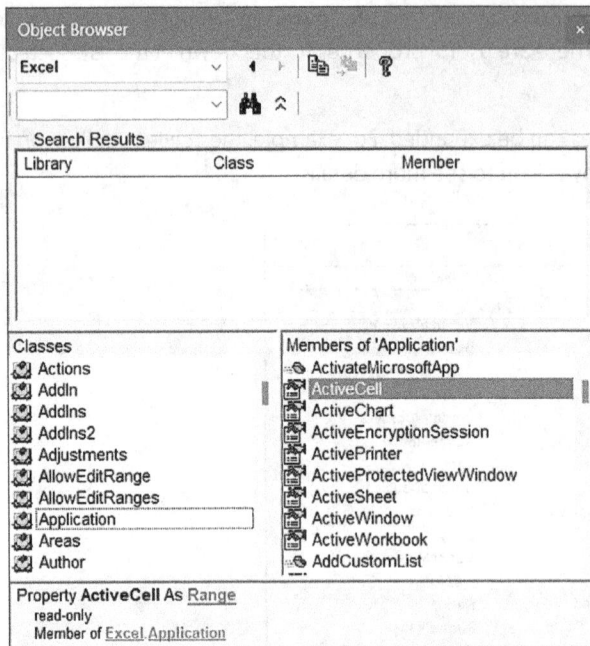

FIGURE 2-16 The Object Browser lets you explore objects, properties, methods, constants, and enumerations available in the VBA environment.

You have learned from the Object Browser that `ActiveCell` returns a range. When you click the hyperlink for `Range` in the bottom window, the Classes and Members windows update to show you all the properties and methods that apply to `Range` objects and, hence, to the `ActiveCell` property. Click any property or method and then click the yellow question mark near the top of the Object Browser to go to the online Help topic for that property or method.

Type any term in the text box in the Search field (next to the binoculars) and press Enter to find all matching members of the Excel library. Methods appear as green books with speed lines. Properties appear as index cards, each with a hand pointing to it.

The search capabilities and hyperlinks available in the Object Browser make it much more valuable than an alphabetic printed listing of all the information. Learn to make use of the Object Browser in the VBA window by pressing F2. To close the Object Browser and return to your code window, click the *X* in the upper-right corner.

> **Tip** If you've maximized the Object Browser and are having trouble returning it to a floating window, try this: Drag it to the left or right edge of the VB Editor to dock it there. Once docked, move it back to the center of the code window—at that point, it should return to a resizable floating window.

Seven tips for cleaning up recorded code

Chapter 1 gave you four tips for recording code. So far, this chapter has covered how to understand the recorded code, how to access VBA help for any word, and how to use the excellent VBA debugging tools to step through your code. The remainder of this chapter presents seven tips to use when cleaning up recorded code.

Tip 1: Don't select anything

Nothing screams "recorded code" more than having code that selects things before acting on them. This makes sense in a way: In the Excel interface, you have to select row 1 before you can make it bold.

However, this is rarely done in VBA. There are a couple of exceptions to this rule. For example, you need to select a point on a chart before you can change its properties.

To streamline the code the macro recorder gives you, in many cases, you can remove the part of the code that performs the selection. The following two lines are macro recorder code before it has been streamlined:

```
Cells.Select
Selection.Columns.AutoFit
```

You can streamline the recorded code so it looks like this:

```
Cells.Columns.AutoFit
```

There are a couple of advantages to doing this streamlining. First, there will be half as many lines of code in your program. Second, the program will run faster because Excel does not have to redraw the screen after the lines that perform the selection.

After recording code, you can do this streamlining by highlighting the code from before the word Select at the end of one line all the way to the dot after the word Selection on the next line. Then, press Delete (see Figures 2-17 and 2-18).

```
    Range("E11:G11").Select
    Rows("1:1").Select
    Selection.Font.Bold = True
    Rows("11:11").Select
    Selection.Font.Bold = True
    Selection.CurrentRegion.Select
    Selection.Columns.AutoFit
End Sub
```

FIGURE 2-17 Select the part of the code highlighted here...

```
        Selection.End(xlDown).Select
        Selection.Offset(1, 0).Select
        Range("A11").FormulaR1C1 = "Total"
        Range("E11").FormulaR1C1 = "=SUM(R[-9]C:R[-1]C)"
        Range("E11").AutoFill Destination:=Range("E11:G11"), Type:=xlFillDefault
        Rows("1:1").Font.Bold = True
        Rows("11:11").Font.Bold = True
        Range("A1").CurrentRegion.Columns.AutoFit
    End Sub
```

FIGURE 2-18 ...and press the Delete key. This is Cleaning Up Recorded Macros 101.

Tip 2: Use `Cells(2,5)` because it's more convenient than `Range("E2")`

The macro recorder uses the `Range()` property frequently. If you follow the macro recorder's example, you will find yourself building a lot of complicated code. For example, if you have the row number for the total row stored in a variable `TotalRow`, you might try to build this code:

```
Range("E" & TotalRow).Formula = "=SUM(E2:E" & TotalRow-1 & ")"
```

In this code, you are using concatenation to join the letter *E* with the current value of the `TotalRow` variable. This works, but eventually, you have to refer to a range where the column is stored in a variable. Say that `FinalCol` is 10, which indicates column J. The column in the `Range` property must always be a letter, so you have to do something like this:

```
FinalColLetter = MID("ABCDEFGHIJKLMNOPQRSTUVWXYZ",FinalCol,1)
Range(FinalColLetter & "2").Select
```

Alternatively, perhaps you could do something like this:

```
FinalColLetter = CHR(64 + FinalCol)
Range(FinalColLetter & "2").Select
```

These approaches work for the first 26 columns but fail for the remaining 99.85 percent of the columns.

You could start to write 10-line functions to calculate that the column letter for column 15896 is WMJ, but it is not necessary. Instead of using `Range("WMJ17")`, you can use the `Cells(Row,Column)` syntax.

Chapter 3, "Referring to ranges, names, and tables," covers this topic in complete detail. However, for now, you need to understand that `Range("E10")` and `Cells(10, 5)` both point to the cell at the intersection of the fifth column and the tenth row. Chapter 3 also shows you how to use `.Resize` to point to a rectangular range. `Cells(11, 5).Resize(1, 3)` is E11:G11.

Tip 3: Use more reliable ways to find the last row

It is difficult to trust data from just anywhere. If you are analyzing data in Excel, remember that the data can come from who-knows-what system written who-knows-how-long-ago. The universal truth is that eventually, some clerk will find a way to break the source system and enter a record without an invoice number. Maybe it will take a power failure to do it, but invariably, you cannot count on having every cell filled in.

This is a problem when you're using the End+down arrow shortcut. This key combination does not take you to the last row with data in the worksheet. It takes you to the last row with data in the current range. In Figure 2-19, pressing End+down arrow would move the cursor to cell A7 rather than the true last row with data.

One better solution is to start at the bottom of the worksheet and look for the first non-blank cell by using this:

```
FinalRow = Cells(Rows.Count, 1).End(xlUp).Row
```

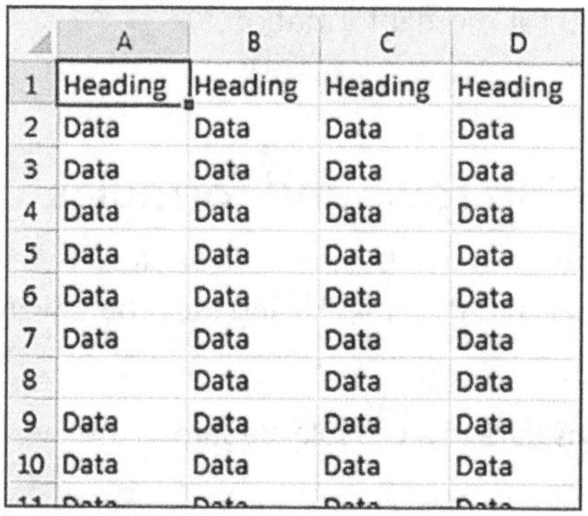

◢	A	B	C	D
1	Heading	Heading	Heading	Heading
2	Data	Data	Data	Data
3	Data	Data	Data	Data
4	Data	Data	Data	Data
5	Data	Data	Data	Data
6	Data	Data	Data	Data
7	Data	Data	Data	Data
8		Data	Data	Data
9	Data	Data	Data	Data
10	Data	Data	Data	Data
11	Data	Data	Data	Data

FIGURE 2-19 End+down arrow fails in the user interface if a record is missing a value. Similarly, End(xlDown) fails in Excel VBA.

This method could fail if the very last record happens to contain the blank row. If the data is dense enough that there will always be a diagonal path of non-blank cells to the last row, you could use this:

```
FinalRow = Cells(1,1).CurrentRegion.Rows.Count
```

If you are sure that there are not any notes or stray activated cells below the data set, you might try this:

```
FinalRow = Cells(1, 1).SpecialCells(xlLastCell).Row
```

The xlLastCell property is often wrong. Say that you have data in A1:F500. If you accidentally press Ctrl+down arrow from A500, you will arrive at A1048576. If you then apply Bold to the empty cell, it becomes activated. Or, if you type **Total** and then clear the cell, it becomes activated. At this point, xlLastCell will refer to F1048576.

Another method is to use the Find method:

```
FinalRow = Cells.Find("*", SearchOrder:=xlByRows, _
    SearchDirection:=xlPrevious).Row
```

You will have to choose from these various methods based on the nature of your data set. If you are not sure, you could loop through all the columns. If you are expecting seven columns of data, you could use this code:

```
FinalRow = 0
For i = 1 to 7
  ThisFinal = Cells(Rows.Count, i).End(xlUp).Row
  If ThisFinal > FinalRow then FinalRow = ThisFinal
Next i
```

> **Note** ListObjects—Excel tables created by selecting Insert | Table—have their own set of properties that make some things, such as finding the last row used in the table, a lot easier. See "Referencing tables aka ListObjects" in Chapter 3 for more information.

Tip 4: Use variables to avoid hard-coding rows and formulas

The macro recorder never records a variable. Variables are easy to use, but just as in BASIC, a variable can remember a value. Variables are discussed in more detail in Chapter 4, "Laying the groundwork with variables and structures."

It is recommended that you set the last row that contains data to a variable. Be sure to use meaningful variable names such as FinalRow:

```
FinalRow = Cells(Rows.Count, 1).End(xlUp).Row
```

When you know the row number of the last record, put the word *Total* in column A of the next row:

```
Cells(FinalRow + 1, 1).Value = "Total"
```

You can even use the variable when building this formula, which totals everything from E2 to the FinalRow of E:

```
Cells(FinalRow + 1, 5).Formula = "=SUM(E2:E" & FinalRow & ")"
```

Tip 5: Use R1C1 formulas that make your life easier

The macro recorder often writes formulas in an arcane R1C1 style. However, most people change the code back to use a regular A1-style formula. After reading Chapter 6, "R1C1 style formulas," you'll understand that there are times when you can build an R1C1 formula that is much simpler than the corresponding A1-style formula. By using an R1C1 formula, you can add totals to all three cells in the total row with the following:

```
Cells(FinalRow+1, 5).Resize(1, 3).FormulaR1C1 = "=SUM(R2C:R[-1]C)"
```

Tip 6: Copy and paste in a single statement

Recorded code is notorious for copying a range, selecting another range, and then doing an `ActiveSheet.Paste`. The Copy method, as it applies to a range, is actually much more powerful. You can specify what to copy and also specify the destination in one statement.

Here's the recorded code:

```
Range("E14").Select
Selection.Copy
Range("F14:G14").Select
ActiveSheet.Paste
```

Here's better code:

```
Range("E14").Copy Destination:=Range("F14:G14")
```

Tip 7: Use `With...End With` to perform multiple actions

If you are making the total row bold with double underline, a larger font, and a special color, you might get recorded code like this:

```
Range("A14:G14").Select
Selection.Font.Bold = True
Selection.Font.Size = 12
Selection.Font.ColorIndex = 5
Selection.Font.Underline = xlUnderlineStyleDoubleAccounting
```

For four of these lines of code, VBA must resolve the expression `Selection.Font`. Because you have four lines that all refer to the same object, you can name the object once at the top of a `With` block. Inside the `With...End With` block, everything that starts with a period is assumed to refer to the `With` object:

```
With Range("A14:G14").Font
    .Bold = True
    .Size = 12
    .ColorIndex = 5
    .Underline = xlUnderlineStyleDoubleAccounting
End With
```

See Chapter 4 for more information on using `With...End With` blocks.

Case study: Putting it all together—Fixing the recorded code

Using the seven tips discussed in the preceding section, you can convert the recorded code from Chapter 1 into efficient, professional-looking code. Here is the code as recorded by the macro recorder at the end of Chapter 1:

```
Sub FormatInvoice3()
'ImportInvoice Macro
Workbooks.OpenText Filename:="C:\Data\invoice.txt", Origin:=437, _
    StartRow:=1, DataType:=xlDelimited, TextQualifier:=xlDoubleQuote, _
    ConsecutiveDelimiter:=False, Tab:=False, Semicolon:=False, _
    Comma:=True, Space:=False, Other:=False, FieldInfo:=Array( _
    Array(1, 3), Array(2, 1), Array(3, 1), Array(4, 1), _
    Array(5, 1), Array(6, 1), Array(7, 1)), TrailingMinusNumbers:=True
Selection.End(xlDown).Select
ActiveCell.Offset(1, 0).Range("A1").Select
ActiveCell.FormulaR1C1 = "Total"
ActiveCell.Offset(0, 4).Range("A1").Select
Selection.FormulaR1C1 = "=SUM(R2C:R[-1]C)"
Selection.AutoFill Destination:=ActiveCell.Range("A1:C1"), Type:= _
    xlFillDefault
ActiveCell.Range("A1:C1").Select
ActiveCell.Rows("1:1").EntireRow.Select
ActiveCell.Activate
Selection.Font.Bold = True
Application.Goto Reference:="R1C1:R1C7"
Selection.Font.Bold = True
Selection.CurrentRegion.Select
Selection.Columns.AutoFit
End Sub
```

Follow these steps to clean up the recorded macro code:

1. Leave the `Workbook.OpenText` lines alone; they are fine as recorded.

2. Note that the following line of code attempts to locate the final row of data so that the program knows where to enter the total row:

   ```
   Selection.End(xlDown).Select
   ```

3. You do not need to select anything to find the last row. It also helps to assign the row number of the final row and the total row to a variable so that they can be used later. To handle the unexpected case in which a single cell in column A is blank, start at the bottom of the worksheet and go up to find the last-used row:

   ```
   'Find the last row with data. This might change every day
   FinalRow = Cells(Rows.Count, 1).End(xlUp).Row
   TotalRow = FinalRow + 1
   ```

   Note that these lines of code enter the word `Total` in column A of the total row:

   ```
   ActiveCell.Offset(1, 0).Range("A1").Select
   ActiveCell.FormulaR1C1 = "Total"
   ```

Better code uses the `TotalRow` variable to locate where to enter the word `Total`. Again, there is no need to select the cell before entering the label:

```
'Build a Total row below this
Cells(TotalRow,1).Value = "Total"
```

4. Note that these lines of code enter the `Total` formula in column E and copy it to the next two columns:

```
ActiveCell.Offset(0, 4).Range("A1").Select
Selection.FormulaR1C1 = "=SUM(R2C:R[-1]C)"
Selection.AutoFill Destination:=ActiveCell.Range("A1:C1"), Type:= _
  xlFillDefault
ActiveCell.Range("A1:C1").Select
```

There is no reason to do all this selecting. The following line enters the formula in three cells:

```
Cells(TotalRow,5).Resize(1, 3).FormulaR1C1 = "=SUM(R2C:R[-1]C)"
```

(The R1C1 style of formulas is discussed in Chapter 6.)

5. Note that the macro recorder selects a range and then applies formatting:

```
ActiveCell.Rows("1:1").EntireRow.Select
ActiveCell.Activate
Selection.Font.Bold = True
Application.Goto Reference:="R1C1:R1C7"
Selection.Font.Bold = True
```

There is no reason to select before applying the formatting. The preceding five lines can be simplified to the two lines below. These two lines perform the same action and do it much more quickly:

```
Cells(1, 1).Resize(1, 7).Font.Bold = True
Cells(TotalRow, 1).Resize(1, 7).Font.Bold = True
```

6. Note that the macro recorder selects all cells before doing the `AutoFit` command:

```
Selection.CurrentRegion.Select
Selection.Columns.AutoFit
```

There is no need to select the cells before doing the `AutoFit`:

```
Cells(1, 1).Resize(TotalRow, 7).Columns.AutoFit
```

(The `Resize` method is discussed in Chapter 3.)

7. Note that the macro recorder adds a short description to the top of each macro:

```
'ImportInvoice Macro
```

You have changed the recorded macro code into something that will actually work, so you should feel free to add your name as author to the description and mention what the macro does:

```
'Written by Bill Jelen. Import invoice.txt and add totals.
```

Here is the final macro with a declaration of variables (see Chapter 4), with all the changes discussed above:

```
Sub FormatInvoiceFixed()
'Written by Bill Jelen. Import invoice.txt and add totals.
Dim TotalRow as Long, FinalRow as Long
Workbooks.OpenText Filename:="C:\Data\invoice.txt", Origin:=437, _
   StartRow:=1, DataType:=xlDelimited, TextQualifier:=xlDoubleQuote, _
   ConsecutiveDelimiter:=False, Tab:=False, Semicolon:=False, _
   Comma:=True, Space:=False, Other:=False, FieldInfo:=Array( _
   Array(1, 3), Array(2, 1), Array(3, 1), Array(4, 1), _
   Array(5, 1), Array(6, 1), Array(7, 1))
FinalRow = Cells(Rows.Count, 1).End(xlUp).Row
TotalRow = FinalRow + 1
Cells(TotalRow, 1).Value = "Total"
Cells(TotalRow, 5).Resize(1, 3).FormulaR1C1 = "=SUM(R2C:R[-1]C)"
Cells(TotalRow, 1).Resize(1, 7).Font.Bold = True
Cells(1, 1).Resize(1, 7).Font.Bold = True
Cells(1, 1).Resize(TotalRow, 7).Columns.AutoFit
End Sub
```

Next steps

By now, you should know how to record a macro. You should also be able to use Help and debugging to figure out how code works. This chapter provides seven tools for making the recorded code look like professional code.

The next chapters go into more detail about referring to ranges, looping, and the crazy but useful R1C1 style of formulas that the macro recorder loves to use.

Referring to ranges, names, and tables

In this chapter, you will:

- Learn how to reference the `Range` object

- Reference a range relative to another range

- Use the `Cells` property to select a range

- Use the `Columns` and `Rows` properties to specify a range

- Use the `Union` and `Intersect` methods to create new ranges based on other ranges

- Use the `IsEmpty` function to check whether a cell is empty

- Use the `CurrentRegion` property to select a data range

- Use the `SpecialCells` property to interact with specific cells in a range

- Use the `Areas` collection to return a noncontiguous range

- Reference ranges in other sheets

- Work with defined names

- Reference tables, also known as `ListObjects`

A range can be a cell, a row, a column, or a grouping of any of these. The `Range` object is probably the most frequently used object in Excel VBA; after all, you're manipulating data on a sheet. Although a range can refer to any grouping of cells on a sheet, it can refer to only one sheet at a time. If you want to refer to ranges on multiple sheets, you must refer to each sheet separately.

A *name,* or *defined name,* is a word you can use to reference a range or hold a formula, string, number, or array. It is particularly useful for holding information between workbook sessions.

An Excel *table* (choose Insert | Table) is a special type of range on a sheet. It shares some properties with defined names but has its own unique methods accessed through the `ListObject` object.

This chapter shows you different ways of referring to ranges, such as specifying a row or column. You'll also find out how to manipulate cells based on the active cell and how to create a new range from overlapping ranges. It also explains different types of names and the various ways you can use them. Finally, you'll learn how to access different parts of tables.

The Range object

The following is the Excel object hierarchy:

```
Application > Workbook > Worksheet > Range
```

The Range object is a property of the Worksheet object. This means it requires that a sheet be active or must reference a worksheet. Both of the following lines mean the same thing if Worksheets(1) is the active sheet:

```
Range("A1")
Worksheets(1).Range("A1")
```

There are several ways to refer to a Range object. Range("A1") is the most identifiable because that is how the macro recorder refers to it. However, all the following are equivalent when referring to cell D5:

```
Range("D5")
[D5]
Range("B3").Range("C3")
Cells(5,4)
Range("A1").Offset(4,3)
Range("MyRange") 'assuming that D5 has a defined name of MyRange
```

Which format you use depends on your needs. Keep reading. It will all make sense soon!

> **Caution**   Using square brackets around a cell address, such as [D5], is a shortcut notation to the Evaluate method, which can convert a string or name to an object or value. While it does allow for shorter code, it can confuse someone else reading your code.

Syntax for specifying a range

The Range object has two acceptable syntaxes. To specify a rectangular range in the first syntax, specify the complete range reference just as you would in a formula in Excel:

```
Range("A1:B5")
```

In the alternative syntax, specify the upper-left corner and lower-right corner of the desired rectangular range. In this syntax, the equivalent statement might be this:

```
Range("A1", "B5")
```

Referencing named ranges

You probably have already used named ranges on your worksheets and in formulas. You can also use them in VBA.

Use the following code to refer to the range "MyRange" in Sheet1:

```
Worksheets("Sheet1").Range("MyRange")
```

Notice the name of the range is in quotes—unlike the use of named ranges in formulas on the sheet itself. If you forget to put the name in quotes, Excel thinks you are referring to a variable in the program.

> **Note** Refer to "Other types of names" later in this chapter to learn how to use names to hold non-range information.

Referencing a range relative to another range

> **Note** Recall that when you recorded a macro in Chapter 1, "Unleashing the power of Excel with VBA," with relative references enabled, the following line was recorded:
>
> ```
> ActiveCell.Offset(0, 4).Range("A1:C1").Select
> ```
>
> I consider this coding style to be very unintuitive. This line of code mentions three addresses, and the actual cell selected is none of them! It seems misleading when you're trying to read this code.
>
> The following information is included because it's how the macro recorder may provide code, and I want you to understand it. The better way of coding would be to use just the Offset property, covered in "Using the Offset property to refer to a range" section later in this chapter.

Typically, the Range object is a property of a worksheet. It is also possible to have Range be the property of another range. In this case, the Range property is relative to the original range, which makes for unintuitive code. Consider this example:

```
Range("B5").Range("C3").Select
```

This code actually selects cell D7, as shown in Figure 3-1. Think about cell C3, which is located two rows below and two columns to the right of cell A1. The preceding line of code starts at cell B5. If we assume that B5 is in the A1 position, VBA finds the cell that would be in the C3 position relative to B5. In other words, VBA finds the cell that is two rows below and two columns to the right of B5, which is D7.

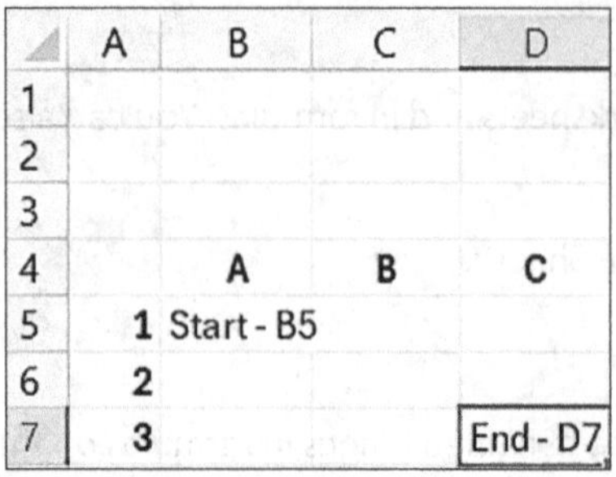

FIGURE 3-1 `Range("B5").Range("C3").Select` selects D7 on the active sheet.

Using the `Cells` property to select a range

The `Cells` property refers to all the cells of the specified `Range` object, which can be a worksheet or a range of cells. For example, this line selects all the cells of the active sheet:

```
Cells.Select
```

> **Note** Using the above line of code isn't recommended because selecting all the cells on a sheet can be very slow.

Using the `Cells` property with the `Range` object is redundant, though it is valid:

```
Range("A1:D5").Cells
```

This line refers to the original `Range` object. However, the `Cells` property has an `Item` property that makes the `Cells` property very useful. The `Item` property enables you to refer to a specific cell using its row and column number, like this:

```
Cells.Item(Row,Column)
```

You must use a numeric value for `Row`, but you may use the numeric value or string value for `Column`. Both of the following lines refer to cell C5:

```
Cells.Item(5,"C")
Cells.Item(5,3)
```

Because the `Item` property is the default property of the `Range` object, you can shorten these lines as follows:

```
Cells(5,"C")
Cells(5,3)
```

The ability to use numeric values for parameters is particularly useful if you need to loop through rows or columns. The macro recorder usually uses something like `Range("A1").Select` for a single cell and `Range("A1:C5").Select` for a range of cells. If you're learning to code only from the recorder, you might be tempted to write code like this:

```
FinalRow = Cells(Rows.Count, 1).End(xlUp).Row
For i = 1 to FinalRow
  Range("A" & i & ":E" & i).Font.Bold = True
Next i
```

This little piece of code, which loops through rows and bolds the cells in columns A through E, is awkward to read and write. But how else can you do it? Like this:

```
FinalRow = Cells(Rows.Count, 1).End(xlUp).Row
For i = 1 to FinalRow
  Cells(i,"A").Resize(,5).Font.Bold = True
Next i
```

Instead of trying to type the range address, the new code uses the `Cells` and `Resize` properties to find the required range based on the active cell. See the "Using the `Resize` property to change the size of a range" section later in this chapter for more information on the `Resize` property.

> **Level Up!**
>
> The examples in this chapter loop through the cells on a sheet. While this method is a good way to learn how to program, it slows Excel down when you're dealing with tens of thousands of rows. To speed up your program, place the range into an array in memory. While you'll still be looping, doing so in memory is much faster.
>
> Refer to Chapter 8, "Arrays," for more information and to level up your programs.

You can use the `Cells` properties for parameters in the `Range` property. The following refers to the range A1:E5:

```
Range(Cells(1,1),Cells(5,5))
```

This is particularly useful when you need to specify variables with a parameter, as in the previous looping example.

Using the `Offset` property to refer to a range

You've already seen a reference to `Offset` when you recorded a relative reference. `Offset` enables you to manipulate a cell based on the location of another cell, such as the active cell. Therefore, you do not need to know the address of the cell you want to manipulate.

The syntax for the `Offset` property is as follows:

```
Range.Offset(RowOffset, ColumnOffset)
```

For example, the following code affects cell F5 from cell A1:

```
Range("A1").Offset(RowOffset:=4, ColumnOffset:=5)
```

Or, shorter yet, you can write this:

```
Range("A1").Offset(4,5)
```

The count of the rows and columns starts at A1 but does not include A1.

If you need to go over only a row or a column but not both, you don't have to enter both the row and the column parameters. To refer to a cell one column over, use one of these lines:

```
Range("A1").Offset(ColumnOffset:=1)
Range("A1").Offset(,1)
```

Both lines have the same meaning, so the choice is yours. If you use the second line, make sure to include the comma so Excel knows that the 1 refers to the ColumnOffset argument. Referring to a cell one row up is similar:

```
Range("B2").Offset(RowOffset:=-1)
Range("B2").Offset(-1)
```

Once again, you can choose which one to use. It's a matter of the readability of the code.

Suppose you have a dataset with ship dates in column C and want to place "Shipped" in column H if there is a ship date and "Pending" if the date hasn't been filled in yet. To do this, loop through column C, looking at the cell value and placing the result five columns to the right of column C, which would place the results in column H.

When used in a Sub and looping through a dataset, it would look like this:

```
Sub MarkShipped()
Dim curCell As Range
For Each curCell In Range("C2:C100")
  If Len(Trim(curCell.Value)) <> 0 Then
    'Trim removes any leading and trailing spaces in the cell
    'Len returns the number of characters after the trim
    curCell.Offset(, 5).Value = "Shipped"
  Else
    curCell.Offset(, 5).Value = "Pending"
  End If
Next curCell
End Sub
```

The status is noted by the program, as shown in Figure 3-2.

Offsetting isn't only for single cells; you can use it with ranges. You can shift the focus of a range over in the same way you can shift the active cell. The following line refers to B2:D4 (see Figure 3-3):

```
Range("A1:C3").Offset(1,1)
```

	A	B	C	D	E	F	G	H
1	Customer Name	Order Date	Ship Date	Product Name	Qty	Price Per	Total	Status
2	John Doe	8/5/2024	8/11/2024	Gadget	37	$2.25	$83.25	Shipped
3	Ashley Taylor	9/29/2024		Doohickey	50	$0.88	$44.00	Pending
4	Emily Davis	8/2/2024	8/14/2024	Thingy 1	47	$1.12	$52.64	Shipped
5	Tom Nguyen	8/27/2024	9/6/2024	Widget B	45	$2.91	$130.95	Shipped
6	Chris Brown	9/7/2024		Doohickey	45	$1.12	$50.40	Pending

FIGURE 3-2 The code enters the shipping status of the order in column H based on whether there is a Ship Date entry in column C.

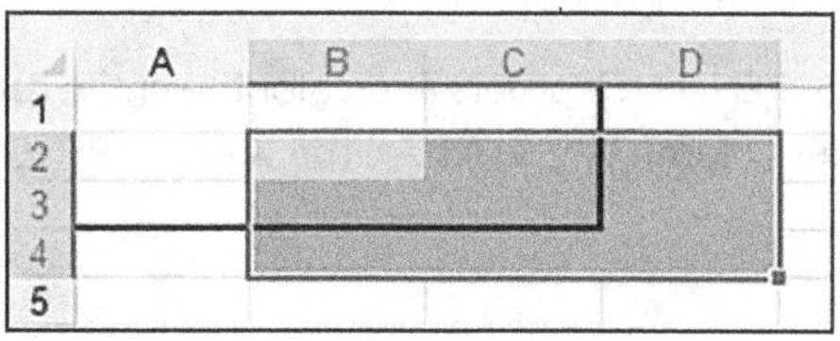

FIGURE 3-3 Offsetting the original range A1:C3 by one row and one column references a new range, B2:D4.

Using the `Resize` property to change the size of a range

The `Resize` property enables you to change the size of a range based on the location of the active cell. For example, if you know the cell a dataset starts in, and you calculate the last used row and column, you can resize the range to encompass the additional rows and columns. This is the syntax for the `Resize` property:

```
Range.Resize(RowSize, ColumnSize)
```

The row and column values include the total number of rows and columns in the final range. To reference the range B3:D13, use the following:

```
Range("B3").Resize(RowSize:=11, ColumnSize:=3)
```

Here's a simpler way to reference this range:

```
Range("B3").Resize(11, 3)
```

But what if you need to resize by only a row or a column—not both? You don't have to enter both the row and the column parameters.

To expand by two columns, use either of the following:

```
Range("B3").Resize(ColumnSize:=2)
```

or

```
Range("B3").Resize(,2)
```

Both lines mean the same thing. The choice is yours. If you use the second line, make sure to include the comma so Excel knows the 2 refers to the `ColumnSize` argument. Resizing just the rows is similar. You can use either of the following:

```
Range("B3").Resize(RowSize:=2)
```

or

```
Range("B3").Resize(2)
```

Once again, the choice is yours. It is a matter of the readability of the code.

From a list of customer orders, you want to find the "PENDING" orders and color the entire row, as shown in Figure 3-4. You would loop through the status column H, and where the value is "PENDING," resize the range to encompass A:H like this:

```
Sub HighlightPending()
Dim curCell As Range
Dim setColor As Integer
For Each curCell In Range("H2:H100")
    'assign the highlight value to a variable
    If UCase(curCell.Value) = "PENDING" Then
        'use UCase or LCase to ensure consistent case
        setColor = 6 'yellow
    Else
        setColor = -4142 'clear color
    End If
    'Resize the selection based on column A
    Cells(curCell.Row, 1).Resize(, 8).Interior.ColorIndex = setColor
Next curCell
End Sub
```

	A	B	C	D	E	F	G	H
1	Customer Name	Order Date	Ship Date	Product Name	Qty	Price Per	Total	Status
2	John Doe	8/5/2024	8/11/2024	Gadget	37	$2.25	$83.25	Shipped
3	Ashley Taylor	9/29/2024		Doohickey	50	$0.88	$44.00	Pending
4	Emily Davis	8/2/2024	8/14/2024	Thingy 1	47	$1.12	$52.64	Shipped
5	Tom Nguyen	8/27/2024	9/6/2024	Widget B	45	$2.91	$130.95	Shipped
6	Chris Brown	9/7/2024		Doohickey	45	$1.12	$50.40	Pending

FIGURE 3-4 You can resize a range to extend the selection.

Because we want the row highlighting to start in column A, the starting cell is set using `Cells(curCell.Row,1)`. From there, we resize the columns to also include columns B to H using `Resize(,8)`. When you're resizing, the starting cell is the upper-left-corner cell of the range.

Resizing isn't only for single cells; you can use it to resize an existing range. For example, if you have a named range consisting of 100 rows but need it and the column next to it, use this:

```
Range("ProductName").Resize(,2)
```

Remember, the number you resize by is the total number of rows/columns you want to include.

Using the `Columns` and `Rows` properties to specify a range

The `Columns` and `Rows` properties refer to the columns and rows of a specified `Range` object, which can be a worksheet or a range of cells. They return a `Range` object referencing the rows or columns of the specified object.

You've seen the following line used, but what is it doing?

```
FinalRow = Cells(Rows.Count, 1).End(xlUp).Row
```

This line of code finds the last row in a sheet in which column A has a value and places the row number of that `Range` object into the variable called `FinalRow`. This can be useful when you need to loop through a sheet row by row; you will know exactly how many rows you need to go through.

> **Note** Some properties of columns and rows require contiguous rows and columns in order to work properly. For example, if you were to use the following line of code, 9 would be the answer because only the first range would be evaluated:
>
> ```
> Range("A1:B9, C10:D19").Rows.Count
> ```
>
> However, if the ranges were grouped separately, the answer would be 19. Excel takes the top-left cell address, A1, and the bottom-right cell address, D19, and counts the rows in the range A1:D19:
>
> ```
> Range("A1:B9", "C10:D19").Rows.Count
> ```

Using the `Union` method to join multiple ranges

The `Union` method enables you to join two or more noncontiguous ranges. It creates a temporary object of the multiple ranges. This enables you to create a single object of multiple ranges you can manipulate efficiently, avoiding the need for repetitive actions on individual ranges:

```
Application.Union(argument1, argument2, etc.)
```

The expression `Application` is not required. The following two procedures use `Union` to create objects of the rows matching particular values. In the first, we're matching the customer name "Bob Johnson," like this:

```
Sub CustomerUnion(ByRef rngUnion As Range)
Dim curCell As Range
For Each curCell In Range("A2:A100")
  If UCase(curCell.Value) = "BOB JOHNSON" Then
    If rngUnion Is Nothing Then
      'the 1st match, we assign to our Union variable
      'because Ranges are objects, we must use Set
      Set rngUnion = Range(Cells(curCell.Row, 1), Cells(curCell.Row, 8))
    Else
```

```
'other matches, we use Union to add it
            Set rngUnion = Union(rngUnion, Range(Cells(curCell.Row, 1), _
                Cells(curCell.Row, 8)))
        End If
    End If
Next curCell
End Sub
```

In the second, we're matching the product name "Widget B," like this:

```
Sub ProductUnion(ByRef rngUnion As Range)
Dim curCell As Range
For Each curCell In Range("D2:D100")
    If UCase(curCell.Value) = "WIDGET B" Then
        If rngUnion Is Nothing Then
            Set rngUnion = Range(Cells(curCell.Row, 1), Cells(curCell.Row, 8))
        Else
            Set rngUnion = Union(rngUnion, Range(Cells(curCell.Row, 1), _
                Cells(curCell.Row, 8)))
        End If
    End If
Next curCell
End Sub
```

In both cases, we're declaring a `ByRef` parameter so we can return the union to the calling proce-dure. Refer to "Controlling argument passing with `ByVal` and `ByRef`" in Chapter 4 to learn about speci-fying how arguments are passed in procedures.

So, what do you do with these separate ranges? Read on to learn how we can generate a report with the common records between the two ranges.

Using the `Intersect` method to create a new range from overlapping ranges

The `Intersect` method returns the cells that overlap between two or more ranges. If there is no over-lap, an error is returned:

```
Application.Intersect(argument1, argument2, etc.)
```

The expression `Application` is not required. In the section "Using the Union method to join multiple ranges," we created two separate ranges with rows that matched specific criteria. Using `Intersect`, we can create a new range with just the rows that are common between the two ranges. Place the results on a sheet and you have a report showing the records where Bob Johnson bought Widget Bs, as shown in Figure 3-5.

Here is the code that brings it all together:

```
Sub Customer_Product_Intersect()
Dim rngCustomer As Range, rngProduct As Range
Dim rngIntersect As Range
```

```
'Call the procedures that will return the ranges with the matching rows
CustomerUnion rngCustomer
ProductUnion rngProduct
'run an Intersect on those two returned ranges
Set rngIntersect = Intersect(rngCustomer, rngProduct)
'check if rngIntersect has a value (Not Nothing means there is something)
If Not rngIntersect Is Nothing Then
   'we have a matching customer and product
   'copy over header, without formatting
   Worksheets("Report").Range("A1:H1").Value = Range("A1:H1").Value
   'place data results
   rngIntersect.Copy Worksheets("Report").Range("A2")
Else
   'no matches, inform user
   MsgBox "No Customer/Product matches found"
End If
'clear the object variables
Set rngIntersect = Nothing
Set rngCustomer = Nothing
Set rngProduct = Nothing
End Sub
```

> **Note** Refer to the section "Using Set to assign object variables" in Chapter 4 to learn more about the Set keyword.

▲	A	B	C	D	E	F	G	H
1	Customer Name	Order Date	Ship Date	Product Name	Qty	Price Per	Total	Status
2	Bob Johnson	9/17/2024		Widget B	21	$1.63	$34.23	Pending
3	Bob Johnson	8/5/2024	8/19/2024	Widget B	16	$1.63	$26.08	Shipped
4	Bob Johnson	8/15/2024	8/24/2024	Widget B	49	$1.63	$79.87	Shipped

FIGURE 3-5 By combining the Union and Intersect methods, a report with only the records where Bob Johnson bought Widget B can be generated.

Using the IsEmpty function to check whether a cell is empty

The IsEmpty function returns a Boolean value that indicates whether a single cell is empty: True if empty, and False if not. The cell must truly be empty for the function to return True:

```
IsEmpty(Cell)
```

The issue arises because Excel's definition of empty differs from yours and mine. For example, if you previously had a formula in a cell that returned a blank ("") and then did a paste values to get rid of the formula—Excel does not see the cell as empty; the "" is something to Excel. To truly clear the contents of a cell, you need to use Clear Contents from the cell context menu or press Delete. Refer to the section "Case Study: Using the SpecialCells method to select specific cells" for code that can help you quickly find these fake empty cells.

If you trust the source of your data, then IsEmpty is a good alternative to using Len and Trim to check if a cell is empty. But if in doubt, stick to Len and Trim, as shown in "Using the Offset property to refer to a range" earlier in this chapter. To use IsEmpty instead, change the If statement, like this:

```
If Not IsEmpty(curCell) Then
  curCell.Offset(, 5).Value = "Shipped"
Else
  curCell.Offset(, 5).Value = "Pending"
End If
```

Using the CurrentRegion property to select a data range

CurrentRegion returns a Range object that represents a set of contiguous data. As long as the data is surrounded by one empty row and one empty column—or the edge of the worksheet—you can select the dataset by using CurrentRegion:

```
RangeObject.CurrentRegion
```

> **Caution** What looks empty to you might not be empty to Excel. This can lead to unexpected results when using CurrentRegion.

The following line selects the dataset in columns A:H—even the hidden columns—because this is the contiguous range of cells around cell A1 (see Figure 3-6). Column I is an empty column, so Excel does not include the data in column J:

```
Range("A1").CurrentRegion.Select
```

This is useful if you have a dataset whose size is in constant flux.

	A	B	E	F	G	H	I	J
1	Customer Name	Order Date	Qty	Price Per	Total	Status		Doohickey
2	John Doe	8/5/2024	37	$2.25	$83.25	Shipped		Gadget
3	Ashley Taylor	9/29/2024	50	$0.88	$44.00	Pending		Gizmo
4	Emily Davis	8/2/2024	47	$1.12	$52.64	Shipped		Widget B
5	Tom Nguyen	8/27/2024	45	$2.91	$130.95	Shipped		Thingy 1
6	Chris Brown	9/7/2024	45	$1.12	$50.40	Pending		Widget A

FIGURE 3-6 You can use CurrentRegion to select a range of contiguous data around the active cell.

Case Study: Using the `SpecialCells` method to select specific cells

Even Excel power users might not have encountered the Go To Special dialog. If you press the F5 key in an Excel worksheet, you get the normal Go To dialog (see Figure 3-7). In the lower-left corner of this dialog is a button labeled Special. Click this button to get to the super-powerful Go To Special dialog (see Figure 3-8).

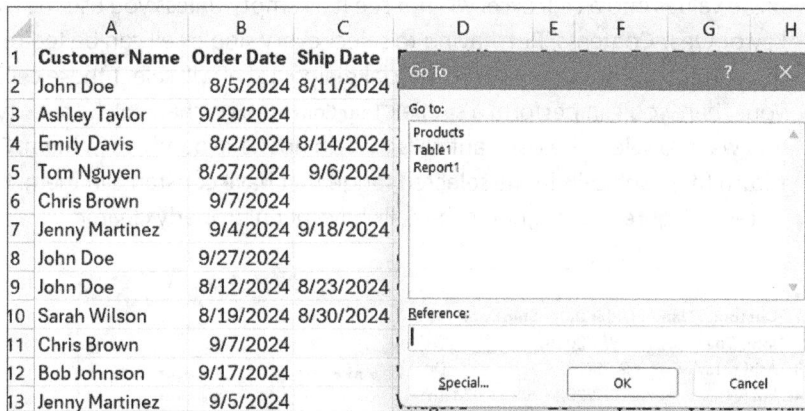

FIGURE 3-7 Although the Go To dialog doesn't seem useful, click the Special button in the lower-left corner to specify what type of cells to select.

In the Excel interface, the Go To Special dialog enables you to select only cells with formulas, only blank cells, or only visible cells. For example, selecting only visible cells is excellent for grabbing the visible results of AutoFiltered data. If you already have a range highlighted, only cells within this range meeting the criteria will be selected. Make sure only one cell is selected to search the entire sheet.

To simulate the Go To Special dialog in VBA, use the `SpecialCells` method. This enables you to act on cells that meet certain criteria, like this:

```
RangeObject.SpecialCells(Type, Value)
```

The `SpecialCells` method has two parameters: `Type` and `Value`. `Type` is one of the `xlCellType` constants:

```
xlCellTypeAllFormatConditions
xlCellTypeAllValidation
xlCellTypeBlanks
xlCellTypeComments
xlCellTypeConstants
xlCellTypeFormulas
xlCellTypeLastCell
xlCellTypeSameFormatConditions
xlCellTypeSameValidation
xlCellTypeVisible
```

Set one of the following optional `Value` constants if you use `xlCellTypeConstants` or `xlCellTypeFormulas`:

```
xlErrors
xlLogical
xlNumbers
xlTextValues
```

In the section on using the `IsEmpty` function, I explained how even when you paste values into a cell, Excel will not see it as empty unless you use the Delete key or Clear Contents. But, having to select every single cell can be tedious. Using the correct options in the Go To Special dialog, Excel will select those cells for you. Then, you can perform a single `ClearContents` on them all. By specifying that you want to select the constant cells that do not have numbers in them, Excel will return the blank cells in the selected range that have constants in them. But, as noted in Figure 3-8, it ignores the cells have been properly cleared.

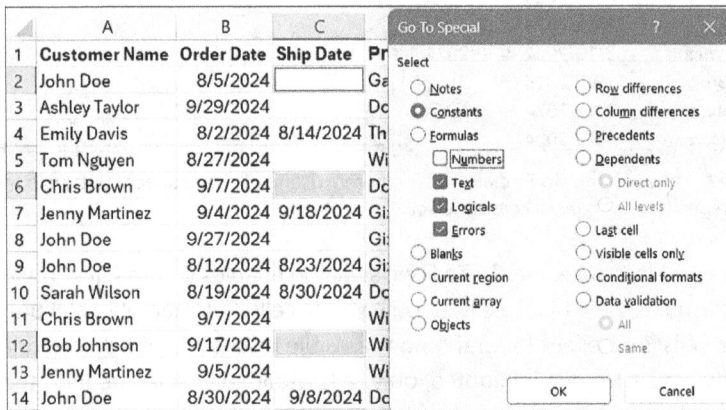

FIGURE 3-8 The Go To Special dialog has many incredibly useful selection tools, such as one for selecting only the fake empty cells on a sheet.

Here is the code to select the cells and then clear the contents, making them truly empty:

```
On Error Resume Next
Set rngFakeEmpty = Range("C2:C100").SpecialCells(xlCellTypeConstants, _
  xlErrors + xlLogical + xlTextValues)
On Error GoTo 0
If Not rngFakeEmpty Is Nothing Then
  rngFakeEmpty.ClearContents
End If
```

Note If you were to record the above steps, instead of xlErrors + xlLogical + xlTextValues, you would see 22 when you review the code. But there isn't a constant with a value of 22 (refer to the section "Using constant values" in Chapter 20 for details on how to get the numerical value behind constants). So where does it come from? By adding up the numerical values of the constants, you get 22: xlErrors(16) + xlLogical (4) + xlTextValues (2).

You can break it out as I did or use the summed value. But keep in mind someone else reading your code may not know what 22 means, or you might forget what you were doing next time you review your code.

Using the Areas collection to return a noncontiguous range

The Areas collection is a collection of noncontiguous ranges within a selection. It consists of individual Range objects representing contiguous ranges of cells within the selection. If a selection contains only one area, the Areas collection contains a single Range object that corresponds to that selection.

You might be tempted to loop through the rows in a sheet and check the properties of a cell in a row, such as its formatting (for example, the font or fill) or whether the cell's value is below a specific number. Then, you could copy the row and paste it into another section. However, there is an easier way. In Figure 3-9, a formula =1/(C2<50) has been entered in column D to identify low inventory items. The formula works like this:

1. C2<50 checks if the quantity in C2 is less than 50.

2. If the quantity is less than 50, indicating a low inventory, the formula returns 1.

3. If the quantity is not less than 50, the formula returns a #DIV/0! error.

We can use the absence of an error to identify the low inventory rows using Specials Cells to copy and paste just the low inventory rows into a report, like this:

```
Set NewDestination = Range("I2")
For Each rng In Range("D1:D16").SpecialCells(xlCellTypeFormulas, _
  xlNumbers).Areas
  'we only want the data, not the helper column
  rng.Offset(, -3).Resize(, 3).Copy Destination:=NewDestination
  'set the variable to the next available row to paste to
  Set NewDestination = NewDestination.Offset(rng.Rows.Count)
Next rng
```

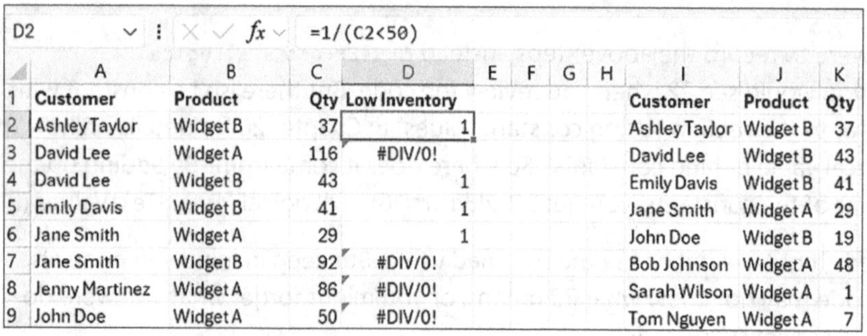

D2 =1/(C2<50)

	A	B	C	D	E	F	G	H	I	J	K
1	Customer	Product	Qty	Low Inventory					Customer	Product	Qty
2	Ashley Taylor	Widget B	37	1					Ashley Taylor	Widget B	37
3	David Lee	Widget A	116	#DIV/0!					David Lee	Widget B	43
4	David Lee	Widget B	43	1					Emily Davis	Widget B	41
5	Emily Davis	Widget B	41	1					Jane Smith	Widget A	29
6	Jane Smith	Widget A	29	1					John Doe	Widget B	19
7	Jane Smith	Widget B	92	#DIV/0!					Bob Johnson	Widget A	48
8	Jenny Martinez	Widget A	86	#DIV/0!					Sarah Wilson	Widget A	1
9	John Doe	Widget A	50	#DIV/0!					Tom Nguyen	Widget A	7

FIGURE 3-9 The `Areas` collection makes it easier to manipulate noncontiguous ranges.

Referencing ranges in other sheets

Switching between sheets by activating the needed sheet slows down your code. To avoid this, refer to a sheet that is not active by first referencing the `Worksheet` object:

```
Worksheets("Sheet1").Range("A1")
```

This line of code references Sheet1 of the active workbook even if Sheet2 is the active sheet.

To reference a range in another workbook, include the `Workbook` object, the `Worksheet` object, and then the `Range` object:

```
Workbooks("InvoiceData.xlsx").Worksheets("Sheet1").Range("A1")
```

To use the `Range` property as an argument within another `Range` property, identify the range fully each time. For example, suppose that Sheet1 is your active sheet and you need to total data from Sheet2:

```
WorksheetFunction.Sum(Worksheets("Sheet2").Range(Range("A1"), _
  Range("A7")))
```

This line does not work. Why not? Although `Range("A1"), Range("A7")` is meant to refer to the sheet at the beginning of the code line (Sheet2), Excel does not assume that you want to carry the `Worksheet` object reference over to these other `Range` objects; instead, Excel assumes that they refer to the active sheet, Sheet1. So, what do you do? Well, you could write this:

```
WorksheetFunction.Sum(Worksheets("Sheet2").Range(Worksheets("Sheet2"). _
  Range("A1"), Worksheets("Sheet2").Range("A7")))
```

However, not only is this a long line of code, but it is also difficult to read! Thankfully, there is a simpler way, using `With...End With`:

```
With Worksheets("Sheet2")
  WorksheetFunction.Sum(.Range(.Range("A1"), .Range("A7")))
End With
```

Notice now there is a `.Range` in your code but without the preceding object reference. That's because `With Worksheets("Sheet2")` implies that the object of the range is that worksheet. Whenever Excel sees a period without an object reference directly to the left of it, it looks up the code for the closest `With` statement and uses that as the object reference. Refer to "Using `With` statements to streamline code" in Chapter 4 for more information.

Working with defined names

You've probably named ranges in a worksheet by highlighting a range and typing a name in the Name box to the left of the formula bar. You also might have created more complicated defined names containing formulas. For example, perhaps you created a name with a formula that finds the last row in a column. The ability to name a range makes it much easier to write formulas.

The ability to create and manipulate defined names is also available in VBA, which provides the same benefits as using names in a workbook. For example, you can store a value in a name. This section will explore the basics of working with defined names in VBA.

Global versus local names

Names that are *global* are available anywhere in a workbook. Names that are *local* are available only on a specific worksheet. With local names, you can have multiple references in the workbook with the same name. Global names must be unique to the workbook. For both types, the name cannot start with a number; it should start with a letter.

> **Caution** While a name may start with an underscore, Excel uses a prefix underscore for names it creates dynamically. These names are not visible from the Name Manager dialog and no error is generated if you reuse the name. To avoid confusion, you may want to avoid starting your names with an underscore. For example, `_DataRange` is a name Excel might create, while `Data_Range` is a perfectly valid name you can define.

The Name Manager dialog (accessed via the Formulas tab) lists all the visible names in a workbook, including queries and listobjects. The Scope column lists the scope of the name, whether it is the workbook or a specific sheet, such as Sheet1.

For example, in Figure 3-10, the Products name is assigned to the Settings sheet and the workbook.

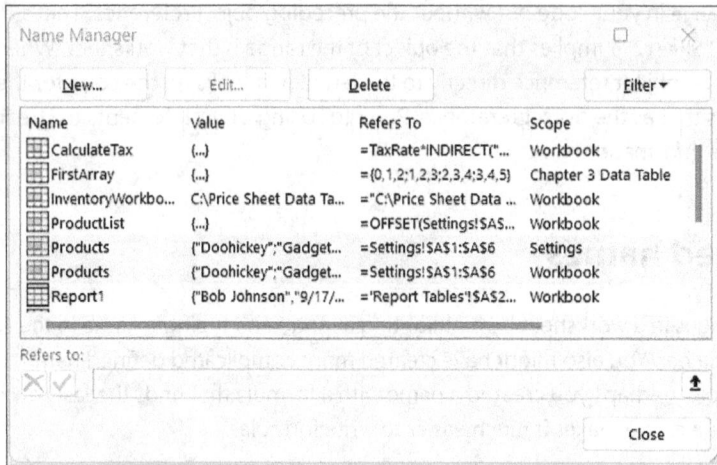

FIGURE 3-10 The Name Manager lists all local and global names.

Creating defined names

The simple syntax for defining a name with code is as follows:

```
Object.Names.Add Name, RefersTo
```

`Object` is not required; if you leave it off, the defined name will default to being a global name. But if you want to create a local name, you must include the sheet object. `Name` is one or more words (no spaces allowed) that you'll use to identify the defined name. `RefersTo` specifies the value associated with the name. It can be a range address, formula, string, number, or an array of values.

> **Tip** Even though the object (for example, `Activeworkbook`) is not required when creating a global name in the active workbook, I include it so there's no doubt where the name is being created.

This section reviews how to add names holding different types of information: ranges, formulas, strings, numbers, and arrays. Reading the information stored in a name depends on the information stored. Refer to "Reading names," later in this chapter, for information on how specific value types are stored.

Adding a named range

If you record the creation of a named range and then view the code, you see something like this:

```
ActiveWorkbook.Names.Add Name:="Products", RefersToR1C1:="=Settings!R1C1:R6C1"
```

This creates a global name `Products`, which includes the range A1:A6 (R1C1:R6C1) on the Settings sheet. The formula is enclosed in quotes, and the equals sign in the range reference must be included.

If the sheet on which the name is created is the active sheet, the sheet reference does not have to be included. However, including the sheet reference can make the code easier to understand.

To create a local name, include the sheet name with the Name argument:

```
ActiveWorkbook.Names.Add Name:="Settings!Products", RefersToR1C1:= _
    "=Settings!R1C1:R6C1"
```

Alternatively, specify that the Names collection belongs to a worksheet:

```
Worksheets("Settings").Names.Add Name:="Products", RefersToR1C1:= _
    "=Settings!R1C1:R6C1"
```

Case Study: Non-absolute references don't always point to the correct range

If a reference is not absolute, the name will be created, but it may not point to the correct range. For example, if you run the following line of code, the name is created in the workbook:

```
ActiveWorkbook.Names.Add Name:="Doohickey", RefersTo:="=Sheet1!A1"
```

However, as you can see in Figure 3-11, the name hasn't been assigned to the correct range. The reference will change depending on which cell is the active cell when the name is viewed or used.

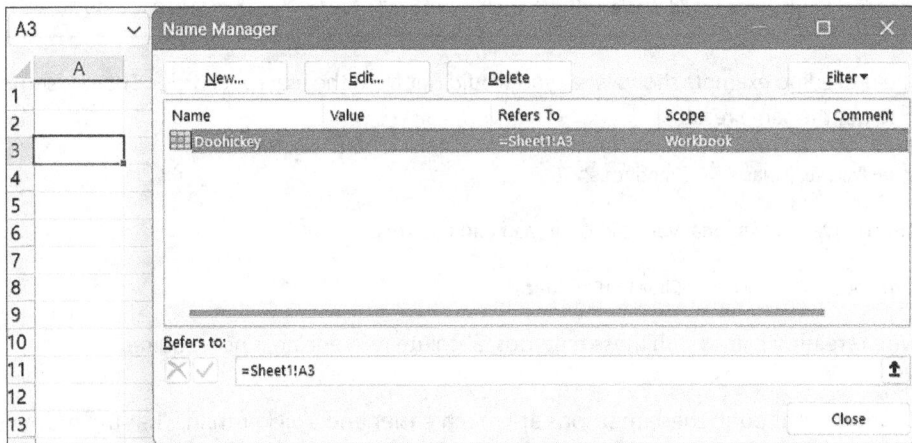

FIGURE 3-11 Despite what was coded, because absolute referencing was not used, Doohickey refers to the active cell.

Why? Because when you're setting up a named range using relative referencing, you have to remember what relative referencing means to Excel. You're telling Excel that *based on the active cell, calculate the relative position of the range I've specified and use that relative positioning from now on.*

Yeah, it was confusing to me the first time I read it. I program in A1 style 99 percent of the time and rarely think in relative referencing. So, I'll break it down.

1. Select B1 on Sheet1.

2. In the Name Manager, create a new Name—**RelName**—and for the RefersTo, enter **=Sheet1!A1.** Click OK and Close.

3. In cell B1, type =**RelName**. It will return what's entered in A1.

4. In cell C5, type =**RelName**. It will return what's entered in B5.

When you typed = `Sheet1!A1` while B1 was selected, Excel interpreted the formula as *always refer to the cell that's one column to the left of the cell where this name is used.* Because by using A1 without dollar signs, you told Excel to store the reference as relative.

So, what does this mean for VBA? Just like in the UI, the selected cell in VBA becomes the anchor point (B1) for Excel to calculate the relative offset. If it helps, consider entering the refers to in R1C1, like this:

```
'Assuming Sheet1 is the active sheet
'This is the anchor cell for the relative reference
Range("B1").Select
'This means: "from wherever it's used, go 0 rows, -1 column"
ThisWorkbook.Names.Add Name:="RelName", RefersToR1C1:="=Sheet1!R[0]C[-1]"
```

The preceding example shows what you would get from the macro recorder. There is some simpler code to get the same result:

```
Range("A1:A6").Name = "Products"
```

Alternatively, for a local variable only, you can use this:

```
Range("A1:A6").Name = "Sheet1!Products"
```

When creating names with these methods, absolute referencing is not required.

> **Caution**   Although these methods are much easier and quicker than what the macro recorder creates, they're limited in that they work only for ranges. Formulas, strings, numbers, and arrays require the use of the Add method, and tables (listobjects) use an entirely different method. Refer to the section "Referencing tables aka ListObjects" for information on working with tables.

Using a named range is fairly straightforward since it's a range. You can use the name directly with the Range object, like this:

```
Set ProductListing = Range("Products")
```

is the same as saying:

```
Set ProductListing = Range("A1:A6")
```

Just remember that if you're accessing a local variable, you must include the sheet name, Settings!Products.

Adding a formula name

The syntax for storing a formula in a name is the same as for a range because the range is essentially a formula. The following code is useful for creating dynamic datasets or for referencing any dynamic listing on which calculations may be performed. This one allows for a dynamic named column with the product listing starting in A2:

```
Names.Add Name:="ProductList", _
   RefersTo:="=OFFSET(Settings!$A$2,0,0,COUNTA(Settings!$A:$A)-1)"
```

> **Tip**   Use the INDIRECT function if you want to create a formula that adjusts as it's copied down. For example, to create the name CalculateTax to calculate tax on items in a table, you might start with =TaxRate*$G2. However, this formula won't work as a defined name because the G2 reference needs to be adjusted. To make it dynamic, use =TaxRate*INDIRECT("G"&ROW()). This way, the formula will reference the correct row as you copy it down.

Just like with named ranges, you can use a named formula directly. To put the formula stored in the CalculateTax name in cells I2:I4, do this:

```
ActiveSheet.Range("I2:I4").Formula = _
   ThisWorkbook.Names("CalculateTax").RefersTo
```

Adding a string name

When using names to hold strings, such as the path to another workbook, enclose the string value in quotation marks. The string being stored cannot have more than 255 characters. Because no formula is involved, an equals sign is not needed. If you were to include an equals sign, Excel would treat the value as a formula. Let Excel include the equals sign shown in the Refers To column of the Name Manager:

```
ThisWorkbook.Names.Add Name:="InventoryWorkbookPath", _
   RefersTo:="C:\Price Sheet Data Tables.xlsm"
```

Figure 3-12 shows how the coded name appears in the Name Manager dialog.

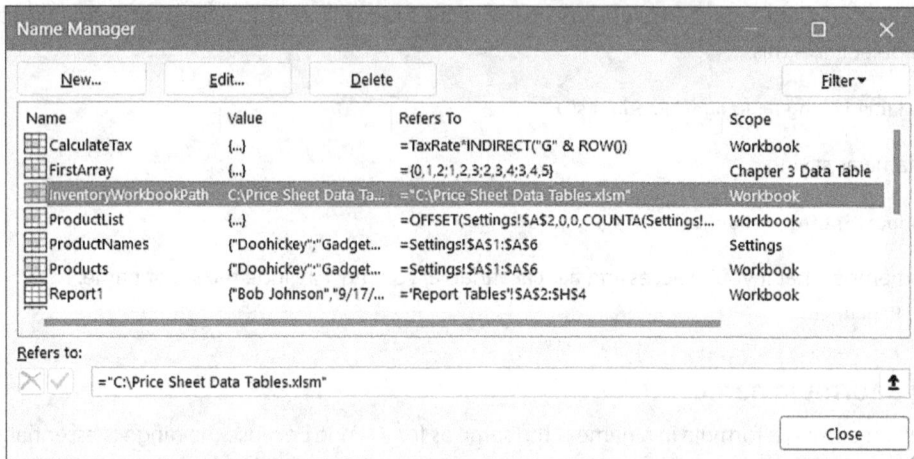

FIGURE 3-12 You can assign a name to a string value.

> **Tip** Because names do not lose their references between sessions, using names is a handy way to store values as opposed to storing values in cells from which the information would have to be retrieved.

For example, if I have a client workbook with a coded path to another file, I make it more flexible by storing the path in a name. Before sending the updated workbook to the client, I update the name to the client's path. I make it even easier by using a program to do the switching, like this:

```
Global Const TracysPC = True
Sub SwitchPaths()
If TracysPC Then
  ThisWorkbook.Names.Add Name:="InventoryWorkbookPath", _
    RefersTo:="C:\Price Sheet\Price Sheet Data Tables.xlsm"
Else
  ThisWorkbook.Names.Add Name:="InventoryWorkbookPath", _
    RefersTo:="C:\Price Sheet Data Tables.xlsm"
End If
End Sub
```

When the constant `TracysPC` is set to `True`, the name is set to a location on my pc, and when it's `False`, it's set to a location specific to the client. I can also reference that constant in other areas where it matters if I'm running the code on my machine or the client's. Refer to Chapter 4, "Laying the groundwork with variables and structures," for more information on `Global Const`.

Unlike with named ranges and formulas, you can't just access and use a string stored in a name. Because Excel wraps the string in quotation marks and precedes it with an equals sign, you'll have to do some cleanup before you can use the string. See "Reading names," later in this chapter, for a function you can use to clean this up.

Adding a number name

You can use names to store numbers between sessions. Here's an example:

```
Names.Add Name:="TaxRate", RefersTo:=0.0425
```

Notice the lack of quotation marks and an equals sign in the `RefersTo` parameter. Using quotation marks changes the number to a string. With the addition of an equals sign in the quotation marks, the number changes to a formula.

But when you attempt to use the number directly from the name, you can't. The preceding equals sign gets included when you extract the `RefersTo` value. See this chapter's "Reading names" section for a function you can use to clean this up.

Adding an array name

A name can hold the data stored in an array. The array size is limited by available memory. See Chapter 8, "Arrays," for more information about coding with arrays.

The following creates an array, `myArray`, and stores it in the name `FirstArray`:

```
Sub NamedArray()
Dim myArray(3,2)
Dim i As Integer, j As Integer
For i = 0 To 3 'by default arrays start at 0
  For j = 0 To 2
    myArray(i, j) = i + j
  Next j
Next i
'The following line takes our array and gives it a name
Names.Add Name:="FirstArray", RefersTo:=myArray
End Sub
```

When you look at the Refers To field in the Name Manager dialog box, you see the following:

```
={0,1,2;1,2,3;2,3,4;3,4,5}
```

You can't do much with the data in this layout. You'll need to reformat it back to a proper array to work with it. Refer to "Reading names," later in this chapter for a function you can use to automate this.

Managing defined names

Once you've created your defined names, you'll want to keep them organized and up-to-date. This section will show you how to rename, comment on, hide, and delete names. It also lists the names reserved for use by Excel.

Renaming names

The name you create becomes an object when referenced like this:

```
ThisWorkbook.Names("Products")
```

The object has many properties, including `Name`, which you can use to rename the existing name, like this:

```
ThisWorkbook.Names("Products").Name = "ProductNames"
```

`Products` no longer exists; `ProductNames` is now the name assigned to the name.

When you are renaming names in which a local reference and a global reference both carry the same name, the previous line renames the local reference if the sheet on which it's defined is the active sheet. Be specific when renaming a local reference.

> **⊖ Caution** If you try to use this method to rename a global and local reference to the same name, Excel will not allow it. No error message is provided.

Adding comments

You can add comments about names, such as why a name was created or where it is used. To insert a comment for the local name `Bob_Johnson`, do this:

```
ThisWorkbook.Worksheets("Widget B Report").Names("Bob_Johnson").Comment = _
   "3rd quarter orders"
```

The comments appear in a column in the Name Manager, as shown in Figure 3-13.

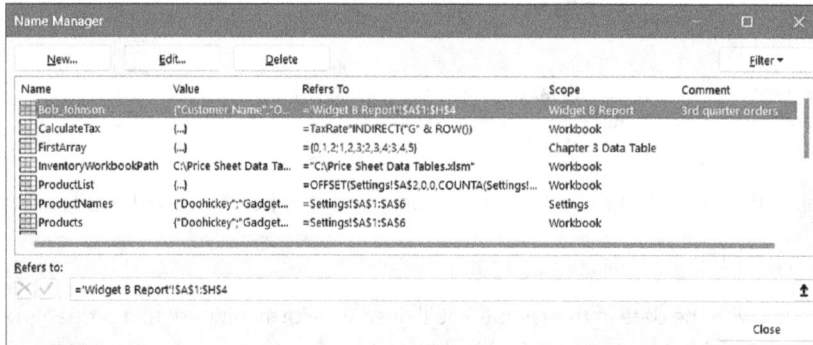

FIGURE 3-13 You can add comments about names to help remember their purpose.

> **⚠ Warning** The name must exist before a comment can be added to it.

Hiding names

Names are incredibly useful, but you don't necessarily want to see all the names you have created. Like many other objects, names have a `Visible` property. To hide a name, set the `Visible` property to `False`. To unhide a name, set the `Visible` property to `True`:

```
ThisWorkbook.Names.Add Name:="Products", RefersTo:="=$A$1:$A$6", Visible:=False
```

Reserved names

Excel uses local names of its own to keep track of information. These local names are considered reserved, and if you use them for your own references, they might cause problems. You should also be careful about mixing numbers and letters in names since they may be cell addresses, such as `LOG2` and `R123C7`. And even though `R123Y` is not a valid cell reference, it's close enough that Excel displays an error message, preventing the creation of the name.

Highlight an area on a sheet. Then, from the Page Layout tab, select Print Area | Set Print Area.

As shown in Figure 3-14, a `Print_Area` listing is in the Name field. Deselect the area and look again in the Name field drop-down menu. The name is still listed there. Select it, and the print area that was previously set is now highlighted. If you save, close, and reopen the workbook, `Print_Area` is still set to the same range. `Print_Area` is a local name reserved by Excel for its own use.

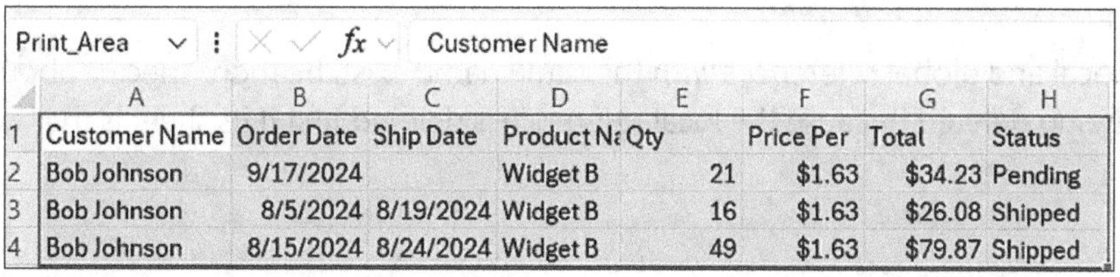

	A	B	C	D	E	F	G	H
1	Customer Name	Order Date	Ship Date	Product Na	Qty	Price Per	Total	Status
2	Bob Johnson	9/17/2024		Widget B	21	$1.63	$34.23	Pending
3	Bob Johnson	8/5/2024	8/19/2024	Widget B	16	$1.63	$26.08	Shipped
4	Bob Johnson	8/15/2024	8/24/2024	Widget B	49	$1.63	$79.87	Shipped

Name box: Print_Area   fx   Customer Name

FIGURE 3-14 Excel creates its own names.

Note   Each sheet has its own print area. In addition, setting a new print area on a sheet that has an existing print area overwrites the original print-area name.

Fortunately, Excel does not have a large list of reserved names:

```
Criteria
Database
Extract
Print_Area
Print_Titles
```

`Criteria` and `Extract` are used when Advanced Filter (on the Data tab, select Advanced from the Sort & Filter group) is configured to extract the results of the filter to a new location.

`Database` is no longer required in Excel. However, some features, such as Data Form, still recognize it. Legacy versions of Excel used it to identify the data you wanted to manipulate in certain functions.

`Print_Area` is used when a print area is set (from the Page Layout tab, select Print Area | Set Print Area) or when Page Setup options that designate the print area (from the Page Layout tab, Scale) are changed.

`Print_Titles` is used when print titles are set (select Page Layout | Print Titles).

You should avoid using these reserved names, and you should use variations on them with caution. For example, if you create the name PrintTitles, you might accidentally code this:

```
Worksheets("Sheet4").Names("Print_Titles").Delete
```

If you do this, you delete the Excel name rather than your custom name.

Deleting names

Use the `Delete` method to delete a name. For example, to delete the global Products name, do this:

```
ThisWorkbook.Names("Products").Delete
```

An error occurs if you attempt to delete a name that does not exist.

> **Note** If both local and global references with the same name exist, be more specific about which name is being deleted because the local reference is deleted first if its sheet is the active sheet.

Reading names

The `RefersTo` property is how you assign a value to your defined name, and it is also how you can read that value back. The problem is you might not be able to use that value until it's cleaned up. When the value is read, it always starts with an equals sign. In the case of ranges and formulas, you want that equals sign. Unless the value is a number, it's wrapped in quotation marks, which you don't want when returning a string since Excel will already wrap a string in quotation marks.

Ranges can be used directly. You don't even have to use the `Names` object like this:

```
Set ProductListing = Range("Products")
```

Formulas can also be used directly, like this:

```
ActiveSheet.Range("I2:I4").Formula = _
    ThisWorkbook.Names("CalculateTax").RefersTo
```

Strings require the removal of the equals sign and quotation marks. When you read the `RefersTo` value, you get `="C:\Price Sheet Data Tables.xlsm"` when what you want is `C:\Price Sheet Data Tables.xlsm`.

Numbers just need the preceding equals sign removed, so you go from `=0.0425` to `0.0425`.

Arrays require more than a simple clean-up. The `RefersTo` for the name `FirstArray` looks like this `={0,1,2;1,2,3;2,3,4;3,4,5}`, which has little use in this format. To extract the array into a variable in your code, you'll need to use the `Evaluate` method, `Evaluate("FirstArray")`, which will put the values into a 4-row by 3-column array.

Now, you could clean up the values as you code, create a function to do the cleanup as needed, or you can add the following function, `GetValueFromName`, to your code library. It has two parameters: the name of the defined name and, optionally, the name of the sheet if the defined name is local. The function will decipher the type of name and return the `RefersTo` value in a format that you can then assign to a variable.

```
Function GetValueFromName(ByVal myName As String, Optional ByVal SheetName As _
    String) As Variant
Dim Defined_Name As Name
Dim NamedRange As Range
Dim NameValue As Variant
Dim hasRefRange As Boolean
If IsEmpty(SheetName) Then
  Set Defined_Name = ThisWorkbook.Names(myName)
Else
  Set Defined_Name = ThisWorkbook.Worksheets(SheetName).Names(myName)
End If
'ignore any error and continue to the next line
On Error Resume Next
Set NamedRange = Defined_Name.RefersToRange
If Err.Number = 0 Then
  hasRefRange = True
Else
  'no RefersToRange value
  hasRefRange = False
End If
On Error GoTo 0
NameValue = Defined_Name.RefersTo
If hasRefRange = True Then
  'is a range, do nothing
Else
  If StrComp(Mid(NameValue, 2, 1), Chr(34), vbBinaryCompare) = 0 Then
    'check if the 2nd character is a quotation mark
    'is a string
    NameValue = Mid(NameValue, 3, Len(NameValue) - 3)
  ElseIf StrComp(Mid(NameValue, 2, 1), "{", vbBinaryCompare) = 0 Then
    'check if the 2nd character is a curly bracket
    'is an array, so use Evaluate to place it in a VBA type array
    NameValue = Evaluate(NameValue)
  ElseIf IsNumeric(Mid(NameValue, 2)) Then
    'check if starting at the 2nd character the value is a number
    'is a number
    NameValue = Mid(NameValue, 2)
  Else
    'is a formula, do nothing
  End If
End If
```

```
GetValueFromName = NameValue
Set NamedRange = Nothing
Set Defined_Name = Nothing
End Function
```

Referencing tables, a.k.a. `ListObjects`

A table is a special type of range that offers the convenience of referencing defined names. However, tables are not created in the same manner as other ranges. They also have their own set of properties and methods that make working with large datasets a lot easier.

Adding a `ListObject`

Excel tables share some of the properties of defined names, but they also have their own unique methods. Unlike defined ranges, you can't manually create tables by assigning the range to a name; you create them in VBA by using `ListObjects.Add`. The syntax for this method is:

```
ListObjects.Add (SourceType, Source, LinkSource, X1ListObjectHasHeaders, _
    Destination, TableStyleName)
```

To create a table from cells A1:H4, and assuming the data table has column headers, as shown in Figure 3-15, use this:

```
Worksheets("Report Tables").ListObjects.Add(xlSrcRange, Range("$A$1:$H$4"), , _
    xlYes).Name = "Report1"
```

	A	B	C	D	E	F	G	H
	Report1	⌄ : ✕ ✓	*fx* ⌄	Bob Johnson				
	Customer Name ⌄	Order Date ⌄	Ship Date ⌄	Product Name ⌄	Qty ⌄	Price Per ⌄	Total ⌄	Status ⌄
2	Bob Johnson	9/17/2024		Widget B	21	$1.63	$34.23	Pending
3	Bob Johnson	8/5/2024	8/19/2024	Widget B	16	$1.63	$26.08	Shipped
4	Bob Johnson	8/15/2024	8/24/2024	Widget B	49	$1.63	$79.87	Shipped

FIGURE 3-15 You can turn a dataset into an Excel table by assigning a name to it using VBA.

xlSrcRange (the SourceType) tells Excel that the source of the data is an Excel range. You then need to specify the range (the Source) of the table. If you have headers in the table, include that row when indicating the range. The next argument is LinkSource, a Boolean indicating whether there is an external data source. This argument is not used in the preceding example because the SourceType is xlSrcRange. xlYes (X1ListObjectHasHeaders) lets Excel know that the data table has column headers; otherwise, Excel automatically generates them. Destination, which is not shown in the preceding example, is used when SourceType is xlSrcExternal, indicating the upper-left cell where the table will begin. The final argument, TableStyleName, is the name of the style to apply to the table. If left off, then the default style based on the workbook theme will be applied.

Working with `ListObjects`

Although you can reference a table's range by using `Activesheet.Range("Report1")`, you have access to more of the properties and methods that are unique to tables if you use the `ListObjects` object, like this:

```
Activesheet.ListObjects("Report1")
```

This exposes the properties and methods of a table, but you can't use that line to select the table. To select the table, you have to specify the part of the table you want to work with. To select the entire table, including the header and total rows, specify the `Range` property:

```
Activesheet.ListObjects("Report1").Range.Select
```

The table part properties include the following:

- `Range`—Returns the entire table.

- `DataBodyRange`—Returns the data part only.

- `HeaderRowRange`—Returns the header row only.

- `TotalRowRange`—Returns the total row only.

- `ListColumns`—Returns the specified column only.

What I really like about coding with tables is the ease of referencing specific columns of a table. You don't have to know how many columns to move in from a starting position or the letter/number of the column, and you don't have to use a `FIND` function. Instead, you can use the header name of the column. For example, to select the data of the Qty column of the table but not the header or total rows, do this:

```
Activesheet.ListObjects("Report1").ListColumns("Qty") _
    .DataBodyRange.Select
```

To add a new row of data to a table, add a new row to the listobject, and then fill in the values. You can fill in each cell one by one, or you can dump an array of values onto the row. Both methods are shown below:

```
Sub AddData()
Dim tblReport As ListObject
Dim newRow As Long
Dim NewValues
Set tblReport = Worksheets("Report Tables").ListObjects("Report1")
With tblReport
    'place the new row at the bottom
    .ListRows.Add
    'get the position of the new row
    newRow = .DataBodyRange.Rows.Count

    'add some values one by one
    .DataBodyRange.Cells(newRow, 1).Value = "Bob Johnson"
    .DataBodyRange.Cells(newRow, 4).Value = "Widget B"
    .DataBodyRange.Cells(newRow, 5).Value = 34
```

```
    'dump an array
    NewValues = Array("Bob Johnson", , , "Widget B", 34, "", "", "")
    .ListRows.Add
    newRow = .DataBodyRange.Rows.Count
    .ListRows(newRow).Range.Value = NewValues
    End With
Set tblReport = Nothing
End Sub
```

> ⊖ **Caution**   In the second method, where we build and dump an array, you'll notice that when building the array, I was able to simply put commas for the first set of skipped columns, but I had to use "" to mark the other empty columns. That's because the array I dump must have the same number of elements as the range.

> 🗒 **Note**   For more details on coding with tables, check out *Excel Tables: A Complete Guide for Creating, Using, and Automating Lists and Tables* by Zack Barresse and Kevin Jones (ISBN: 9781615470280).

Next steps

The foundation laid in this chapter, covering ranges, names, and listobjects, is crucial for Excel programming. The next chapter builds on this knowledge, exploring essential programming techniques to enhance code clarity and efficiency. By mastering variable declaration, parameter passing, object assignment, and constant definition, you'll write code that is easier to understand and execute.

CHAPTER 4

Laying the groundwork with variables and structures

In this chapter, you will:

- Learn how to declare variables and control where they can be used and how long they keep their values.

- Understand the difference between `Sub` and `Function` procedures and how to define and use each one correctly.

- Use `ByVal` and `ByRef` to control whether procedures work with a copy or the original variable.

- Return values or objects from a function and use `Set` and parentheses properly when calling them.

- Write cleaner, more efficient code using `With...End With` blocks.

- Simplify your code by using meaningful names instead of numbers—especially useful for things like column headers or custom settings.

- Write flexible code for different environments using compiler directives like `#Const` and `#If...Then`.

This chapter holds the tidbits of programming that don't quite fit anywhere else—but they matter. These are the small distinctions that separate the skilled programmer from the just-get-it-working programmer. Some of them make your code easier to write. Others make it easier to read. All of them help you write cleaner, more reliable code that's easier to maintain when things get complicated.

Declaring and assigning variables

A *variable* is a name you assign to hold a value in your code, similar to Excel's defined names that can hold a value. That value can be a number, a string, a date, an object—pretty much anything you work with in code. You declare variables to give yourself a place to store and manipulate data as your program runs. Declaring them is not required, but I recommend them to help the compiler catch errors.

An example of declaring a variable to hold a row number would look like this:

```
Dim FinalRow as Long
```

- **Dim** The declaration type that sets the scope

- **FinalRow** The variable name

  - Must be one word; spaces not allowed

  - Must start with a letter

  - Can include underscores (_) but no other punctuation

- **Long** The variable type

Keep reading to learn about the different data types and how you control the lifetime and scope of variables.

> **Tip** By default, Excel does not require variable declaration. Under Tools | Options | Editor is the setting Require Variable Declaration. Selecting this option forces the compiler to stop if it finds a variable that it does not recognize, which reduces misspelled variable names. Declaring variables with certain data types is important to catch data type-related errors. Option Explicit will appear at the top of every module if this option is turned on. Note that for existing modules, you'll have to type Option Explicit at the top of a module.

Variable data types

A *data type* is a rule that defines what kind of data the variable can hold. When you declare a variable, you also define its data type. There was a time when computers were slower, and you had to carefully consider what data type you needed. With today's faster computers, speed isn't as much of a factor, but you still have to apply the correct type. Here are some of the commonly used data types:

- **Long** Whole numbers within the range –2,147,483,648 to 2,147,483,647

- **Integer** Whole number within the range –32,768 to 32,767

- **Double** Decimal numbers with high precision. It can handle much larger (and smaller) values than Long, and keeps about 15 digits of accuracy, even with decimals

- **String** Text

- **Boolean** True or False

- **Object** Excel structures such as Workbook, Range, etc.

> **Note** While you'll still see Integer used, it's becoming less common. Long allows for a wider range of values and performs just as fast. If you assign Long now, you won't have to worry about your variables unexpectedly exceeding the limits of Integer in the future.

Variable lifetime and scope

When you declare a variable, you're not just picking a name and a type—you're also deciding where it's visible and how long it lasts. Scope controls which parts of your code can access the variable. Lifetime controls whether it disappears when a procedure ends or whether it stays in memory and keeps its value until the workbook closes. A variable might exist only inside a single procedure, across an entire module, or throughout the whole workbook. The table below shows how your declaration type determines both scope and lifetime.

TABLE 4-1 Variable visibility and duration in VBA

Declaration Type	Valid Declaration Location(s)	Scope	Lifetime
Dim (inside procedure)	Inside procedures	Only in that procedure	Only while the procedure runs
Static	Inside procedures	Only in that procedure	Retains value between calls to that procedure
Dim (at module level)	Top of a standard or class module	Only inside that module	As long as the module is loaded
Private (module level)	Top of a standard or class module	Only inside that module	As long as the workbook is open
Public (module level)	Top of a standard module only	All procedures in the project	As long as the workbook is open
Const	Inside procedures or at the module level	Matches location: procedure or module	Fixed value, persists for session duration
Global (legacy, replaced by Public)	Top of a standard module only	All procedures in the project	As long as the workbook is open

Declaration Do's and Don'ts

Some keywords can be combined when declaring variables, but not all combinations make sense or even work. The rules are simple once you know them, and they help avoid unnecessary errors or confusion. Below are some common combinations, along with a couple that can cause issues if you're not paying attention:

- Create a constant available anywhere in the project.

  ```
  Public Const AppVersion As String = "1.0"
  ```

- Limit the constant to any procedure within the current module.

  ```
  Private Const CompanyName As String = "Acme Corp"
  ```

- The following is not valid. You can't combine Static and Const—Const values don't change, and Static implies a changing value that's remembered.

  ```
  Static Const something = 5
  ```

- The following is redundant. Just use Private—Dim is implied and unnecessary at the module level.

  ```
  Private Dim total As Long
  ```

Declaring constants for safety and clarity

Constants are exactly what they sound like—fixed values that never change while the code runs. You can declare them inside a procedure or at the top of a module. At the module level, they can be `Private` or `Public`, depending on whether you want them to be used just within a specific module or available anywhere in the workbook. (Refer to Table 4-1, "Variable visibility and duration in VBA.")

You'll often see constants declared without a data type. VBA will infer the type based on the value you assign:

```
Const TaxRate = 0.075
Const AppName = "Inventory Tracker"
```

This works, but it's not always the best approach. In some cases, especially with numeric values, VBA might not infer the type you actually want. To make your intent clear and avoid surprises, it's better to specify the type explicitly:

```
Const TaxRate As Double = 0.075
Const AppName As String = "Inventory Tracker"
```

One common beginner mistake is using a constant when you need a variable, usually in loops or counters. If you're planning to change the value, it can't be a constant. The following would generate an error:

```
Const Total = 0
Total = Total + 1
```

Constants are a great way to lock down values that shouldn't be touched and make your code easier to read. Once you get in the habit of using them for things like version names, default settings, and calculation thresholds, they become second nature.

> ## Level Up!
>
> When I'm working with a client who's comfortable in the VB Editor, I'll put any constants they may want to change at the very top of a module (after any `Option` statements). That way, they're easy to find and update without digging through the rest of the code. I also like to make my public constants stand out visually. I used to use all caps, but these days, I prefer multiple words separated by an underscore, like this:
>
> ```
> Public Const Troubleshooting_Mode = True
> ```
>
> It keeps things legible without shouting at you.

Using `Set` to assign object variables

At this point, you've seen a variable that contains a single value, like `TotalSales = 0`. That's a normal variable; it stores one value, like a number or a string. But there's another kind of variable: an *object variable*. Instead of holding a simple value, it holds a reference to an entire structure, such as a worksheet, a range, or a chart. These variables don't hold just a value; they hold access to the object itself, along with its properties (`Worksheet.Name`) and methods (`Worksheet.Copy`).

To work with object variables, you need to do two things:

1. Declare the variable with a specific object type, such as Worksheet.

2. Use the `Set` keyword to assign it to a real object.

For example, to assign a worksheet and range to object variables, do this:

```
'Declare the object types
Dim mySheet as Worksheet
Dim myRange as Range
'Assign the variables to real objects
Set mySheet = ThisWorkbook.Worksheets("Report")
Set myRange = mySheet.Range("A1:D5")
```

As you can see in the above example, once we assign the Report sheet to the variable `mySheet`, we can use that object variable in our code instead of typing out the full sheet reference. Not only does this make code easier to read, but it's also faster to type.

And you don't lose anything by using an object variable instead of the full reference—you still get tool tips, autocomplete, and full access to the object's properties and methods while writing your code.

Level Up!

You can declare an object variable outside a procedure, but you can only assign the object within a procedure. For example, if you have multiple procedures that need to work with the same sheet, you can do something like this:

```
'At the top of a module
Public curSheet As Worksheet

Sub InitializeSheet(ByVal SheetName As String)
'initialize the object to the specific sheet
Set curSheet = ThisWorkbook.Worksheets(SheetName)
End Sub

Sub DoSomethingToSheet()
'good coding behavior : check if the variable is assigned
If curSheet Is Nothing Then
  MsgBox "Current sheet Not Set"
Else
  With curSheet
    'do things to the sheet
  End With
End If
End Sub
```

Notice that neither procedure includes `Set curSheet = Nothing` (see "Releasing object variables"). That's intentional—there may be other procedures that need to reference the object. Instead, you'll want to either clear the object at the end of your main routine or create a cleanup procedure that releases any public variables once your program is finished running.

Releasing object variables

After you're done working with an object variable, you release it by setting it to `Nothing`:

```
Set mySheet = Nothing
```

This tells VBA to release the object reference and free the memory. In small projects, this isn't always necessary—VBA will clean up when the procedure ends or the workbook closes. But in larger projects, especially ones that hold on to lots of object references (like open workbooks, ranges, or pivot tables), clearing them explicitly is good practice.

It's not always mandatory—but it is smart housekeeping.

Controlling argument passing with `ByVal` and `ByRef`

When you call a procedure like a `Sub` or `Function`, you can send it extra information to work with—this is called "passing an argument." The variables you send are called *parameters*, and they let the procedure perform its task using the data you provide.

In this example, the `Test` procedure declares a variable, `userName`, and passes it to `SayHello`, which uses the value in a message:

```
Sub Test()
Dim userName As String
userName = "Tracy"
SayHello userName
End Sub

Sub SayHello(ByVal name As String)
MsgBox "Hello, " & name
End Sub
```

Whether the procedure can modify that variable depends on how you pass it:

- `ByVal` (by value): The procedure gets a copy.

- `ByRef` (by reference): The procedure gets a pointer to the original.

- If you omit both, VBA assumes `ByRef`—so it's safer to explicitly use `ByVal` when you want to protect the original.

The following example demonstrates what happens when a variable is passed `ByVal` versus `ByRef`:

```
Sub Test()
Dim ourNumber As Integer
ourNumber = 5
PassByVal ourNumber
Debug.Print ourNumber 'Still 5
PassByRef ourNumber
Debug.Print ourNumber 'Now 15
End Sub

Sub PassByVal(ByVal num As Integer)
num = num + 10
End Sub

Sub PassByRef(ByRef num As Integer)
num = num + 10
End Sub
```

In `PassByVal`, the procedure changes its own copy of the value, so the original stays the same. In `PassByRef`, the procedure is given a pointer to the original variable, so the change affects the original.

> **Note** Always match the parameter type to the variable type you're passing. VBA will try to convert types, but with `ByRef`, unexpected changes can occur.

Why object variables are different

With regular variables like numbers and strings, `ByVal` truly means "hands off the original." But with object variables, such as collections, ranges, worksheets, or custom objects, it's different. Passing an object `ByVal` does not copy the object. It just protects the reference (the envelope), not the contents.

> **Note** Arrays aren't declared as objects, but when passed to a procedure, they behave the same way as object variables: only the reference (pointer) is protected by `ByVal`, not the contents.

```
Sub Test_ByVal ()
Dim myList As Collection
Set myList = New Collection 'Initialize the collection
myList.Add "One"
AddItem myList
Debug.Print myList.Count 'Now 2
End Sub

Sub AddItem (ByVal myList As Collection)
myList.Add "Two"
End Sub
```

Even though `myList` is passed `ByVal`, the `AddItem` procedure can still add to the original collection because it holds a pointer to the same object. However, if you reassign the object entirely, then that change won't affect the original:

```
Sub ChangeCollection(ByVal myList As Collection)
Set myList = New Collection 'new object
myList.Add "Test"
End Sub
```

Setting `myList` to a new collection creates a new object in memory. The original collection in the calling procedure remains unchanged.

If passing an object `ByVal` still lets you change its contents, what's the point of using `ByRef`? Because `ByRef` allows you to replace the entire object—not just modify its contents. The following procedure compares two collections. If `newCollection` has more entries in it, then it replaces `curCollection`:

```
Sub ReplaceIfBetter(ByRef curCollection As Collection, _
  ByVal newCollection As Collection)
If newCollection.Count > curCollection.Count Then
  Set curCollection = newCollection
End If
End Sub
```

You can think of it like this:

- `ByVal`—hands off the envelope, but you can change what's inside

- `ByRef`—you can swap the envelope and its contents

If you really need to protect the contents, you must build protections into your code—such as creating your own collection object. That technique is shown in the next case study.

Case Study: Creating a read-only collection

If you want to pass a `Collection` into a procedure and guarantee that it won't be modified, VBA doesn't have a built-in way to enforce that. But you build a read-only version of a collection using a class module.

> **Note** Refer to Chapter 9, "Creating custom objects and collections," for more information on custom objects.

Here's a basic outline of a read-only custom collection:

1. Create a class module named `ReadOnlyCollection`

2. Enter the following code:

   ```
   Private pItems As Collection

   Public Sub Init(ByVal inputCol As Collection)
   ```

```
            Set pItems = inputCol
            End Sub

            Public Property Get Count() As Long
            Count = pItems.Count
            End Property

            Public Property Get Item(ByVal index As Long) As Variant
            Item = pItems(index)
            End Property
```

This class stores a reference to a `Collection`, but does not expose any way to modify it—only to read its contents. You can use the class like this:

```
Dim rawData As New Collection
rawData.Add "Apple"
rawData.Add "Banana"
'declare and call the class module
Dim safeData As New ReadOnlyCollection
safeData.Init rawData
'safeData points to the same collection as rawData
'but only exposes read-only access through the custom properties
'in ReadOnlyCollection
Debug.Print safeData.Item(1) 'Apple
Debug.Print safeData.Count '2
```

In this case, `safeData` gives you access to the original data—but without any ability to call `.Add`, `.Remove`, or reassign the contents. If you hand `safeData` to another procedure or object, it can read the collection, but not change it. This is a simple but powerful way to protect important data structures while still making them accessible where needed.

Managing code variations with compiler directives

Have you ever seen `#Const` or `#If...Then` in VBA code and wondered what the `#` meant?

These are compiler directives—special instructions to VBA that affect how code is compiled before it runs. Unlike regular `If...Then` statements, compiler directives decide which blocks of code to include at compile time, instead of while the code is running, which is how it's normally done. This means that the excluded code might not even be part of the final compiled version.

This is especially useful when you want to:

■ Test different versions of your code.

■ Show extra messages or logging while debugging.

■ Hide sensitive or environment-specific logic from production.

In the following example, if `Debug_Mode` is set to `True`, the procedure prints a message to the Immediate window. If it's set to `False`, it shows a message box instead. This allows you to maintain one set of code, but toggle specific sections depending on your current needs.

```
#Const Debug_Mode = True

Sub RunTask()
#If Debug_Mode Then
  Debug.Print "Debug mode active"
#Else
  MsgBox "Production mode"
#End If
End Sub
```

Does # Always Mean Compiler Directive?

Not always! In VBA, the # symbol has multiple meanings, and it's only a compiler directive in certain cases.

Compiler directives begin with # at the start of a line and include:

```
#Const
#If...Then
#ElseIf
#Else
#End If
```

These are instructions for the compiler. They control whether specific blocks of code are included when your project is compiled.

Other uses of # are not directives:

- Date literals —Dates are wrapped in # signs:
  ```
  If myDate = #7/4/2025# Then MsgBox "Happy 4th!"
  ```
- # used with a number (0#)—A legacy method of declaring variables as doubles. Nowadays, we use `CDbl(0)`, `Dim DollarsAndCents as Double`, or `Function DoSomething() As Double`.

So, unless it's the first non-space character on the line, # doesn't signal a compiler directive.

> **Note** See "Supporting users with different feature needs" in Chapter 13, "Excel power," for an example of how a compiler directive was used to include QuickBooks integration only for users who had the required third-party service installed.
>
> "Making 32-bit- and 64-bit-compatible API declarations" in Chapter 23, "The Windows Application Programming Interface (API)," has an example of compiling code based on the user's Windows and Office versions.

Understanding Subs and Functions

In VBA, there are two core types of procedures:

- **Subroutines (Subs)**   Perform an action but don't return a value.

- **Functions**   Perform a task and usually return a result (either a value or an object).

If you've ever recorded a macro, you've seen a Sub—it's the default type VBA creates. For example:

```
Sub Macro1()
Selection.FormulaR1C1 = "Hello!"
End Sub
```

A Function looks similar to a Sub but is designed to return a result. You define one like this:

```
Function name(parameters) As data type
```

That means the function has a name, can take parameters, and ends with As followed by the type of result it will return—such as String, Boolean, or Object. You assign the return value by setting the function's name equal to the result, like this:

```
Function GetGreeting() As String
  GetGreeting = "Hello!"
End Function
```

This one returns a string that you can assign to a variable:

```
Dim msg As String
msg = GetGreeting()
```

> **Tip**   Always include parentheses when calling a function, even if it takes no parameters. It helps avoid confusion and ensures VBA treats it as a function.

If the function returns an object, use Set, and include parentheses—even if there are no arguments. Without parentheses, VBA assumes you're calling a Sub and ignores the return value, so be sure to include them, like this:

```
Dim dBar As FormatCondition
Set dBar = Range("A1:A10").FormatConditions.AddDatabar()
```

> **Note**   Some built-in functions—like MsgBox or InputBox—accept multiple optional parameters. You can assign those by name using :=, like this:
>
> ```
> MsgBox Prompt:="Done", Buttons:=vbInformation, Title:="Complete"
> ```
>
> This improves readability and avoids errors in parameter order.
>
> For more details, see "Understanding the parts of VBA "speech" in Chapter 2, "This sounds like BASIC, so why doesn't it look familiar?"

Using Enum to create custom constants

Sometimes your code needs to reference a list of predefined options, such as columns in a report, types of errors, or system modes. While you could define a series of Const values, VBA offers a cleaner option: the Enum statement. Short for enumeration, an Enum lets you create a named group of constants that you can assign numbers to or that you can allow Excel to assign numbers in numeric order.

Here's the basic structure, with Excel assigning the numbers:

```
Enum ReportColumns
  colDate
  colProduct
  colQuantity
  colPrice
End Enum
```

By default, Enum values start at 0 and increase by 1. You can also set the starting number yourself:

```
Enum DataTypes
  dtText = 1
  dtNumber = 2
  dtDate = 3
End Enum
```

Or skip numbers intentionally:

```
Enum ErrorCodes
  errNone = 0
  errMissingData = 10
  errInvalidFormat = 20
  errAccessDenied = 99
End Enum
```

Once declared, you can refer to these values in your code like this:

```
If myColumn = ReportColumns.colQuantity Then
  'Handle quantity column
End If
```

> **Note** Enums only support numeric values—you can't assign text to them. That's often confusing at first because the names you use in your Enum look like string values, but they're really just labels for numbers.

When using an Enum to define things like worksheet headers or column positions, it's helpful to know how many values are in your list. You can do this by adding a final entry at the end, like this:

```
Enum ReportColumns
    colDate = 1
    colProduct
    colQty
    colPricePer
    colTotal
    [_last]
End Enum
```

This special [_last] entry gives you a built-in count of the items in your Enum. For example:

```
Dim colCount As Long
colCount = ReportHeaders.[_last] - 1
```

The - 1 is required because [_last] returns its position in the list. The underscore (_) hides the entry from the tooltip; I use it just in case there is a column label "Last." The square brackets are required because VBA won't allow keywords to start with an underscore. You can name it whatever you like, but [_last] is a popular convention for good reason.

Declaring parameters using an Enum

Another usage of Enum is in procedure parameters. You can declare a parameter to be of your custom Enum type, which guarantees the caller must pass one of the defined values:

```
Sub CreateReport(ByVal colType As ReportColumns)
    Select Case colType
        Case colDate
            Debug.Print "Working with Date column"
        Case colProduct
            Debug.Print "Working with Product column"
        Case Else
            Debug.Print "Other column"
    End Select
End Sub
```

Now, when someone calls CreateReport, the tooltips guide them to use one of the defined constants:

```
CreateReport colProduct   'Clean, readable, safe
```

This eliminates hardcoded values like CreateReport(1) and makes your code much easier to read and maintain.

Using `With` statements to streamline code

When you're writing multiple lines of code that act on the same object, you might find yourself repeating that object's name again and again:

```
ActiveSheet.Range("A1").Value = "Total"
ActiveSheet.Range("A1").Font.Bold = True
ActiveSheet.Range("A1").Font.Size = 14
```

That works, but it's repetitive and harder to maintain, especially if you ever need to change the reference to a different object. Instead, you can use a `With...End With` block to simplify things:

```
With ActiveSheet.Range("A1")
  .Value = "Total"
  .Font.Bold = True
  .Font.Size = 14
End With
```

Inside the `With...End With` block, every line that starts with a period (.) refers to the object named on the previous `With` line, in this case, `ActiveSheet.Range("A1")`.

This doesn't just make your code shorter—it makes it easier to read and update.

> **Note**   For a detailed example of using `With...End With` to clean up code, refer to "Tip 7: Use `With...End` with to perform multiple actions" in Chapter 2.

Nesting `With...End With` statements

You can also use a `With...End With` block inside another when working with related objects, like a cell and its font:

```
With ActiveSheet.Range("A1")
  .Value = "Total"
  With .Font
    .Bold = True 'refers to Font
    .Size = 14 'refers to Font
  End With 'Font
End With 'ActiveSheet
```

Just be careful not to lose track of which object each period refers to because the inner `With` resets the reference. In this case, the `With .Font` is a reference to the previous `With ActiveSheet.Range("A1")`. Once the `End With` statement for the `.Font` is reached, the reference resets to `ActiveSheet.Range("A1")`.

Switching objects within `With...End With` blocks

Sometimes, you want to work your way down through related objects—for example, starting at the workbook level, then drilling into a sheet, then into a specific cell. You can do this cleanly by nesting `With...End With` blocks:

```
With ThisWorkbook
  With .Worksheets("Data")
    .Name = "Old Data"
    With .ListObjects("myTable")
      .HeaderRowRange(1, 1).Value = "Date Updated"
    End With 'Table
    With .Range("C2")
      .Value = Now
      .Font.Italic = True
    End With ' Cell
    .PageSetup.LeftFooter = "Expired Data"
  End With 'Worksheet
End With 'Workbook
```

Each `With...End With` focuses on one object, and everything inside refers back to it using a leading period. This keeps the code clean and shows clearly how the objects relate to each other.

> **Tip** Use comments and indentation to make nested `With...End With` blocks easier to follow, especially when you're working across multiple object levels.

Next steps

In this chapter, you were introduced to key coding concepts you'll keep seeing throughout the book—like variables, functions, and code structure. Don't worry if it didn't all click right away; you can always return to this chapter as needed. Now that you're getting an idea of how Excel works, it's time to learn about a fundamental component of any programming language: loops. If you have taken a programming class, you will be familiar with basic loop structures. VBA supports all the usual loops. Chapter 5 also describes a special loop, `For Each...Next`, which is unique to object-oriented programming, such as VBA.

CHAPTER 5

Looping and flow control

In this chapter, you will:

- Work with `For...Next` loops

- Get to know `Do` loops

- Be introduced to the VBA loop: `For Each`

- Use `If...Then...Else` and `Select Case` for flow control

Loops make your life easier. You might have 20 lines of macro code that do something cool one time. Add a line of code above and below, and suddenly, your macro fixes a million rows instead of one row. Loops are a fundamental component of any programming language. If you've taken any programming classes—even BASIC—you've likely encountered a `For...Next` loop. Fortunately, VBA supports all the usual loops, plus a special loop that is excellent to use with VBA.

This chapter covers the basic loop constructs:

- `For...Next`

- `Do...While`

- `Do...Until`

- `While...Wend`

- `Do Until...Loop`

This chapter also discusses the useful loop construct that is unique to object-oriented languages: `For Each...Next`.

> **Level Up!**
>
> The examples in this chapter loop through the cells on the sheet. This is fine for small data sets and a good way to learn looping and flow control since you can see what's happening on the sheet. But if you have a large data set, looping on a sheet is very slow. Instead, place the data in an array and then perform your loop—it's much faster. See Chapter 8, "Arrays," to learn more about this powerful tool for data automation.

For...Next loops

For and Next are common loop constructs. Everything between For and the Next is run multiple times. Each time the code runs, a certain counter variable, specified in the For statement, has a different value.

Consider this code:

```
For i = 1 to 10
  Cells(i, i).Value = i
Next i
```

As this program starts to run, you need to give the counter variable a name. In this example, the name of the variable is i. The first time through the code, the variable i is set to 1. The first time the loop is executed, i is equal to 1, so the cell in row 1, column 1 is set to 1 (see Figure 5-1).

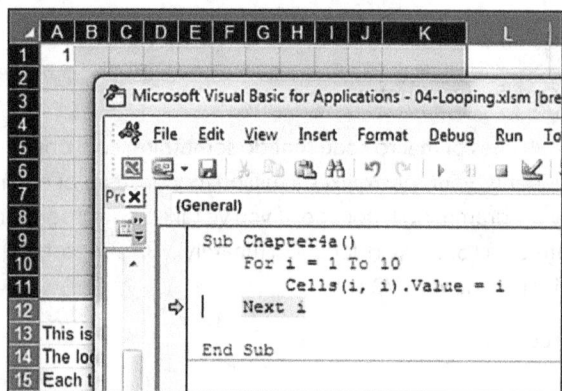

FIGURE 5-1 After the first iteration through the loop, the cell in row 1, column 1 has the value 1.

> **Note** To improve readability, you should always indent lines of code inside of a loop. It is your preference whether you use 1, 2, 3, or 4 spaces for the indent.

Let's take a close look at what happens as VBA gets to the line that says Next i. Before this line is run, the variable i is equal to 1. During the execution of Next i, VBA must make a decision. VBA adds 1 to the variable i and compares it to the maximum value in the To clause of the For statement. If it is within the limits specified in the To clause, the loop is not finished. In this case, the value of i is incremented to 2. Code execution then moves back to the first line of code after the For statement. Figure 5-2 shows the state of the program before it runs the Next line. Figure 5-3 shows what happens after the Next line is executed.

The second time through the loop, the value of i is 2. The cell in row 2, column 2 (that is, cell B2) gets the value 2.

As the process continues, the Next i statement advances i up to 3, 4, and so on. On the tenth pass through the loop, the cell in row 10, column 10 is assigned the value 10.

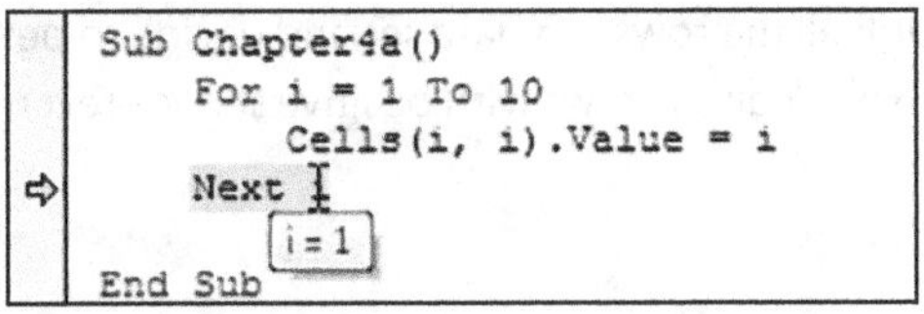
Sub Chapter4a()
For i = 1 To 10
Cells(i, i).Value = i
Next i
i = 1
End Sub

FIGURE 5-2 Before the Next `i` statement is run, `i` is equal to 1. VBA can safely add 1 to `i`, and it will be less than or equal to the 10 specified in the To clause of the For statement.

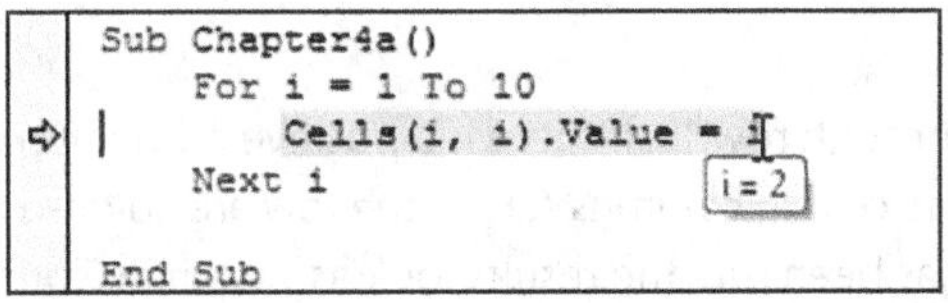
Sub Chapter4a()
For i = 1 To 10
Cells(i, i).Value = i
Next i
i = 2
End Sub

FIGURE 5-3 After the Next `i` statement is run, `i` is incremented to 2. Code execution continues with the line of code immediately following the For statement, which writes a 2 to cell B2.

It is interesting to watch what happens to the variable `i` on the last pass through `Next i`. Before running the `Next i` line, the variable contains `10`. VBA is now at a decision point. It adds 1 to the variable `i`. The value stored in `i` is now equal to `11`, which is greater than the limit in the `For...Next` loop. VBA then moves execution to the next line in the macro after the `Next` statement (see Figure 5-4). In case you are tempted to use the variable `i` later in the macro, it is important to realize that it will be incremented beyond the limit specified in the `To` clause of the `For` statement.

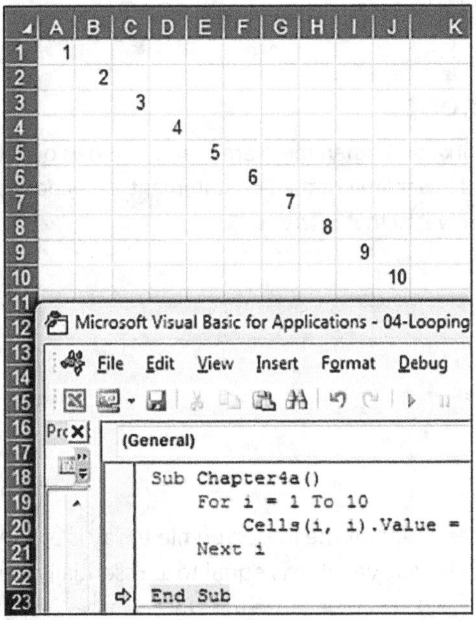
Microsoft Visual Basic for Applications - 04-Looping
File
Edit
View
Insert
Format
Debug
(General)
Sub Chapter4a()
For i = 1 To 10
Cells(i, i).Value =
Next i
End Sub

FIGURE 5-4 After incrementing `i` to 11, code execution moves to the line after the Next statement.

The common use for such a loop is to walk through all the rows in a data set and decide to perform some action based on some criteria. For example, to mark all the rows with positive service revenue in column F, you could use this loop:

```
For i = 2 to 10
  If Cells(i, 6).Value > 0 Then
    Cells(i, 8).Value = "Service Revenue"
    Cells(i, 1).Resize(1, 8).Interior.ColorIndex = 4
  End If
Next i
```

This loop checks each item of data from row 2 through row 10. If there is a positive number in column F, column H of that row has a new label, and the cells in columns A:H of the row are colored using the color index 4, which is green. After this macro has been run, the results look as shown in Figure 5-5.

	A	B	C	D	E	F	G	H	I
1	InvoiceDate	InvoiceNumber	SalesRepNumber	CustomerNumber	ProductRevenue	ServiceRevenue	ProductCost		
2	6/8/2015	123829 S21		C8754	21000	0	9875		
3	6/8/2015	123834 S54		C7796	339000	0	195298		
4	6/8/2015	123835 S21		C1654	161000	0	90761		
5	6/8/2015	123836 S45		C6460	275500	10000	146341	Service Revenue	
6	6/8/2015	123837 S54		C5143	925400	0	473515		
7	6/8/2015	123841 S21		C8361	94400	0	53180		
8	6/8/2015	123842 S45		C1842	36500	55000	20696	Service Revenue	
9	6/8/2015	123843 S54		C4107	599700	0	276718		
10	6/8/2015	123844 S21		C5205	244900	0	143393		
11									

FIGURE 5-5 After the loop completes all nine iterations, any rows with positive values in column F are colored green and have the label Service Revenue added to column H.

Using variables in the For statement

The previous example is not very useful in that it works only when there are exactly 10 rows of data. It is possible to use a variable to specify the upper and lower limit of the For statement. This code sample identifies FinalRow with data and then loops from row 2 to that row:

```
FinalRow = Cells(Rows.Count, 1).End(xlUp).Row
For i = 2 to FinalRow
  If Cells(i, 6).Value > 0 Then
    Cells(i, 8).Value = "Service Revenue"
    Cells(i, 1).Resize(1, 8).Interior.ColorIndex = 4
  End If
Next i
```

> **Warning** Exercise caution when using variables. What if the imported file today is empty and has only a heading row? In this case, the FinalRow variable is equal to 1. Essentially, this makes the first statement of the loop say For i = 2 to 1. Because the start number is higher than the end number, the loop does not execute at all. The variable i is equal to 2, and code execution jumps to the line after Next.

Variations on the For...Next loop

In a For...Next loop, it is possible to have the loop variable jump up by something other than 1. For example, you might use it to apply greenbar formatting to every other row in a data set. In this case, you want to have the counter variable i examine every other row in the data set. Indicate this by adding the Step clause to the end of the For statement:

```
FinalRow = Cells(Rows.Count, 1).End(xlUp).Row
For i = 2 to FinalRow Step 2
  Cells(i, 1).Resize(1, 7).Interior.ColorIndex = 35
Next i
```

While running this code, VBA adds a light green shading to rows 2, 4, 6, and so on (see Figure 5-6).

	A	B	C	D	E
1	InvoiceDate	InvoiceNumber	SalesRepNumber	CustomerNumber	ProductRevenue
2	6/7/2011	123829 S21		C8754	21000
3	6/7/2011	123830 S45		C3390	188100
4	6/7/2011	123831 S54		C2523	510600
5	6/7/2011	123832 S21		C5519	86200
6	6/7/2011	123833 S45		C3245	800100
7	6/7/2011	123834 S54		C7796	339000
8	6/7/2011	123835 S21		C1654	161000

FIGURE 5-6 The Step clause in the For statement of the loop causes the action to occur on every other row.

The Step clause can be any number. You might want to check every tenth row of a data set to extract a random sample and place the results in an area starting five rows below the last row of data. In this case, you would use Step 10:

```
FinalRow = Cells(Rows.Count, 1).End(xlUp).Row
NextRow = FinalRow + 5
Cells(NextRow-1, 1).Value = "Random Sample of Above Data"
For i = 2 to FinalRow Step 10
  Cells(i, 1).Resize(1, 8).Copy Destination:=Cells(NextRow, 1)
  NextRow = NextRow + 1
Next i
```

You can also have a For...Next loop run backward from the end of the data set to the beginning. This is particularly useful if you are selectively deleting rows. If you run forward through the loop and two sequential records need to be deleted, the loop will miss the second one as it slides upward after deleting the first record. By going backward, both records will be deleted.

To do this, reverse the order of the For statement and have the Step clause specify a negative number:

```
'Delete all rows where column C is Sales Rep S54
FinalRow = Cells(Rows.Count, 1).End(xlUp).Row
For i = FinalRow to 2 Step -1
  If Cells(i, 3).Value = "S54" Then
    Rows(i).Delete
  End If
Next i
```

Exiting a loop early after a condition is met

Sometimes, you don't need to execute a whole loop. Perhaps you just need to read through a data set until you find one record that meets certain criteria. In this case, you want to find the first record and then stop the loop. A statement called `Exit For` does this.

The following sample macro looks for a row in the data set where service revenue in column F is positive and product revenue in column E is 0. If such a row is found, you might display a message that the file needs manual processing today and move the cell pointer to that row:

```
'Are there any special processing situations in the data?
FinalRow = Cells(Rows.Count, 1).End(xlUp).Row
ProblemFound = False
For i = 2 to FinalRow
  If Cells(i, 6).Value > 0 Then
    If cells(i, 5).Value = 0 Then
      Cells(i, 6).Select
      ProblemFound = True
      Exit For
    End If
  End If
Next i
If ProblemFound Then
  MsgBox "There is a problem at row " & i
  Exit Sub
End If
```

Nesting one loop inside another loop

It is okay to run a loop inside another loop. The following code has the first loop run through all the rows in a record set while the second loop runs through all the columns:

```
'Loop through each row and column
'Add a checkerboard format
FinalRow = Cells(Rows.Count, 1).End(xlUp).Row
FinalCol = Cells(1, Columns.Count).End(xlToLeft).Column
For i = 2 To FinalRow
  'For even numbered rows, start in column 1
  'For odd numbered rows, start in column 2
  If i Mod 2 = 1 Then 'Divide i by 2 and keep remainder
    StartCol = 1
  Else
```

```
    StartCol = 2
  End If
  For j= StartCol To FinalCol Step 2
    Cells(i, j).Interior.ColorIndex = 35
  Next j
Next i
```

In this code, the outer loop uses the i counter variable to loop through all the rows in the data set. The inner loop uses the j counter variable to loop through all the columns in that row. Because Figure 5-7 has seven data rows, the code runs through the i loop seven times. Each time through the i loop, the code runs through the j loop six or seven times. This means that the line of code that is inside the j loop ends up being executed several times for each pass through the i loop. Figure 5-7 shows the result.

◢	A	B	C	D	E
1	Item	January	February	March	April
2	Hardware Revenue	1,972,637	1,655,321	1,755,234	1,531,060
3	Software Revenue	236,716	198,639	210,628	183,727
4	Service Revenue	473,433	397,277	421,256	367,454
5	Cost of Good Sold	1,084,951	910,427	965,379	842,083
6	Selling Expense	394,527	331,064	351,047	306,212
7	G&A Expense	150,000	150,000	150,000	150,000
8	R&D	125,000	125,000	125,000	125,000

FIGURE 5-7 The result of nesting one loop inside the other; VBA can loop through each row and then each column.

Do loops

There are several variations of the Do loop. The most basic Do loop is useful for doing a bunch of mundane tasks. For example, suppose that someone sends you a list of addresses going down a column, as shown in Figure 5-8.

In this case, you might need to rearrange these addresses into a database with name in column B, street in column C, and city and state in column D. By setting relative recording (see Chapter 1, "Unleashing the power of Excel with VBA") and using the shortcut Ctrl+A, you can record this bit of useful code:

```
Sub FixOneRecord()
'Keyboard Shortcut: Ctrl+Shift+A
ActiveCell.Offset(1, 0).Range("A1").Select
Selection.Cut
ActiveCell.Offset(-1, 1).Range("A1").Select
ActiveSheet.Paste
ActiveCell.Offset(2, -1).Range("A1").Select
Selection.Cut
ActiveCell.Offset(-2, 2).Range("A1").Select
ActiveSheet.Paste
ActiveCell.Offset(1, -2).Range("A1:A3").Select
```

```
Selection.EntireRow.Delete
ActiveCell.Select
End Sub
```

5	
6	John Smith
7	123 Main Street
8	Akron OH 44308
9	
10	Jane Doe
11	245 State Street
12	Merritt Island FL 32953
13	
14	Ralph Emerson
15	345 2nd Ave
16	New York NY 10011
17	
18	George Washington
19	456 3rd St
20	Philadelphia PA 12345
21	

FIGURE 5-8 It would be more useful to have these addresses in a database format to use in a mail merge.

This code is designed to copy one single address into a database format. The code also navigates the cell pointer to the name of the next address in the list. Each time you press Ctrl+A, one address is reformatted.

> **Note** Do not assume that the preceding code is suitable for a professional application. Remember that you don't need to select something before acting on it. However, sometimes, macros are written just to automate a one-time mundane task.

Without a macro, a lot of manual copying and pasting would be required. However, with the preceding recorded macro, you can simply place the cell pointer on a name in column A and press Ctrl+A. That one address is copied into three columns, and the cell pointer moves to the start of the next address (see Figure 5-9).

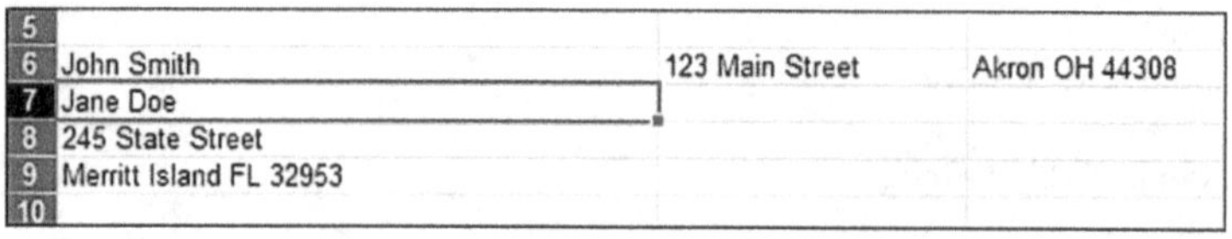

5			
6	John Smith	123 Main Street	Akron OH 44308
7	Jane Doe		
8	245 State Street		
9	Merritt Island FL 32953		
10			

FIGURE 5-9 After the macro is run once, one address is moved into the proper format, and the cell pointer is positioned to run the macro again.

When you use this macro, you are able to process an address every second using the shortcut. However, when you need to process 5,000 addresses, you do not want to keep running the same macro over and over. In this case, you can use a Do...Loop to set up the macro to run continuously. You can have VBA run this code continuously by enclosing the recorded code with `Do` at the top and `Loop` at the end. Now, you can sit back and watch the code perform this insanely boring task in minutes rather than hours.

> **Caution** This particular `Do...Loop` will run forever because there is no mechanism to stop it. This works for the task at hand because you can watch the progress on the screen and press Esc to stop execution when the program advances past the end of this database.

This code uses a `Do` loop to fix the addresses:

```
Sub FixAllRecords()
Do
  ActiveCell.Offset(1, 0).Range("A1").Select
  Selection.Cut
  ActiveCell.Offset(-1, 1).Range("A1").Select
  ActiveSheet.Paste
  ActiveCell.Offset(2, -1).Range("A1").Select
  Selection.Cut
  ActiveCell.Offset(-2, 2).Range("A1").Select
  ActiveSheet.Paste
  ActiveCell.Offset(1, -2).Range("A1:A3").Select
  Selection.EntireRow.Delete
  ActiveCell.Select
Loop
End Sub
```

These examples have shown quick-and-dirty loops that are great for when you need to accomplish a task quickly. The `Do...Loop` provides a number of options that enable you to have the program stop automatically when it accomplishes the end of the task.

The first option is to have a line in the `Do...Loop` that detects the end of the data set and exits the loop. In the current example, this could be accomplished by using the `Exit Do` command in an `If` statement. If the current cell is on a cell that is empty, you can assume that you have reached the end of the data and stopped processing the loop:

```
Sub LoopUntilDone()
Do
  If Selection.Value = "" Then Exit Do
  ActiveCell.Offset(1, 0).Range("A1").Select
  Selection.Cut
  ActiveCell.Offset(-1, 1).Range("A1").Select
  ActiveSheet.Paste
  ActiveCell.Offset(2, -1).Range("A1").Select
  Selection.Cut
  ActiveCell.Offset(-2, 2).Range("A1").Select
  ActiveSheet.Paste
  ActiveCell.Offset(1, -2).Range("A1:A3").Select
  Selection.EntireRow.Delete
  ActiveCell.Select
Loop
End Sub
```

Using the `While` or `Until` clause in `Do` loops

There are four variations of using `While` or `Until`. These clauses can be added to either the `Do` statement or the `Loop` statement. In each case, the `While` or `Until` clause includes some test that evaluates to `True` or `False`.

With a `Do While <test expression>...Loop` construct, the loop is never executed if `<test expression>` is false. If you are reading records from a text file, you cannot assume that the file has one or more records. Instead, you need to test to see whether you are already at the end of the file with the `EOF` function before you enter the loop:

```
'Read a text file, skipping the Total lines
Open "C:\Invoice.txt" For Input As #1
r = 1
Do While Not EOF(1)
  Line Input #1, Data
  If Not Left (Data, 5) = "TOTAL" Then
    'Import this row
    r = r + 1
    Cells(r, 1).Value = Data
  End If
Loop
Close #1
```

In this example, the `Not` keyword `EOF(1)` evaluates to `True` after there are no more records to be read from Invoice.txt. Some programmers think it is hard to read a program that contains a lot of instances of `Not`. To avoid the use of `Not`, use the `Do Until <test expression>...Loop` construct:

```
'Read a text file, skipping the Total lines
Open "C:\Invoice.txt" For Input As #1
r = 1
Do Until EOF(1)
  Line Input #1, Data
  If Not Left(Data, 5) = "TOTAL" Then
    'Import this row
    r = r + 1
    Cells(r, 1).Value = Data
  End If
Loop
Close #1
```

In other examples, you might always want the loop to be executed the first time. In these cases, move the `While` or `Until` instruction to the end of the loop. This code sample asks the user to enter sales amounts made that day; it continually asks for sales amounts until the user enters a zero:

```
TotalSales = 0
Do
  x = InputBox( _
    Prompt:="Enter Amount of Next Invoice. Enter 0 when done.", _
    Type:=1)
```

```
    TotalSales = TotalSales + x
Loop Until x = 0
MsgBox "The total for today is $" & TotalSales
```

In the following loop, a check amount is entered, and then it looks for open invoices to which the check can be applied. However, it is often the case that a single check is received that covers several invoices. The following program sequentially applies the check to each invoice until 100 percent of the check has been applied:

```
'Ask for the amount of check received. Add zero to convert to numeric.
AmtToApply = InputBox("Enter Amount of Check") + 0
'Loop through the list of open invoices.
'Apply the check to the invoice and Decrement AmtToApply
NextRow = 2
Do While AmtToApply > 0
  OpenAmt = Cells(NextRow, 3)
  If OpenAmt > AmtToApply Then
    'Apply total check to this invoice
    Cells(NextRow, 4).Value = AmtToApply
    AmtToApply = 0
  Else
    Cells(NextRow, 4).Value = OpenAmt
    AmtToApply = AmtToApply - OpenAmt
  End If
  NextRow = NextRow + 1
Loop
```

Because you can construct the `Do...Loop` with the `While` or `Until` qualifiers at the beginning or end, you have a great deal of subtle control over whether the loop is always executed once, even when the condition is true at the beginning.

While...Wend loops

`While...Wend` loops are included in VBA for backward compatibility. In the VBA help file, Microsoft suggests that the `Do...Loop` construction is more flexible. However, because you might encounter `While...Wend` loops in code written by others, this chapter includes a quick example. In this loop, the first line is always `While <condition>`. The last line of the loop is always `Wend`. Note that there is no `Exit While` statement. In general, these loops are okay, but the `Do...Loop` construct is more robust and flexible. Because the `Do` loop offers either the `While` or the `Until` qualifier, you can use this qualifier at the beginning or the end of the loop, and you can exit a `Do` loop early:

```
'Read a text file, adding the amounts
Open "C:\Invoice.txt" For Input As #1
TotalSales = 0
While Not EOF(1)
  Line Input #1, Data
  TotalSales = TotalSales + Data
Wend
MsgBox "Total Sales=" & TotalSales
Close #1
```

The VBA loop: For Each

Even though the VBA loop is an excellent loop, the macro recorder never records this type of loop. VBA is an object-oriented language. It is common to have a collection of objects in Excel, such as a collection of worksheets in a workbook, cells in a range, pivot tables on a worksheet, or data series on a chart.

This special type of loop is great for looping through all the items in a collection. It uses object variables, which we discussed in Chapter 4, "Laying the groundwork with variables and structures." Unlike simple variables that store single values (like TotalSales), object variables, such as ThisWorkbook, represent complex entities with multiple properties and methods.

The For Each loop employs an object variable rather than a counter variable. The following code loops through all the cells in column A:

```
For Each myCell in Range("A1").CurrentRegion.Resize(, 1)
  If myCell.Value = "Total" Then
    myCell.Resize(1,8).Font.Bold = True
  End If
Next myCell
```

This code uses the .CurrentRegion property to define the current region and then uses the .Resize property to limit the selected range to a single column. The object variable is called myCell. Any name could be used for the object variable, but myCell seems more appropriate than something arbitrary like Fred.

The following code sample searches all open workbooks, looking for a workbook in which the first worksheet is called Menu. When the sheet is found, Exit For is used to leave the loop:

```
For Each wb in Workbooks
  If wb.Worksheets(1).Name = "Menu" Then
    WBFound = True
    WBName = wb.Name
    Exit For
  End If
Next wb
```

This code sample deletes all pivot tables on the current sheet:

```
For Each pt in ActiveSheet.PivotTables
  pt.TableRange2.Clear
Next pt
```

Flow control: Using If...Then...Else and Select Case

Another aspect of programming that the macro recorder will never record is the concept of flow control. Sometimes, you do not want every line of a program to be executed every time you run a macro. VBA offers two excellent choices for flow control: the If...Then...Else and Select Case constructs.

Basic flow control: `If...Then...Else`

The most common device for program flow control is the `If` statement. For example, suppose you have a list of products, as shown in Figure 5-10. You want to loop through each product in the list and copy it to either a Fruits list or a Vegetables list. Beginning programmers might be tempted to loop through the rows twice—once to look for fruit and a second time to look for vegetables. However, there is no need to loop through twice because you can use an `If...Then...Else` construct on a single loop to copy each row to the correct place.

⬛	A	B	C
1	Class	Product	Quantity
2	Fruit	Apples	1
3	Fruit	Apricots	3
4	Vegetable	Asparagus	62
5	Fruit	Bananas	55
6	Fruit	Blueberry	17
7	Vegetable	Broccoli	56
8	Vegetable	Cabbage	35
9	Fruit	Cherries	59
10	Herbs	Dill	91
11	Vegetable	Eggplant	94
12	Fruit	Kiwi	86

FIGURE 5-10 A single loop can look for fruits or vegetables.

Using conditions

Any `If` statement needs a condition that is being tested. The condition should always evaluate to TRUE or FALSE. Here are some examples of simple and complex conditions:

- `If Range("A1").Value = "Title" Then`

- `If Not Range("A1").Value = "Title" Then`

- `If Range("A1").Value = "Title" And Range("B1").Value = "Fruit" Then`

- `If Range("A1").Value = "Title" Or Range("B1").Value = "Fruit" Then`

Using `If...Then...End If`

After the `If` statement, you can include one or more program lines that will be executed only if the condition is met. You should then close the `If` block with an `End If` line. Here is a simple example of an `If` statement:

```
Sub ColorFruitRedBold()
FinalRow = Cells(Rows.Count, 1).End(xlUp).Row
For i = 2 To FinalRow
  If Cells(i, 1).Value = "Fruit" Then
    Cells(i, 1).Resize(1, 3).Font.Bold = True
    Cells(i, 1).Resize(1, 3).Font.ColorIndex = 3
  End If
```

```
Next i
MsgBox "Fruit is now bold and red"
End Sub
```

Either/or decisions: `If...Then...Else...End If`

Sometimes, you will want to do one set of statements if a condition is true and another set of statements if the condition is not true. To do this with VBA, the second set of conditions would be coded after the `Else` statement. There is still only one `End If` statement associated with this construct. For example, you could use the following code to color the fruit red and the vegetables green:

```
Sub FruitRedVegGreen()
FinalRow = Cells(Rows.Count, 1).End(xlUp).Row
For i = 2 To FinalRow
  If Cells(i, 1).Value = "Fruit" Then
    Cells(i, 1).Resize(1, 3).Font.ColorIndex = 3
  Else
    Cells(i, 1).Resize(1, 3).Font.ColorIndex = 50
  End If
Next i
MsgBox "Fruit is red / Veggies are green"
End Sub
```

Using `If...ElseIf...End If` for multiple conditions

Notice that the product list in Figure 5-10 includes one item that is classified as an herb. Three conditions can be used to test items on the list. It is possible to build an `If...End If` structure with more than two conditions. First, test to see whether the record is a fruit. Next, use an `ElseIf` to test whether the record is a vegetable. Then, test to see whether the record is an herb. Finally, if the record is none of those, highlight the record as an error. Here's the code that does all this:

```
Sub MultipleIf()
FinalRow = Cells(Rows.Count, 1).End(xlUp).Row
For i = 2 To FinalRow
  If Cells(i, 1).Value = "Fruit" Then
    Cells(i, 1).Resize(1, 3).Font.ColorIndex = 3
  ElseIf Cells(i, 1).Value = "Vegetable" Then
    Cells(i, 1).Resize(1, 3).Font.ColorIndex = 50
  ElseIf Cells(i, 1).Value = "Herbs" Then
    Cells(i, 1).Resize(1, 3).Font.ColorIndex = 5
  Else
    'This must be a record in error
    Cells(i, 1).Resize(1, 3).Interior.ColorIndex = 6
  End If
Next i
MsgBox "Fruit is red / Veggies are green / Herbs are blue"
End Sub
```

Using `Select Case...End Select` for multiple conditions

When you have many different conditions, it becomes unwieldy to use many `ElseIf` statements. For this reason, VBA offers another construct known as the `Select Case` construct. In your running example, always check the value of the class in column A. This value is called the *test expression*. The basic syntax of this construct starts with the words `Select Case` followed by the test expression:

```
Select Case Cells(i, 1).Value
```

Thinking about this problem in English, you might say, "In cases in which the record is fruit, color the record with red." VBA uses a shorthand version of this. You write the word `Case` followed by the literal `"Fruit"`. Any statements that follow `Case "Fruit"` are executed whenever the test expression is a fruit. After these statements, you have the next `Case` statement: `Case "Vegetable"`. You continue in this fashion, writing a `Case` statement followed by the program lines that are executed if that case is true.

After you have listed all the possible conditions you can think of, you can optionally include a `Case Else` section at the end. The `Case Else` section includes what the program should do if the test expression matches none of your cases. Below, the macro adds a note in column D if an unexpected value is found in A. Finally, you close the entire construct with the `End Select` statement.

The following program does the same operation as the previous macro but uses a `Select Case` statement:

```
Sub SelectCase()
FinalRow = Cells(Rows.Count, 1).End(xlUp).Row
For i = 2 To FinalRow
  Select Case Cells(i, 1).Value
    Case "Fruit"
      Cells(i, 1).Resize(1, 3).Font.ColorIndex = 3
    Case "Vegetable"
      Cells(i, 1).Resize(1, 3).Font.ColorIndex = 50
    Case "Herbs"
      Cells(i, 1).Resize(1, 3).Font.ColorIndex = 5
    Case Else
       Cells(i, 4).Value = "Unexpected value!"
  End Select
Next i
MsgBox "Fruit is red / Veggies are green / Herbs are blue"
End Sub
```

Complex expressions in `Case` statements

It is possible to have fairly complex expressions in `Case` statements. For example, say that you want to perform the same actions for all berry records:

```
Case "Strawberry", "Blueberry", "Raspberry"
  AdCode = 1
```

If it makes sense to do so, you might code a range of values in the Case statement:

```
Case 1 to 20
  Discount = 0.05
Case 21 to 100
  Discount = 0.1
```

You can include the keyword Is and a comparison operator, such as > or <:

```
Case Is < 10
  Discount = 0
Case Is > 100
  Discount = 0.2
Case Else
  Discount = 0.10
```

Nesting If statements

It is not only possible but also common to nest an If statement inside another If statement. In this situation, it is important to use proper indentation. You often will find that you have several End If lines at the end of the construct. With proper indentation, it is easier to tell which End If is associated with a particular If.

The final macro in this chapter contains a lot of logic that handles the following discount rules:

- For fruit, quantities less than 5 cases get no discount.

- Quantities of fruit from 5 to 20 cases get a 10 percent discount.

- Quantities of fruit greater than 20 cases get a 15 percent discount.

- For herbs, quantities less than 10 cases get no discount.

- Quantities of herbs from 10 cases to 15 cases get a 3 percent discount.

- Quantities of herbs greater than 15 cases get a 6 percent discount.

- For vegetables except asparagus, quantities of 5 cases and greater earn a 12 percent discount.

- Asparagus requires 20 cases for a discount of 12 percent.

- None of the discounts apply if the product is on sale this week. The sale price is 25 percent off the normal price. This week's sale items are strawberries, lettuce, and tomatoes.

The code to execute this logic follows:

```
Sub ComplexIf()
FinalRow = Cells(Rows.Count, 1).End(xlUp).Row
For i = 2 To FinalRow
  ThisClass = Cells(i, 1).Value
  ThisProduct = Cells(i, 2).Value
  ThisQty = Cells(i, 3).Value
```

```vba
'First, figure out if the item is on sale
Select Case ThisProduct
  Case "Strawberry", "Lettuce", "Tomatoes"
    Sale = True
  Case Else
    Sale = False
End Select
'Figure out the discount
If Sale Then
  Discount = 0.25
ElseIf ThisClass = "Fruit" Then
  Select Case ThisQty
    Case Is < 5
      Discount = 0
    Case 5 To 20
      Discount = 0.1
    Case Is > 20
      Discount = 0.15
    End Select
ElseIf ThisClass = "Herbs" Then
  Select Case ThisQty
    Case Is < 10
      Discount = 0
    Case 10 To 15
      Discount = 0.03
    Case Is > 15
      Discount = 0.06
  End Select
ElseIf ThisClass = "Vegetable" Then
  'There is a special condition for asparagus
  If ThisProduct = "Asparagus" Then
    If ThisQty < 20 Then
      Discount = 0
    Else
      Discount = 0.12
    End If
  Else
    If ThisQty < 5 Then
      Discount = 0
    Else
      Discount = 0.12
    End If 'Is the product asparagus or not?
  End If 'Is the product on sale?
  Cells(i, 4).Value = Discount
  If Sale Then
    Cells(i, 4).Font.Bold = True
  End If
End if
Next i
Range("D1").Value = "Discount"
MsgBox "Discounts have been applied"
End Sub
```

Next steps

Loops add a tremendous amount of power to your recorded macros. Any time you need to repeat a process over all worksheets or all rows in a worksheet, using a loop is the way to go. Excel VBA supports the traditional programming loops of For...Next and Do...Loop and the object-oriented loop For Each...Next. Chapter 6, "R1C1 style formulas," discusses the seemingly arcane R1C1 style of formulas and shows why it is important in Excel VBA.

R1C1 style formulas

In this chapter, you will:

- Understand A1 versus R1C1 references
- Toggle to R1C1 style references
- Witness the miracle of Excel formulas
- Examine the R1C1 reference style

Understanding R1C1 formulas will make your job easier in VBA. You could skip this chapter, but if you do, your code will be harder to write. Taking 30 minutes to understand R1C1 will make every macro you write for the rest of your life easier to code.

We can trace the A1 style of referencing back to VisiCalc. Dan Bricklin and Bob Frankston used A1 to refer to the cell in the upper-left corner of the spreadsheet. Mitch Kapor used this same addressing scheme in Lotus 1-2-3. Upstart Multiplan from Microsoft attempted to buck the trend and used something called R1C1 style addressing. In R1C1 addressing, the cell known as A1 is referred to as R1C1 because it is in row 1, column 1.

With the dominance of Lotus 1-2-3 in the 1980s and early 1990s, the A1 style became the standard. Microsoft realized it was fighting a losing battle and eventually offered either R1C1 style addressing or A1 style addressing in Excel. When you open Excel today, the A1 style is used by default. Officially, however, Microsoft supports both styles of addressing.

You would think that this chapter would be a non-issue. Anyone who uses the Excel interface would agree that the R1C1 style is dead. However, we have what, on the face of it, seems to be an annoying problem: The macro recorder records formulas in the R1C1 style. So, you might be thinking that you just need to learn R1C1 addressing so that you can read the recorded code and switch it back to the familiar A1 style.

I have to give Microsoft credit. R1C1 style formulas, you'll grow to understand, are actually more efficient, especially when you are dealing with writing formulas in VBA. Using R1C1 style addressing enables you to write more efficient code.

Toggling to R1C1 style references

You don't need to switch to the R1C1 style in order to use `.FormulaR1C1` in your code. However, while you're learning about R1C1, it helps to temporarily switch to the R1C1 style.

To switch to R1C1 style addressing, select Options from the File menu. In the Formulas category, select the R1C1 Reference Style checkbox (see Figure 6-1).

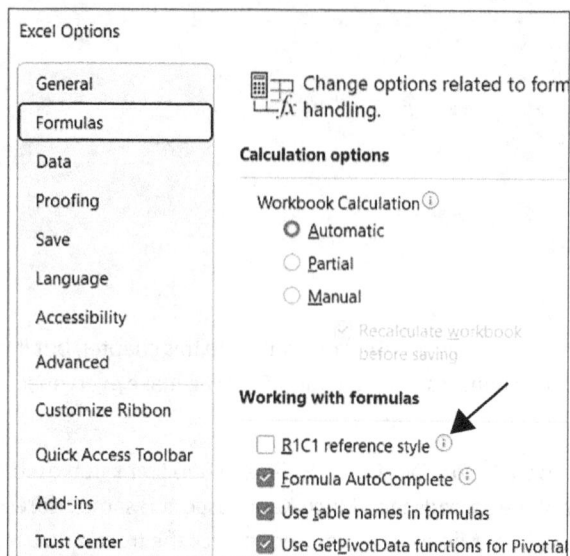

FIGURE 6-1 Selecting the R1C1 reference style in the Formulas category of the Excel Options dialog causes Excel to use R1C1 style in the Excel user interface.

After you switch to R1C1 style, the column letters A, B, C, and D across the top of the worksheet are replaced by the numbers 1, 2, 3, and 4 (see Figure 6-2).

FIGURE 6-2 In R1C1 style, the column letters are replaced by numbers.

In this format, the cell that you know as B5 is called R5C2 because it is in row 5, column 2.

Every couple of weeks, someone manages to turn on this option accidentally, and we get an urgent forum post at MrExcel.com. This style is foreign to 99 percent of spreadsheet users.

Witnessing the miracle of Excel formulas

Automatically recalculating thousands of cells is the main benefit of electronic spreadsheets over the green ledger paper used up until 1979. However, a close second-prize award would be that you can enter one formula and copy that formula to thousands of cells.

Entering a formula once and copying 1,000 times

Switch back to A1 style referencing. Consider the worksheet shown in Figure 6-3. Enter a simple formula such as =B4*C4 in cell D4, double-click the AutoFill handle, and the formula intelligently changes as it is copied down the range.

D4			×	✓	fx	=B4*C4
	A	B	C	D	E	
1	Tax Rate	6.25%				
2						
3	SKU	Quantity	Unit Price	Total Price	Taxable?	
4	217	12	12.45	149.4	TRUE	
5	123	144	1.87		TRUE	
6	329	18	19.95		TRUE	
7	616	1	642		FALSE	
8	909	64	17.5		TRUE	
9	527	822	0.12		TRUE	
10	Total					

FIGURE 6-3 Double-click the AutoFill handle, and Excel intelligently copies this relative-reference formula down the column.

The formula is rewritten for each row, eventually becoming =B9*C9. It seems intimidating to consider having a macro enter all these different formulas. Figure 6-4 shows how the formulas change when you copy them down columns D, F, and G.

> **Note** Press Ctrl+` to switch to showing formulas rather than their results. Press it again to toggle back to seeing values. The backtick (`) symbol is usually in the upper-left corner of the keyboard, next to the number 1 key.

D	E	F	G
it Total e Price	Taxable?	Tax	Total
=B4*C4	TRUE	=IF(E4,ROUND(D4*$B$1,2),0)	=F4+D4
=B5*C5	TRUE	=IF(E5,ROUND(D5*$B$1,2),0)	=F5+D5
=B6*C6	TRUE	=IF(E6,ROUND(D6*$B$1,2),0)	=F6+D6
=B7*C7	FALSE	=IF(E7,ROUND(D7*$B$1,2),0)	=F7+D7
=B8*C8	TRUE	=IF(E8,ROUND(D8*$B$1,2),0)	=F8+D8
=B9*C9	TRUE	=IF(E9,ROUND(D9*$B$1,2),0)	=F9+D9
=C10*B10		=SUM(G4:G9)	

FIGURE 6-4 Amazingly, Excel adjusts the cell references in each formula as you copy down the column.

The formula in cell F4 includes both relative and absolute formulas: =IF(E4,ROUND(D4*$B$1,2),0). Thanks to the dollar signs inserted in the reference to cell B1, you can copy down this formula, and it always multiplies the total price in this row by the tax rate in cell B1.

The secret: It's not that amazing

Excel actually uses R1C1 style formulas behind the scenes. Excel shows addresses and formulas in A1 style merely because it needs to adhere to the standard made popular by VisiCalc and Lotus.

If you switch the worksheet in Figure 6-4 to use R1C1 notation, you can see that the "different" formulas in D4:D9 are all actually identical formulas in R1C1 notation. The same is true of F4:F9 and G4:G9.

Use the Options dialog to change the sample worksheet to R1C1 style addresses. If you examine the formulas in Figure 6-5, you see that in R1C1 language, every formula in column 4 is identical. Given that Excel is storing the formulas in R1C1 style, copying them, and then merely translating them to A1 style for us to understand, its ability to manipulate A1 style formulas as easily as it does isn't so amazing.

	4	5	6
it e	Total Price	Taxable?	Tax
	=RC[-2]*RC[-1]	TRUE	=IF(RC[-1],ROUND(RC[-2]*R1C2,2),0)
	=RC[-2]*RC[-1]	TRUE	=IF(RC[-1],ROUND(RC[-2]*R1C2,2),0)
	=RC[-2]*RC[-1]	TRUE	=IF(RC[-1],ROUND(RC[-2]*R1C2,2),0)
	=RC[-2]*RC[-1]	FALSE	=IF(RC[-1],ROUND(RC[-2]*R1C2,2),0)
	=RC[-2]*RC[-1]	TRUE	=IF(RC[-1],ROUND(RC[-2]*R1C2,2),0)
	=RC[-2]*RC[-1]	TRUE	=IF(RC[-1],ROUND(RC[-2]*R1C2,2),0)
	=RC[-1]*RC[-2]		=SUM(R[-6]C[1]:R[-1]C[1])

FIGURE 6-5 The same formulas as in Figure 6-4 are shown in R1C1 style. Note that every formula in column 4 is the same, and every formula in column 6 is the same.

This is one of the reasons R1C1 style formulas are more efficient than A1 style formulas in VBA. When you have the same formula being entered in an entire range, it is less confusing.

Case study: Entering A1 versus R1C1 in VBA

Think about how you would set up this spreadsheet in the Excel interface. First, you enter a formula in cells D4, F4, and G4. Next, you copy these cells and paste them the rest of the way down the column. By using R1C1 style formulas, you can enter the same formula in the entire column at once.

The equivalent code in R1C1 style allows the formulas to be entered for the entire column in a single statement. Remember, the advantage of R1C1 style formulas is that all the formulas in columns D, F, and most of G are identical:

```
Sub R1C1Style()
'Locate the FinalRow
FinalRow = Cells(Rows.Count, 2).End(xlUp).Row
'Enter the first formula
Range("D4:D" & FinalRow).FormulaR1C1 = "=RC[-2]*RC[-1]"
Range("F4:F" & FinalRow).FormulaR1C1 = _
  "=IF(RC[-1],ROUND(RC[-2]*R1C2,2),0)"
Range("G4:G" & FinalRow).FormulaR1C1 = "=RC[-1]+RC[-3]"
'Enter the Total Row
Cells(FinalRow + 1, 1).Value = "Total"
Cells(FinalRow + 1, 6).FormulaR1C1 = "=SUM(R4C:R[-1]C)"
End Sub
```

> **Note** It seems counterintuitive, but when you specify an A1 style formula, Microsoft internally converts the formula to R1C1 and then enters that formula in the entire range. Thus, you can actually add the "same" A1 style formula to an entire range by using a single line of code:
>
> ```
> Range("D4:D" & FinalRow).Formula = "=B4*C4"
> ```
>
> Although you are asking for the formula =B4*C4 to be entered in D4:D1000, Excel enters this formula in row 4 and appropriately adjusts the formula for the additional rows.

Understanding the R1C1 reference style

An R1C1 style reference includes the letter *R* to refer to *row* and the letter *C* to refer to *column*. Because the most common reference in a formula is a relative reference, let's first look at relative references in R1C1 style.

Using R1C1 with relative references

Imagine that you are entering a formula in a cell. To point to a cell in a formula, you use the letters *R* and *C*. After each letter, enter the number of rows or columns in square brackets.

The following list explains the "rules" for using R1C1 relative references:

- For columns, a positive number means to move to the right a certain number of columns, and a negative number means to move to the left a certain number of columns. For example, from cell E5, use RC[1] to refer to F5 and RC[-1] to refer to D5.

- For rows, a positive number means to move down the spreadsheet a certain number of rows. A negative number means to move toward the top of the spreadsheet a certain number of rows. For example, from cell E5, use R[1]C to refer to E6 and use cell R[-1]C to refer to E4.

- If you leave off the number for either the R or the C, it means that you are pointing to a cell in the same row or column as the cell with the formula. For example, the R in RC[3] means that you are pointing to the current row.

- If you enter =R[-1]C[-1] in cell E5, you are referring to a cell one row up and one column to the left: cell D4.

- If you enter =RC[1] in cell E5, you are referring to a cell in the same row but one column to the right: cell F5.

- If you enter =RC in cell E5, you are referring to a cell in the same row and column, which is cell E5 itself. You would generally not do this because it would create a circular reference.

Figure 6-6 shows how you would enter a reference in cell E5 to point to various cells around E5.

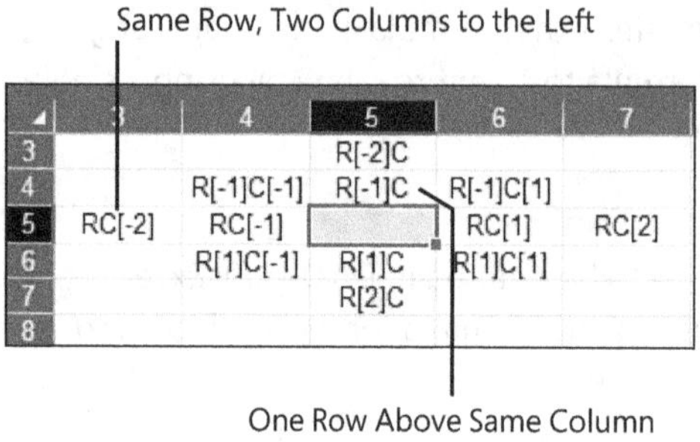

FIGURE 6-6 Various relative references, which would be entered in cell E5 to describe each cell around E5.

You can use R1C1 style to refer to a range of cells. If you want to add up the 12 cells to the left of the current cell, you use this formula:

=SUM(RC[-12]:RC[-1])

Using R1C1 with absolute references

An *absolute reference* is a reference in which the row and column remain fixed when the formula is copied to a new location. In A1 style notation, Excel uses a $ before the row number or column letter to keep that row or column absolute as the formula is copied.

To always refer to an absolute row or column number, just leave off the square brackets. This reference refers to cell $B$3, no matter where it is entered:

=R3C2

Using R1C1 with mixed references

A *mixed reference* is a reference in which the row is fixed, and the column is allowed to be relative, or in which the column is fixed, and the row is allowed to be relative. This is useful in many situations.

Imagine that you have written a macro to import Invoice.txt into Excel. Using `.End(xlUp)`, you find where the total row should go. As you are entering totals, you know that you want to sum from the row above the formula up to row 2. The following code would handle that:

```
Sub MixedReference()
TotalRow = Cells(Rows.Count, 1).End(xlUp).Row + 1
Cells(TotalRow, 1).Value = "Total"
Cells(TotalRow, 5).Resize(1, 3).FormulaR1C1 = "=SUM(R2C:R[-1]C)"
End Sub
```

In this code, the reference `R2C:R[-1]C` indicates that the formula should add from row 2 in the same column to the row just above the formula in the current column. Do you see the advantage of using R1C1 formulas in this case? You can use a single R1C1 formula with a mixed reference to easily enter a formula to handle an indeterminate number of rows of data (see Figure 6-7).

	1	2	3	4	5	6	7	8
1	InvoiceDate	InvoiceNumber	SalesRepNumber	CustomerNumber	ProductRevenue	ServiceRevenue	ProductCost	
2	6/9/2014	123829	S21	C8754	538400	0	299897	
3	6/9/2014	123830	S45	C4056	588600	0	307563	
4	6/9/2014	123831	S54	C8323	882200	0	521726	
5	6/9/2014	123832	S21	C6026	830900	0	494831	
6	6/9/2014	123833	S45	C3025	673600	0	374953	
7	6/9/2014	123834	S54	C8663	966300	0	528575	
8	6/9/2014	123835	S21	C1508	467100	0	257942	
9	6/9/2014	123836	S45	C7366	658500	10000	308719	
10	6/9/2014	123837	S54	C4533	191700	0	109534	
11	Total				5797300	10000	=SUM(R2C:R[-1]C)	
12								

FIGURE 6-7 After the macro has run, the formulas in columns 5–7 of the total row will have a reference to a range that is locked to row 2, but all other aspects are relative.

Referring to entire columns or rows with R1C1 style

You will occasionally write a formula that refers to an entire column. For example, you might want to know the maximum value in column G. If you don't know how many rows you will have in G, you can write =MAX($G:$G) in A1 style or =MAX(C7) in R1C1 style. To find the minimum value in row 1, use =MIN($1:$1) in A1 style or =MIN(R1) in R1C1 style. You can use relative references for either rows or columns. To find the average of the row above the current cell, use =AVERAGE(R[-1]).

Replacing many A1 formulas with a single R1C1 formula

When you get used to R1C1 style formulas, they actually seem a lot more intuitive to build. One classic example to illustrate R1C1 style formulas is building a multiplication table. It is easy to build a multiplication table in Excel using a single mixed-reference formula.

Building the table

Enter the numbers **1** through **12** going across B1:M1. Copy and transpose these so that the same numbers are going down A2:A13. Now, the challenge is to build a single formula that works in all cells of B2:M13 and shows the multiplication of the number in row 1 by the number in column 1. Using A1 style formulas, you must press the F4 key five times to get the dollar signs in the proper locations. The following is a far simpler formula in R1C1 style:

```
Sub MultiplicationTable()
'Build a multiplication table using a single formula
Range("B1:M1").Value = Array(1, 2, 3, 4, 5, 6, 7, 8, 9, 10, 11, 12)
Range("B1:M1").Font.Bold = True
Range("B1:M1").Copy
Range("A2:A13").PasteSpecial Transpose:=True
Range("B2:M13").FormulaR1C1 = "=RC1*R1C"
Cells.EntireColumn.AutoFit
End Sub
```

The R1C1 style reference =RC1*R1C could not be simpler. In English, it is saying, "Take this row's column 1 and multiply it by row 1 of this column." It works perfectly to build the multiplication table shown in Figure 6-8.

FIGURE 6-8 The macro creates a multiplication table. The formula in B2 uses two mixed references: =$A2*B$1.

> ⊖ **Caution** After running the macro and producing the multiplication table shown in Figure 6-8, note that Excel still has the copied range from line 2 of the macro as the active Clipboard item. If the user of this macro selects a cell and presses Enter, the contents of those cells copy to the new location. However, this is generally not desirable. To get Excel out of Cut/Copy mode, add this line of code before your program ends:
>
> ```
> Application.CutCopyMode = False
> ```

An interesting twist

Try this experiment: Move the cell pointer to F6. Turn on macro recording using the Record Macro button on the Developer tab. Click the Use Relative Reference button on the Developer tab. Enter the formula =**A1** and press Ctrl+Enter to stay in F6. Click the Stop Recording button on the floating toolbar. You get this single-line macro, which enters a formula that points to a cell five rows up and five columns to the left:

```
Sub Macro1()
    Selection.FormulaR1C1 = "=R[-5]C[-5]"
End Sub
```

Now, move the cell pointer to cell B1 and run the macro that you just recorded. You might think that pointing to a cell five rows above B1 would lead to the ubiquitous Run Time Error 1004. But it doesn't! When you run the macro, the formula in cell B1 is pointing to =XFA1048572, as shown in Figure 6-9, meaning that R1C1 style formulas actually wrap from the left side of the workbook to the right side. I cannot think of any instance in which this would actually be useful, but for those of you who rely on Excel to error out when you ask for something that does not make sense, be aware that your macro will happily provide a result that's probably not the one that you expected!

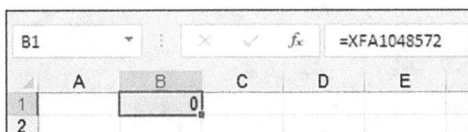

FIGURE 6-9 The formula to point to five rows above B1 wraps around to the bottom of the worksheet.

Remembering column numbers associated with column letters

I like R1C1 style formulas enough to use them regularly in VBA. I don't like them enough to change my Excel interface over to R1C1 style numbers. So, I routinely have to know that the cell known as U21, for example, is really R21C21.

Knowing that *U* is the twenty-first letter of the alphabet is not something that comes naturally. We have 26 letters, so *A* is 1, and *Z* is 26. *M* is the halfway point of the alphabet and is column 13. The rest of the letters are not particularly intuitive. A quick way to get the column number for any column is to enter =COLUMN() in any empty cell in that column. The result tells you that, for example, DGX is column 2910 (see Figure 6-10).

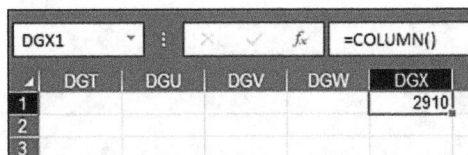

FIGURE 6-10 Use the temporary formula =COLUMN() to learn the column number of any cell.

You could also select any cell in DGX, switch to VBA, press Ctrl+G for the Immediate window, type **? ActiveCell.Column**, and press Enter.

Next steps

This chapter covered a great technique of using R1C1 formulas to make your code easier to understand. In Chapter 7, you find out how you can write code to run automatically based on a user's actions, such as activating a sheet or selecting a cell. This is done with events, which are actions in Excel that you can capture and use to your advantage.

Event programming

In this chapter, you will:

- Learn what events are and how to use them
- Review the different types of workbook-, worksheet-, chart-, and application-level events
- Use a sheet event to quickly enter 24-hour time into a cell

An event allows you to automatically trigger a procedure to run based on something a user or another procedure does in Excel. For example, if a person changes the contents of a cell after they press Enter or Tab, you can have the code run automatically. The event that triggers the code is the changing of the contents of the cell.

Levels of events

You can find events at the following levels:

- **Application level**—Control based on application actions, such as `Application_NewWorkbook`.
- **Workbook level**—Control based on workbook actions, such as `Workbook_Open`.
- **Worksheet level**—Control based on worksheet actions, such as `Worksheet_SelectionChange`.
- **Chart sheet level**—Control based on chart actions, such as `Chart_Activate`.

These are the places where you should put different types of events:

- Workbook events go into the ThisWorkbook module.
- Worksheet events go into the module of the sheet they affect, such as Sheet1.
- Chart sheet events go into the module of the chart sheet they affect, such as Chart1.
- Pivot table events go into the module of the sheet with the pivot table, or they can go into the ThisWorkbook module.
- Embedded chart and application events go into class modules.

The events can still make procedure or function calls outside their own modules. Therefore, if you want the same action to take place for two different sheets, you don't have to copy the code. Instead, place the code in a module and have each sheet event call the procedure.

This chapter explains different levels of events, where to find them, and how to use the events.

> **Note** Userform and control events are discussed in Chapter 10, "Userforms: An introduction," and Chapter 22, "Advanced userform techniques."

Using events

Each level consists of several types of events, and memorizing the syntax of them all would be a feat. Excel makes it easy to view and insert the available events in their proper modules right from the VB Editor.

When a ThisWorkbook, Sheet, Chart Sheet, or Class module is active, the corresponding events are available through the Object and Procedure dropdown, as shown in Figure 7-1.

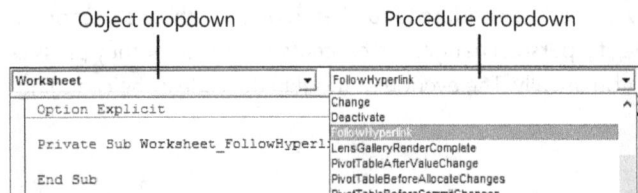

FIGURE 7-1 The different events are easy to access from the VB Editor Object and Procedure dropdown.

After an object is selected, the Procedure dropdown updates to list the events available for that object. Selecting a procedure automatically places the procedure header (`Private Sub`) and footer (`End Sub`) in the editor, as shown in Figure 7-2.

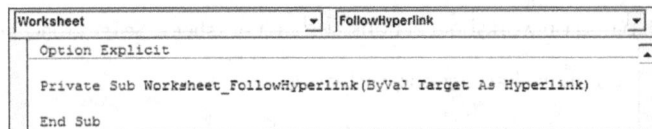

FIGURE 7-2 The procedure header and footer are automatically placed when you make selections from the dropdown.

Event parameters

Some events have parameters, such as `Target` or `Cancel`, that allow values to be passed into the procedure. For example, some procedures are triggered before the actual event, such as `BeforeRightClick`. Assigning `True` to the `Cancel` parameter prevents the default action from taking place. In this case, the shortcut menu is prevented from appearing:

```
Private Sub Worksheet_BeforeRightClick(ByVal Target As Range, Cancel As Boolean)
Cancel = True
End Sub
```

Disabling and enabling events

Some events can trigger other events, including themselves. For example, the Worksheet_Change event is triggered by a change in a cell. If the event is triggered and the procedure itself changes a cell, the event gets triggered again, which changes a cell, triggering the event, and so on. The procedure gets stuck in an endless loop.

To prevent an endless loop, disable the events and then re-enable them at the end of the procedure:

```
Private Sub Worksheet_Change(ByVal Target As Range)
Application.EnableEvents = False 'disable
Range("A1").Value = Target.Value
Application.EnableEvents = True 'enable
End Sub
```

> **Tip**   To interrupt a macro, press Esc or Ctrl+Break. To continue it, use Run on the toolbar or press F5.

Workbook events

Table 7-1 lists event procedures that are available at the workbook level. Some events, such as Workbook_SheetActivate, are sheet events that are available at the workbook level. This means you don't have to copy and paste the code in each sheet in which you want it to run.

> **Note**   Table 7-1 does not include the sheet and pivot table events that are also available at the sheet level. To learn more about such events, such as Workbook_SheetChange, look up the Change event in Table 7-2.

TABLE 7-1 Workbook events

Event Name	Description
Workbook_Activate	Occurs when the workbook containing this event becomes the active workbook.
Workbook_Deactivate	Occurs when the active workbook is switched from the workbook containing the event to another workbook.
Workbook_Open	The default workbook event; occurs when a workbook is opened; no user interface is required.
Workbook_BeforeSave	Occurs when the workbook is saved. SaveAsUI is set to True if the Save As dialog is to be displayed. Setting Cancel to True prevents the workbook from being saved.
Workbook_AfterSave	Occurs after the workbook is saved. Success returns True if the file was saved successfully and False if the save was not successful.

Event Name	Description
Workbook_BeforePrint	Occurs when any print command is used, whether it is in the ribbon, on the keyboard, or in a macro. Setting Cancel to True prevents the workbook from being printed.
Workbook_BeforeClose	Occurs when the user closes a workbook. Setting Cancel to True prevents the workbook from closing.
Workbook_NewSheet	Occurs when a new sheet is added to the active workbook. Sh is the new worksheet or chart sheet object.
Workbook_NewChart	Occurs when the user adds a new chart to the active workbook. Ch is the new chart object. The event is not triggered if a chart is moved from one location to another unless it is moved between a chart sheet and a chart object. In that case, the event is triggered because a new chart sheet or object is being created.
Workbook_WindowResize	Occurs when the user resizes the active workbook's window. Wn is the window.
Workbook_WindowActivate	Occurs when the user activates any workbook window. Wn is the window. Only activating the workbook window starts this event.
Workbook_WindowDeactivate	Occurs when the user deactivates any workbook window. Wn is the window. Only deactivating the workbook window starts this event.
Workbook_AddInInstall	Occurs when the user installs the workbook as an add-in (by selecting File, Options, Add-ins). Double-clicking an .xlam file (an add-in) to open it does not activate the event.
Workbook_AddInUninstall	Occurs when the user uninstalls the workbook (add-in). The add-in is not automatically closed.
Workbook_Sync	Occurs when the user synchronizes the local copy of a sheet in a workbook that is part of a Document Workspace with the copy on the server. SyncEventType is the status of the synchronization.
Workbook_ PivotTableCloseConnection	Occurs when a pivot table report closes its connection to its data source. Target is the pivot table that has closed the connection.
Workbook_ PivotTableOpenConnection	Occurs when a pivot table report opens a connection to its data source. Target is the pivot table that has opened the connection.
Workbook_RowsetComplete	Occurs when the user drills through a record set or calls on the row set action on an OLAP pivot table. Description is a description of the event; Sheet is the name of the sheet on which the record set is created; Success indicates success or failure.
Workbook_BeforeXmlExport	Occurs when the user exports or saves XML data. Map is the map used to export or save the data; Url is the location of the XML file; setting Cancel to True cancels the export operation.
Workbook_AfterXmlExport	Occurs after the user exports or saves XML data. Map is the map used to export or save the data; Url is the location of the XML file; Result indicates success or failure.
Workbook_BeforeXmlImport	Occurs when the user imports or refreshes XML data. Map is the map used to import the data; Url is the location of the XML file; IsRefresh returns True if the event was triggered by refreshing an existing connection and False if triggered by importing from a new data source; setting Cancel to True cancels the import or refresh operation.
Workbook_AfterXmlImport	Occurs when the user exports or saves XML data. Map is the map used to export or save the data; IsRefresh returns True if the event was triggered by refreshing an existing connection and False if triggered by importing from a new data source; Result indicates success or failure.

Event Name	Description
Workbook_ModelChange	Occurs when the user changes the Data Model. Changes is the type of change, such as columns added, changed, or deleted, that was made to the Data Model.
Workbook_BeforeRemoteChange	Occurs before changes by a remote user are merged into the workbook.
Workbook_AfterRemoteChange	Occurs after changes by a remote user are merged into the workbook.

Workbook-level sheet events

Table 7-2 lists sheet and pivot table events that are available at the workbook level. These events affect all sheets and pivot tables in the workbook.

TABLE 7-2 Workbook-level sheet and pivot table events

Event Name	Description
Workbook_SheetActivate	Occurs when the user activates any chart sheet or worksheet in the workbook. Sh is the active sheet.
Workbook_SheetBeforeDelete	Occurs before any worksheet in the workbook is deleted. Sh is the sheet being deleted.
Workbook_SheetBeforeDoubleClick	Occurs when the user double-clicks any chart sheet or worksheet in the active workbook. Sh is the active sheet; Target is the object that's double-clicked; setting Cancel to True prevents the default action from taking place.
Workbook_SheetBeforeRightClick	Occurs when the user right-clicks any worksheet in the active workbook. Sh is the active worksheet; Target is the object that's right-clicked; setting Cancel to True prevents the default action from taking place.
Workbook_SheetCalculate	Occurs when any worksheet is recalculated, or any updated data is plotted on a chart. Sh is the sheet that triggers the calculation.
Workbook_SheetChange	Occurs when the user changes any range in a worksheet. Sh is the worksheet; Target is the changed range.
Workbook_SheetDeactivate	Occurs when the user deactivates any chart sheet or worksheet in the workbook. Sh is the sheet being switched from.
Workbook_SheetFollowHyperlink	Occurs when the user clicks any hyperlink in Excel. Sh is the active worksheet; Target is the hyperlink.
Workbook_SheetSelectionChange	Occurs when the user selects a new range on any sheet. Sh is the active sheet; Target is the affected range.
Workbook_SheetTableUpdate	Occurs after a query table (not a list object) connected to a data model is updated. Sh is the sheet with the query table; Target is the query table that was updated.
Workbook_SheetLensGalleryRenderComplete	Occurs when the user selects the Quick Analysis tool. Sh is the active sheet.
Workbook_SheetPivotTableUpdate	Occurs when the user updates a pivot table. Sh is the sheet with the pivot table; Target is the updated pivot table.
Workbook_SheetPivotTableAfterValueChange	Occurs after the user edits cells inside a pivot table or the user recalculates them if they contain a formula. Sh is the sheet the pivot table is on; TargetPivotTable is the pivot table with the changed cells; TargetRange is the range that was changed.

Event Name	Description
Workbook_SheetPivotTableBeforeAllocateChanges	Occurs before a pivot table is updated from its OLAP data source. Sh is the sheet the pivot table is on; TargetPivotTable is the updated pivot table; ValueChangeStart is the index number of the first change; and ValueChangeEnd is the index number of the last change. Setting Cancel to True prevents the changes from being applied to the pivot table.
Workbook_SheetPivotTableBeforeCommitChanges	Occurs before an OLAP pivot table updates its data source. Sh is the sheet the pivot table is on; TargetPivotTable is the updated pivot table; ValueChangeStart is the index number of the first change; and ValueChangeEnd is the index number of the last change. Setting Cancel to True prevents the changes from being applied to the data source.
Workbook_SheetPivotTableBeforeDiscardChanges	Occurs before an OLAP pivot table discards changes from its data source. Sh is the sheet the pivot table is on; TargetPivotTable is the pivot table with changes to discard; ValueChangeStart is the index number of the first change; and ValueChangeEnd is the index number of the last change.
Workbook_SheetPivotTableChangeSync	Occurs after the user changes a pivot table. Sh is the sheet the pivot table is on; Target is the pivot table that has been changed.

Worksheet events

Table 7-3 lists worksheet and pivot table event procedures that are available at the worksheet level.

TABLE 7-3 Worksheet events

Event Name	Description
Worksheet_Activate	Occurs when the sheet on which the event is located becomes the active sheet.
Worksheet_BeforeDelete	Occurs before the sheet on which the event is located is deleted.
Worksheet_Deactivate	Occurs when another sheet becomes the active sheet. If a Deactivate event is on the active sheet and you switch to a sheet with an Activate event, the Deactivate event runs first, followed by the Activate event.
Worksheet_BeforeDoubleClick	Allows control over what happens when the user double-clicks the sheet. Target is the selected range on the sheet. Cancel is set to False by default, but if set to True, it prevents the default action, such as entering a cell, from happening.
Worksheet_BeforeRightClick	Occurs when the user right-clicks a range. Target is the object that's right-clicked; setting Cancel to True prevents the default action from taking place.
Worksheet_Calculate	Occurs after a sheet is recalculated.
Worksheet_Change	Triggered by a change to a cell's value, such as when the user enters, edits, deletes, or pastes text. Recalculation of a value does not trigger the event. Target is the cell that has been changed.
Worksheet_SelectionChange	Occurs when the user selects a new range. Target is the newly selected range.
Worksheet_FollowHyperlink	Occurs when the user clicks a hyperlink. Target is the hyperlink.
Worksheet_LensGalleryRenderComplete	Occurs when the user selects the Quick Analysis tool.

Event Name	Description
Worksheet_PivotTableUpdate	Occurs when the user updates a pivot table. Target is the updated pivot table.
Worksheet_PivotTableAfterValueChange	Occurs after the user edits cells inside a pivot table or the user recalculates them if they contain a formula. TargetPivotTable is the pivot table with the changed cells; TargetRange is the range that was changed.
Worksheet_PivotTableBeforeAllocateChanges	Occurs before a pivot table is updated from its OLAP data source. Sh is the sheet the pivot table is on; TargetPivotTable is the updated pivot table; ValueChangeStart is the index number of the first change; ValueChangeEnd is the index number of the last change; setting Cancel to True prevents the changes from being applied to the pivot table.
Worksheet_PivotTableBeforeCommitChanges	Occurs before an OLAP pivot table updates its data source. TargetPivotTable is the updated pivot table; ValueChangeStart is the index number of the first change; ValueChangeEnd is the index number of the last change; setting Cancel to True prevents the changes from being applied to the data source.
Worksheet_PivotTableBeforeDiscardChanges	Occurs before an OLAP pivot table discards changes from its data source. TargetPivotTable is the pivot table with changes to discard; ValueChangeStart is the index number of the first change; ValueChangeEnd is the index number of the last change.
Worksheet_PivotTableChangeSync	Occurs after a pivot table has been changed. Target is the pivot table that has been changed.
Worksheet_TableUpdate	Occurs after a query table (not a list object) connected to a data model is updated. Target is the query table that has been changed.

Case study: Quickly entering 24-hour time into a cell

Say that you're entering arrival and departure times and want the times to be formatted with a 24-hour clock. You have tried formatting the cells, but no matter how you enter the times, they are displayed as 0:00.

The only way to get the time to appear as 24-hour time, such as 23:45, is to have the time entered in the cell in that manner. Because typing the colon is time-consuming, it would be more efficient to enter the numbers and let Excel format the time for you.

The solution is to use a Change event to take what is in the cell and insert the colon for you:

```
Private Sub Worksheet_Change(ByVal Target As Range)
Dim UserInput As String, NewInput As String
If Target.Count > 1 Then Exit Sub 'more than 1 cell selected
If Target.Column < 3 Then
  UserInput = Target.Value
  If IsNumeric(UserInput) Then
    If Len(UserInput) > 2 Then
      NewInput = Left(UserInput, Len(UserInput) - 2) & ":" & _
        Right(UserInput, 2)
    Else 'midnight hour, since Excel drops the leading zeroes
      NewInput = "00:" & Format(UserInput, "00")
    End If
    Application.EnableEvents = False
    Target = NewInput
```

```
    Application.EnableEvents = True
    End If
End If
End Sub
```

An entry of 2345 displays as 23:45. Note that the code limits this format change to columns A and B (`If ThisColumn < 3`). Without this limitation, entering numbers anywhere on a sheet, such as in a totals column, would force the numbers to be reformatted.

> ⊖ **Caution** Use `Application.EnableEvents = False` to prevent the procedure from calling itself when the value in the target is updated.

Chart events

Chart events occur when a chart is changed or activated. Embedded charts (charts on a worksheet) require the use of a class module to access the events. For more information about class modules, see Chapter 9, "Creating custom objects and collections."

Embedded charts

Because embedded charts do not create chart sheets, the chart events are not as readily available as those of chart sheets. However, you can make them available by adding a class module, as described here:

1. Insert a class module.

2. Rename the module to something that will make sense to you, such as `cl_ChartEvents`.

3. Enter the following line of code in the class module:

    ```
    Public WithEvents myChartClass As Chart
    ```

    The chart events are now available to the chart, as shown in Figure 7-3. They are accessed in the class module rather than on a chart sheet.

4. Insert a standard module.

5. Enter the following lines of code in the standard module, making sure the `Dim myClassModule` line is placed at the top of the module after any `Option` statements you may have:

    ```
    Dim myClassModule As New cl_ChartEvents
    Sub InitializeChart()
        Set myClassModule.myChartClass = Worksheets(1).ChartObjects(1).Chart
    End Sub
    ```

These lines initialize the embedded chart to be recognized as a chart object. The procedure must be run once per Excel session.

> **Tip** You can use `Workbook_Open` to automatically run the `InitializeChart` procedure.

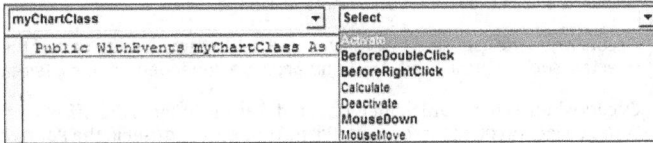

FIGURE 7-3 Embedded chart events are now available in the class module.

Embedded chart and chart sheet events

Whether a chart is embedded on a worksheet or is its own chart sheet, the same events are available. The only difference will be that the procedure heading for an embedded chart replaces Chart with the class object you created. For example, to trigger the BeforeDoubleClick event on a chart sheet, the procedure header would be this: `Chart_BeforeDoubleClick`.

To trigger the BeforeDoubleClick event on an embedded chart (using the class object created in the previous section), the procedure header would be this: `myChartClass_BeforeDoubleClick`.

Table 7-4 lists the various chart events available to both embedded charts and chart sheets.

TABLE 7-4 Chart events

Event Name	Description
Chart_Activate	Occurs when a chart sheet is activated or changed.
Chart_BeforeDoubleClick	Occurs when any part of a chart is double-clicked. ElementID is the part of the chart that is double-clicked, such as the legend. Arg1 and Arg2 are dependent on the ElementID; setting Cancel to True prevents the default double-click action from occurring.
Chart_BeforeRightClick	Occurs when the user right-clicks a chart. Setting Cancel to True prevents the default right-click action from occurring.
Chart_Calculate	Occurs when the user changes a chart's data.
Chart_Deactivate	Occurs when the user makes another object (such as another chart or sheet) the active object.
Chart_MouseDown	Occurs when the cursor is over the chart, and the user presses any mouse button. Button is the mouse button that was clicked; Shift is whether the Shift, Ctrl, or Alt keys were pressed; X is the X coordinate of the cursor when the button is pressed; Y is the Y coordinate of the cursor when the button is pressed.
Chart_MouseMove	Occurs as the user moves the cursor over a chart. Button is the mouse button being held down, if any; Shift is whether the Shift, Ctrl, or Alt keys were pressed; X is the X coordinate of the cursor on the chart; Y is the Y coordinate of the cursor on the chart.

Event Name	Description
Chart_MouseUp	Occurs when the user releases any mouse button while the cursor is on the chart. Button is the mouse button that was clicked; Shift is whether the Shift, Ctrl, or Alt keys were pressed; X is the X coordinate of the cursor when the button is released; Y is the Y coordinate of the cursor when the button is released.
Chart_Resize	Occurs when the user resizes a chart using the resize handles. However, this does not occur when the size is changed using the size controls on the Chart Tools, Format tab or in the Format Chart Area task pane.
Chart_Select	Occurs when the user selects a chart element. ElementID is the part of the chart selected, such as the legend. Arg1 and Arg2 are dependent on the ElementID.
Chart_SeriesChange	Occurs when a chart data point is updated. SeriesIndex is the offset in the Series collection of updated series; PointIndex is the offset in the Point collection of updated points.

Application-level events

Application-level events, listed in Table 7-5, affect all open workbooks in an Excel session. You need a class module to access them. This is similar to the class module used to access events for embedded charts. For more information about class modules, see Chapter 9.

Follow these steps to create the class module:

1. Insert a class module.

2. Rename the module to something that makes sense to you, such as cl_AppEvents.

3. Enter the following line of code in the class module:

   ```
   Public WithEvents AppEvent As Application
   ```

   The application events are now available to the workbook, as shown in Figure 7-4. They are accessed in the class module rather than in a standard module.

4. Insert a standard module.

5. Enter the following lines of code in the standard module, making sure the Dim myAppEvent line is placed at the top of the module after any Option statements you may have:

   ```
   Dim myAppEvent As New cl_AppEvents
   Sub InitializeAppEvent()
   Set myAppEvent.AppEvent = Application
   End Sub
   ```

These lines initialize the application to recognize application events. The procedure must be run once per session.

> **Tip** You can use Workbook_Open to automatically run the InitializeAppEvent procedure.

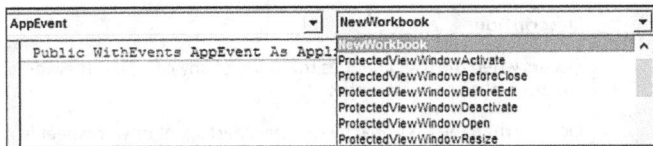

FIGURE 7-4 Application events are now available through the class module.

> 📝 **Note** The object in front of the event, such as AppEvent, is dependent on the name given in the class module.

TABLE 7-5 Application events

Event Name	Description
AppEvent_AfterCalculate	Occurs after all calculations are complete, after AfterRefresh, and SheetChange events, and after Application.CalculationState is set to xlDone, and there aren't any outstanding queries or incomplete calculations.
AppEvent_NewWorkbook	Occurs when the user creates a new workbook. Wb is the new workbook.
AppEvent_ProtectedViewWindowActivate	Occurs when the user activates a workbook in Protected View mode. Pvw is the workbook being activated.
AppEvent_ProtectedViewWindowBeforeClose	Occurs when the user closes a workbook in Protected View mode. Pvw is the workbook being deactivated; Reason is why the workbook closed; setting Cancel to True prevents the workbook from closing.
AppEvent_ProtectedViewWindowDeactivate	Occurs when the user deactivates a workbook in Protected View mode. Pvw is the workbook being deactivated.
AppEvent_ProtectedViewWindowOpen	Occurs when a workbook is open in Protected View mode. Pvw is the workbook being opened.
AppEvent_ProtectedViewWindowResize	Occurs when the user resizes the window of the protected workbook. However, this does not occur in the application itself. Pvw is the workbook that's being resized.
AppEvent_ProtectedViewWindowBeforeEdit	Occurs when the user clicks the Enable Editing button in a protected workbook. Pvw is the protected workbook; setting Cancel to True prevents the workbook from being enabled.
AppEvent_SheetActivate	Occurs when the user activates a sheet. Sh is the worksheet or chart sheet.
AppEvent_SheetBeforeDelete	Occurs before any worksheet in a workbook is deleted. Sh is the sheet being deleted.
AppEvent_SheetBeforeDoubleClick	Occurs when the user double-clicks a worksheet. Target is the selected range on the sheet; Cancel is set to False by default. However, when set to True, it prevents the default action, such as entering a cell, from happening.
AppEvent_SheetBeforeRightClick	Occurs when the user right-clicks any worksheet. Sh is the active worksheet; Target is the object that's right-clicked; setting Cancel to True prevents the default action from taking place.
AppEvent_SheetCalculate	Occurs when the user recalculates any worksheet or plots any updated data on a chart. Sh is the active sheet.

Event Name	Description
AppEvent_SheetChange	Occurs when the user changes the value of any cell. Sh is the worksheet; Target is the changed range.
AppEvent_SheetDeactivate	Occurs when the user deactivates any chart sheet or worksheet in a workbook. Sh is the sheet being deactivated.
AppEvent_SheetFollowHyperlink	Occurs when the user clicks any hyperlink in Excel. Sh is the active worksheet; Target is the hyperlink.
AppEvent_SheetSelectionChange	Occurs when the user selects a new range on any sheet. Sh is the active sheet; Target is the selected range.
AppEvent_SheetTableUpdate	Occurs after a query table (not a list object) connected to a data model is updated. Sh is the active sheet; Target is the query table that has been updated.
AppEvent_ SheetLensGalleryRenderComplete	Occurs when the user selects the Quick Analysis tool. Sh is the active sheet.
AppEvent_SheetPivotTableUpdate	Occurs when the user updates a pivot table. Sh is the active sheet; Target is the updated pivot table.
AppEvent_ SheetPivotTableAfterValueChange	Occurs after the user edits cells inside a pivot table or, if the cells contain a formula, the user recalculates them. Sh is the sheet the pivot table is on; TargetPivotTable is the pivot table with the changed cells; TargetRange is the range that was changed.
AppEvent_ SheetPivotTableBeforeAllocateChanges	Occurs before a pivot table is updated from its OLAP data source. Sh is the sheet the pivot table is on; TargetPivotTable is the updated pivot table; ValueChangeStart is the index number of the first change; ValueChangeEnd is the index number of the last change; setting Cancel to True prevents the changes from being applied to the pivot table.
AppEvent_ SheetPivotTableBeforeCommitChanges	Occurs before an OLAP pivot table updates its data source. Sh is the sheet the pivot table is on; TargetPivotTable is the updated pivot table; ValueChangeStart is the index number of the first change; ValueChangeEnd is the index number of the last change; setting Cancel to True prevents the changes from being applied to the data source.
AppEvent_ SheetPivotTableBeforeDiscardChanges	Occurs before an OLAP pivot table discards changes from its data source. Sh is the sheet the pivot table is on; TargetPivotTable is the pivot table with changes to discard; ValueChangeStart is the index number of the first change; ValueChangeEnd is the index number of the last change.
AppEvent_WindowActivate	Occurs when the user activates any workbook window. Wb is the workbook that's being deactivated; Wn is the window. This only works if there are multiple windows.
AppEvent_WindowDeactivate	Occurs when the user deactivates any workbook window. Wb is the active workbook; Wn is the window. This only works if there are multiple windows.
AppEvent_WindowResize	Occurs when the user resizes the active workbook. Wb is the active workbook; Wn is the window.
AppEvent_WorkbookActivate	Occurs when the user activates any workbook. Wb is the workbook being activated.
AppEvent_WorkbookDeactivate	Occurs when the user switches between workbooks. Wb is the workbook that's being switched away from.

Event Name	Description
AppEvent_WorkbookAddinInstall	Occurs when the user installs a workbook as an add-in (via File, Options, Add-ins). Double-clicking an .xlam file to open it does not activate the event. Wb is the workbook being installed.
AppEvent_WorkbookAddinUninstall	Occurs when the user uninstalls a workbook (add-in). The add-in is not automatically closed. Wb is the workbook being uninstalled.
AppEvent_WorkbookBeforeClose	Occurs when the user closes a workbook. Wb is the workbook; setting Cancel to True prevents the workbook from closing.
AppEvent_WorkbookBeforePrint	Occurs when the user uses any print command (via the ribbon, keyboard, or a macro). Wb is the workbook; setting Cancel to True prevents the workbook from being printed.
AppEvent_Workbook_BeforeSave	Occurs when the user saves the workbook. Wb is the workbook; SaveAsUI is set to True if the Save As dialog is to be displayed; setting Cancel to True prevents the workbook from being saved.
AppEvent_WorkbookAfterSave	Occurs after the user has saved the workbook. Wb is the workbook; Success returns True if the file was saved successfully and returns False if the save was not successful.
AppEvent_WorkbookNewSheet	Occurs when the user adds a new sheet to the active workbook. Wb is the workbook; Sh is the new worksheet.
AppEvent_WorkbookNewChart	Occurs when the user adds a new chart to the active workbook. Wb is the workbook; Ch is the new chart object. The event is not triggered if the user moves a chart from one location to another unless the user moves it between a chart sheet and a chart object. In that case, the event is triggered because a new chart sheet or object is being created.
AppEvent_WorkbookOpen	Occurs when the user opens a workbook. Wb is the workbook that was just opened.
AppEvent_WorkbookPivotTableCloseConnection	Occurs when a pivot table report closes its connection to its data source. Wb is the workbook containing the pivot table that triggered the event; Target is the pivot table that has closed the connection.
AppEvent_WorkbookPivotTableOpenConnection	Occurs when a pivot table report opens a connection to its data source. Wb is the workbook containing the pivot table that triggered the event; Target is the pivot table that has opened the connection.
AppEvent_WorkbookRowsetComplete	Occurs when the user drills through a record set or calls upon the row set action on an OLAP pivot table. Wb is the workbook that triggered the event; Description is a description of the event; Sheet is the name of the sheet on which the record set is created; Success indicates success or failure.
AppEvent_WorkbookSync	Occurs when the user synchronizes the local copy of a sheet in a workbook that is part of a document workspace with the copy on the server. Wb is the workbook that triggered the event; SyncEventType is the status of the synchronization.
AppEvent_WorkbookBeforeXmlExport	Occurs when the user exports or saves XML data. Wb is the workbook that triggered the event; Map is the map used to export or save the data; Url is the location of the XML file; Cancel set to True cancels the export operation.
AppEvent_WorkbookAfterXmlExport	Occurs after the user exports or saves XML data. Wb is the workbook that triggered the event; Map is the map used to export or save the data; Url is the location of the XML file; Result indicates success or failure.

Event Name	Description
AppEvent_WorkbookBeforeXmlImport	Occurs when the user imports or refreshes XML data. Wb is the workbook that triggered the event; Map is the map used to import the data; Url is the location of the XML file; IsRefresh returns True if the event was triggered by refreshing an existing connection and False if triggered by importing from a new data source; setting Cancel to True cancels the import or refresh operation.
AppEvent_WorkbookAfterXmlImport	Occurs after the user imports or refreshes XML data. Wb is the workbook that triggered the event; Map is the map used to import the data; IsRefresh returns True if the event was triggered by refreshing an existing connection and False if triggered by importing from a new data source; Result indicates success or failure.
AppEvent_WorkbookModelChange	Occurs when the user changes the Data Model. Wb is the workbook that triggered the event; Changes is the type of change, such as columns added, changed, or deleted, that the user made to the Data Model.
AppEvent_ WorkbookAfterRemoteChange	Occurs after changes by a remote user are merged into the workbook. Wb is the workbook that triggered the event.
AppEvent_ WorkbookBeforeRemoteChange	Occurs before changes by a remote user are merged into the workbook. Wb is the workbook that triggered the event.

Next steps

In this chapter, you've learned more about interfacing with Excel. In Chapter 8, "Arrays," you find out how to use multidimensional arrays. Reading data into a multidimensional array, performing calculations on the array, and then writing the array back to a range can speed up your macros dramatically.

CHAPTER 8

Arrays

In this chapter, you will:

- Learn how to declare an array

- Fill an array

- Retrieve data from an array

- Place code in memory for faster processing

- Extract a single element from an array

- Resize arrays while looping

- Pass an array to another procedure or function

An *array* is a type of variable that can be used to hold more than one piece of data. For example, if you have to work with the name and address of a client, your first thought might be to assign one variable for the name and another for the address of the client. Instead, consider using an array, which can hold both pieces of information—and not for just one client but for thousands.

> **Note** I consider this chapter the first step in leveling up your programming skills. By learning to work with arrays, you'll not only speed up your code but also open up a whole new world of possibilities.

Declaring an array

You declare an array by adding parentheses after the array name and specifying the number of array elements in the parentheses:

```
Dim myArray(2)
```

This creates an array, myArray, that contains three elements holding the values 10, apples, and 30:

```
myArray(0) = 10
myArray(1) = "apples"
myArray(2) = 30
```

Three elements are included because, by default, the index count starts at 0. If the counter needs to start at 1, use `Option Base 1` to force the count to start at 1. To do this, place the `Option Base` statement in the declarations section at the top of the module:

```
Option Base 1
Sub MyFirstArray()
Dim myArray(2)
```

This forces any arrays in the current module to start at 1. This array now has only two elements.

> **Note**   Unlike other variables, arrays in VBA don't require a specific data type declaration because they can hold various types of data, such as integers, strings, or even other arrays. But if you want to limit the data type, such as to strings only, then do this:
>
> ```
> Dim myArray(2) as String
> ```

You also can create an array independently of the `Option Base` statement by declaring its lower and upper bounds:

```
Dim myArray(1 to 10)
Dim BigArray(100 to 200)
```

Every array has a lower bound (`LBound`) and an upper bound (`UBound`). When you declare `Dim myArray(2)`, you are declaring the upper bound and allowing the `Option Base` statement to declare the lower bound. By declaring `Dim myArray(1 to 10)`, you declare the lower bound, 1, and the upper bound, 10.

> **Note**   Unless otherwise noted, all samples in this chapter are Option Base 0.

Declaring a multidimensional array

The arrays just discussed are considered one-dimensional arrays because only one number designates the location of an element of the array. Such an array is like a single row of data, but because there can be only one row, you do not have to worry about the row number—only the column number. For example, to retrieve the second element (column) use `myArray(1)`.

In some cases, a single dimension is not enough. This is where multidimensional arrays come in. Whereas a one-dimensional array is like a single row of data, a two-dimensional array contains rows and columns.

To declare another dimension to an array, you add another argument. The following creates an array of 10 rows and 20 columns:

```
Dim myArray(1 to 10, 1 to 20)
```

Note Another word for an array is *matrix*, which is what a spreadsheet is. The `Cells` object refers to elements of a spreadsheet—and a cell consists of a row and a column. You've been using arrays all along!

You can create additional dimensions by including additional arguments. For example, to create a three-dimensional array, do this:

```
Dim myArray (1 to 4, 1 to 10, 1 to 4)
```

Caution When working with arrays, remember that:

1D arrays are like a single row of data. The index refers to the position within that row—that is, the column.
2D arrays are like a data set with rows and columns. The first index refers to the row, and the second index refers to the column.

Always double-check your array dimensions and indexing to ensure you're accessing the correct elements.

Assume you have the data shown in Figure 8-1, and you want to place it, without the headers, into an array. Place the values in the first two columns of the first row of data, and the VBE Watch window updates as shown in Figure 8-2:

```
Dim arrData (1 to 8, 1 to 100)
arrData (1,1) = "John Doe"
arrData (1,2) = "8/5/2024"
```

	A	B	C	D	E	F	G	H
1	**Customer Name**	**Order Date**	**Ship Date**	**Product Name**	**Qty**	**Price Per**	**Total**	**Status**
2	John Doe	8/5/2024	8/11/2024	Gadget	37	$2.25	$83.25	
3	Ashley Taylor	9/29/2024		Doohickey	50	$0.88	$44.00	
4	Emily Davis	8/2/2024	8/14/2024	Thingy 1	47	$1.12	$52.64	
5	Tom Nguyen	8/27/2024	9/6/2024	Widget B	45	$2.91	$130.95	
6	Chris Brown	9/7/2024		Doohickey	45	$1.12	$50.40	
7	Jenny Martinez	9/4/2024	9/18/2024	Gizmo	5	$2.25	$11.25	

FIGURE 8-1 Order data that will be placed into an array.

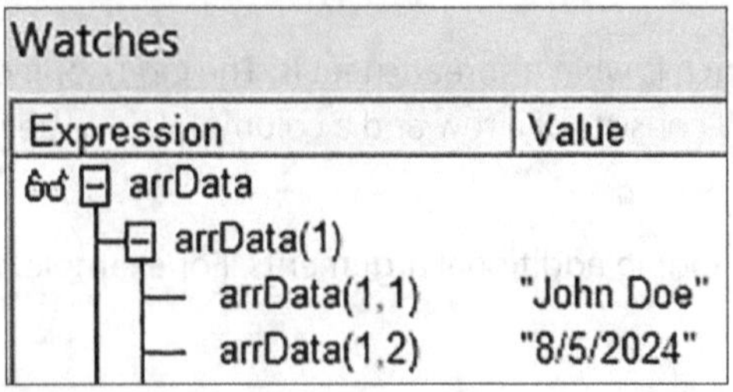

FIGURE 8-2 The VB Editor Watch window shows the first row of the array being filled from the previous lines of code.

The following code places values in the first two columns of the second row:

```
arrData(2,1) = "Ashley Taylor"
arrData(2,2) = "9/29/2024"
```

And so on. Of course, this is time-consuming and can require many lines of code. Other ways to fill an array are discussed in the next section.

Filling an array

Now that you can declare an array, you need to fill it. So far, we've entered a value for each element of the array individually, which can be a slow process when you have a lot of data. If you're filling from a sheet, you may be tempted to loop it. However, there are quicker ways, depending on your situation.

Using the `Array` function

If you just need a single row in an array, like the header shown in Figure 8-3, you can use the `Array` function to shove the data into the array. Notice that, in this case, you don't have to declare the size of the array when you fill it, as shown in the following example.

```
Dim arrHeader()
'Fill the variable with array data
arrHeader = Array("Customer Name", "Product Name", "Qty")
'Unload the array onto a sheet by placing it in a range of the same size
Worksheets("Report1").Range("A1").Resize(, UBound(arrHeader )+1).Value _
   = arrHeader
```

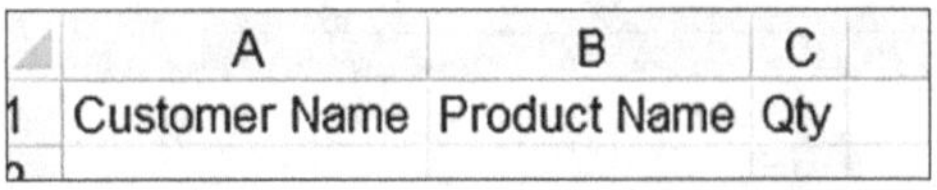

	A	B	C
1	Customer Name	Product Name	Qty

FIGURE 8-3 Use an array to create column headers quickly.

Instead of explicitly stating the entire range when placing the array, the first cells, A1, is noted, but then the range is resized. When you resize a range using `UBound`, you're determining the size of the array and ensuring that the range is large enough to accommodate all the elements, in this case, increasing the number of columns. The +1 adjustment accounts for the 0-based indexing of arrays in VBA.

> **Note** You can still use the Array function if you need to fill a single column. You'll just have to transpose the array as you place it on the sheet. See the section "Transposing an array" if you need to place the data in a column instead of a row.

Filling from a sheet or listobject

If the information needed in the array is on the sheet already, use the following to place the data into the array. By calculating the last row and column used by the data set, you can place any size data set quickly into an array, like this:

```
Dim arrData()
Dim FinalRow As Long, FinalColumn As Long
'data only, -1 so we don't include header
FinalRow = Cells(Rows.Count, 1).End(xlUp).Row - 1
FinalColumn = Cells(1, Columns.Count).End(xlToLeft).Column
arrData = Range("A2").Resize(FinalRow, FinalColumn).Value
```

If the data is in a listobject, thanks to the DataBodyRange property, it's even easier to dump the data into an array, like this:

```
Dim arrData()
arrData = ActiveSheet.ListObjects(1).DataBodyRange.Value2
```

Thanks to the listobject's properties, the five lines of code used for the data set become just two for the listobject.

Either way, when you look at the array in the Watch Window, shown in Figure 8-4, you'll notice the LBound is 1, instead of 0, because sheets start in row 1. Keep this in mind when looping — or use LBound(arrData) to start your loop on the correct element.

Watches	
Expression	Value
𝟞𝟞 ⊟ arrData	
⊟ arrData(1)	
— arrData(1,1)	"John Doe"
— arrData(1,2)	45509
— arrData(1,3)	45515
— arrData(1,4)	"Gadget"

FIGURE 8-4 Despite the fact that the module is 0-based, because the data comes directly from a sheet, the lower bound of arrData is 1.

> **Tip** In the previous code, we used `DataBodyRange.Value2` instead of `DataBodyRange.Value`. So what's the difference?
>
> The `Value` property includes formatting, such as currency symbols or date types. The `Value2` property skips all formatting and returns the unformatted value, making your code slightly faster. For example, when using `Value`, a date is held as #8/5/2024#, a date variable. When using `Value2`, it's held as 45509, a double.

Using the `Split` function

If you have delimited data, for example, a comma-delimited list, you can use the `Split` function to parse the data into a 0-based array (even if the module is 1-based). The list will be broken up into string values and placed into a one-dimensional array, as shown in Figure 8-5.

When dimming the array value, if you want to force all values to be treated as strings, do this:

```
Dim arrData() as String
```

Then, using `Split`, assign the results to the variable. So, if `myList` is a comma-delimited list, do this:

```
arrData = Split(myList, ",")
```

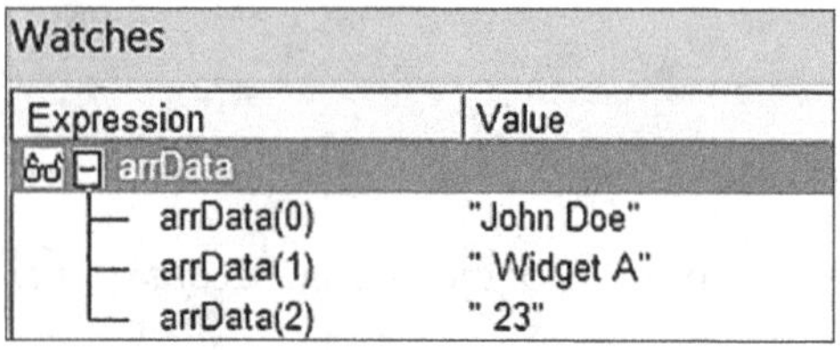
Watches
Expression
Value
arrData
arrData(0)
"John Doe"
arrData(1)
" Widget A"
arrData(2)
" 23"

FIGURE 8-5 Use the Split function to parse a delimited string into an array.

> **Tip** If you know what element in the delimited string you need, you can extract it directly. If you have a delimited string called `myList` and you want the product name, which is the second element, do this:
>
> ```
> Dim ProductName as String
> ProductName = Split(myList, ",")(1)
> ```

Working with data in an array

Now that the data is in memory, you can work with it, such as extracting specific information or performing calculations. To do this, loop through the array, just as you would on a sheet. Except when you do it in memory, it is significantly faster. This is what makes arrays so powerful.

In the examples in Chapter 3, "Referring to ranges, names, and tables," we looped through the rows when placing results on the sheet. You could do this with arrays, writing results as you process each row, but why slow down your program? You've started using arrays—let's keep using them.

Updating existing array fields

In this first example, we're going to update the Status column with "Shipping" or "Pending," depending on whether there is or isn't a date in the Ship Date column. Because the column already exists and is part of the array, we'll write the value directly to the array column, like this:

```
'data only, don't include header
FinalRow = Cells(Rows.Count, 1).End(xlUp).Row - 1
FinalColumn = Cells(1, Columns.Count).End(xlToLeft).Column
arrData = Range("A2").Resize(FinalRow, FinalColumn).Value
For eaRow = LBound(arrData) To UBound(arrData)
  'Ship Date is column C (3)
  If Len(Trim(arrData(eaRow, 3))) = 0 Then
   arrData(eaRow, 8) = "Pending"
  Else
    arrData(eaRow, 8) = "Shipping"
  End If
Next eaRow
```

To place the updated array back on the sheet, do this:

```
Range("A2").Resize(FinalRow, FinalColumn).Value = arrData
```

> **Note** Why use `Len` and `Trim` instead of `IsEmpty`? In Chapter 3, we learned that sometimes an empty cell isn't really empty as far as Excel is concerned. This applies to data that's been transferred to memory.

Using a second array to hold results

But what if there isn't already a column setup in the array? In that case, create a second array to hold the results. Because you don't know the number of rows until the code runs, you'll have to set the size as the code runs. See "Using dynamic arrays" in this chapter for more information on using the `ReDim` statement.

In the following example, we want to calculate the tax and final total for each order, as shown in Figure 8-6. To do this, we declare a new array, `arrTaxTotal`, and once we put the original data into `arrData`, we'll use the upper bound of `arrData`'s first dimension to figure out the number of rows `arrTaxTotal` needs.

Note To get the upper or lower bounds of another dimension, you have to specify the dimension. For example, to retrieve the upper bound of the second dimension, do this: UBound(arrData,2).

As we loop through `arrData`, calculating the tax and final total, the results are placed in `arrTaxTotal`. To finish, we add headers to two new columns and then dump our results, like this:

```
Sub CalculateTax_DataSet()
Dim FinalRow As Long, FinalColumn As Long
Dim arrData(), arrTaxTotal()
Dim TaxRate As Double
Dim eaRow As Long
'data only, don't include header
FinalRow = Cells(Rows.Count, 1).End(xlUp).Row - 1
FinalColumn = Cells(1, Columns.Count).End(xlToLeft).Column
arrData = Range("A2").Resize(FinalRow, FinalColumn).Value
TaxRate = 0.042
'resize based on arrData
ReDim arrTaxTotal(1 To UBound(arrData), 1 To 2)
For eaRow = LBound(arrData) To UBound(arrData)
  arrTaxTotal(eaRow, 1) = arrData(eaRow, 7) * TaxRate
  arrTaxTotal(eaRow, 2) = arrTaxTotal(eaRow, 1) + arrData(eaRow, 7)
Next eaRow
'place the results on the sheet
Cells(1, FinalColumn + 1).Resize(, 2).Value = Array("Tax", "Final Total")
Cells(2, FinalColumn + 1).Resize(FinalRow, UBound(arrTaxTotal, 2)).Value = _
  arrTaxTotal
End Sub
```

	A	B	C	D	E	F	G	H	I	J
1	Customer Name	Order Date	Ship Date	Product Name	Qty	Price Per	Total	Status	Tax	Final Total
2	John Doe	8/5/2024	8/11/2024	Gadget	37	$2.25	$83.25	Shipping	$3.50	$86.75
3	Ashley Taylor	9/29/2024		Doohickey	50	$0.88	$44.00	Pending	$1.85	$45.85
4	Emily Davis	8/2/2024	8/14/2024	Thingy 1	47	$1.12	$52.64	Shipping	$2.21	$54.85
5	Tom Nguyen	8/27/2024	9/6/2024	Widget B	45	$2.91	$130.95	Shipping	$5.50	$136.45
6	Chris Brown	9/7/2024		Doohickey	45	$1.12	$50.40	Pending	$2.12	$52.52
7	Jenny Martinez	9/4/2024	9/18/2024	Gizmo	5	$2.25	$11.25	Shipping	$0.47	$11.72

FIGURE 8-6 You can run two arrays side by side, creating a new array you can dump anywhere in the workbook, including next to the original data set.

If you're working with data in a listobject, placing the results will require you to expand the table first, assigning new (and unique) column headers; then, you can dump the data into the new columns like this:

```
'add new columns to table
For i = 1 To 2 '2 new headers
  curHeader = Choose(i, "Tax", "Final Total")
  ActiveSheet.ListObjects(1).ListColumns.Add
  ActiveSheet.ListObjects(1).ListColumns(LastColumn + i).Name = curHeader
Next i
```

```
'place the results in the table
ActiveSheet.ListObjects(1).ListColumns(LastColumn + 1).DataBodyRange. _
    Resize(, UBound(arrTaxTotal, 2)) = arrTaxTotal
```

> **Level Up!**
>
> These are basic examples of using an array to speed up code. The data is already in an easy-to-read format, so you can simply place it in the array. But what if the data wasn't so well formatted, such as a report you need to convert to a data table? "Converting a fixed-width report to a data set" in Chapter 13 shows how to use a custom object, collection, and array to reorganize the data.

Extracting a single element from a 2D array

Excel doesn't have a specific VBA function for pulling a single element from an array, but it can be done by using the Application.Index function:

```
Application.Index(Array, Row_Number, Column_Number)
```

As shown in Figure 8-7, you can pull an entire row, an entire column, or a single value if you know where in the data it is. When pulling an entire row or column, place the result in an array. When pulling a single value, place it in a variable of the correct data type, such as a string, like this:

```
Dim arrData(), CustomerRow(), ProductColumn()
Dim Product As String
arrData = Worksheets("ListObject").ListObjects("Table1").DataBodyRange.Value2
'pull row 6
CustomerRow = Application.Index(arrData, 6, 0)
'pull column D (4)
ProductColumn = Application.Index(arrData, 0, 4)
'pull the value from row 6, column 4
Product = Application.Index(arrData, 6, 4)
```

Watches	
Expression	**Value**
&d ⊟ CustomerRow	
— CustomerRow(1)	"Jenny Martinez"
— CustomerRow(2)	45539
— CustomerRow(3)	45553
— CustomerRow(4)	"Gizmo"
— CustomerRow(5)	5
— CustomerRow(6)	2.25
— CustomerRow(7)	11.25
— CustomerRow(8)	Empty

FIGURE 8-7 Application.Index is used to pull a specific row from arrData into the array, CustomerRow.

Using dynamic arrays

You don't always know how big an array needs to be. You could create an array based on how big it could ever need to be, but that's a waste of memory—and what if it turns out that it needs to be even bigger? To avoid this problem, you can use a dynamic array. A dynamic array is an array that does not have a set size. In other words, you declare the sizeless array like this:

```
Dim myArray()
```

> **Note** If you want to specify a data type for the elements in the array, include empty parentheses, like this:
>
> ```
> Dim myArray() as String
> ```

Later, as the program needs to use the array, ReDim is used to set the size of the array, like we did when we resized arrTaxTotal in the section "Working with data in an array."

```
Dim arrData(), arrTaxTotal()
arrData = ActiveSheet.ListObjects(1).DataBodyRange.Value2
ReDim arrTaxTotal(1 To UBound(arrData), 1 To 2)
```

Using ReDim reinitializes the array. Therefore, if you use it many times, such as in a loop, you lose all the data it holds. To prevent this from happening, use Preserve. The Preserve keyword enables you to resize the last array dimension while keeping existing data. There are limitations to resizing an array: you cannot use it to change the number of dimensions, and you can only resize the last dimension.

The following example looks for all the Excel files in a directory and puts the results in an array. Because you do not know how many files there will be until you actually look at them, you can't size the array before the program is run:

```
Sub XLFiles()
Dim FName As String
Dim arNames() as String
Dim myCount As Integer
'Dir returns the first filename that matches the argument. To get the rest of
'the filenames, call Dir again, but with no arguments. When no more
'filenames match, Dir returns an empty string ("").
FName = Dir("C:\Excel VBA 2024\*.xls*")
Do Until FName = ""
  myCount = myCount + 1
  ReDim Preserve arNames(1 to 1, 1 To myCount)
  arNames(myCount) = FName
  FName = Dir
Loop
Worksheets("Excel Files").Range("A1").Resize(, myCount).Value = arNames
End Sub
```

Transposing an array

In the previous example, the list of Excel files was placed in a row. To place the list in a column, use the `Application.Transpose` function when dumping the array onto the sheet, like this:

```
Worksheets("Excel Files").Range("A1").Resize(,myCount).Value = _
    Application.Transpose(arNames)
```

This method can be used for any size array, as long as it doesn't exceed the actual number of rows and columns on the sheet.

Tip Assume you have a dynamic array where you need to update the first element (rows). Since that's not allowed, you switch the first two element sizes when you create the array, and then transpose the data when placing the results on a sheet. For example, this is what you want to do, but Excel will not allow it:

```
ReDim myArray(1 to myCount, 1 to 1)
```

Instead, do this:

```
ReDim myArray(1 to 1, 1 to myCount)
'fill array
Range("A1").Resize(myCount).Value = Application.Transpose(myArray)
```

Passing an array

Just like strings, integers, and other variables, arrays can be passed into other procedures. The array must be declared `ByRef` when setting up the procedure's parameters, even if you're not planning to make changes to it. The following sub, `PassAnArray`, passes the array `arrData` into the function `CustomerTotal`. The data in the array is summed for the specified customer, and the result is returned to the sub:

```
Sub PassAnArray()
Dim arrData()
Dim CustomerName As String
```

```
'place the data in the table into the array
arrData = Worksheets("Sales Data").ListObjects("tblSales").DataBodyRange.Value2
CustomerName = InputBox("Enter the customer name")
If CustomerName <> "" Then   'user didn't Cancel or leave blank
  MsgBox CustomerName & "'s purchase total is: " & _
     Format(CustomerTotal(arrData, CustomerName), "$#,#00.00 ")
End If
End Sub
Function CustomerTotal(ByRef AllData, ByVal CustName As String) As Double
Dim eaRow As Long
Dim tmpAmount As Double
tmpAmount = 0
For eaRow = LBound(AllData) To UBound(AllData)
   'customer name is in column 1
   If UCase(AllData(eaRow, 1)) = UCase(CustName) Then
      'The data to sum is the 7th column in the data
      tmpAmount = AllData(eaRow, 7) + tmpAmount
   End If
Next eaRow
CustomerTotal = tmpAmount
End Function
```

> **Tip** Instead of using the specific number 7, there are two other ways you can identify the column to retrieve:
>
> - If you're dealing with a listobject, as we are here, you can return the index number of the column if you know the header text, like this:
>
>   `Worksheets("Sales Data").ListObjects("tblSales").ListColumns("Total").Index`
>
>   This can be useful if the column order may change but not the headers.
>
> - Use the Enum value type. This allows you to specify an integer for a named value, making code easier to read. See "Using Enum to create custom constants" in Chapter 4, "Laying the groundwork with variables and structures."

> **Warning** You can't assign the values of one array to be the values of another unless both arrays are the same size or the second array doesn't have declared dimensions. To append values from one array to another or to pass values between arrays of differing sizes, you have to loop through the arrays.

Next steps

Arrays are a type of variable used for holding more than one piece of data. In Chapter 9, "Creating custom objects and collections," you discover the powerful technique of setting up your own custom object. With this technique, you can create your own object with its own methods and properties.

Creating custom objects and collections

In this chapter, you will:

- Learn how to insert a class module

- Create and use a custom object

- Use collections to hold values or custom objects

- Learn how to use custom objects, collections, and arrays together to write efficient code

- Learn about dictionaries and how they differ from collections

- Define and use user-defined types (UDTs) to organize and store related values

Excel already has many objects available, such as Worksheet, but there are times when the job at hand requires a custom object. You can create custom objects that you use in the same way as Excel's built-in objects. These special objects are created in *class modules*.

Class modules are used to create custom objects with custom properties and methods. They can also be used to trap application events, embedded chart events, ActiveX control events, and more.

Collections are a variable type that can hold groups of similar items, including custom objects. Each item in a collection has a unique key, which can be used to retrieve a value, including all the properties of an object, from the collection.

Inserting a class module

From the VB Editor, select Insert | Class Module. A new module, Class1, is added to the VBAProject workbook and is visible in the Project Explorer window (see Figure 9-1). Here are two things to keep in mind concerning class modules:

- Each custom object must have its own module. (Event trapping can share a module.)

- The class module should be renamed to reflect the custom object.

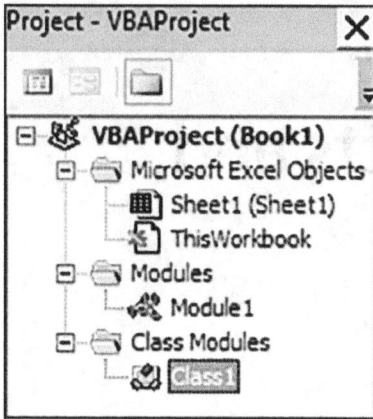

FIGURE 9-1 Custom objects are created in class modules.

> **Note** Chapter 7, "Event programming," explains how certain actions in workbooks, worksheets, and nonembedded charts can be trapped and used to activate code. Refer to that chapter for setting up a class module to trap application and chart events.

Creating a custom object

Class modules are useful for trapping events, but they also are valuable because you can use them to create custom objects. When you are creating a custom object, the class module becomes a template of the object's properties and methods.

Properties are variables in the object that you can assign a value to or read a value from. They can be private, in which case they are accessible only within the class module itself. If they're public, they're available from any module once access to the custom object has been set up.

Methods are procedures in the object that will perform an action, just like the subs and functions in standard modules. Subs do not return values, while functions return values of the specified type. They also can be private or public.

Consider the Worksheet object. When you refer to it in your code, as soon as you hit the period (.) on the keyboard, a tooltip appears listing several items, as shown in Figure 9-2. These are the various properties and methods available in the Worksheet object.

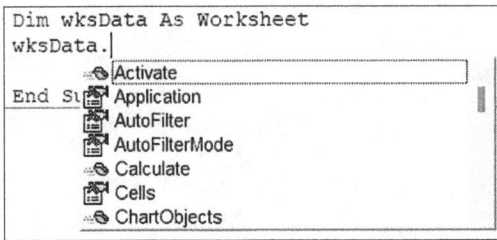

```
Dim wksData As Worksheet
wksData.|
          Activate
End Su    Application
          AutoFilter
          AutoFilterMode
          Calculate
          Cells
          ChartObjects
```

FIGURE 9-2 The properties and methods of standard objects are easily accessible via a tooltip while coding.

Tip If the tooltip doesn't appear, it's possible there's something wrong with the code somewhere in the workbook, and it won't compile. Go to the Debug menu, select Compile VBAProject, and resolve any issues the compiler finds. Repeat until all issues are resolved. Then, go back to your original position, delete the period, and type it again. The tooltip should appear.

The tooltip identifies properties, such as `Application`, with one icon and methods, such as `Calculate`, with a different one. These icons will also be used with custom objects so you can quickly differentiate between properties and methods.

To demonstrate custom object creation and usage, we'll create an object for the sales data shown in Figure 9-3. It will include 12 properties: six that are read (`Get`) and write (`Let`), one that is read-only (`Get`), five of which will be write-only (`Let`), and one private method and two public methods to calculate values for some of the properties.

	A	B	C	D	E	F
1	Customer Name ˅	Order Date ˅	Ship Date ˅	Product Name ˅	Qty ˅	Price Per ˅
2	John Doe	8/5/2024	8/11/2024	Gadget	37	$2.25
3	John Doe	8/5/2024	8/11/2024	Gadget	3	$2.25
4	Ashley Taylor	9/29/2024		Doohickey	50	$0.88
5	Emily Davis	8/2/2024	8/14/2024	Thingy 1	47	$1.12
6	Tom Nguyen	8/27/2024	9/6/2024	Widget B	45	$2.91
7	Chris Brown	9/7/2024		Doohickey	45	$1.12

FIGURE 9-3 Sample data used in the following code examples. This data set consists of sales records, including customer names, order and ship dates, product names, quantities, and prices.

To get started, insert a class module and rename it `clsSalesData`, as shown in Figure 9-4. To rename it, do the following:

1. Select the class module in the VBAProject window.

2. Press F4 to ensure the Properties window is open.

3. In the Properties window, change the Name property to `clsSalesData`, and then press Enter to get out of the field.

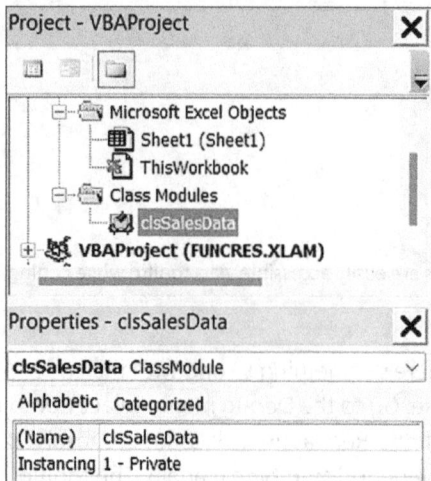

FIGURE 9-4 Rename the class module to something easier to identify and differentiate it from other class modules you may add later.

Adding properties

At the very top of the class module, place the following private variables. Notice that each line begins with the word `Private`. These variables will be used only within the class module itself. They receive their values from properties or methods within the class module:

```
'fields in data
Private m_CustomerName As String
Private m_OrderDate As Variant
Private m_ShipDate As Variant
Private m_ProductName As String
Private m_Quantity As Long
Private m_PricePer As Double
'user entered
Private m_TaxPerc As Double
'other calculated fields
Private m_Status As Double
Private m_SubTotal As Double
Private m_Discount As Double
Private m_TaxAmount As Double
Private m_PreTaxTotal As Double
Private m_FinalTotal As Double
'boolean to track calculation status
Private m_Calculate As Boolean
```

> **Tip** Prefixing private variables with `m_` is something I picked up from another programmer. It's called Hungarian notation and is used to indicate data types, such as `iCounter` being an integer for counting. Such notation is not required, but I do use it to differentiate between private module-level variables and procedure-level variables.

Property Let

Property Let procedures are used to assign values to properties (let the property be this value). The syntax is:

```
Public Property Let PropertyName (ByVal Variable as Datatype)
'code, such as:
m_PropertyName = Variable
End Property
```

These properties are public so that the values can be assigned from outside the class module. Add the following after the private variables:

```
Public Property Let CustomerName(ByVal RHS As String): m_CustomerName = RHS: _
    End Property

Public Property Let OrderDate(ByVal RHS As Variant)
If IsValidDate(RHS) Then
   m_OrderDate = Format(RHS, "mm/dd/yyyy")
Else
   m_OrderDate = 0
End If
End Property

Public Property Let ShipDate(ByVal RHS As Variant)
If IsValidDate(RHS) Then
   m_ShipDate = Format(RHS, "mm/dd/yyyy")
Else
   m_ShipDate = 0
End If
End Property

Public Property Let ProductName(ByVal RHS As String): m_ProductName = RHS: _
    End Property

Public Property Let Quantity(ByVal RHS As Long): m_Quantity = RHS: End _
    Property

Public Property Let PricePer(ByVal RHS As Double): m_PricePer = RHS: End _
    Property
```

The following column isn't in the data set, but the value is needed for calculations:

```
Public Property Let TaxPerc(ByVal RHS As Double): m_TaxPerc = RHS: End _
    Property
```

> **Tip** Because the properties are just assigning the variable to a private variable, I prefer to minimize the lines of code and have it all in one row, such as the `PricePer` property. To do this, use a colon (:) as the line separator, replacing the line break. But if code needs more than just one line, like the `ShipDate` property, I write it in a typical manner, one line at a time.

These seven properties are writable. The argument, RHS, is the value being assigned to the property, which is then assigned to one of the private variables. I like to use RHS (Right Hand Side—easy to remember!) as a common argument name for consistency, but you can use what you want.

A private function, IsValidDate, is used to validate the date fields. Technically, this is considered a method, even though it's only used within the object itself. The method is discussed in the "Adding methods" section. If the entry is a valid date, then it is formatted as mm/dd/yyyy before being stored in the corresponding private variable.

Property Get

Property Get procedures are the read-only properties of the class module (get the value of this property). You don't have to configure a Get for every Let. Why? Imagine that you have another routine that reads all the values from a database into the program's memory. A programmer using your class module doesn't need to see this raw data. Using the Get property, you can control what data the programmer can access but still have the data available to the program. The syntax for using Get is:

```
Public Property Get PropertyName() as Datatype
'code, such as
PropertyName = m_PropertyName
End Property
```

In our working example, we have more Get properties than Let properties because we're performing calculations and outputting additional data. The first six properties are for the existing columns in the data set:

```
Public Property Get CustomerName() As String: CustomerName = m_CustomerName: End
Property

Public Property Get OrderDate() As Date: OrderDate = m_OrderDate: End Property

Public Property Get ShipDate() As Variant: ShipDate = m_ShipDate: End Property

Public Property Get ProductName() As String: ProductName = m_ProductName: End
Property

Public Property Get Quantity() As Long: Quantity = m_Quantity: End Property

Public Property Get PricePer() As Double: PricePer = m_PricePer: End Property
```

The next four properties are for new columns in the data set (or in a report if that's what you're working on). Notice that additional code can be included when writing properties; it doesn't have to be a basic assignment of variable values.

```
Public Property Get Discount() As Double: Discount = m_Discount: End Property

Public Property Get Status() As Double
If IsDate(m_ShipDate) Then
  Status = "Shipped"
Else
  Status = "Pending"
End If
End Property
```

```
Public Property Get SubTotal() As Double
'in case the user didn't run Calculate, run it here
If Not m_Calculate Then Calculate
SubTotal = m_SubTotal
End Property

Public Property Get TaxAmount() As Double
If Not m_Calculate Then Calculate
TaxAmount = m_TaxAmount
End Property

Public Property Get FinalTotal() As Double
FinalTotal = m_PreTaxTotal + m_TaxAmount
End Property
```

> **Caution**   The data types of Let, Set, and Get properties of the same name must be the
> same. If you know you'll need to change the data type, then they'll have to have different
> property names. For example, if the code is reading in numbers, such as Social Security
> numbers, but they're supposed to be strings, you could do this:
>
> ```
> Private m_rawSSN as string
>
> Public Property Let rawSSN(ByVal RHS As Long)
> 'leading zeroes would be dropped, so format back in
> If IsNumeric(RHS) Then
>   m_rawSSN = Format(RHS, "000-##-####")
> Else
>   m_rawSSN = "Invalid SSN"
> End If
> End Property
>
> Public Property Get cleanSSN () as String: cleanSSN = m_rawSSN: End Property
> ```

Property Set

Property Set procedures, much like Let procedures, allow you to set the value of a property in the
module. These procedures are used to assign an object to a property. For example, if you want to
create a worksheet property that gets passed a worksheet object, do this:

```
Property Set DataWorksheet (ByVal RHS as Worksheet): _
   Set m_DataSheet = RHS: End Property
```

You would use Get to retrieve:

```
Property Get DataWorksheet() As Worksheet: Set DataWorksheet = m_DataSheet: _
   End Property
```

Adding methods

Two of the Let properties reference a function, isValidDate, while two of the Get properties reference a sub, Calculate. Those two procedures and ApplyDiscount are methods for our custom objects. isValidDate is a private function because it's only used within the object; the other two procedures are public because the user will call them.

> **Note** A Calculate sub is not required. I wrote the code this way to ensure the user sets the values first.

isValidDate is used to ensure the values in the date fields can be interpreted as dates. This private function is called by the Let properties of the date fields, which, if the data is a date, reformats the value. Here is the code for the function:

```
Private Function IsValidDate(ByVal PossibleDate As Variant) As Boolean
'ensures the entry is a date
If PossibleDate = "" Or PossibleDate = 0 Then
  IsValidDate = False
ElseIf IsNumeric(PossibleDate) Then
  'check if numeric value falls within valid Excel date range
  '2958465 is equivalent to 12/31/9999
  If PossibleDate >= 1 And PossibleDate <= 2958465 Then
    IsValidDate = True
  Else
    IsValidDate = False
  End If
ElseIf IsDate(DateValue(PossibleDate)) Then
  'check if string date
  IsValidDate = True
Else
  IsValidDate = False
End If
End Function
```

ApplyDiscount is called if the user wants to apply a discount to the data being processed. It updates the variable m_Discount:

```
Public Sub ApplyDiscount()
'applies discount based on quantity purchased
'not product dependent
'if user doesn't want to apply any discounts then don't call this sub
Select Case m_Quantity
  Case Is <= 10
    m_Discount = 0
  Case 11 To 20
    m_Discount = 0.05
  Case 21 To 40
    m_Discount = 0.1
  Case Is > 50
    m_Discount = 0.15
```

```
    Case Else
        m_Discount = 0
    End Select
End Sub
```

Calculate is called once all the data has been input and forces the custom object to perform the required calculations:

```
Public Sub Calculate()
'forces the class to perform the various calculations; filling the other _
    variables
'doing it this ways ensures the calculations are done in the correct order
m_Calculate = True
m_SubTotal = m_Quantity * m_PricePer
'get tax amount
'subtract any discount first
m_PreTaxTotal = m_SubTotal - (m_SubTotal * m_Discount)
m_TaxAmount = m_PreTaxTotal * m_TaxPerc
End Sub
```

The object is now complete. The next step is to use the object in an actual program.

Using a custom object

When a custom object is properly configured in a class module, it can be referenced from other modules. To access the properties and methods of the object, first declare a variable as the class module and then set a new instance of the object. You can then write the code, referencing the custom object and taking advantage of IntelliSense to access its properties and methods, as shown in Figure 9-5.

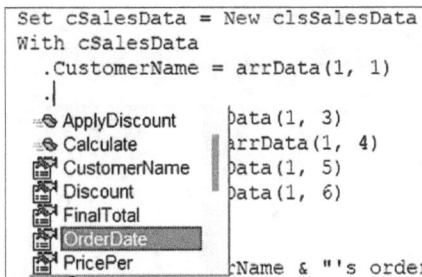

FIGURE 9-5 The properties and method of the custom object are just as easily accessible as they are for standard objects.

The following example uses the custom object created in the previous section, "Creating a custom object." It reads the values of the properties from an array and then generates a message box, retrieving the values from the first record:

```
Sub SingleSalesTotal()
'Reads in a single record
Dim cSalesData As clsSalesData 'declare the variable
Dim arrData()
```

```
arrData = _
  Worksheets("SalesRecords_Table").ListObjects("tblSalesRecords")._
    DataBodyRange.Value2
Set cSalesData = New clsSalesData 'set a new instance
With cSalesData
  .CustomerName = arrData(1, 1)
  .OrderDate = arrData(1, 2)
  .ShipDate = arrData(1, 3)
  .ProductName = arrData(1, 4)
  .Quantity = arrData(1, 5)
  .PricePer = arrData(1, 6)
  .ApplyDiscount
  .Calculate
  MsgBox .CustomerName & "'s order total for " & .OrderDate & " is " & _
    Format(.FinalTotal, "$#,##0.00")
End With
Set cSalesData = Nothing
End Sub
```

The line `Set cSalesData = New clsSalesData` is how we initialize a new instance of the custom object. It's a fresh, empty copy waiting for you to fill it with information. You must include that line for every record you create. Figure 9-6 shows what the object looks like once you've filled it. Figure 9-7 shows the message box generated by the program.

cSalesData		clsSalesData/clsSalesData
CustomerName	"John Doe"	String
Discount	0.1	Double
FinalTotal	74.925	Double
m_Calculate	True	Boolean
m_CustomerName	"John Doe"	String
m_Discount	0.1	Double
m_FinalTotal	0	Double

FIGURE 9-6 A custom object can hold many different variables of differing types.

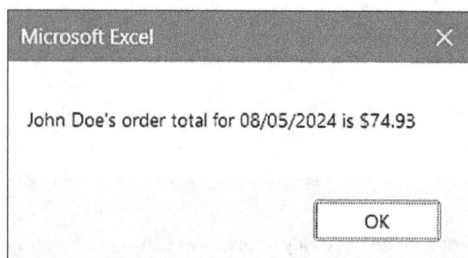

Microsoft Excel

John Doe's order total for 08/05/2024 is $74.93

OK

FIGURE 9-7 Individual records in a collection can be easily accessed.

`Set cSalesData = Nothing` releases the reference to the variable, allowing the memory it occupies to be made available for other processes.

Working with one record isn't that useful. You could loop each row and display a message box, but that's not very practical. What you need to do is store each new instance of the custom object as you process all the data. And that's where collections come in.

Using collections

A *collection* is a group of items that, while it can include a mix of data types, is usually of a single type. For example, `Worksheet` is a member of the `Worksheets` collection. The collection object has two methods and two properties. For a collection called `AllRecords`, the syntax for the methods and properties would be as follows:

- `Add` is used to add an item to the collection (see "Add and retrieve an item to/from a collection" for details):

  `AllRecords.Add Item, Key, Before, After`

- `Remove` is used to remove an item from the collection:

  `AllRecords.Remove Key`

- `Count` returns the number of items in the collection:

  `AllRecords.Count`

- `Item` is used to refer to a specific item in a collection:

  `AllRecords(Key)`

> **Level Up!**
>
> If you're already familiar with collections and are just looking for an example of how they work with custom objects, feel free to jump to "Case Study: Creating a collection to hold custom objects" at the end of this section. The case study brings together the information in this section to fill a collection and empty it onto a sheet.

Declare and initialize a collection

To use a collection, you first declare a variable as the collection and then initialize it by creating a new instance of the collection like this:

```
Dim AllRecords as Collection
Set AllRecords = New Collection
```

> **Note**   You may see code where the two lines are combined, `Dim AllRecords as New Collection`. While there is nothing inherently wrong with this code, keeping the lines separate aids in readability and gives you more control over the code.

Add and retrieve an item to/from a collection

Once you've initialized the collection, you can use the `Add` method to add items to it:

```
AllRecords.Add Item, Key, Before, After
```

The Add method has four arguments. Item is whatever information the collection holds. It can be anything from a string to an object, such as a worksheet or custom object. The optional second value is Key, which is used to look up a member of the collection. It must be a unique string value. You can use Key to directly reference an item in a collection. If you don't know Key, then the only way to find an item in a collection is to loop through the collection.

Before and After are optional arguments you can use to position an item in a collection. You can refer to the key or position of the item.

The following example creates a collection with two items. The first item is added with a key; the second item is not.

```
AllRecords.Add "apples", "Key1" 'with a key
AllRecords.Add 456 'without a key
```

Notice that the key is a string. If you want to use numbers for the key, then force the number (1) to be treated as a string by wrapping it in the conversion function CStr, like this:

```
AllRecords.Add "A 3rd value", CStr(1)
```

The Item property is how you retrieve an item from a collection—but you don't actually have to use the term. For single values held in a collection, you just assign the item to a variable:

```
myItem = AllRecords("Key1")
```

But what if keys weren't used? Then that's when you use a counter loop on the collection:

```
For icounter = 1 to AllRecords.Count
   Debug.print AllRecords(icounter)
Next icounter
```

If the values in the collections are custom objects, refer to the following case study for a step-by-step example of filling and emptying the collection.

> **Tip**   You never know when a string made of numbers, such as an invoice number, will show up in the data you're using for your keys. To prevent errors, it's a good idea to always wrap your key with CStr.

Case Study: Creating a collection to hold custom objects

In the section "Using a custom object," we filled a single instance of the custom object, but the data set had 100 rows. While it's possible to create a separate variable for each instance, this would result in managing 100 individual variables—an inefficient solution. A better approach is to store each object instance in a collection.

To do this, initialize a new instance of the custom object before you fill it with the row's data. Once it's filled, add the object to the collection and repeat until all 100 rows are in the collection.

In this case study, we're going to fill the collection with the data and then generate a new report that includes calculated data from the object.

```
Sub ProcessAllData()
Dim cSalesData As clsSalesData 'declare the custom object
Dim AllRecords As Collection 'declare the collection
Dim rawData(), reportData()
Dim eaRow As Long, eaRecord As Long
rawData = _
  Worksheets("SalesRecords_Table").ListObjects("tblSalesRecords"). _
    DataBodyRange.Value2
'initialize the collection
Set AllRecords = New Collection
```

For each row in the array, initialize a new instance of the object (Set cSalesData = New clsSalesData), fill in the properties, and then call the two methods. Once that's done, add the object to the collection (AllRecords.Add cSalesData) and then repeat until the entire array has been processed into the collection:

```
For eaRow = 1 To UBound(rawData)
  Set cSalesData = New clsSalesData
  With cSalesData
    'fill the properties
    .CustomerName = rawData(eaRow, 1)
    .OrderDate = rawData(eaRow, 2)
    .ShipDate = rawData(eaRow, 3)
    .ProductName = rawData(eaRow, 4)
    .Quantity = rawData(eaRow, 5)
    .PricePer = rawData(eaRow, 6)
    .TaxPerc = 0.0425
    'call the methods
    .ApplyDiscount
    .Calculate
  End With
  'add the custom object to the collection, no key
  AllRecords.Add cSalesData
Next eaRow
```

Now that all the data is in the collection, resize the reportData array to hold all the records and fields we need. Then, loop through the collection and fill the array. There are two ways to do this, depending on why you're looping through the collection. One method would be to loop through the objects in the collection; this method will be covered at the end of the case study. For this report, we're looping to fill an array. We'll need a row counter (eaRecord) to correspond with the array, so do a counting loop:

```
ReDim reportData(1 To AllRecords.Count, 1 To 8)
For eaRecord = 1 To UBound(reportData)
  'load the object from the collection to an object variable
  Set cSalesData = AllRecords(eaRecord)
  'unload the desired variables into the array
  With cSalesData
    reportData(eaRecord, 1) = .CustomerName
    reportData(eaRecord, 2) = .OrderDate
```

```
      reportData(eaRecord, 3) = .ProductName
      reportData(eaRecord, 4) = .Quantity
      reportData(eaRecord, 5) = Format(.SubTotal, $#,##0.00")
      reportData(eaRecord, 6) = Format(.TaxAmount, "$#,##0.00")
      reportData(eaRecord, 7) = Format(.FinalTotal, "$#,##0.00")
      reportData(eaRecord, 8) = .Status
    End With
  Next eaRecord
```

Now that we have the data in an array, we can dump it into a sheet:

```
With Worksheets("SalesReport")
  'place the column headers on the sheet
  .Range("A1").Resize(, UBound(reportData, 2)) = Array("Customer", _
    "Order Date", "Product", "Quantity", "SubTotal", "Tax", "Total", "Status")
  .Range("A2").Resize(UBound(reportData), UBound(reportData, 2)) = reportData
End With
'free up memory
Set AllRecords = Nothing
Set cSalesData = Nothing
End Sub
```

> **Tip** It's always a good idea to free up memory, even with today's powerful computers. One big reason is that if you leave global variables initialized, they might hang on to old or incorrect values. That can cause unexpected issues later in your program. If you get into the habit of uninitializing them, you don't have to worry about whether they're global or not—it just becomes part of your routine.

In the above sample, a counting loop was used to extract the data from the objects to the array. This method was used so the counter could also be used for the array's row location. An alternative method is to loop through the objects in the collection directly, like this:

```
eaRecord = 1
For Each cSalesData In AllRecords
  With cSalesData
    'same as previous code
  End With
  eaRecord = eaRecord + 1
Next cSalesData
```

In this case, the object is automatically loaded into cSalesData. Since the data goes into an array, a counter variable, eaRecord, needs to be used. But if there's no need for a counter, such as the data going directly onto a unique report, consider using this method.

Checking for an item in a collection

You can only check if an item already exists in a collection if you've set a unique key. Since keys must be unique, it's a good idea to check for the existence of the key before adding it to the collection. If you don't and you try to add an existing key, you'll get an error message. There are two ways to check for an existing key:

- Add the key to the collection. If there's an error message, it already exists. If it doesn't exist, the item will be added to the collection:

```
On Error Resume Next
AllRecords.Add myValue, "myKey"
If Err.Number <> 0 Then
   'there was an error message
   MsgBox "Key already exists"
Else
   'no error message
   MsgBox "New Item Added"
End If
'reset error handling
On Error GoTo 0
```

- Load the item (using the key) into a variable. Again, if you get an error message, then it doesn't exist. If there's no error, you can then decide what you want to do next:

```
On Error Resume Next
myValue = AllRecords("myKey")
If Err.Number <> 0 Then
   'there was an error message
   MsgBox "Key doesn't exist"
   'key doesn't exist, so you can choose to add it
   AllRecords.Add myValue, "myKey"
Else
   'error message
   MsgBox "Key already exists"
End If
'reset error handling
On Error GoTo 0
```

In either case, you'll have to precede the check with On Error Resume Next so that the code doesn't cause an error. Then, you'll want to check using Err.Number to see if there's an error.

Level Up!

I test for items in a collection by loading the item into a temporary variable. This allows me to choose what my next steps will be: either adding the item or loading it to work with it. Since it's something I do quite often, I've added a function to my code library that also provides the flexibility of checking for a single value, as in the preceding examples, or checking a custom object by loading it into an object type variable. Here's the code for my function:

```
Function CollectionKeyExists(ByVal KeyName As String, ByVal _
   CollectionToSearch As Collection, ByVal isObject As Boolean) As Boolean
'isObject True means need to use Set, else the code will error, even if the _
   Key exists
Dim tmpValue As Variant
CollectionKeyExists = False
On Error Resume Next
If isObject Then
   Set tmpValue = CollectionToSearch(KeyName)
```

```
    Else
        tmpValue = CollectionToSearch(KeyName)
    End If
    If Err.Number = 0 Then CollectionKeyExists = True
    On Error GoTo 0
    Set tmpValue = Nothing
    End Function
```

Using the function would look like this:

```
If CollectionKeyExists(myKey, AllRecords, False) Then
    MsgBox "Key " & myKey & " already exists"
    Else
    MsgBox myKey & " doesn't exist"
    'key doesn't exist, so you can choose to add it
    AllRecords.Add myValue, myKey
End If
```

By using a separate function, I keep the status of the error handling in the calling sub alone; the error handling in the function affects only it.

Updating a custom object with an existing key

If the collection value is a single value, then to update that value, you just have to remove the existing key and add the new value. However, to update the custom object linked to an existing key, you have to follow these steps:

1. Load the existing object into a temporary variable of the object type:

    ```
    Dim tmpObject As clsSalesData
    Set tmpObject = AllRecords("Bob Johnson")
    ```

2. Delete the existing value and key from the collection:

    ```
    AllRecords.Remove ("Bob Johnson")
    ```

3. Update the temporary object's properties:

    ```
    tmpObject.Quantity = tmpObject.Quantity + 5
    ```

4. Add the temporary object to the collection:

    ```
    AllRecords.Add tmpObject, "Bob Johnson"
    ```

That's a lot of steps, especially if you include the code to check whether the key exists. If the code often updates existing collections, you don't need to loop through the collection often, and you don't have to worry about Excel for Mac, then you may want to consider using a dictionary instead of a collection.

> **Note** "Should I use a collection or a dictionary?" You'll see that question posted online often, and I sometimes ask myself the same thing. (I usually use collections, but that's mainly habit.)

Collections

- do not require keys
- are built into VBA and do not require reference to an external library
- can be looped with a counter
- cannot directly update an existing object

Dictionaries

- require unique keys
- require a reference to an external library, currently unavailable on Macs
- can update an existing value
- have a built-in function to check for a key's existence
- cannot be looped with a counter to access items directly

Keep reading to learn more about dictionaries and decide which you'll choose—unless the project specifications have already decided for you.

Using dictionaries

The ability to use a key to look up values in a collection is a major plus. I often parallel collections and arrays to help find information in an array. For example, I use the key in the collection to look up the location of a record in the array.

But a major downside to collections is that after you add an item to a collection with a key, you can't change it. You have to load it into a temporary variable to update it, delete the original, and then add the updated variable as a new element of the collection.

So, if you need the advantages of a collection but also need to change the value, you can use a dictionary. A *dictionary* does almost everything a collection does and more, but it needs a little more setup because it's part of the Microsoft Scripting Runtime Library. The dictionary object has six methods and four properties:

- Add is used to add an item to the dictionary. Note that the parameters are the reverse of collections. With dictionaries, specify the key first:

  ```
  dictData.Add Key, Item
  ```

- Exists returns True if a key is already in use; False if it is not:

  ```
  dictData.Exists (Key)
  ```

- Items returns an array (0-based) of all keys in the dictionary:

  ```
  dictData.Items
  ```

- Keys returns an array (0-based) of all keys in the dictionary:

  ```
  dictData.Keys
  ```

- Remove is used to remove a specific item from the dictionary:

  `dictData.Remove Key`

- RemoveAll removes all items in the dictionary:

  `dictData.RemoveAll`

- Count returns the number of items in the dictionary:

  `AllRecords.Count`

- Item sets or returns the value of an item in the dictionary. Since it's the default property, you don't have to explicitly specify it:

  - Return an item like this: `dictData(Key)`
  - Assign a new value to an existing key like this: `dictData(Key) = newValue`

- Key assigns a new name to an existing key in the dictionary:

  `dictData.Key (oldKey) = newKey`

- CompareMode sets or returns the comparison mode for keys in the dictionary allowing keys to be case sensitive (by default, they are):

  - To make key case sensitive: `dictData.CompareMode = vbBinaryCompare`
  - To make key case insensitive: `dictData.CompareMode = vbTextCompare`

Some of the other differences between collections and dictionaries include the following:

- A dictionary key can be any variable type except for an array.
- A dictionary key can be changed.
- You can retrieve an array of all the keys or all items.

In the following example, which declares the dictionary using late binding, data is placed into an array and processed using the product name as the key. The summed quantities are then placed on the sheet, with the dictionary keys as labels, as shown in Figure 9-8.

Customer Name	Product Name	Qty	Price Per
Jane Smith	Gadget	17	$0.88
Ashley Taylor	Widget B	37	$0.88
Jane Smith	Doohickey	14	$0.88
Gadget		233	
Doohickey		476	
Thingy 2		431	
Widget B		572	
Gizmo		511	
Widget A		337	

FIGURE 9-8 You can use a dictionary to hold values that could change multiple times as the code runs.

Tip See Chapter 20, "Automating Word," for information on early versus late binding.

```
Sub UsingADictionary()
Dim dictData As Object
Dim tblSales As ListObject
Dim arrData(), arrReport(), arrHeaders()
Dim eaRow As Long
Dim rng As Range
'create the dictionary object
Set dictData = CreateObject("Scripting.Dictionary")
Set tblSales = _
  Worksheets("SalesRecords_Table").ListObjects("tblSalesRecords")
'put the data into an array for faster processing
arrData = tblSales.DataBodyRange.Value2
'loop through the array
For eaRow = 1 To UBound(arrData)
  'if key exists, add to it
  'else create and add to it
  If dictData.Exists(arrData(eaRow, 4)) Then
    dictData(arrData(eaRow, 4)) = dictData(arrData(eaRow, 4)) + arrData(eaRow, 5)
  Else
    dictData.Add arrData(eaRow, 4), arrData(eaRow, 5)
  End If
Next eaRow
'rename a key, just for the heck of it
dictData.Key("Thingy 1") = "Thingy 2"
'the location 2 rows beneath the table
Set rng = tblSales.Range.Offset(tblSales.Range.Rows.Count + 2).Resize(1, 1)
'put the dictionary keys and values each into an array
'then dump them on the sheet
arrHeaders = dictData.Keys
rng.Resize(dictData.Count, 1).Value = Application.Transpose(arrHeaders)
arrReport = dictData.Items
rng.Offset(, 1).Resize(dictData.Count, 1).Value = Application.Transpose(arrReport)
Set dictData = Nothing
Set tblSales = Nothing
Set rng = Nothing
End Sub
```

The previous example is one use of dictionaries, taking advantage of the ease of updating values. But, just like with collections, you can also store custom objects in dictionaries. Much of the code is the same as that of collections, but there are some differences:

- Initializing the dictionary:

  ```
  Set dictData = CreateObject("Scripting.Dictionary")
  ```

- Creating a key:

  ```
  UniqueKey = Replace(.CustomerName & .ProductName, " ", "")
  ```

- Checking for the existence of the key and either updating the existing quantity or adding the new record:

```
If AllRecords.Exists(UniqueKey) Then
  AllRecords(UniqueKey).Quantity = AllRecords(UniqueKey).Quantity + .Quantity
Else
  AllRecords.Add UniqueKey, cSalesData
End If
```

- Looping through the Items property to access all records:

  - The loop object variable, LoopObject, must be declared as a variant because the Items property returns an array that can hold any type of data, including custom objects. Anything could be in that array position, so we initially assign it to a variant.

    ```
    Dim LoopObject as Variant
    ```

  - As we loop through the objects, load the record into a variable of the custom object so we can access the properties and methods more easily with tooltips:

    ```
    For Each LoopObject In AllRecords.Keys
        Set cSalesData = LoopObject
        With cSalesData ...
    ```

- Include a loop counter for placing the data in the array:

  ```
  eaRecord = eaRecord + 1
  ```

Using user-defined types to create custom properties

User-defined types (UDTs) offer a simple way to group related data without requiring a class module. Unlike custom objects, UDTs can only hold properties and cannot define methods. While they are more limited, UDTs are sufficient for scenarios where organizing data is the primary requirement. I think of them as data packets—you assign values to the properties, then place the packet into an array or pass the packet to another procedure.

As shown in Figure 9-9, a UDT is declared with a Type...End Type statement. It can be public or private. A name that is treated like a data type, such as SalesOrder, is given to the UDT. Within Type, individual variables are declared that become the properties of the UDT.

Within a procedure, a variable of the custom type is defined (SingleOrder as SalesOrder). When that variable is used, the properties are available, just as they are in a custom object.

> **Caution**   You cannot place UDTs into collections or dictionaries. Also, their values persist until explicitly changed. For example, if the CustomerName property is set to 'John Doe,' it will retain that value until you overwrite it. To avoid using outdated data, you can create a reset function that initializes all properties to their default values, such as assigning an empty string ("") to text fields and 0 to numeric fields.

```
Option Explicit

Public Type SalesOrder
  CustomerName As String
  OrderDate As Date
  ShipDate As Variant
  ProductName As String
  Quantity As Long
  PricePerUnit As Double
End Type

Private Function ReadSalesDataFromSheet() As SalesOrder()
Dim arrData()
Dim AllOrders() As SalesOrder, SingleOrder As SalesOrder
Dim eaRow As Long, orderIndex As Long

arrData = _
  Worksheets("SalesRecords_Table").ListObjects("tblSalesRecords").DataBodyRange.Value2
ReDim AllOrders(1 To UBound(arrData))
'loop through the sales, filling the SalesOrder UDT with the row's values
For eaRow = 1 To UBound(arrData)
  SingleOrder.|
              CustomerName
              OrderDate
              PricePerUnit
              ProductName
              Quantity
              ShipDate
```

FIGURE 9-9 The properties of a UDT are available as they are in a custom object.

In the following example, we're going to calculate the total revenue for the shipped items. First, we'll put each data row into the SalesOrder UDT, which is then placed in an array, AllOrders. That array of AllOrders is then passed to another function that will "open" each packet, check if the product has been shipped, and then calculate the total cost. There is one sub that will call these functions.

To start, we create the UDT, SalesOrder, at the top of the module:

```
Private Type SalesOrder
  CustomerName As String
  OrderDate As Date
  ShipDate As Variant
  ProductName As String
  Quantity As Long
  PricePerUnit As Double
End Type
```

The function ReadSalesDataFromSheet processes each data row, filling an instance of the SalesOrder UDT (SingleOrder). Each SingleOrder is then placed in the array AllOrders, which is used to store all SalesOrder instances, as shown in Figure 9-10. When all the rows have been processed, the function returns the AllOrders array to the calling sub.

```
Private Function ReadSalesDataFromSheet() As SalesOrder()
Dim arrData()
Dim AllOrders() As SalesOrder, SingleOrder As SalesOrder
Dim eaRow As Long, orderIndex As Long
arrData = _
  Worksheets("SalesRecords_Table").ListObjects("tblSalesRecords"). _
    DataBodyRange.Value2
ReDim AllOrders(1 To UBound(arrData))
'loop through the sales, filling the SalesOrder UDT with the row's values
```

```
   For eaRow = 1 To UBound(arrData)
     SingleOrder.CustomerName = arrData(eaRow, 1)
     SingleOrder.OrderDate = arrData(eaRow, 2)
     SingleOrder.ShipDate = arrData(eaRow, 3)
     SingleOrder.ProductName = arrData(eaRow, 4)
     SingleOrder.Quantity = arrData(eaRow, 5)
     SingleOrder.PricePerUnit = arrData(eaRow, 6)
     'place the filled UDT into an array that will hold all the UDTs
     'it's always a good idea to use a temporary variable, in this case AllOrders,
     'then when it has the final result, you pass it to the function
     AllOrders(orderIndex + 1) = SingleOrder
     orderIndex = orderIndex + 1 'location counter
   Next eaRow
   'return array to calling sub
   ReadSalesDataFromSheet = AllOrders
   End Function
```

The function `CalculateShippedRevenue` calculates the total revenue from a list of sales orders where the goods have been shipped. It takes an array of `SalesOrder` objects (`AllOrders`) as input and returns a `Double` value representing the total revenue.

```
Private Function CalculateShippedRevenue(AllOrders() As SalesOrder) As Double
Dim totalRevenue As Double
Dim eaRow As Long
For eaRow = LBound(AllOrders) To UBound(AllOrders)
  If Len(Trim(AllOrders(i).ShipDate)) <> 0 Then
    totalRevenue = totalRevenue + (AllOrders(eaRow).Quantity * _
      AllOrders(eaRow).PricePerUnit)
  End If
Next eaRow
CalculateShippedRevenue = totalRevenue
End Function
```

ReadSalesDataFromSheet		SalesOrder(1 to 100)
ReadSalesDataFromSheet(1)		SalesOrder
CustomerName	"John Doe"	String
OrderDate	#8/5/2024#	Date
PricePerUnit	2.25	Double
ProductName	"Gadget"	String
Quantity	37	Long
ShipDate	45515	Variant/Double

FIGURE 9-10 By declaring the function ReadSalesDataFromSheet to return an array of type `SalesOrder`, each element of the array can represent an instance of `SalesOrder` and hold its properties.

Next steps

Class modules are needed to capture application-level and embedded chart events. They can also be used to organize data, making the data easier to work with, especially when stored in a collection. Chapter 10 introduces the tools you can use to interact with users. You'll find out how to prompt people for information to use in your code, warn them of illegal actions, and provide them with an interface to work with other than the spreadsheet.

CHAPTER 10

Userforms: An introduction

In this chapter, you will:

- Use an input box to request user input

- Use a message box to display information

- Learn how to create a userform

- Add controls to the userform

- Verify a required field has an entry

- Prevent a user from closing a form

- Prompt the user to select a file

Userforms enable you to display information and allow the user to input information. Using `InputBox` and `MsgBox` controls are simple ways of doing this. You can use the userform controls in the VB Editor to create more complex forms.

This chapter covers simple user interfaces using input boxes and message boxes and the basics of creating userforms in the VB Editor.

> **Note** To learn more about advanced userform programming, see Chapter 22, "Advanced userform techniques."

Input boxes

The `InputBox` function is used to create a basic interface element that requests input from the user before the program can continue. You can configure the prompt, the title for the window, a default value, the window position, and user help files. The only two buttons provided are the OK and Cancel buttons. The returned value is a string.

The following code asks the user for the number of months to be averaged. Figure 10-1 shows the resulting input box.

```
AveMos = InputBox(Prompt:="Enter the number of months to average", _
    Title:="Enter Months", Default:="3")
```

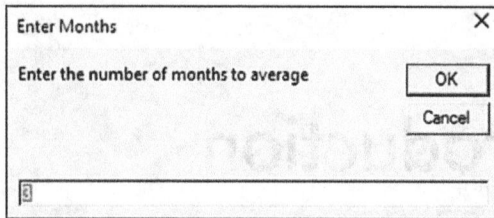

FIGURE 10-1 An input box can be simple but still effective.

> **Tip** If you need to force the entry of a variable type other than string, use `Application.InputBox`. This method allows you to specify the return data type: formula (0), number (1), text (2), True or False (4), cell reference (8), error value (16), or array of values (64). If you want to allow numbers and text, set the `Type` to `1 + 2`.

Message boxes

The `MsgBox` function creates a message box that displays information and waits for the user to click a button before continuing. Whereas `InputBox` has only OK and Cancel buttons, the `MsgBox` function enables you to choose from several configurations of buttons, including Yes, No, OK, and Cancel. You also can configure the prompt, the window title, and help files. The following code produces a prompt to find out whether the user wants to continue. You use a `Select Case` statement to continue the program with the appropriate action:

```
myTitle = "Report Finalized"
MyMsg = "Do you want to save changes and close?"
Response = MsgBox(myMsg, vbExclamation + vbYesNoCancel, myTitle)
Select Case Response
  Case Is = vbYes
    ActiveWorkbook.Close SaveChanges:=True
  Case Is = vbNo
    ActiveWorkbook.Close SaveChanges:=False
  Case Is = vbCancel
    Exit Sub
End Select
```

Figure 10-2 shows the resulting customized message box.

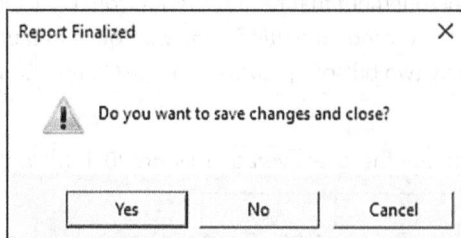

FIGURE 10-2 The `MsgBox` function is used to display information and obtain a basic response from the user.

Tip You can combine an icon option and a buttons option for the `buttons` argument by separating them with the plus (+) symbol. In the previous example, `vbExclamation + vbYesNoCancel` instructed Excel to show the exclamation symbol and the Yes, No, and Cancel buttons.

Creating a userform

Userforms combine the capabilities of `InputBox` and `MsgBox` to create a more efficient way of interacting with the user. For example, rather than have the user fill out personal information on a sheet, you can create a userform that prompts for the required data (see Figure 10-3).

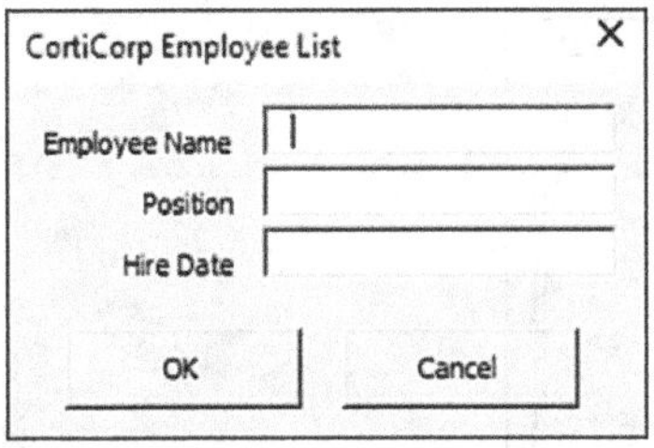

FIGURE 10-3 Create a custom userform to get more information from the user.

Level Up!

The userforms in this chapter are intentionally simple to keep the focus on core concepts. The bonus workbook, `ProjectFilesChapter10_BonusUserform.xlsm`, shows a more practical example with a multipage form, smarter field handling, and better use of table-based data.

Insert a userform in the VB Editor by selecting Insert, UserForm from the main menu. When a UserForm module is added to the Project Explorer, a blank form appears in the window where your code usually is, and the Controls toolbox appears. If the toolbox does not appear, select View | Toolbox from the main menu.

To change the userform's codename, select the form and change the (`Name`) property from the Properties window. The userform's codename is used to refer to the form, as shown in the following sections. You can resize a userform by grabbing and dragging the handles on its right side, bottom edge, or lower-right corner. To add controls to the form, click the desired control in the toolbox and draw it on the form. You can move and resize controls at any time.

> **Note** By default, the toolbox displays the most common controls. To access more controls, right-click the area of the toolbox near the current tools and select Additional Controls. However, be careful; other users might not have the same additional controls as you do. If you send users a form with a control they do not have installed, the program generates an error.

After you add a control to a form, you can change its properties from the Properties window. (Or, if you don't want to set the properties manually now, you can set them later programmatically.) If the Properties window is not visible, you can bring it up by selecting View | Properties Window. Figure 10-4 shows the Properties window for a text box.

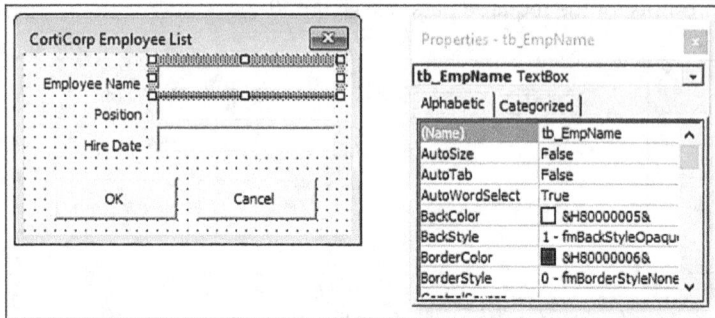

FIGURE 10-4 Use the Properties window to change the properties of a control.

Calling and hiding a userform

A userform can be called from any module. The syntax `FormName.Show` causes a form for the user to pop up:

```
frm_AddEmp.Show
```

The `Load` method can also be used to call a userform to place it in memory. It allows a form to be loaded while remaining hidden:

```
Load frm_AddEmp
```

To hide a userform, use the `Hide` method. When you do, the form is still active but is hidden from the user. However, the controls on the form can still be accessed programmatically:

```
frm_AddEmp.Hide
```

The `Unload` method unloads a form from memory and removes it from the user's view, which means the form cannot be accessed by the user or programmatically:

```
Unload Me
```

> **Tip** Me is a keyword that can be used to refer to the userform. It can be used in the code of any control to refer to the parent form.

Programming userforms

The code for a control goes in the form's module. Unlike with the other modules, double-clicking the form's module opens the form in Design view. To view the code, you can right-click either the module or the userform in Design view and select View Code.

Userform events

Just like a worksheet, a userform has events that are triggered by actions. After the userform has been added to a project, the events are available in the Properties dropdown menu at the top right of the code window (see Figure 10-5); to access them, select UserForm from the Object dropdown menu on the left.

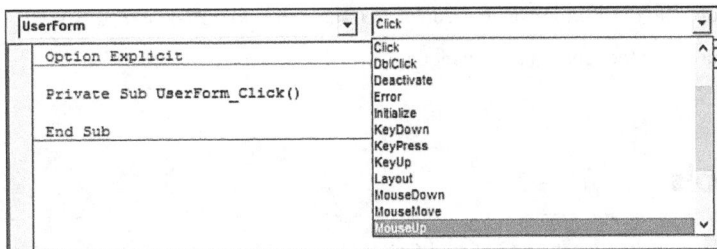

FIGURE 10-5 Various events for a userform can be selected from the dropdown menu at the top of the code window.

The available events for userforms are described in Table 10-1.

TABLE 10-1 Userform events

Event	Description
Activate	Occurs when a userform is either loaded or shown. This event is triggered after the Initialize event.
AddControl	Occurs when a control is added to a userform at runtime. Does not run at design time or upon userform initialization.
BeforeDragOver	Occurs while the user drags and drops data onto the userform.
BeforeDropOrPaste	Occurs right before the user is about to drop or paste data into the userform.
Click	Occurs when the user clicks the userform with the mouse.
DblClick	Occurs when the user double-clicks the userform with the mouse. If a click event is also in use, the double-click event will not work.
Deactivate	Occurs when a userform is deactivated.

Event	Description
Error	Occurs when the userform runs into an error and cannot return the error information.
Initialize	Occurs when the userform is first loaded before the Activate event.
KeyDown	Occurs when the user presses a key on the keyboard.
KeyPress	Occurs when the user presses an ANSI key. An ANSI key is a typeable character, such as the letter A. An example of a nontypeable character is the Tab key.
KeyUp	Occurs when the user releases a key on the keyboard.
Layout	Occurs when the control changes size.
MouseDown	Occurs when the user presses the mouse button within the borders of the userform.
MouseMove	Occurs when the user moves the mouse within the borders of the userform.
MouseUp	Occurs when the user releases the mouse button within the borders of the userform.
QueryClose	Occurs before a userform closes. It allows you to recognize the method used to close a form and have code respond accordingly.
RemoveControl	Occurs when a control is deleted from within the userform.
Resize	Occurs when the userform is resized.
Scroll	Occurs when a visible scrollbar box is repositioned.
Terminate	Occurs after the userform has been unloaded. This is triggered after QueryClose.
Zoom	Occurs when the zoom value is changed.

Programming controls

To program a control, select the control and go to View | Code. The footer, header, and default action for the control are entered in the programming field automatically. To see the other actions that are available for a control, select the control from the Object dropdown menu and view the actions in the Properties dropdown menu, as shown in Figure 10-6.

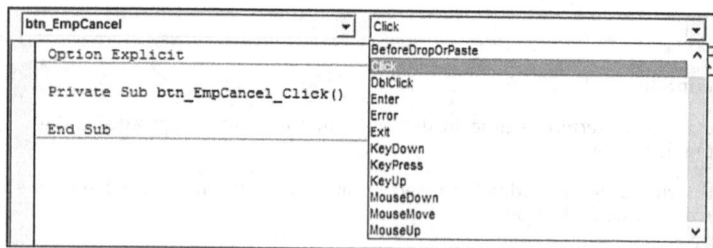

FIGURE 10-6 You can select various actions for a control from the VB Editor dropdown menus.

Controls are objects, like ActiveWorkbook. They have properties and methods that depend on the type of control. Most of the programming for the controls is done in the form's module. However, if another module needs to refer to a control, the parent (the form) needs to be included with the object. Here's an example of a button event that closes the form:

```
Private Sub btn_EmpCancel_Click()
Unload Me
End Sub
```

The preceding code can be broken down into three sections:

- Btn_EmpCancel—Name given to the control

- Click—The control's action

- Unload Me—Code behind the control, which, in this case, is unloading the form

Tip Change the (Name) property in the control's Properties window to rename a control from the default assigned by the editor.

Case study: Bug fix when adding controls to an existing form

If you've been using a userform for some time and later try to add a new control, you might find that Excel seems to get confused about the control. You will see that the control is added to the form, but when you right-click the control and select View Code, the code module does not seem to acknowledge that the control exists. The control name is not available in the left dropdown menu at the top of the code module.

To work around this situation, follow these steps:

1. Add all the controls you need to add to the existing userform.

2. In the Project Explorer, right-click the userform and select Export File. Select Save to save the file in the default location.

3. In the Project Explorer, right-click the userform and select Remove. Because you just exported the userform, click No to the question about exporting.

4. Right-click anywhere in the Project Explorer and select Import File. Select the file name that you saved in step 2.

   The new controls are now available in the userform's code window.

Using basic form controls

Each control has different events associated with it, so you can code what happens based on the user's actions. A table reviewing the control events is available at the end of each of the sections that follow.

Using labels, text boxes, and command buttons

A label control is used to display text with information for the user.

A text box control is used to get a manual entry from the user.

A command button control is used to create a button a user can press to have the program perform an action.

The basic form shown in Figure 10-7 consists of labels, text boxes, and command buttons. Using such a form is a simple yet effective method of requesting information from the user. After the text boxes have been filled in, the user clicks OK, your code reformats the data if needed, and then adds the information to a sheet (see Figure 10-8), as shown in the following code:

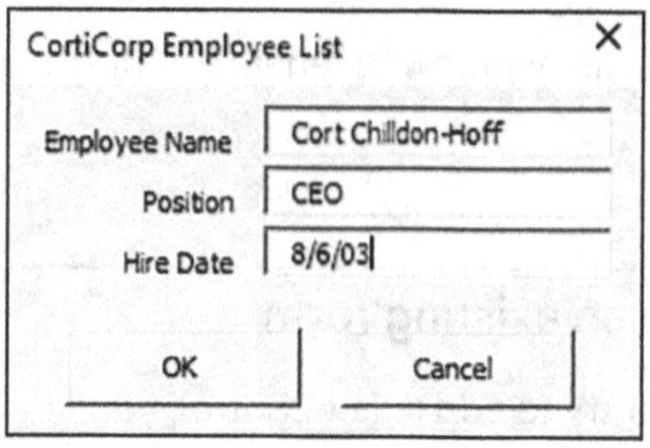

FIGURE 10-7 You can use a simple form like this to collect information from the user.

Name	Position	Hire Date
Tracy Syrstad	Developer	20-Jul-03
Cort Chilldon_Hoff	CEO	6-Aug-03

FIGURE 10-8 The information from the form is added to the sheet.

```
Private Sub btn_EmpOK_Click()
Dim LastRow As Long
Dim tblEmployees As ListObject
Set tblEmployees = Worksheets("Employees").ListObjects("tblEmployees")
With tblEmployees
   .ListRows.Add 'add a new row
   With .DataBodyRange
      LastRow = .Rows.Count 'get the new row
      .Cells(LastRow, 1).Value = tb_EmpName.Value
      .Cells(LastRow, 2).Value = tb_EmpPosition.Value
      .Cells(LastRow, 3).Value = tb_EmpHireDate.Value
   End With
End With
Set tblEmployees = Nothing
End Sub
```

By changing the code as shown in the following sample, you can use the same form design to retrieve information. The following code retrieves the position and hire date after the employee's name is entered:

```
Private Sub btn_EmpOK_Click()
Dim EmpFound As Range
Dim tblEmployees As ListObject
Set tblEmployees = Worksheets("Employees").ListObjects("tblEmployees")
With tblEmployees.ListColumns("Name").DataBodyRange
  Set EmpFound = .Find(tb_EmpName.Value)
  If EmpFound Is Nothing Then
    Msgbox ("Employee not found!")
    tb_EmpName.Value = ""
  Else
    With .Cells(EmpFound.Row - 1, 1)
      tb_EmpPosition = .Offset(0, 1)
      tb_HireDate = .Offset(0, 2)
    End With
  End If
End With
Set EmpFound = Nothing
Set tblEmployees = Nothing
End Sub
```

EmpFound returns the location of the match as it pertains to the sheet, not the listobject. To return the correct location as it pertains to the listobject's databodyrange, subtract 1 from Emfound.Row (assuming the top left cell of your table is in row 1).

The available events for Label, TextBox, and CommandButton controls are described in Table 10-2.

TABLE 10-2 Label, TextBox, and CommandButton control events

Event	Description
AfterUpdate[1]	Occurs after the control's data has been changed by the user.
BeforeDragOver	Occurs while the user drags and drops data onto the control.
BeforeDropOrPaste	Occurs right before the user is about to drop or paste data into the control.
BeforeUpdate[1]	Occurs before the data in the control is changed.
Change[1]	Occurs when the value of the control is changed.
Click[2]	Occurs when the user clicks the control with the mouse.
DblClick	Occurs when the user double-clicks the control with the mouse.
DropButtonClick[1]	Occurs when the user presses F4 on the keyboard. This is similar to the dropdown control on the combo box, but there is no dropdown feature on a text box.
Enter[3]	Occurs right before the control receives the focus from another control on the same userform.
Error	Occurs when the control runs into an error and cannot return the error information.
Exit[3]	Occurs right after the control loses focus to another control on the same userform.

1 TextBox control only

2 Label and CommandButton controls

3 TextBox and CommandButton controls

Event	Description
KeyDown[3]	Occurs when the user presses a key on the keyboard.
KeyPress[3]	Occurs when the user presses an ANSI key. An ANSI key is a typeable character, such as the letter A. An example of a nontypeable character is the Tab key.
KeyUp[3]	Occurs when the user releases a key on the keyboard.
MouseDown	Occurs when the user presses the mouse button within the control's border.
MouseMove	Occurs when the user moves the mouse within the control's border.
MouseUp	Occurs when the user releases the mouse button within the control's border.

1 TextBox control only

2 Label and CommandButton controls

3 TextBox and CommandButton controls

Deciding whether to use list boxes or combo boxes in forms

You can let users type employee names to search for, but what if they misspell a name? You need a way to make sure that names are typed correctly. Which do you use for this, a list box or a combo box? As explained below, the two are similar, but the combo box has an additional feature that you may or may not need.

A list box displays a list of values from which the user can choose.

A combo box displays a list of values from which the user can choose and allows the user to enter a new value.

In this case, when you want to limit user options, you should use a list box to list the employee names, as shown in Figure 10-9.

FIGURE 10-9 You can use a list box to control user input and selections.

Use the following `Initialize` event to fill the list box with names:

```
Private Sub UserForm_Initialize()
Dim tblEmployees As ListObject
Set tblEmployees = Worksheets("Employees").ListObjects("tblEmployees")
Me.lb_EmpName.RowSource = tblEmployees.ListColumns(1).DataBodyRange.Address
Set tblEmployees = Nothing
End Sub
```

Use the `Click` event to fill in the position and hire date fields when a name is selected:

```
Private Sub lb_EmpName_Click()
Dim EmpFound As Range
Dim tblEmployees As ListObject
Set tblEmployees = Worksheets("Employees").ListObjects("tblEmployees")
With tblEmployees.ListColumns("Name").DataBodyRange
  Set EmpFound = .Find(lb_EmpName.Value)
  With .Cells(EmpFound.Row - 1, 1)
    tb_EmpPosition.Value = .Offset(0, 1)
    tb_HireDate.Value = .Offset(0, 2)
  End With
End With
Set EmpFound = Nothing
Set tblEmployees = Nothing
End Sub
```

Using the `MultiSelect` property of a list box

List boxes have a `MultiSelect` property, which enables the user to select multiple items from the choices in the list box (see Figure 10-10):

- `fmMultiSelectSingle`—The default setting allows only a single item selection at a time.

- `fmMultiSelectMulti`—This allows an item to be deselected when it is clicked again; multiple items can also be selected.

- `fmMultiSelectExtended`—This allows the Ctrl and Shift keys to be used to select multiple items.

If multiple items are selected, the `Value` property cannot be used to retrieve the items. Instead, check to see whether the item is selected and then manipulate it as needed. The following code processes the job positions list box, adding selected positions to the table:

```
Private Sub btn_EmpOK_Click()
Dim LastRow As Integer, i As Integer
Dim tblEmployees As ListObject

Set tblEmployees = Worksheets("Employees").ListObjects("tblEmployees")
With tblEmployees
  .ListRows.Add 'add a new row
  With .DataBodyRange
    LastRow = .Rows.Count 'get the new row
    .Cells(LastRow, 1).Value = tb_EmpName.Value
    For i = 0 To lb_EmpPosition.ListCount - 1
      'if the item is selected, add it to the sheet
      If lb_EmpPosition.Selected(i) = True Then
        .Cells(LastRow, 2).Value = .Cells(LastRow, 2).Value & _
          lb_EmpPosition.List(i) & ","
      End If
    Next i
    .Cells(LastRow, 3).Value = tb_HireDate.Value
    'remove excess comma
    .Cells(LastRow, 2).Value = Left(.Cells(LastRow, 2).Value, _
```

```
      Len(.Cells(LastRow, 2).Value) - 1)
   End With
End With
Set tblEmployees = Nothing
End Sub
```

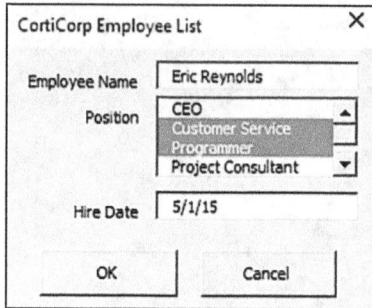

FIGURE 10-10 The `MultiSelect` property enables the user to select multiple items from a list box.

The items in a list box start counting at zero. For this reason, if you use the `ListCount` property, you must subtract one from the result:

```
For i = 0 To lb_EmpPosition.ListCount - 1
```

The available events for `ListBox` controls and `ComboBox` controls are described in Table 10-3.

TABLE 10-3 `ListBox` and `ComboBox` control events

Event	Description
AfterUpdate	Occurs after the control's data has been changed by the user.
BeforeDragOver	Occurs while the user drags and drops data onto the control.
BeforeDropOrPaste	Occurs right before the user is about to drop or paste data into the control.
BeforeUpdate	Occurs before the data in the control is changed.
Change	Occurs when the value of the control is changed.
Click	Occurs when the user selects a value from the list box or combo box.
DblClick	Occurs when the user double-clicks the control with the mouse.
DropButtonClick[1]	Occurs when the dropdown menu appears after the user clicks the dropdown arrow of the combo box or presses F4 on the keyboard.
Enter	Occurs right before the control receives the focus from another control on the same userform.
Error	Occurs when the control runs into an error and can't return the error information.
Exit	Occurs right after the control loses focus to another control on the same userform.
KeyDown	Occurs when the user presses a key on the keyboard.
KeyPress	Occurs when the user presses an ANSI key. An ANSI key is a typeable character, such as the letter A. An example of a nontypeable character is the Tab key.
KeyUp	Occurs when the user releases a key on the keyboard.

Event	Description
MouseDown	Occurs when the user presses the mouse button within the control's border.
MouseMove	Occurs when the user moves the mouse within the control's border.
MouseUp	Occurs when the user releases the mouse button within the control's border.

1 ComboBox control only

Adding option buttons to a userform

⊙ Option buttons are similar to checkboxes in that they can be used to make selections. However, unlike checkboxes, option buttons can be configured to allow only one selection out of a group.

▣ Using the Frame tool, draw a frame to separate the next set of controls from the other controls on the userform. The frame is used to group option buttons, as shown in Figure 10-11.

FIGURE 10-11 You can use a frame to group option buttons together.

Option buttons have a GroupName property. If you assign the same group name, Buildings, to a set of option buttons, you force them to act collectively as a toggle so that only one button in the set can be selected. Selecting an option button automatically deselects the other buttons in the same group or frame. To prevent this behavior, either leave the GroupName property blank or enter a unique name for each option button.

Note For users who prefer to select the option button's label rather than the button itself, create a separate label and add code to the label, like this, to trigger the option button:

```
Private Sub Lbl_Bldg1_Click()
  Obtn_Bldg1.Value = True
End Sub
```

The available events for OptionButton controls and Frame controls are described in Table 10-4.

TABLE 10-4 `OptionButton` and `Frame` control events

Event	Description
AfterUpdate[1]	Occurs after the control's data has been changed by the user.
AddControl[2]	Occurs when a control is added to a frame on a form at runtime. Does not run at design time or upon userform initialization.
BeforeDragOver	Occurs while the user drags and drops data onto the control.
BeforeDropOrPaste	Occurs right before the user is about to drop or paste data into the control.
BeforeUpdate[1]	Occurs before the data in the control is changed.
Change[1]	Occurs when the value of the control is changed.
Click	Occurs when the user clicks the control with the mouse.
DblClick	Occurs when the user double-clicks the control with the mouse.
Enter	Occurs right before the control receives the focus from another control on the same userform.
Error	Occurs when the control runs into an error and cannot return the error information.
Exit	Occurs right after the control loses focus to another control on the same userform.
KeyDown	Occurs when the user presses a key on the keyboard.
KeyPress	Occurs when the user presses an ANSI key. An ANSI key is a typeable character, such as the letter A. An example of a nontypeable character is the Tab key.
KeyUp	Occurs when the user releases a key on the keyboard.
Layout[2]	Occurs when the frame changes size.
MouseDown	Occurs when the user presses the mouse button within the control's border.
MouseMove	Occurs when the user moves the mouse within the control's border.
MouseUp	Occurs when the user releases the mouse button within the control's border.
RemoveControl[2]	Occurs when a control is deleted from within the frame control.
Scroll[2]	Occurs when the scrollbar box, if visible, is repositioned.
Zoom[2]	Occurs when the zoom value is changed.

1 OptionButton control only

2 Frame control only

Adding graphics to a userform

A list on a form can be even more helpful if a corresponding graphic is added to the form. The following code displays a photograph corresponding to the selected employee from the list box:

```
Private Sub lb_EmpName_Change()
Dim EmpFound As Range
Dim tblEmployees As ListObject
Set tblEmployees = Worksheets("Employees").ListObjects("tblEmployees")
With tblEmployees
   Set EmpFound = .ListColumns("Name").DataBodyRange.Find(lb_EmpName.Value)
   If EmpFound Is Nothing Then
```

```
        MsgBox "Employee not found!"
        lb_EmpName.Value = ""
        Exit Sub
      Else
        With .DataBodyRange.Cells(EmpFound.Row - 1, .ListColumns("Name").Index)
          tb_EmpPosition = .Offset(0, 1).Value
          tb_HireDate = .Offset(0, 2).Value
          On Error Resume Next
          Img_Employee.Picture = LoadPicture _
            (ThisWorkbook.Path & "\" & EmpFound.Value & ".jpg")
          On Error GoTo 0
        End With
      End If
    End With
    Set EmpFound = Nothing
    Set tblEmployees = Nothing
    End Sub
```

The available events for Graphic controls are described in Table 10-5.

TABLE 10-5 Graphic control events

Event	Description
BeforeDragOver	Occurs while the user drags and drops data onto the control.
BeforeDropOrPaste	Occurs right before the user is about to drop or paste data into the control.
Click	Occurs when the user clicks the image with the mouse.
DblClick	Occurs when the user double-clicks the image with the mouse.
Error	Occurs when the control runs into an error and can't return the error information.
MouseDown	Occurs when the user presses the mouse button within the borders of the image.
MouseMove	Occurs when the user moves the mouse within the borders of the image.
MouseUp	Occurs when the user releases the mouse button within the control's border.

Using a spin button on a userform

In the example we've been working with, the Hire Date field allows the user to enter the date in any format, such as 1/1/25 or January 1, 2025. This possible inconsistency can create problems later on if you need to use or search for dates. The solution? Force users to enter dates in a unified manner.

Spin buttons allow the user to increment/decrement through a series of numbers. In this way, the user is forced to enter numbers rather than text. Draw a spin button for a Month entry on the form. In the Properties window, set Min to 1 for January and Max to 12 for December. For the Value property, enter 1, the first month. Next, draw a text box next to the spin button. This text box reflects the value of the spin button. Place the code below behind the month's spin button control:

```
Private Sub SpBtn_Month_Change()
tb_Month.Value = SpBtn_Month.Value
End Sub
```

Finish building the form. Use a `Min` of 1 and `Max` of 31 for Day, and a `Min` of 1900 and a `Max` of 2100 for Year:

```
Private Sub btn_EmpOK_Click()
Dim LastRow As Integer, i As Integer
Dim tblEmployees As ListObject
Set tblEmployees = Worksheets("Employees").ListObjects("tblEmployees")
If tb_EmpName.Value = "" Then
  frm_AddEmp.Hide
  MsgBox ("Please enter an Employee Name")
  frm_AddEmp.Show
  Exit Sub
End If
With tblEmployees
  .ListRows.Add 'add a new row
  With .DataBodyRange
    LastRow = .Rows.Count 'get the new row
    .Cells(LastRow, 1).Value = tb_EmpName.Value
    For i = 0 To lb_EmpPosition.ListCount - 1
      If lb_EmpPosition.Selected(i) = True Then
        .Cells(LastRow, 2).Value = _
          .Cells(LastRow, 2).Value & lb_EmpPosition.List(i) & ","
      End If
    Next i
    'Concatenate the values from the textboxes to create the date
    .Cells(LastRow, 3).Value = tb_Month.Value & "/" & tb_Day.Value & _
      "/" & tb_Year.Value
  End With
End With
End Sub
```

The available events for `SpinButton` controls are described in Table 10-6.

TABLE 10-6 `SpinButton` control events

Event	Description
AfterUpdate	Occurs after the control's data has been changed by the user.
BeforeDragOver	Occurs while the user drags and drops data onto the control.
BeforeDropOrPaste	Occurs right before the user is about to drop or paste data into the control.
BeforeUpdate	Occurs before the data in the control is changed.
Change	Occurs when the value of the control is changed.
Enter	Occurs right before the control receives the focus from another control on the same userform.
Error	Occurs when the control runs into an error and cannot return the error information.
Exit	Occurs right after the control loses focus to another control on the same userform.
KeyDown	Occurs when the user presses a key on the keyboard.

Event	Description
KeyPress	Occurs when the user presses an ANSI key. An ANSI key is a typeable character, such as the letter A. An example of a nontypeable character is the Tab key.
KeyUp	Occurs when the user releases a key on the keyboard.
SpinDown	Occurs when the user clicks the lower or left spin button, decreasing the value.
SpinUp	Occurs when the user clicks the upper or right spin button, increasing the value.

Using the MultiPage control to combine forms

The MultiPage control provides a neat way of organizing multiple forms. Instead of having one form for personal employee information and one for on-the-job information, combine the information into one multipage form, as shown in Figures 10-12 and 10-13.

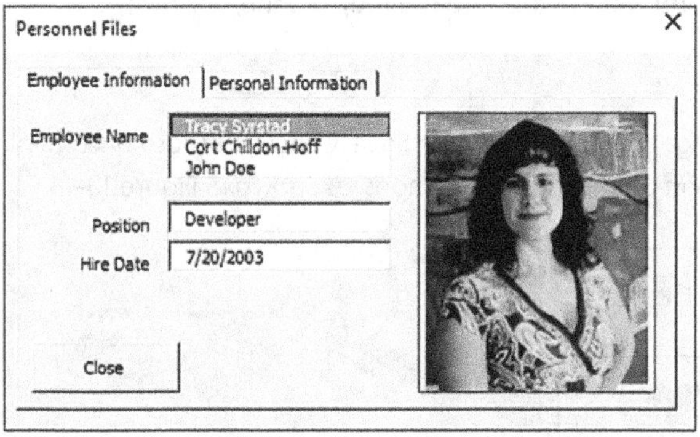

FIGURE 10-12 Use the MultiPage control to combine multiple forms. This is the first page of the form.

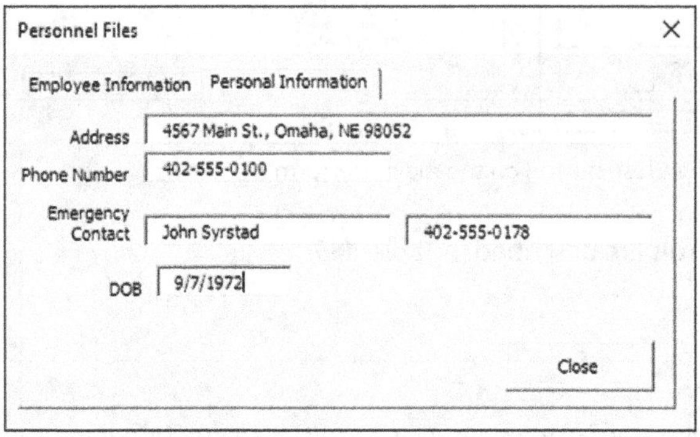

FIGURE 10-13 This is the second page of the form.

You can modify a page by right-clicking the page's tab and choosing one of the following menu options: New Page, Delete Page, Rename, or Move.

Tip Adding multipage forms after the rest of the form has been created is not an easy task. Therefore, plan multipage forms from the beginning. If you decide later that you need a multipage form, insert a new form, draw the MultiPage control, and copy/paste the controls from the other forms to the new form.

Note Do not right-click on the multipage tab headers (the tab area) to view the MultiPage code. Instead, right-click anywhere within the body of the MultiPage control (the main area where other controls go) to get the View Code option.

Unlike many of the other controls in which the Value property holds a user-entered or user-selected value, the MultiPage control uses the Value property to hold the active page's number, starting at zero. For example, if you have a five-page form and want to activate the fourth page, use this:

```
MultiPage1.Value = 3
```

If you have a control you want all the pages to share, such as a Save, Cancel, or Close button, place the control on the main userform rather than on the individual pages, as shown in Figure 10-14.

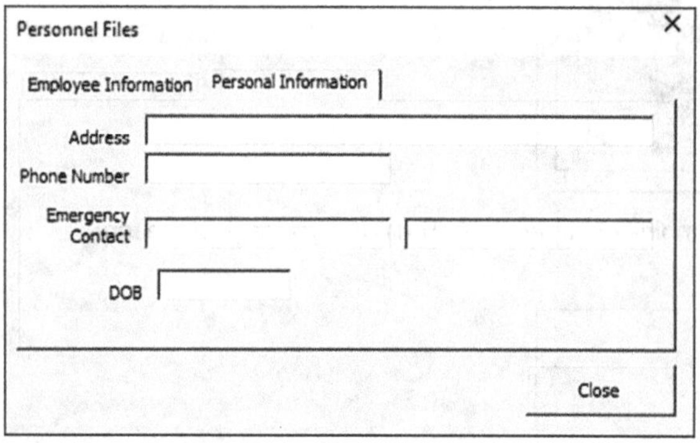

FIGURE 10-14 Place common controls such as the Close button on the main userform.

The available events for MultiPage controls are described in Table 10-7.

TABLE 10-7 MultiPage control events

Event	Description
AddControl	Occurs when a control is added to a page of the MultiPage control. Does not run at design time or upon userform initialization.
BeforeDragOver	Occurs while the user drags and drops data onto a page of the MultiPage control.
BeforeDropOrPaste	Occurs right before the user is about to drop or paste data onto a page of the MultiPage control.
Change	Occurs when the user changes pages of a MultiPage control.

Event	Description
Click	Occurs when the user clicks on a page of the MultiPage control.
DblClick	Occurs when the user double-clicks a page of the MultiPage control.
Enter	Occurs right before the MultiPage control receives the focus from another control on the same userform.
Error	Occurs when the MultiPage control runs into an error and cannot return the error information.
Exit	Occurs right after the MultiPage control loses focus to another control on the same userform.
KeyDown	Occurs when the user presses a key on the keyboard.
KeyPress	Occurs when the user presses an ANSI key. An ANSI key is a typeable character, such as the letter A. An example of a nontypeable character is the Tab key.
KeyUp	Occurs when the user releases a key on the keyboard.
Layout	Occurs when the MultiPage control changes size.
MouseDown	Occurs when the user presses the mouse button within the control's border.
MouseMove	Occurs when the user moves the mouse within the control's borders.
MouseUp	Occurs when the user releases the mouse button within the control's border.
RemoveControl	Occurs when a control is removed from a page of the MultiPage control.
Scroll	Occurs when the scrollbar box, if visible, is repositioned.
Zoom	Occurs when the zoom value is changed.

Verifying field entry

Even when users are told to fill in all the fields, they don't always do it. With a paper form, there is no way to force them to do so. As a programmer, you can ensure that all required fields are filled in by not allowing the user to continue until all requirements are met. Here's how to do this:

```
If tb_EmpName.Value = "" Then
   frm_AddEmp.Hide
   MsgBox "Please enter an Employee Name"
   frm_AddEmp.Show
   Exit Sub
End If
```

Illegal window closing

The userforms created in the VB Editor are not that different from normal dialogs; they also include the X close button in the upper-right corner. Although using the button is not wrong, it can cause problems, depending on the objective of the userform. In cases like this, you might want to control what happens if the user clicks the button. Use the `QueryClose` event of the userform to find out what method is used to close the form and code an appropriate action:

```
Private Sub UserForm_QueryClose(Cancel As Integer, CloseMode As Integer)
If CloseMode = vbFormControlMenu Then
  MsgBox "Please use the OK or Cancel buttons to close the form", _
    vbCritical
  Cancel = True 'prevent the form from closing
End If
End Sub
```

When you know which method the user used to try to close the form, you can create a message box similar to the one shown in Figure 10-15 to warn the user that the method was illegal.

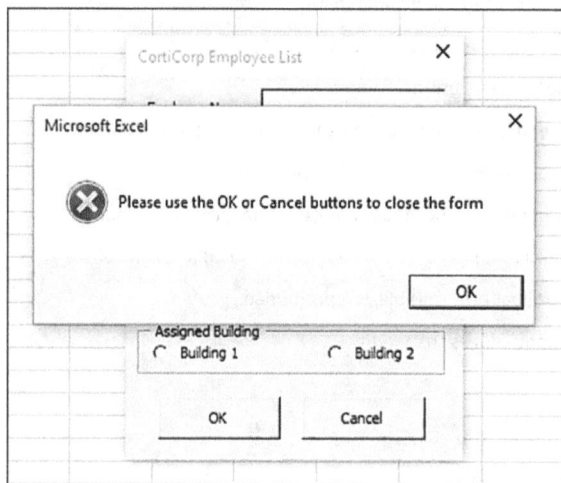

FIGURE 10-15 You can control what happens when the user clicks the X button.

The `QueryClose` event can be triggered in four ways:

- `vbFormControlMenu`—The user either right-clicks on the form's title bar and selects the Close command or clicks the X in the upper-right corner of the form.

- `vbFormCode`—The `Unload` statement is used.

- `vbAppWindows`—Windows shuts down.

- `vbAppTaskManager`—The Task Manager shuts down the application.

Getting a file name

One of the most common client interactions occurs when you need the client to specify a path and file name. Excel VBA has a built-in function to display the File Open dialog, as shown in Figure 10-16. The client browses to and selects a file. When the client clicks the Open button, instead of opening the file, Excel VBA returns the full path and file name to the code:

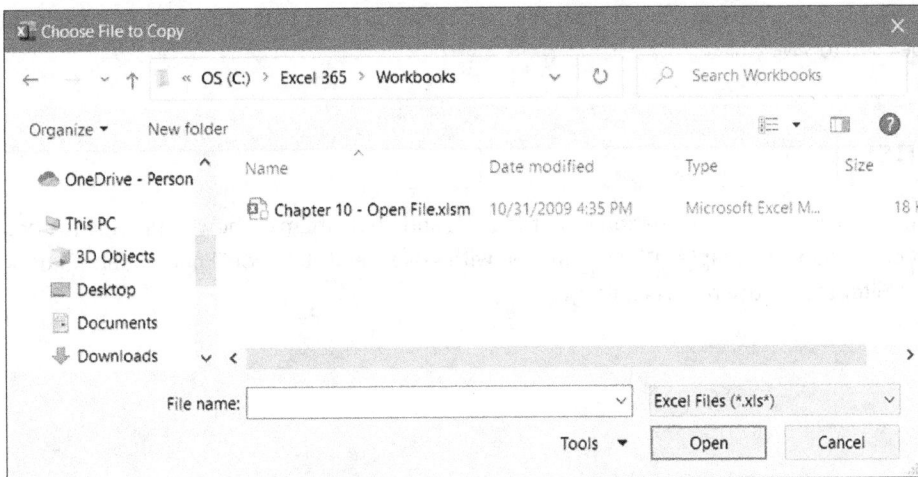

FIGURE 10-16 You can customize the File Open dialog to have the user select a file.

```
Sub SelectFile()
Dim x As String
'Ask which file to copy
x = Application.GetOpenFilename(FileFilter:="Excel Files (*.xls*), *.xls*", _
  Title:="Choose File to Copy", MultiSelect:=False)
'check in case no files were selected
If x = "False" Then Exit Sub
MsgBox "You selected " & x
End Sub
```

The preceding code allows the client to select one file. If you want the user to specify multiple files, use this code:

```
Sub ManyFiles()
Dim x As Variant
Dim i As Integer
x = Application.GetOpenFilename(FileFilter:="Excel Files (*.xls*), *.xls*", _
  Title:="Choose Files", MultiSelect:=True)
On Error Resume Next
If Ubound(x) > 0 Then
  For i = 1 To UBound(x)
    MsgBox "You selected " & x(i)
  Next i
ElseIf x = "False" Then
  Exit Sub
End If
On Error GoTo 0
End Sub
```

In a similar fashion, you can use `Application.GetSaveAsFileName` to find the path and file name that should be used to save a file.

Next steps

Userforms allow you to get information from the users and guide them on how to provide the program with that information. In Chapter 11, "Data mining with Advanced Filter," you'll find out about using Advanced Filter to produce reports quickly.

Data mining with Advanced Filter

In this chapter, you will:

- Replace a loop by using AutoFilter
- Get to know Advanced Filter
- Use Advanced Filter to extract a unique list of values
- Use Advanced Filter with criteria ranges
- Use Filter In Place in Advanced Filter
- Use Advanced Filter to return all records that match the criteria
- Learn the ways you can sort your data

Read this chapter.

Although very few people use Advanced Filter in Excel, it is a workhorse in Excel VBA. I estimate that I end up using one of these filtering techniques as the core of a macro in 80% of the macros I develop for clients. Given that Advanced Filter is used in fewer than 1% of Excel sessions, this is a dramatic statistic.

So, even if you hardly ever use Advanced Filter in regular Excel, you should study this chapter to learn some powerful VBA techniques.

Replacing a loop with AutoFilter

In Chapter 5, "Looping and flow control," you read about several ways to loop through a data set to format records that match certain criteria. By using Filter (Microsoft's name for what was originally AutoFilter), you can achieve the same result much faster. While other examples in this chapter use Advanced Filter, this example can be solved with the simpler Filter. Although Microsoft changed the name of AutoFilter to Filter in Excel 2007, the VBA code still refers to AutoFilter.

When AutoFilter was added to Excel, the team at Microsoft added extra care and attention to it. Items hidden because of AutoFilter are not simply treated like other hidden rows. AutoFilter gets special treatment. You've likely run into a frustrating situation where you have applied formatting to visible rows, and the formatting has been applied to the hidden rows. This is certainly a problem when you've hidden rows by clicking the #2 Group and Outline button after using the Subtotal command. This is always a problem when you manually hide rows, but it is never a problem when the rows are hidden because of AutoFilter.

After you've applied AutoFilter to hide rows, any action performed on the CurrentRegion is applied only to the visible rows. You can apply bold formatting. You can change the font to red. You can even use CurrentRegion.EntireRow.Delete to delete the visible rows and not affect the rows hidden by the filter.

Let's say that you have a data set like the one shown in Figure 11-1, and you want to perform some action on all the records that match certain criteria, such as all Ford records.

	A	B	C	D	E	F	G	H
1	Region	Product	Date	Customer	Quantity	Revenue	COGS	Profit
83	Central	R537	10-Sep-23	Magnificent Eggbeater Corporation	500	11525	5621	5904
84	East	R537	11-Sep-23	Mouthwatering Notebook Inc.	1000	20940	11242	9698
85	East	R537	12-Sep-23	Trustworthy Flagpole Partners	100	2257	1082	1175
86	Central	W435	13-Sep-23	Ford	900	20610	9742	10868
87	Central	R537	13-Sep-23	Distinctive Wax Company	700	17367	7869	9498
88	West	M556	13-Sep-23	Guarded Aerobic Corporation	700	12145	6522	5623
89	Central	R537	13-Sep-23	Magnificent Eggbeater Corporation	1000	25140	11242	13898

FIGURE 11-1 Find and mark all Ford records.

In Chapter 6, "R1C1 style formulas," you learned to write code like the following, which you could use to color all the Ford records green:

```
Sub OldLoop()
FinalRow = Cells(Rows.Count, 1).End(xlUp).Row
For I = 2 To FinalRow
  If Cells(i, 4).Value = "Ford" Then
    Cells(i, 1).Resize(1, 8).Interior.Color = RGB(0,255,0)
  End If
Next i
End Sub
```

If you needed to delete records, you had to be careful to run the loop from the bottom of the data set to the top, using code like this:

```
Sub OldLoopToDelete()
FinalRow = Cells(Rows.Count, 1).End(xlUp).Row
For i = FinalRow To 2 Step -1
  If Cells(i, 4).Value = "Ford" Then
    Rows(i).Delete
  End If
Next i
End Sub
```

The AutoFilter method, however, enables you to isolate all the Ford records in a single line of code:

```
Range("A1").AutoFilter Field:=4, Criteria1:= "Ford"
```

After isolating the matching records, you do not need to use the `VisibleCellsOnly` setting to format the matching records. Instead, you can use the following line of code to make all the matching records green:

```
Range("A1").CurrentRegion.Interior.Color = RGB(0,255,0)
```

There are two problems with the current two-line macro. First, the program leaves the AutoFilter dropdown menus in the data set. Second, the heading row is also formatted in green.

> **Note**   The `.CurrentRegion` property extends the A1 reference to include the entire data set.

This single line of code turns off the AutoFilter dropdown menus and clears the filter:

```
Range("A1").AutoFilter
```

If you want to leave the AutoFilter dropdown menus on but clear the column D dropdown menu from showing Ford, you can use this line of code:

```
ActiveSheet.ShowAllData
```

Addressing the second problem is a bit more difficult. After you apply the filter and select `Range("A1").CurrentRegion`, the selection automatically includes the headers in the selection. Any formatting is also applied to the header row.

If you do not care about the first blank row below the data, you can simply add `OFFSET(1)` to move the current region down to start in A2. This would be fine if your goal were to delete all the Ford records:

```
Sub DeleteFord()
'skips header, but also deletes blank row below
Range("A1").AutoFilter Field:=4, Criteria1:="Ford"
Range("A1").CurrentRegion.Offset(1).EntireRow.Delete
Range("A1").AutoFilter
End Sub
```

> **Note**   Refer to "Using the `Offset` property to refer to a range" in Chapter 3, "Referring to ranges, names, and tables," for more information on using `Offset`.

The preceding code works when you do not mind if the first blank row below the data is deleted. However, when you apply a green format to those rows, the code applies the green format to the blank row below the data set, and that would not look right.

If you will be doing some formatting, you can determine the height of the data set and use `.Resize` to reduce the height of the current region while you use `Offset`:

```
Sub ColorFord()
DataHt = Range("A1").CurrentRegion.Rows.Count
```

```
Range("A1").AutoFilter Field:=4, Criteria1:="Ford"
With Range("A1").CurrentRegion.Rows("2:" & DataHt)
  'No need to use VisibleCellsOnly for formatting
  .Interior.Color = RGB(0,255,0)
  .Font.Bold = True
End With
'Clear the AutoFilter & remove dropdowns
Range("A1").AutoFilter
End Sub
```

Using AutoFilter techniques

Excel's AutoFilter feature supports numerous filter types: selecting multiple items, searching for values, filtering by top or bottom values or percentages, filtering by color or icon, and more. While the interface has evolved over time, the VBA code continues to use the same properties, including `Field`, `Criteria1`, `Operator`, and `Criteria2`.

Selecting multiple items

You can filter a column for multiple values by using the `xlOr` or `xlAnd` operators when selecting two values:

```
Range("A1").AutoFilter Field:=4, _
  Criteria1:="Ford", _
  Operator:=xlOr, _
  Criteria2:="General Motors"
```

If you need to filter three or more values, use `Operator:=xlFilterValues`, and provide an array of items for `Criteria1`, like this:

```
Range("A1").AutoFilter Field:=4, _
  Criteria1:=Array("General Motors", "Ford", "Sure Door Inc."), _
  Operator:=xlFilterValues
```

Filtering by Top or Bottom Values

You can return the top or bottom records by either item count or percentage by using one of the following operators:

- xlTop10Items

- xlTop10Percent

- xlBottom10Items

- xlBottom10Percent

Despite their names, you can specify any number, not just 10. For example, to return the top 12 rows by Revenue, do this:

```
Range("A1").AutoFilter Field:=6, _
    Criteria1:="12", _
    Operator:=xlTop10Items
```

This code is broken out as follows:

- `Field:=6` tells Excel to target the sixth column in the range, which is Revenue.

- `Criteria:="12"` tells Excel how many items to return.

- `Operator:=xlTop10Items` tells Excel which operator to use.

> **Note** Notice that we entered the 12 as a string. Always use quotation marks for the criteria entries.

Selecting using the Search box

The Excel interface lets you filter a column using the Search Box in the AutoFilter dropdown. As you type, Excel matches your entry to any part of the cell, similar to using TextFilters | Contains.

You can replicate this behavior in VBA by using wild cards. For example, to filter the Customer column for any names that contain at, do this:

```
Range("A1").AutoFilter Field:=4, Criteria1:="*at*"
```

> **Note** If you try to record this type of search with the macro recorder, Excel simply records a filter for the matched names—the specific letter combination you typed is not captured.

Filtering by color

To find records that have a particular font color, use the operator `xlFilterFontColor` and specify a particular RGB value as the criteria. This code finds all cells with a red font in column F:

```
Sub FilterByFontColor()
Range("A1").AutoFilter Field:=6, _
  Criteria1:=RGB(255, 0, 0), Operator:=xlFilterFontColor
End Sub
```

To find records that have no particular font color, use the operator `xlFilterAutomaticFillColor` and do not specify criteria:

```
Sub FilterNoFontColor()
Range("A1").AutoFilter Field:=6, _
  Operator:=xlFilterAutomaticFontColor
End Sub
```

To find records that have a particular fill color, use the operator `xlFilterCellColor` and specify a particular RGB value as the criteria. This code finds all red cells in column F:

```
Sub FilterByFillColor()
Range("A1").AutoFilter Field:=6, _
  Criteria1:=RGB(255, 0, 0), Operator:=xlFilterCellColor
End Sub
```

To find records that have no fill color, use the operator `xlFilterNoFill` and do not specify criteria.

Filtering by icon

If you are expecting a data set to have an icon set applied, you can filter to show only records with one particular icon by using the `xlFilterIcon` operator.

For the criteria, you have to know which icon set has been applied, as well as which icon within the set you want to filter by. The icon sets are identified using the names shown in column A in Figure 11-2. The icons within each set range from 1 through 5. The following code filters the Revenue column to show the rows containing an upward-pointing arrow in the 5 Arrows Gray icon set:

```
Sub FilterByIcon()
'filter the icon set x15ArrowsGray by the upward-pointing arrow
'which is the fifth icon (Item) in the set
Range("A1").AutoFilter Field:=6, _
  Criteria1:=ActiveWorkbook.IconSets(x15ArrowsGray).Item(5), _
  Operator:=xlFilterIcon
End Sub
```

To find records that have no conditional formatting icon, use the operator `xlFilterNoIcon` and do not specify criteria.

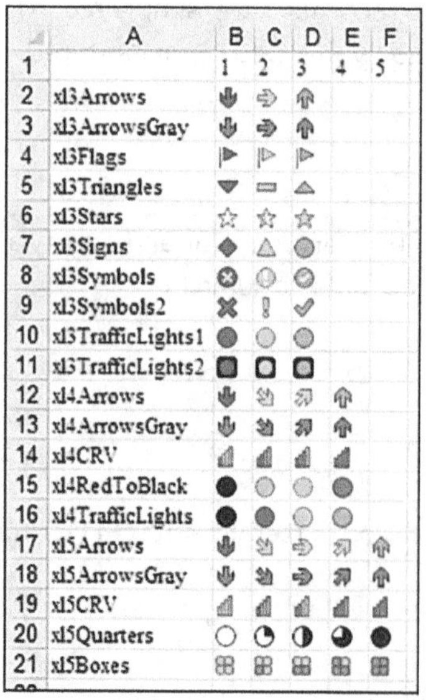

FIGURE 11-2 To search for a particular icon, you need to know the icon set from column A and the item number from row 1.

Selecting a dynamic date range using Dynamic Filters

Perhaps the most powerful feature in the world of Excel filters is the dynamic filters. These filters enable you to choose records that are above average or with a date field to select virtual periods, such as next week or last year.

To use a dynamic filter, specify xlFilterDynamic as the operator and then use 1 of 34 values as Criteria1. The following code finds all dates that are in the next year:

```
Sub DynamicAutoFilter()
Range("A1").AutoFilter Field:=3, _
  Criteria1:=xlFilterNextYear, _
  Operator:=xlFilterDynamic
End Sub
```

The following are all the dynamic filter criteria options, which you specify as Criteria1 in the AutoFilter method:

- **Criteria for values**—Use xlFilterAboveAverage or xlFilterBelowAverage to find all the rows that are above or below average.

- **Criteria for future periods**—Use xlFilterTomorrow, xlFilterNextWeek, xlFilterNextMonth, xlFilterNextQuarter, or xlFilterNextYear to find rows that fall in a certain future period. Note that "next week" starts on Sunday and ends on Saturday.

- **Criteria for current periods**—Use xlFilterToday, xlFilterThisWeek, xlFilterThisMonth, xlFilterThisQuarter, or xlFilterThisYear to find rows that fall within the current period. Excel uses the system clock to find the current day.

- **Criteria for past periods**—Use xlFilterYesterday, xlFilterLastWeek, xlFilterLastMonth, xlFilterLastQuarter, xlFilterLastYear, or xlFilterYearToDate to find rows that fall within a previous period.

- **Criteria for specific quarters**—Use xlFilterAllDatesInPeriodQuarter1, xlFilterAll _ DatesInPeriodQuarter2, xlFilterAllDatesInPeriodQuarter3, or xlFilterAllDates _ InPeriodQuarter4 to filter to rows that fall within a specific quarter. Note that these filters do not differentiate based on a year. If you ask for quarter 1, you might get records from this January, last February, and next March.

- **Criteria for specific months**—Use xlFilterAllDatesInPeriodJanuary through xlFilterAll _ DatesInPeriodDecember to filter records that fall during a certain month. As with quarters, the filter does not filter to any particular year.

Unfortunately, you cannot combine criteria. You might think that you can specify xlFilterDates _ InPeriodJanuary as Criteria1 and xlFilterDatesNextYear as Criteria2. Even though this is a brilliant thought, Microsoft does not support this syntax (yet).

You can use Criteria2 as a single criteria on date fields filtering by date, month, or year by providing an array detailing the filtering as Array(Level, Date) with xlFilterValues operator. Level is 0-2 (year,month,date), and `Date` is one valid date inside the filtering period. The following code finds all dates that are in December 2024 and all months in 2025:

```
Sub AutoFilterByCriteria2()
Range("A1").AutoFilter Field:=3, _
  Criteria2:=Array(1, "12/01/2024", 0, "01/01/2025"), _
  Operator:=xlFilterValues
End Sub
```

Selecting visible cells only

After you apply a filter, most commands operate only on the visible rows in the selection. If you need to delete the records, format the records, or apply a conditional format to the records, you can simply refer to the `.CurrentRegion` of the first heading cell and perform the command.

For example, after you've filtered your table, copy the results to a new sheet, like this:

```
Range("A1").CurrentRegion.Copy Destination:=Worksheets("Report").Range("A1")
```

However, if you have a data set in which the rows have been hidden using the Hide Rows command, any formatting applied to `.CurrentRegion` applies to the hidden rows, too. To work with only the visible cells in these cases, refer to "Selecting with SpecialCells" in Chapter 13, "Excel Power."

Advanced Filter—easier in VBA than in Excel

Advanced filters in Excel can be tricky to learn, especially when setting up criteria ranges, but they're a powerful tool once you get the hang of them. Still, they can be frustrating.

However, in VBA, advanced filters are a joy to use. With a single line of code, you can rapidly extract a subset of records from a database or quickly get a unique list of values in any column. This is critical when you want to run reports for a specific region or customer. Two advanced filters are used most often in the same procedure—one to get a unique list of customers and a second to filter to each customer, as shown in Figure 11-3. The rest of this chapter builds toward such a routine.

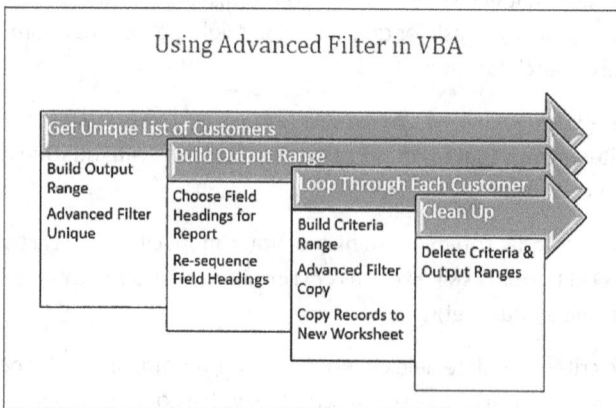

FIGURE 11-3 A typical macro uses two advanced filters.

Using the Excel interface to build an advanced filter

Because not many people use the Advanced Filter feature, this section walks you through examples using the user interface to build an advanced filter and then shows you the analogous code. You will be amazed at how complex the user interface seems and yet how easy it is to program a powerful advanced filter to extract records.

One reason Advanced Filter is hard to use is that you can use it in several different ways. Every Advanced Filter has to have a List Range. You must make three basic choices in the Advanced Filter dialog. Because each choice has two options, there are eight (2 × 2 × 2) possible combinations of these choices. The three basic choices are shown in Figure 11-4 and described here:

- **Action**—You can select Filter The List, In-Place, or you can select Copy To Another Location. If you choose to filter the records in place, the nonmatching rows are hidden. Choosing to copy to a new location copies the records that match the filter to a new range.

- **Criteria**—You can filter with or without criteria. Filtering with criteria is appropriate for getting a subset of rows. Filtering without criteria is still useful when you want a subset of columns or when you are using the Unique Records Only option.

- **Unique**—You can choose to request Unique Records Only or request all matching records. The Unique option makes using the Advanced Filter command one of the fastest ways to find a unique list of values in one field. By placing the Customer heading in the output range, you get a unique list of values for that one column.

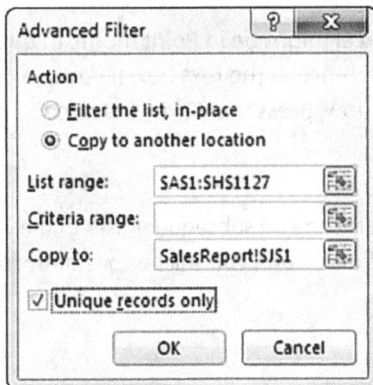

FIGURE 11-4 The Advanced Filter dialog is complicated to use in the Excel user interface. Fortunately, it is much easier in VBA.

Using Advanced Filter to extract a unique list of values

One of the simplest uses of Advanced Filter is to extract a unique list of a single field from a data set. In this example, you want to get a unique list of customers from a sales report. You know that Customer is in column D of the data set. You have an unknown number of records starting in cell A2, and row 1 is the header row. There is nothing located to the right of the data set.

Extracting a unique list of values with the user interface

When using Advanced Filter to extract a unique list, Excel doesn't check just one column. It looks at all the columns you want to extract. If even one value in a selected column is different, it treats that row as unique. To extract a unique list of values from a data set with duplicate rows, follow these steps:

1. With the cursor anywhere in the data range, select Advanced from the Sort & Filter group on the Data tab. The first time you use the Advanced Filter command on a worksheet, Excel automatically populates the List Range field with the entire data set. On subsequent uses of the Advanced Filter command, this dialog remembers the settings from the prior advanced filter.

2. Select the Unique Records Only checkbox at the bottom of the dialog.

3. In the Action section, select Copy To Another Location.

4. Type J1 in the Copy To text box.

By default, Excel copies all the columns in the data set. You can filter just the Customer column either by limiting List Range to include only column D or by specifying one or more headings in the Copy To range. Each method has its own drawbacks.

Changing the list range to a single column

Edit List Range to point to the Customer column. In this case, you need to change the default $A$1:$H$1127 to $D$1:$D$1127. The Advanced Filter dialog should appear.

> **Note** When you initially edit any range in the dialog, Excel might be in Point mode. In this mode, pressing a left- or right-arrow key inserts a cell reference in the text box. If you see the word **Point** in the lower-left corner of your Excel window, press the F2 key to change from Point mode to Edit mode.

The drawback of this method is that Excel remembers the list range on subsequent uses of the Advanced Filter command. If you later want to get a unique list of regions, you will be constantly specifying the list range.

Copying the customer heading before filtering

With a little thought before invoking the Advanced Filter command, you can allow Excel to keep the default list range $A$1:$H$1127. In cell J1, type the Customer heading, as shown in Figure 11-5. Leave the List Range field pointing to columns A through H. Because the Copy To range of J1 already contains a valid heading from the list range, Excel copies data only from the Customer column. This is the preferred method, particularly if you will be using multiple advanced filters. Because Excel remembers the settings from the preceding advanced filter, it is more convenient to always filter the entire columns of the list range and limit the columns by setting up headings in the Copy To range.

After you use either of these methods to perform the advanced filter, a concise list of the unique customers appears in column J (see Figure 11-5).

J	K	L	M
Customer			
Trustworthy Flagpole Partners			
Amazing Shoe Company			
Mouthwatering Notebook Inc.			
Cool Saddle Traders			
Tasty Shovel Company			
Distinctive Wax Company			
Guarded Aerobic Corporation			
Tasty Yogurt Corporation			
Agile Aquarium Inc.			
Magnificent Eggbeater Corporation			
User-Friendly Luggage Corporation			
Guarded Umbrella Traders			

FIGURE 11-5 The advanced filter extracted a unique list of customers from the data set and copied it to column J.

Extracting a unique list of values with VBA code

In VBA, you use the AdvancedFilter method to carry out the Advanced Filter command. Again, you have three choices to make:

- **Action**—Choose to either filter in place with the parameter Action:=xlFilterInPlace or copy with Action:=xlFilterCopy. If you want to copy, you also have to specify the parameter CopyToRange:=Range("J1").

- **Criteria**—To filter with criteria, include the parameter CriteriaRange:=Range("L1:L2"). To filter without criteria, omit this optional parameter.

- **Unique**—To return only unique records, specify the parameter Unique:=True.

The following code sets up a single-column output range two columns to the right of the listobject holding the data:

```
Sub GetUniqueCustomers()
Dim Lo As ListObject
Dim WSD As Worksheet
Dim IRange As Range, ORange As Range
Dim colReport As Long
Set WSD = Worksheets("SalesReport")
With WSD
    Set Lo = .ListObjects("tblSales")
    'Find what column to place the results in
    colReport = Lo.HeaderRowRange.Cells(1, Lo.ListColumns.Count).Offset(, 2).Column
    'Clear out results of previous macros
    .Range(.Cells(1, colReport), .Cells(1, Columns.Count)).EntireColumn.Delete
    'Set up output range. Copy heading from Customer column
    Set ORange = .Cells(1, colReport)
```

```
  ORange.Value = Lo.ListColumns("Customer").Name
  'Define the Input Range
  Set IRange = Lo.ListColumns("Customer").Range
  'Do the Advanced Filter to get unique list of customers
  IRange.AdvancedFilter Action:=xlFilterCopy, CopyToRange:=ORange, Unique:=True
End With
'cleanup memory
Set IRange = Nothing: Set ORange = Nothing
Set Lo = Nothing
Set WSD = Nothing
End Sub
```

By default, an advanced filter copies all columns. If you want just one particular column, use that column heading as the heading in the output range.

Level Up!

The fact that our data is in a listobject affords us (and our client) a bit of flexibility. For example, the column headers do not need to remain in the same order. You can quickly reference the desired column using the header. And if the reverse were true—headers would change, but not order, then you could specify the header's address.

Often, when a client sends me a data set, my first question is if I can change it to a listobject. It makes coding so much easier!

The first bit of the preceding code is a good example of how listobjects make coding easier. We find the column we're going to place the results in with a line of code that has no static references in it. Then, we use that information to clean up the sheet. Although it is not necessary to do so, you can define an object variable for the output range (ORange) and for the input range (IRange).

Tip
If you find yourself referencing the same column header multiple times, consider creating a constant (Const) either at the module level or at least within the sub. This reduces the chance of typos and gives you a single location from which to update it.

To really impress a client with your forethought, create a Settings sheet where the columns are configured, and the client can update the information themselves. See Chapter 13, "Excel Power," for an example of this setup.

This code is generic enough that it will not have to be rewritten if new columns are added to the table later. Setting up the object variables for the input and output range is done for readability rather than out of necessity. The previous code could be written just as easily like this shortened version:

```
Sub UniqueCustomerRedux()
'Copy a heading to create an output range
Range("J1").Value = Range("D1").Value
'Use the Advanced Filter
```

```
Range("D1").EntireColumn.AdvancedFilter xlFilterCopy, _
    CopyToRange:=Range("J1"), Unique:=True
End Sub
```

When you run either of the previous blocks of code on the sample data set, you get a unique list of customers off to the right of the data. The key to getting a unique list of customers is copying the header from the Customer field to a blank cell and specifying this cell as the output range.

Sorting the list and adding a revenue summary

After you have the unique list of customers, you can sort the list and add a SUMIF formula to get total revenue by customer. The following code gets the unique list of customers, sorts it, and then builds a formula for total revenue by customer. Figure 11-6 shows the results:

```
Sub RevenueByCustomers()
Dim Lo As ListObject
Dim WSD As Worksheet
Dim IRange As Range, ORange As Range
Dim colReport As Long
Dim Results As Range
Dim LastRow As Long
Dim CustomerCol As Long, RevenueCol As Long
Dim FirstRow As Long, FinalRow As Long
Set WSD = Worksheets("SalesReport")
Set Lo = WSD.ListObjects("tblSales")
With Lo
   'Get the column numbers for the "Customer" and "Revenue" fields
   CustomerCol = .ListColumns("Customer").Range.Column
   RevenueCol = .ListColumns("Revenue").Range.Column
   FirstRow = .DataBodyRange.Cells(1, 1).Row
   FinalRow = .ListRows.Count + .HeaderRowRange.Row
   'Find what column to place the results in
   colReport = .HeaderRowRange.Cells(1, .ListColumns.Count).Offset(, 2).Column
   'Clear out results of previous macros
   With WSD
     .Range(.Cells(1, colReport), .Cells(1, Columns.Count)).EntireColumn.Delete
   End With
   'Set up output range. Copy heading from Customer column
   Set ORange = WSD.Cells(1, colReport)
   ORange.Value = .ListColumns(CustomerCol).Name
   'Define the Input Range
   Set IRange = .ListColumns(CustomerCol).Range
End With
'Do the Advanced Filter to get unique list of customers
IRange.AdvancedFilter Action:=xlFilterCopy, CopyToRange:=ORange, Unique:=True
With WSD
   'Determine how many unique customers we have
   LastRow = .Cells(.Rows.Count, colReport).End(xlUp).Row
   'Sort the resulting data
   'Refer to "Sorting data" in this chapter for details
   With ORange.Resize(LastRow, 1)
      .Worksheet.Sort.SortFields.Clear
```

```
   .Worksheet.Sort.SortFields.Add Key:=.Columns(1), Order:=xlAscending
   With .Worksheet.Sort
      .SetRange ORange.Resize(LastRow, 1)
      .Header = xlYes
      .Apply
   End With
 End With
 'Add a SUMIF formula to get totals
 .Cells(1, colReport + 1).Value = "Revenue"
 .Cells(2, colReport + 1).Resize(LastRow - 1).FormulaR1C1 = "=SUMIF(R" & _
    (FirstRow) & "C" & CustomerCol & ":R" & FinalRow & "C" & CustomerCol & "," & _
    "RC[-1],R" & (FirstRow) & "C" & RevenueCol & ":R" & FinalRow & "C" & _
    RevenueCol & ")"
End With
'cleanup memory
Set IRange = Nothing: Set ORange = Nothing
Set Lo = Nothing
Set WSD = Nothing
End Sub
```

> **Note** This code is written to be flexible when it comes to the size of the data and the place-ment of the results. While the table definitely gives us that flexibility, for readability, we have more variables defined. For example, it's easier to do `FirstRow = .DataBodyRange.Cells(1, _ 1).Row` once, and then after that, simply type `FirstRow`. Don't let a few extra lines deter you from designs that are easier to maintain.

=SUMIF($D$2:$D$1127,J2,$F$2:$F$1127)

J	K	L	M
Customer	Revenue		
Agile Aquariun	97107		
Amazing Shoe	820384		
Appealing Eggl	92544		
Cool Saddle Tr	53170		
Distinctive Wax	947025		
Enhanced Egg	1543677		
First-Rate Glas	106442		
First-Rate Note	104205		

FIGURE 11-6 This macro produced a summary report by customer from a lengthy data set. Using `AdvancedFilter` is the key to powerful macros such as these.

Using the unique list to fill a userform's list box

Another use of a unique list of values is to quickly populate a list box or a combo box on a userform. For example, suppose that you have a macro that can run a report for any one specific customer. To allow your clients to choose which customers to report, create a simple userform and name it `frmReport`. Add a list box (`lbCust`) to the userform and set the list box's `MultiSelect` property to `1-fmMulti _ SelectMulti`. In addition to the list box, there are four command buttons: OK (`btnOK`), Cancel (btnCancel), Mark All (btnMarkAll), and Clear All (btnClearAll). The code to run the form follows. Note that the Userform_Initialize procedure includes an advanced filter to get the unique list of customers from the data set:

> **Note** Refer to Chapter 10, "Userforms: An introduction," if you've never created a userform before and need more detailed assistance.

```
Private Sub btnCancel_Click()
Unload Me
End Sub

Private Sub btnMarkAll_Click()
Dim i As Integer
For I = 0 To lbCust.ListCount - 1
  Me.lbCust.Selected(i) = True
Next i
End Sub

Private Sub btnClearAll_Click()
Dim i As Integer
For i = 0 To lbCust.ListCount - 1
  Me.lbCust.Selected(i) = False
Next i
End Sub

Private Sub btnOK_Click()
Dim i As Integer
For i = 0 To lbCust.ListCount - 1
  If Me.lbCust.Selected(i) = True Then
    'Call a routine (discussed later) to produce this report
    RunCustReport WhichCust:=Me.lbCust.List(i)
  End If
Next i
Unload Me
End Sub

Private Sub UserForm_Initialize()
Dim Lo As ListObject
Dim WSD As Worksheet
Dim IRange As Range, ORange As Range
Dim colReport As Long, LastRow As Long
Set WSD = Worksheets("SalesReport")
Set Lo = WSD.ListObjects("tblSales")
With Lo
  'Find what column to place the results in
  colReport = .HeaderRowRange.Cells(1, .ListColumns.Count).Offset(, 2).Column
  With WSD
    'Clear out results of previous macros
    .Range(.Cells(1, colReport), .Cells(1, Columns.Count)).EntireColumn.Delete
  End With
  'Set up output range. Copy heading from Customer column
```

```
    Set ORange = WSD.Cells(1, colReport)
    ORange.Value = .ListColumns("Customer").Name
     'Define the Input Range
    Set IRange = .ListColumns("Customer").Range
End With
'Do the Advanced Filter to get unique list of customers
IRange.AdvancedFilter Action:=xlFilterCopy, CopyToRange:=ORange, Unique:=True
With WSD
    'Determine how many unique customers we have
    LastRow = .Cells(.Rows.Count, colReport).End(xlUp).Row
    'Sort the data using Range.Sort
    'see "Sorting data" for details
    ORange.Resize(LastRow, 1).Sort Key1:=.Cells(1, colReport), _
        Order1:=xlAscending, Header:=xlYes
End With
'place list in listbox
With Me.lbCust
    .RowSource = ""
    .List = WSD.Cells(2, colReport).Resize(LastRow - 1, 1).Value
End With
'Erase the temporary list of customers
WSD.Cells(1, colReport).Resize(LastRow, 1).Clear

'cleanup memory
Set IRange = Nothing: Set ORange = Nothing
Set Lo = Nothing
Set WSD = Nothing
End Sub
```

Launch the form from a standard module, like this:

```
Sub ShowCustForm()
    frmReport.Show
End Sub
```

Your clients are presented with a list of all valid customers from the data set. Because the list box's `MultiSelect` property is set to allow it, the clients can select any number of customers. We'll expand on this userform later in the chapter.

Getting unique combinations of two or more fields

To get all unique combinations of two or more fields, build the output range to include the additional fields by adding their headers to the range. This code sample builds a list of unique combinations of two fields—`Customer` and `Product`—and then sorts it by `Customer`:

```
Sub UniqueCustomerProduct()
Dim Lo As ListObject
Dim WSD As Worksheet
Dim IRange As Range, ORange As Range
Dim colReport As Long, LastRow As Long
Set WSD = Worksheets("SalesReport")
With WSD
```

```
    Set Lo = .ListObjects("tblSales")
    'Find what column to place the results in
    colReport = Lo.HeaderRowRange.Cells(1, Lo.ListColumns.Count).Offset(, 2).Column
    'Clear out results of previous macros
    .Range(.Cells(1, colReport), .Cells(1, Columns.Count)).EntireColumn.Delete
    'Set up output range. Copy heading from Customer column
    Set ORange = .Cells(1, colReport).Resize(, 2)
    ORange.Cells(1, 1).Value = Lo.ListColumns("Customer").Name
    ORange.Cells(1, 2).Value = Lo.ListColumns("Product").Name
    'Define the Input Range - headers and databody
    Set IRange = Lo.Range
    'Do the Advanced Filter to get unique list of customers
    IRange.AdvancedFilter Action:=xlFilterCopy, CopyToRange:=ORange, Unique:=True
  End With
  With WSD
    'Determine how many unique customers and products we have and sort
    'see "Sorting data" for more details on Range.Sort
    LastRow = .Cells(.Rows.Count, colReport).End(xlUp).Row
    Orange.Resize(LastRow, 2).Sort Key1:=.Cells(1, colReport), _
      Order1:=xlAscending, Key2:=.Cells(1, colReport + 1), Order2:=xlAscending, _
      Header:=xlYes
  End With
  'cleanup memory
  Set IRange = Nothing: Set ORange = Nothing
  Set Lo = Nothing
  Set WSD = Nothing
  End Sub
```

In the result shown in Figure 11-7, you can see that Enhanced Eggbeater buys only one product, and Distinctive Wax buys three products. This might be useful as a guide in running reports on either customer by product or product by customer.

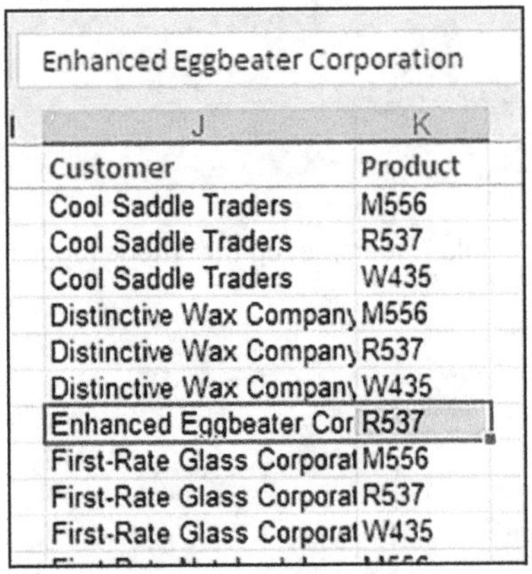

Customer	Product
Cool Saddle Traders	M556
Cool Saddle Traders	R537
Cool Saddle Traders	W435
Distinctive Wax Company	M556
Distinctive Wax Company	R537
Distinctive Wax Company	W435
Enhanced Eggbeater Cor	R537
First-Rate Glass Corporat	M556
First-Rate Glass Corporat	R537
First-Rate Glass Corporat	W435

FIGURE 11-7 By including two column headers in the output range on a Unique Values query, you get every combination of customer and product.

Using Advanced Filter with criteria ranges

As the name implies, Advanced Filter is usually used to filter records—in other words, to get a subset of data. You specify the subset by setting up a criteria range.

> **Note** Even if you are familiar with criteria, be sure to check out using the powerful Boolean formula in criteria ranges later in this chapter, in the section, "The most complex criteria: Replacing the list of values with a condition created as the result of a formula."

Set up a criteria range in a blank area of a worksheet. It's easier if you set it up to the right of your data, but it's not required. A criteria range always includes two or more rows. The first row of the criteria range contains one or more field header values to match the one(s) in the data range you want to filter. The second row contains a value showing which records to extract. In Figure 11-8, J1:J2 is the criteria range, and L1 is the output range.

In the Excel user interface, to extract a unique list of products that a particular customer purchased, select Advanced Filter and set up the Advanced Filter dialog, as shown in Figure 11-8. Figure 11-9 shows the results.

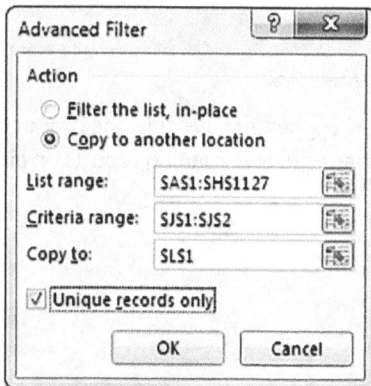

FIGURE 11-8 To create a unique list of products purchased by Cool Saddle Traders, set up the criteria range in J1:J2.

J	K	L
Customer		Product
Cool Saddle Traders		R537
		M556
		W435

FIGURE 11-9 Here is the result of the advanced filter that uses a criteria range and asks for a unique list of products. Of course, more complex and interesting criteria can be built.

You can use the following VBA code to perform an equivalent advanced filter:

```vba
Sub UniqueProductsOneCustomer()
Dim Lo As ListObject
Dim WSD As Worksheet
Dim IRange As Range, ORange As Range, CRange As Range
Dim NextCol As Long, LastRow As Long
Set WSD = Worksheets("SalesReport")
With WSD
    Set Lo = .ListObjects("tblSales")
    'Find what column to place the criteria in
    NextCol = Lo.HeaderRowRange.Cells(1, Lo.ListColumns.Count).Offset(, 2).Column
    'Clear out results of previous macros
    .Range(.Cells(1, NextCol), .Cells(1, .Columns.Count)).EntireColumn.Delete
    'Set up criteria range
    Set CRange = .Cells(1, NextCol).Resize(2)
    CRange.Cells(1, 1).Value = Lo.ListColumns("Customer").Name
    CRange.Cells(2, 1).Value = "Cool Saddle Traders"
    'setup output range 2 columns to the right of the criteria
    Set ORange = CRange.Offset(, 2).Resize(1)
    ORange.Value = Lo.ListColumns("Product").Name
    'Define the Input Range - headers and databody
    Set IRange = Lo.Range
    'Do the Advanced Filter to get unique list of Products for the Customer
    IRange.AdvancedFilter Action:=xlFilterCopy, CriteriaRange:=CRange, _
        CopyToRange:=ORange, Unique:=True
End With
With WSD
    'Determine how many unique customers and products we have and sort
    LastRow = .Cells(.Rows.Count, ORange.Column).End(xlUp).Row
    ORange.Resize(LastRow).Sort Key1:=.Cells(1, ORange.Column), _
        Order1:=xlAscending, Header:=xlYes
End With
'cleanup memory
Set IRange = Nothing: Set ORange = Nothing: Set CRange = Nothing
Set Lo = Nothing
Set WSD = Nothing
End Sub
```

Joining multiple criteria with a logical OR

You might want to filter records that match one criteria or another. For example, you can extract customers who purchased either product M556 *or* product W435. This is called a *logical OR* criteria.

When your criteria should be joined by a logical OR, place the criteria on subsequent rows of the criteria range. For example, the criteria range shown in J1:J3 in Figure 11-10 tells you which customers order product M556 or product W435.

J
Product
M556
W435

FIGURE 11-10 Place criteria on successive rows to join them with an OR. This criteria range gets customers who ordered either product M556 or product W435.

Joining two criteria with a logical AND

Sometimes, you will want to filter records that match one criteria *and* another criteria. For example, you might want to extract records in which the product sold was W435 *and* the region was the West region. This is called a *logical AND.*

To join two criteria with AND, put both criteria on the same row of the criteria range. For example, the criteria range shown in J1:K2 in Figure 11-11 gets the customers who ordered product W435 in the West region.

J	K
Product	Region
W435	West

FIGURE 11-11 Place criteria on the same row to join them with an AND. The criteria range in J1:K2 gets customers from the West region who ordered product W435.

Other slightly complex criteria ranges

The criteria range shown in Figure 11-12 is based on two different fields that are joined with an OR. The query finds all records that are from the West region or whose product is W435.

J	K
Region	Product
West	
	W435

FIGURE 11-12 The criteria range in J1:K3 returns records in which either the region is West or the product is W435.

The most complex criteria: Replacing the list of values with a condition created as the result of a formula

It is possible to have a criteria range with multiple logical AND and logical OR criteria joined together. Although this might work in some situations, in other scenarios, it quickly gets out of hand. Fortunately, Excel allows for criteria in which the records are selected as the result of a formula to handle this situation.

Case study: Working with very complex criteria

Your clients so loved the "Create a Customer" report that they hired you to write a new report. In this case, they could select any customer, any product, any region, or any combination of them. You can quickly adapt the frmReport userform to show three list boxes, as shown in Figure 11-13.

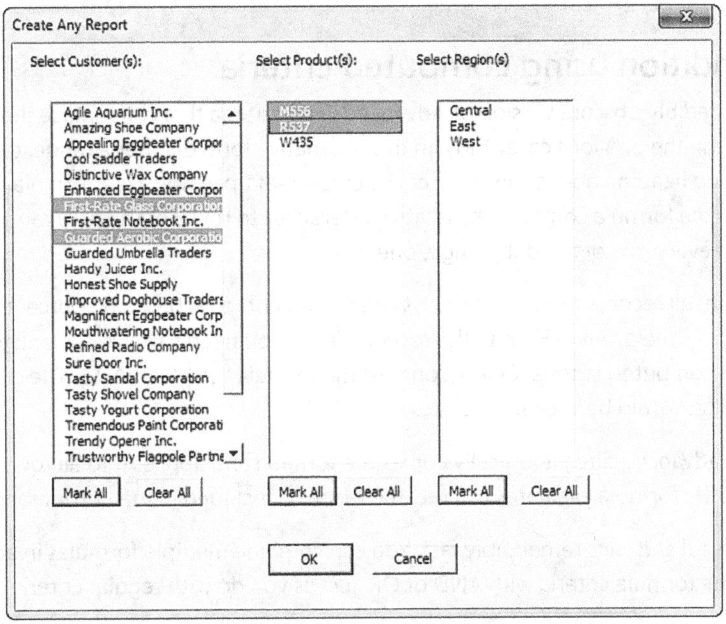

FIGURE 11-13 This super-flexible form lets clients run any type of report that they can imagine. It creates some nightmarish criteria ranges, though, unless you know the way out.

In your first test, imagine that you select two customers and two products. In this case, your program has to build a five-row criteria range, as shown in Figure 11-14. This isn't too bad.

J	K
Customer	Product
First-Rate Glass Corporation	R537
First-Rate Glass Corporation	M556
Guarded Aerobic Corporation	R537
Guarded Aerobic Corporation	M556

FIGURE 11-14 This criteria range returns any records for which the two selected customers ordered any of the two selected products.

This gets crazy if someone selects 10 products, all regions except the house region, and all customers except the internal customer. Your criteria range would need unique combinations of the selected fields. This could easily be 10 products times 9 regions times

499 customers—or more than 44,000 rows of the criteria range. You could quickly end up with a criteria range that spans thousands of rows and three columns. I was once foolish enough to actually try running an advanced filter with such a criteria range. It would still be trying to compute if I hadn't rebooted the computer.

The solution for this report is to replace the lists of values with a formula-based condition.

Setting up a condition using computed criteria

Amazingly, there is an incredibly obscure version of Advanced Filter criteria that can replace the 44,000-row criteria range in the previous case study. In this alternative form of criteria range, the top row is left blank. There is no heading above the criteria. The criteria set up in row 2 is a formula that results in True or False. If the formula contains any relative references to row 2 of the data range, Excel compares that formula to every row of the data range, one by one.

For example, if you want all records in which the Gross Profit Percentage is below 53 percent, the formula built in J2 references the profit in H2 and the revenue in F2. You need to leave J1 blank to tell Excel that you are using a computed criteria. Cell J2 contains the formula =(H2/F2)<0.53. The criteria range for the advanced filter would be specified as J1:J2.

As Excel performs the advanced filter, it logically copies the formula and applies it to all rows in the database. Anywhere that the formula evaluates to True, the record is included in the output range.

This is incredibly powerful and runs remarkably fast. You can combine multiple formulas in adjacent columns or rows to join the formula criteria with AND or OR, just as you do with regular criteria.

> **Note**   Row 1 of the criteria range doesn't have to be blank, but it cannot contain words that are headings in the data range. You could perhaps use that row to explain that someone should look to this page in this book for an explanation of these computed criteria.

Case study: Using formula-based conditions in the Excel user interface

You can use formula-based conditions to solve the report introduced in the previous case study. Figure 11-15 shows the flow involved in setting up a formula-based condition.

To illustrate, off to the right of the criteria range, set up a column of cells with the list of selected customers. Assign a name to the range, such as MyCust. In cell J2 of the criteria range, enter a formula such as =NOT(ISNA(Match(D2, MyCust,0))).

To the right of the MyCust range, set up a range with a list of selected products. Assign this range the name MyProd. In K2 of the criteria range, add this formula to check products: =NOT(ISNA(Match(B2,MyProd,0))).

To the right of the MyProd range, set up a range with a list of selected regions. Assign this range the name MyRegion. In L2 of the criteria range, add this formula to check for selected regions: =NOT(ISNA(Match(A2, MyRegion,0))).

Now, with a criteria range of J1:L2, you can effectively retrieve records that match any combination of selections from the userform.

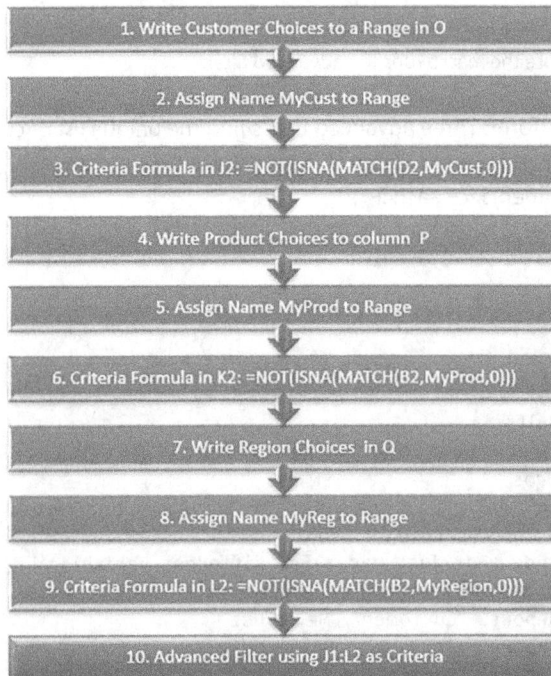

1. Write Customer Choices to a Range in O
↓
2. Assign Name MyCust to Range
↓
3. Criteria Formula in J2: =NOT(ISNA(MATCH(D2,MyCust,0)))
↓
4. Write Product Choices to column P
↓
5. Assign Name MyProd to Range
↓
6. Criteria Formula in K2: =NOT(ISNA(MATCH(B2,MyProd,0)))
↓
7. Write Region Choices in Q
↓
8. Assign Name MyReg to Range
↓
9. Criteria Formula in L2: =NOT(ISNA(MATCH(B2,MyRegion,0)))
↓
10. Advanced Filter using J1:L2 as Criteria

FIGURE 11-15 Here are the logical steps in using formula-based conditions to solve the problem.

Using formula-based conditions with VBA

Referring back to the userform shown in Figure 11-13, you can use formula-based conditions to filter the report using the userform. The following is the code for this userform. Note the logic in btnOK_Click that builds the formula. Figure 11-16 shows the Excel sheet just before the advanced filter is run.

| fx | | =NOT(ISNA(MATCH($D2,$O$2:$O$11,0))) | | | | | | | |

H	I	J	K	L	M N	O	P	Q
S Profit								
2 11568		TRUE	FALSE	TRUE		Amazing Shoe Company M556		Central
9 5586						Distinctive Wax Company W435		East
2 1175						First-Rate Notebook Inc.		
1 5619						Handy Juicer Inc.		
7 4655						Improved Doghouse Traders		
9 9893						Refined Radio Company		
7 4707						Sure Door Inc.		
7 3133						Tasty Shovel Company		
7 4729						Tremendous Paint Corporation		
5 7061						Trustworthy Flagpole Partners		
4 10906								
4 8962								

FIGURE 11-16 Here is the worksheet just before the macro runs the advanced filter.

The following code initializes the userform. Three advanced filters find the unique list of customers, products, and regions. Because the filters are almost identical, a separate sub, FilterAndFill_ListBox, is called from the initialize sub with arguments for each list:

```
Private Sub UserForm_Initialize()
Dim Lo As ListObject
Dim WSD As Worksheet
Dim colReport As Long
Set WSD = Worksheets("SalesReport")
Set Lo = WSD.ListObjects("tblSales")
'Find what column to place the results in
colReport = Lo.HeaderRowRange.Cells(1, Lo.ListColumns.Count).Offset(, 2).Column
'Clear out results of previous macros
WSD.Range(WSD.Cells(1, colReport), WSD.Cells(1, Columns.Count)).EntireColumn.Delete
'Create a unique list and fill the corresponding listbox
'don't repeat identical and long code that just has a few different variables
'instead, create a sub or function and call that with arguments
FilterAndFill_ListBox WSD, Lo, colReport, "Customer", Me.lbCust
FilterAndFill_ListBox WSD, Lo, colReport, "Product", Me.lbProduct
FilterAndFill_ListBox WSD, Lo, colReport, "Region", Me.lbRegion

'Erase the temporary list of customers
WSD.Range(WSD.Cells(1, colReport), WSD.Cells(1, Columns.Count)).EntireColumn.Delete
'cleanup memory
Set Lo = Nothing
Set WSD = Nothing
End Sub

Private Sub FilterAndFill_ListBox(ByVal WSD As Worksheet, ByVal Lo As ListObject, _
  ByVal colReport As Long, ByVal HeaderName As String, ByVal curListBox As _
MSForms.ListBox)
'never repeat code where just variables differ!
'create a sub or function and send the arguments that make each call uniuqe
'Set up output range. Copy heading from desired column
Dim ORange As Range, IRange As Range
Dim LastRow As Integer
```

```
Set ORange = WSD.Cells(1, colReport)
ORange.Value = Lo.ListColumns(HeaderName).Name
'Define the Input Range
Set IRange = Lo.Range 'includes the data and headers
'Do the Advanced Filter to get unique list of items
IRange.AdvancedFilter Action:=xlFilterCopy, CopyToRange:=ORange, Unique:=True
'Determine how many unique items we have
LastRow = WSD.Cells(WSD.Rows.Count, colReport).End(xlUp).Row
'Sort the data using Range.Sort
'see "Sorting Data" for details
ORange.Resize(LastRow, 1).Sort Key1:=Cells(1, colReport), _
  Order1:=xlAscending, Header:=xlYes
'place list in listbox
With curListBox
  .RowSource = ""
  .List = WSD.Cells(2, colReport).Resize(LastRow - 1, 1).Value
End With
'clean memory
Set ORange = Nothing: Set IRange = Nothing
End Sub
```

These tiny procedures run when someone clicks Cancel, Mark All, or Clear All in the userform in Figure 11-13:

```
Private Sub btnCancel_Click()
  Unload Me
End Sub


Private Sub cbMarkAll_Click()
Dim i As Integer
For I = 0 To lbCust.ListCount - 1
  Me.lbCust.Selected(i) = True
Next i
End Sub


Private Sub cbClearAll_Click()
Dim i As Integer
For i = 0 To lbCust.ListCount - 1
  Me.lbCust.Selected(i) = False
Next i
End Sub


Private Sub pbClearAll_Click()
Dim i As Integer
'Clear all products
For i = 0 To lbProduct.ListCount - 1
  Me.lbProduct.Selected(i) = False
Next i
End Sub


Private Sub pbMarkAll_Click()
Dim i As Integer
Mark all products
```

```
   For i = 0 To lbProduct.ListCount - 1
     Me.lbProduct.Selected(i) = True
   Next i
   End Sub

   Private Sub rbClearAll_Click()
   Dim i As Integer
   'Clear all regions
   For i = 0 To lbRegion.ListCount - 1
     Me.lbRegion.Selected(i) = False
   Next i
   End Sub

   Private Sub rbMarkAll_Click()
   Dim i As Integer
   'Mark all regions
   For i = 0 To lbRegion.ListCount - 1
     Me.lbRegion.Selected(i) = True
   Next i
   End Sub
```

The following code is attached to the OK button. This code builds three ranges in O, P, and Q that list the selected customers, products, and regions. The actual criteria range is composed of three blank cells in J1:L1 and then three formulas in J2:L2:

```
   Private Sub btnOK_Click()
   'Build a Complex Criteria that ANDS all choices together
   Dim WSD As Worksheet
   Dim Lo As ListObject
   Dim rngCriteria As Range, rngLists As Range, rngResults As Range
   Dim CRange As Range, IRange As Range, ORange As Range
   Dim ListCol As Integer
   Dim MyColumn As Integer
   Dim MyControl As String, MyFormula As String
   Dim NextRow As Long
   Dim eaListbox As Integer, eaListItem As Integer
   Set WSD = Worksheets("SalesReport")
   Set Lo = WSD.ListObjects("tblSales")
   'Find what columns to place the criteria in
   'Remember to include the blank row above
   Set rngCriteria = Lo.HeaderRowRange.Cells(1, Lo.ListColumns.Count). _
     Offset(, 2).Resize(2, 3)
   'put the selections 2 columns over
   Set rngLists = rngCriteria.Offset(1, rngCriteria.Columns.Count + 2). _
     Resize(1, 3)
   'we're using all the columns in the results, so just setup 1 blank cell
   Set rngResults = rngLists.Offset(-1, rngLists.Columns.Count + 3).Resize(1,1)
   For eaListbox = 1 To 3
     Select Case eaListbox
       Case 1
         MyControl = "lbCust"
         MyColumn = 4
         ListCol = rngLists.Cells(1, 1).Column
```

```
      Case 2
        MyControl = "lbProduct"
        MyColumn = 2
        ListCol = rngLists.Cells(1, 2).Column
      Case 3
        MyControl = "lbRegion"
        MyColumn = 1
        ListCol = rngLists.Cells(1, 3).Column
    End Select
    NextRow = 2
    'Check to see what was selected in each listbox
    For eaListItem = 0 To Me.Controls(MyControl).ListCount - 1
      If Me.Controls(MyControl).Selected(eaListItem) = True Then
        WSD.Cells(NextRow, ListCol).Value = Me.Controls(MyControl).List(eaListItem)
        NextRow = NextRow + 1
      End If
    Next eaListItem
    'If anything was selected, build a new criteria formula
    If NextRow > 2 Then
      'the reference to Row 2 must be relative in order to work
      MyFormula = "=NOT(ISNA(MATCH(RC" & MyColumn & ",R2C" & ListCol & _
          ":R" & NextRow - 1 & "C" & ListCol & ",0)))"
      WSD.Cells(2, rngCriteria.Cells(1, eaListbox).Column).FormulaR1C1 = _
          MyFormula
    End If
  Next eaListbox
Unload Me
'Figure 11-16 shows the worksheet at this point
'if we built any criteria, define the criteria range
If WorksheetFunction.CountA(rngCriteria) >= 1 Then
  Set CRange = rngCriteria
  Set IRange = Lo.Range
  Set ORange = rngResults
  IRange.AdvancedFilter xlFilterCopy, CRange, ORange
End If
'Clear out the criteria
rngCriteria.EntireColumn.ClearContents
rngLists.EntireColumn.ClearContents
'At this point, the matching records are in T1
MsgBox "The matching records are in T1"
'memory cleanup
Set CRange = Nothing: Set IRange = Nothing: Set ORange = Nothing
Set rngCriteria = Nothing: Set rngLists = Nothing: Set rngResults = Nothing
Set WSD = Nothing
Set Lo = Nothing
End Sub
```

Figure 11-16 shows the worksheet just before the AdvancedFilter method is called. The user has selected customers, products, and regions. The macro has built temporary tables in columns O, P, and Q to show which values the user selected. The criteria range is J1:L2. The criteria formula in J2 looks to see whether the value in $D2 is in the list of selected customers in O. The formulas in K2 and L2 compare $B2 to column P and $A2 to column Q.

Using formula-based conditions to return above-average records

The formula-based conditions formula criteria are cool but are a rarely used feature in a rarely used function. Some interesting business applications use this technique. For example, this criteria formula would find all the above-average rows in the data set:

```
=$A2>Average($A$2:$A$1048576)
```

Using Filter In Place in Advanced Filter

It is possible to filter a large data set in place. In this case, you do not need an output range. You normally specify a criteria range; otherwise, you return 100% of the records, and there is no need to use the advanced filter!

In the user interface of Excel, running Filter In Place makes sense: You can easily peruse the filtered list, looking for something in particular.

Running a filter in place in VBA is a little less convenient. The only good way to programmatically peruse the filtered records is to use the xlCellTypeVisible option of the SpecialCells method. In the Excel user interface, the equivalent action is to select Home | Find & Select | Go To Special. In the Go To Special dialog, select Visible Cells Only.

To run a Filter In Place, use the constant xlFilterInPlace as the Action parameter in the AdvancedFilter command and remove the CopyToRange from the command:

```
iRange.AdvancedFilter Action:=xlFilterInPlace, CriteriaRange:=cRange, _
    Unique:=False
```

Then you use this programmatic equivalent to looping by using Visible Cells Only:

```
For Each myCell In Range("A2:A" & FinalRow).SpecialCells(xlCellTypeVisible)
  Ctr = Ctr + 1
Next myCell
MsgBox Ctr & " cells match the criteria"
```

If you know that there will be no blanks in the visible cells, you can eliminate the loop with this:

```
Ctr = Application.Counta(Range("A2:A" & FinalRow). _
    SpecialCells(xlCellTypeVisible))
```

Catching no records when using a filter in place

Just as when using Copy, you have to watch out for the possibility of having no records match the criteria. However, in this case, it is more difficult to realize that nothing is returned. You generally find out when the .SpecialCells method returns a runtime error 1004, which indicates that no cells were found.

To catch this condition, you have to set up an error trap to anticipate the 1004 error with the `SpecialCells` method. Try to set a range that holds the visible cells. If the range is created, you know you have results. If it is not, then you know there were no matches.

```
Dim myResults as Range
On Error Resume Next
Set myResults = Lo.ListColumns(1).DataBodyRange.SpecialCells(xlCellTypeVisible)
On Error GoTo 0
If Not myResults Is Nothing Then
  MsgBox myResults.Cells.Count & " cells match the criteria"
Else
  MsgBox "No records match the criteria"
End If
```

> **Note** See Chapter 24, "Handling errors," for more information on catching errors.

This error trap works because it specifically excludes the header row from the `SpecialCells` range. The header row is always visible after an advanced filter. Including it in the range would prevent the 1004 error from being raised.

Showing all records after running a filter in place

After filtering in place, you can get all records to show again by using the `ShowAllData` method:

```
ActiveSheet.ShowAllData
```

The real workhorse: `xlFilterCopy` with all records rather than unique records only

The examples at the beginning of this chapter talk about using `xlFilterCopy` to get a unique list of values in a field. You used unique lists of customers, regions, and products to populate the list boxes in your report-specific userforms.

However, a more common scenario is to use an advanced filter to return all records that match the criteria. After the client selects which customer to report, an advanced filter can extract all records for that customer.

In all the examples in the following sections, you want to keep the Unique Records Only check-box cleared. You do this in VBA by specifying `Unique:=False` as a parameter to the `AdvancedFilter` method. This is not difficult to do, and you have some powerful options. If you need only a subset of fields for a report, copy only those field headings to the output range. If you want to resequence the fields to appear exactly as you need them in the report, you can do this by changing the sequence of the headings in the output range.

The next sections walk you through three quick examples to show the options available.

Copying all columns

To copy all columns, specify a single blank cell as the output range. You get all columns for those records that match the criteria, as shown in Figure 11-17:

```
Sub AllColumnsOneCustomer()
Dim Lo As ListObject
Dim WSD As Worksheet
Dim IRange As Range, ORange As Range, CRange As Range
Dim NextCol As Long
Set WSD = Worksheets("SalesReport")
With WSD
  Set Lo = .ListObjects("tblSales")
  'Find what column to place the criteria in
  NextCol = Lo.HeaderRowRange.Cells(1, Lo.ListColumns.Count).Offset(, 2).Column
  'Clear out results of previous macros
  .Range(.Cells(1, NextCol), .Cells(1, .Columns.Count)).EntireColumn.Delete
  'Set up criteria range
  Set CRange = .Cells(1, NextCol).Resize(2)
  CRange.Cells(1, 1).Value = Lo.ListColumns("Customer").Name
  'in reality, this value should be passed from the userform
  CRange.Cells(2, 1).Value = "Trustworthy Flagpole Partners"
  'setup output range. It is a single blank cell
  Set ORange = CRange.Offset(, 2).Resize(1)
  'Define the Input Range - headers and databody
  Set IRange = Lo.Range
  'Do the Advanced Filter to get a list of all customer records
  IRange.AdvancedFilter Action:=xlFilterCopy, CriteriaRange:=CRange, _
    CopyToRange:=ORange, Unique:=False
End With
'cleanup memory
Set IRange = Nothing: Set ORange = Nothing: Set CRange = Nothing
Set Lo = Nothing
Set WSD = Nothing
End Sub
```

J	K	L	M	N	O
Customer		Region	Product	Date	Customer
Trustworthy Flagpole F	East	R537		19-Jul-23	Trustworth
		East	W435		3-Sep-23 Trustworth
		West	M556		7-Sep-23 Trustworth
		Central	W435		9-Sep-23 Trustworth

FIGURE 11-17 When using xlFilterCopy with a blank output range, you get all columns in the same order as they appear in the original list range.

Copying a subset of columns and reordering

If you are doing an advanced filter to send records to a report, it is likely that you might need only a subset of columns, and you might need them in a different sequence.

This example finishes the `frmReport` example that was presented earlier in this chapter. As you recall, `frmReport` allows the client to select a customer. Pressing the OK button then calls the `RunCustReport` routine, passing a parameter to identify for which customer to prepare a report.

Imagine that this is a report being sent to the customer. The customer really does not care about the surrounding region, and you do not want to reveal your cost of goods sold or profit. Assuming that you will put the customer's name in the title of the report, the fields that you need in order to produce the report are Date, Quantity, Product, and Revenue.

The following code copies those headings to the output range:

```
Sub RunCustReport(WhichCust As Variant)
Dim Lo As ListObject
Dim WBN As Workbook
Dim WSN As Worksheet
Dim WSD As Worksheet
Dim IRange As Range, ORange As Range, CRange As Range
Dim NextCol As Long, TotalRow As Long
Set WSD = Worksheets("SalesReport")
With WSD
  Set Lo = .ListObjects("tblSales")
  'Find what column to place the criteria in
  NextCol = Lo.HeaderRowRange.Cells(1, Lo.ListColumns.Count).Offset(, 2).Column
  'Clear out results of previous macros
  .Range(.Cells(1, NextCol), .Cells(1, .Columns.Count)).EntireColumn.Delete

  'Set up criteria range
  Set CRange = .Cells(1, NextCol).Resize(2)
  CRange.Cells(1, 1).Value = Lo.ListColumns("Customer").Name
  CRange.Cells(2, 1).Value = WhichCust
  'setup output range. We want Date (C), Quantity (E), Product (B), Revenue (F)
  Set ORange = CRange.Offset(, 2).Resize(1, 4)
  With Lo
    ORange.Value = Array(.ListColumns(3).Name, .ListColumns(5).Name, _
        .ListColumns(2).Name, .ListColumns(6).Name)
  End With
  'Define the Input Range - headers and databody
  Set IRange = Lo.Range
  'Do the Advanced Filter to get a list of all the customer's records
  IRange.AdvancedFilter Action:=xlFilterCopy, CriteriaRange:=CRange, _
      CopyToRange:=ORange, Unique:=False
End With
'Create a new workbook with one blank sheet to hold the output
'xlWBATWorksheet is the template name for a single worksheet
Set WBN = Workbooks.Add(xlWBATWorksheet)
Set WSN = WBN.Worksheets(1)
With WSN
  'Set up a title on WSN
  .Cells(1, 1).Value = "Report of Sales to " & WhichCust
  'Copy data from WSD to WSN
  ORange.CurrentRegion.Copy Destination:=.Cells(3, 1)
  TotalRow = .Cells(Rows.Count, 1).End(xlUp).Row + 1
```

```
       .Cells(TotalRow, 1).Value = "Total"
       .Cells(TotalRow, 2).FormulaR1C1 = "=SUM(R2C:R[-1]C)" 'sum Quantity
       .Cells(TotalRow, 4).FormulaR1C1 = "=SUM(R2C:R[-1]C)" 'sum Revenue
       'Format the new report with bold
       .Cells(3, 1).Resize(1, 4).Font.Bold = True
       .Cells(TotalRow, 1).Resize(1, 4).Font.Bold = True
       .Cells(1, 1).Font.Size = 18
   End With
   WBN.SaveAs ThisWorkbook.Path & Application.PathSeparator & _
       WhichCust & "2.xlsx", 51
   WBN.Close SaveChanges:=False
   WSD.Activate
   'clear the output range, etc.
   WSD.Range("J1:Z1").EntireColumn.Clear
   'cleanup memory
   Set IRange = Nothing: Set ORange = Nothing: Set CRange = Nothing
   Set Lo = Nothing
   Set WSD = Nothing: Set WSN = Nothing
   Set WBN = Nothing
   End Sub
```

The call to run this report for a specific customer looks like this:

```
RunCustReport WhichCust:="Cool Saddle Traders"
```

The advanced filter produces data, as shown in Figure 11-18. The program then goes on to copy the matching records to a new workbook. A title and a total row are added, and the report is saved with the customer's name. Figure 11-19 shows the final report.

	J	K	L	M	N	O
	Customer		Date	Quantity	Product	Revenue
	Cool Saddle Traders		22-Jul-23	400	R537	9152
			25-Jul-23	600	R537	13806
			16-Aug-23	400	M556	7136
			23-Sep-23	100	R537	2358
			29-Sep-23	100	R537	1819
			21-Oct-23	100	R537	2484
			3-Mar-24	200	W435	4270
			18-Aug-24	700	W435	12145

FIGURE 11-18 Immediately after the advanced filter, you have just the columns and records needed for the report.

	A	B	C	D	E	F
1	Report of Sales to Cool Saddle Traders					
2						
3	Date	Quantity	Product	Revenue		
4	22-Jul-23	400	R537	9152		
5	25-Jul-23	600	R537	13806		
6	16-Aug-23	400	M556	7136		
7	23-Sep-23	100	R537	2358		
8	29-Sep-23	100	R537	1819		
9	21-Oct-23	100	R537	2484		
10	3-Mar-24	200	W435	4270		
11	18-Aug-24	700	W435	12145		
12	Total	2600		53170		

FIGURE 11-19 After copying the filtered data to a new sheet and applying some formatting, you have a good-looking report to send to each customer.

Case study: Utilizing two kinds of advanced filters to create a report for each customer

The final advanced filter example for this chapter uses two advanced filter techniques. Let's say that after importing invoice records, you want to send a purchase summary to each customer. The process is similar to creating the single customer report from the previous section. But this time, we need to create the list of customers and then loop through the list to generate their reports. The process looks like this:

1. Run an advanced filter that requests unique values to get a list of customers in column J. This AdvancedFilter specifies the Unique:=True parameter and uses a CopyToRange that includes a single heading, Customer:

```
'Find what column to place the criteria in
NextCol = Lo.HeaderRowRange.Cells(1, Lo.ListColumns.Count).Offset(, 2).Column
'Define the Input Range - the customer column
Set IRange = Lo.ListColumns("Customer").Range
'define output range
Set ORange = WSD.Cells(1, NextCol)
'Use the Advanced Filter to get a unique list of customers
IRange.AdvancedFilter Action:=xlFilterCopy, CopyToRange:=ORange, Unique:=True
```

2. Place the list of customers into an array. See Chapter 8, "Arrays," for more details on arrays:

```
LastRow = .Cells(.Rows.Count, ORange.Column).End(xlUp).Row
'this is a 2D array, the 2nd name in the list is allCustomers(2,1)
allCustomers = .Cells(2, ORange.Column).Resize(LastRow - 1).Value
```

3. For each customer in the array of unique customers, perform steps 4 through 8. Find the number of customers in the output range from step 1. Then use a For eaCustomer loop to loop through the customers:

```
'loop through the array of Customer Names
For eaCustomer = 1 To UBound(allCustomers)
  'Steps 4 through 8 here
'Next eaCustomer
```

4. Build a criteria range in J1:J2 to be used in a new advanced filter. The criteria range would include the heading Customer in J1 and the customer name from this iteration of the loop in cell J2:

```
'Set up criteria range for current Customer
Set CRange = WSD.Cells(1, NextCol).Resize(2)
CRange.Cells(1, 1).Value = Lo.ListColumns("Customer").Name
'Customer array is a single column with multiple rows
'technically, we're looping through the rows
CRange.Cells(2, 1).Value = allCustomers(eaCustomer, 1)
```

5. Use an advanced filter to copy matching records for this customer to column N. This Advanced Filter statement specifies the Unique:=False parameter. Because you want only the columns Date, Quantity, Product, and Revenue, the CopyToRange specifies a four-column range with those headings copied in the proper order:

```
'setup output range. We want Date (C), Quantity (E), Product (B), Revenue (F)
Set ORange = CRange.Offset(, 2).Resize(1, 4)
With Lo
  ORange.Value = Array(.ListColumns(3).Name, .ListColumns(5).Name, _
    .ListColumns(2).Name, .ListColumns(6).Name)
End With
'Do the Advanced Filter to get a list of all the customer's records
IRange.AdvancedFilter Action:=xlFilterCopy, CriteriaRange:=CRange, _
  CopyToRange:=ORange, Unique:=False
```

6. Copy the customer records to a report sheet in a new workbook. The VBA code uses the Workbooks.Add method to create a new workbook. Using the template name xlW-BATWorksheet is the way to specify that you want a workbook with a single worksheet. The extracted records from step 5 are copied to cell A3 of the new workbook:

```
'Create a new workbook with one blank sheet to hold the output
Set WBN = Workbooks.Add(xlWBATWorksheet)
Set WSN = WBN.Worksheets(1)
'Copy data from WSD to WSN
ORange.CurrentRegion.Copy Destination:=.Cells(3, 1)
```

7. Format the report with a title and totals. In VBA, add a title that reflects the customer's name in cell A1. Make the headings bold and add a total below the final row:

```
'Set up a title on WSN
WSN.Cells(1, 1).Value = "Report of Sales to " & allCustomers(eaCustomer, 1)
TotalRow = WSN.Cells(Rows.Count, 1).End(xlUp).Row + 1
WSN.Cells(TotalRow, 1).Value = "Total"
WSN.Cells(TotalRow, 2).FormulaR1C1 = "=SUM(R2C:R[-1]C)"
WSN.Cells(TotalRow, 4).FormulaR1C1 = "=SUM(R2C:R[-1]C)"
```

```
'Format the new report with bold
WSN.Cells(3, 1).Resize(1, 4).Font.Bold = True
WSN.Cells(TotalRow, 1).Resize(1, 4).Font.Bold = True
WSN.Cells(1, 1).Font.Size = 18
```

8. Use Save As to save the workbook based on the customer's name. After the workbook is saved, close the new workbook. Return to the original workbook and clear the output range to prepare for the next pass through the loop:

```
WBN.SaveAs ThisWorkbook.Path & Application.PathSeparator & _
    allCustomers(eaCustomer, 1) & ".xlsx", 51
WBN.Close SaveChanges:=False
'Free up memory by setting object variables to nothing
Set WSN = Nothing
Set WBN = Nothing
'clear the output range, etc.
CRange.EntireColumn.Clear
ORange.EntireColumn.Clear
```

The complete code is as follows:

```
Sub RunReportForEachCustomer()
Dim Lo As ListObject
Dim WBN As Workbook
Dim WSN As Worksheet
Dim WSD As Worksheet
Dim IRange As Range, ORange As Range, CRange As Range
Dim NextCol As Long, TotalRow As Long, LastRow As Long
Dim allCustomers()
Dim eaCustomer As Integer
'turn off screenflicker = faster run
Application.ScreenUpdating = False
Set WSD = Worksheets("SalesReport")
With WSD
  Set Lo = .ListObjects("tblSales")
  'Find what column to place the criteria in
  NextCol = Lo.HeaderRowRange.Cells(1, Lo.ListColumns.Count).Offset(, 2).Column
  'Clear out results of previous macros
  .Range(.Cells(1, NextCol), .Cells(1, .Columns.Count)).EntireColumn.Delete
  'Define the Input Range - the customer column
  Set IRange = Lo.ListColumns("Customer").Range
  'define output range
  Set ORange = .Cells(1, NextCol)
  'Use the Advanced Filter to get a unique list of customers
  IRange.AdvancedFilter Action:=xlFilterCopy, CopyToRange:=ORange, Unique:=True
  'put the customer list into an array
  LastRow = .Cells(.Rows.Count, ORange.Column).End(xlUp).Row
  'see the Array chapters for more info on using arrays
  'this is a 2D array, the 2nd name in the list is allCustomers(2,1)
```

```
        allCustomers = .Cells(2, ORange.Column).Resize(LastRow - 1).Value
        'clean up the sheet
        .Range(.Cells(1, NextCol), .Cells(1, .Columns.Count)).EntireColumn.Delete
    End With   'wsd
    'loop through the array of Customer Names
    For eaCustomer = 1 To UBound(allCustomers)
        'Set up criteria range for current Customer
        Set CRange = WSD.Cells(1, NextCol).Resize(2)
        CRange.Cells(1, 1).Value = Lo.ListColumns("Customer").Name
        'Customer array is a single column with multiple rows
        'technically, we're looping through the rows
        CRange.Cells(2, 1).Value = allCustomers(eaCustomer, 1)
        'Define the Input Range - headers and databodyrange
        Set IRange = Lo.Range
        'setup output range. We want Date (C), Quantity (E), Product (B), Revenue (F)
        Set ORange = CRange.Offset(, 2).Resize(1, 4)
        With Lo
            ORange.Value = Array(.ListColumns(3).Name, .ListColumns(5).Name, _
                .ListColumns(2).Name, .ListColumns(6).Name)
        End With
        'Do the Advanced Filter to get a list of all the customer's records
        IRange.AdvancedFilter Action:=xlFilterCopy, CriteriaRange:=CRange, _
            CopyToRange:=ORange, Unique:=False
        'Create a new workbook with one blank sheet to hold the output
        'xlWBATWorksheet is the template name for a single worksheet
        Set WBN = Workbooks.Add(xlWBATWorksheet)
        Set WSN = WBN.Worksheets(1)
        With WSN
            'Set up a title on WSN
            .Cells(1, 1).Value = "Report of Sales to " & allCustomers(eaCustomer, 1)
            'Copy data from WSD to WSN
            ORange.CurrentRegion.Copy Destination:=.Cells(3, 1)
            TotalRow = .Cells(Rows.Count, 1).End(xlUp).Row + 1
            .Cells(TotalRow, 1).Value = "Total"
            .Cells(TotalRow, 2).FormulaR1C1 = "=SUM(R2C:R[-1]C)"   'sum Quantity
            .Cells(TotalRow, 4).FormulaR1C1 = "=SUM(R2C:R[-1]C)"   'sum Revenue
            'Format the new report with bold
            .Cells(3, 1).Resize(1, 4).Font.Bold = True
            .Cells(TotalRow, 1).Resize(1, 4).Font.Bold = True
            .Cells(1, 1).Font.Size = 18
        End With
        WBN.SaveAs ThisWorkbook.Path & Application.PathSeparator & _
            allCustomers(eaCustomer, 1) & ".xlsx", 51
        WBN.Close SaveChanges:=False
        'free up memory
        Set WSN = Nothing
        Set WBN = Nothing
        'clear output range, etc.
        CRange.EntireColumn.Clear
        ORange.EntireColumn.Clear
```

```
Next eaCustomer
WSD.Activate
MsgBox UBound(allCustomers) & " Reports have been created!"
'cleanup memory
Set IRange = Nothing: Set ORange = Nothing: Set CRange = Nothing
Set Lo = Nothing
Set WSD = Nothing: Set WSN = Nothing
Application.ScreenUpdating = True
End Sub
```

This is a remarkable 63 lines of code. By incorporating a couple of advanced filters and not much else, you have managed to produce a tool that created 27 reports in less than 1 minute. Even an Excel power user would normally take 2 to 3 minutes per report to create these manually. In less than 60 seconds, this code will save someone a few hours every time these reports need to be created. Imagine a real scenario in which there are hundreds of customers. Undoubtedly, there are people in every city who are manually creating these reports in Excel because they simply don't realize the power of Excel VBA.

Excel in practice: Turning off a few dropdown menus in the AutoFilter

A really cool trick is possible only in Excel VBA. When you AutoFilter a list in the Excel user interface, every column in the data set gets a field dropdown arrow in the heading row. Sometimes, you have a field that does not make a lot of sense to AutoFilter. For example, in your current data set, you might want to provide AutoFilter dropdown menus for Region, Product, and Customer but not the numeric or date fields. After setting up the AutoFilter, you need one line of code to turn off each dropdown menu that you do not want to appear. The following code turns off the dropdown menus for columns C, E, F, G, and H:

```
Sub AutoFilterCustom()
Set Lo = Worksheets("SalesReport2").ListObjects("tblSales")
With Lo.Range.Cells(1, 1)
    .AutoFilter Field:=3, VisibleDropDown:=False
    .AutoFilter Field:=5, VisibleDropDown:=False
    .AutoFilter Field:=6, VisibleDropDown:=False
    .AutoFilter Field:=7, VisibleDropDown:=False
    .AutoFilter Field:=8, VisibleDropDown:=False
End With
End Sub
```

Using this tool is a fairly rare treat. Most of the time, Excel VBA lets you do things that are possible in the user interface—and lets you do them rapidly. The VisibleDropDown parameter actually enables you to do something in VBA that is generally not available in the Excel user interface. Your knowledgeable clients will be scratching their heads, trying to figure out how you set up the cool automatic filter with only a few filterable columns (see Figure 11-20).

	A	B	C	D	E	F	G	H
1	Region	Product	Date	Customer	Quantity	Revenue	COGS	Profit
2	East	R537	19-Jul-23	Trustworthy Flagpole Partners	1000	22810	11242	11568
3	East	M556	20-Jul-23	Amazing Shoe Company	500	10245	4659	5586
4	Central	W435	20-Jul-23	Amazing Shoe Company	100	2257	1082	1175
5	Central	R537	21-Jul-23	Mouthwatering Notebook Inc.	500	11240	5621	5619
6	East	R537	22-Jul-23	Cool Saddle Traders	400	9152	4497	4655
7	East	W435	22-Jul-23	Tasty Shovel Company	800	18552	8659	9893

FIGURE 11-20 Using VBA, you can set up an automatic filter in which only certain columns have the AutoFilter dropdown arrow.

> **Tip** If you need another reason to start using listobjects—it doesn't matter where the table starts on the sheet. I have a few clients who like to start their data sets in cell B2. With listobjects, it doesn't matter since the top left cell of the data is based on the position of the table, `Lo.Range.Cells(1, 1)`.

To clear the filter from the customer column, use this code:

```
Sub SimpleFilter()
Dim Lo As ListObject
Set Lo = Worksheets("SalesReport2").ListObjects("tblSales")
With Lo.Range.Cells(1, 1)
   .AutoFilter
   .AutoFilter Field:=4, VisibleDropDown:=False
End With
End Sub
```

Sorting data

While this chapter focuses on filtering, sorting often goes hand in hand with it. Depending on how the data is structured or your needs, there are three ways you can sort your data—`Range.Sort`, `Worksheet.Sort`, `ListObject.Sort`.

> **Note** The following subsections are referring to the data in Figure 11-20.

Using Range.Sort

The `Range.Sort` method is a single-line solution for sorting up to three column. Best for simple data sets, it may cause issues when used on tables or filtered ranges. Its parameters define:

- Key column(s) used to sort the data

- Key's sort order — ascending or descending

- Whether or not the data has a header in the first row

- Sort orientation — by rows (default) or column

- Sort method, such as text, values, or cell color

`Range.Sort` remembers the most recent settings, including those from manual sorts. Unless you explicitly change them, those prior settings can carry over and give you unexpected results.

The following code sorts by column F (Revenue) in descending order:

```
Sub LegacySort()
Dim rng As Range
Set rng = Worksheets("SalesReport_dataset").Range("A1:H1127") 'includes header
'the key is the first data cell, NOT the header
rng.Sort Key1:=Range("F2"), Order1:=xlDescending, Header:=xlYes
Set rng = Nothing
End Sub
```

Using Worksheet.Sort

The `Worksheet.Sort` object can be used to sort by more than three columns. It allows you to reuse your settings or just change a few of them. How? A `With` block is used to create the `Sort` object, which has properties and methods you can access and edit as needed. It's more structured than `Range.Sort` but allows for more complex operations.

Here is the code from `Range.Sort`, but using `Worksheet.Sort`:

```
Sub ModernSort()
Dim ws As Worksheet
Set ws = Worksheets("SalesReport_dataset")
With ws.Sort
  .SortFields.Clear 'clear previous sort keys to prevent stacking
  .SortFields.Add Key:=ws.Range("F2:F1127"), _
      SortOn:=xlSortOnValues, Order:=xlDescending, DataOption:=xlSortNormal
  .SetRange ws.Range("A1:H1127") 'the entire data set, including header
  .Header = xlYes 'Required if using a header
  .MatchCase = False
  .Apply
End With
Set ws = Nothing
End Sub
```

- `.SortFields.Clear` must be called each time before adding new keys or you'll stack the new key on top of the old one(s).

- `.SetRange` is required. If you don't specify the full range, the sort may behave unexpectedly. Must include the header row.

- `.Header` is required if you have a header row.

- `.Apply` runs the sort once you have it configured.

Once you've set up a `Worksheet.Sort` object, it persists until the workbook is closed. This allows you to change just the parts you need.

To sort the same data set by two different columns, do this:

```
With ws.Sort
  .SortFields.Clear 'clear previous sort columns
  'First sort key: Customer (column D), ascending
  .SortFields.Add Key:=ws.Range("D2:D1127"), _
    SortOn:=xlSortOnValues, Order:=xlAscending, DataOption:=xlSortNormal
  'Second sort key: Revenue (column F), descending
  .SortFields.Add Key:=ws.Range("F2:F1127"), _
    SortOn:=xlSortOnValues, Order:=xlDescending, DataOption:=xlSortNormal
  .Apply ' all other settings from previous run are reused
End With
```

If you're sorting a different range on another sheet, then you do need to set up a new `Worksheet.Sort` object.

Using ListObject.Sort

If the data set is in a listobject, then you don't sort the worksheet or range. Listobjects have their `Sort` object. It's very similar to `Worksheet.Sort`:

```
Sub ListObjectSort()
Dim tbl As ListObject
Set tbl = Worksheets("SalesReport").ListObjects("tblSales")
With tbl.Sort
  .SortFields.Clear
  .SortFields.Add _
      Key:=tbl.ListColumns("Revenue").Range, _
      SortOn:=xlSortOnValues, _
      Order:=xlDescending, _
      DataOption:=xlSortNormal
  .Header = xlYes
  .Apply
End With
Set tbl = Nothing
End Sub
```

- `.Key` is set by specifying the column using the `ListColumns` property. If you don't want to use the column name (Revenue), you can use the index (6) instead.

- `.Header` is required.

- `.SortFields.Clear` must be called each time before adding new keys, or you'll stack the new key on top of the old one(s).

- `.Apply` runs the sort once you have it configured.

- SetRange? There is no such property here. It's part of the listobject.

You aren't obligated to use `ListObject.Sort` on a listobject. Instead, you can treat it as a normal data set and use `Worksheet.Sort`. Just remember to configure the `.SetRange` property of `Worksheet.Sort` for the listobject's range.

Next steps

The techniques from this chapter give you many reporting techniques available via the arcane Advanced Filter tool. Chapter 12, "Using VBA to create pivot tables," introduces a powerful feature in Excel: the pivot table. The combination of advanced filters and pivot tables can help you create reporting tools that enable amazing applications.

Using VBA to create pivot tables

In this chapter, you will:

- Build a pivot table
- Use advanced pivot table features
- Filter a data set
- Use the Data Model in Excel
- Use other pivot table features
- Compare VBA to Office Scripts

Pivot tables are a powerful tool in Excel. The concept was first put into practice by Lotus, with its Improv product.

I love pivot tables because they help you very quickly summarize massive amounts of data. The name *pivot table* comes from the ability you have to drag fields in the PivotTable Field list and have them recalculate. You can use a basic pivot table to produce a concise summary in seconds. However, pivot tables come in so many varieties that they can be the tools of choice for many different uses. You can build pivot tables to act as the calculation engine to produce reports by store or by style or to find the top 5 or bottom 10 of anything quickly.

I don't suggest that you use VBA to build pivot tables for a user; rather, I suggest that you use pivot tables as a means to an end—to extract a summary of data that you can then take on to better uses.

> **Level Up!**
>
> Instead of coding the creation of a pivot table in that program you have to run every week, design the pivot table and attach it to a small sample of data stored in a table. Your code updates the data, refreshes the pivot table and you're done! Refer to Chapter 13, "Excel Power," for an example of how to do this.

As Microsoft invests in making Excel the premier choice in business intelligence, pivot tables continue to evolve. They were introduced in Excel 5 and perfected in Excel 97. In Excel 2000, pivot table creation in VBA was dramatically altered. Microsoft has continued to make improvements over the years. Because of all the changes from version to version, you need to be extremely careful when writing code in Excel that might be run in other versions.

> **Note** Much of the code in this chapter works with Excel 2010 and newer, but compatibility isn't guaranteed. Be sure to test your version carefully. The code listings from this chapter are available for download at *microsoftpressstore.com/XLVBAAuto/downloads*.

Building a pivot table in Excel VBA

As I mentioned earlier, this chapter does not mean to imply that you should use VBA to build pivot tables. Instead, the purpose of this chapter is to remind you that you can use pivot tables as a means to an end: You can use a pivot table to extract a summary of data and then use that summary elsewhere.

> **Note** Although the Excel user interface has names for the various sections of a pivot table, VBA code continues to refer to the old names. Microsoft made this choice because, otherwise, millions of lines of code would stop working in Excel 2007 because they would refer to, say, a *page field* rather than a *filter field*. Today, the four sections of a pivot table in the Excel user interface are Filters, Columns, Rows, and Values, but VBA continues to use the old terms: Page fields, Column fields, Row fields, and Data fields.

ManualUpdate versus RefreshTable versus PivotCache.Refresh

Throughout the code in this chapter, you'll see `ManualUpdate`, `RefreshTable`, and `PivotCache.Refresh` used—sometimes sparingly, other times, profusely. But what's the difference, and why are they important?

Before you can build your pivot table, you need to define your pivot cache. This holds the data for the pivot table. It doesn't automatically update when the source data changes; rather, it updates under specific circumstances, and you can control this with `PivotCache.Refresh`. This is also useful to reinforce the connection between the cache and pivot tables built from it, especially when using `ShowPages`.

Once you've updated the pivot cache, you want to ensure your pivot table is also updated. To force that, you use `RefreshTable`, which refreshes the pivot table's fields and data from the pivot cache. There's also `RefreshAll`, but that refreshes all connections in Excel, which can slow down your workbook. Be selective when possible.

Finally, there's `ManualUpdate`. In Listing 12-3, you'll see me constantly toggling it—setting it to `True` so the pivot table doesn't recalculate, then to `False`, so it does. Frankly, it makes me uncomfortable; it's like toggling `Application.Calculation` between `xlManual` and `xlAutomatic`. But sometimes, it's necessary.

You usually want `ManualUpdate = True` so that your code runs faster. However, when building a pivot table from scratch, there are cases, such as grouping or sorting, when the pivot table must update before proceeding. In those cases:

1. First set `ManualUpdate = False`.

2. Perform the action (such as grouping).

3. Then, set `ManualUpdate = True` and continue building the pivot table.

You don't need to toggle it when applying formatting since formatting changes don't require recalculating.

Defining the pivot cache

Figure 12-1 shows a sample data table that includes sales information organized by region, product, date, and customer. The macros create a regular pivot table from the table's data. Near the end of the chapter, an example shows how to build a pivot table based on the Data Model and Power Pivot.

	A	B	C	D	E	F	G	H
1	Region	Product	Date	Customer	Quantity	Revenue	COGS	Profit
2	West	D625	1/4/2023	Guarded Kettle Corporatic	430	10937	6248	4689
3	Central	A292	1/4/2023	Mouthwatering Jewelry Cc	400	8517	4564	3953
4	West	B722	1/4/2023	Agile Glass Supply	940	23188	11703	11485
5	Central	E438	1/4/2023	Persuasive Kettle Inc.	190	5520	2958	2562
6	East	E438	1/4/2023	Safe Saddle Corporation	130	3933	2024	1909
7	West	C409	1/4/2023	Agile Glass Supply	440	11304	5936	5368

FIGURE 12-1 You can create summary reports from this data table.

You first create a pivot cache object to describe the input area of the data, like this:

```
Dim WSD As Worksheet
Dim Lo As ListObject
Dim PTCache As PivotCache
Dim PT As PivotTable
Dim Prange As Range
Set WSD = Worksheets("PivotTable")
Set Lo = WSD.ListObjects("tblPT_Data")
'Delete any prior pivot tables
For Each PT In WSD.PivotTables
    PT.TableRange2.Clear
Next PT
'Define input area and set up a pivot cache
Set PRange = Lo.Range 'headers and databodyrange
```

```
Set PTCache = ThisWorkbook.PivotCaches.Create( _
    SourceType:=xlDatabase, _
    SourceData:=Lo.Name, _
    Version:=xlPivotTableVersion15)
```

When defining the pivot cache (`PivotCaches.Create`), the first thing you do is let Excel know the SourceType—where you're pulling the data from:

xlDatabase	Uses a worksheet range or table
xlExternal	Connects to an external data source, such as a Data Model
xlConsolidation	Uses multiple ranges

Next is the SourceData, a specific reference to the data. Each point below correlates to the SourceType used:

SourceType:=xlDatabase	Table name or a range reference
SourceType:=xlExternal	An existing WorkbookConnection
SourceType:=xlConsolidation	A reference to two or more identically sized ranges on multiple sheets

Finally, you specify the Version. The default—if you leave it off—is xlPivotTablesVersion12, which is Excel 2007. For Excel 2013 to the current version of Excel, use xlPivotTableVersion15.

> **Note** If you aren't using a listobject, calculate the size of the data range, including headers, and assign it to the PRange object, then create the pivot cache like this:
>
> ```
> Set PTCache = ThisWorkbook.PivotCaches.Create( _
>     SourceType:=xlDatabase, _
>     SourceData:=PRange.Address, _
>     Version:=xlPivotTableVersion15)
> ```
>
> The SourceData is a string variable holding the address of the data set.

> **Caution** If you've coded pivot tables before, you may have used `PivotCaches.Add` to create your pivot cache. This method still works, but since it dates back to at least 2003, it creates an older-style pivot cache that may not be compatible with new methods, such as `PivotFilters.Add2`.
>
> If you run into issues using newer methods or properties, check that you're using `PivotCaches.Create`. Note that in some cases, the reverse is true: If you need to use `PivotFields.AutoShow` (which has been replaced by `PivotFilters.Add2`), you must use `PivotCaches.Add`. Keep in mind `PivotCaches.Add` limits your code to the pre-Excel 2013 object model.

Creating and configuring the pivot table

After defining the pivot cache, use the CreatePivotTable method to create a blank pivot table based on the defined pivot cache. When defining the pivot table, you first tell it the TableDestination, which is the top left cell of the pivot table. Next, you assign a unique TableName to your pivot table. Finally, you specify the DefaultVersion, which is x1PivotTableVersion15.

```
Set PT = PTCache.CreatePivotTable(TableDestination:=Lo.Range.Cells(2, _
    Lo.ListColumns.Count + 2), TableName:="PivotTable1", _
    DefaultVersion:=x1PivotTableVersion15)
```

After running the preceding code, you have a strange-looking blank pivot table like the one shown in Figure 12-2. You need to use code to drop fields onto the table.

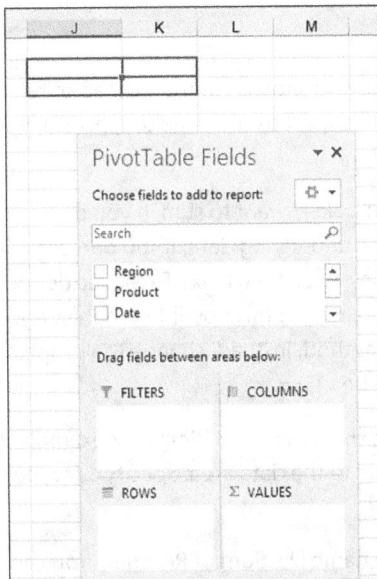

FIGURE 12-2 When you use the CreatePivotTable method, Excel gives you a four-cell blank pivot table that is not very useful.

Adding fields using the AddFields method

You can now run through the steps needed to lay out the pivot table. In the .AddFields method, you can specify one or more fields that should be in the row, column, or filter area of the pivot table.

The RowFields parameter enables you to define fields that appear in the Rows area of the PivotTable Fields list. The ColumnFields parameter corresponds to the Columns area. The PageFields parameter corresponds to the Filters area.

The following line of code populates a pivot table with two fields in the row area and one field in the column area. To specify two or more fields in a single parameter, such as RowFields, wrap those fields in the Array function, like this:

```
PT.AddFields RowFields:=Array("Region", "Customer"), ColumnFields:="Product"
```

To add a field such as Revenue to the Values area of the table, you change the Orientation property of the field to xlDataField, as explained in the next section.

Adding fields with direct property assignment

When adding fields by setting the properties, there are settings you should control instead of relying on Excel's defaults. This is done by accessing and adjusting the properties of the field, specifically setting the Orientation property for the area it should be added to.

For example, you're building a report with revenue that you'll likely want to sum. If you don't explicitly specify the calculation, Excel scans through the values in the underlying data. If 100 percent of the revenue columns are numeric, Excel sums those columns. If one cell contains text, Excel decides on that day to count the revenue, which produces confusing results. Because of this possible variability, you should never use the DataFields argument in the AddFields method. Instead, change the property of the field to xlDataField. You can then specify the Function to be xlSum.

You can change several other properties within the same With...End With block. For example, the Position property is useful when you are adding multiple fields to the data area. Specify 1 for the first field, 2 for the second field, and so on.

By default, Excel renames a Revenue field to have a strange name like Sum of Revenue. You can use the .Name property to change that heading back to something more useful.

Note You cannot reuse the word Revenue as a name. Instead, you can add a trailing space after the word Revenue.

You are not required to specify a number format for data fields, but doing so can make the resulting pivot table easier to understand and takes only one extra line of code:

```
'Set up the data fields
With PT.PivotFields("Revenue")
    .Orientation = xlDataField
    .Function = xlSum
    .Position = 1
    .NumberFormat = "#,##0"
    .Name = "Revenue "
End With
```

Removing fields from an area

Removing a field requires the `Orientation` property to be set to `xlHidden`. If the area is grouped, you must reference the grouped date name like this:

```
PT.PivotFields("Days (Date)").Orientation = xlHidden
```

See the section "Grouping daily dates to months, quarters, or years" in this chapter for more information on grouping dates.

Controlling subtotals

As soon as you have more than one row field, Excel automatically adds subtotals for all but the innermost row field. These subtotal rows can get in the way if you plan to reuse the results of the pivot table as a new data set. Although accomplishing this task manually can be relatively simple, the VBA code to suppress subtotals is surprisingly complex.

Most users are unaware that it's possible to show multiple types of subtotals for a single row field. The code to create the table in Figure 12.3, which displays both sum and count subtotals for the Region field, is as follows:

```
'Set up the data fields
With PT.PivotFields("Revenue")
   .Orientation = xlDataField
   .Function = xlSum
   .Position = 1
   .NumberFormat = "#,##0"
   .Name = "Total Revenue"
End With
With PT.PivotFields("Revenue")
   .Orientation = xlDataField
   .Function = xlCount
   .Position = 2
   .Name = "Revenue Count"
End With
'suppress all subtotals except xlSum and xlCount
PT.PivotFields("Region").Subtotals = Array(False, True, True, False, _
   False, False, False, False, False, False, False, False)
```

Region	Product	Customer	Total Revenue
Central	A292	Enhanced Toothpick Corporation	293,017
		Inventive Clipboard Corporation	410,968
		Matchless Yardstick Inc.	476,223
		Mouthwatering Jewelry Company	374,000
		Persuasive Kettle Inc.	1,565,368
		Remarkable Umbrella Company	362,851
		Tremendous Bobsled Corporation	560,759
	A292 Sum		4,043,186
	A292 Count		328

FIGURE 12-3 Use the `Subtotals` property to configure more than one subtotal for a field.

To suppress subtotals for a field, you must set the `Subtotals` property to an array of 12 `False` values—each corresponding to a different subtotal type. The first `False` turns off automatic subtotals, the second `False` turns off the `Sum` subtotal, the third `False` turns off the `Count` subtotal, and so on. This code suppresses the `Region` subtotals:

```
PT.PivotFields("Region").Subtotals = Array(False, False, False, False, _
    False, False, False, False, False, False, False, False)
```

A different technique is to turn on the first subtotal, automatic, which will disable the other 11 subtotals. You then turn off the first subtotal, which ensures all subtotals are suppressed. If you want to reuse the data from the pivot table in our current example, turn off the grand totals and subtotals, like this:

```
With PT
    .ColumnGrand = False
    .RowGrand = False
    .PivotFields("Region").Subtotals(1) = True
    .PivotFields("Region").Subtotals(1) = False
End With
```

Formatting the pivot table

Your pivot table inherits the table style settings selected as the default on whatever computer happens to run the code. If you want control over the final format, you can explicitly choose a table style. The following code applies banded rows and a light table style:

```
'Format the pivot table
PT.ShowTableStyleRowStripes = True
PT.TableStyle2 = "PivotStyleLight1"
```

You can also fill in the labels along the left column, like this:

```
PT.RepeatAllLabels xlRepeatLabels
```

At this point, you have a complete pivot table like the one shown in Figure 12-4.

Region	Customer	A292	B722	C409	D625	E438
Central	Enhanced Toothpick Corporation	293,017	403,764	364,357	602,380	635,402
Central	Inventive Clipboard Corporation	410,968	440,937	422,647	292,109	346,605
Central	Matchless Yardstick Inc.	476,223	352,550	260,833	392,890	578,970
Central	Mouthwatering Jewelry Company	374,000	446,290	471,812	291,793	522,434
Central	Persuasive Kettle Inc.	1,565,368	1,385,296	1,443,434	1,584,759	2,030,578
Central	Remarkable Umbrella Company	362,851	425,325	469,054	653,531	645,140
Central	Tremendous Bobsled Corporation	560,759	711,826	877,247	802,303	1,095,329
East	Excellent Glass Traders	447,771	386,804	723,888	522,227	454,540
East	Magnificent Patio Traders	395,186	483,856	484,067	430,971	539,616
East	Mouthwatering Tripod Corporation	337,100	310,841	422,036	511,184	519,701
East	Safe Saddle Corporation	646,559	857,573	730,463	1,038,371	1,053,369
East	Unique Marble Company	1,600,347	1,581,665	1,765,305	1,707,140	2,179,242
East	Unique Saddle Inc.	408,114	311,970	543,737	458,428	460,826
East	Vibrant Tripod Corporation	317,953	368,601	313,807	499,055	519,112
West	Agile Glass Supply	628,204	652,845	905,059	712,285	978,745
West	Functional Shingle Corporation	504,818	289,670	408,567	505,071	484,777
West	Guarded Kettle Corporation	1,450,110	1,404,742	1,889,149	1,842,751	2,302,023
West	Innovative Oven Corporation	452,320	364,200	420,624	539,300	582,773
West	Persuasive Yardstick Corporation	268,394	426,882	441,914	257,998	402,987
West	Tremendous Flagpole Traders	446,799	557,376	237,439	554,595	564,562
West	Trouble-Free Eggbeater Inc.	390,917	520,048	508,324	370,819	515,235

FIGURE 12-4 Running fewer than 50 lines of code created this pivot table in less than a second.

Listing 12-1 shows the complete code used to generate this pivot table.

Listing 12-1   Code to generate the pivot table shown in Figure 12-4

```
Sub CreatePivot()
Dim WSD As Worksheet
Dim Lo As ListObject
Dim PTCache As PivotCache
Dim PT As PivotTable
Set WSD = ThisWorkbook.Worksheets("PivotTable")
Set Lo = WSD.ListObjects("tblPT_Data")
'Delete any prior pivot tables
For Each PT In WSD.PivotTables
   PT.TableRange2.Clear
Next PT
'Define input area and set up a Pivot Cache
Set PTCache = ThisWorkbook.PivotCaches.Create(SourceType:=xlDatabase, _
   SourceData:=Lo.Name)
'Create the Pivot Table from the Pivot Cache
Set PT = PTCache.CreatePivotTable(TableDestination:=Lo.Range.Cells(2, _
   Lo.ListColumns.Count + 2), TableName:="PivotTable1")
With PT
   'Turn off updating while building the table
   .ManualUpdate = True
   'explicitly set the layout
   .RowAxisLayout xlTabularRow
   'Set up the row & column fields
   .AddFields RowFields:=Array("Region", "Customer"), ColumnFields:="Product"
   'Set up the data fields
   With .PivotFields("Revenue")
      .Orientation = xlDataField
      .Function = xlSum
      .Position = 1
      .NumberFormat = "#,##0"
      .Name = "Revenue "
   End With
   'Format the pivot table
   .ShowTableStyleRowStripes = True
   .TableStyle2 = "PivotStyleLight1"
   .ColumnGrand = False
   .RowGrand = False
   .RepeatAllLabels xlRepeatLabels
   .PivotFields("Region").Subtotals(1) = True
   .PivotFields("Region").Subtotals(1) = False
   WSD.Activate
   .TableRange2.Cells(1, 1).Select 'to activate field list
   .ManualUpdate = False
End With
'release memory
Set Lo = Nothing
Set PT = Nothing
Set WSD = Nothing
Set PtCache = Nothing
End Sub
```

Adding multiple pivot tables with the same data source

If you need to add another pivot table that uses the same data source as the previous pivot table, you don't add a new cache. Instead, you create the new pivot table using the same cache as the existing pivot table, like this:

```
'get the pivot cache used by previous pivot table
Set PTCache = WSPS.PivotTables("PivotTable1").PivotCache
'Create the Pivot Table from the Pivot Cache
Set PT2 = PTCache.CreatePivotTable(TableDestination:=WSPS.Range("F20"), _
   TableName:="PivotTable2")
With PT2
   'Set up the row & column fields
   .AddFields RowFields:=Array("Customer")
   'Set up the data fields
   With .PivotFields("Quantity")
     .Orientation = xlDataField
     .Function = xlSum
     .Position = 1
     .NumberFormat = "#,##0"
     .Name = "Quantity "
   End With
End With
```

Learning why you cannot move or change part of a pivot report

Although pivot tables are incredible, they have annoying limitations; for example, you cannot move or change just part of a pivot table. Try to run a macro that clears row 2. The macro comes to a screeching halt with error 1004, as shown in Figure 12-5. To get around this limitation, you can copy the pivot table and paste it as values, as explained in the following section.

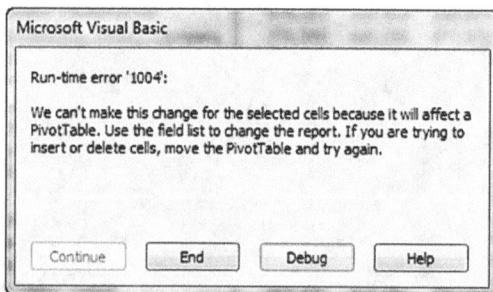

FIGURE 12-5 You cannot delete just part of a pivot table.

Determining the size of a finished pivot table to convert the pivot table to values

Knowing the size of a pivot table in advance is difficult. If you run a report of transactional data on one day, you might or might not have sales from the West region, for example. This could cause your table to be either six or seven columns wide. Therefore, you should use the special property `TableRange2` to refer to the entire pivot table.

`PT.TableRange2` includes the entire pivot table. In Figure 12-6, `TableRange2` includes the extra row at the top with the field heading Revenue. To eliminate that row, the code copies `PT.TableRange2` but offsets this selection by one row by using `.Offset(1, 0)`. Depending on the nature of your pivot table, you might need to use an offset of two or more rows to get rid of extraneous information at the top of the pivot table.

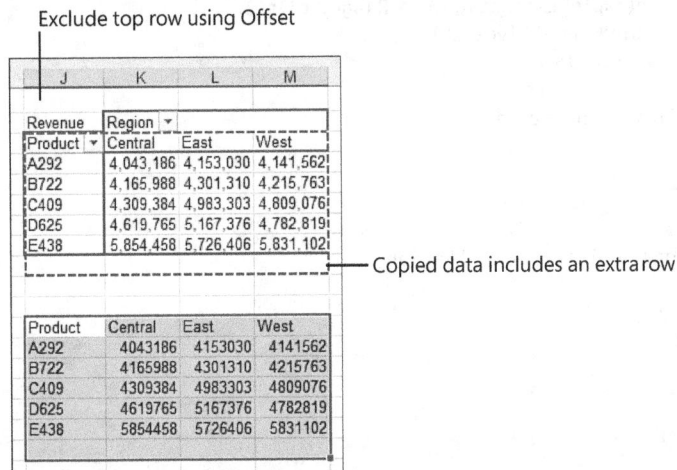

FIGURE 12-6 This figure shows an intermediate result of the macro. Only the summary in J12:M17 will remain after the macro finishes.

The code copies `PT.TableRange2` and uses `PasteSpecial` on a cell four rows below the current pivot table. At that point in the code, your worksheet looks as shown in Figure 12-6. The data set at the top is a live pivot table, and the data set below it is the copied results.

You can then eliminate the pivot table by applying the `Delete` method to the entire table. If your code is then going on to do additional formatting, you should remove the pivot cache from memory by setting `PTCache` equal to `Nothing`.

The code in Listing 12-2 uses a pivot table to produce a summary from the underlying data. At the end of the code, the pivot table is copied to static values, and the pivot table and cache are cleared.

Listing 12-2   Code to produce a static summary from a pivot table

```
Sub CreateSummaryReportUsingPivot()
'Use a Pivot Table to create a static summary report
'with model going down the rows and regions across
Dim WSD As Worksheet
Dim Lo As ListObject
Dim PtCache As PivotCache
Dim PT As PivotTable
Set WSD = Worksheets("PivotTable")
```

```vba
Set Lo = WSD.ListObjects("tblPT_Data")
'Delete any prior pivot tables
For Each PT In WSD.PivotTables
   PT.TableRange2.EntireColumn.Delete xlShiftToLeft
Next PT
'Define input area and set up a Pivot Cache
Set PtCache = ThisWorkbook.PivotCaches.Create(SourceType:=xlDatabase, _
      SourceData:=Lo.Name, Version:=xlPivotTableVersion15)
'Create the Pivot Table from the Pivot Cache
'Two columns to the right of the table
Set PT = PtCache.CreatePivotTable(TableDestination:=Lo.Range.Cells(2, _
      Lo.ListColumns.Count + 2), TableName:="PivotTable1", _
      DefaultVersion:=xlPivotTableVersion15)
With PT
   'Turn off updating while building the table
   .ManualUpdate = True
   'explicitly set the layout
   .RowAxisLayout xlTabularRow
   'Set up the row & column fields
   .AddFields RowFields:="Product", ColumnFields:="Region"
   'Set up the data fields
   With PT.PivotFields("Revenue")
      .Orientation = xlDataField
      .Function = xlSum
      .Position = 1
      .NumberFormat = "#,##0"
      .Name = "Revenue "
   End With

   'hide grand totals
   .ColumnGrand = False
   .RowGrand = False
   'display 0 for empty data cells
   .NullString = "0"
   'Calc the pivot table
   .ManualUpdate = False
   .ManualUpdate = True
   'PT.TableRange2 contains the results. Move these to J12
   'as just values and not a real pivot table.
   PT.TableRange2.Offset(1, 0).Copy
   Lo.Range.Cells(5 + PT.TableRange2.Rows.Count, _
      Lo.ListColumns.Count + 2).PasteSpecial xlPasteValues
   'At this point, the worksheet looks like Figure 12-6
   WSD.Activate
   Selection.Cells(1, 1).Select
   .ManualUpdate = False
   'Delete the original Pivot Table & the Pivot Cache
   .TableRange2.Delete xlShiftToLeft
   Set PtCache = Nothing
End With
'release memory
```

```
Set Lo = Nothing
Set PT = Nothing
Set WSD = Nothing
Set PtCache = Nothing
End Sub
```

The code in Listing 12-2 creates the pivot table. It then copies the results and pastes them as values in J12:M17. Figure 12-6, which was shown previously, includes an intermediate result just before the original pivot table is cleared.

So far, this chapter has walked you through building very simple pivot table reports. Pivot tables offer far more flexibility, though. The sections that follow present more complex reporting examples.

Using advanced pivot table features

In this section, you use detailed transactional data to produce a series of reports for each product line manager. This section covers the following advanced pivot table steps that are required in these reports:

1. Group the daily dates up to yearly dates.

2. Change the Show Values As (Calculation) option.

3. Control the sort order so the largest customers are listed first.

4. Use the ShowPages feature to replicate the report for each product line manager.

5. After producing the pivot tables, copy each pivot table as values to a new sheet in a separate workbook and do some basic formatting.

Figure 12-7 shows the report for one product line manager to give you an idea of the final goal.

	A	B	C	D	E
1	Product report for A292				
2					
3					
4		2023			2024
5	Customer	# of Orders	Revenue	% of Total	# of Orders
6	Unique Marble Company	59	716,631	12.4%	70
7	Persuasive Kettle Inc.	64	860,540	14.9%	54
8	Guarded Kettle Corporation	63	710,732	12.3%	56
9	Safe Saddle Corporation	15	184,144	3.2%	37

FIGURE 12-7 Using pivot tables simplifies the creation of the report.

Adding fields to the filters area, aka PageFields

As mentioned earlier, the name of the field areas in the PivotTable Fields list has changed, but the VBA version has not. So, while the UI labels the area as Filters, in VBA, the parameter is called

`PageFields`. You can set up the filters in the same `AddFields` method you use for rows and columns, like this:

```
'Set up the row, column and filter fields
PT.AddFields RowFields:="Customer", ColumnFields:="Date", PageFields:="Product"
```

When you are creating a pivot table for someone to use, you should know that the fields in `PageFields` allow for easy ad hoc analysis. In this case, the value in `PageFields` is going to make it easy to replicate the report for every product line manager.

Counting the number of records

So far, the `Function` property of the Data fields has always been `xlSum`. A total of 11 functions are available: `xlSum`, `xlCount`, `xlAverage`, `xlStdDev`, `xlMin`, `xlMax`, and so on.

`Count` is the only function that works for text fields. To count the number of records, and hence the number of orders, add a text field to the data area and choose `xlCount` as the function:

```
With PT.PivotFields("Region")
   .Orientation = xlDataField
   .Function = xlCount
   .Position = 1
   .NumberFormat = "#,##0"
   .Name = "# of Orders "
End With
```

> **Note** This is a count of the number of records. It is not a count of the distinct values in a field. A count of distinct values was previously difficult to do in a pivot table. It is now possible with the Data Model. See the "Using the Data Model in Excel" section later in this chapter for details.

Grouping daily dates to months, quarters, or years

Pivot tables have the amazing capability to group daily dates up to months, quarters, and years. There are seven choices for grouping times or dates: Seconds, Minutes, Hours, Days, Months, Quarters, and Years. Note that you can group a field by multiple items. To do so, you specify a series of `True/False` values corresponding to Seconds, Minutes, and so on.

> **Caution** When you group dates in a pivot table, Excel creates a new field instead of modifying the original date field. While referencing the original field name sometimes works, such as `PT.PivotFields("Date").ClearAllFilters`, it often doesn't. It's best to get into the habit of referencing the new grouped `Date` field names, such as `"Months (Date)"` and `"Years (Date)"`.

For example, to group by Months, Quarters, and Years, you would use the following:

```
PT.PivotFields("Date").LabelRange.Group _
    Periods:= Array(False, False, False, False, True, True, True)
```

> **Note** Never choose to group by only months without including years. If you do this, Excel combines January from all years in the data into a single item called January. Although this is great for seasonality analyses, it is rarely what you want in a summary. Always choose Years and Months in the Grouping dialog.

If you want to group by week, you group only by day and use 7 as the value for the By parameter:

```
PT.PivotFields("Date").LabelRange.Group _
    Start:=True, End:=True, By:=7, _
    Periods:=Array(False, False, False, True, False, False, False)
```

Specifying `True` for `Start` and `End` starts the first week at the earliest date in the data. If you want to show only the weeks from Monday, January 2, 2023, to Monday, January 1, 2024, use this code:

```
With PT
    With .PivotFields("Date")
        .LabelRange.Cells(2,1).Group _
            Start:=DateSerial(2023, 1, 2), _
            End:=DateSerial(2024, 1, 1), _
            By:=7, _
            Periods:=Array(False, False, False, True, False, False, False)
    End With '.PivotFields
    With .PivotFields("Days (Date)") 'new Field name
        .PivotItems("<1/2/2023").Visible = False
        .PivotItems(">1/1/2024").Visible = False
    End With 'Days (Date)
End With
```

> **Note** There is one limitation to grouping by week. When you group by week, you cannot group by any other measure. For example, grouping by both week and quarter is not valid. You don't get an error message, and the table is generated. But the days won't be grouped into weeks.

For this report, you need to group only by year, so the code is as follows:

```
'Group daily dates up to years
PT.PivotFields("Date").LabelRange.Cells(2,1).Group _
    Periods:=Array(False, False, False, False, False, False, True)
```

A new field, Years (Date) is added to the pivot table.

> **Tip** Before grouping the daily dates up to years, you had about 500 date columns across this report. After grouping, you have two date columns plus a total. I prefer to group the dates as soon as possible in the macro. If you added the other two data fields to the report before grouping, your report would be 1,500 columns wide. Although this is not a problem since Excel 2007 increased the column limit from 256 to 16,384, it still creates an unusually large report when you ultimately need only a few columns. Allowing the pivot table to grow to 1,500 columns, even for a few lines of code, would make the worksheet's last cell column BER.

Changing the calculation to show percentages

Excel offers 15 choices on the Show Values As tab of the Value Field Settings dialog. These calculations enable you to change how a field is displayed in the report. Instead of showing sales, you could show sales as a percentage of total sales. You could show a running total. You could show each day's sales as a percentage of the previous day's sales.

All these settings are controlled through the pivot field's .Calculation property. Each calculation has its own unique set of rules. Some, such as % Of Column, work without any further settings. Others, such as Running Total In, require a base field. Others, such as % Of, require a base field and a base item.

To get the percentage of the total, specify xlPercentOfTotal as the .Calculation property for the page field:

```
.Calculation = xlPercentOfTotal
```

To set up a running total, you have to specify a BaseField. If you need a running total along a Date column, use this:

```
'Set up Running Total
.Calculation = xlRunningTotal
.BaseField = "Date"
'If days are grouped into weeks, use this instead:
'.BaseField = "Days (Date)"
```

With ship months (Date field grouped by month) going down the rows, you might want to see the percentage of revenue growth from month to month. You can set up this arrangement with the xlPercentDifferenceFrom setting. In this case, you must specify that the BaseField is "Months (Date)" and that the BaseItem is something called "(previous)":

```
'Set up % change from prior month
With PT.PivotFields("Revenue")
   .Orientation = xlDataField
   .Function = xlSum
   .Caption = "%Change"
   .Calculation = xlPercentDifferenceFrom
   .BaseField = "Months (Date)"
```

```
   .BaseItem = "(previous)"
   .NumberFormat = "#0.0%"
End With
```

Note that with positional calculations, you cannot use the AutoShow or AutoSort methods. This is too bad; it would be interesting to sort the customers from high to low and see their sizes in relation to each other.

You can use the xlPercentDifferenceFrom setting to express revenues as a percentage of the West region sales:

```
'Show revenue as a percentage of California
With PT.PivotFields("Revenue")
   .Orientation = xlDataField
   .Function = xlSum
   .Caption = "% of West"
   .Calculation = xlPercentDifferenceFrom
   .BaseField = "State"
   .BaseItem = "California"
   .Position = 3
   .NumberFormat = "#0.0%"
End With
```

Table 12-1 shows the complete list of .Calculation options and whether you need a base field or a base item.

TABLE 12-1 Complete list of .Calculation options

Calculation	BaseField/BaseItem
xlDifferenceFrom	Both required
xlIndex	Neither
xlPercentDifferenceFrom	Both required
xlPercentOf	Both required
xlPercentOfColumn	Neither
xlPercentOfParent	BaseField only
xlPercentOfParentColumn	Both required
xlPercentOfParentRow	Both required
xlPercentOfRow	Neither
xlPercentOfTotal	Neither
xlPercentRunningTotal	BaseField only
xlRankAscending	BaseField only
xlRankDescending	BaseField only
xlRunningTotal	BaseField only

After that long explanation of the `.Calculation` property, you can build the other two pivot table fields for the product line report.

Add Revenue to the report twice. The first time, there is no calculation. The second time, calculate the percentage of total:

```
'Set up the data fields - Revenue
With PT.PivotFields("Revenue")
   .Orientation = xlDataField
   .Function = xlSum
   .Position = 2
   .NumberFormat = "#,##0"
   .Name = "Revenue " 'Note the trailing space!
End With
'Set up the data fields - % of total Revenue
With PT.PivotFields("Revenue")
   .Orientation = xlDataField
   .Function = xlSum
   .Position = 3
   .NumberFormat = "0.0%"
   .Name = "% of Total "
   .Calculation = xlPercentOfColumn
End With
```

> **Note** Take careful note of the name of the first field in the preceding code. By default, Excel would use Sum of Revenue. If you think this is a goofy title (as I do), you can change it. However, you cannot change it to Revenue because there is already a field in the PivotTable Fields list with that name.
>
> In the preceding code, I use the name Revenue with a trailing space. This works fine, and no one notices the extra space. However, in the rest of the macro, when you refer to this field, remember to refer to it as Revenue with a trailing space.

Eliminating blank cells in the Values area

If you have some customers who were new in year 2, their sales will appear blank in year 1. You can replace blank cells with zeros. In the Excel interface, you find the setting for this on the Layout & Format tab of the PivotTable Options dialog. Select the For Empty Cells Show option, and type **0** in the box.

The equivalent operation in VBA is to set the `NullString` property for the pivot table to "0":

```
PT.NullString = "0"
```

> **Note** Although the proper code is to set this value to a text zero, Excel puts a real zero in the empty cells.

Controlling the sort order with AutoSort

The Excel interface offers an AutoSort option that enables you to show customers in descending order based on total revenue. The equivalent code in VBA to sort the customer field by descending revenue uses the AutoSort method:

```
PT.PivotFields("Customer").AutoSort Order:=xlDescending, Field:="Revenue "
```

After applying some formatting in the macro, you now have one report with totals for all products, as shown in Figure 12-8.

J	K		T	U	V
Product	(All)	▾			
	Years (Date)	▾			
			Total # of	Total	Total %
	2023		Orders	Revenue	of Total
Customer	▾ # of Orders				
Unique Marble Company	307		627	8,899,187	12.5%
Guarded Kettle Corporation	316		606	8,888,775	12.5%
Persuasive Kettle Inc.	268		563	8,009,435	11.2%
Safe Saddle Corporation	135		295	4,326,335	6.1%

FIGURE 12-8 The Product dropdown menu in column K enables you to filter the report to certain products.

Replicating the report for every product

As long as your pivot table was not built on an OLAP data source, you now have access to one of the most powerful but least well-known features in pivot tables. The command, found under the Pivot Table Options dropdown, is called Show Report Filter Pages, and it replicates your pivot table for every item in one of the fields in the Filters area.

Because you built the report in this example with Product as a filter field, it takes only the following code to replicate the pivot table for every product:

```
'Replicate the pivot table for each product
PT.ShowPages PageField:="Product"
```

After running this code, you have a new worksheet with a pivot table for every product in the data set. From there, you copy each sheet to its own workbook and then apply some simple formatting and calculations. Check the end of the macro, shown in Listing 12-3, for these techniques, which should be second nature by this point in the book.

Listing 12-3 Code to produce one report per product

```
Sub CustomerByProductReport()
Dim WSD As Worksheet, WS As Worksheet, curWks As Worksheet
Dim wkbReports As Workbook
Dim Lo As ListObject
Dim PTCache As PivotCache
Dim PT As PivotTable, PT2 As PivotTable
```

```vba
Dim CalcRows As Long
Dim Ctr As Integer
Dim PTAddress As String
Set WSD = ThisWorkbook.Worksheets("PivotTable")
Set Lo = WSD.ListObjects("tblPT_Data")
With Application
  .ScreenUpdating = False
  .Calculation = xlCalculationManual
End With
'Delete any prior pivot tables
For Each PT In WSD.PivotTables
  PT.TableRange2.Delete xlShiftToLeft
Next PT
'Define input area and set up a Pivot Cache
Set PTCache = ThisWorkbook.PivotCaches.Create(SourceType:=xlDatabase, _
    SourceData:=Lo.Name)
'if using a dataset, SourceData has to be more detailed.
'PRange would be your entire dataset
'Set PTCache = ThisWorkbook.PivotCaches.Create _
 (SourceType:=xlDatabase, SourceData:=PRange.Address)
'Create the Pivot Table from the Pivot Cache
Set PT = PTCache.CreatePivotTable(TableDestination:=Lo.Range.Cells _
    (2, Lo.ListColumns.Count + 2), TableName:="PivotTable1")
With PT
  'Turn off recalculation while building the table
  .ManualUpdate = True
  'explicitly set the layout
  .RowAxisLayout xlTabularRow
  'Set up the row and columns fields
  .AddFields RowFields:="Customer", ColumnFields:="Date", PageFields:="Product"
  'Set up the data fields - count of orders
  With .PivotFields("Region")
    .Orientation = xlDataField
    .Function = xlCount
    .Position = 1
    .NumberFormat = "#,##0"
    .Name = "# of Orders "
  End With
  'force Excel to update so we have dates to group
  .ManualUpdate = False
  'Group daily dates up to years
  .PivotFields("Date").LabelRange.Cells(2, 1).Group _
      Periods:=Array(False, False, False, False, False, False, True)
  'turn updates off
  .ManualUpdate = True
  'Set up the data field - Revenue
  With .PivotFields("Revenue")
    .Orientation = xlDataField
    .Function = xlSum
    .Position = 2
    .NumberFormat = "#,##0"
    .Name = "Revenue "  'notice the trailing space
  End With
```

```vba
    'Set up the data field - % of total Revenue
    With .PivotFields("Revenue")
        .Orientation = xlDataField
        .Function = xlSum
        .Position = 3
        .NumberFormat = "0.0%"
        .Name = "% of Total "
        .Calculation = xlPercentOfColumn
    End With
    'force updates so we have the data to sort
    .ManualUpdate = False
    'Sort the customers so the largest revenue is at the top
    .PivotFields("Customer").AutoSort Order:=xlDescending, Field:="Revenue "
    'formatting doesn't require calculations, so we can turn off updates
    .ManualUpdate = True
    'format the pivot table
    .ShowTableStyleColumnStripes = True
    .ShowTableStyleRowStripes = True
    .TableStyle2 = "PivotStyleLight8"
    .NullString = "0"
    'turn manual off so the new tables update properly
    .ManualUpdate = False
    'Replicate the pivot table for each product
    .ShowPages PageField:="Product"
    'Refresh PivotCache to stabilize updates
    'new pivot tables will be refreshed later
    ThisWorkbook.PivotCaches(1).Refresh
    PTAddress = .TableRange2.Address
End With
'Create a new blank workbook
'specifying xlWBATWorksheet ensure there's only 1 sheet
Set wkbReports = Workbooks.Add(xlWBATWorksheet)
'format the reports
Ctr = 0
For Each WS In ThisWorkbook.Worksheets
    If WS.PivotTables.Count > 0 And WS.Cells(1, 1).Value = "Product" Then
        With WS
            Ctr = Ctr + 1
            Set PT2 = .PivotTables(1)
            CalcRows = PT2.TableRange1.Rows.Count - 3
            'add a new sheet if the 1st report is already done
            If Ctr = 1 Then
                Set curWks = wkbReports.Sheets(1)
            Else
                wkbReports.Worksheets.Add _
                    After:=wkbReports.Worksheets(wkbReports.Worksheets.Count)
                Set curWks = wkbReports.Worksheets(wkbReports.Worksheets.Count)
            End If
            PT2.RefreshTable
            PT2.TableRange2.Copy
            curWks.Range("A1").PasteSpecial xlPasteValuesAndNumberFormats
            Application.CutCopyMode = False
            DoEvents
```

```vba
    With curWks
        .Name = WS.Name
        .Range("A1:B2").Clear  'clear values & formatting
        .Range("A1:C3").ClearContents  'clear values only
        .Range("A1").Value = "Product report for " & WS.Name
        .Range("A1").Style = "Title"
        'Copy some headings
        .Range("B5:D5").Copy Destination:=.Range("H5:J5")
        Application.CutCopyMode = False
        DoEvents
        .Range("H4").Value = "Total"
        .Range("I4:J4").Clear
        'Copy the format
        .Range("J1").Resize(CalcRows + 5, 1).Copy
        .Range("K1").Resize(CalcRows + 5, 1).PasteSpecial xlPasteFormats
        Application.CutCopyMode = False
        DoEvents
        .Range("K5").Value = "% Rev Growth"
        .Range("K6").Resize(CalcRows, 1).FormulaR1C1 = "=IFERROR(RC6/RC3-1,1)"
        'force calculation update
        .Calculate
        'get rid of formulas
        .Range("K6").Resize(CalcRows, 1).Value = .Range("K6").Resize(CalcRows, _
            1).Value
        .Range("A2:K5").Style = "Heading 4"
        .Range("A2").Resize(CalcRows + 4, 11).Columns.AutoFit
        'select a cell so the paste ranges are no longer selected
        'but without having to activate the sheet
        Application.GoTo Reference:=.Range("A1"), Scroll:=False
    End With 'curwks
    DoEvents
    'delete the pivot table
    PT2.TableRange2.Delete xlShiftToLeft
End With   'WS
    'delete the sheet
    Application.DisplayAlerts = False
    WS.Delete
    Application.DisplayAlerts = True
End If
Next WS
'some final cleanup
PT.TableRange2.Delete xlShiftToLeft
'clean up sheet
WSD.Range(PTAddress).EntireColumn.Delete xlShiftToLeft
'activate 1st report sheet
wkbReports.Sheets(1).Activate
MsgBox Ctr & " product reports created."
With Application
    .ScreenUpdating = True
    .Calculation = xlCalculationAutomatic
End With
'release memory
'the ':' allows separate lines of code to share a line of code
Set PT = Nothing: Set PT2 = Nothing
```

```
Set WS = Nothing: Set curWks = Nothing: Set WSD = Nothing
Set PTCache = Nothing
Set wkbReports = Nothing
End Sub
```

Filtering a data set

There are many ways to filter a pivot table—from using the slicers to the conceptual filters to simply selecting and clearing items from one of the many field dropdown menus.

Manually filtering two or more items in a pivot field

When you open a field heading dropdown menu and select or clear items from the list, you are applying a manual filter (see Figure 12-9).

For example, say that you have a client who sells cleaning materials to various companies. In the report showing sales of brooms, they want to see specific customers. The code to hide a particular customer is as follows:

```
PT.PivotFields("Customer").PivotItems("Agile Glass Supply").Visible = False
```

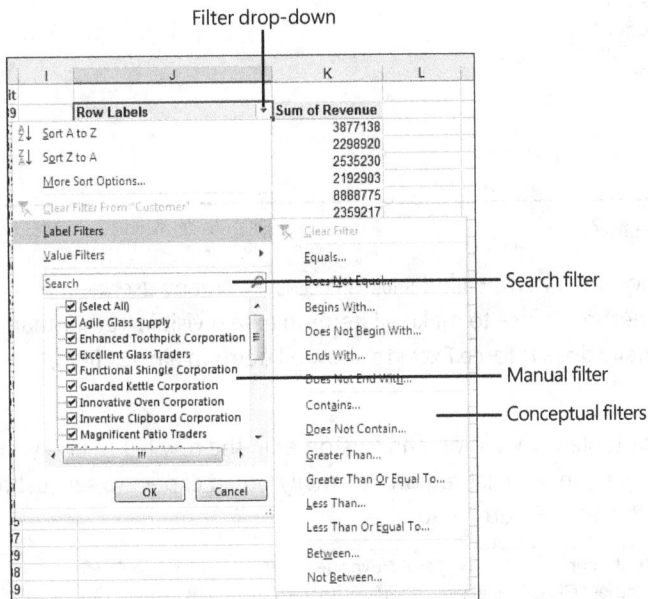

FIGURE 12-9 This filter dropdown menu offers manual filters, a search box, and conceptual filters.

This process is easy in VBA. After building the table with Customer in the rows field, loop through the field's items to change the Visible property to show only certain customers.

To be safe, ensure all items are visible before hiding any, as Excel doesn't allow all items to be hidden. Doing so will result in an error. And since Excel (still) doesn't provide a single function to toggle visibility for all items in a field, you'll need to first loop through and make all items visible, then loop again to hide the ones you don't want.

```
Dim PvtItem As PivotItem
Dim hiddenCount As Integer
PT.ManualUpdate = True
'Make sure all Customers are visible
For Each PvtItem In PT.PivotFields("Customer").PivotItems
  PvtItem.Visible = True
Next PvtItem
'Loop and keep certain items visible
For Each PvtItem In PT.PivotFields("Customer").PivotItems
  Select Case PvtItem.Name
    Case "Guarded Kettle Corporation", "Safe Saddle Corporation"
      PvtItem.Visible = True
      visibleCount = visibleCount + 1
    Case Else
      If hiddenCount = PT.PivotFields("Customer").PivotItems.Count - 1 Then
        'no customers matched what we were looking for
        'the last customer will be left visible
        MsgBox "Selected Customers not found", vbCritical
      Else
        PvtItem.Visible = False
        hiddenCount = hiddenCount + 1
      End If
  End Select
  Next PvtItem
PT.ManualUpdate = False
```

What about .ShowAllItems?

There's a misleading method for pivot items called ShowAllItems. For many users—me included—this looks like the method to use to make all items in a field visible, rather than looping. However, what it actually does is force Excel to show all items in a pivot field, even if they don't have data.

For example, you create a pivot table with Region and Customer in the row fields, and you've filtered for "Excellent Glass Traders" in the East region. Normally, you'd expect to see just the data relevant to your filter, as shown in Figure 12-10.

Region	Customer	Total Revenue
⊟East	Excellent Glass Traders	2,535,230
East Total		2,535,230
Grand Total		2,535,230

FIGURE 12-10 You expect the Excellent Glass Traders to appear only in the East region.

But if you add the following line to the code PT.PivotFields("Region").ShowAllItems = _
True, "Excellent Glass Traders" displays under each region, with empty cells where there are
no data, as shown in Figure 12-11.

Region	▼	Customer	▼	Total Revenue
⊟ Central		Excellent Glass Traders		
Central Total				
⊟ East		Excellent Glass Traders		2,535,230
East Total				**2,535,230**
⊟ West		Excellent Glass Traders		
West Total				
Grand Total				**2,535,230**

FIGURE 12-11 Using ShowAllItems forces Excellent Glass Traders to appear under each region, even though there is only revenue for the East region.

Perhaps someday Microsoft will provide a method or property that duplicates the Select All checkbox, but that time isn't now. Until then, we loop.

Using the conceptual filters

The dropdown menus for any date, numeric, or text field label in a pivot table include conceptual filters: Label Filters, Date Filters, or Value Filters. For example, the date filters offer the capability to filter to a conceptual period, such as last month or next year (see Figure 12-12). To apply these filters, use the .Add2 method.

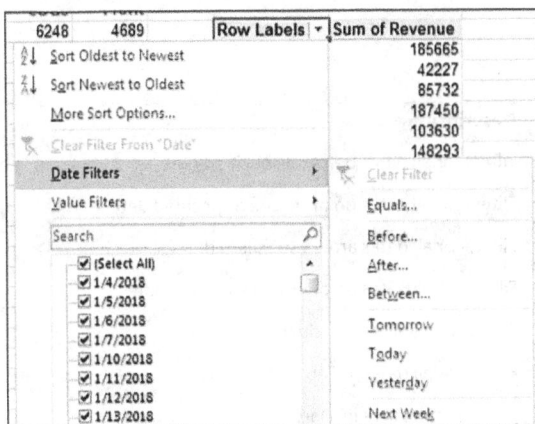

FIGURE 12-12 The Date Filter flyout menu provides many options for filtering a date field.

To apply a label filter in VBA, use the PivotFilters.Add2 method. The following code filters to the customers that start with the letter *E*:

```
PT.PivotFields("Customer").PivotFilters.Add2 _
    Type:=xlCaptionBeginsWith, Value1:="E"
```

To clear the filter from the Customer field, use the ClearAllFilters method:

```
PT.PivotFields("Customer").ClearAllFilters
```

To apply a date filter to the date field to find records from this week, use this code:

```
PT.PivotFields("Date").PivotFilters.Add2 Type:= xlDateThisWeek
```

> **Note** If the dates used in the filter do not exist or the filter has already been applied, an error message is generated. The best practice is to clear the filters from the pivot field before applying a filter.

The value filters enable you to filter one field based on the value of another field. For example, to find all the customers where the total revenue is more than $3,000,000, use this code:

```
PT.PivotFields("Customer").PivotFilters.Add2 Type:=xlValueIsGreaterThan, _
    DataField:=PT.PivotFields("Sum of Revenue"), Value1:=3000000
```

Other value filters might enable you to specify, for example, that you want customers where the revenue is between $1,000,000 and $2,000,000. In this case, you specify one limit as Value1 and the second limit as Value2:

```
PT.PivotFields("Customer").PivotFilters.Add Type:=xlValueIsBetween, _
    DataField:=PT.PivotFields("Sum of Revenue"), Value1:=1000000, Value2:=2000000
```

Table 12-2 lists all the possible filter types.

TABLE 12-2 Filter types

Filter type	Description
xlBefore	Filters for all dates before a specified date
xlBeforeOrEqualTo	Filters for all dates on or before a specified date
xlAfter	Filters for all dates after a specified date
xlAfterOrEqualTo	Filters for all dates on or after a specified date
xlAllDatesInPeriodJanuary	Filters for all dates in January
xlAllDatesInPeriodFebruary	Filters for all dates in February
xlAllDatesInPeriodMarch	Filters for all dates in March
xlAllDatesInPeriodApril	Filters for all dates in April
xlAllDatesInPeriodMay	Filters for all dates in May
xlAllDatesInPeriodJune	Filters for all dates in June
xlAllDatesInPeriodJuly	Filters for all dates in July
xlAllDatesInPeriodAugust	Filters for all dates in August
xlAllDatesInPeriodSeptember	Filters for all dates in September

Filter type	Description
xlAllDatesInPeriodOctober	Filters for all dates in October
xlAllDatesInPeriodNovember	Filters for all dates in November
xlAllDatesInPeriodDecember	Filters for all dates in December
xlAllDatesInPeriodQuarter1	Filters for all dates in Quarter 1
xlAllDatesInPeriodQuarter2	Filters for all dates in Quarter 2
xlAllDatesInPeriodQuarter3	Filters for all dates in Quarter 3
xlAllDatesInPeriodQuarter4	Filters for all dates in Quarter 4
xlBottomCount	Filters for the specified number of values from the bottom of a list
xlBottomPercent	Filters for the specified percentage of values from the bottom of a list
xlBottomSum	Sums the values from the bottom of the list
xlCaptionBeginsWith	Filters for all captions, beginning with the specified string
xlCaptionContains	Filters for all captions that contain the specified string
xlCaptionDoesNotBeginWith	Filters for all captions that do not begin with the specified string
xlCaptionDoesNotContain	Filters for all captions that do not contain the specified string
xlCaptionDoesNotEndWith	Filters for all captions that do not end with the specified string
xlCaptionDoesNotEqual	Filters for all captions that do not match the specified string
xlCaptionEndsWith	Filters for all captions that end with the specified string
xlCaptionEquals	Filters for all captions that match the specified string
xlCaptionIsBetween	Filters for all captions that are within a specified range of values
xlCaptionIsGreaterThan	Filters for all captions that are greater than the specified value
xlCaptionIsGreaterThanOrEqualTo	Filters for all captions that are greater than or match the specified value
xlCaptionIsLessThan	Filters for all captions that are less than the specified value
xlCaptionIsLessThanOrEqualTo	Filters for all captions that are less than or match the specified value
xlCaptionIsNotBetween	Filters for all captions that are not within a specified range of values
xlDateBetween	Filters for all dates that are within a specified range of dates
xlDateLastMonth	Filters for all dates that apply to the previous month
xlDateLastQuarter	Filters for all dates that apply to the previous quarter
xlDateLastWeek	Filters for all dates that apply to the previous week
xlDateLastYear	Filters for all dates that apply to the previous year
xlDateNextMonth	Filters for all dates that apply to the next month
xlDateNextQuarter	Filters for all dates that apply to the next quarter

Filter type	Description
xlDateNextWeek	Filters for all dates that apply to the next week
xlDateNextYear	Filters for all dates that apply to the next year
xlDateNotBetween	Filters for all dates that are not within the specified range
xlDateThisMonth	Filters for all dates that apply to the current month
xlDateThisQuarter	Filters for all dates that apply to the current quarter
xlDateThisWeek	Filters for all dates that apply to the current week
xlDateThisYear	Filters for all dates that apply to the current year
xlDateToday	Filters for all dates that apply to the current date
xlDateTomorrow	Filters for all dates that apply to the next day
xlDateYesterday	Filters for all dates that apply to the previous day
xlNotSpecificDate	Filters for all dates that do not match a specified date
xlSpecificDate	Filters for all dates that match a specified date
xlTopCount	Filters for the specified number of values from the top of a list
xlTopPercent	Filters for the specified percentage of values from the top of a list
xlTopSum	Sums the values from the top of the list
xlValueDoesNotEqual	Filters for all values that do not match the specified value
xlValueEquals	Filters for all values that match the specified value
xlValueIsBetween	Filters for all values that are within a specified range of values
xlValueIsGreaterThan	Filters for all values that are greater than the specified value
xlValueIsGreaterThanOrEqualTo	Filters for all values that are greater than or match the specified value
xlValueIsLessThan	Filters for all values that are less than the specified value
xlValueIsLessThanOrEqualTo	Filters for all values that are less than or match the specified value
xlValueIsNotBetween	Filters for all values that are not within a specified range of values
xlYearToDate	Filters for all values that are within one year of a specified date

Using the search filter

The Excel interface includes a Search box in the filter dropdown menu. Although this is a slick feature in the Excel interface, there is no equivalent functionality in VBA that automatically selects matching results. Whereas the dropdown menu offers the Select All Search Results checkbox, VBA requires manually applying a filter to achieve similar results. To do this, use the xlCaptionContains filter as the Type argument in the code samples shown in the section "Using the conceptual filters."

Case study: Filtering to the top 5 or top 10 by using a filter

If you're building an executive dashboard, you may want to highlight the top 5 customers. Even experienced users may not have explored the Top 10 option, which is found under Value Filters in the filter dropdown menu. This setting allows you to filter for the top or bottom *n* records based on any data field in the report.

In VBA, use the `PivotFilters.Add2` method to apply this conceptual filter, as shown below:

```
'Show only the top 5 customers
PT.PivotFields("Customer").PivotFilters.Add2 _
    Type:=xlTopCount, DataField:=PT.PivotFields("Total Revenue"), Value1:="5"
```

When you create a report showing the top or bottom *n* records, it's often helpful to copy the data and then go back to the original pivot report to get the totals for all markets. In the code, this is achieved by removing the Customer field from the pivot table and copying the grand total to the report. The code that follows produces the report shown in Figure 12-13.

	A	B	C	D	E	F	G
1	Top 5 Customers						
2							
3	Customer	A292	B722	C409	D625	E438	Grand Total
4	Guarded Kettle Corporation	1,450,110	1,404,742	1,889,149	1,842,751	2,302,023	8,888,775
5	Unique Marble Company	1,600,347	1,581,665	1,765,305	1,707,140	2,179,242	8,833,699
6	Persuasive Kettle Inc.	1,565,368	1,385,296	1,443,434	1,584,759	2,030,578	8,009,435
7	Safe Saddle Corporation	646,559	857,573	730,463	1,038,371	1,053,369	4,326,335
8	Tremendous Bobsled Corporation	560,759	711,826	877,247	802,303	1,095,329	4,047,464
9	Top 5 Total	5,823,143	5,941,102	6,705,598	6,975,324	8,660,541	34,105,708
10							
11	Total Company	12,337,778	12,683,061	14,101,763	14,569,960	17,411,966	71,104,528
12							

FIGURE 12-13 The Top 5 Customers report was created from two pivot tables.

```
Sub Top5Customers()
'Produce a report of the top 5 customers
Dim wkbReports As Workbook
Dim curWks As Worksheet
Dim WSD As Worksheet
Dim Lo As ListObject
Dim PTCache As PivotCache
Dim PT As PivotTable
Dim PRange As Range
Set WSD = ThisWorkbook.Worksheets("PivotTable")
Set Lo = WSD.ListObjects("tblPT_Data")
'Delete any prior pivot tables
For Each PT In WSD.PivotTables
  PT.TableRange2.Delete xlShiftToLeft
Next PT
'Define input area and set up a Pivot Cache
Set PRange = Lo.Range   'headers and databodyrange
Set PTCache = ThisWorkbook.PivotCaches.Create(SourceType:=xlDatabase, _
```

```
      SourceData:=Lo.Name)
   'Create the Pivot Table from the Pivot Cache
   Set PT = PTCache.CreatePivotTable(TableDestination:=PRange.Cells(2, _
      Lo.ListColumns.Count + 2), TableName:="PivotTable1")
   With PT
      'Turn off updating while building the table
      .ManualUpdate = True
      'explicitly set the layout
      .RowAxisLayout xlTabularRow
      'Set up the row fields
      .AddFields RowFields:="Customer", ColumnFields:="Product"
      'Set up the data fields
      With .PivotFields("Revenue")
         .Orientation = xlDataField
         .Function = xlSum
         .Position = 1
         .NumberFormat = "#,##0"
         .Name = "Total Revenue"
      End With
      'Ensure that we get zeros instead of blanks in the data area
      .NullString = "0"
      'Recalculate so there's data to sort and show
      PT.ManualUpdate = False
      'Sort customers descending by sum of revenue
      .PivotFields("Customer").AutoSort Order:=xlDescending, Field:="Total Revenue"
      'Show only the top 5 customers
      .PivotFields("Customer").PivotFilters.Add2 Type:=xlTopCount, _
         DataField:=.PivotFields("Total Revenue"), Value1:=5
      'Create a new blank workbook with one worksheet
      Set wkbReports = Workbooks.Add(xlWBATWorksheet)
      Set curWks = wkbReports.Worksheets(1)
      With curWks
         .Name = "Report"
         'Set up title for report
         With .Range("A1")
            .Value = "Top 5 Customers"
            .Font.Size = 14
         End With
         'Copy the pivot table data to row 3 of the report sheet
         'Use offset to eliminate the title row of the pivot table
         PT.TableRange2.Offset(1, 0).Copy
         .Range("A3").PasteSpecial xlPasteValuesAndNumberFormats
         LastRow = .Cells(Rows.Count, 1).End(xlUp).Row
         .Cells(LastRow, 1).Value = "Top 5 Total"
         'Go back to the pivot table to get totals
         With PT
            .PivotFields("Customer").Orientation = xlHidden
            .ManualUpdate = False
            .ManualUpdate = True
            .TableRange2.Offset(2, 0).Copy
```

```
        End With
        'paste the values two rows below the main report
        .Cells(LastRow + 2, 1).PasteSpecial xlPasteValuesAndNumberFormats
        .Cells(LastRow + 2, 1).Value = "Total Company"
      End With  'curwks
      'Delete the pivot table
      PT.TableRange2.Delete xlShiftToLeft
    End With
    'Do some basic formatting
    'Autofit columns, bold the headings, right-align
    With curWks
      With .Range("A3")
        .Resize(LastRow + 2, 7).Columns.AutoFit
        .EntireRow.Font.Bold = True
        .EntireRow.HorizontalAlignment = xlRight
        .HorizontalAlignment = xlLeft
      End With
      .Range("A2").Select
    End With
    MsgBox "CEO Report has been Created"
    'clean up to free up memory
    Set PTCache = Nothing
    Set PRange = Nothing
    Set PT = Nothing
    Set wkbReports = Nothing
    Set curWks = Nothing
    Set WSD = Nothing
    Set Lo = Nothing
    End Sub
```

The Top 5 Customers report includes two snapshots of a pivot table. First, a filter is applied to capture the top five customers along with their total revenue by product. Then, the macro removes the customer field, leaving only product totals to generate the Total Company row.

Setting up slicers to filter a pivot table

A *slicer* is a visual pivot table filter that you can resize and reposition. You can control the color of a slicer and control the number of columns in it. You can also select or unselect items from a slicer by using VBA.

Figure 12-14 shows a pivot table with two slicers. Both slicers have been modified to show multiple columns.

A slicer consists of a slicer cache and a slicer. To define a slicer cache, you need to specify a pivot table as the Source and a field name as the SourceField. The slicer cache is defined at the workbook level, allowing multiple pivot tables from the same data source to be attached to the same slicer. The exception is when pivot tables are based on the Data Model or an OLAP source; in that case, data sources can still share a slicer if they are properly related.

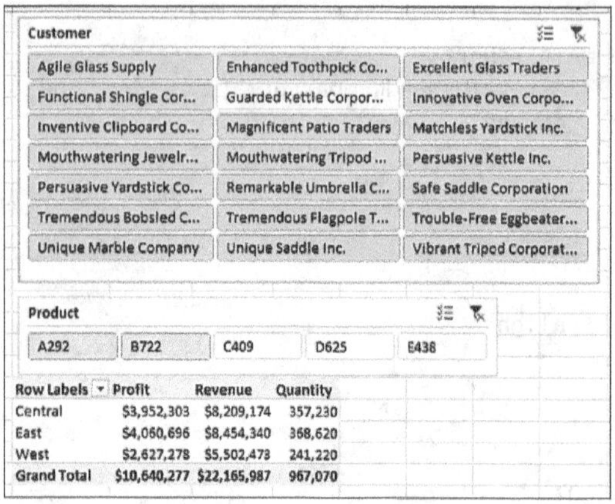

FIGURE 12-14 Slicers provide a visual filter of several fields.

Assuming PT is our Source, and Product is the SourceField, the following code would set up the slicer cache:

```
Dim SCP as SlicerCache 'Product slicercache
Set SCP = ThisWorkbook.SlicerCaches.Add2(PT, SourceField:="Product")
```

When Named Arguments Work—And When They Don't

Certain named arguments, like Source:=PT, are not allowed in SlicerCaches.Add2, even though others, like SourceField:="Product", work fine. The cause of this is unclear, and Microsoft's documentation does not fully explain it.

The previous line of code doesn't include the Source argument name because doing so would cause an error. If named arguments worked as expected, the line would be:
ThisWorkbook.SlicerCaches.Add2(Source:=PT, SourceField:="Product")

Instead, you have to pass the first argument without naming it, like this:
ThisWorkbook.SlicerCaches.Add2(PT, SourceField:="Product")

Slicers.Add throws in its own twist to this special case. The SlicerDestination argument accepts either the sheet object or the sheet name—but how you enter the argument determines whether you can use the named argument.

If you want to use the named argument, use either of these:
Slicers.Add(SlicerDestination:=WSD.Name, …)
Slicers.Add(SlicerDestination:=Worksheets("Data"), …)

If you don't want to use named arguments, either of these will work:
Slicers.Add(WSD, …)
Slicers.Add(WSD.Name, …)

It's fine to be in the habit of not naming your arguments, especially for common properties and methods. I usually don't. They're included in most of the code here to make it easier for you to understand.

After you've defined the slicer cache, you can add the slicer. The slicer is defined as an object of the slicer cache. Specify a worksheet as the `SlicerDestination`. It can be the sheet object or the sheet's name. The `Name` argument controls the internal name for the slicer. The `Caption` argument is the heading that is visible in the slicer. This might be useful if you would like to show the name Region, but the IT department defined the field as `IDKRegn`. Specify the size of the slicer by entering `Height` and `Width` in points. Specify the location by entering `Top` and `Left` in points.

The following code sets up a Product slicer. The values for `Top`, `Left`, `Height`, and `Width` are assigned to be equal to the location or size of certain cell ranges:

```
Dim SLP as Slicer 'Product slicer
Set SLP = SCP.Slicers.Add(WSD, Name:="Product", _
 Caption:="Product", _
 Top:=WSD.Range("O14").Top + 5, _
 Left:=WSD.Range("O14").Left , _
 Width:= WSD.Range("O14:Q14").Width, _
 Height:=WSD.Range("O14:O18").Height)
```

> ### Level Up!
>
> I first showed you how to set up the slicer cache. Then, I added the slicer separately because there are a lot of parameters involved, and it's easier to follow this way. Plus, you may one day need to add multiple slicers to the same cache—for example, to generate multiple reports using the same data.
>
> But you don't have to use separate lines. Instead, you can combine the creation of both cache and slicer into one call. Assume we want to add a Customer slicer above the Product slicer. The code would look like this:
>
> ```
> Dim SLC As Slicer
> 'the skipped Slicer parameter is Level, used only by OLAP data sources
> Set SLC = ThisWorkbook.SlicerCaches.Add2(PT, "Customer").Slicers.Add(WSD, , _
>     "Customer", "Customer Name", WSD.Range("O1").Top + 5, WSD.Range("O1").Left, _
>     WSD.Range("O1:W1").Width, WSD.Range("O1:W13").Height)
> ```
>
> The order of parameters remains the same, but in this case, we're able to combine the two methods. Note that this creates a slicer object (`Dim SLC As Slicer`), not a slicer cache.

Every slicer starts out as one column. You can change the style and number of columns code like this:

```
'Format the color and number of columns
With SLP
  .Style = "SlicerStyleLight6"
  .NumberOfColumns = 5
End With
```

After the slicer is defined, you can use VBA to choose which items are activated in the slicer. It seems counterintuitive, but to choose items in the slicer, you have to change `SlicerItem`, which is a member of the `SlicerCache`, not a member of the `Slicer`:

```
With SCP
   .ClearManualFilter 'clear any current filters
   .SlicerItems("C409").Selected = False
   .SlicerItems("D625").Selected = False
   .SlicerItems("E438").Selected = False
End With
```

Listing 12-4 shows how to build a pivot table with two slicers.

Listing 12-4 Code to build a pivot table with two slicers

```
Sub PivotWithTwoSlicers()
Dim Lo As ListObject
Dim SL As Slicer, SLP As Slicer, SLC As Slicer
Dim SC As SlicerCache
Dim WSD As Worksheet, WSPS As Worksheet
Dim PT As PivotTable
Dim PTCache As PivotCache
Dim sCount As Integer
Set WSD = Worksheets("Data")
Set WSPS = Worksheets("Pivots and Slicers")
Set Lo = WSD.ListObjects("tblPT_Data")
With Application
   .ScreenUpdating = False
   .Calculation = xlCalculationManual
End With
'Delete any prior slicers and caches
For Each SC In ThisWorkbook.SlicerCaches
   For Each SL In SC.Slicers
     SL.Delete
   Next SL
   'deleting the slicers should get rid of the cache, but just in case
   'Excel has a problem with "ghost" caches
   On Error Resume Next
   SC.Delete
   On Error GoTo 0
Next SC
'Delete any prior pivot tables
For Each PT In WSPS.PivotTables
   PT.TableRange2.Delete xlShiftToLeft
Next PT
'Define input area and set up a Pivot Cache
Set PTCache = ThisWorkbook.PivotCaches.Create(SourceType:=xlDatabase, _
    SourceData:=Lo.Name)
'Create the Pivot Table from the Pivot Cache
Set PT = PTCache.CreatePivotTable(TableDestination:=WSPS.Range("A20"), _
    TableName:="PivotTable1")
```

```
With PT
  'Set up the row & column fields
  .AddFields RowFields:=Array("Region")
  'Set up the data fields
  With .PivotFields("Quantity")
    .Orientation = xlDataField
    .Function = xlSum
    .Position = 1
    .NumberFormat = "#,##0"
    .Name = "Quantity "
  End With
  With .PivotFields("Revenue")
    .Orientation = xlDataField
    .Function = xlSum
    .Position = 1
    .NumberFormat = "$#,##0"
    .Name = "Revenue "
  End With
  With .PivotFields("Profit")
    .Orientation = xlDataField
    .Function = xlSum
    .Position = 1
    .NumberFormat = "$#,##0"
    .Name = "Profit "
  End With
End With  'PT
'Define the Slicer Caches and slicers
Set SLC = ThisWorkbook.SlicerCaches.Add2(PT, "Customer").Slicers.Add(WSPS, , _
    Name:="Customer", Caption:="Customer", Top:=WSPS.Range("A1").Top + 5, _
    Left:=WSPS.Range("A1").Left + 5, Width:=415, Height:=184)
With SLC
  .Style = "SlicerStyleLight1"
  .NumberOfColumns = 3
End With
'The skipped parameter is 'Level' used only by OLAP data sources
Set SLP = ThisWorkbook.SlicerCaches.Add2(PT, "Product").Slicers.Add(WSPS, , _
    Name:="Product", Caption:="Product", Top:=WSPS.Range("A14").Top + 5, _
    Left:=WSPS.Range("A14").Left + 5, Width:=343, Height:=54)
With SLP
  .Style = "SlicerStyleLight4"
  .NumberOfColumns = 5
End With
'Unselect some products
'since we never set a slicer cache, we can get it from the slicer properties
With SLP.SlicerCache
  .ClearManualFilter  'clear any current filters
  .SlicerItems("C409").Selected = False
  .SlicerItems("D625").Selected = False
  .SlicerItems("E438").Selected = False
End With
'Unselect One Customer
With SLC.SlicerCache
  .ClearManualFilter
```

```
      .SlicerItems("Guarded Kettle Corporation").Selected = False
  End With
  WSPS.Activate
  'clean up and release memory
  With Application
     .ScreenUpdating = False
     .Calculation = xlAutomatic
  End With
  'memory clean up
  'using ":" allows combining multiple lines
  Set Lo = Nothing
  Set SLC = Nothing: Set SLP = Nothing: Set SL = Nothing
  Set WSD = Nothing: Set WSPS = Nothing
  Set PT = Nothing
  Set PTCache = Nothing: Set SC = Nothing
  End Sub
```

Modifying an existing slicer

The preceding code assigned the newly created slicer to an object variable so you could easily format the slicer. What if a slicer was created before your macro starts running? You can easily figure out the name of the slicer. If a slicer is created for the Product field, for example, the name of the SlicerCache is "Slicer_Product". The following code formats an existing slicer:

```
  Sub MoveAndFormatSlicer()
  Dim SCP As SlicerCache
  Dim SLP As Slicer
  Dim WSPS As Worksheet
  Set WSPS = Worksheets("Pivots and Slicers")
  Set SCP = ThisWorkbook.SlicerCaches("Slicer_Product")
  Set SLP = SCP.Slicers("Product")
  With SLP
     .Style = "SlicerStyleLight6"
     .NumberOfColumns = 1
     .Top = WSPS.Range("J1").Top + 5
     .Left = WSPS.Range("J1").Left
     .Width = WSPS.Range("J1:K1").Width
     .Height = WSPS.Range("J1:L10").Height
  End With
  Set SCP = Nothing
  Set SLP = Nothing
  Set WSPS = Nothing
  End Sub
```

> **Note** You can set a custom name for the slicer cache using the third parameter when creating it. For example, to name it BestCustomers, you'd use:
>
> ```
> ThisWorkbook.SlicerCaches.Add2(PT, "Customer", "BestCustomers"). _
>   Slicers.Add (WSPS, , Name:="Customer", Caption:="Customer", _
> ```

```
    Top:=WSPS.Range("A1").Top + 5, Left:=WSPS.Range("A1").Left + 5, _
    Width:=415, Height:=184)
```

The catch? Excel doesn't prefix custom cache names with Slicer. So, if someone else is modifying your code, they may not know that you're using custom names. Unless you have a real need for custom names, it's best to let Excel generate them.

Attaching another pivot table to an existing slicer

Pivot tables that share the same source can also share the same slicer. In this way, they can all be filtered from a single selection. To attach a pivot table to an existing slicer, do this:

```
'Get the existing slicer cache
Set SC = ThisWorkbook.SlicerCaches("Slicer_Product")
'Attach the second pivot table to the slicer cache
SC.PivotTables.AddPivotTable PT2
'Force a reset of the filters, just in case there's issues
SC.ClearManualFilter
```

> **Note** You can create a separate cache and slicer for the new pivot table, even if it's for the same field. When this happens, Excel appends a number to the slicer cache name, such as "Slicer_Product1," to ensure uniqueness.
>
> This can also happen if you delete a slicer, but the cache doesn't clear as it should. If you add the slicer again, the expected name "Slicer_Product" will be "Slicer_Product1." See the following section for a code sample that attempts to prevent the creation of ghost caches.

Deleting slicer caches

Excel usually deletes a slicer cache when all attached slicers are removed, but this doesn't always happen. If a "ghost cache" lingers, Excel renames the next slicer cache for that field, which can break code expecting the original name.

If you're programmatically deleting slicers, minimize ghost caches by explicitly deleting the cache after the slicers, like this:

```
For Each SC In ThisWorkbook.SlicerCaches
    For Each SL In SC.Slicers 'delete the slicers
        SL.Delete
    Next SL
    'deleting the slicers should get rid of the cache, but just in case
    'Excel has a problem with "ghost" caches
    On Error Resume Next
    SC.Delete
    On Error GoTo 0
Next SC
```

If the ghost persists after running this and reopening the workbook, update your code to use the new name or start fresh in a new workbook.

Setting up a timeline to filter an Excel pivot table

A Timeline slicer is just like a regular slicer, but it only works with date fields. It lets you filter a pivot table by years, quarters, months, or days using a simple, scrollable interface. Regular slicers work with any field, but if you want a time-based filter, you'll need a Timeline.

After generating the pivot table, you define the slicer cache, using the 4th parameter to specify the type as xlTimeLine:

```
Set SC = ThisWorkbook.SlicerCaches.Add2(PT, "ShipDate", , xlTimeline)
```

Then you add the slicer to the slicer cache:

```
Set SL = ThisWorkbook.SlicerCaches.Add2(PT, "ShipDate", , _
    xlTimeline).Slicers.Add(WSD, , Name:="ShipDate", Caption:="Quarter", _
    Top:=PTTopLeft.Offset(-9).Top + 5, Left:=PTTopLeft.Offset(-9).Left, _
    Width:=230, Height:=108)
```

Timelines can exist at the day, month, quarter, or year level. To change the level of a timeline, use the TimelineViewState.Level property:

```
SL.TimelineViewState.Level = xlTimelineLevelQuarters
```

To filter a timeline to certain dates, you have to use the TimelineState.SetFilterDataRange property, which applies to the slicer cache:

```
SC.TimelineState.SetFilterDateRange "1/1/2023", "3/31/2023"
```

Listing 12-5 shows the complete macro to build a pivot table and add a quarter-based Timeline slicer.

Listing 12-5 Code to build a pivot with a timeline

```
Sub PivotWithQuarterSlicer()
Dim Lo As ListObject
Dim SL As Slicer
Dim SC As SlicerCache
Dim WSD As Worksheet
Dim PT As PivotTable
Dim PTCache As PivotCache
Dim PTTopLeft As Range
Set WSD = Worksheets("Data")
Set Lo = WSD.ListObjects("tblPTData")
With Application
  .ScreenUpdating = False
  .Calculation = xlCalculationManual
End With
'Delete any prior slicers and caches
```

```
For Each SC In ThisWorkbook.SlicerCaches
  For Each SL In SC.Slicers
    SL.Delete
  Next SL
  'deleting the slicers should get rid of the cache, but just in case
  'Excel has a problem with "ghost" caches
  On Error Resume Next
  SC.Delete
  On Error GoTo 0
Next SC
'Delete any prior pivot tables
For Each PT In WSD.PivotTables
  PT.TableRange2.Delete xlShiftToLeft
Next PT
'Define input area and set up a Pivot Cache
Set PTCache = ThisWorkbook.PivotCaches.Create(SourceType:=xlDatabase, _
  SourceData:=Lo.Name)
'Create the Pivot Table from the Pivot Cache
Set PT = PTCache.CreatePivotTable(TableDestination:=WSD.Cells(10, _
  Lo.DataBodyRange.Columns.Count + 2), TableName:="PivotTable1")
With PT
  'Set up the row & column fields
  .AddFields RowFields:=Array("Customer")
  'Set up the data fields
  With .PivotFields("Revenue")
    .Orientation = xlDataField
    .Function = xlSum
    .Position = 1
    .NumberFormat = "#,##0"
    .Name = "Revenue "
  End With
  Set PTTopLeft = .TableRange1.Cells(1, 1)
End With
Set SL = ThisWorkbook.SlicerCaches.Add2(PT, "ShipDate", , _
  xlTimeline).Slicers.Add(WSD, , Name:="ShipDate", Caption:="Quarter", _
  Top:=PTTopLeft.Offset(-9).Top + 5, Left:=PTTopLeft.Offset(-9).Left, _
  Width:=230, Height:=108)
'Set the timeline to show quarters
SL.TimelineViewState.Level = xlTimelineLevelQuarters
'Set the dates for the timeline default filter range
SL.SlicerCache.TimelineState.SetFilterDateRange "4/1/2023", "6/30/2023"
'cleanup
Set PTTopLeft = Nothing
Set Lo = Nothing
Set PTCache = Nothing
Set PT = Nothing
Set SC = Nothing
Set SL = Nothing
Set WSD = Nothing
End Sub
```

Figure 12-15 shows the Timeline slicer built by the code in Listing 12-5.

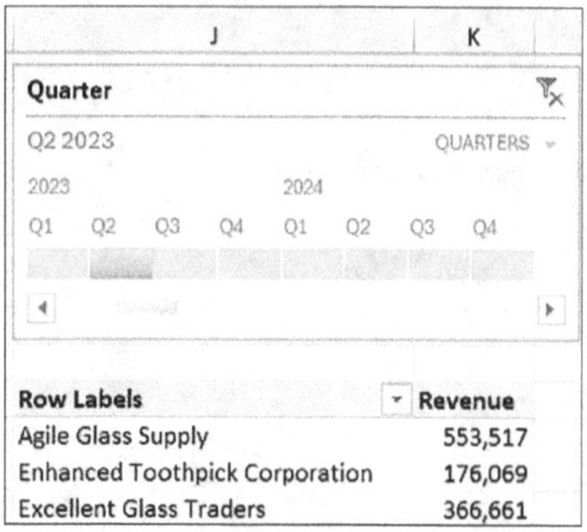

FIGURE 12-15 Timelines are a unique visualization for filtering dates.

Formatting the intersection of values in a pivot table

Excel 365 allows you to assign a formatting rule to the intersection of labels in a pivot table. Let's say you have a pivot table with Customers in rows and Product in columns. If you add a fill color to the cell at the intersection of customer Agile Glass Supply and product A292, the fill color will follow Agile Glass Supply and A292 as the pivot table is rearranged. If you add a new inner row field, such as Years, then all of the A292 cells for the Agile Glass Supply will have the same fill color.

You can work with just the data field by using the `DataBodyRange.Cells` property of the pivot table. If the data field starts in L4 and the intersection of Agile Glass Supply and A292 is in L18, you would use the following to apply a fill color:

```
With With PT.DataBodyRange.Cells(15, 1).Interior.Interior
   .Pattern = xlSolid
    .PatternColorIndex = xlAutomatic
   .ThemeColor = xlThemeColorAccent4
   .TintAndShade = -0.249946592608417
   .PatternTintAndShade = 0
End With
```

Using the Data Model in Excel

Excel incorporates most parts of Power Pivot into the core Excel product. This means you can add two tables to the Data Model, create a relationship, build a measure, and then build a pivot table from the Data Model.

To follow along with this example, open the `ProjectFiles12c-BeforeDataModel.xlsm` file from the sample download files. This workbook has two tables: `tblSales` and `tblSector`. `tblSector` is a lookup table that is related to `tblSales` via a customer field. To build the pivot table, follow these general steps:

1. Add the main table to the Data Model.

2. Add the lookup table to the Data Model.

3. Link the two tables with a relationship.

4. Create a pivot cache from `ThisWorkbookDataModel`.

5. Create a pivot table from the cache.

6. Add row fields.

7. Define a measure. Add the measure to the pivot table.

Adding both tables to the Data Model

You should already have a data set in the workbook that has been converted to a table using the Ctrl+T shortcut. On the Table Design tab, ensure the table name is `tblSales`. To link this table to the Data Model, use this code:

```
Dim WBT As Workbook
Dim TableName As String
Set WBT = ThisWorkbook
TableName = "tblSales"
'Build Connection to the main Sales table
WBT.Connections.Add2 Name:="LinkedTable_" & TableName, _
  Description:="", _
  ConnectionString:="WORKSHEET;" & WBT.FullName, _
  CommandText:=WBT.Name & "!" & TableName, _
  lCmdType:=7, _
  CreateModelConnection:=True, _
  ImportRelationships:= False
```

Several variables in this code use the table name, the workbook path, or the workbook name. By storing the table name in a variable at the top of the code, you can use the variable to build the connection name, connection string, and command text.

Adapting the preceding code to link to the lookup table then requires only changing the `TableName` variable:

```
TableName = "tblSector"
WBT.Connections.Add2 Name:="LinkedTable_" & TableName, _
  Description:="", _
  ConnectionString:="WORKSHEET;" & WBT.FullName, _
  CommandText:=WBT.Name & "!" & TableName, _
  lCmdType:=7, _
  CreateModelConnection:=True, _
  ImportRelationships:=False
```

Creating a relationship between the two tables

When working with multiple tables, you need to define how they relate to each other. A one-to-many relationship is the most common setup: one table contains unique values (the primary key), while another contains duplicate values (the foreign key) that link back to it.

For example, in our Sales table, each sale lists a Customer, but that customer's name appears only once in the tblSector. Creating a relationship between the tblSales.Customer column (foreign key) and the tblSector.Customer column (primary key) allows you to analyze data from both tables in a pivot table.

To create a relationship in VBA, use the ModelRelationships.Add method, specifying the two columns that should be linked:

```
'Create relationship
Dim MO As Model
Set MO = WBT.Model
'Relate the two tables (Customer field must exist in both)
MO.ModelRelationships.Add _
  ForeignKeyColumn:= _
  MO.ModelTables("tblSales").ModelTableColumns("Customer"), _
  PrimaryKeyColumn:= _
  MO.ModelTables("tblSector").ModelTableColumns("Customer")
```

Now that Excel knows how the tables are related, it will be able to combine information from both.

Defining the pivot cache and building the pivot table

The code to define the pivot cache specifies that the data is external. Even though the linked tables are in your workbook, and even though the Data Model is stored as a binary large object within the workbook, this is still considered an external data connection. The connection is always called ThisWorkbookDataModel. To set up the pivot cache, use this code:

```
'Define the PivotCache
Set PTCache = WBT.PivotCaches.Create(SourceType:=xlExternal, _
    SourceData:=WBT.Connections("ThisWorkbookDataModel"), _
    Version:=xlPivotTableVersion15)
'Create the pivot table from the pivot cache
Set PT = PTCache.CreatePivotTable(TableDestination:=WSD.Cells(1, 1), _
    TableName:="PivotTable1", DefaultVersion:=xlPivotTableVersion15)
```

Adding model fields to the pivot table

There are two types of fields you need to add to the pivot table. Text fields such as Customer, Sector, and Product are simply fields that can be added to the row or column area of the pivot table. No calculation has to happen to these fields. The code for adding text fields is shown in this section. When you add a numeric field to the Values area in the Excel interface, you are implicitly defining a new calculated field. To do this in VBA, you must explicitly define the field and then add it.

First, let's look at the simpler example of adding a text field to the row area. The VBA code generically looks like this:

```
With PT.CubeFields("[TableName].[FieldName]")
    .Orientation = xlRowField
    .Position = 1
End With
```

In the current example, add the Sector field from tblSector by using this code:

```
With PT.CubeFields("[tblSector].[Sector]")
    .Orientation = xlRowField
    .Position = 1
End With
```

Adding numeric fields to the Values area

When you manually create a measure in the Data Model, you set a caption and number format, and Excel will carry those settings into the pivot table that uses the measure.

But when you create a measure programmatically, Excel handles it differently. Instead of adding the measure at the model level, you're inserting it directly into the pivot table. You specify the hierarchy and function, but the caption is ignored. If you need to reference the measure, like changing the number format, you have to use the name Excel assigns it, which is stored in the measure's Value property.

To make it easier to refer to this measure later, assign the new measure to an object variable:

```
'Before you can add Revenue to the pivot table, you have to define the measure.
'This happens using the GetMeasure method.
'Assign the cube field to the CFRevenue object
Dim CFRevenue As CubeField
Set CFRevenue = _
    PT.CubeFields.GetMeasure(AttributeHierarchy:="[tblSales].[Revenue]", _
    Function:=xlSum)
'Add the field to the pivot table
PT.AddDataField Field:=CFRevenue, Caption:="Total Revenue"
PT.PivotFields(CFRevenue.Value).NumberFormat = "$#,##0,K"
```

The following measure uses the xlDistinctCount function to count the number of unique customers in each sector:

```
'Add distinct count of customer as a cube field
Dim CFCustCount As CubeField
Set CFCustCount = PT.CubeFields.GetMeasure( _
    AttributeHierarchy:="[tblSales].[Customer]", _
    Function:=xlDistinctCount)
'Add the field to the pivot table
PT.AddDataField Field:=CFCustCount, Caption:="Customer Count"
```

Now that Power Pivot ships with every copy of Excel for desktop PC, you can use DAX formulas to create new measures. Unlike the previous measures, DAX formula measures are added to the Data Model and then to the pivot table. The following code adds a field for Median Sales:

```
'Add Median Sales using DAX
Dim MedianSales As ModelMeasure
Set MedianSales = MO.ModelMeasures.Add(MeasureName:="Median Sales", _
    AssociatedTable:=MO.ModelTables("tblSales"), Formula:="Median([Revenue])", _
    FormatInformation:=MO.ModelFormatCurrency("Default", 2))
PT.AddDataField PT.CubeFields("[Measures].[" & MedianSales.Name & "]")
```

GetMeasure **versus** ModelMeasures.Add

Could we have used ModelMeasures.Add for CFRevenue and CFCustCount? Yes. Instead of GetMeasure, we could have used DAX functions like SUM([Revenue]) and DISTINCTCOUNT([Customer]). This would also let us set the caption and number format directly in the Data Model.

So, why didn't we? It comes down to style and flexibility. This approach shows you both options for some measurements—you can let the pivot table handle what it can or define everything in the Data Model. And, you may not want to clutter the Measures dialog with calculations that the pivot table itself can easily handle.

Putting it all together

Figure 12-16 shows the Data Model pivot table created using the code in Listing 12-6.

	A	B	C	D
1	Sector	Total Revenue	Customer Count	Median Sales
2	Apparel	$758K	2	$10,752.50
3	Chemical	$569K	1	$10,137.50
4	Consumer	$2,195K	7	$12,756.00
5	Electronics	$222K	4	$14,554.00
6	Food	$750K	1	$12,743.50
7	Hardware	$2,179K	11	$11,547.50
8	Textiles	$35K	1	$8,908.00
9	Grand Total *	$6,708K	27	$11,858.00

FIGURE 12-16 Two tables are linked with a pivot table and two measures via a macro.

Listing 12-6   Code to create a Data Model pivot table

```
Sub BuildModelPivotTable()
Dim WBT As Workbook
Dim WSD As Worksheet
Dim MO As Model
Dim MedianSales As ModelMeasure
Dim PTCache As PivotCache
Dim PT As PivotTable
Dim CFRevenue As CubeField, CFCustCount As CubeField
Dim SalesTable As String, SectorTable As String
Set WBT = ActiveWorkbook
Set WSD = WBT.Worksheets("Report")
SalesTable = "tblSales"
SectorTable = "tblSector"
'Build Connection to the main Sales table
WBT.Connections.Add2 Name:="LinkedTable_" & SalesTable, Description:="MainTable", _
   ConnectionString:="WORKSHEET;" & WBT.FullName, CommandText:=WBT.Name & "!" & _
   SalesTable, lCmdType:=7, CreateModelConnection:=True, _
   ImportRelationships:=False
'Build Connection to the Sector lookup table
WBT.Connections.Add2 Name:="LinkedTable_" & SectorTable, _
   Description:="LookupTable", ConnectionString:="WORKSHEET;" & WBT.FullName, _
   CommandText:=WBT.Name & "!" & SectorTable, lCmdType:=7, _
   CreateModelConnection:=True, ImportRelationships:=False
'Relate the two tables
Set MO = WBT.Model
'Relate the two tables (Customer field must exist in both)
MO.ModelRelationships.Add _
   ForeignKeyColumn:=MO.ModelTables("tblSales").ModelTableColumns("Customer"), _
   PrimaryKeyColumn:=MO.ModelTables("tblSector").ModelTableColumns("Customer")
'Delete any prior pivot tables
For Each PT In WSD.PivotTables
   PT.TableRange2.Clear
Next PT
'Define the PivotCache
Set PTCache = WBT.PivotCaches.Create(SourceType:=xlExternal, _
```

```
    SourceData:=WBT.Connections("ThisWorkbookDataModel"), _
    Version:=xlPivotTableVersion15)
'Create the pivot table from the pivot cache
Set PT = PTCache.CreatePivotTable(TableDestination:=WSD.Cells(1, 1), _
    TableName:="PivotTable1", DefaultVersion:=xlPivotTableVersion15)
'Add the Sector field from the Sector table to the Row areas
With PT.CubeFields("[" & SectorTable & "].[Sector]")
    .Orientation = xlRowField
    .Position = 1
End With
'Before you can add Revenue to the pivot table, you have to define the measure
'This happens using the GetMeasure method
'Assign the cube field to CFRevenue object
Set CFRevenue = PT.CubeFields.GetMeasure(AttributeHierarchy:= _
    "[" & SalesTable & "].[Revenue]", Function:=xlSum)
'Add the field to the pivot table
PT.AddDataField Field:=CFRevenue, Caption:="Total Revenue"
PT.PivotFields(CFRevenue.Value).NumberFormat = "$#,##0,K"
'Add Distinct Count of Customer as a Cube Field
Set CFCustCount = PT.CubeFields.GetMeasure(AttributeHierarchy:= _
    "[" & SalesTable & "].[Customer]", Function:=xlDistinctCount)
'Add the newly created cube field to the pivot table
PT.AddDataField Field:=CFCustCount, Caption:="Customer Count"
'Add Median Sales using DAX
Set MedianSales = MO.ModelMeasures.Add(MeasureName:="Median Sales", _
    AssociatedTable:=MO.ModelTables(SalesTable), Formula:="Median([Revenue])", _
    FormatInformation:=MO.ModelFormatCurrency("Default", 2))
PT.AddDataField PT.CubeFields("[Measures].[" & MedianSales.Name & "]")
'cleanup
Set WBT = Nothing
Set WSD = Nothing
Set MO = Nothing
Set MedianSales = Nothing
Set PT = Nothing
Set PTCache = Nothing
Set CFRevenue = Nothing
Set CFCustCount = Nothing
End Sub
```

Using other pivot table features

This section covers a few additional features in pivot tables that you might need to code with VBA.

Calculated data fields

Pivot tables offer two types of formulas. The more useful type creates a calculated field. This adds a
new field to the pivot table. Calculations for calculated fields are always done at the summary level. If
you define a calculated field for the average price as revenue divided by units sold, Excel first adds the
total revenue and total quantity, and then it divides these totals to get the result. In many cases, this is

exactly what you need. If your calculation does not follow the associative law of mathematics, it might not work as you expect.

To set up a calculated field, use the Add method with the CalculatedFields object. You have to specify a field name and a formula, as shown here:

```
'Define calculated fields
PT.CalculatedFields.Add Name:="ProfitPercent", Formula:="=Profit/Revenue"
With PT.PivotFields("ProfitPercent")
  .Orientation = xlDataField
  .Function = xlSum
  .Position = 3
  .NumberFormat = "#0.0%"
  .Name = "GP Pct"
End With
```

> **Note** If you create a field called Profit Percent, the default pivot table produces a field called Sum of Profit Percent. This title is misleading. To prevent this, use the Name property when defining the Data field to replace Sum of Profit Percent with something such as GP Pct. Keep in mind that this name must differ from the name for the calculated field.

Calculated items

Calculated items allow you to create custom calculations within an existing field by grouping individual items. The new calculated item appears alongside the other in the pivot table, calculating results based on the defined formula.

For example, we want to group two specific products, A292 and C409, into the new category, MyDivision. The code to do this is:

```
PT.PivotFields("Product").CalculatedItems.Add "MyDivision", "='A292' + 'C409'"
```

Once we add the Revenue field to the Values area, the pivot table is updated, as shown in Figure 12-17.

Product ⌄	Sum of Revenue
A292	12,365,722
C409	14,133,525
MyDivision	26,499,247
B722	12,683,061
D625	14,600,282
E438	17,469,488
Grand Total	**97,751,325**

FIGURE 12-17 The Grand Total row includes the revenues from A292 and C409 twice – as individual products and as part of MyDivision.

Did you see the problem?

The grand total of the Revenue column is exaggerated as it double-counts A292 and C409 because they're already included along with MyDivision. The solution is to hide the individual products, like this:

```
With PT.PivotFields("Product")
  .PivotItems("A292").Visible = False
  .PivotItems("C409").Visible = False
End With
```

By hiding the individual products, they aren't included in the grand total and we won't get the boss in trouble with corporate.

> **Note** In the previous example, I'm summing the two products, but you can create just about any formula you want. For example, if A292 was an old product and C409 a new product and you wanted to see how the revenue changed, you could do this:
>
> ```
> PT.PivotFields("Product").CalculatedItems.Add "Revenue Change", "='C409' - 'A292'"
> ```

Using `ShowDetail` to filter a record set

When you double-click any number in the Values area of a pivot table on a sheet, Excel inserts a new sheet in the workbook and copies all the source records that represent that number. This is a great way to manually perform a drill-down query into a data set.

The equivalent VBA property is `ShowDetail`. Setting this property to `True` for any data cell in the pivot table generates a new worksheet with all the underlying records. You can target the data field by using `DataBodyRange.Cell`.

The top left cell of `DataBodyRange` acts like A1, so you'll need to offset from it to reference a specific cell. For example, if the data field starts in L4 and you want details of the value in L18, the following would generate a sheet with all the rows making up that value:

```
PT.DataBodyRange.Cells(15, 1).ShowDetail = True
```

Changing the layout from the Design tab

The Layout group on the Design tab contains four dropdown menus that control the following:

- The location of subtotals (top or bottom)

- The presence of grand totals

- The report layout, including whether outer row labels are repeated

- The presence of blank rows

Subtotals can appear either at the top or at the bottom of a group of pivot items. The SubtotalLocation property applies to the entire pivot table; valid values are xlAtBottom and xlAtTop:

```
PT.SubtotalLocation:=xlAtTop
```

Grand totals can be turned on or off for rows or columns. Because these two settings can be confusing, remember that at the bottom of a report, there is a total line that most people would call the grand total row. To turn off that row, you have to use the following:

```
PT.ColumnGrand = False
```

You need to turn off ColumnGrand when you want to suppress the total row because Microsoft calls that row the "grand total for columns." Get it? In other words, Microsoft is saying that the row at the bottom contains the total of the columns above it. It is one of the more awkward phrases in the Excel ribbon. It confuses me every time.

To suppress what you would call the grand total column along the right side of the report, you have to suppress what Microsoft calls the "total for rows" by using the following code:

```
PT.RowGrand = False
```

Settings for the report layout

There are three settings for the report layout:

- **Tabular layout**— Displays each field in its own column.

- **Outline layout**— Organizes data hierarchically, with subtotals above grouped items.

- **Compact layout**— Nests row fields within a single column, reducing horizontal width.

By default, when you create a pivot table, you get the Compact layout. A user can change this for all new pivot tables by going to File, Options, Data, and modifying the Edit Default Layout settings. With VBA, you can override the user's layout preference with one of these lines:

```
PT.RowAxisLayout xlTabularRow
PT.RowAxisLayout xlOutlineRow
PT.RowAxisLayout xlCompactRow
```

You can also add a blank line to the layout after each group of pivot items. Although the Design tab offers a single setting to affect the entire pivot table, the setting is actually applied individually to each pivot field. The macro recorder responds by recording a dozen lines of code for a pivot table with 12 fields. You can intelligently add a single line of code for the outer row fields:

```
PT.PivotFields("Customer").LayoutBlankLine = True
```

Case study: Applying a data visualization

Excel offers data visualizations such as icon sets, color gradients, and in-cell data bars. When you apply a data bar to a pivot table, you should exclude the total rows from the visualization.

For example, if 20 customers each averaged $3 million in revenue, the total for the 20 customers is $60 million. If you include the total in the data visualization, the total gets the largest bar, and all the customer records have tiny bars.

In the Excel user interface, when applying a data bar via the Add Rule or Edit Rule Excel options, be sure to select the option All Cells Showing "Sum of Revenue" values for "Customer" (or whatever your fields are called).

The code to add a data bar to the Revenue field is as follows:

```
'Apply a data bar
With PT.DataBodyRange.Columns(1) 'Revenue is the first value field
  .FormatConditions.AddDatabar
  .FormatConditions(1).ShowValue = True
  .FormatConditions(1).SetFirstPriority
  With .FormatConditions(1)
    .MinPoint.Modify newtype:=xlConditionValueLowestValue
    .MaxPoint.Modify newtype:=xlConditionValueHighestValue
  End With
  With .FormatConditions(1).BarColor
    .ThemeColor = xlThemeColorAccent3
    .TintAndShade = -0.5
  End With
  'Ensures formatting applies only to the field, not totals
  .FormatConditions(1).ScopeType = xlFieldsScope
End With
```

Columns(1) refers to the first field in the Values area, in this case, the Revenue field. After configuring the data bar for the first cell, we set the ScopeType to xlFieldsScope, so that it applies it to all Revenue cells and columns.

Office Scripts for pivot tables

Pivot tables are a popular tool for summarizing data, and Excel users often want to automate their creation—even in Excel Online. Since you can't use VBA online, this is where Office Scripts come in. This section provides a brief look at which parts of pivot table creation can currently be automated with this scripting language, keeping in mind that Office Scripts are still evolving and gaining new capabilities. Refer to Chapter 27, "An introduction to creating Office Add-ins," for a brief overview of the scripting tools available for Excel Online.

Scripts are accessed locally or online through the Automate tab, not to be mistaken with Power Automate, a separate service. They are stored in your OneDrive account, not in a workbook. This means they're available to all workbooks you open but cannot be shared by simply sending a file.

The Office Scripts macro recorder can successfully record these pivot table actions:

- Add a new pivot table to the right of your data set.

- Add Product to the Rows area.

- Add Revenue to the Values area.

- Add Region to the Columns area.

The recorded macro is short, relatively easy to understand, and runs successfully.

On the downside, the macro recorder does not (yet) support:

- Changing the number format of a numeric field.

- Replacing blanks in the Values area with zero.

- Using the suggested pivot tables from the Ideas feature.

Figure 12-18 shows the recorded Office Scripts code.

```
Script 4
1    function main(workbook: ExcelScript.Workbook) {
2      let tblPT_Data = workbook.getTable("tblPT_Data");
3      let selectedSheet = workbook.getActiveWorksheet();
4      // Add a new pivot table on selectedSheet
5      let newPivotTable = workbook.addPivotTable("PivotTable1", tblPT_Data, selectedSheet.
          getRange("N4"));
6      // Add pivot field to a hierarchy in newPivotTable
7      newPivotTable.addRowHierarchy(newPivotTable.getHierarchy("Product"));
8      // Add pivot field to a hierarchy in newPivotTable
9      newPivotTable.addDataHierarchy(newPivotTable.getHierarchy("Revenue"));
10     // Add pivot field to a hierarchy in newPivotTable
11     newPivotTable.addColumnHierarchy(newPivotTable.getHierarchy("Region"));
12     // Change pivot position in a hierarchy in newPivotTable
13     newPivotTable.getColumnHierarchy("Region").setPosition(0);
14   }
```

FIGURE 12-18 A 14-line script adds Product to the Rows, Revenue to Values, and Region to Columns in a new pivot table in Excel Online.

Here is a description of the recorded code with suggested changes:

The script is named Script 4. In the Script Details, click on the name and type a better name, such as CreatePTByProductAndRegion.

Comment lines start with // instead of an apostrophe like in VBA.

selectedSheet is an object variable. Where VBA would do:

```
Set selectedSheet = ActiveSheet
```

Typescript does:

```
let selectedSheet = workbook.getActiveWorksheet()
```

The code is case-sensitive. You have to use getActiveWorksheet and not getactiveworksheet or GetActiveWorksheet. If you don't use the case correctly, the editor will flag it as an error but then suggest that you could change the spelling to getActiveWorksheet.

When the macro recorder creates the pivot table using .addPivotTable, it specifies a name, source data, and destination data. If your data isn't in a table, you can use Office Scripts' equivalent of .CurrentRegion, which is .getSurroundingRegion() like this:

```
selectedSheet.getRange("A1").getSurroundingRegion()
```

The modified code to create a pivot table called PTOne, based on A:H and starting in cell N2, is shown here. Note that the results are stored in an object variable called newPivotTable for easy reference later in the script:

```
let newPivotTable = workbook.addPivotTable("PTOne",
selectedSheet.getRange("A1").getSurroundingRegion(),
selectedSheet.getRange("N2"));
```

Once the pivot table is created, you can add fields to the Rows area with the following:

```
newPivotTable.addRowHierarchy(newPivotTable.getHierarchy("Product"));
```

For a column field, instead of .addRowHierarchy, use .addColumnHierarchy. For a Values field, use .AddDataHierarchy.

Near the end of the script, the macro recorder added a stray line:

```
newPivotTable.getColumnHierarchy("Region").setPosition(0);
```

This would have been needed if you had multiple fields in the Columns area. But with only one field in the Columns area, that line can be deleted.

Documentation for everything shows up when you hover over any word in the script. This is better than VBA, where you have to press F1 and then wait for a web page to load.

After seeing the recorded code, it should be relatively easy to edit it. The following code in Listing 12-7 creates a pivot table with Product in rows, Region in columns, and Revenue in values. And because there are times you have to use a range instead of listobject, it's using .getSurroundingRegion.

Listing 12-7   Office Script code to create a pivot table in Excel Online

```
function main(workbook: ExcelScript.Workbook) {
  let tblPT_Data = workbook.getTable("tblPT_Data");
  let selectedSheet = workbook.getActiveWorksheet();
  // Add a new pivot table on selectedSheet
  //let newPivotTable = workbook.addPivotTable("PTOne", tblPT_Data, _
    selectedSheet.getRange("N2"));
  let newPivotTable = workbook.addPivotTable("PTOne", _
    selectedSheet.getRange("A1").getSurroundingRegion(), _
```

```
        selectedSheet.getRange("N2"));
    // Add Sector to Rows
    newPivotTable.addRowHierarchy(newPivotTable.getHierarchy("Product"));
    // Add Revenue to Data
    newPivotTable.addDataHierarchy(newPivotTable.getHierarchy("Revenue"));
    // Add Region to Columns
    newPivotTable.addColumnHierarchy(newPivotTable.getHierarchy("Region"));
}
```

The resulting pivot table is shown in Figure 12-19.

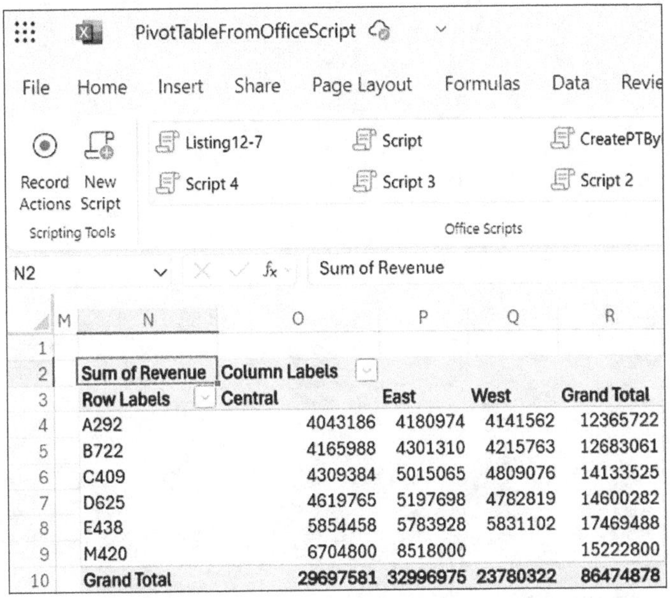

FIGURE 12-19 A pivot table created in Excel Online from an Office Scripts macro.

There are still gaps. When you look at Figure 12-19, you might want to change "For Empty Cells, Show" to zero. There is a setting in Excel Online for this. But when you try to record a macro for how to make that change, the macro recorder tells you that this is not yet supported in TypeScript:

```
// This action currently can't be recorded.
```

You can learn more about working with pivot tables in Office Scripts at the following Microsoft page: *https://learn.microsoft.com/en-us/office/dev/scripts/develop/pivottables*.

Next steps

You may be able to tell that pivot tables are my favorite feature in Excel. They are incredibly powerful and flexible. Combined with VBA, they provide an excellent calculation engine and power many of the reports I build for clients. Chapter 13, "Excel power," offers multiple techniques for handling various tasks in VBA. It also includes a section with ideas to solve various project design issues.

Excel power

In this chapter, you will:

- List all files in a folder

- Import data from a CSV file

- Learn methods of splitting and merging data

- Export data to an XML file

- Create a log file

- Clean a report so you can analyze the data

- Learn the favorite techniques of various VBA pros

A major secret of successful programmers is to never waste time writing the same code twice. They all have little bits—or even big bits—of code that they use over and over again. Another big secret is to never take 8 hours doing something that can be done in 10 minutes—which is what this book is about!

This chapter features contributed programs from Excel power users—tools they found useful and hope you will, too. In addition to saving time, these examples can teach new techniques. We left the original code intact, so you'll see a variety of programming styles and approaches, such as different ways to reference ranges. The final section of this chapter highlights sample projects I've tackled and walks through how each might be approached and solved.

File operations

The utilities shown in the following sections deal with handling files in folders. Being able to loop through a list of files in a folder is a useful task.

Listing files in a directory

This utility was submitted by our good friend Nathan P. Oliver of Minneapolis, Minnesota.

This program returns the file name, size, and date modified of all specified file types in the selected directory and its subfolders:

> **Note** This example uses Let to assign values to variables. It's valid VBA syntax, but rarely needed. In modern code, simple assignments like x = 5 work without it.

```vba
Sub ExcelFileSearch()
Dim srchExt As Variant, srchDir As Variant
Dim i As Long, j As Long, strName As String
Dim varArr(1 To 1048576, 1 To 3) As Variant
Dim strFileFullName As String
Dim ws As Worksheet
Dim fso As Object
Let srchExt = Application.InputBox("Please Enter File Extension", "Info Request")
If srchExt = False And Not TypeName(srchExt) = "String" Then
  Exit Sub
End If
Let srchDir = BrowseForFolderShell
If srchDir = False And Not TypeName(srchDir) = "String" Then
  Exit Sub
End If
Application.ScreenUpdating = False
Set ws = ThisWorkbook.Worksheets.Add(Sheets(1))
On Error Resume Next
Application.DisplayAlerts = False
ThisWorkbook.Worksheets("FileSearch Results").Delete
Application.DisplayAlerts = True
On Error GoTo 0
ws.Name = "FileSearch Results"
Let strName = Dir$(srchDir & "\*" & srchExt)
Do While strName <> vbNullString
 Let i = i + 1
  Let strFileFullName = srchDir & strName
  Let varArr(i, 1) = strFileFullName
  Let varArr(i, 2) = FileLen(strFileFullName) \ 1024
  Let varArr(i, 3) = FileDateTime(strFileFullName)
  Let strName = Dir$()
Loop
Set fso = CreateObject("Scripting.FileSystemObject")
Call recurseSubFolders(fso.GetFolder(srchDir), varArr(), i, CStr(srchExt))
Set fso = Nothing
ThisWorkbook.Windows(1).DisplayHeadings = False
With ws
  If i > 0 Then
    .Range("A2").Resize(i, UBound(varArr, 2)).Value = varArr
    For j = 1 To i
      .Hyperlinks.Add anchor:=.Cells(j + 1, 1), Address:=varArr(j, 1)
    Next
  End If
  .Range(.Cells(1, 4), .Cells(1, .Columns.Count)).EntireColumn.Hidden = _
    True
  .Range(.Cells(.Rows.Count, 1).End(xlUp)(2), _
    .Cells(.Rows.Count, 1)).EntireRow.Hidden = True
  With .Range("A1:C1")
```

```
          .Value = Array("Full Name", "Kilobytes", "Last Modified")
          .Font.Underline = xlUnderlineStyleSingle
          .EntireColumn.AutoFit
          .HorizontalAlignment = xlCenter
      End With
End With
Application.ScreenUpdating = True
End Sub


Private Sub recurseSubFolders(ByRef Folder As Object, _
    ByRef varArr() As Variant, _
    ByRef i As Long, _
    ByRef srchExt As String)
Dim SubFolder As Object
Dim strName As String, strFileFullName As String
For Each SubFolder In Folder.SubFolders
    Let strName = Dir$(SubFolder.Path & "\*" & srchExt)
    Do While strName <> vbNullString
      Let i = i + 1
      Let strFileFullName = SubFolder.Path & "\" & strName
      Let varArr(i, 1) = strFileFullName
      Let varArr(i, 2) = FileLen(strFileFullName) \ 1024
      Let varArr(i, 3) = FileDateTime(strFileFullName)
      Let strName = Dir$()
    Loop
    If i > 1048576 Then Exit Sub
    Call recurseSubFolders(SubFolder, varArr(), i, srchExt)
Next
End Sub


Private Function BrowseForFolderShell() As Variant
Dim objShell As Object, objFolder As Object
Set objShell = CreateObject("Shell.Application")
Set objFolder = objShell.BrowseForFolder(0, "Please select a folder", 0, "C:\")
If Not objFolder Is Nothing Then
  On Error Resume Next
  If IsError(objFolder.Items.Item.Path) Then
    BrowseForFolderShell = CStr(objFolder)
  Else
    On Error GoTo 0
    If Len(objFolder.Items.Item.Path) > 3 Then
      BrowseForFolderShell = objFolder.Items.Item.Path & _
        Application.PathSeparator
    Else
      BrowseForFolderShell = objFolder.Items.Item.Path
    End If
  End If
Else
  BrowseForFolderShell = False
End If
Set objFolder = Nothing: Set objShell = Nothing
End Function
```

Importing and deleting a CSV file

This utility was submitted by Masaru Kaji of Kobe, Japan. Masaru is a computer systems administrator.

If you find yourself importing a lot of comma-separated value (CSV) files and then having to go back and delete them, this program is for you. It quickly opens a CSV file in Excel and permanently deletes the original file:

```
Option Base 1
Sub OpenLargeCSVFast()
Dim buf(1 To 16384) As Variant
Dim i As Long
'Change the file location and name here
Const strFilePath As String = "C:\temp\Sales.CSV"
Dim strRenamedPath As String
strRenamedPath = Split(strFilePath, ".")(0) & "txt"
With Application
  .ScreenUpdating = False
  .DisplayAlerts = False
End With
'Setting an array for FieldInfo to open CSV
For i = 1 To 16384
  buf(i) = Array(i, 2)
Next
Name strFilePath As strRenamedPath
Workbooks.OpenText Filename:=strRenamedPath, DataType:=xlDelimited, _
  Comma:=True, FieldInfo:=buf
Erase buf
ActiveSheet.UsedRange.Copy ThisWorkbook.Sheets(1).Range("A1")
ActiveWorkbook.Close False
Kill strRenamedPath
With Application
  .ScreenUpdating = True
  .DisplayAlerts = True
End With
End Sub
```

Reading a text file into memory and parsing

This utility was submitted by Rory Archibald, a reinsurance analyst residing in East Sussex, United Kingdom. A self-admitted geek by inclination, he also maintains the website *exceljunkie.wordpress.com*.

This utility takes a different approach to reading a text file than you might have used in the past. Instead of reading one record at a time, the macro loads the entire text file into memory in a single string variable. The macro then parses the string into individual records, all still in memory. It then places all the records on the sheet at one time (what I like to call "dumping" the data onto the sheet). The advantage of this method is that you access the file on disk only once. All subsequent processing occurs in memory and is very fast. Without further ado, here's the utility:

```
Sub LoadLinesFromCSV()
Dim sht As Worksheet
```

```
Dim strtxt As String
Dim textArray() As String
'Add new sheet for output
Set sht = Sheets.Add
'open the csv file
With CreateObject("Scripting.FileSystemObject") _
  .GetFile("c:\temp\sales.csv").OpenAsTextStream(1)
  'read the contents into a variable
  strtxt = .ReadAll
  'close it!
  .Close
End With
'split the text into an array using carriage return and line feed
'separator
textArray = VBA.Split(strtxt, vbCrLf)
sht.Range("A1").Resize(UBound(textArray) + 1).Value = _
  Application.Transpose(textArray)
End Sub
```

Handling comma-delimited lines after splitting on line breaks

If your file is comma-delimited, splitting on vbCrLf gives you individual rows, but each row still contains multiple fields. You can use Excel's Text to Columns at this point, or you can split each line by commas before dumping it into the sheet. Here's the code you can insert into the previous sub to do this:

```
Dim tempSplit() As String
Dim outputArray() As String
Dim i As Long, j As Long, maxCols As Long
'this would go AFTER textArray = VBA.Split(strtxt, vbCrLf)
'First, find the maximum number of columns
tempSplit = Split(textArray(1), ",")
maxCols = UBound(tempSplit)
'Resize output array: (rows, columns)
ReDim outputArray(LBound(textArray) To UBound(textArray), 0 To maxCols)
'Fill output array with split values
For i = LBound(textArray) To UBound(textArray)
  tempSplit = Split(textArray(i), ",")
  For j = LBound(tempSplit) To UBound(tempSplit)
    outputArray(i, j) = tempSplit(j)
  Next j
Next i
'output Split commas, replacing the original output
sht.Range("A1").Resize(UBound(outputArray) + 1, UBound(outputArray, 2)).Value _
  = outputArray
```

Checking cloud-based file paths

This function is becoming a must nowadays as more of my clients are storing workbooks in the cloud. Modern Excel files can be opened directly from platforms like SharePoint, OneDrive, or Teams. When that happens, Excel often returns a URL instead of a file path, which breaks many file-related VBA routines, especially those that rely on `ThisWorkbook.Path` or try to open, save, or browse relative to the current workbook's location.

For example:

- `ThisWorkbook.Path` may be empty.

- `ThisWorkbook.FullName` may return a URL like *https://....*

- `ChDir`, `Dir`, or `Application.GetSaveAsFilename` will fail if passed a URL or an empty string.

To safely handle this possibility, use the function below to detect cloud-hosted workbooks before running file-based logic.

```
Public Function IsCloudHosted(wb As Workbook) As Boolean
Dim fullPath As String
fullPath = wb.FullName
IsCloudHosted = (wb.Path = "") Or (LCase(Left(fullPath, 4)) = "http")
End Function
```

You could use this function in a routine like this:

```
Sub BrowseForFile()
Dim startPath As String
Dim selectedFile As Variant
If IsCloudHosted(ThisWorkbook) Then
  MsgBox "This workbook appears to be cloud-hosted." & Chr(10) & _
    "File-related operations may not work properly.", vbExclamation
    Exit Sub
End If
startPath = ThisWorkbook.Path
'change the current directory to the current path
ChDir startPath 'safe only if workbook is local
selectedFile = Application.GetOpenFilename("Excel Files (*.xls*), *.xls*")
If selectedFile <> False Then
  MsgBox "You selected: " & selectedFile
End If
End Sub
```

Combining and separating workbooks

The utilities in the following sections demonstrate how to combine worksheets into a single workbook, separate a single workbook into individual worksheets, or export data on a sheet to an XML file.

Separating worksheets into workbooks

This utility was submitted by Tommy Miles of Houston, Texas.

This sample goes through the active workbook and saves each sheet as its own workbook in the same path as the original workbook. It names the new workbooks based on the sheet name, and it overwrites files without prompting. Notice that you need to choose whether you save the file as .xlsm (macro-enabled) or .xlsx (with macros stripped). In the following code, both lines are included—xlsm and xlsx—but the xlsx lines are commented out to make them inactive:

```
Sub SplitWorkbook()
Dim ws As Worksheet
Dim DisplayStatusBar As Boolean
DisplayStatusBar = Application.DisplayStatusBar
Application.DisplayStatusBar = True
Application.ScreenUpdating = False
Application.DisplayAlerts = False
For Each ws In ThisWorkbook.Sheets
  Dim NewFileName As String
  Application.StatusBar = ThisWorkbook.Sheets.Count & " Remaining Sheets"
  If ThisWorkbook.Sheets.Count <> 1 Then
    NewFileName = ThisWorkbook.Path & "\" & ws.Name & ".xlsm" 'Macro-Enabled
    'NewFileName = ThisWorkbook.Path & "\" & ws.Name & ".xlsx" 'Not Macro-Enabled
    ws.Copy
    ActiveWorkbook.Sheets(1).Name = "Sheet1"
    ActiveWorkbook.SaveAs Filename:=NewFileName, _
      FileFormat:=xlOpenXMLWorkbookMacroEnabled
    'ActiveWorkbook.SaveAs Filename:=NewFileName, _
      FileFormat:=xlOpenXMLWorkbook
    ActiveWorkbook.Close SaveChanges:=False
  Else
    NewFileName = ThisWorkbook.Path & "\" & ws.Name & ".xlsm"
    'NewFileName = ThisWorkbook.Path & "\" & ws.Name & ".xlsx"
    ws.Name = "Sheet1"
  End If
Next
Application.DisplayAlerts = True
Application.StatusBar = False
Application.DisplayStatusBar = DisplayStatusBar
Application.ScreenUpdating = True
End Sub
```

Combining workbooks

This utility was submitted by Tommy Miles.

This sample goes through all the Excel files in a specified directory and combines them into a single workbook. It renames the sheets based on the name of the original workbook:

```
Sub CombineWorkbooks()
Dim CurFile As String, DirLoc As String
Dim DestWB As Workbook
Dim ws As Object 'allows for different sheet types
DirLoc = ThisWorkbook.Path & "\tst\" 'location of files
CurFile = Dir(DirLoc & "*.xls*")
Application.ScreenUpdating = False
Application.EnableEvents = False
Set DestWB = Workbooks.Add(xlWorksheet)
```

```
    Do While CurFile <> vbNullString
      Dim OrigWB As Workbook
      Set OrigWB = Workbooks.Open(Filename:=DirLoc & CurFile, ReadOnly:=True)
      'Limits to valid sheet names and removes ".xls*"
      CurFile = Left(Left(CurFile, Len(CurFile) - 5), 29)
      For Each ws In OrigWB.Sheets
        ws.Copy After:=DestWB.Sheets(DestWB.Sheets.Count)
        If OrigWB.Sheets.Count > 1 Then
          DestWB.Sheets(DestWB.Sheets.Count).Name = CurFile & ws.Index
        Else
          DestWB.Sheets(DestWB.Sheets.Count).Name = CurFile
        End If
      Next
      OrigWB.Close SaveChanges:=False
      CurFile = Dir
    Loop
    Application.DisplayAlerts = False
    DestWB.Sheets(1).Delete
    Application.DisplayAlerts = True
    Application.ScreenUpdating = True
    Application.EnableEvents = True
    Set DestWB = Nothing
    End Sub
```

Copying data to separate worksheets without using `Filter`

This utility was submitted by Zack Barresse from Boardman, Oregon. Zack is an Excel ninja and VBA nut, and he's a former firefighter and paramedic. He co-authored one of my favorite books, *Excel Tables: A Complete Guide for Creating, Using, and Automating Lists and Tables* (Holy Macro! Books, 2014), with Kevin Jones. The fundamentals covered in this book are still relevant today.

You can use `Filter` to select specific records and then copy them to another sheet. But if you are dealing with a lot of data or have formulas in the data set, it can take a while to run. Instead of using `Filter`, consider using a formula to mark the desired records and then sort by that column to group the desired records together. Combine this with `SpecialCells`, and you could have a procedure that runs up to 10 times faster than code that uses `Filter`. Here's how it looks:

```
Sub CriteriaRange_Copy()
Dim Table As ListObject
Dim SortColumn As ListColumn
Dim CriteriaColumn As ListColumn
Dim FoundRange As Range
Dim TargetSheet As Worksheet
Dim HeaderVisible As Boolean
Set Table = ActiveSheet.ListObjects(1) 'Set as desired
HeaderVisible = Table.ShowHeaders
Table.ShowHeaders = True
On Error GoTo RemoveColumns
Set SortColumn = Table.ListColumns.Add(Table.ListColumns.Count + 1)
Set CriteriaColumn = Table.ListColumns.Add (Table.ListColumns.Count + 1)
On Error GoTo 0
'Add a column to keep track of the original order of the records
```

```
SortColumn.Name = " Sort"
CriteriaColumn.Name = " Criteria"
SortColumn.DataBodyRange.Formula = "=ROW(A1)"
SortColumn.DataBodyRange.Value = SortColumn.DataBodyRange.Value
'add the formula to mark the desired records
'the records not wanted will have errors
CriteriaColumn.DataBodyRange.Formula = "=1/(([@Units]<10)*([@Cost]<5))"
CriteriaColumn.DataBodyRange.Value = CriteriaColumn.DataBodyRange.Value
Table.Range.Sort Key1:=CriteriaColumn.Range(1, 1), _
  Order1:=xlAscending, Header:=xlYes
On Error Resume Next
Set FoundRange = Intersect(Table.Range, CriteriaColumn.DataBodyRange. _
  SpecialCells(xlCellTypeConstants, xlNumbers).EntireRow)
On Error GoTo 0
If Not FoundRange Is Nothing Then
  Set TargetSheet = ThisWorkbook.Worksheets.Add(After:=ActiveSheet)
  FoundRange(1, 1).Offset(-1, 0).Resize(FoundRange.Rows.Count + 1, _
    FoundRange.Columns.Count - 2).Copy
  TargetSheet.Range("A1").PasteSpecial xlPasteValuesAndNumberFormats
  Application.CutCopyMode = False
End If
Table.Range.Sort Key1:=SortColumn.Range(1, 1), Order1:=xlAscending, _
  Header:=xlYes
RemoveColumns:
If Not SortColumn Is Nothing Then SortColumn.Delete
If Not CriteriaColumn Is Nothing Then CriteriaColumn.Delete
Table.ShowHeaders = HeaderVisible
End Sub
```

Exporting data to an XML file

This utility was submitted by Livio Lanzo. Livio is currently working as a business analyst in finance in Luxembourg. His main task is to develop Excel/Access tools for a bank. Livio is also active on the *MrExcel.com* forum under the handle VBA Geek.

This program exports the data from a table to an XML file. It uses early binding, so a reference must be established in the VB Editor using Tools, References to the Microsoft XML, v6.0 library:

```
Const ROOT_ELEMENT_NAME = "SAMPLEDATA"
Const GROUPS_NAME = "EMPLOYEES"
Const XML_EXPORT_PATH = "C:\temp\myXMLFile.xml"
Sub CreateXML()
Dim xml_DOM As MSXML2.DOMDocument60
Dim xml_El As MSXML2.IXMLDOMElement
Dim xRow As Long
Dim xCol As Long
Set xml_DOM = CreateObject("MSXML2.DOMDocument.6.0")
xml_DOM.appendChild xml_DOM.createElement(ROOT_ELEMENT_NAME)
With Sheet1.ListObjects("TableEmployees")
  For xRow = 1 To .ListRows.Count
    CREATE_APPEND_ELEMENT xml_DOM, ROOT_ELEMENT_NAME, GROUPS_NAME, 0, NODE_ELEMENT
    For xCol = 1 To .ListColumns.Count
      CREATE_APPEND_ELEMENT xml_DOM, GROUPS_NAME, _
```

```
        .HeaderRowRange(1, xCol).Text, (xRow - 1), NODE_ELEMENT
      CREATE_APPEND_ELEMENT xml_DOM, .HeaderRowRange(1, xCol).Text, _
        .DataBodyRange(xRow, xCol).Text, (xRow - 1), NODE_TEXT
    Next xCol
  Next xRow
End With
xml_DOM.Save XML_EXPORT_PATH
MsgBox "File Created: " & XML_EXPORT_PATH, vbInformation
End Sub


Private Sub CREATE_APPEND_ELEMENT(xmlDOM As MSXML2.DOMDocument60, _
  ParentElName As String, _
  NewElName As String, _
  ParentElIndex As Long, _
  ELType As MSXML2.tagDOMNodeType)
Dim xml_ELEMENT As Object
If ELType = NODE_ELEMENT Then
  Set xml_ELEMENT = xmlDOM.createElement(NewElName)
ElseIf ELType = NODE_TEXT Then
  Set xml_ELEMENT = xmlDOM.createTextNode(NewElName)
End If
xmlDOM.getElementsByTagName(ParentElName)(ParentElIndex).appendChild _
  xml_ELEMENT
End Sub
```

Placing a chart in a cell note

This utility was submitted by Tom Urtis of San Francisco, California. Tom is the principal owner of Atlas Programming Management, an Excel consulting firm in the Bay Area.

A live chart cannot exist in a shape, but you can take a picture of a chart and load it into the note shape, as shown in Figure 13-1.

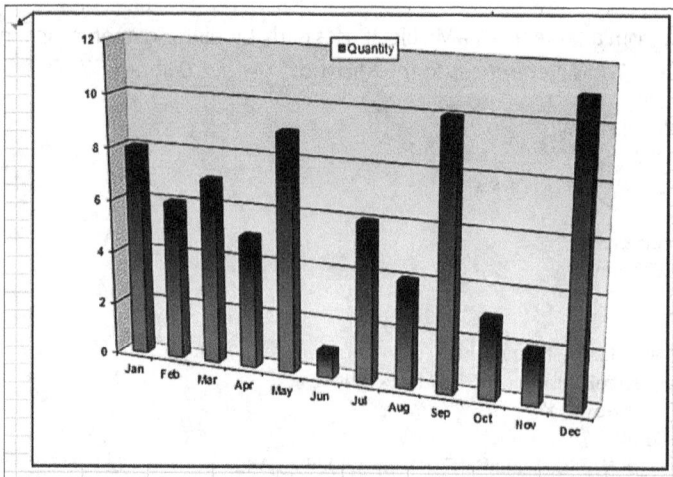

FIGURE 13-1 Place a chart in a cell note.

These are the steps to do this manually:

1. Create and save the image you want the note to display.

2. If you have not already done so, create the note and select the cell in which the note is located.

3. From the Review tab, select Notes | Edit Note, or right-click the cell and select Edit Note.

4. Right-click the note border and select Format Comment.

5. Select the Colors And Lines tab and click the down arrow belonging to the Color field of the Fill section.

6. Select Fill Effects, select the Picture tab, and then click the Select Picture button.

7. Navigate to your desired image, select the image, and click OK twice.

The effect of having a "live chart" in a note can be achieved if, for example, the code is part of a SheetChange event when the chart's source data is being changed. In addition, business charts are updated often, so you might want a macro to keep the note updated and to avoid repeating the same steps.

The following utility does just that—and you can use it by simply modifying the file pathname, chart name, destination sheet, cell, and size of the note shape, depending on the size of the chart:

```
Sub PlaceGraph()
Dim x As String, z As Range
Application.ScreenUpdating = False
'assign a temporary location to hold the image
x = ThisWorkbook.Path & Application.PathSeparator & "XWMJGraph.gif"
'assign the cell to hold the note
Set z = Worksheets("ChartInNote").Range("A3")
'delete any existing note in the cell
On Error Resume Next
z.Comment.Delete
On Error GoTo 0
'select and export the chart
ActiveSheet.ChartObjects("Chart 1").Activate
ActiveChart.Export x
'add a new note to the cell, set the size and insert the chart
With z.AddComment
  With .Shape
    .Height = 322
    .Width = 465
    .Fill.UserPicture x
  End With
End With
'delete the temporary image
On Error Resume Next
Kill x
If Err.Number <> 0 Then
  MsgBox "Can't delete file: " & x
```

```
    Err.Clear
    End If
    Range("A1").Activate
    Application.ScreenUpdating = True
    Set z = Nothing
    End Sub
```

Tracking user changes

The Change event is a code solution posted often at Excel forums, primarily because it fills a void that formulas alone can't manage (for example, inserting a date and time stamp when a user changes a specific range). The following utility takes advantage of the Change event in order to create a log file that tracks the cell address, new value, date, time, and username for changes made to column A of the sheet in which the code is placed.

This utility was submitted by our good friend Chris "Smitty" Smith of Redmond, Washington:

```
Private Sub Worksheet_Change(ByVal Target As Range)
'Code goes in the Worksheet specific module
Dim ws As Worksheet
Dim lr As Long
Dim rng As Range
'Set the Destination worksheet
Set ws = Sheets("Log Sheet")
'Get the first unused row on the Log sheet
lr = ws.Cells(Rows.Count, "A").End(xlUp).Row
'Set Target Range, i.e. Range("A1, B2, C3"), or Range("A1:B3")
Set rng = Target.Parent.Range("A:A")
'Only look at single cell changes
If Target.Count > 1 Then Exit Sub
'Only look at that range
If Intersect(Target, rng) Is Nothing Then Exit Sub
'Action if Condition(s) are met (do your thing here...)
'Put the Target cell's Address in Column A
ws.Cells(lr + 1, "A").Value = Target.Address
'Put the Target cell's value in Column B
ws.Cells(lr + 1, "B").Value = Target.Value
'Put the Date in Column C
ws.Cells(lr + 1, "C").Value = Date
'Put the Time in Column D
ws.Cells(lr + 1, "D").Value = Format(Now, "HH:MM:SS AM/PM")
'Put the Date in Column E
ws.Cells(lr + 1, "E").Value = Environ("UserName")
End Sub
```

Using a settings table

I include a settings sheet in almost every project. It might just store file paths or column headers, but in larger projects, it becomes a full configuration table that lets clients control things like logos, report names, sheet selections, and value substitutions. This makes the code more flexible and maintainable, and clients can expand it on their own. I've seen setups grow from three to over a hundred customers without a single support call.

The setup is easy. I use the first column to hold my lookup value. The rest of the columns are the values returned. The lookup column is specified in the arguments; if a match is found, the row number is returned. You can then look up the specific column and row needed. The code for the function is:

```
Function TableMatchLookup(ByVal LookupColumn As ListColumn, _
    ByVal LookupValue As Variant, ByRef MatchFound As Variant) As Boolean
On Error Resume Next
MatchFound = Application.Match(LookupValue, LookupColumn.DataBodyRange, 0)
On Error GoTo 0
If IsError(MatchFound) Then
    TableMatchLookup = False
Else
    TableMatchLookup = True
End If
End Function
```

This is how I use it to look up a specific setting, Data Workbook:

```
Function GetDataWorkbook(ByRef FileName As String, ByRef errMessage As String) As
Boolean
Dim tblSettings As ListObject
Dim MatchFound As Variant, SettingValue As Variant
On Error GoTo errHandler
Set tblSettings = Worksheets("Settings").ListObject("tblSettings")
If Not TableMatchLookup(tblSettings.ListColumn(1), "Data Workbook", MatchFound) Then
    'label not found
    errMessage = "Setting not found"
    GoTo errHandler
Else
    'label found, now check for actual setting
    SettingValue = Trim(tblSettings.DataBodyRange.Cells(MatchFound, 2))
    If SettingValue = "" Then
        'it's blank
        errMessage = "Data Workbook not configured"
        GoTo errHandler
    Else
        'Entry there, is it valid?
        'Dir$ returns the filename if found
        'the $ forces a string be returned
        If Len(Dir$(SettingValue)) > 0 Then
            'valid
            FileName = SettingValue
        Else
            'not valid
            errMessage = "Invalid path" & Chr(10) & SettingValue
            GoTo errHandler
        End If
    End If
End If
errHandler:
```

```
If Err.Number <> 0 Then
  errMessage = "Unexpected error - " & Err.Number & ": " & Err.Description
  Err.Clear
End If
If Len(errMessage) > 0 Then
  GetDataWorkbook = False
Else
  GetDataWorkbook = True
End If
Set tblSettings = Nothing
End Function
```

Techniques for VBA pros

The utilities provided in the following sections amaze me. In the various message board communities on the Internet, VBA programmers are constantly coming up with new ways to do things faster and better. When someone posts some new code that obviously runs circles around the prior generally accepted best code, everyone benefits.

Creating an Excel state class module

This utility was submitted by Juan Pablo Gonzàlez Ruiz of Bogotà, Colombia.

The following class module is one of my favorites, and I use it in almost every project I create. Before Juan shared the module with me, I used to enter the eight lines of code to turn off and back on screen updating, events, alerts, and calculations. At the beginning of a sub, I would turn them off, and at the end, I would turn them back on. That was quite a bit of typing. Now, I just place the class module in a new workbook I create and call it as needed.

Insert a class module named cAppState and place the following code in it:

```
Private m_su As Boolean
Private m_ee As Boolean
Private m_da As Boolean
Private m_calc As Long
Private m_cursor As Long
Private m_except As StateEnum
Public Enum StateEnum
  None = 0
  ScreenUpdating = 1
  EnableEvents = 2
  DisplayAlerts = 4
  Calculation = 8
  Cursor = 16
End Enum

Public Sub SetState(Optional ByVal except As StateEnum = StateEnum.None)
m_except = except
```

```
With Application
  If Not m_except And StateEnum.ScreenUpdating Then
    .ScreenUpdating = False
  End If

  If Not m_except And StateEnum.EnableEvents Then
    .EnableEvents = False
  End If

  If Not m_except And StateEnum.DisplayAlerts Then
    .DisplayAlerts = False
  End If

  If Not m_except And StateEnum.Calculation Then
    .Calculation = xlCalculationManual
  End If

  If Not m_except And StateEnum.Cursor Then
    .Cursor = xlWait
  End If
End With
End Sub

Private Sub Class_Initialize()
With Application
  m_su = .ScreenUpdating
  m_ee = .EnableEvents
  m_da = .DisplayAlerts
  m_calc = .Calculation
  m_cursor = .Cursor
End With
End Sub

Private Sub Class_Terminate()
With Application
  If Not m_except And StateEnum.ScreenUpdating Then
    .ScreenUpdating = m_su
  End If
  If Not m_except And StateEnum.EnableEvents Then
    .EnableEvents = m_ee
  End If
  If Not m_except And StateEnum.DisplayAlerts Then
    .DisplayAlerts = m_da
  End If
  If Not m_except And StateEnum.Calculation Then
    .Calculation = m_calc
  End If
  If Not m_except And StateEnum.Cursor Then
    .Cursor = m_cursor
  End If
End With
End Sub
```

The following code is an example of calling the class module to turn off the various states, running your code, and then setting the states back:

```
Sub RunFasterCode
Dim appState As cAppState
Set appState = New cAppState
appState.SetState None
'run your code
'if you have any formulas that need to update, use
'Application.Calculate
'to force the workbook to calculate
Set appState = Nothing
End Sub
```

Filtering an OLAP pivot table by a list of items

This utility was submitted by Jerry Sullivan of San Diego, California. Jerry is an operations manager for exp (*www.exp.com*), a building engineering consulting firm.

This procedure filters an OLAP pivot table to show items in a separate list, regardless of whether an item in that list has a matching record.

The code converts user-friendly items into MDX member references—for example, from "banana" to "[tblSales].[product_name].&[banana]"]":

```
Sub FilterOLAP_PT()
'example showing call to function sOLAP_FilterByItemList
Dim pvt As PivotTable
Dim sErrMsg As String, sTemplate As String
Dim vItemsToBeVisible As Variant
On Error GoTo ErrProc
With Application
   .EnableCancelKey = xlErrorHandler
   .ScreenUpdating = False
   .DisplayStatusBar = False
   .EnableEvents = False
End With
'read filter items from worksheet table
vItemsToBeVisible = Application.Transpose( _
   wksPivots.ListObjects("tblVisibleItemsList").DataBodyRange.Value)
Set pvt = wksPivots.PivotTables("PivotTable1")
'call function
sErrMsg = sOLAP_FilterByItemList( _
   pvf:=pvt.PivotFields("[tblSales].[product_name].[product_name]"), _
   vItemsToBeVisible:=vItemsToBeVisible, _
   sItemPattern:="[tblSales].[product_name].&[ThisItem]")
ExitProc:
On Error Resume Next
With Application
   .EnableEvents = True
   .DisplayStatusBar = True
   .ScreenUpdating = True
```

```
End With
If Len(sErrMsg) > 0 Then MsgBox sErrMsg
Exit Sub
ErrProc:
sErrMsg = Err.Number & " - " & Err.Description
Resume ExitProc
End Sub


Private Function sOLAP_FilterByItemList(ByVal pvf As PivotField, _
    ByVal vItemsToBeVisible As Variant, _
    ByVal sItemPattern As String) As String
'filters an OLAP pivot table to display a list of items,
'where some of the items might not exist
'works by testing whether each pivotitem exists, then building an
'array of existing items to be used with the VisibleItemsList property

'Input Parameters:
'pvf - pivotfield object to be filtered
'vItemsToBeVisible - 1-D array of strings representing items to be visible
'sItemPattern - string that has MDX pattern of pivotItem reference
'where the text "ThisItem" will be replaced by each
'item in vItemsToBeVisible to make pivotItem references.
'e.g.: "[tblSales].[product_name].&[ThisItem]"
Dim lFilterItemCount As Long, lNdx As Long
Dim vFilterArray As Variant
Dim vSaveVisibleItemsList As Variant
Dim sReturnMsg As String, sPivotItemName As String
'store existing visible items
vSaveVisibleItemsList = pvf.VisibleItemsList
If Not (IsArray(vItemsToBeVisible)) Then _
    vItemsToBeVisible = Array(vItemsToBeVisible)
ReDim vFilterArray(1 To _
    UBound(vItemsToBeVisible) - LBound(vItemsToBeVisible) + 1)
pvf.Parent.ManualUpdate = True
'check if pivotitem exists then build array of items that exist
For lNdx = LBound(vItemsToBeVisible) To UBound(vItemsToBeVisible)
    'create MDX format pivotItem reference by substituting item into
    'pattern
    sPivotItemName = Replace(sItemPattern, "ThisItem", vItemsToBeVisible(lNdx))
    'attempt to make specified item the only visible item
    On Error Resume Next
    pvf.VisibleItemsList = Array(sPivotItemName)
    On Error GoTo 0
    'if item doesn't exist in field, this will be false
    If LCase$(sPivotItemName) = LCase$(pvf.VisibleItemsList(1)) Then
        lFilterItemCount = lFilterItemCount + 1
        vFilterArray(lFilterItemCount) = sPivotItemName
    End If
Next lNdx
'if at least one existing item found, filter pivot using array
If lFilterItemCount > 0 Then
    ReDim Preserve vFilterArray(1 To lFilterItemCount)
    pvf.VisibleItemsList = vFilterArray
Else
```

```
    sReturnMsg = "No matching items found."
    pvf.VisibleItemsList = vSaveVisibleItemsList
End If
pvf.Parent.ManualUpdate = False
sOLAP_FilterByItemList = sReturnMsg
End Function
```

Creating a custom sort order

This utility was submitted by Wei Jiang of Wuhan City, China.

By default, Excel enables you to sort lists numerically or alphabetically, but sometimes that is not what is needed. For example, a client might need each day's sales data sorted by the default division order of belts, handbags, watches, wallets, and everything else. Although you can manually set up a custom series and sort using it, if you're creating an automated workbook for other users, that might not be an option. This utility uses a custom sort order list to sort a range of data into the default division order and then deletes the custom sort order. Figure 13-2 shows the results before deleting the list:

▲	A	B	C	D	E	F	G	H	I
1	Date	Category	# sold						Belts
2	1/1/2018	Belts	15						Handbags
3	1/1/2018	Wallets	17						Watches
4	1/2/2018	Belts	17						Wallets
5	1/2/2018	Wallets	18						Everything Else
6	1/3/2018	Wallets	19						
7	1/3/2018	Handbags	20						

FIGURE 13-2 When you use the macro, the list in A:C is sorted first by date and then by the custom sort list in column I.

```
Sub CustomSort()
'add the custom list to Custom Lists
Application.AddCustomList ListArray:=Range("I1:I5")
'get the list number
nIndex = Application.GetCustomListNum(Range("I1:I5").Value)
'Now, we could sort a range with the custom list.
'Note, we should use nIndex + 1 as the custom list number here,
'for the first one is Normal order
Range("A2:C16").Sort Key1:=Range("B2"), Order1:=xlAscending, _
    Header:=xlNo, Orientation:=xlSortColumns, _
    OrderCustom:=nIndex + 1
Range("A2:C16").Sort Key1:=Range("A2"), Order1:=xlAscending, _
    Header:=xlNo, Orientation:=xlSortColumns
'At the end, we should remove this custom list...
Application.DeleteCustomList nIndex
End Sub
```

Creating a cell progress indicator

Here is another utility submitted by the prolific Tom Urtis.

I have to admit, the conditional formatting options in Excel, such as data bars, are fantastic. However, there still isn't an option for a visual like the example shown in Figure 13-3. The following utility builds a progress indicator in column C, based on entries in columns A and B:

```
Private Sub Worksheet_Change(ByVal Target As Range)
If Target.Column > 2 Or Target.Cells.Count > 1 Then Exit Sub
If Application.IsNumber(Target.Value) = False Then
  Application.EnableEvents = False
  Application.Undo
  Application.EnableEvents = True
  MsgBox "Numbers only please."
  Exit Sub
End If
Select Case Target.Column
  Case 1
    If Target.Value > Target.Offset(0, 1).Value Then
      Application.EnableEvents = False
      Application.Undo
      Application.EnableEvents = True
      MsgBox "Value in column A may not be larger than value " & _
        "in column B."
      Exit Sub
    End If
  Case 2
    If Target.Value < Target.Offset(0, -1).Value Then
      Application.EnableEvents = False
      Application.Undo
      Application.EnableEvents = True
      MsgBox "Value in column B may not be smaller " & _
        "than value in column A."
      Exit Sub
    End If
End Select
Dim x As Long
x = Target.Row
Dim z As String
z = Range("B" & x).Value - Range("A" & x).Value
With Range("C" & x)
  .Formula = "=IF(RC[-1]<=RC[-2],REPT(""n"",RC[-1])&" & _
    "REPT(""n"",RC[-2]-RC[-1]),REPT(""n"",RC[-2])&" & _
    "REPT(""o"",RC[-1]-RC[-2]))"
  .Value = .Value
  .Font.Name = "Wingdings"
  .Font.ColorIndex = 1
  .Font.Size = 10
  If Len(Range("A" & x)) <> 0 Then
    .Characters(1, (.Characters.Count - z)).Font.ColorIndex = 3
    .Characters(1, (.Characters.Count - z)).Font.Size = 12
  End If
End With
End Sub
```

A	B	C
Progress made	Progress required	Visual representation of progress made vs progress completed
11	15	■■■■■■■■■■■□□□□
14	20	■■■■■■■■■■■■■■□□□□□□
1	5	■□□□□
4	10	■■■■□□□□□□
4	10	■■■■□□□□□□
10	10	■■■■■■■■■■
8	10	■■■■■■■■□□
	10	□□□□□□□□□□

FIGURE 13-3 You can use indicators in cells to show progress.

Using a protected password box

This utility was submitted by Daniel Klann of Sydney, Australia. Daniel works mainly with VBA in Excel and Access but dabbles in all sorts of languages.

Using an input box for password protection has a major security flaw: The characters being entered are easily viewable. This program changes the characters to asterisks as they are entered—just like a real password field (see Figure 13-4). Note that the code that follows does not work in 64-bit Excel. Refer to Chapter 23, "The Windows Application Programming Interface (API)," for information on modifying the code for 64-bit Excel.

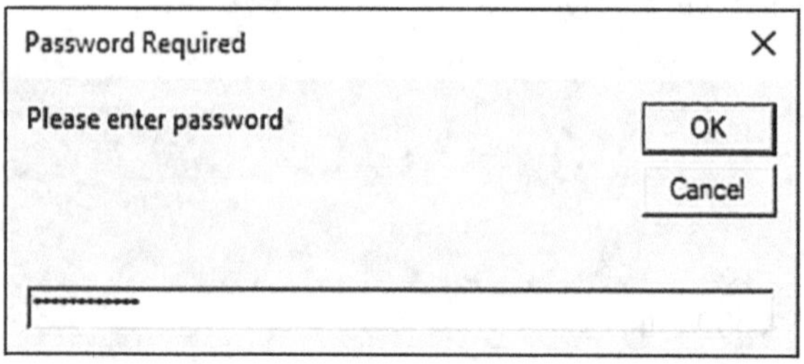

FIGURE 13-4 You can use an input box as a secure password field.

Here is the utility:

```
Private Declare PtrSafe Function CallNextHookEx Lib "user32" (ByVal hHook As _
   LongPtr, ByVal ncode As Long, ByVal wParam As LongPtr, lParam As Any) _
   As LongPtr

Private Declare PtrSafe Function GetModuleHandle Lib "kernel32" Alias _
   "GetModuleHandleA" (ByVal lpModuleName As String) As LongPtr

Private Declare PtrSafe Function SetWindowsHookEx Lib "user32" Alias _
   "SetWindowsHookExA" (ByVal idHook As Long, ByVal lpfn As LongPtr, ByVal hmod As _
   LongPtr, ByVal dwThreadId As Long) As LongPtr
```

```
Private Declare PtrSafe Function UnhookWindowsHookEx Lib "user32" (ByVal hHook _
    As LongPtr) As Long

Private Declare PtrSafe Function SendDlgItemMessage Lib "user32" Alias _
    "SendDlgItemMessageA" (ByVal hDlg As LongPtr, ByVal nIDDlgItem As Long, ByVal _
    wMsg As Long, ByVal wParam As Long, ByVal lParam As Long) As Long

Private Declare PtrSafe Function GetClassName Lib "user32" Alias _
    "GetClassNameA" (ByVal hwnd As LongPtr, ByVal lpClassName As String, ByVal _
    nMaxCount As Long) As Long

Private Declare PtrSafe Function GetCurrentThreadId Lib "kernel32" () As Long

'Constants to be used in our API functions
Private Const EM_SETPASSWORDCHAR = &HCC
Private Const WH_CBT = 5
Private Const HCBT_ACTIVATE = 5
Private Const HC_ACTION = 0
Private hHook As LongPtr

Public Function NewProc(ByVal lngCode As Long, ByVal wParam As Long, ByVal _
    lParam As Long) As LongPtr
Dim RetVal
Dim strClassName As String, lngBuffer As Long
If lngCode < HC_ACTION Then
    NewProc = CallNextHookEx(hHook, lngCode, wParam, lParam)
    Exit Function
End If
strClassName = String$(256, " ")
lngBuffer = 255
If lngCode = HCBT_ACTIVATE Then    'A window has been activated
    RetVal = GetClassName(wParam, strClassName, lngBuffer)
    'Check for class name of the Inputbox
    If Left$(strClassName, RetVal) = "#32770" Then
        'Change the edit control to display the password character *.
        'You can change the Asc("*") as you please.
        SendDlgItemMessage wParam, &H1324, EM_SETPASSWORDCHAR, Asc("*"), &H0
    End If
End If
'This line will ensure that any other hooks that may be in place are
'called correctly.
CallNextHookEx hHook, lngCode, wParam, lParam
End Function


Public Function InputBoxDK(Prompt, Optional Title, Optional Default, Optional _
    XPos, Optional YPos, Optional HelpFile, Optional Context) As String
Dim lngModHwnd As LongPtr, lngThreadID As Long
lngThreadID = GetCurrentThreadId
lngModHwnd = GetModuleHandle(vbNullString)

hHook = SetWindowsHookEx(WH_CBT, AddressOf NewProc, lngModHwnd, lngThreadID)
On Error Resume Next
InputBoxDK = InputBox(Prompt, Title, Default, XPos, YPos, HelpFile, Context)
UnhookWindowsHookEx hHook
End Function
```

```
Sub HiddenPassword()
If InputBoxDK("Please enter password", "Password Required") <> "password" Then
  MsgBox "Sorry, that was not a correct password."
Else
  MsgBox "Correct Password! Come on in."
End If
End Sub
```

Selecting with `SpecialCells`

This utility was submitted by Ivan F. Moala of Auckland, New Zealand.

Typically, when you want to find certain values, text, or formulas in a range, the range is selected, and each cell is tested. The following utility shows how you can use `SpecialCells` to select only the desired cells. Having fewer cells to check speeds up your code.

The following code ran in the blink of an eye on my machine. However, the version that checked each cell in the range (A1:Z20000) took 14 seconds—an eternity in the automation world!

```
Sub SpecialRange()
Dim TheRange As Range
Dim oCell As Range
Set TheRange = Range("A1:Z20000").SpecialCells(xlCellTypeConstants, xlTextValues)
For Each oCell In TheRange
  If oCell.Text = "Your Text" Then
    MsgBox oCell.Address
    MsgBox TheRange.Cells.Count
  End If
Next oCell
End Sub
```

Resetting a table's format

Here's another utility submitted by Zack Barresse.

Tables are great tools to use, but they're not perfect. One issue you'll eventually run into is a table's formatting acting up. For example, formatting might suddenly no longer be applied to new rows. The following procedure resets a table's format so it functions properly:

```
Sub ResetFormat(ByVal Table As ListObject, _
  Optional ByVal RetainNumberFormats As Boolean = True)
Dim Formats() As Variant
Dim ColumnStep As Long
If Table.Parent.ProtectContents = True Then
  MsgBox "The worksheet is protected.", vbExclamation, "Whoops!"
  Exit Sub
End If
If RetainNumberFormats Then
  ReDim Formats(Table.ListColumns.Count - 1)
  For ColumnStep = 1 To Table.ListColumns.Count
```

```
      On Error Resume Next
      Formats(ColumnStep - 1) = Table.ListColumns(ColumnStep). _
        DataBodyRange.NumberFormat
      On Error GoTo 0
      If IsEmpty(Formats(ColumnStep - 1)) Then
        Formats(ColumnStep - 1) = "General"
      End If
    Next ColumnStep
  End If
  Table.Range.Style = "Normal"
  If RetainNumberFormats Then
    For ColumnStep = 1 To Table.ListColumns.Count
      On Error Resume Next
      Table.ListColumns(ColumnStep).DataBodyRange.NumberFormat = _
        Formats(ColumnStep - 1)
      On Error GoTo 0
      If Err.Number <> 0 Then
        Table.ListColumns(ColumnStep).DataBodyRange.NumberFormat = _
          "General"
        Err.Clear
      End If
    Next ColumnStep
  End If
End Sub
```

Using VBA Extensibility to add code to new workbooks

Say that you have a macro that moves data to a new workbook for the regional managers. What if you also need to copy macros to the new workbook? You can use VBA Extensibility to import modules to a workbook or to actually write lines of code to the workbook.

To use any of the following examples, you must trust access to VBA by going to the Developer tab, choosing Macro Security, and checking Trust Access To The VBA Project Object Model.

> **Note** Changing this setting is a matter of trust, since it gives your code permission to modify other projects—a potential security risk if misused. An alternative solution would be to create a template workbook with the required code in it and transfer the data to new workbooks based on that template.

The easiest way to use VBA Extensibility is to export a complete module or userform from the current project and import it into the new workbook. Perhaps you have an application with thousands of lines of code, and you want to create a new workbook with data for the regional manager and give her three macros to enable custom formatting and printing. Place all of these macros in a module called modToRegion. Macros in this module also call the frmRegion userform. The following code transfers this code from the current workbook to the new workbook:

```
Sub MoveDataAndMacro()
Dim WSD as worksheet
```

```
Set WSD = Worksheets("Report")
'Copy Report to a new workbook
WSD.Copy
'The active workbook is now the new workbook
'Delete any old copy of the module from C
On Error Resume Next
'Delete any stray copies from hard drive
Kill ("C:\temp\ModToRegion.bas")
Kill ("C:\temp\frmRegion.frm")
On Error GoTo 0
'Export module & form from this workbook
ThisWorkbook.VBProject.VBComponents("ModToRegion").Export _
  ("C:\temp\ModToRegion.bas")
ThisWorkbook.VBProject.VBComponents("frmRegion").Export _
  ("C:\temp\frmRegion. frm")
'Import to new workbook
ActiveWorkbook.VBProject.VBComponents.Import ("C:\temp\ModToRegion.bas")
ActiveWorkbook.VBProject.VBComponents.Import ("C:\temp\frmRegion.frm")
On Error Resume Next
Kill ("C:\temp\ModToRegion.bas")
Kill ("C:\temp\frmRegion.bas")
On Error GoTo 0
End Sub
```

This method works if you need to move modules or userforms to a new workbook. However, what if you need to write some code for the Workbook_Open macro in the ThisWorkbook module? There are two tools to use. The Lines method enables you to return a particular set of code lines from a given module. The InsertLines method enables you to insert code lines into a new module.

> **Note** With each call to InsertLines, you must insert a complete macro. Excel attempts to compile the code after each call to InsertLines. If you insert lines that do not completely compile, Excel might crash with a general protection fault (GPF).

```
Sub MoveDataAndMacro()
Dim WSD as worksheet
Dim WBN as Workbook
Dim WBCodeMod1 As Object, WBCodeMod2 As Object
Set WSD = Worksheets("Report")
'Copy Report to a new workbook
WSD.Copy
'The active workbook is now the new workbook
Set WBN = ActiveWorkbook
'Copy the Workbook level Event handlers
Set WBCodeMod1 = ThisWorkbook.VBProject.VBComponents("ThisWorkbook") _
  .CodeModule
Set WBCodeMod2 = WBN.VBProject.VBComponents("ThisWorkbook").CodeModule
WBCodeMod2.InsertLines 1, WBCodeMod1.Lines(1, WBCodeMod1.countoflines)
End Sub
```

Converting a fixed-width report to a data set

This is my own submission. I've been writing a lot of cleaning programs for clients lately and realized this was a good example of using a custom object, collection, and array to accomplish the task. Also included is a function for checking if a record exists in a collection.

Imagine you request customer information and receive the data in a report format, as shown in Figure 13-5. Each customer record consists of two rows, some information is missing, and there are duplicate records.

	A			
Name	Email	Address	City	Company	State
1	Name	Email	Address	City	Company	State
2	Ahmed Barrera		442-4673 Egestas. Road	Indianapolis		IN
3						
4	Alana Brooks		P.O. Box 356, 7377 Erat St.	Henderson		NV
5		dapibus.rutrum@cursus.com			Scelerisque Inc.	
6	Alice Sharp		8548 Ac Rd.	Cleveland		OH
7		gravida.molestie@Cras.net			Integer Sem Elit Ltd	
8	Ahmed Barrera			Indianapolis		IN
9		Cras@eu.net				
10	Ahmed Barrera			Indianapolis		IN
11					Adipiscing Lobortis Risus Consulting	
12	Allegra Silva		Ap #168-1770 Fusce Avenue	Hartford		CT
13		tincidunt@blanditNamnulla.ca			Metus In LLP	

FIGURE 13-5 Extracting data from a report may seem nearly impossible, but with a little ingenuity and code, it can be done.

The custom object is used to clean and organize the customer data. The collection is used to ensure I only have unique records, but also allows me to merge duplicate records. Finally, the array is sized for just the unique records and quickly places the results on the sheet.

Place the following in a class module named clsRecord:

```
Private m_UserName As String
Private m_StreetAddress As String
Private m_City As String
Private m_State As String
Private m_Company As String
Private m_Email As String

Public Property Let currentRecord(RHS As String)
'the 2 row record is broken up when it's passed in
CleanRecord RHS
End Property
Public Property Get UserName() As String
UserName = m_UserName
End Property
Public Property Get StreetAddress() As String
StreetAddress = m_StreetAddress
End Property
Public Property Get City() As String
City = m_City
End Property
```

```vba
Public Property Get State() As String
State = m_State
End Property
Public Property Get Company() As String
Company = m_Company
End Property
Public Property Get Email() As String
Email = m_Email
End Property


Private Sub CleanRecord(ByVal curRecord As String)
If Len(Trim(curRecord)) = 0 Then Exit Sub 'no data
'if some data is missing, it can throw off the Mid statements
'so we use On Error Resume Next to keep the code moving
On Error Resume Next
If Trim(Left(curRecord, 1)) <> "" Then
  'if there's data in position 1, we have a 1st row record
  If m_UserName = "" Then m_UserName = Trim(Left(curRecord, 34))
  If m_StreetAddress = "" Then m_StreetAddress = Trim(Mid(curRecord, 35, 45))
  If m_City = "" Then m_City = Trim(Mid(curRecord, 80, 37))
  If m_State = "" Then m_State = _
    Trim(Mid(curRecord, 117, Len(curRecord) - 116))
Else
  'else, it's a 2nd row record
  If m_Email = "" Then m_Email = Trim(Mid(curRecord, 18, 83))
  If m_Company = "" Then m_Company = _
    Trim(Mid(curRecord, 101, Len(curRecord) - 100))
End If
On Error GoTo 0
End Sub
```

Place the following in a standard module:

```vba
Enum Report
  UserName = 1
  StreetAddress
  City
  State
  Email
  Company
End Enum
'see Chapter 4, "Laying the groundwork with variables and structures,"
'for information on using Enum

Sub CleanReport()
Dim cRecord As clsRecord
Dim AllRecords As Collection: Set AllRecords = New Collection
Dim rawData, FinalData
Dim errMessage As String, UserNameKey As String
Dim eaRecord As Long
rawData = Worksheets("Data").Range("A1:A203")
On Error GoTo errHandler
```

```
      For eaRecord = 2 To UBound(rawData) Step 2
        UserNameKey = Trim(Left(rawData(eaRecord, 1), 34))
        'check if we already have the record in the collection
        If GetFromCollection(UserNameKey, AllRecords, cRecord, True, errMessage) Then
          'delete the original
          AllRecords.Remove UserNameKey
        Else
          'initialize a new Record
          Set cRecord = New clsRecord
        End If
        'send current record set to class for cleaning
        cRecord.currentRecord = rawData(eaRecord, 1)
        cRecord.currentRecord = rawData(eaRecord + 1, 1)
        'save the record to the collection
        AllRecords.Add cRecord, CStr(UserNameKey)
      Next eaRecord
      'place final records into array
      ReDim FinalData(1 To AllRecords.Count, 1 To 6)
      For eaRecord = 1 To AllRecords.Count
        Set cRecord = AllRecords(eaRecord)
        FinalData(eaRecord, Report.UserName) = cRecord.UserName
        FinalData(eaRecord, Report.StreetAddress) = cRecord.StreetAddress
        FinalData(eaRecord, Report.City) = cRecord.City
        FinalData(eaRecord, Report.State) = cRecord.State
        FinalData(eaRecord, Report.Email) = cRecord.Email
        FinalData(eaRecord, Report.Company) = cRecord.Company
      Next eaRecord
      With Worksheets("Report")
        .Range("A1").Resize(, 6).Value = _
          Array("Name", "Address", "City", "State", "Email", "Company")
        .Range("A2").Resize(UBound(FinalData), UBound(FinalData, 2)).Value = FinalData
      End With
errHandler:
      If Err.Number <> 0 Then
        MsgBox Err.Number & ": " & Err.Description
      End If
      Set AllRecords = Nothing
      Set cRecord = Nothing
End Sub


Function GetFromCollection(ByVal KeyName As String, _
        ByVal CollectionToSearch As Collection, ByRef ReturnedValue As Variant, _
        ByVal ReturnObject As Boolean, ByRef errMessage As String) As Boolean
      GetFromCollection = True
      On Error Resume Next
      If ReturnObject Then
        Set ReturnedValue = CollectionToSearch(KeyName)
      Else
        ReturnedValue = CollectionToSearch(KeyName)
      End If
      If Err.Number <> 0 Then GetFromCollection = False
      On Error GoTo 0
End Function
```

Leveling up: Real project issues, real solutions

Every Excel project has multiple ways to reach a solution. This section walks you through how I approach specific challenges, based on my style, priorities, and what I've found effective in the real world. These aren't the only solutions, but they're solid ones that demonstrate practical application of the techniques covered in this book.

You won't find full code listings here. Instead, I'll point you to the relevant chapters where the concepts are explained in detail. For the more advanced examples where I've provided sample code, check out the ProjectFilesChapter13-ExcelPower.xlsm workbook. The Discussion sheet in that file will guide you to the appropriate workbook.

Filtering out large numbers of rows efficiently

When I'm handed a massive data set, my first instinct is "Can I make this smaller?" Sure, putting it in memory really speeds it up, but eventually, the decrease in speed is noticed. One of my favorite tools for removing unwanted rows is the Advanced Filter. It's built-in and optimized for speed—I can't think of a coding method that would be faster.

You could also use Power Query, especially if you're already working with raw M code and controlling queries through VBA. Power Query is well-suited for scenarios where filtering needs to happen before the data hits the worksheet—especially when pulling from external sources. It's a different layer of control: more about shaping the import logic than managing what's already on the sheet. But I'll admit it: I'm old school. For now, Advanced Filter is still my go-to when I want quick, no-fuss row reduction directly from VBA.

Refer to Chapter 11, "Data mining with Advanced Filter," for more information on setting up criteria ranges and extracting filtered results. Refer to Chapter 18, "Reading from the web using M and VBA," for more information on creating queries in Power Query and using VBA to control certain variables.

Importing daily report data into an existing table

You receive a report every day and want to make it easy for the user to press a button and have the data imported directly into an existing table in Excel—no manual copy and paste, no reformatting. The file is always structured the same way, and the goal is simply to append new data cleanly.

If the report file always has the same name and location, the easiest approach is to store the full file path in a settings table. This way, the user can update the path if the report ever moves, and your code stays flexible. If the file name changes daily or is manually selected, you can still store the most recent folder path in the settings table and have the program start the file picker there. See this chapter's section "Using a settings table" for more information on how I set up and retrieve data from lookup tables.

Once the path is established, use `OpenText` to bring the file into memory, then dump the results into the table that holds all records. The idea is to fully automate the import so that the user doesn't have to touch the worksheet structure at all.

You'll find examples of bringing the data into memory in this chapter's sections "Importing and deleting a CSV file" and "Reading a text file into memory and parsing."

Transposing array data before writing to the worksheet

When you're building a dynamic 2D array in VBA, you typically want to add rows as you go. But since VBA only allows you to apply `ReDim Preserve` on the last dimension, that means you have to size your array as (`ColumnCount, RowCount`). In other words, columns come first because they're fixed, and rows go second so they can expand.

This works fine for processing in memory, but when it comes time to write the array to a worksheet, Excel expects the opposite: (`Row, Column`). If you skip the transpose, you'll end up with rotated data. The solution is simple—use `Application.Transpose` right before dumping the array to the sheet.

See "Transposing an array" in Chapter 8, "Arrays," for an example of this approach and how to structure the array correctly from the beginning.

Tracking dynamic columns

In some projects, you need to track only specific columns from a data table, but those columns might move or have their headers changed over time. Instead of hardcoding their positions or names, you can let the user define which columns to track by using a settings table. This table typically has two columns: Data Header (the actual header from the raw data) and Code Header (the internal name your code expects). This setup allows your code to remain stable while giving users the flexibility to update mappings as needed.

The program reads this list into memory and loops through each entry. As each Data Header match is found, the column number is stored in a collection using the Code Header as the key.

From that point on, any time the code needs to reference a specific field, it pulls the position from the collection using the key. This keeps the logic clean and flexible, even if the source file changes layout.

See Chapter 9, "Creating custom objects and collections," for information on creating and using collections.

In situations where the client doesn't need this kind of flexibility, I still plan for the future. In those cases, I use an `Enum` to track the locations of the headers. It's also useful to track the headers for my final report. The setup for raw data, where I may only care about some columns, might look like this:

```
Enum colsRawData
  SKU = 1
  prodDescription
  prodValue
  'skip columns not needed
  InStock = 8
  LastOrderDate = 25
  [_last] 'count marker
End Enum
```

Then, when I need to refer to a column, I don't have to remember where the column is, just the code name—like this:

```
ProductValue = myArray(curRow, colsRawData.prodValue)
```

Refer to "Using `Enum` to create custom constants" in Chapter 4, "Laying the groundwork with variables and structures," for an explanation of how `Enum` can help structure your code.

Converting a data set with multi-row records into a clean data set

Some reports span multiple rows per record, contain duplicate entries, or have missing values that need to be filled in. Others require combining fields from multiple partial records into a single complete one. These are the kinds of problems best handled with full control in VBA.

Here's my usual approach to projects like this:

1. Put the data set into an array for looping (Chapter 8, "Arrays").

2. While looping, store each record in a custom object (Chapter 9, "Creating custom objects and collections").

3. Put each custom object into a collection.

Once the data has been processed, I generate the report:

4. Create an empty array based on the number of objects in the collection and the number of columns in the report.

5. Loop through the collection, placing each value from the collection into the array.

6. Dump the array into a table on a sheet.

For example, in "Converting a fixed-width report to a data set," the data is loaded into memory and parsed line by line. As each line is processed, the code either creates or updates a custom object—depending on whether the record is new, incomplete, or a duplicate that needs merging. These objects are stored in a collection for easy access.

Once all lines are processed and the final records are assembled, the collection is converted into an array matching the output structure, and that array is written to a table in the workbook.

This method gives you complete flexibility to reshape fragmented data or inconsistent data into complete, clean records, whether that means combining totals, filling gaps, or restructuring messy input. A good code sample of this can be found in Chapter 9's case study, "Creating a collection to hold custom objects."

Using templates to generate reports

I rarely code the creation of charts or pivot tables. Instead, I use a template with two sheets: one containing a small sample data table, the other containing the report object (chart or pivot table) already connected to that table. I copy both sheets, update the table with the real data, and refresh the workbook so the report object reflects the new data.

This method allows me to set up things like a logo, contact info, and any other elements the client wants on every report. It also gives the client full control over the final layout. For example, they can change the chart type or adjust the fields used in the pivot table.

There are two ways you can set this up:

- **Use a template workbook and open a copy of it**   This is my preferred method when I'm generating multiple reports at one time, for example, individual sales rep reports that will be emailed out separately.

- **Use template sheets stored in the program workbook**   I make copies of these sheets either within the same workbook or into a new one. I usually use this approach when the report is for a single user.

Refer to this chapter's downloadable workbook for an example method.

Copying existing charts to a new workbook

Templates make things easier, especially when working with structured tables, but they aren't always an option. I had a client who needed to copy a specific chart to a report workbook and attach it to that workbook's data. The catch? His data wasn't always in the same location or in a listobject. Luckily, the series labels and data rows were consistent. But I had to figure out the data columns to use. Because of the inconsistencies, I had to rebuild the full SERIES formula manually.

Each series in a collection has a formula. The basic SERIES formula format is:

```
=SERIES(Name, XValues, YValues, PlotOrder)
```

A simple SERIES formula is when you have a single consecutive range for each parameter, like this:

```
=SERIES(Sheet1!$A$1, Sheet1!$B$2:$B$5, Sheet1!$C$2:$C$5, 1)
```

But my project included more complex parameters with non-consecutive ranges. Parameters containing multiple ranges are wrapped in parentheses:

```
=SERIES(Sheet1!$N$13,(Sheet1!$L$16:$M$18, Sheet1!$L$21:$M$22), _
  (Sheet1!$N$16:$N$18, Sheet1!$N$21:$N$22),1)
```

In that case:

- Name = Sheet1!$N$13

- XValues = Sheet1!$L$16:$M$18, Sheet1!$L$21:$M$22

- YValues = Sheet1!$N$16:$N$18, Sheet1!$N$21:$N$22

- PlotOrder = 1

I had to do the following to update the data source for a chart copied to a new workbook:

1. Remove the external workbook name by using REPLACE.

2. Extract the sheet name. I'll be putting one back, but I found it easier to work with the range addresses without a sheet name included.

3. Remove =Series(from the start and the formula's closing parenthesis.

4. Split the remaining formula using a comma delimiter. Some parameters—like XValues or YValues—may include multiple ranges wrapped in parentheses, which also contain commas. We'll handle those next.

5. Loop through the array you just created. If you find a value starting with a left parenthesis, loop forward to find the closing parenthesis and join the parts back together. You'll end up with a new array where each value is a parameter of the formula (Name, XValues, YValues, and PlotOrder).

6. Loop through those parameters. If a parameter has multiple ranges, use Split with a comma delimiter. If it's a single range, store it in a single-element array so you can process everything the same way.

7. Update the ranges as needed. For example:

   - Pie chart: YValues only

   - Line chart: both X and Y

   - Stacked column: possibly all three

8. Rebuild the SERIES formula string by joining the final parameter values. Make sure to preserve parentheses around grouped ranges.

9. Apply the new formula back to the chart:

```
.SeriesCollection(i).Formula = newFormula
```

10. If working with multiple series, loop through SeriesCollection.

Refer to this chapter's project workbook for a detailed example. But here's a simplified example of the code for breaking apart and rebuilding the formula:

```
Sub RebuildSeriesFormula_bookVersion()
Dim oldFormula As String, newFormula As String
Dim primaryParts(0 To 3) As String
Dim paramParts() As String
Dim rawParts() As String
Dim tempParam As String, temp As String
Dim i As Long, j As Long, k As Long
'Original formula with workbook and sheet name already removed
oldFormula = _
   "=SERIES($N$13,($L$16:$M$18, $L$21:$M$22), ($N$16:$N$18, $N$21:$N$22),1)"
'Remove =SERIES( and the closing parenthesis
oldFormula = Replace(oldFormula, "=SERIES(", "")
oldFormula = Left(oldFormula, Len(oldFormula) - 1)
'Split formula into raw parts using commas
rawParts = Split(oldFormula, ",")
k = 0
i = 0
'Group broken pieces of multi-range parameters back together
Do While i <= UBound(rawParts) And k <= 3
  temp = Trim(rawParts(i))
  If Left(temp, 1) = "(" Then
    Do While InStr(temp, ")") = 0 And i < UBound(rawParts)
      i = i + 1
      temp = temp & "," & Trim(rawParts(i))
    Loop
  End If
  primaryParts(k) = temp
  k = k + 1
  i = i + 1
Loop
'Loop through the four main parameters
For i = 0 To UBound(primaryParts)
  tempParam = Trim(primaryParts(i))
  'Check for multi-range parameter (wrapped in parentheses)
  If Left(tempParam, 1) = "(" And Right(tempParam, 1) = ")" Then
    tempParam = Mid(tempParam, 2, Len(tempParam) - 2)
    paramParts = Split(tempParam, ",")
  Else
    ReDim paramParts(0)
    paramParts(0) = tempParam
  End If
  'Update each sub-range
  'in this case, just removing spaces
  For j = 0 To UBound(paramParts)
    paramParts(j) = Trim(paramParts(j))
  Next j
```

```
    'Reassemble the parameter, rewrap with parentheses if needed
    If UBound(paramParts) > 0 Then
        primaryParts(i) = "(" & Join(paramParts, ",") & ")"
    Else
        primaryParts(i) = paramParts(0)
    End If
Next i
'Rebuild the full SERIES formula
newFormula = "=SERIES(" & Join(primaryParts, ",") & ")"
'Preview result
Debug.Print newFormula
End Sub
```

Your actual process may differ from mine, but hopefully this review will emphasize what you need to watch out for and where those issues might be. This project was difficult because the data sets were not in an optimal layout—set columns, rows growing, no blank rows or columns between data. Having data in a listobject makes it easier for programmers and Excel to work with. Blank rows and columns, and transposed data should be left to reports, not data sets.

> **Note** Pie charts are an exception. They should always be built from summarized data. If your source is a well-structured table, that means summarizing the data first—such as pulling totals for a specific month or category—and then charting that result. You're not charting the data set directly; you're charting a summary drawn from it.

Reducing API access token requests

In Chapter 18, "Reading from the web using M and VBA," the queries retrieved a new access token with every call. That means every time you search for an artist, album, or track:

- You're requesting a new token every time, even if the old one still works.

- This can waste your free token quota, especially when testing.

> **Note** The following steps work in conjunction with the workbook created in Chapter 18.

To handle these issues, let's cache the token in memory for about an hour:

- Create a blank query called `shared_token`:

    1. In Power Query, go to the Home tab.

    2. Click New Source | Blank Query.

    3. In the formula bar, type: **= fnGetToken()**.

    4. Rename this query to **shared_token**.

- Create a second query called `shared_time`:

   1. Click New Source | Blank Query.

   2. In the formula bar, type: = **DateTime.LocalNow()**

   3. Rename this query to **shared_time**.

Open the existing `config` query and modify it so it looks like this:

```
let
  current = DateTime.LocalNow(),
  duration = try Duration.From(current - shared_time) otherwise #duration(1,0,0,0),
  isValid = duration < #duration(0,0,55,0),
  cachedToken = if isValid then shared_token else fnGetToken(),
  Settings = [
    clientId = "YOUR_APP_CLIENT_ID,
    clientSecret = "YOUR_APP_CLIENT_SECRET",
    Token = cachedToken,
    time = current
  ]
in
  Settings
```

Update your other queries so that wherever you have:

```
Token = fnGetToken()
```

Replace it with:

```
Token = config[Token]
```

That's it! Now, Power Query will check if the last token is less than 55 minutes old. If it is, it will be reused; otherwise, a new one will be obtained.

Generating reports in Word

Sometimes, a report is too complex for basic Word mail merge—maybe the layout is too intricate, or the user wants more control over the formatting and placement of the data. In these cases, an option is to automate Word using VBA and insert data into predefined bookmarks. This approach gives you full control over where and how data appears in the document. For details on using bookmarks and controlling Word from Excel, see Chapter 20, "Automating Word."

Since the method of insertion in Word depends on what you're inserting, such as text or a chart, projects that give clients the ability to add or change bookmarks should include a Type column in the configuration table. This lets the code handle each bookmark appropriately, based on whether it's inserting plain text, a chart, or something else. Refer to Table 13-1 for a general reference for common types and how they're typically handled in Word automation:

TABLE 13-1 Common insertion methods in Word

Type	Default Insertion/Paste Method	Notes
Text	`Bookmark.Range.Text = Value.`	Replaces the entire bookmark range. No formatting preserved.
Chart	Copy the Excel chart object, and then use `PasteSpecial`.	Usually, paste as Enhanced Metafile. Anchor inline or floating.
Picture	Insert via `.InlineShapes.AddPicture`.	Consider resizing or anchoring the layout.
Table	`PasteSpecial` as RTF or insert cell-by-cell.	Depends on whether formatting is preserved or built into Word.
Range Name	Use `Range("NamedRange").Copy`, and then paste.	Can be text or a table, depending on the range. Handle like a separate type if needed.
HTML	`PasteSpecial` as HTML format.	Requires Word to interpret formatting properly.
File	Insert as a linked or embedded object.	Use `.InlineShapes.AddOLEObject` if embedding.

Supporting users with different feature needs

Sometimes you're building one workbook for multiple users, but not all of them need the same features. One might require integration with a third-party system, while another doesn't. Rather than maintain separate versions, you can use compiler directives to include or exclude feature-specific code as needed. See the Chapter 4 section, "Managing code variations with compiler directives," for more information on compiler directives.

In one case, a user needed to connect to QuickBooks Desktop through a third-party service. To avoid issues for other users, I wrapped that logic in a compiler directive and used late binding to avoid triggering compile errors:

```
#Const QB = True 'Change to False for non-QuickBooks version
Public Sub ImportData()
#If QB Then
  'QuickBooks integration via third-party service
  Dim qbAPI As Object
  Set qbAPI = CreateObject("QuickBooksThirdParty.API.Handler")
  MsgBox "Starting import process..."
  'Example function
  qbAPI.ImportSales
  MsgBox "QuickBooks import completed."
#Else
  MsgBox "QuickBooks integration is not enabled for this version."
  Exit Sub
#End If
End Sub
```

This works because the project doesn't include an implicit reference to the QuickBooks library. Using late binding keeps the project portable and safe to compile. See Chapter 20, "Automating Word," for more information on libraries and early versus late binding.

Note Compiler directives are useful when you're maintaining separate builds of a workbook—such as enabling QuickBooks integration for one user, but leaving it out for others. But this approach isn't ideal if you're distributing the same workbook to numerous users. Every time you have to distribute an update, the `Const` value would have to be set for the users. For that reason, it's often better to use runtime logic (such as checking for a configuration file) when you want more flexibility without modifying the code itself.

Next steps

The utilities in this chapter aren't Excel's only source of programming power. User-defined functions (UDFs) enable you to create complex custom formulas to cover what Excel's functions don't. In Chapter 14, "Sample user-defined functions," you'll find out how to create and share your own functions.

Sample user-defined functions

In this chapter, you will:

- Learn how to create and share user-defined functions

- Review useful custom functions

- Learn how to create and share LAMBDA functions

Excel provides many built-in functions. However, sometimes, you need a complex custom function that Excel doesn't offer, such as a function that sums a range of cells based on their interior color.

So, what do you do? You could use the calculator next to you as you work your way down your list—but be careful not to enter the same number twice! Or, you could convert the data set to a table, set a SUBTOTAL function for visible cells in the total row, and filter by color. Both methods are time-consuming and prone to accidents. What to do?

You could write a procedure to solve this problem—after all, that's what this book is about. However, you have other options: *user-defined functions* (UDFs) and LAMBDA.

> **Note** If you plan on distributing LAMBDA functions, the user must be in Excel 365, preferably the latest build.

Creating user-defined functions

A User Defined Function (UDF) is just a standard VBA Function procedure—but one that's intended to be used directly on a worksheet, like a built-in Excel formula. Because of this, UDFs come with practical limitations: they must return a value that Excel can display, they shouldn't have side effects, such as deleting rows or triggering events, and while they can access external libraries, that's uncommon. In most cases, UDFs are designed to be simple, fast, and safe for cell-level use.

Once you've written a custom function in VBA, you can use it on the worksheet just like Excel's built-in functions, such as SUM. The user doesn't need to know anything about the code—just the function name and its required arguments.

> **Note** You can enter UDFs only into standard modules. `Sheet` and `ThisWorkbook` modules are a special type of module. If you enter a UDF in either of those modules, Excel does not recognize that you are creating a UDF.

Building a simple custom function

To learn the basics of UDFs, you'll build a custom function to add two values. After you've created it, you'll use it on a worksheet.

Insert a new module in the VB Editor. Type the following ADD function into the module to total the values in two different cells. The function has two arguments:

```
Add(Number1,Number2)
```

Number1 is the first number to add; Number2 is the second number to add:

```
Function Add(ByVal Number1 As Integer, ByVal Number2 As Integer) As Integer
Add = Number1 + Number2
End Function
```

Let's break this down:

- The function name is ADD.

- Arguments are placed in parentheses after the name of the function. This example has two arguments: Number1 and Number2. They are both of type integer. If you were to enter decimal values, such as 3.4 and 6.62, Excel will round them before they're even used in the calculation.

- `As Integer` defines the variable type of the result as a whole number.

- `ADD = Number1 + Number2` is the result of the function that is returned.

Here is how to use the function on a worksheet:

1. Type numbers into cells A1 and A2.

2. Select cell A3.

3. Press Shift+F3 to open the Insert Function dialog, or choose Formulas | Insert Function.

4. In the Insert Function dialog, select the User Defined category (see Figure 14-1).

5. Select the ADD function.

6. In the first argument box, select cell A1 (see Figure 14-2).

7. In the second argument box, select cell A2.

8. Click OK.

Congratulations! You have created your first custom function.

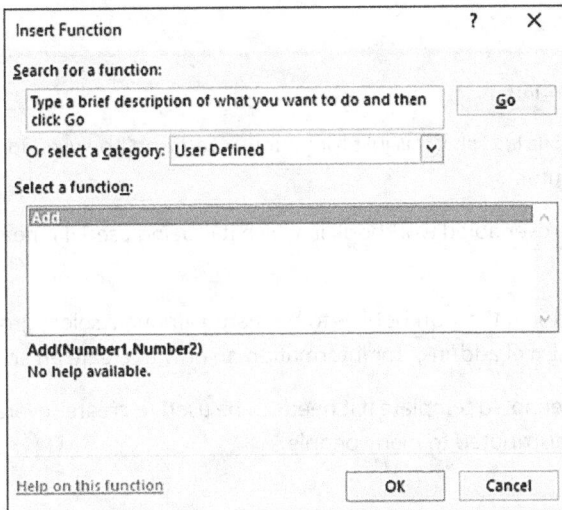

FIGURE 14-1 You can find your UDFs under the User Defined category of the Insert Function dialog.

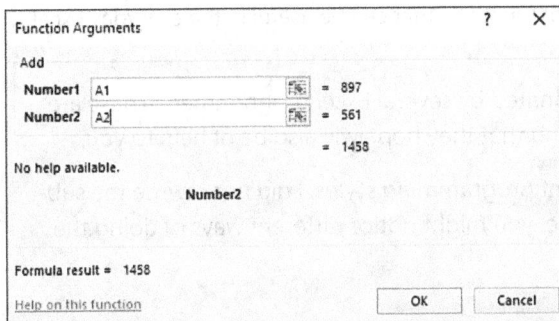

FIGURE 14-2 You can use the Function Arguments dialog to enter your arguments.

📝 **Note** You can easily share custom functions because users are not required to know how the function works. See the next section, "Sharing UDFs," for more information.

Most of the functions used on sheets can also be used in VBA and vice versa. However, in VBA, you call the UDF (ADD) from a procedure (Addition) like this:

```
Sub Addition ()
Dim Total as Integer
Total = Add (1,10) 'we use a user-defined function Add
MsgBox "The answer is: " & Total
End Sub
```

Sharing UDFs

Where you store a UDF affects how you can share it:

- **Personal.xlsb**—Store a UDF in `Personal.xlsb` if it is just for your use and won't be used in a workbook opened on another computer.

- **Workbook**—Store a UDF in the macro-enabled workbook in which it is being used if it needs to be distributed to many people.

- **Add-in**—Distribute a UDF via an add-in if the workbook is to be shared among a select group of people. See Chapter 26, "Creating Excel add-ins," for information on how to create an add-in.

- **Template**—Store a UDF in a macro-enabled template if it needs to be used to create several workbooks, and the workbooks are distributed to many people.

Useful custom Excel functions

The sections that follow include a sampling of functions that can be useful in the everyday Excel world.

> **Note** This chapter shows functions donated by several Excel programmers. These are functions that they have found useful and that they hope will also be of help to you.
>
> Different programmers have different programming styles. I did not rewrite the submissions. As you review the lines of code, you might notice different ways of doing the same task, such as referring to ranges.

Checking whether a workbook is open

There might be times when you need to check whether a workbook is open in the current Excel session. The following function returns `True` if a workbook is open and `False` if it is not:

```
BookOpen(Bk)
```

The argument is `Bk`, which is the name of the workbook being checked:

```
Function BookOpen(Bk As String) As Boolean
Dim T As Excel.Workbook
Err.Clear 'clears any errors
On Error Resume Next 'if the code runs into an error, it skips it and
'continues
Set T = Application.Workbooks(Bk)
BookOpen = Not T Is Nothing
'If the workbook is open, then T will hold the workbook object and
```

```
'therefore will NOT be Nothing
Err.Clear
On Error GoTo 0
End Function
```

Here is an example of using the function:

```
Sub OpenAWorkbook()
Dim IsOpen As Boolean
Dim BookName As String
BookName = "ProjectFilesChapter14.xlsm"
IsOpen = BookOpen(BookName) 'calling our function - don't forget the parameter
If IsOpen Then
    MsgBox BookName & " is already open!"
Else
    Workbooks.Open BookName
End If
End Sub
```

Checking whether a sheet in an open workbook exists

This function requires that the workbook(s) it checks be open. It returns `True` if the sheet is found and `False` if it is not:

```
WorksheetExists(SheetName, Optional TargetBook)
```

These are the arguments:

- SheetName—The name of the sheet being searched.

- TargetBook—(Optional) The name of the workbook that contains the sheet.

Here is the function. If the workbook argument is not provided, it uses the active workbook:

```
Function WorksheetExists(ByVal SheetName As String, _
    Optional TargetBook As Workbook) As Boolean
If TargetBook Is Nothing Then
    If ActiveWorkbook Is Nothing Then Exit Function
    Set TargetBook = ActiveWorkbook
End If
On Error Resume Next
WorksheetExists = CBool(Len(TargetBook.Worksheets(SheetName).Name) <> 0)
On Error GoTo 0
End Function
```

> **Note** CBool is a function that converts the expression between the parentheses to a Boolean value.

Here is an example of using this function:

```
Sub CheckForSheet()
'notice that only one parameter is passed; the workbook name is optional
If Not WorksheetExists("Sheet9") Then
  MsgBox "The worksheet exists!"
Else
  MsgBox "The worksheet does NOT exist!"
End If
End Sub
```

Counting the number of workbooks in a directory

This function searches the current directory and its subfolders if you want, counting all Excel macro workbook files (.xlsm), including hidden files, or just the ones starting with a string of letters:

```
NumFilesInCurDir (LikeText, Subfolders)
```

These are the arguments:

- LikeText—(Optional) A string value to search for; must include an asterisk (*), such as Mr*.

- Subfolders—(Optional) True to search subfolders, False (default) not to.

> **Note** FileSystemObject requires the Microsoft Scripting Runtime reference library. To enable this setting, go to Tools | References and check Microsoft Scripting Runtime.

This function is a recursive function, which means it calls itself until a specific condition is met—in this case, until all subfolders are processed. Here is the function:

```
Function NumFilesInCurDir(Optional strInclude As String = "", _
  Optional blnSubDirs As Boolean = False)
Dim fso As FileSystemObject
Dim fld As Folder
Dim fil As File
Dim subfld As Folder
Dim intFileCount As Integer
Dim strExtension As String
strExtension = "XLSM"
Set fso = New FileSystemObject
Set fld = fso.GetFolder(ThisWorkbook.Path)
For Each fil In fld.Files
  If Left(fil.Name, 2) <> "~$" And _
    UCase(fil.Name) Like "*" & UCase(strInclude) & "*." & _
    UCase(strExtension) Then
    intFileCount = intFileCount + 1
  End If
```

```
Next fil
If blnSubDirs Then
  For Each subfld In fld.Subfolders
    intFileCount = intFileCount + NumFilesInCurDir(strInclude, True)
  Next subfld
End If
NumFilesInCurDir = intFileCount
Set fso = Nothing
End Function
```

Here is an example of using this function:

```
Sub CountMyWkbks()
Dim MyFiles As Integer
MyFiles = NumFilesInCurDir("MrE*", True)
MsgBox MyFiles & " file(s) found"
End Sub
```

Retrieving the user ID

Ever need to keep a record of who saves changes to a workbook? With the USERID function, you can retrieve the name of the user who is logged in to a computer. Combine it with the function discussed in the "Retrieving permanent date and time" section later in this chapter, and you have a nice log file. You can also use the USERID function to set up user rights to a workbook:

```
WinUserName ()
```

No arguments are used with this function.

> **Note** The USERID function is an advanced function that uses the *application programming interface* (API), which is reviewed in Chapter 23, "The Windows Application Programming Interface (API)." The code is specific to 32-bit Excel. If you are running 64-bit Excel, refer to Chapter 23 for instructions on making necessary changes to ensure it works.

This first section (`Private` declarations) must be at the top of the module:

```
Private Declare Function WNetGetUser Lib "mpr.dll" Alias "WNetGetUserA" _
  (ByVal lpName As String, ByVal lpUserName As String, _
  lpnLength As Long) As Long
Private Const NO_ERROR = 0
Private Const ERROR_NOT_CONNECTED = 2250&
Private Const ERROR_MORE_DATA = 234
Private Const ERROR_NO_NETWORK = 1222&
Private Const ERROR_EXTENDED_ERROR = 1208&
Private Const ERROR_NO_NET_OR_BAD_PATH = 1203&
```

You can place the following section of code anywhere in the module, as long as it is below the preceding section:

```
Function WinUsername() As String
'variables
Dim strBuf As String, lngUser As Long, strUn As String
'clear buffer for user name from api func
strBuf = Space$(255)
'use api func WNetGetUser to assign user value to lngUser
'strBuf will have lots of blank spaces
lngUser = WNetGetUser("", strBuf, 255)
'if no error from function call
If lngUser = NO_ERROR Then
  'clear out blank space in strBuf and assign val to function
  strUn = Left(strBuf, InStr(strBuf, vbNullChar) - 1)
  WinUsername = strUn
Else
  'error, give up
  WinUsername = "Error :" & lngUser
End If
End Function
```

Here's an example of using this function:

```
Sub CheckUserRights()
Dim UserName As String
UserName = WinUsername
Select Case UserName
  Case "Administrator"
    MsgBox "Full Rights"
  Case "Guest"
    MsgBox "You cannot make changes"
  Case Else
    MsgBox "Limited Rights"
End Select
End Sub
```

Retrieving the date and time of the last save

This function retrieves the saved date and time of any workbook, including the current one:

```
LastSaved(FullPath)
```

Note The cell must be formatted for date and time to display the date/time correctly.

The argument is FullPath, a string showing the full path and file name of the file in question:

```
Function LastSaved(FullPath As String) As Date
LastSaved = FileDateTime(FullPath)
End Function
```

Retrieving permanent date and time

Because of the volatility of the NOW function, it isn't very useful for stamping a worksheet with the creation or editing date. Every time the workbook is opened or recalculated, the result of the NOW function is updated. The following UDF uses the NOW function. However, because you need to reenter the cell to update the function, it is much less volatile (see Figure 14-3).

No arguments are used with this function:

DateTime()

| 6/1/25 2:41 PM =NOW() |
| 6/1/25 2:40 PM =DateTime() |

FIGURE 14-3 Even after forcing a recalculation, the DateTime() cell shows the time when it was originally placed in the cell, whereas NOW() shows the current system time.

> **Note** The cell must be formatted correctly to display the date and time.

Here is the function:

```
Function DateTime()
DateTime = Now
End Function
```

Validating an email address

If you manage an email subscription list, you might receive invalid email addresses, such as addresses with a space before the "at" symbol (@). The IsEmailValid function can check addresses and confirm that they are proper email addresses (see Figure 14-4):

IsEmailValid (strEmail)

Tracy@ MrExcel.com	FALSE	<-a space after the @
ExcelGGirl@gmail.com	TRUE	
consult$@MrExcel.com	FALSE	<-invalid characters

FIGURE 14-4 Validating email addresses.

> **Note** This function cannot verify that an email address is already in use. It only checks the syntax to verify that the address might be legitimate.

The function's only argument is strEmail, an email address:

```
Function IsEmailValid(strEmail As String) As Boolean
Dim strArray As Variant
Dim strItem As Variant
Dim i As Long
Dim c As String
Dim blnIsItValid As Boolean
blnIsItValid = True
'count the @ in the string
i = Len(strEmail) - Len(Application.Substitute(strEmail, "@", ""))
'if there is more than one @, invalid email
If i <> 1 Then IsEmailValid = False: Exit Function
ReDim strArray(1 To 2)
'the following two lines place the text to the left and right
'of the @ in their own variables
strArray(1) = Left(strEmail, InStr(1, strEmail, "@", 1) - 1)
strArray(2) = Application.Substitute(Right(strEmail, Len(strEmail) - _
  Len(strArray(1))), "@", "")
For Each strItem In strArray
  'verify there is something in the variable.
  'If there isn't, then part of the email is missing
  If Len(strItem) <= 0 Then
    blnIsItValid = False
    IsEmailValid = blnIsItValid
    Exit Function
  End If
  'verify only valid characters in the email
  For i = 1 To Len(strItem)
    'lowercases all letters for easier checking
    c = LCase(Mid(strItem, i, 1))
    If InStr("abcdefghijklmnopqrstuvwxyz_-.", c) <= 0 _
      And Not IsNumeric(c) Then
      blnIsItValid = False
      IsEmailValid = blnIsItValid
      Exit Function
    End If
  Next i
  'verify that the first character of the left and right aren't periods
  If Left(strItem, 1) = "." Or Right(strItem, 1) = "." Then
    blnIsItValid = False
    IsEmailValid = blnIsItValid
    Exit Function
  End If
Next strItem
'verify there is a period in the right half of the address
If InStr(strArray(2), ".") <= 0 Then
  blnIsItValid = False
  IsEmailValid = blnIsItValid
  Exit Function
End If
i = Len(strArray(2)) - InStrRev(strArray(2), ".") 'locate the period
'verify that the number of letters corresponds to a valid domain
'extension
```

```
If i <> 2 And i <> 3 And i <> 4 Then
  blnIsItValid = False
  IsEmailValid = blnIsItValid
  Exit Function
End If
'verify that there aren't two periods together in the email
If InStr(strEmail, "..") > 0 Then
  blnIsItValid = False
  IsEmailValid = blnIsItValid
  Exit Function
End If
IsEmailValid = blnIsItValid
End Function
```

Summing cells based on interior color

Let's say you have created a list of how much each of your clients owes. From this list, you want to sum just the cells to which you have applied a cell fill to indicate clients who are 30 days past due. This function sums cells based on their fill color:

```
SumColor(CellColor, SumRange)
```

> **Note** Cells colored by conditional formatting will not work with this function; the cells must have an interior color.

These are the arguments:

- `CellColor`—The address of a cell with the target color.

- `SumRange`—The range of cells to be searched.

Here is the function's code:

```
Function SumByColor(CellColor As Range, SumRange As Range)
Dim myCell As Range
Dim iCol As Integer
Dim myTotal
iCol = CellColor.Interior.ColorIndex 'get the target color
For Each myCell In SumRange 'look at each cell in the designated range
  'if the cell color matches the target color
  If myCell.Interior.ColorIndex = iCol Then
    'add the value in the cell to the total
    myTotal = WorksheetFunction.Sum(myCell, myTotal)
  End If
Next myCell
SumByColor = myTotal
End Function
```

Figure 14-5 shows a sample worksheet using this function.

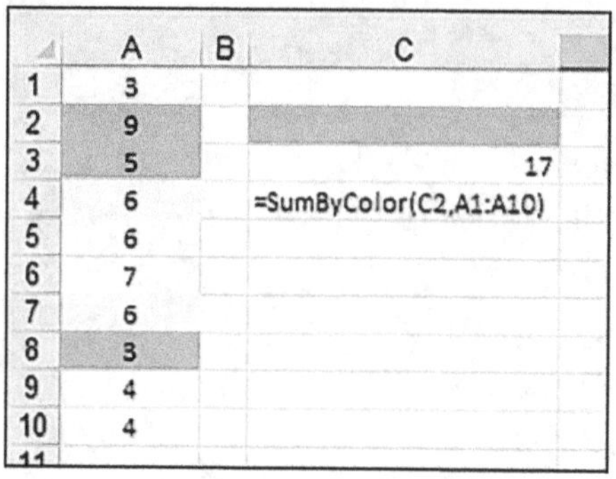

FIGURE 14-5 The function sums cells based on interior color.

Finding the first nonzero-length cell in a range

Suppose you have imported a large list of data with many empty cells. Here is a function that evaluates a range of cells and returns the value of the first nonzero-length cell:

```
FirstNonZeroLength(Rng)
```

The argument is Rng, the range to search.

Here's the function:

```
Function FirstNonZeroLength(Rng As Range)
Dim myCell As Range
'the 0# initializes FirstNonZeroLength as a Double
'this is an older way of coding;now we declare type using Dim
FirstNonZeroLength = 0#
For Each myCell In Rng
    If Not IsNull(myCell) And myCell <> "" Then
        FirstNonZeroLength = myCell.Value
        Exit Function
    End If
Next myCell
FirstNonZeroLength = myCell.Value
End Function
```

Figure 14-6 shows the function on a sample worksheet.

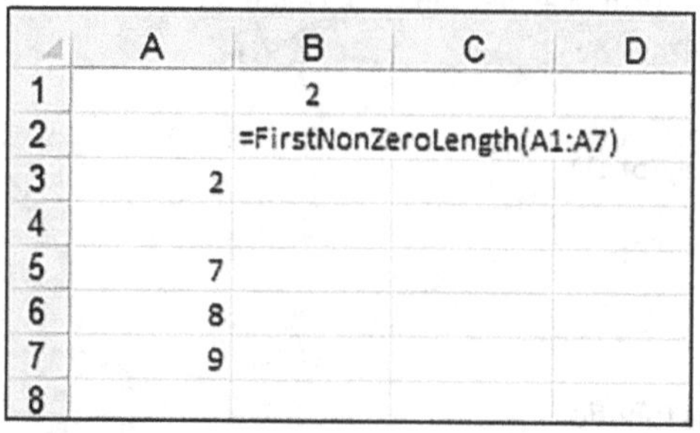

FIGURE 14-6 You can use a user-defined function to find the value of the first nonzero-length cell in a range.

> **Note** FirstNonZeroLength can be replaced with the following formula, which you can also convert to a LAMBDA function.
>
> ```
> =INDEX(FILTER(TOCOL(A1:A7, 1), TOCOL(A1:A7, 1) <> ""), 1)
> ```
>
> Refer to "Creating LAMBDA functions" later in this chapter for more information on creating and using LAMBDA functions.

Substituting multiple characters

Excel has a substitute function, but it is a value-for-value substitution. What if you have several characters you need to substitute? Figure 14-7 shows several examples of how this function works:

```
MSubstitute(trStr, frStr, toStr)
```

	A	B	C
1	1 Introduction	Introduction	=MSubstitute(B1,"1","")
2	This wam a test	This was a test	=MSubstitute(B2,"wam", "was")
3	123abc456	abc	=MSubstitute(B3,"1234567890","")
4	Adnothyer Tuiest	Another Test	=MSubstitute(B4,"dyui","")

FIGURE 14-7 You can substitute multiple characters in a cell.

These are the arguments:

- trStr—The string to be searched.

- frStr—The text being searched for.

- toStr—The replacement text.

Here's the function's code:

```
Function MSubstitute(ByVal trStr As Variant, frStr As String, _
   toStr As String) As Variant
Dim iCol As Integer
Dim j As Integer
Dim Ar As Variant
Dim vfr() As String
Dim vto() As String
ReDim vfr(1 To Len(frStr))
ReDim vto(1 To Len(frStr))
'place the strings into an array
For j = 1 To Len(frStr)
   vfr(j) = Mid(frStr, j, 1)
   If Mid(toStr, j, 1) <> "" Then
     vto(j) = Mid(toStr, j, 1)
   Else
     vto(j) = ""
   End If
```

```
  Next j
  'compare each character and substitute if needed
  If IsArray(trStr) Then
    Ar = trStr
    For iRow = LBound(Ar, 1) To UBound(Ar, 1)
      For iCol = LBound(Ar, 2) To UBound(Ar, 2)
        For j = 1 To Len(frStr)
          Ar(iRow, iCol) = Application.Substitute(Ar(iRow, iCol), _
            vfr(j), vto(j))
        Next j
      Next iCol
    Next iRow
  Else
    Ar = trStr
    For j = 1 To Len(frStr)
      Ar = Application.Substitute(Ar, vfr(j), vto(j))
    Next j
  End If
  MSUBSTITUTE = Ar
  End Function
```

> **Note** The toStr argument is assumed to be the same length as frStr. If it isn't, the remaining characters are considered null (""). The function is case-sensitive. To replace all instances of a, use a and A. You cannot replace one character with two characters. For example, this:
>
> ```
> =MSUBSTITUTE("This is a test","i","$@")
> ```
>   results in this:
>
> ```
> "Th$s $s a test"
> ```

Sorting and concatenating

The following function enables you to sort the column of data by numbers and then by letters and concatenate it using a comma (,) as the delimiter (see Figure 14-8). Note that since the numbers are treated as strings, they are sorted lexicographically (for example, all numbers that start with 1, then numbers that start with 2, and so on). For example, if sorting 1,2,10, you would actually get 1,10,2 because 10 starts with a 1, which comes before 2:

```
SortConcat(Rng)
```

	A	B
1	**Unsorted List**	**Sorted String**
2	q	1,14,50,9,a,f,gg,q,r,rrrrr
3	r	=sortConcat(A2:A11)
4	f	
5	a	
6	gg	
7	1	
8	9	
9	50	
10	14	
11	rrrrr	
12		

FIGURE 14-8 This function sorts and concatenates a range of variables.

The argument is Rng, the range of data to be sorted and concatenated. SortConcat calls another procedure, BubbleSort, that must be included.

Here's the main function:

```
Function SortConcat(Rng As Range) As Variant
Dim MySum As String, arr1() As String
Dim j As Integer, i As Integer
Dim cl As Range
Dim concat As Variant
On Error GoTo FuncFail:
'initialize output
SortConcat = 0#
'avoid user issues
If Rng.Count = 0 Then Exit Function
'get range into variant variable holding array
ReDim arr1(1 To Rng.Count)
'fill array
i = 1
For Each cl In Rng
  arr1(i) = cl.Value
  i = i + 1
Next
'sort array elements
Call BubbleSort(arr1)
'create string from array elements
For j = UBound(arr1) To 1 Step -1
  If Not IsEmpty(arr1(j)) Then
    MySum = arr1(j) & ", " & MySum
  End If
Next j
'assign value to function
SortConcat = Left(MySum, Len(MySum) - 1)
'exit point
concat_exit:
Exit Function
```

```
'display error in cell
FuncFail:
SortConcat = Err.Number & " - " & Err.Description
Resume concat_exit
End Function
```

The following function is the ever-popular BubbleSort. Many developers use this program to do a simple sort of data:

```
Sub BubbleSort(List() As String)
'Sorts the List array in ascending order
Dim First As Integer, Last As Integer
Dim i As Integer, j As Integer
Dim Temp
First = LBound(List)
Last = UBound(List)
For i = First To Last - 1
  For j = i + 1 To Last
    If List(i) > List(j) Then
        Temp = List(j)
        List(j) = List(i)
        List(i) = Temp
    End If
  Next j
Next i
End Sub
```

Sorting numeric and alpha characters

This function takes a mixed range of numeric and alpha characters and sorts them—first numerically and then alphabetically:

```
sorter(Rng)
```

The result is placed in an array that can be displayed on a worksheet, as shown in Figure 14-9. Excel will automatically resize the results range as needed.

	fx	=Sorter($B$88:$B$100)	
B	**C**	**D**	
start data	data sorted		
E	2		
B	3		
Y	6		
T	9		
R	9d		
F	B		
SS	DD		
DD	E		
9	F		
3	R		
2	SS		
6	T		
9d	Y		

FIGURE 14-9 This function sorts a mixed alphanumeric list.

The argument is `Rng`, which is the range to be sorted. The function uses the following two procedures to sort the data in the range:

```vba
Public Sub QuickSort(ByRef vntArr As Variant, _
    Optional ByVal lngLeft As Long = -2, _
    Optional ByVal lngRight As Long = -2)
Dim i, j, lngMid As Long
Dim vntTestVal As Variant
If lngLeft = -2 Then lngLeft = LBound(vntArr)
If lngRight = -2 Then lngRight = UBound(vntArr)
If lngLeft < lngRight Then
  lngMid = (lngLeft + lngRight) \ 2
  vntTestVal = vntArr(lngMid)
  i = lngLeft
  j = lngRight
  Do
    Do While vntArr(i) < vntTestVal
      i = i + 1
    Loop
    Do While vntArr(j) > vntTestVal
      j = j - 1
    Loop
    If i <= j Then
      Call SwapElements(vntArr, i, j)
      i = i + 1
      j = j - 1
    End If
  Loop Until i > j
  If j <= lngMid Then
    Call QuickSort(vntArr, lngLeft, j)
    Call QuickSort(vntArr, i, lngRight)
  Else
    Call QuickSort(vntArr, i, lngRight)
    Call QuickSort(vntArr, lngLeft, j)
  End If
End If
End Sub

Private Sub SwapElements(ByRef vntItems As Variant, _
    ByVal lngItem1 As Long, _
    ByVal lngItem2 As Long)
Dim vntTemp As Variant
vntTemp = vntItems(lngItem2)
vntItems(lngItem2) = vntItems(lngItem1)
vntItems(lngItem1) = vntTemp
End Sub
```

Here's an example of using this function:

```vba
Function sorter(Rng As Range) As Variant
'returns an array
Dim arr1() As Variant
If Rng.Columns.Count > 1 Then Exit Function
arr1 = Application.Transpose(Rng)
```

```
QuickSort arr1
sorter = Application.Transpose(arr1)
End Function
```

Searching for a string within text

Have you ever needed to find out which cells contain a specific string of text? This function can search strings in a range, looking for specified text:

```
ContainsText(Rng,Text)
```

It returns a result that identifies which cells contain the text, as shown in Figure 14-10.

	A	B	C	D
1	This is an apple		A3	=ContainsText(A1:A3,"banana")
2	This is an orange		A1,A2	=ContainsText(A1:A3,"This is")
3	Here is a banana			
4				

FIGURE 14-10 The ContainsText function returns a result that identifies which cells contain a specified string.

These are the arguments:

- Rng—The range in which to search.

- Text—The text for which to search.

Here's the function's code:

```
Function ContainsText(Rng As Range, Text As String) As String
Dim T As String
Dim myCell As Range
For Each myCell In Rng 'look in each cell
  If InStr(myCell.Text, Text) > 0 Then 'look in the string for the text
    If Len(T) = 0 Then
      'if the text is found, add the address to my result
      T = myCell.Address(False, False)
    Else
      T = T & "," & myCell.Address(False, False)
    End If
  End If
Next myCell
ContainsText = T
End Function
```

Returning the addresses of duplicate maximum values

MAX finds and returns the maximum value in a range, but it doesn't tell you whether there is more than one maximum value. This function returns the addresses of the maximum values in a range, as shown in Figure 14-11:

```
ReturnMaxs(Rng)
```

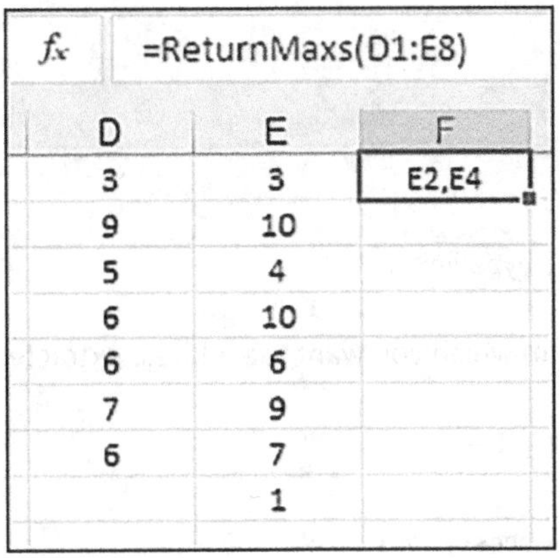

f_x	=ReturnMaxs(D1:E8)

D	E	F
3	3	E2,E4
9	10	
5	4	
6	10	
6	6	
7	9	
6	7	
	1	

FIGURE 14-11 This function returns the addresses of all maximum values in a range.

The argument is Rng, the range to search for the maximum values.

Here's the function's code:

```
Function ReturnMaxs(Rng As Range) As String
Dim Mx As Double
Dim myCell As Range
'if there is only one cell in the range, then exit
If Rng.Count = 1 Then ReturnMaxs = Rng.Address(False, False): _
  Exit Function
Mx = Application.Max(Rng) 'uses Excel's MAX to find the max in the range
'Because you now know what the max value is,
'search the range to find matches and return the address
For Each myCell In Rng
  If myCell = Mx Then
    If Len(ReturnMaxs) = 0 Then
      ReturnMaxs = myCell.Address(False, False)
    Else
      ReturnMaxs = ReturnMaxs & ", " & myCell.Address(False, False)
    End If
  End If
Next myCell
End Function
```

Returning a hyperlink address

Let's say that you've received a spreadsheet containing a list of hyperlinked information. You want to see the actual links, not the descriptive text. You could just right-click a hyperlink and select Edit Hyperlink, but you want something more permanent. This function extracts the hyperlink address, as shown in Figure 14-12:

```
GetAddress(HyperlinkCell)
```

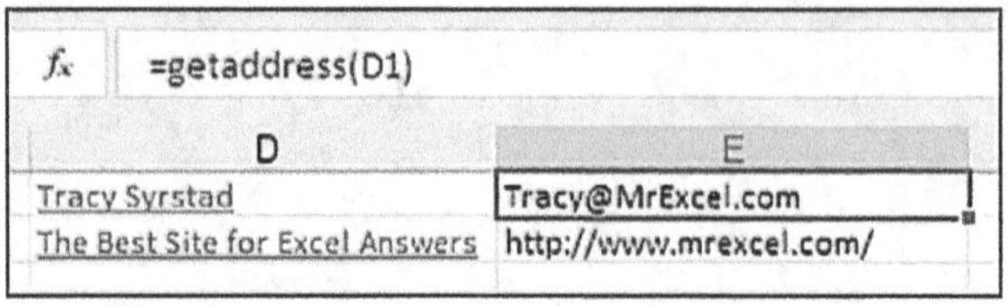

f_x	=getaddress(D1)

D	E
Tracy Syrstad	Tracy@MrExcel.com
The Best Site for Excel Answers	http://www.mrexcel.com/

FIGURE 14-12 You can extract the hyperlink address from behind a hyperlink.

The argument is `HyperlinkCell`, the hyperlinked cell from which you want the address extracted.

Here's the function's code:

```
Function GetAddress(HyperlinkCell As Range)
  GetAddress = Replace(HyperlinkCell.Hyperlinks(1).Address, "mailto:", "")
End Function
```

Creating LAMBDA functions

While UDFs are very useful, you might need to create and distribute custom formulas in a macro-free workbook. You could create the formula and then instruct users on how to copy and paste it where needed, modifying the correct cell references. Alternatively, you can create a LAMBDA function and provide users with the function name and the required arguments.

LAMBDA allows you to design a custom function in the Name Manager using Excel's native functions and other custom LAMBDA functions. You then call that function similarly to how you would call a UDF—but there is no VBA needed.

> **Note** Unlike VBA, multiple lines and spacing don't matter in formulas. Therefore, in the following code blocks, lines wrap naturally, and underscores are not used to join multiple lines together.

> **Caution** While LAMBDA functions are powerful for formula-based logic, they can't replace all UDFs. Lambdas can't interact with Excel's object model—they can't reference workbooks, worksheets, or ranges. They also don't support error handling (On Error, Err.Number), side effects (such as triggering events), or calls to external libraries. If you need these abilities, you'll have to stick to UDFs or, in some cases, move the logic into standard VBA procedures triggered by events or buttons.

Building a simple LAMBDA function

To learn the basics of LAMBDA functions, you'll build a custom function that returns the parent worksheet name of a referenced cell. The structure of the function is:

```
=LAMBDA(parameters, calculation)
```

You can have up to 253 comma-delimited parameters—just make sure the calculation is the last argument.

In Excel, open the Name Manager, located in the Formulas tab, and click the New button. In the Name field, enter the name of the function, SHEETNAME. In the Refers To field, enter the following:

```
=LAMBDA(reference, LET(name, CELL("filename",reference),RIGHT(name, LEN(name) -
FIND("]", name))))
```

Figure 14-13 shows the fields filled in. Click OK to save your changes and return to Excel.

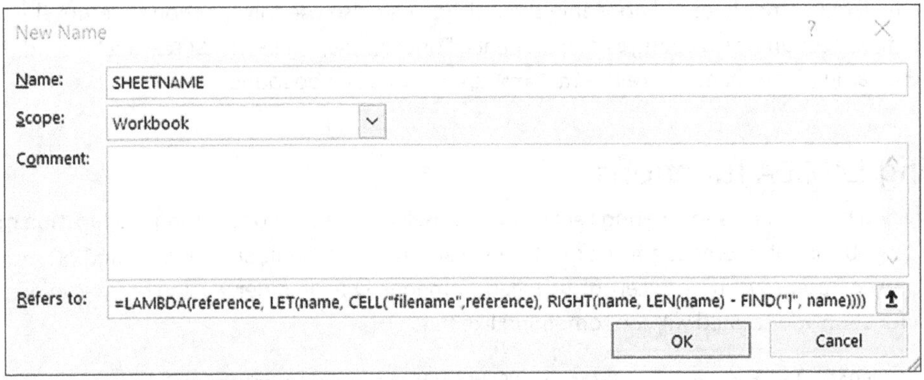

New Name		?	×
<u>N</u>ame:	SHEETNAME		
<u>S</u>cope:	Workbook ⌄		
C<u>o</u>mment:			
<u>R</u>efers to:	=LAMBDA(reference, LET(name, CELL("filename",reference), RIGHT(name, LEN(name) - FIND("]", name)))) ⬆		
		OK	Cancel

FIGURE 14-13 LAMBDA functions are defined in the Name Manager.

Let's break down the previous formula:

- LAMBDA is the Excel function that makes this all work.

- reference is the parameter used by the calculation; in this case, it will be a cell reference. You could simply use x if you wanted to, but helpful terms make it easier when you come back later and review the function.

- LET(name, CELL("filename",reference),RIGHT(name, LEN(name) - FIND("]", name))) is the actual calculation being done.

> **Note** LET is an Excel function that allows you to assign values to names that are then used in a calculation, all within the LET function itself. In the previous formula, name is the variable name, CELL("filename",reference) is the value of that variable, and RIGHT(name, LEN(name) - FIND("]", name)) is the calculation using the variable.

Here's how to use the function on a worksheet:

> **Note** This function requires the workbook to be saved; otherwise, CELL has no file name to return.

1. Select the cell on the sheet where you want the sheet name to be.

2. Type = and then the function name, just as you would one of Excel's built-in functions, like this: =SHEETNAME.

3. Type the opening parenthesis, select a cell on the sheet from which you want to return the sheet name, then type the closing parenthesis. Your formula should look something like this: =SHEETNAME(Sheet2!C18).

4. Press the Enter key.

5. The name of the sheet will appear in the cell. You can also use this function to return the name of the sheet on which a range name appears. For example, =SHEETNAME(TaxRate) would return the name of the sheet where the TaxRate range name can be found.

Sharing LAMBDA functions

There are two requirements for sharing LAMBDA functions. First, the workbook using the function must include it—you cannot reference a function stored in another workbook, such as Personal.xlsb. Second, the end user must have Excel 365 installed. Someone with an older version of Excel looking at a LAMBDA function you created will see something like this:

```
=_xlfn.LAMBDA(_xlpm.reference, LET(name, CELL("filename",_xlpm.reference),
RIGHT(name, LEN(name) - FIND("]", name))))
```

Useful LAMBDA functions

The previous SHEETNAME function and the following two functions were written by Suat Ozgur. Suat is a Full-stack Web Developer and a certified Database Administrator. These functions and many others can be found in the Excel LAMBDA Functions forum at the MrExcel message board *(www.mrexcel.com/board/forums/excel-lambda-functions.40/)*.

> **Note** Reading long LAMBDA functions can be challenging, especially when they contain nested functions with multiple parameters. To make them easier to follow, try copying the formula into Notepad++ and then selecting the Show Symbol menu and choosing Show Indent Guide. The vertical lines can help you track where functions like IF begin and end or which arguments belong with which function. It's a great way to visually untangle complex logic.

SLUGIFY.PLUS

SLUGIFY.PLUS takes text and replaces non-alphanumeric characters with dashes, allowing the text to be used as the URL slug in a web address, as shown in Figure 14-14. It uses recursion and branching to remove any multiple adjacent dashes that may appear. *Recursion* is when a program (or formula, in this case) calls itself. In the following code, you'll notice there are calls to SLUGIFY.PLUS within the formula itself.

Branching is when a statement, such as an IF statement, instructs the code on what to do based on the value of an expression. In this function, the value of the subroutine argument is used to initialize the start of the branch (IF(subroutine=1)). A recursion call sets this argument's value to 0, instructing the code to follow another branch of logic:

```
SLUGIFY.PLUS(reference, ndx, subroutine)
```

B2	∨ : × ✓ *fx* ∨	=SLUGIFY.PLUS('Excel 365 Chapter Slugs'!$A2,1,1)	
	A	B
1	Chapter Names	Slug
2	Referring to Ranges, Names, and Listobjects	referring-to-ranges-names-and-listobjects
3	Laying the Groundwork with Variables and Structures	laying-the-groundwork-with-variables-and-structures
4	Looping and Flow Control	looping-and-flow-control
5	R1C1-Style Formulas	r1c1-style-formulas
6	Event Programming	event-programming
7	Arrays	arrays
8	Creating Custom Objects and Collections	creating-custom-objects-and-collections
9	Userforms: An Introduction	userforms-an-introduction

FIGURE 14-14 SLUGIFY.PLUS renders a usable URL slug from text.

These are the arguments:

- reference—The cell reference (or string value) that contains the string to be converted to a URL slug.

- ndx—The starting character index. Enter 1 to convert the entire string.

- subroutine—The subroutine index of the process that we want to call. The initial value must be 1.

Here is the function's formula:

```
=LAMBDA(reference,ndx,subroutine,
  IF(subroutine=1,
    IF(ndx > LEN(reference),
      SLUGIFY.PLUS(reference, 0,2),
      SLUGIFY.PLUS(
        LET(
          character, LOWER(MID(reference, ndx, 1)),
          charcode, CODE(character),
          LEFT(reference, ndx - 1) &
            IF(OR(
              AND(charcode > 96, charcode < 123),
              AND(charcode > 47, charcode < 58))
              ,character,"-") &
            RIGHT(reference, LEN(reference) - ndx)),
        ndx + 1,1
    )),
```

```
IF(LEN(reference)-LEN(SUBSTITUTE(reference, "--", "")) = 0,
   LET(
      clearleft, IF(LEFT(reference, 1)="-", RIGHT(reference, LEN(reference)-1),
reference),
      clearright, IF(RIGHT(clearleft, 1)="-", LEFT(clearleft, LEN(clearleft)-1),
clearleft),
      clearright),
   SLUGIFY.PLUS(
      SUBSTITUTE(reference, "--", "-"), 0, 2
   )))))
```

TOC2HTML

TOC2HTML creates the HTML code for a table of contents, as shown in Figure 14-15. This function uses recursion and looping to accomplish this task. To create the loop, the argument `loopCounter` is used to initialize the counter within the code, `i`, to 0. The LET function is then used to increment the `i` (LET(i, i+1, ...), and the variable is then used as the `loopCounter` value in the recursive call:

```
TOC2HTML(reference, chapterKeyword, loopCounter)
```

B1	⌄ : ✕ ✓ *fx* ⌄ =TOC2HTML(A2:A26,"Chapter",)	
	A	B
1		\<li>Referring to Ranges, Names, and Listobjects \</li>\<li>Laying the Groundwork with Variables and Structures\</li>\<li>Looping and Flow Control\</li>\<li>R1C1-Style Formulas\</li>\<li>Event Programming\</li>\<li>Arrays\</li>\<li>Creating Custom Objects and Collections\</li>\<li>Userforms: An Introduction\</li>\<li>Data Mining with Advanced
2	Referring to Ranges, Names, and Listobjects	
3	Laying the Groundwork with Variables and Structures	
4	Looping and Flow Control	
5	R1C1-Style Formulas	
6	Event Programming	
7	Arrays	
8	Creating Custom Objects and Collections	
9	Userforms: An Introduction	

FIGURE 14-15 TOC2HTML takes a range and generates an HTML list.

These are the arguments:

- reference—The range consisting of multiple rows and a single column containing the table of contents list.

- chapterKeyword—The repeating keyword defines the main chapters to create the nested sections.

- loopCounter—The counter to create the loop. The initial value should be 0 or blank.

Here is the function's formula:

```
=LAMBDA(rng,chapterKeyword,i,
  LET(
    rows, ROWS(rng),
    IF(i = rows,
      "",
      LET(
        i, i + 1,
        cll, INDEX(rng, i),
        isFirstLevel, IFERROR(FIND(chapterKeyword, cll), 0),
        IF(
          isFirstLevel,
          IF(i = 1,
            "<ul>",
            "</ul></li>"
          ) & "<li><p>" & cll & "</p><ul>",
          "<li>" & cll & "</li>"
        ) &
        TOC2HTML(rng, chapterKeyword, i) &
        IF(
          i = rows - 1,
          "</ul></li></ul>",
          ""
        )
      )
    )
  )
)
```

Case Study: Converting Select...Case in VBA to LAMBDA and SWITCH

At some point, you've probably nested an If...Then...Else on a worksheet to return a value. The Select...Case statement available in VBA makes this a lot easier. And if you need to use a LAMBDA function, SWITCH offers the same flexibility (see Figure 14-16).

The syntax for the SWITCH function is:

```
SWITCH(expression, value1, result1, [value2, result2], ..., [default])
```

The SWITCH function in Excel is similar to the Select Case statement in VBA. Both evaluate a single expression and return a result based on matching values. In Select Case, each Case represents a possible match, followed by the code to execute. Similarly, SWITCH takes the expression to evaluate, followed by a series of value/result pairs. If the expression matches a value, the corresponding result is returned. You can also include an optional final argument (similar to Case Else) to act as a default if no values match. While Select Case can handle ranges and complex logic, SWITCH is best for exact, simple comparisons.

f_x	=ExcelExperience(E3)					
D	E	F	G	H		I

1. Have you ever created a Pivot Table with VBA?						
	Yes	Well done!	Please continue to question 2			

FIGURE 14-16 The ExcelExperience function uses the Select...Case structure rather than nested If...Then statements.

To demonstrate how SWITCH works, we'll convert a Select...Case that takes the user input and returns a response to a LAMBDA using SWITCH.

Since both Select...Case and SWITCH are case-sensitive, I've developed the habit of always using uppercase (UCase) when comparing strings. Here is the code for the UDF using Select...Case:

```
Function ExcelExperience(ByVal UserResponse As String) As String
Select Case UCase(UserResponse)
  Case Is = "YES"
    ExcelExperience = "Well done! Please continue to question 2"
  Case Is = "NO"
    ExcelExperience = "Check out Chapter 12 for some help. " & _
      "Please skip to question 10"
  Case Is = "MAYBE"
    ExcelExperience = "Please clarify your response " & _
      "in the box below"
  Case Else
    ExcelExperience = "Invalid response"
End Select
End Function
```

And here is the formula for the LAMBDA. Response is the cell address (or string value) that contains the user's response:

```
=LAMBDA(response,
  SWITCH(
    UPPER(response),
    "YES", "Well done! Please continue to question 2",
    "NO", "Check out Chapter 12 for some help. Please skip to question 10",
    "MAYBE", "Please clarify your response in the box below",
    "Invalid response"
  )
)
```

Next steps

User-defined and LAMBDA functions allow you to simplify potentially complex formulas, making them easier for users to apply. Now that you've learned how to work the data, it's time to visualize it. In Chapter 15, "Creating charts," you'll find out how spreadsheet charting has become highly customizable and capable of handling large amounts of data.

Creating charts

In this chapter, you will:

- Use `.AddChart2` to create a chart

- Understand chart styles

- Format a chart

- Create a combo chart, map chart, and waterfall chart

- Export a chart as a graphic

They say a picture is worth a thousand words. And for a picture of numbers, nothing works better than a well-conceived chart that draws data from an Excel table. Charts linked with data have been in use from the early spreadsheet days. Over this period, spreadsheet charting has evolved tremendously, morphing from a rudimentary graphical spreadsheet tool to a highly customizable resource capable of handling large amounts of data.

In the beginning, all charts in Excel were chart sheets—standalone sheets that displayed only the chart. In the mid-1990s, Excel introduced embedded charts, allowing charts to appear alongside the data.

This shift required programmers to navigate two separate object models. A chart sheet is represented by the `Chart` object directly. An embedded chart, however, is contained inside a `ChartObject`, which holds the actual `Chart`.

Fortunately, modern VBA has simplified things. No matter which type of chart you're working with, you can declare and configure it using the same variable:

```
Dim CH As Chart
```

Behind the scenes, you might still access it differently—but once you've got a reference to the `Chart`, nearly all chart-related code works the same way.

> **Note** I don't often create charts with VBA. My preferred method is to design a chart template in the workbook and copy it as needed. This gives clients the flexibility to adjust chart types or colors on their own. That said, there are times when you'll want more control—such as applying a brand color to the series or fine-tuning layout elements that aren't exposed through the UI. In those cases, building or customizing the chart programmatically becomes worthwhile.
>
> This chapter focuses on formatting charts—things like fonts, colors, and layout. But when you're reusing a chart in a new context, appearance isn't always the problem. If you're copying the chart to a different workbook, the series may still reference the original data. Excel stores those links inside each series formula, and updating the chart means rewriting them. I cover how to handle that, along with an example of using a chart template, in Chapter 13, "Excel power."

Using .AddChart2 to create a chart

With the .AddChart2 method, you can specify a chart style, type, size, and location. There's even a property, NewLayout, which, when set to True, can avoid having a legend in a single-series chart.

The following code takes the data from A3:G6 and creates an embedded chart to fill B8:G20:

```
Sub CreateChartUsingAddChart2()
'Create a Clustered Column Chart in B8:G20 from data in A3:G6
'Set a sheet object because with AddChart2, you don't have to
'have the sheet your embedding the chart into as the active sheet.
Dim wks As Worksheet
Dim CH As Chart
Dim ChartLocation As Range
Dim chObj As ChartObject
Set wks = Worksheets("Sheet1")
'delete any existing charts on the sheet
For Each chObj In wks.ChartObjects
    chObj.Delete
Next chObj
Set ChartLocation = wks.Range("B8:G20")
Set CH = wks.Shapes.AddChart2( _
    Style:=203, _
    XlChartType:=xlColumnClustered, _
    Left:=ChartLocation.Cells(1, 1).Left, _
    Top:=ChartLocation.Cells(1, 1).Top, _
    Width:=ChartLocation.Width, _
    Height:=ChartLocation.Height, _
    NewLayout:=False).Chart
CH.SetSourceData wks.Range("A3:G6")
'cleanup memory
Set CH = Nothing
Set chObj = Nothing
```

```
Set wks = Nothing
Set ChartLocation = Nothing
End Sub
```

The values for Left, Top, Width, and Height are in pixels. By finding the .Left property of cell B8 and using that as the Left of the chart, you don't have to try to guess that column B is 27.34 pixels from the left edge of the worksheet.

Figure 15-1 shows the resulting chart.

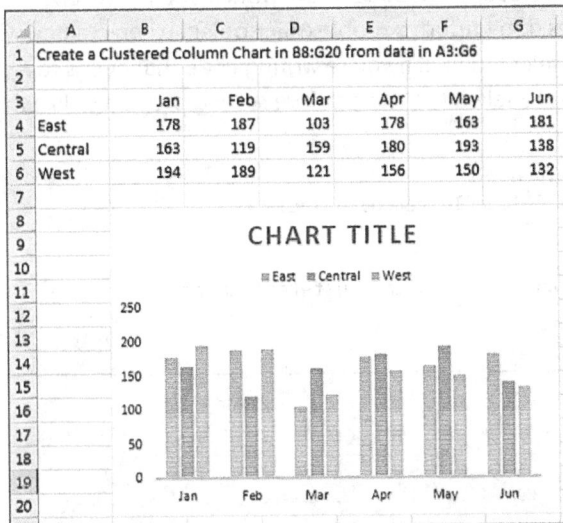

FIGURE 15-1 Create a chart to fill a specific range.

If you need to create a chart sheet, the code's a little shorter. One thing to keep in mind is that the chart sheet is both a chart and a sheet—they share the same object. So, if you want to modify the chart, you use the CH object variable, but you also use it if you want to make changes to the sheet aspect, such as CH.Protect ChartSheetPassword if you want to protect the sheet. Here's the code to create the previous chart as a chart sheet:

```
Sub CreateChartSheet()
'Create a Clustered Column chart as a chart sheet from data in A3:G6
Dim CH As Chart
Set CH = Charts.Add
With CH
   .ChartType = xlColumnClustered
   .ChartStyle = 203
   .SetSourceData Worksheets("Sheet1").Range("A3:G6")
   'rename the chart sheet; the chart IS the sheet and vice versa
   .Name = "MyChartSheet"
End With
'cleanup memory
Set CH = Nothing
End Sub
```

> **Caution** Note that the embedded chart uses the `Style` property to set the style, but the chart sheet uses `ChartStyle`. But then, to really confuse us, if you want to change the style of an existing embedded chart, you have to use `ChartStyle`.

Handling chart creation in Excel 2013 and 2016

Traditionally, well-written VBA avoids selecting anything in the worksheet. However, in Excel 2013 and 2016, some chart types don't return a usable `Chart` object when created with `AddChart2` unless the chart is actively selected first. If you're writing code that needs to support these versions, you may need to select the chart before setting properties like this:

```
Dim ch As Chart
If Val(Application.Version) < =16 Then
  ActiveSheet.Shapes.AddChart2(, xlColumnClustered).Select
  Set ch = ActiveChart
Else
  Set ch = ActiveSheet.Shapes.AddChart2(, xlColumnClustered).Chart
End If
ch.SetSourceData Range("A1:B7")
```

Understanding chart styles

The Chart Styles gallery shows professionally designed chart styles on the ribbon's Chart Design tab. These innovative designs use combinations of properties that have been in Excel for years, but they allow you to apply a group of properties in a single command. The `AddChart2` method enables you to specify the style number to use when creating the chart. Unfortunately, the style numbering system is fairly complex.

Figure 15-2 shows the Chart Styles gallery for a clustered column chart.

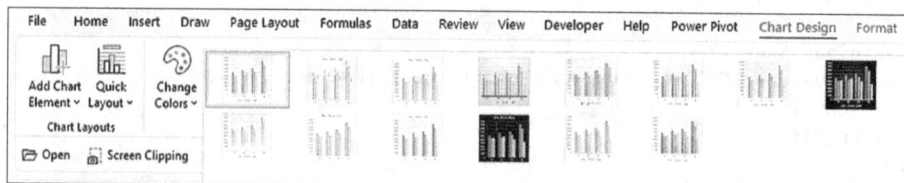

FIGURE 15-2 Apply a chart style to quickly format a chart.

In Figure 15-2, the chart styles are numbered 201–215. However, if you switch to a bar chart, the similar chart styles are numbered 216–230.

The styles for the old chart types run from 201–353. Styles 354–497 are for the eight new chart types.

Follow these steps to learn the style number associated with your favorite style:

1. Create a chart in the Excel user interface.

2. Open the Chart Styles gallery on the Design tab and choose the chart style you want to use. Keep the chart selected before moving to Step 3.

> **Caution** You might tend to click away from the chart to admire the newly selected style. If you do unselect the chart, be certain to reselect the chart before continuing with the following steps.

3. Switch to VBA by pressing Alt+F11.

4. Open the Immediate window by pressing Ctrl+G.

5. Type **? ActiveChart.ChartStyle** in the Immediate window and press Enter. The resulting number shows you the value to use for the `.Style` argument in the `.AddChart2` method.

6. If you don't care what chart style you will get, specify –1 as the `.Style` argument. This gives you the default style for that chart type.

It is strange that the `.AddChart2` method uses an argument called `Style:=201`, but if you want to change the chart style later, you have to use the `.ChartStyle` property.

Table 15-1 lists the `ChartType` argument values.

TABLE 15-1 Chart types for use in VBA

Chart Type	Enumerated Constant
Clustered column	xlColumnClustered
Stacked column	xlColumnStacked
100% stacked column	xlColumnStacked100
3-D clustered column	xl3DColumnClustered
Stacked column in 3-D	xl3DColumnStacked
100% stacked column in 3-D	xl3DColumnStacked100
3-D column	xl3DColumn
Waterfall	xlWaterfall
Tree map	xlTreeMap
Sunburst	xlSunburst
Histogram	xlHistogram
Pareto	xlPareto
Box and whisker	xlBoxWhisker
Funnel	xlFunnel

Chart Type	Enumerated Constant
Filled Region Map	xlRegionMap
Line	xlLine
Stacked line	xlLineStacked
100% stacked line	xlLineStacked100
Line with markers	xlLineMarkers
Stacked line with markers	xlLineMarkersStacked
100% stacked line with markers	xlLineMarkersStacked100
Pie	xlPie
Pie in 3-D	xl3DPie
Pie of pie	xlPieOfPie
Exploded pie	xlPieExploded
Exploded pie in 3-D	xl3DPieExploded
Bar of pie	xlBarOfPie
Clustered bar	xlBarClustered
Stacked bar	xlBarStacked
100% stacked bar	xlBarStacked100
Clustered bar in 3-D	xl3DBarClustered
Stacked bar in 3-D	xl3DBarStacked
100% stacked bar in 3-D	xl3DBarStacked100
Area	xlArea
Stacked area	xlAreaStacked
100% stacked area	xlAreaStacked100
3-D area	xl3DArea
Stacked area in 3-D	xl3DAreaStacked
100% stacked area in 3-D	xl3DAreaStacked100
Scatter with only markers	xlXYScatter
Scatter with smooth lines and markers	xlXYScatterSmooth
Scatter with smooth lines	xlXYScatterSmoothNoMarkers
Scatter with straight lines and markers	xlXYScatterLines
Scatter with straight lines	xlXYScatterLinesNoMarkers
High-low-close	xlStockHLC
Open-high-low-close	xlStockOHLC
Volume-high-low-close	xlStockVHLC

Chart Type	Enumerated Constant
Volume-open-high-low-close	xlStockVOHLC
3-D surface	xlSurface
Wireframe 3-D surface	xlSurfaceWireframe
Contour	xlSurfaceTopView
Wireframe contour	xlSurfaceTopViewWireframe
Doughnut	xlDoughnut
Exploded doughnut	xlDoughnutExploded
Bubble	xlBubble
Bubble with a 3-D effect	xlBubble3DEffect
Radar	xlRadar
Radar with markers	xlRadarMarkers
Filled radar	xlRadarFilled

Excel supports a few other chart types that misrepresent your data, such as the cone and pyramid charts. For backward compatibility, these are still in VBA, but they are omitted from Table 15-1. If your manager forces you to create those old chart types, you can find them by searching for **xlChartType enumeration** in your favorite search engine.

Formatting a chart

After creating a chart, you will often want to add or move elements of the chart. The following sections describe code to control the myriad chart elements.

Referring to a specific chart

The macro recorder has an unsatisfactory way of writing code for chart creation. The macro recorder uses the .AddChart2 method and adds a .Select to the end of the line to select the chart. The rest of the chart settings then apply to the ActiveChart object. This approach is a bit frustrating because you are required to do all the chart formatting before you select anything else in the worksheet. The macro recorder does this because chart names are unpredictable. The first time you run a macro, the chart might be called Chart 1. But if you run the macro on another day or on a different worksheet, the chart might be called Chart 3 or Chart 5.

If you need to modify a preexisting chart—such as a chart that you did not create—and there is only one shape on the worksheet, you can use this line of code:

```
Set CH = ActiveSheet.ChartObjects(1).Chart
```

If there are many charts, and you need to find the one with the upper-left corner located in cell B8, you can loop through all the ChartObjects objects until you find one in the correct location, like this:

```
Dim ChObj As ChartObject
Dim CH As Chart
For Each ChObj In ActiveSheet.ChartObjects
  If ChObj.TopLeftCell.Address = "$B$8" Then
    Set CH = ChObj.Chart
  End If
Next ChObj
```

Specifying a chart title

Every chart created with NewLayout:=True has a chart title. When the chart has two or more series, that title is "Chart Title." You should plan on changing the chart title to something useful.

> **Note** The following examples work with a chart assigned to the CH object—whether it's a newly created embedded chart using AddChart2, an existing embedded chart accessed via ChartObject.Chart, or a chart sheet assigned directly to CH.

To specify a chart title, use this code:

```
CH.ChartTitle.Text  = "Sales by Region"
```

This code only works if your chart already has a title. If you are not sure that the selected chart style has a title, you can use the following code to ensure that one is placed at the top:

```
CH.SetElement msoElementChartTitleAboveChart
```

Although it is relatively easy to add a chart title and specify its wording, it becomes increasingly complex to change the formatting of the chart title. The following code changes the font, size, and color of the title:

```
With CH.ChartTitle.Format.TextFrame2.TextRange.Font
  .Name = "Rockwell"
  .Fill.ForeColor.ObjectThemeColor = msoThemeColorAccent2
  .Size = 14
End With
```

The two axis titles operate the same as the chart title. To change the words, use the .Text property. To format the words, use the .Format.TextFrame2.TextRange.Font object. The following code changes the axis title along the category axis:

```
CH.SetElement msoElementPrimaryCategoryAxisTitleHorizontal
CH.Axes(xlCategory, xlPrimary).AxisTitle.Text = "Months"
CH.Axes(xlCategory, xlPrimary).AxisTitle. _
  Format.TextFrame2.TextRange.Font.Fill. _
  ForeColor.ObjectThemeColor = msoThemeColorAccent2
```

Applying a chart color

The `Chart.ChartColor` property assigns 1 of 26 color themes to a chart. Assign a value from 1 to 26, but be aware that the order of the colors in the Chart Styles fly-out menu (see Figure 15-3) has nothing to do with the 26 values.

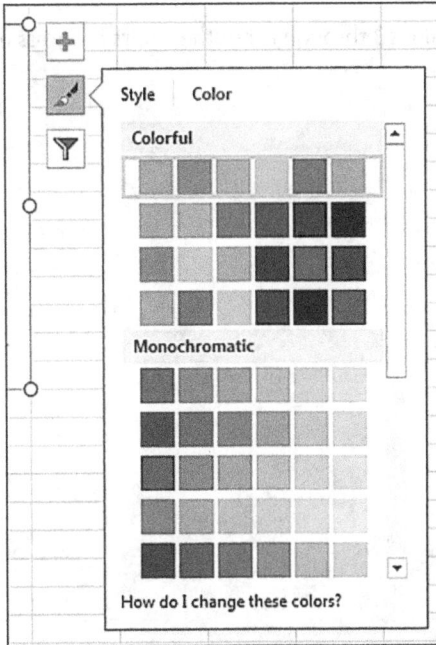

FIGURE 15-3 Color schemes in the menu are called Color 1, Color 2, and so on but have nothing to do with the VBA settings.

To understand the `ChartColor` values in VBA, consider the color dropdown menu shown in Figure 15-4. This dropdown menu offers 10 columns of colors: Background 1, Text 1, Background 2, Text 2, and then Theme 1 through Theme 6.

Here is a synopsis of the 26 values you can use for `ChartColor`:

- VBA `ChartColor` 1, 9, and 20 use grayscale colors from column 3 of Figure 15-4. A `ChartColor` value of 1 starts with a dark gray, then a light gray, and then a medium gray. A `ChartColor` value of 9 starts with a light gray and moves to a darker gray. A `ChartColor` value of 20 starts with three medium grays, then black, then very light gray, and then medium gray.

- VBA `ChartColor` 2 uses the six theme colors in the top row of Figure 15-4, from left to right.

- VBA `ChartColor` values 3 through 8 use a single column of colors. For example, `ChartColor = 3` uses the six colors in Theme 1, from dark to light. `ChartColor` values of 4 through 8 correspond to Themes 2 through 6.

- `ChartColor` value 10 repeats value 2 but adds a light border around the chart element.

- Values 11 through 13 are the most inventive. They use three theme colors from the top row combined with the same three theme colors from the bottom row. This produces light and dark versions of three different colors. ChartColor 11 uses the odd-numbered themes (1, 3, and 5). ChartColor 12 uses the even-numbered themes. ChartColor 13 uses Themes 4, 5, and 6.

- ChartColor values 14 through 19 repeat values 3 through 8 but add a light border.

- ChartColor values 21 through 26 are similar to values 3 through 8, but the colors progress from light to dark.

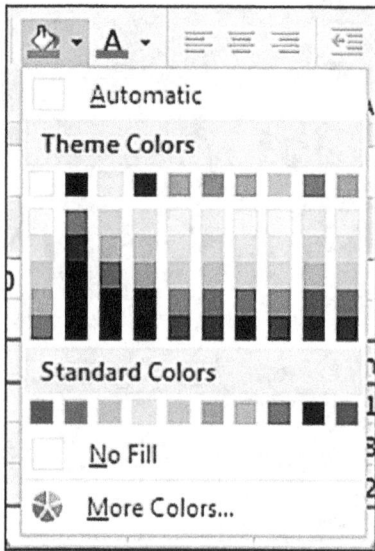

FIGURE 15-4 ChartColor combinations include a mix of colors from the current theme.

The following code changes the chart to use varying shades of Themes 4, 5, and 6:

```
CH.ChartColor = 13
```

Filtering a chart

In real life, creating charts from tables of data is not always simple. Tables frequently have totals or subtotals. The table in Figure 15-5 has quarterly total columns intermixed with monthly values. When you create a chart from this data, the total columns create a bad chart.

To filter a row or column in VBA, you set the new .IsFiltered property to True. The following code removes the total columns:

```
CH.ChartGroups(1).FullCategoryCollection(4).IsFiltered = True
CH.ChartGroups(1).FullCategoryCollection(8).IsFiltered = True
CH.ChartGroups(1).FullCategoryCollection(12).IsFiltered = True
CH.ChartGroups(1).FullCategoryCollection(16).IsFiltered = True
```

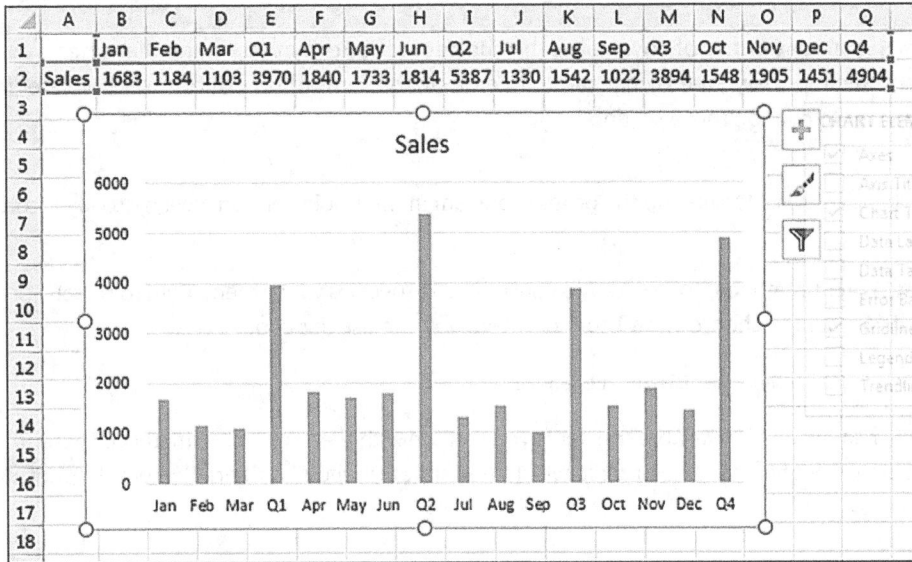

⊿	A	B	C	D	E	F	G	H	I	J	K	L	M	N	O	P	Q
1		Jan	Feb	Mar	Q1	Apr	May	Jun	Q2	Jul	Aug	Sep	Q3	Oct	Nov	Dec	Q4
2	Sales	1683	1184	1103	3970	1840	1733	1814	5387	1330	1542	1022	3894	1548	1905	1451	4904

FIGURE 15-5 The subtotals in this table cause a bad-looking chart.

Level Up!

The previous example wrote out each line to make the logic easy to follow. But what if you had twice as many columns? 10 times more? Having to write a line of code for each column to filter would be tedious. Instead, consider the following two routines.

If the columns are a consistent number apart (in our case, every fourth column), do a `For` loop containing `Step 4`, like this:

```
For i = 4 To 16 Step 4
  CH.ChartGroups(1).FullCategoryCollection(i).IsFiltered = True
Next i
```

If the columns are more random, you put them into an array and loop through the array, like this:

```
Dim idx As Variant
For Each idx In Array(3, 7, 11, 15)
  CH.ChartGroups(1).FullCategoryCollection(idx).IsFiltered = True
Next idx
```

Using `SetElement` to emulate changes from the plus icon

When you select a chart, three icons appear to the right of the chart. The top icon is a plus sign. All the choices in this Chart Elements menu, including the options in the fly-outs, use the `SetElement` method in VBA. Note that the Add Chart Element dropdown menu on the Chart Design tab includes all these settings, plus Lines and Up/Down Bars.

> **Note** SetElement does not cover all of the choices in the Format task pane that often appears. See the "Using the Format tab to micromanage formatting options" section later in this chapter to change those settings.

If you do not feel like looking up the proper constant in this book, you can always quickly record a macro.

The SetElement method is followed by a constant that specifies which menu item to select. For example, if you want to choose Show Legend At Left, you can use this code:

```
ActiveChart.SetElement msoElementLegendLeft
```

Table 15-2 shows all the available constants you can use with the SetElement method. These constants are in roughly the same order in which they appear in the Add Chart Element dropdown menu.

TABLE 15-2 Constants available with SetElement

Element Group	SetElement Constant
Axes	msoElementPrimaryCategoryAxisNone
Axes	msoElementPrimaryCategoryAxisShow
Axes	msoElementPrimaryCategoryAxisWithoutLabels
Axes	msoElementPrimaryCategoryAxisReverse
Axes	msoElementPrimaryCategoryAxisThousands
Axes	msoElementPrimaryCategoryAxisMillions
Axes	msoElementPrimaryCategoryAxisBillions
Axes	msoElementPrimaryCategoryAxisLogScale
Axes	msoElementSecondaryCategoryAxisNone
Axes	msoElementSecondaryCategoryAxisShow
Axes	msoElementSecondaryCategoryAxisWithoutLabels
Axes	msoElementSecondaryCategoryAxisReverse
Axes	msoElementSecondaryCategoryAxisThousands
Axes	msoElementSecondaryCategoryAxisMillions
Axes	msoElementSecondaryCategoryAxisBillions
Axes	msoElementSecondaryCategoryAxisLogScale
Axes	msoElementPrimaryValueAxisNone
Axes	msoElementPrimaryValueAxisShow
Axes	msoElementPrimaryValueAxisThousands
Axes	msoElementPrimaryValueAxisMillions

Element Group	SetElement Constant
Axes	msoElementPrimaryValueAxisBillions
Axes	msoElementPrimaryValueAxisLogScale
Axes	msoElementSecondaryValueAxisNone
Axes	msoElementSecondaryValueAxisShow
Axes	msoElementSecondaryValueAxisThousands
Axes	msoElementSecondaryValueAxisMillions
Axes	msoElementSecondaryValueAxisBillions
Axes	msoElementSecondaryValueAxisLogScale
Axes	msoElementSeriesAxisNone
Axes	msoElementSeriesAxisShow
Axes	msoElementSeriesAxisReverse
Axes	msoElementSeriesAxisWithoutLabeling
Axis Titles	msoElementPrimaryCategoryAxisTitleNone
Axis Titles	msoElementPrimaryCategoryAxisTitleBelowAxis
Axis Titles	msoElementPrimaryCategoryAxisTitleAdjacentToAxis
Axis Titles	msoElementPrimaryCategoryAxisTitleHorizontal
Axis Titles	msoElementPrimaryCategoryAxisTitleVertical
Axis Titles	msoElementPrimaryCategoryAxisTitleRotated
Axis Titles	msoElementSecondaryCategoryAxisTitleAdjacentToAxis
Axis Titles	msoElementSecondaryCategoryAxisTitleBelowAxis
Axis Titles	msoElementSecondaryCategoryAxisTitleHorizontal
Axis Titles	msoElementSecondaryCategoryAxisTitleNone
Axis Titles	msoElementSecondaryCategoryAxisTitleRotated
Axis Titles	msoElementSecondaryCategoryAxisTitleVertical
Axis Titles	msoElementPrimaryValueAxisTitleAdjacentToAxis
Axis Titles	msoElementPrimaryValueAxisTitleBelowAxis
Axis Titles	msoElementPrimaryValueAxisTitleHorizontal
Axis Titles	msoElementPrimaryValueAxisTitleNone
Axis Titles	msoElementPrimaryValueAxisTitleRotated
Axis Titles	msoElementPrimaryValueAxisTitleVertical
Axis Titles	msoElementSecondaryValueAxisTitleBelowAxis
Axis Titles	msoElementSecondaryValueAxisTitleHorizontal
Axis Titles	msoElementSecondaryValueAxisTitleNone
Axis Titles	msoElementSecondaryValueAxisTitleRotated

Element Group	SetElement Constant
Axis Titles	msoElementSecondaryValueAxisTitleVertical
Axis Titles	msoElementSeriesAxisTitleHorizontal
Axis Titles	msoElementSeriesAxisTitleNone
Axis Titles	msoElementSeriesAxisTitleRotated
Axis Titles	msoElementSeriesAxisTitleVertical
Axis Titles	msoElementSecondaryValueAxisTitleAdjacentToAxis
Chart Title	msoElementChartTitleNone
Chart Title	msoElementChartTitleCenteredOverlay
Chart Title	msoElementChartTitleAboveChart
Data Labels	msoElementDataLabelCallout
Data Labels	msoElementDataLabelCenter
Data Labels	msoElementDataLabelInsideEnd
Data Labels	msoElementDataLabelNone
Data Labels	msoElementDataLabelInsideBase
Data Labels	msoElementDataLabelOutSideEnd
Data Labels	msoElementDataLabelTop
Data Labels	msoElementDataLabelBottom
Data Labels	msoElementDataLabelRight
Data Labels	msoElementDataLabelLeft
Data Labels	msoElementDataLabelShow
Data Labels	msoElementDataLabelBestFit
Data Table	msoElementDataTableNone
Data Table	msoElementDataTableShow
Data Table	msoElementDataTableWithLegendKeys
Error Bars	msoElementErrorBarNone
Error Bars	msoElementErrorBarStandardError
Error Bars	msoElementErrorBarPercentage
Error Bars	msoElementErrorBarStandardDeviation
GridLines	msoElementPrimaryCategoryGridLinesNone
GridLines	msoElementPrimaryCategoryGridLinesMajor
GridLines	msoElementPrimaryCategoryGridLinesMinor
GridLines	msoElementPrimaryCategoryGridLinesMinorMajor
GridLines	msoElementSecondaryCategoryGridLinesNone
GridLines	msoElementSecondaryCategoryGridLinesMajor

Element Group	SetElement Constant
GridLines	msoElementSecondaryCategoryGridLinesMinor
GridLines	msoElementSecondaryCategoryGridLinesMinorMajor
GridLines	msoElementPrimaryValueGridLinesNone
GridLines	msoElementPrimaryValueGridLinesMajor
GridLines	msoElementPrimaryValueGridLinesMinor
GridLines	msoElementPrimaryValueGridLinesMinorMajor
GridLines	msoElementSecondaryValueGridLinesNone
GridLines	msoElementSecondaryValueGridLinesMajor
GridLines	msoElementSecondaryValueGridLinesMinor
GridLines	msoElementSecondaryValueGridLinesMinorMajor
GridLines	msoElementSeriesAxisGridLinesNone
GridLines	msoElementSeriesAxisGridLinesMajor
GridLines	msoElementSeriesAxisGridLinesMinor
GridLines	msoElementSeriesAxisGridLinesMinorMajor
Legend	msoElementLegendNone
Legend	msoElementLegendRight
Legend	msoElementLegendTop
Legend	msoElementLegendLeft
Legend	msoElementLegendBottom
Legend	msoElementLegendRightOverlay
Legend	msoElementLegendLeftOverlay
Lines	msoElementLineNone
Lines	msoElementLineDropLine
Lines	msoElementLineHiLoLine
Lines	msoElementLineDropHiLoLine
Lines	msoElementLineSeriesLine
Trendline	msoElementTrendlineNone
Trendline	msoElementTrendlineAddLinear
Trendline	msoElementTrendlineAddExponential
Trendline	msoElementTrendlineAddLinearForecast
Trendline	msoElementTrendlineAddTwoPeriodMovingAverage
Up/Down Bars	msoElementUpDownBarsNone
Up/Down Bars	msoElementUpDownBarsShow
Plot Area	msoElementPlotAreaNone

Element Group	SetElement Constant
Plot Area	msoElementPlotAreaShow
Chart Wall	msoElementChartWallNone
Chart Wall	msoElementChartWallShow
Chart Floor	msoElementChartFloorNone
Chart Floor	msoElementChartFloorShow

Note If you attempt to format an element that is not present, Excel returns a -2147467259 `Method Failed` error.

Using `SetElement` enables you to change chart elements quickly. As an example, charting gurus say that the legend should always appear to the left or above the chart. A few of the built-in styles show the legend above the chart. I also prefer to show the values along the axis in thousands or millions when appropriate. This is better than displaying three or six zeros on every line.

The following code handles these settings after you create the chart:

```
Sub UseSetElement()
Dim WS As Worksheet
Dim CH As Chart
Set WS = ActiveSheet
Set CH = WS.Shapes.AddChart2(Style:=201, _
  XlChartType:=xlColumnClustered, _
  Left:=[B6].Left, Top:=[B6].Top, _
  NewLayout:=False).Chart
CH.SetSourceData WS.Range("A3:G6")
'Set value axis to display thousands
CH.SetElement msoElementPrimaryValueAxisThousands
'move the legend to the top
CH.SetElement msoElementLegendTop
Set CH = Nothing
End Sub
```

Using the Format tab to micromanage formatting options

The Format tab offers icons for changing colors and effects for individual chart elements. Although some people may call the Shadow, Glow, Bevel, and Material settings "chart junk," there are ways in VBA to apply these formats.

Excel includes an object called the ChartFormat object that contains the settings for Fill, Glow, Line, PictureFormat, Shadow, SoftEdge, TextFrame2, and ThreeD. You can access the ChartFormat object by using the Format method on many chart elements. Table 15-3 lists a sampling of chart elements you can format using the Format method.

TABLE 15-3 Chart elements to which formatting applies

Chart Element	VBA to Refer to This Chart Element
Chart Title	`ChartTitle`
Axis Title–Category	`Axes(xlCategory, xlPrimary).AxisTitle`
Axis Title–Value	`Axes(xlValue, xlPrimary).AxisTitle`
Legend	`Legend`
Data Labels For Series 1	`SeriesCollection(1).DataLabels`
Data Labels For Point 2	`SeriesCollection(1).DataLabels(2) or` `SeriesCollection(1).Points(2).DataLabel`
Data Table	`DataTable`
Axes–Horizontal	`Axes(xlCategory, xlPrimary)`
Axes–Vertical	`Axes(xlValue, xlPrimary)`
Axis–Series (Surface Charts Only)	`Axes(xlSeries, xlPrimary)`
Major Gridlines	`Axes(xlValue, xlPrimary).MajorGridlines`
Minor Gridlines	`Axes(xlValue, xlPrimary).MinorGridlines`
Plot Area	`PlotArea`
Chart Area	`ChartArea`
Chart Wall	`Walls`
Chart Back Wall	`BackWall`
Chart Side Wall	`SideWall`
Chart Floor	`Floor`
Trendline For Series 1	`SeriesCollection(1).TrendLines(1)`
Droplines	`ChartGroups(1).DropLines`
Up/Down Bars	`ChartGroups(1).UpBars`
Error Bars	`SeriesCollection(1).ErrorBars`
Series(1)	`SeriesCollection(1)`
Series(1) DataPoint(3)	`SeriesCollection(1).Points(3)`

The `Format` method is the gateway to settings for `Fill`, `Glow`, and so on. Each of those objects has different options. The following sections provide examples of how to set up each type of format.

Changing an object's fill

The Shape Fill dropdown menu on the Format tab enables you to choose a single color, a gradient, a picture, or a texture for the fill.

To apply a specific color, you can use the RGB (red, green, blue) setting. To create a color, you specify a value from 0 to 255 for levels of red, green, and blue. The following code applies a simple blue fill:

```
Dim cht As Chart
Dim upb As UpBars
Set cht = ActiveSheet.ChartObjects(1).Chart
Set upb = cht.ChartGroups(1).UpBars
upb.Format.Fill.ForeColor.RGB = RGB(0, 0, 255)
```

If you would like an object to pick up the color from a specific theme accent color, you use the ObjectThemeColor property. The following code changes the bar color of the first series to accent color 6, which is an orange color in the Office theme (but might be another color if the workbook is using a different theme):

```
Sub ApplyThemeColor()
Dim cht As Chart
Dim ser As Series
Set cht = ActiveSheet.ChartObjects(1).Chart
Set ser = cht.SeriesCollection(1)
ser.Format.Fill.ForeColor.ObjectThemeColor = msoThemeColorAccent6
Set ser = Nothing
Set cht = Nothing
End Sub
```

To apply a built-in texture, you use the PresetTextured method. The following code applies a green marble texture to the second series. However, you can apply any of the 20 textures:

```
Sub ApplyTexture()
Dim cht As Chart
Dim ser As Series
Set cht = ActiveSheet.ChartObjects(1).Chart
Set ser = cht.SeriesCollection(2)
ser.Format.Fill.PresetTextured msoTextureGreenMarble
Set ser = Nothing
Set cht = Nothing
End Sub
```

> **Note** When you type **.PresetTextured** followed by a space, the VB Editor offers a complete list of possible texture values.

To fill the bars of a data series with a picture, you use the UserPicture method and specify the path and file name of an image on the computer, as in the following example:

```
Sub FormatWithPicture()
Dim cht As Chart
Dim ser As Series
Set cht = ActiveSheet.ChartObjects(1).Chart
Set ser = cht.SeriesCollection(1)
```

```
MyPic = "C:\PodCastTitle1.jpg"
ser.Format.Fill.UserPicture MyPic
End Sub
```

You can apply a pattern by using the `.Patterned` method. Patterns have a type such as `msoPatternPlain`, as well as foreground and background colors. The following code formats the third series with dark red vertical lines on a white background:

```
Sub FormatWithPattern()
Dim cht As Chart
Dim ser As Series
Set cht = ActiveSheet.ChartObjects(1).Chart
Set ser = cht.SeriesCollection(3)
With ser.Format.Fill
   .Patterned msoPatternDarkVertical
   .BackColor.RGB = RGB(255,255,255)
   .ForeColor.RGB = RGB(255,0,0)
End With
Set ser = Nothing
Set cht = Nothing
End Sub
```

Gradients are more difficult to specify than fills. Excel provides three methods that help you set up the common gradients. The `OneColorGradient` and `TwoColorGradient` methods require that you specify a gradient direction, such as `msoGradientFromCorner`. You can then specify one of four styles, numbered 1 through 4, depending on whether you want the gradient to start at the top left, top right, bottom left, or bottom right. After using a gradient method, you need to specify the `ForeColor` and the `BackColor` settings for the object. The following code sets up a two-color gradient using two theme colors:

```
Sub TwoColorGradient()
Dim cht As Chart
Dim ser As Series
Set cht = ActiveSheet.ChartObjects(1).Chart
Set ser = cht.SeriesCollection(1)
With ser.Format.Fill
   .TwoColorGradient msoGradientFromCorner, 3
   .ForeColor.ObjectThemeColor = msoThemeColorAccent6
   .BackColor.ObjectThemeColor = msoThemeColorAccent2
End With
Set ser = Nothing
Set cht = Nothing
End Sub
```

When using the `OneColorGradient` method, you specify a direction, a style (1 through 4), and a darkness value between 0 and 1 (0 for darker gradients to 1 for lighter gradients).

When using the `PresetGradient` method, you specify a direction, a style (1 through 4), and the type of gradient, such as `msoGradientBrass`, `msoGradientLateSunset`, or `msoGradientRainbow`. Again, as you are typing this code in the VB Editor, tooltips provide a complete list of the available preset gradient types.

Formatting line settings

The LineFormat object formats either a line or the border around an object. You can change numerous properties of a line, such as the color, arrows, and dash style.

The following macro formats the trendline for the first series in a chart:

```
Sub FormatLineOrBorders()
Dim cht As Chart
Set cht = ActiveSheet.ChartObjects(1).Chart
With cht.SeriesCollection(1).Trendlines(1).Format.Line
    .DashStyle = msoLineLongDashDotDot
    .ForeColor.RGB = RGB(50, 0, 128)
    .BeginArrowheadLength = msoArrowheadShort
    .BeginArrowheadStyle = msoArrowheadOval
    .BeginArrowheadWidth = msoArrowheadNarrow
    .EndArrowheadLength = msoArrowheadLong
    .EndArrowheadStyle = msoArrowheadTriangle
    .EndArrowheadWidth = msoArrowheadWide
End With
Set cht = Nothing
End Sub
```

When you are formatting a border, the arrow settings are not relevant, so the code is shorter than the code for formatting a line. The following macro formats the border around a chart:

```
Sub FormatBorder()
Dim cht As Chart
Set cht = ActiveSheet.ChartObjects(1).Chart
With cht.ChartArea.Format.Line
 .DashStyle = msoLineLongDashDotDot
. ForeColor.RGB = RGB(50, 0, 128)
End With
Set cht = Nothing
End Sub
```

Creating a combo chart

Sometimes, you need to chart a series of data that are of differing orders of magnitude. Normal charts do a lousy job of showing smaller series. Combo charts can save the day.

Consider the data and chart in Figure 15-6. Here you want to plot the number of sales per month and also show two quality ratings. Perhaps this is a fictitious car dealer that sells 80–100 cars a month, and customer satisfaction usually runs in the 80–90 percent range. When you try to plot this data on a regular line chart, the column for 90 cars sold dwarfs the column for 80 percent customer satisfaction.

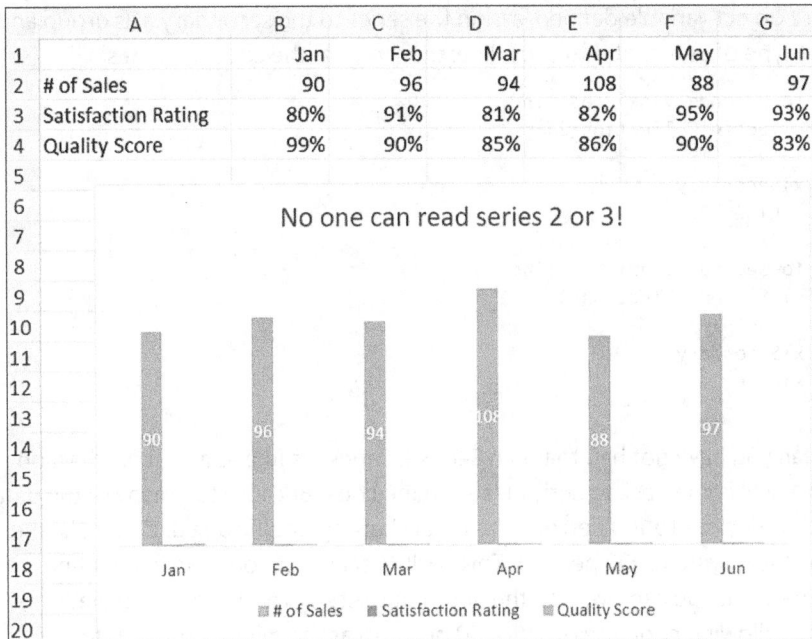

	A	B	C	D	E	F	G
1		Jan	Feb	Mar	Apr	May	Jun
2	# of Sales	90	96	94	108	88	97
3	Satisfaction Rating	80%	91%	81%	82%	95%	93%
4	Quality Score	99%	90%	85%	86%	90%	83%

No one can read series 2 or 3!

FIGURE 15-6 The values for series 2 and 3 are too small to be visible.

Case study: Creating a combo chart

Let's look at an example of the VBA needed to create a combo chart. You want to create a chart that shows the number of sales and also two percentage measurements. In this process, you have to format each of the three series. At the top of the macro, declare object variables for the worksheet, chart, and each series:

```
Dim WS As Worksheet
Dim CH As Chart
Dim Ser1 As Series, Ser2 As Series, Ser3 As Series
```

Create the chart as a regular clustered column chart:

```
Set WS = ActiveSheet
Set CH = WS.Shapes.AddChart2(Style:=201, _
  XlChartType:=xlColumnClustered, _
  Left:=[B6].Left, _
  Top:=[B6].Top, _
  NewLayout:=False).Chart
CH.SetDataSource WS.Range("A1:G4")
```

To work with a series, assign `FullSeriesCollection` to an object variable, such as `Ser2`. You could get away with a single object variable called `Ser` that you use over and over. This code enables you to come back later in the macro to refer to any of the three series. After you have the Ser2 object variable defined, assign the series to the secondary axis group and change the chart type of only that series to a line; then, repeat the code for Series 3:

```
'Move Series 2 to secondary axis as line
Set Ser2 = CH.FullSeriesCollection(2)
With Ser2
   .AxisGroup = xlSecondary
   .ChartType = xlLine
End With
'Move Series 3 to secondary axis as line
Set Ser3 = CH.FullSeriesCollection(3)
With Ser3
   .AxisGroup = xlSecondary
   .ChartType = xlLine
End With
```

Note that so far, you have not had to touch Series 1. Series 1 is fine as a column chart on the primary axis. You'll come back to Series 1 later in the code. Because too many of the data points in Series 3 were close to 100 percent, the Excel charting engine decided to make the right axis span all the way up to 120 percent. This is silly because no one can get a rating higher than 100 percent. You can override the automatic settings and choose a scale for the right axis. The following code uses 0.6 (for 60 percent) as the minimum and 1 (for 100 percent) as the maximum:

```
'Set the secondary axis to go from 60% to 100%
CH.Axes(xlValue, xlSecondary).MinimumScale = 0.6
CH.Axes(xlValue, xlSecondary).MaximumScale = 1
```

When you override the scale values, Excel automatically guesses where you want the gridlines and axis labels. Rather than leave this to chance, you can use MajorUnit and MinorUnit:

```
'Labels every 10%, secondary gridline at 5%
CH.Axes(xlValue, xlSecondary).MajorUnit = 0.1
CH.Axes(xlValue, xlSecondary).MinorUnit = 0.05
CH.Axes(xlValue, xlSecondary).TickLabels.NumberFormat = "0%"
```

Axis labels and major gridlines appear at the increment specified by MajorUnit. Minor gridlines appear at the increment specified by the MinorUnit. This is only important if you plan to show minor gridlines.

At this point, there are numbers on the left axis and numbers on the right axis. I instantly went to the percentages on the right side and tried to follow the gridlines across, but this didn't work because the gridlines didn't line up with the numbers on the right side. Instead, they line up with the numbers on the left side. You can't really tell this for sure, though, because the gridlines coincidentally happen to line up with 100, 80, and 60 percent.

At this point, you might decide to get creative. You could use the following code to delete the gridlines for the left axis, add major and minor gridlines for the right axis, delete the numbers along the left axis, and replace the numbers on the axis with a data label in the center of each column:

```
'Turn off the gridlines for left axis
CH.Axes(xlValue).HasMajorGridlines = False
'Add gridlines for right axis
CH.SetElement msoElementSecondaryValueGridLinesMajor
CH.SetElement msoElementSecondaryValueGridLinesMinorMajor
'Hide the labels on the primary axis
CH.Axes(xlValue).TickLabelPosition = xlNone
'Replace axis labels with a data label on the column
Set Ser1 = CH.FullSeriesCollection(1)
Ser1.ApplyDataLabels
Ser1.DataLabels.Position = xlLabelPositionCenter
```

Now you almost have it. Because the book is printed in monochrome, change the color of the Series 1 data label to white:

```
'Data Labels in white
With Ser1.DataLabels.Format.TextFrame2.TextRange.Font.Fill
   .Visible = msoTrue
   .ForeColor.ObjectThemeColor = msoThemeColorBackground1
   .Solid
End With
```

Because my charting mentors drilled it into my head, the legend has to be at the top or left. Here's how you move it to the top:

```
'Legend at the top, per Gene Z.
CH.SetElement msoElementLegendTop
```

The resulting chart is shown in Figure 15-7. Thanks to the minor gridlines, you can easily tell if each rating was in the 80–85 percent, 85–90 percent, or 90–95 percent range. The columns show the sales; the labels stay out of the way but are still readable.

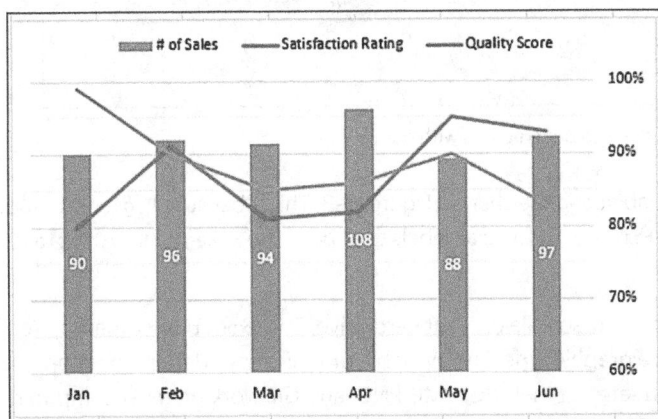

FIGURE 15-7 The gridlines and the two series represented by a line correspond to the axis labels on the right side.

Creating map charts

The filled map chart offers some settings unique to map charts. Say that you have data for six states in the southeast United States. By default, the map chart shows 48 of the 50 states. Set the `.GeoMappingLevel` to `xlGeoMappingDataOnly` to limit the map to only states with data, as shown in Figure 15-8:

```
Sub RegionMapChart()
Dim CH As Chart
Set CH = ActiveSheet.Shapes.AddChart2(-1, xlRegionMap).Chart
CH.SetSourceData Source:=ActiveSheet.Range("A1:B7")
'the following properties are specific to filled map charts
With CH.FullSeriesCollection(1)
    .GeoMappingLevel = xlGeoMappingLevelDataOnly
    .RegionLabelOption = xlRegionLabelOptionsBestFitOnly
End With
CH.ChartTitle.Text = "Filled Region Map Example"
Set CH = Nothing
End Sub
```

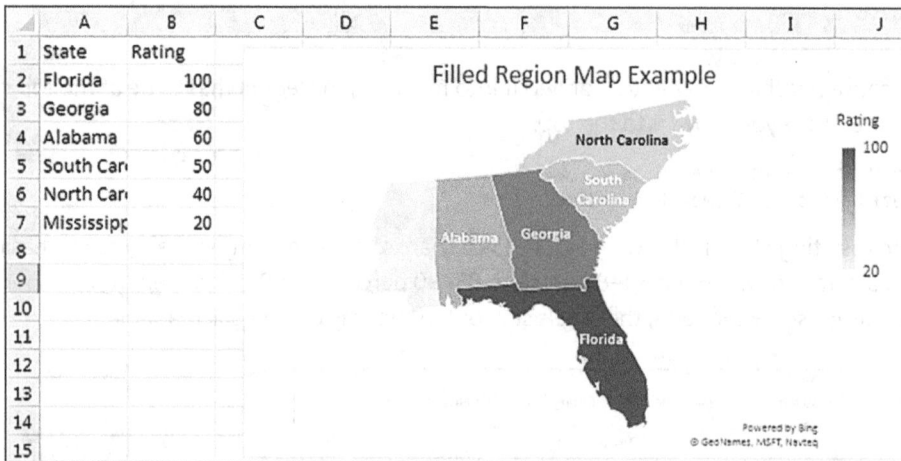

FIGURE 15-8 Limit the filled map chart to only regions with data.

Note that Mississippi is not labeled in the chart in Figure 15-8. This is because `RegionLabelOption` is set to `xlRegionLabelOptionsBestFitOnly`. To force all labels to appear, use `xlRegionLabelOptionsShowAll` instead.

You can export any chart to an image file on your hard drive. The `ExportChart` method requires you to specify a file name and a graphic type. The available graphic types depend on graphic file filters installed in your Registry. It is a safe bet that JPG, BMP, PNG, and GIF work on most computers.

Creating waterfall charts

Waterfall charts use floating columns to visualize how sequential values contribute to a total—like how discounts and fees affect a sale price. By default, each column starts where the previous one ended. However, if a column represents a subtotal or final value, such as a list price or net price, you can use .IsTotal to force that column to the horizontal axis instead of letting it float, as shown in Figure 15-9. The code to create the chart is as follows:

```
Sub WaterfallChart()
Dim CH As Chart
Set CH = ActiveSheet.Shapes.AddChart2(-1, xlWaterfall).Chart
CH.SetSourceData Source:=ActiveSheet.Range("A1:B7")
'Mark certain points as totals
With CH.FullSeriesCollection(1)
  .Points(1).IsTotal = True
  .Points(3).IsTotal = True
  .Points(7).IsTotal = True
End With
Set CH = Nothing
End Sub
```

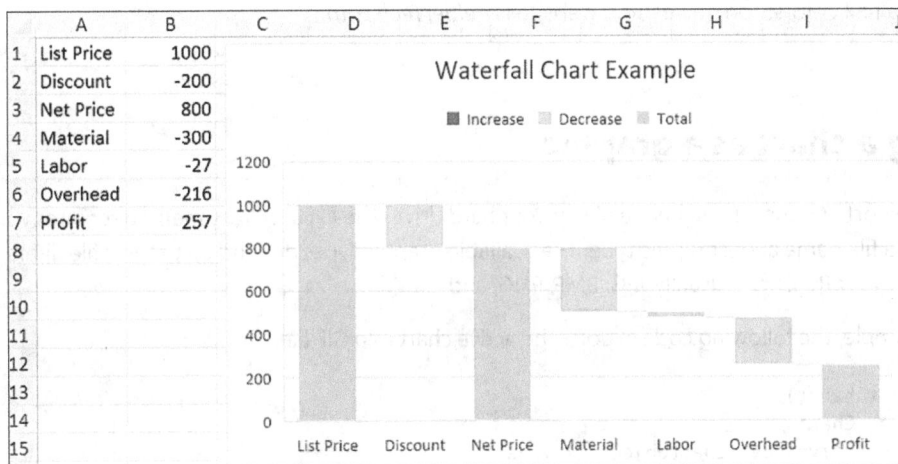

FIGURE 15-9 Any column marked as a total will touch the x-axis.

One of the frustrations with the Ivy charting engines is that it is often difficult to figure out how to change the colors. In the waterfall chart in Figure 15-9, there are colors for Increase, Decrease, and Total. The only way to format those colors is to do the following:

1. Click the legend to select the legend.

2. Click the Increase legend entry to select that one single legend entry.

3. Right-click to see a menu with a choice to change the fill for Increase.

The equivalent VBA doesn't always work in Excel. Sometimes, the formatting won't apply, Excel may hang, or it might crash. This might be a temporary bug, and it might be fixed by the time you are reading this:

```
Sub FormatWaterfall()
Dim cht As Chart
Dim lg As Legend
Dim lgentry As LegendEntry
Dim iLegEntry As Long
Set cht = ActiveChart
Set lg = cht.Legend
For iLegEntry = 1 To lg.LegendEntries.Count
  Set lgentry = lg.LegendEntries(iLegEntry)
  lgentry.Format.Fill.ForeColor.ObjectThemeColor = _
    msoThemeColorAccent1 + (iLegEntry-1)
Next
Set cht = Nothing
Set lg = Nothing
End Sub
```

> **Note** Thanks to charting legend Jon Peltier for discovering this obscure way to change the waterfall fill colors. Jon's awesome website is *PeltierTech.com*.

Exporting a chart as a graphic

You can export any chart to an image file on your hard drive. The ExportChart method requires you to specify a file name and a graphic type. The available graphic types depend on graphic file filters installed in your Registry—usually JPG, BMP, PNG, and GIF.

For example, the following code exports the active chart as a GIF file:

```
Sub ExportChart()
Dim cht As Chart
Set cht = ActiveSheet.ChartObjects(1).Chart
cht.Export Filename:="C:\Chart.gif", Filtername:="GIF"
Set cht = Nothing
End Sub
```

Next steps

This chapter showed how to control a chart's appearance using VBA—from setting titles and colors to adjusting legends and axis labels. In Chapter 16, "Data visualizations and conditional formatting," you'll shift from charts to worksheet-based visuals like icon sets, color scales, and data bars—and see how to automate those just as effectively.

Data visualizations and conditional formatting

In this chapter, you will:

- Use VBA methods and properties for data visualizations
- Add data bars to a range
- Add color scales to a range
- Add icon sets to a range
- Use visualization tricks
- Use other conditional formatting methods

Data visualization tools are used to enhance reports by using icon sets, data bars, color scales, and sparklines. Unlike SmartArt graphics, Microsoft has exposed the entire object model for these tools, so you can use VBA to add data visualizations to your reports.

> **Note** See Chapter 17, "Dashboarding with sparklines in Excel," for more information about sparklines.

> **Caution** Conditional formatting rules in listobjects (tables) have been known to break when sorting or modifying the table. Keep this in mind when applying rules to a listobject.

Excel provides a variety of data visualizations accessible through the Conditional Formatting dropdown on the Home tab. The options described here and shown in Figure 16-1 are also available through VBA:

- **Data bars**—A data bar adds an in-cell bar chart to each cell in a range. The largest numbers have the longest bars, and the smallest numbers have the shortest bars. You can control the bar color as well as the values that should receive the shortest and longest bars. Data bars can be solid or a gradient. The gradient bars can have borders.

- **Color scales**—Excel applies a color to each cell from among a two- or three-color gradient. The two-color gradients are best for reports that are presented in monochrome. The three-color gradients require a presentation in color but can represent a report in a traditional traffic light color combination of red–yellow–green. You can control the points along the continuum where each color begins, and you can choose two or three colors.

- **Icon sets**—Excel assigns an icon to each number. Icon sets can contain three icons, such as the red–yellow–green traffic lights, four icons, or five icons (as with cellphone signal bars). With icon sets, you can control the numeric limits for each icon, reverse the order of the icons, or choose to show only the icons.

- **Above/below average**—These rules, which are under the Top/Bottom Rules flyout menu, make it easy to highlight all the cells that are above or below average. You can choose the formatting to apply to the cells. Note in column G of Figure 16-1 that only 30 percent of the cells are above average. Contrast this with the top 50 percent in column K.

- **Duplicate values**—Excel highlights any values that are repeated within a data set. Because the Remove Duplicates command on the Data tab of the ribbon is so destructive, you might prefer to highlight the duplicates and then intelligently decide which records to delete. This also can be used to highlight values that appear only once in the data. Microsoft refers to this as "Unique Values," although I disagree with that term. I prefer an option that highlights the values that would be left after applying Remove Duplicates. If the word "Apple" appears twice in a column, neither cell will be marked as a unique value.

- **Top/bottom rules**—Excel highlights the top or bottom n percent of cells or highlights the top or bottom n cells in a range.

- **Highlight cells**— Under this flyout menu, you'll find various options such as Greater Than, Between, and Text That Contains, which can now be quickly applied with a selection rather than needing formulas.

	Data Bar		Color Scale		Icon Set		Above Average		Duplicates		Top 50%
2	46		39		41		70		65		70
3	37		74		62		26		73		26
4	67		20		33		83		10		83
5	32		60		63		23		80		23
6	43		79		26		19		38		19
7	50		10		72		10		81		10
8	38		27		73		34		71		34
9	36		43		31		17		81		17
10	56		63		70		12		86		12
11	12		88		17		88		78		88

FIGURE 16-1 Visualizations such as data bars, color scales, icon sets, and top/bottom rules are controlled in the Excel user interface from the Conditional Formatting dropdown menu on the Home tab of the ribbon.

VBA methods and properties for data visualizations

All data visualization settings in VBA are managed through the `FormatConditions` collection. The original method for adding conditional formatting is `FormatConditions.Add`, which is mostly used for formula-based rules. While it can also create data bars, icon sets, and color scales, those options have their own methods: `AddDataBar`, `AddIconSetCondition`, `AddColorScale`, `AddTop10`, `AddAboveAverage`, and `AddUniqueValues`. However, `FormatConditions.Add` is still required by these newer methods when modifying advanced properties.

You can apply several different conditional formatting conditions to the same range. For example, you can apply a two-color color scale, an icon set, and a data bar to the same range. Excel includes a `Priority` property to specify which conditions should be calculated first. Methods such as `SetFirstPriority` and `SetLastPriority` ensure that a new format condition is executed before or after all others.

The `stopIfTrue` property works in conjunction with the `Priority` property. Say that you are highlighting duplicates but want to check only text cells. Create a new formula-based condition that uses `=ISNUMBER()` to find numeric values. Give the `ISNUMBER` condition a higher priority and apply `StopIfTrue` to prevent Excel from ever reaching the duplicates condition for numeric cells.

Use the `Type` property of the `.FormatConditions.Add` method to specify the type of conditional formatting rule to apply, such as a cell value comparison, formula, or data bar. Table 16-1 shows the valid values for this property. The Excel team must have had plans for more conditions; items 7, 14, and 15 do not exist, so they must have been on the drawing board at one time but then removed. One of these was likely the ill-fated "highlight entire table row" feature that was in the Excel 2007 beta but removed in the final version.

TABLE 16-1 Valid types for a format condition

Value	Description	VBA Constant
1	Cell value	xlCellValue
2	Formula	xlExpression
3	Color scale	xlColorScale
4	Data bar	xlDatabar
5	Top 10 values	xlTop10
6	Icon set	xlIconSets
8	Unique values	xlUniqueValues
9	Text string	xlTextString
10	Blanks condition	xlBlanksCondition
11	Time period	xlTimePeriod
12	Above average condition	xlAboveAverageCondition
13	No blanks condition	xlNoBlanksCondition
16	Errors condition	xlErrorsCondition
17	No errors condition	xlNoErrorsCondition

Adding data bars to a range

The Data Bars command adds an in-cell bar chart to each cell in a range. The three columns in Figure 16-2 illustrate different ways you can format data bars. The left column has gradient bars with outlines, while the right column has gradient bars without outlines. The middle column has solid data bars that display negative numbers, which run right to left from the center line.

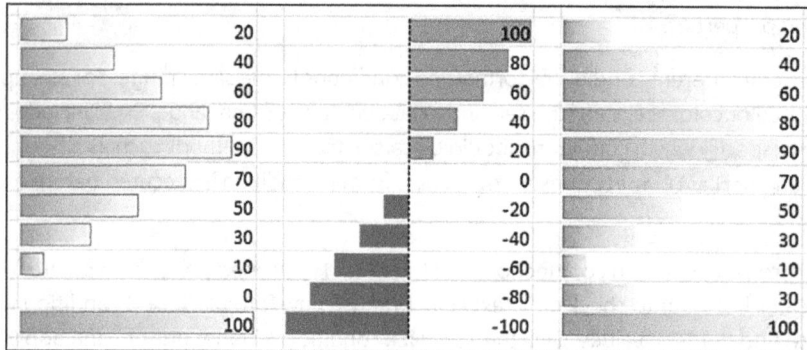

	20	100		20
	40	80		40
	60	60		60
	80	40		80
	90	20		90
	70	0		70
	50	-20		50
	30	-40		30
	10	-60		10
	0	-80		30
	100	-100		100

FIGURE 16-2 Excel offers many variations on data bars.

To add a data bar, you apply the `FormatConditions.AddDataBar` method to a range that contains your numbers. This method requires no arguments, and it returns an object of the `DataBar` type.

After you add the data bar, you will most likely need to change some of its properties. One method of referring to the data bar is to assume that the recently added data bar is the last item in the collection of format conditions. This code would add a data bar, identify the data bar by counting the conditions, and then change the color:

```
Range("A2:A11").FormatConditions.AddDatabar
ThisCond = Range("A2:A11").FormatConditions.Count
With Range("A2:A11").FormatConditions(ThisCond).BarColor
  .Color = RGB(255, 0, 0) 'Red
  .TintAndShade = -0.5 'Darker than normal
End With
```

A safer way to go is to define an object variable of type `DataBar`. Then, you can assign the newly created data bar to the variable:

```
Dim DB As Databar
'Add the data bars
Set DB = Range("A2:A11").FormatConditions.AddDatabar()
'Use a red that is 25% darker
With DB.BarColor
  .Color = RGB(255, 0, 0)
  .TintAndShade = -0.25
End With
```

When specifying colors for the data bar or the border, you should use the RGB function to assign a color. You can modify the color by making it darker or lighter using the TintAndShade property. Valid values are from –1 to 1. Negative values make the color darker, a value of 0 means no modification, and positive values make the color lighter.

By default, Excel assigns the shortest data bar to the minimum value and the longest data bar to the maximum value. If you want to override the defaults, use the Modify method for either the MinPoint or MaxPoint properties. Specify a type from those shown in Table 16-2. Types 0, 3, 4, and 5 require a value. Table 16-2 shows valid types.

TABLE 16-2 MinPoint and MaxPoint types

Value	Description	VBA Constant
0	Number is used.	xlConditionValueNumber
1	Lowest value from the list of values.	xlConditionValueLowestValue
2	Highest value from the list of values.	xlConditionValueHighestValue
3	Percentage is used.	xlConditionValuePercent
4	Formula is used.	xlConditionValueFormula
5	Percentile is used.	xlConditionValuePercentile
6	Lowest number in range is used.	xlConditionValueAutomaticMin
7	Highest number in range is used.	xlConditionValueAutomaticMax
–1	No conditional value.	xlConditionValueNone

Use the following code to have the shortest bar assigned to values of 0 and below:

```
DB.MinPoint.Modify Newtype:=xlConditionValueNumber, NewValue:=0
```

To give the top 20% of the bars the longest bar, use this code:

```
DB.MaxPoint.Modify Newtype:=xlConditionValuePercent, NewValue:=80
```

An interesting alternative is to show only the data bars and not the value. To do this, use this code:

```
DB.ShowValue = False
```

To show negative data bars in Excel, use this line:

```
DB.AxisPosition = xlDataBarAxisAutomatic
```

When you allow negative data bars, you can specify an axis color, a negative bar color, and a negative bar border color. The following code shows samples of how to change the various colors. Figure 16-3 shows the data bars in column C:

```
Sub DataBar2()
'Add a Data bar
'Include negative data bars
'Control the min and max point
```

```
Dim DB As Databar
With Range("C4:C11")
   .FormatConditions.Delete
   'Add the data bars
   Set DB = .FormatConditions.AddDatabar()
End With
'Set the lower limit using xlConditionNumber
DB.MinPoint.Modify newtype:=xlConditionNumber, NewValue:="-600"
'Set the upper limit using a formula; number could be used instead
DB.MaxPoint.Modify newtype:=xlConditionValueFormula, NewValue:="600"
'Change the data bar to Green
With DB.BarColor
   .Color = RGB(0, 255, 0)
   .TintAndShade = -0.15
End With
With DB
   'Use a gradient
   .BarFillType = xlDataBarFillGradient
   'Left to Right for direction of bars
   .Direction = xlLTR
   'Assign a different color to negative bars
   .NegativeBarFormat.ColorType = xlDataBarColor
   'Use a border around the bars
   .BarBorder.Type = xlDataBarBorderSolid
   'Assign a different border color to negative
   .NegativeBarFormat.BorderColorType = xlDataBarSameAsPositive
   'All borders are solid black
   With .BarBorder.Color
      .Color = RGB(0, 0, 0)
   End With
   'Axis where it naturally would fall, in black
   .AxisPosition = xlDataBarAxisAutomatic
   With .AxisColor
      .Color = 0
      .TintAndShade = 0
   End With
   'Negative bars in red
   With .NegativeBarFormat.Color
      .Color = 255
      .TintAndShade = 0
   End With
End With
End Sub
```

In Excel, you have a choice of showing a gradient or a solid bar. To show a solid bar, use the following:

```
DB.BarFillType = xlDataBarFillSolid
```

The following code sample produces the solid bars shown in column E in Figure 16-3:

```
Sub DataBar3()
'Add a Data bar
'Show solid bars
```

```
'Allow negative bars
'hide the numbers, show only the data bars
Dim DB As Databar
With Range("E4:E11")
  .FormatConditions.Delete
  'Add the data bars
  Set DB = .FormatConditions.AddDatabar()
End With
With DB.BarColor
  .Color = RGB(0, 0, 255)
  .TintAndShade = 0.1
End With
'Hide the numbers
DB.ShowValue = False
DB.BarFillType = xlDataBarFillSolid
DB.NegativeBarFormat.ColorType = xlDataBarColor
With DB.NegativeBarFormat.Color
  .Color = RGB(255, 0, 0)
  .TintAndShade = 0
End With
'Allow negatives
DB.AxisPosition = xlDataBarAxisAutomatic
'Negative border color is different
DB.NegativeBarFormat.BorderColorType = xlDataBarColor
With DB.NegativeBarFormat.BorderColor
  .Color = RGB(127, 127, 0)
  .TintAndShade = 0
End With
End Sub
```

By default, the bars go left to right, with lower numbers on the left and increasing values to the right. To make the bars go from right to left, use this code:

```
DB.Direction = xlRTL 'Right to Left
```

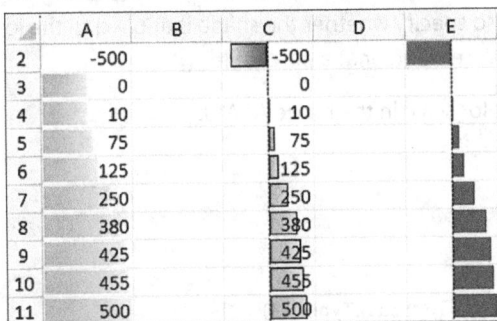

FIGURE 16-3 Data bars created by the macros in this section.

Adding color scales to a range

You can add color scales in either two-color or three-color scale varieties. Figure 16-4 shows the available settings in the Excel user interface for a color scale using three colors.

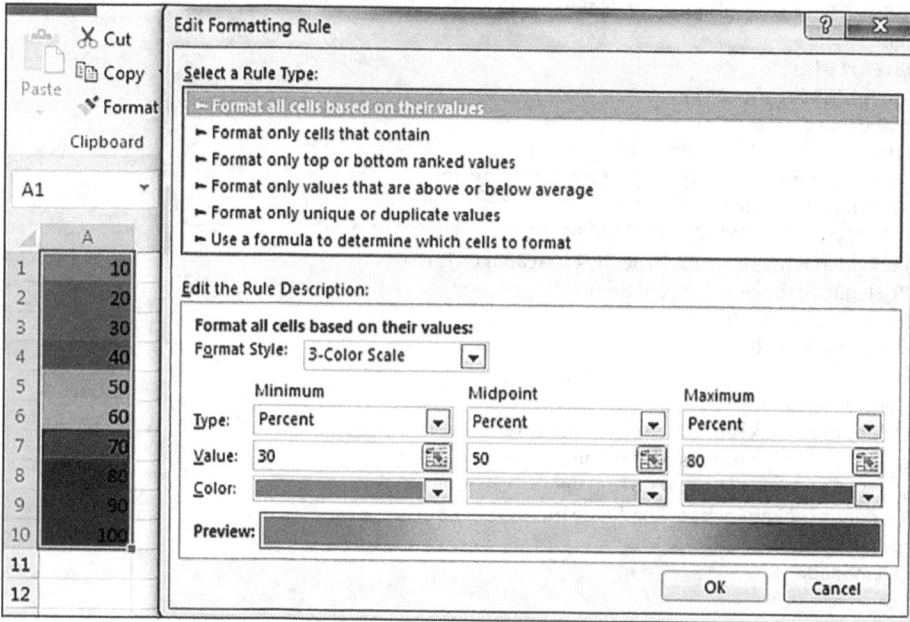

FIGURE 16-4 Color scales enable you to show hot spots in your data set.

As with data bars, you apply a color scale to a range object by using the AddColorScale method. You should specify a ColorScaleType of either 2 or 3 as the only argument of the AddColorScale method.

Next, you can indicate a color and tint for both or all three of the color scale criteria. Using the values shown previously in Table 16-2, you can also specify whether the shade is applied to the lowest value, the highest value, a particular value, or a percentage or at a percentile.

The following code generates a three-color color scale in the range A1:A10:

```
Sub Add3ColorScale()
Dim CS As ColorScale
With Range("A1:A10")
   .FormatConditions.Delete
   'Add the Color Scale as a 3-color scale
   Set CS = .FormatConditions.AddColorScale(ColorScaleType:=3)
End With
'Format the first color as light red
With CS.ColorScaleCriteria(1)
   .Type = xlConditionValuePercent
   .Value = 30
   .FormatColor.Color = RGB(255, 0, 0)
   .FormatColor.TintAndShade = 0.25
```

```
End With
'Format the second color as green at 50%
 With CS.ColorScaleCriteria(2)
   .Type = xlConditionValuePercent
   .Value = 50
   .FormatColor.Color = RGB(0, 255, 0)
   .FormatColor.TintAndShade = 0
End With
'Format the third color as dark blue
With CS.ColorScaleCriteria(3)
   .Type = xlConditionValuePercent
   .Value = 80
   .FormatColor.Color = RGB(0, 0, 255)
   .FormatColor.TintAndShade = -0.25
End With
End Sub
```

Adding icon sets to a range

Icon sets in Excel come with three, four, or five different icons in the set. Figure 16-5 shows the settings for an icon set with five different icons.

To add an icon set to a range, use the AddIconSet method. No arguments are required. You can adjust three properties that apply to the icon set, and you can use several additional lines of code to specify the icon set in use and the limits for each icon.

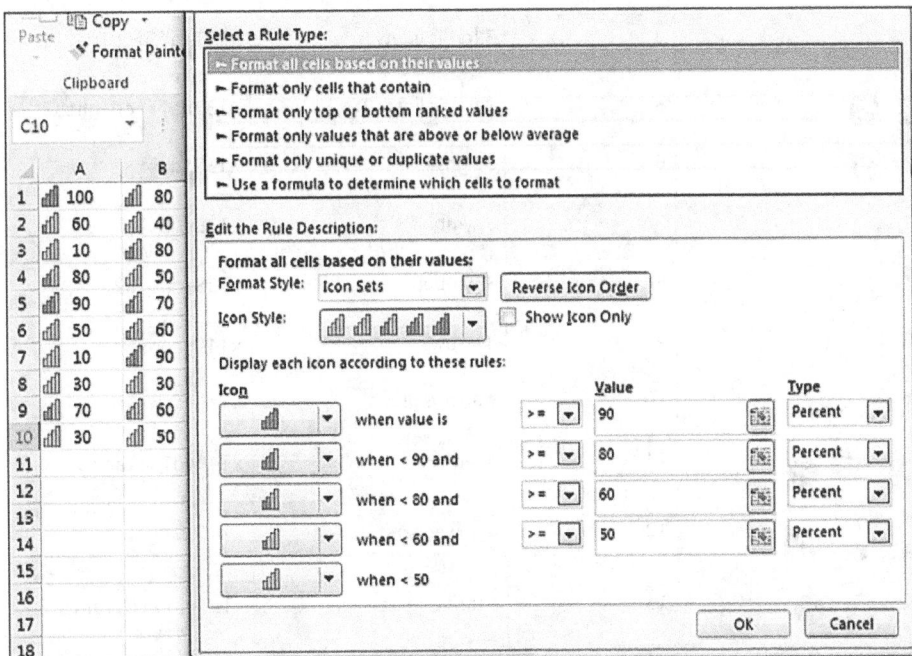

FIGURE 16-5 With additional icons, the complexity of the code increases.

Specifying an icon set

After adding an icon set, you can control whether the icon order is reversed and whether Excel shows only the icons. You can also specify 1 of the 20 built-in icon sets like this:

```
Dim ICS As IconSetCondition
With Range("A1:C10")
  .FormatConditions.Delete
  Set ICS = .FormatConditions.AddIconSetCondition()
End With
'Global settings for the icon set
With ICS
  .ReverseOrder = False
  .ShowIconOnly = False
  .IconSet = ActiveWorkbook.IconSets(xl5CRV)
End With
```

Table 16-3 shows the complete list of icon sets.

TABLE 16-3 Available icon sets and their VBA constants

Icon Set	Value	Description	Constant
	1	3 arrows	xl3Arrows
	2	3 arrows gray	xl3ArrowsGray
	3	3 flags	xl3Flags
	4	3 traffic lights 1	xl3TrafficLights1
	5	3 traffic lights 2	xl3TrafficLights2
	6	3 signs	xl3Signs
	7	3 symbols	xl3Symbols
	8	3 symbols 2	xl3Symbols2
	9	4 arrows	xl4Arrows
	10	4 arrows gray	xl4ArrowsGray
	11	4 red to black	xl4RedToBlack
	12	4 power bars	xl4CRV
	13	4 traffic lights	xl4TrafficLights

Icon Set	Value	Description	Constant
	14	5 arrows	x15Arrows
	15	5 arrows gray	x15ArrowsGray
	16	5 power bars	x15CRV
	17	5 quarters	x15Quarters
	18	3 stars	x13Stars
	19	3 triangles	x13Triangles
	20	5 boxes	x15Boxes
	-1	assign icons to values	x1CustomSet

Specifying ranges for each icon

After specifying the type of icon set, you can specify ranges for each icon within the set. By default, the first icon starts at the lowest value. You can adjust the settings for each of the additional icons in the set, as shown here:

```
'The first icon always starts at 0
'Settings for the second icon - start at 50%
With ICS.IconCriteria(2)
   .Type = x1ConditionValuePercent
   .Value = 50
   .Operator = x1GreaterEqual
End With
With ICS.IconCriteria(3)
   .Type = x1ConditionValuePercent
   .Value = 60
   .Operator = x1GreaterEqual
End With
With ICS.IconCriteria(4)
   .Type = x1ConditionValuePercent
   .Value = 80
   .Operator = x1GreaterEqual
End With
With ICS.IconCriteria(5)
   .Type = x1ConditionValuePercent
   .Value = 90
   .Operator = x1GreaterEqual
End With
```

Valid values for the Operator property are x1Greater or x1GreaterEqual.

> **Note** Reversing the order of the icons (`.ReverseOrder = True`) only affects how they're displayed. When referencing an icon in a set using `IconCriteria`, the lowest value is still assigned 1.

> **Caution** With VBA, it is easy to create overlapping ranges, such as icon 1 from 0 to 50 and icon 2 from 30 to 90. Even though the Edit Formatting Rule dialog prevents overlapping ranges, VBA allows them. However, keep in mind that your icon set will display unpredictably if you create invalid ranges.

Using visualization tricks

If you use an icon set or a color scale, Excel applies a color to all cells in the data set. Two tricks in this section enable you to apply an icon set to only a subset of the cells or to apply two different colors of data bars to the same range. The first trick is available in the user interface, but the second trick is available only in VBA.

Creating an icon set for a subset of a range

Sometimes, you might want to apply a red X only to the bad cells in a range. This is tricky to do in the Excel user interface.

In the user interface, follow these steps to apply a red X to values greater than or equal to 66:

1. Add a three-symbols icon set to the range.

2. Choose Home | Conditional Formatting | Manage Rules and edit the rule. You see the default settings that appear in Figure 16-6.

3. Specify no cell icon for the first two groups.

4. Specify that the top group's Type is Number and >=80.

5. Specify that the second group's Type is Number and >66. Excel defaults the Red X group to be used for <=66 (see Figure 16-7).

The code to create this effect in VBA is straightforward. A great deal of the code makes sure that the icon set has the red X symbols on the cells with values less than or equal to 66. To hide the icons for rules 1 and 2, set the Icon property to `xlIconNoCellIcon`.

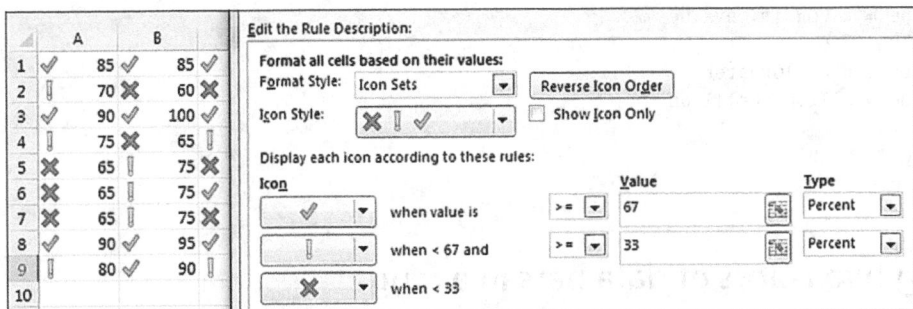

FIGURE 16-6 These default rules appear when you add a three-icon set.

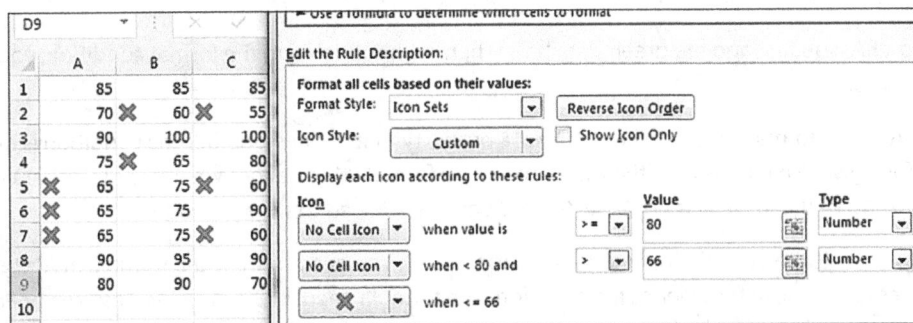

FIGURE 16-7 Although the first two ranges have no cell icon, use the number values to force the red X to show when the value is <=66.

The code to highlight values less than or equal to 66 with a red X is shown here:

```
Sub TrickyFormatting()
'mark the bad cells
Dim ICS As IconSetCondition
Dim FC As FormatCondition
With Range("A1:D9")
  .FormatConditions.Delete
  Set ICS = .FormatConditions.AddIconSetCondition()
End With
With ICS
  .ShowIconOnly = False
  .IconSet = ActiveWorkbook.IconSets(xl3Symbols2)
End With
'Remember, the first icon starts at the lowest value, so the X is criteria 1
With ICS.IconCriteria(3) 'exclamation point
  .Type = xlConditionValue
  .Value = 80
  .Operator = xlGreater
  .Icon = xlIconNoCellIcon
End With
'The threshold for this icon doesn't really matter,
'but you have to make sure that it does not overlap the 3rd icon
With ICS.IconCriteria(2) 'green checkmark
```

```
    .Type = xlConditionValue
    .Value = 66
    .Operator = xlGreater
    .Icon = xlIconNoCellIcon
  End With
  Set ICS = Nothing
  End Sub
```

Using two colors of data bars in a range

This trick is particularly cool because it can be achieved only with VBA. Say that values greater than 90 are acceptable, and those 90 and below indicate trouble. You would like acceptable values to have a green bar and others to have a red bar.

Using VBA, you first add the green data bars. Then, without deleting the format condition, you add red data bars.

In VBA, every format condition has a `Formula` property that defines whether the condition is displayed for a given cell. Therefore, the trick is to write a formula that defines when the green bars are displayed. When the formula is not `True`, the red bars are allowed to show through.

In Figure 16-8, the effect is applied to the range A1:D10. You need to write the formula in A1 style as if it applies to the top-left corner of the selection. The formula needs to be evaluated as `True` or `False`. Excel automatically copies the formula to all the cells in the range. The formula for this condition is =A1>90.

> **Note** The formula is evaluated relative to the current cell pointer location. Even though it is not usually necessary to select cells before adding a `FormatCondition`, in this case, selecting the range ensures that the formula will work.

	A	B	C	D
1	92	96	81	88
2	88	84	82	99
3	99	85	92	88
4	84	84	82	84
5	90	90	82	99
6	90	80	98	88
7	81	97	81	85
8	89	89	91	93
9	81	94	88	83
10	87	82	86	85

FIGURE 16-8 The dark bars are red, and the lighter bars are green. VBA was used to create two overlapping data bars, and then the Formula property hid the top bars for cells 90 and below.

The following code creates the two-color data bars:

```
Sub AddTwoDataBars()
'passing values in green, failing in red
Dim DB As Databar
Dim DB2 As Databar
With Range("A1:D10")
  .FormatConditions.Delete
  'Add a Light Green Data Bar
  Set DB = .FormatConditions.AddDatabar()
  DB.BarColor.Color = RGB(0, 255, 0)
  DB.BarColor.TintAndShade = 0.25
  'Add a Red Data Bar
  Set DB2 = .FormatConditions.AddDatabar()
  DB2.BarColor.Color = RGB(255, 0, 0)
  'Make the green bars only
  .Select 'Required to make the next line work
  .FormatConditions(1).Formula = "=A1>90"
  DB.Formula = "=IF(A1>90,True,False)" 'reinforces the formula
  DB.MinPoint.Modify newtype:= xlConditionValueFormula, NewValue:="60"
  DB.MaxPoint.Modify newtype:=xlConditionValueFormula, NewValue:="100"
  DB2.MinPoint.Modify newtype:= xlConditionValueFormula, NewValue:="60"
  DB2.MaxPoint.Modify newtype:=xlConditionValueFormula, NewValue:="100"
End With
End Sub
```

The `Formula` property works for all the conditional formats, which means you could potentially create some obnoxious combinations of data visualizations. In Figure 16-9, five different icon sets are combined in a single range. No one will be able to figure out whether a red flag is worse than a gray down arrow. Even so, this ability opens interesting combinations for those with a little creativity.

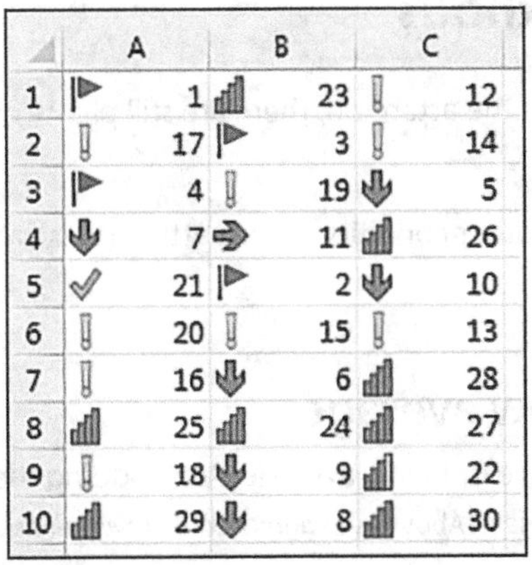

FIGURE 16-9 VBA created this mixture of five different icon sets in a single range. The `Formula` property in VBA is the key to combining icon sets.

Use the following code to create the crazy icon set shown in Figure 16-9:

```
Sub AddCrazyIcons()
With Range("A1:C10")
  .Select 'The .Formula lines below require .Select here
  .FormatConditions.Delete
  'First icon set
  .FormatConditions.AddIconSetCondition
  .FormatConditions(1).IconSet = ActiveWorkbook.IconSets(xl3Flags)
  .FormatConditions(1).Formula = "=IF(A1<5,TRUE,FALSE)"
  'Next icon set
  .FormatConditions.AddIconSetCondition
  .FormatConditions(2).IconSet = _
    ActiveWorkbook.IconSets(xl3ArrowsGray)
  .FormatConditions(2).Formula = "=IF(A1<12,TRUE,FALSE)"
  'Next icon set
  .FormatConditions.AddIconSetCondition
  .FormatConditions(3).IconSet = _
    ActiveWorkbook.IconSets(xl3Symbols2)
  .FormatConditions(3).Formula = "=IF(A1<22,TRUE,FALSE)"
  'Next icon set
  .FormatConditions.AddIconSetCondition
  .FormatConditions(4).IconSet = ActiveWorkbook.IconSets(xl4CRV)
  .FormatConditions(4).Formula = "=IF(A1<27,TRUE,FALSE)"
  'Next icon set
  .FormatConditions.AddIconSetCondition
  .FormatConditions(5).IconSet = ActiveWorkbook.IconSets(xl5CRV)
End With
End Sub
```

Using other conditional formatting methods

Although the icon sets, data bars, and color scales get most of the attention, there are still plenty of other uses for conditional formatting.

The remaining examples in this chapter show some of the other conditional formatting rules and methods available.

Formatting cells that are above or below average

Use the AddAboveAverage method to format cells that are above or below average. After adding the conditional format, specify whether the AboveBelow property is xlAboveAverage or xlBelowAverage.

The following two macros highlight cells that are above and below average:

```
Sub FormatAboveAverage()
With Range("A1:C10")
  .FormatConditions.Delete
  .FormatConditions.AddAboveAverage
  .FormatConditions(1).AboveBelow = xlAboveAverage
```

```
  .FormatConditions(1).Interior.Color = RGB(255, 0, 0)
End With
End Sub

Sub FormatBelowAverage()
With Range("A1:C10")
  .FormatConditions.Delete
  .FormatConditions.AddAboveAverage
  .FormatConditions(1).AboveBelow = xlBelowAverage
  .FormatConditions(1).Interior.Color = RGB(255, 0, 0)
End With
End Sub
```

Formatting cells in the top 10 or bottom 5

Four of the choices on the Top/Bottom Rules flyout menu are controlled with the AddTop10 method. After you add the format condition, you need to set three properties that control how the condition is calculated:

- TopBottom—Set this to either xlTop10Top or xlTop10Bottom.

- Rank—Set this to 5 for the top 5, 6 for the top 6, and so on.

- Percent—Set this to False if you want the top 10 items. Set this to True if you want the top 10 percent of the items.

The following code highlights the top or bottom cells:

```
Sub FormatTop10Items()
With Range("A1:C10")
  .FormatConditions.Delete
  .FormatConditions.AddTop10
  .FormatConditions(1).TopBottom = xlTop10Top
  .FormatConditions(1).Rank = 10
  .FormatConditions(1).Percent = False
  .FormatConditions(1).Interior.Color = RGB(255, 0, 0)
End With
End Sub

Sub FormatBottom5Items()
With Range("A1:C10")
  .FormatConditions.Delete
  .FormatConditions.AddTop10
  .FormatConditions(1).TopBottom = xlTop10Bottom
  .FormatConditions(1).Rank = 5
  .FormatConditions(1).Percent = False
  .FormatConditions(1).Interior.Color = RGB(255, 0, 0)
End With
End Sub

Sub FormatTop12Percent()
With Range("A1:C10")
```

```
        .FormatConditions.Delete
        .FormatConditions.AddTop10
        .FormatConditions(1).TopBottom = xlTop10Top
        .FormatConditions(1).Rank = 12
        .FormatConditions(1).Percent = True
        .FormatConditions(1).Interior.Color = RGB(255, 0, 0)
    End With
    End Sub
```

Formatting unique or duplicate cells

The Remove Duplicates command on the Data tab of the ribbon is destructive. Instead of using it, you might want to mark the duplicates without removing them. If so, you can use the AddUniqueValues method to mark the duplicate or unique cells. After you call this method, set the DupeUnique property to either xlUnique or xlDuplicate.

I do not really like either of these options. Choosing duplicate values marks both cells that contain the duplicate, as shown in column A in Figure 16-10. For example, both A2 and A8 are marked when A8 is really the only duplicate value.

Choosing unique values marks only the cells that do not have duplicates, as shown in column C in Figure 16-10. This leaves several cells unmarked. For example, none of the cells containing 17 is marked.

	A	B	C	D	E
1	Duplicate		Unique		Wishful
2	17		17		17
3	11		11		11
4	7		7		7
5	7		7		7
6	10		10		10
7	10		10		10
8	17		17		17
9	11		11		11
10	14		14		14
11	10		10		10
12	12		12		12
13	14		14		14
14	2		2		2
15	18		18		18
16	4		4		4

FIGURE 16-10 The AddUniqueValues method can mark cells such as those in columns A and C. Unfortunately, it cannot mark the truly useful pattern in column E.

As any data analyst knows, the truly useful option would be to mark any values that appear once and the first instance of any values that appear multiple times. In this wishful state, Excel would mark one instance of each value. In this case, the 17 in E2 would be marked, but any subsequent cells that contain 17, such as E8, would remain unmarked.

The code to mark duplicates or unique values is shown here:

```
Sub FormatDuplicate()
With Range("A2:A16")
  .FormatConditions.Delete
  .FormatConditions.AddUniqueValues
  .FormatConditions(1).DupeUnique = xlDuplicate
  .FormatConditions(1).Interior.Color = RGB(255, 0, 0)
End With
End Sub

Sub FormatUnique()
With Range("C2:C16")
  .FormatConditions.Delete
  .FormatConditions.AddUniqueValues
  .FormatConditions(1).DupeUnique = xlUnique
  .FormatConditions(1).Interior.Color = RGB(255, 0, 0)
End With
End Sub

Sub HighlightFirstUnique()
With Range("E2:E16")
  .FormatConditions.Delete
  .FormatConditions.Add Type:=xlExpression, Formula1:="=COUNTIF(E$2:E2,E2)=1"
  .FormatConditions(1).Interior.Color = RGB(255, 0, 0)
End With
End Sub
```

Formatting cells based on their value

The value conditional formats have been around for several versions of Excel. Use the Add method with the following arguments:

- Type—Because this section deals with formatting based on the cell value, the type is xlCellValue.

- Operator—This argument can be xlBetween, xlEqual, xlGreater, xlGreaterEqual, xlLess, xlLessEqual, xlNotBetween, or xlNotEqual.

- Formula1—Formula1 is used with each of the operators specified to provide a numeric value.

- Formula2—This argument is used for xlBetween and xlNotBetween.

The following code sample highlights cells based on their values:

```
Sub FormatBetween10And20()
With Range("A2:C15")
  .FormatConditions.Delete
  .FormatConditions.Add Type:=xlCellValue, Operator:=xlBetween, _
    Formula1:="=10", Formula2:="=20"
  .FormatConditions(1).Interior.Color = RGB(255, 0, 0)
End With
End Sub
```

```
Sub FormatLessThan15()
With Range("E2:G15")
  .FormatConditions.Delete
  .FormatConditions.Add Type:=xlCellValue, Operator:=xlLess, Formula1:="=15"
  .FormatConditions(1).Interior.Color = RGB(255, 0, 0)
End With
End Sub
```

Formatting cells that contain text

When you are trying to highlight cells that contain a certain bit of text, you use the Add method, the xlTextString type, and an operator of xlBeginsWith, xlContains, xlDoesNotContain, or xlEndsWith.

The following code highlights all cells that contain an upper- or lowercase letter *A*:

```
Sub FormatContainsA()
With Range("M2:O15")
  .FormatConditions.Delete
  .FormatConditions.Add Type:=xlTextString, String:="A", _
    TextOperator:=xlContains
  'other choices: xlBeginsWith, xlDoesNotContain, xlEndsWith
  .FormatConditions(1).Interior.Color = RGB(255, 0, 0)
End With
End Sub
```

Formatting cells that contain dates

Conditional formatting allows you to filter to a virtual date filter. The list of available date operators is a subset of the date operators available in the pivot table filters. Use the Add method, the xlTimePeriod type, and one of these DateOperator values: xlYesterday, xlToday, xlTomorrow, xlLastWeek, xlLast7Days, xlThisWeek, xlNextWeek, xlLastMonth, xlThisMonth, or xlNextMonth.

The following code highlights all dates in the past week:

```
Sub FormatDatesLastWeek()
With Range("I2:K15")
  .FormatConditions.Delete
  'DateOperator choices include xlYesterday, xlToday, xlTomorrow,
  'xlLastWeek, xlThisWeek, xlNextWeek, xlLast7Days
  'xlLastMonth, xlThisMonth, xlNextMonth,
  .FormatConditions.Add Type:=xlTimePeriod, DateOperator:=xlLastWeek
  .FormatConditions(1).Interior.Color = RGB(255, 0, 0)
End With
End Sub
```

Formatting cells that contain blanks or errors

Buried deep within the Excel interface are options to format cells that contain blanks, that contain errors, that do not contain blanks, or that do not contain errors. If you use the macro recorder, Excel uses the complicated xlExpression version of conditional formatting. For example, to look for a blank,

Excel tests to see whether =LEN(TRIM(A1))=0. Instead, you can use any of these four self-explanatory types:

```
.FormatConditions.Add Type:=xlBlanksCondition
.FormatConditions.Add Type:=xlErrorsCondition
.FormatConditions.Add Type:=xlNoBlanksCondition
.FormatConditions.Add Type:=xlNoErrorsCondition
```

You are not required to use any other arguments with these types.

Using a formula to determine which cells to format

The most powerful conditional format is the xlExpression type. With this type, you provide a formula for the active cell that evaluates to True or False. Make sure to write the formula with relative or absolute references so that the formula is correct when Excel copies it to the remaining cells in the selection.

An infinite number of conditions can be identified with a formula. Two popular conditions are shown here.

Highlighting the first unique occurrence of each value in a range

Say that in column A in Figure 16-11, you would like to highlight the first occurrence of each value in the column. The highlighted cells will then contain a complete list of the unique numbers found in the column.

	A	B	C	D	E	F
1	17			Region	Invoice	Sales
2	11			West	1001	112
3	7			East	1002	321
4	7	7 is duplicate of A3		Central	1003	332
5	10			West	1004	596
6	10	10 is duplicate of A5		East	1005	642
7	17	17 appears in A1		West	1006	700
8	11	11 appears in A2		West	1007	253
9	14			Central	1008	529
10	10	10 is duplicate		East	1009	122
11	12			West	1010	601
12	14	Duplicate of A9		Central	1011	460
13	2			East	1012	878
14	18			West	1013	763
15	4			Central	1014	193

FIGURE 16-11 A formula-based condition can mark the first unique occurrence of each value, as shown in column A, or the entire row with the largest sales, as shown in D:F.

The macro should select cells A1:A15. The formula should be written to return a True or False value for cell A1. Because Excel logically copies this formula to the entire range, you should use a careful combination of relative and absolute references.

The formula can use the COUNTIF function. Check to see how many times the range from A$1 to A1 contains the value A1. If the result is equal to 1, the condition is True, and the cell is highlighted. The first formula is =COUNTIF(A$1:A1,A1)=1. As the formula is copied down to, say A12, the formula changes to =COUNTIF(A$1:A12,A12)=1.

The following macro creates the formatting shown in column A in Figure 16-11:

```
Sub HighlightFirstUnique()
With Range("A1:A15")
  .FormatConditions.Delete
  .FormatConditions.Add Type:=xlExpression, Formula1:="=COUNTIF(A$1:A1,A1)=1"
  .FormatConditions(1).Interior.Color = RGB(255, 0, 0)
End With
End Sub
```

Highlighting the entire data set row for the largest sales value

Another example of a formula-based condition involves highlighting the entire row of a data set in response to a value in one column. Consider the data set in cells D2:F15 of Figure 16-11. If you want to highlight the entire row that contains the largest sale, you select cells D2:F15 and write a formula that works for cell D2: =$F2=MAX($F$2:$F$15). The code required to format the row with the largest sales value is as follows:

```
Sub HighlightWholeRow()
With Range("D2:F15")
  .FormatConditions.Delete
  .FormatConditions.Add Type:=xlExpression, Formula1:="=$F2=MAX($F$2:$F$15)"
  .FormatConditions(1).Interior.Color = RGB(255, 0, 0)
End With
End Sub
```

Using the NumberFormat property

Just like you apply a number format to a value in a cell, you can use conditional formatting to selectively change the number format used to display the values. For example, you might want to display numbers greater than 999 in thousands, numbers greater than 999,999 in hundred-thousands, and numbers greater than 9,999,999 in millions.

If you turn on the macro recorder and attempt to record, setting the conditional format to a custom number format, the Excel VBA macro recorder actually records the action of executing an XL4 macro! Instead, skip the recorded code and use the NumberFormat property, as shown here:

```
Sub NumberFormat()
With Range("E1:G26")
  .FormatConditions.Delete
  .FormatConditions.Add Type:=xlCellValue, Operator:=xlGreater, _
    Formula1:="=9999999"
  .FormatConditions(1).NumberFormat = "$#,##0,,""M"""
  .FormatConditions.Add Type:=xlCellValue, Operator:=xlGreater, _
    Formula1:="=999999"
```

```
    .FormatConditions(2).NumberFormat = "$#,##0.0,""M"""
    .FormatConditions.Add Type:=xlCellValue, Operator:=xlGreater, _
      Formula1:="=999"
    .FormatConditions(3).NumberFormat = "$#,##0,K"
End With
End Sub
```

Figure 16-12 shows the original numbers in columns A:C. The results of running the macro are shown in columns E:G. The dialog shows the conditional format rules that are applied.

A	B	C	D	E	F	G
308	957	16120718		308	957	$16,121M
908703	908	17530178		$909K	908	$17,530M
19520474	536510	682		$19,520M	$537K	682
517	919134	1100234		517	$919K	$1,100.2M

Conditional Formatting Rules Manager

Show formatting rules for: Current Selection

New Rule...   Edit Rule...   Delete Rule   Duplicate Rule

Rule (applied in order shown)	Format	Applies to		Stop If True
Cell Value > 9999999	$39M	=$E$1:$G$26	↕	☑
Cell Value > 999999	$38.7M	=$E$1:$G$26	↕	☑
Cell Value > 999	$39K	=$E$1:$G$26	↕	☑

FIGURE 16-12 Specify a number format using conditional formatting.

Next steps

Conditional formatting allows you to add data visualizations to cells, making it easier to quickly grasp the significance of the data. But there's more—what if you could put a chart inside a cell? Professor Edward Tufte first wrote about sparklines in 2006. These graphics are essentially word-sized charts. Chapter 17 shows you how to create dashboards from tiny charts called sparklines.

Dashboarding with sparklines in Excel

In this chapter, you will:

- Create sparklines
- Scale sparklines
- Format sparklines
- Create a dashboard

Sparklines let you create tiny, word-sized charts directly within cells. If you are creating dashboards, you will want to leverage these charts.

The concept of sparklines was first introduced by Professor Edward Tufte, who promoted sparklines as a way to show a maximum amount of information with a minimal amount of ink.

Microsoft supports three types of sparklines:

- **Line**—A sparkline shows a single series on a line chart within a single cell. On a sparkline, you can add markers for the highest point, the lowest point, the first point, and the last point. Each of those points can have a different color. You can also choose to mark all the negative points or even all points.

- **Column**—A spark column shows a single series on a column chart. You can choose to show a different color for the first column, the last column, the lowest column, the highest column, or all negative points.

- **Win/loss**—This is a special type of column chart in which every positive point is plotted at 100 percent height, and every negative point is plotted at –100 percent height. The theory is that positive columns represent wins, and negative columns represent losses. With these charts, you always want to change the color of the negative columns. It is possible to highlight the highest/lowest point based on the underlying data.

Creating sparklines

Microsoft figures that you will usually be creating a group of sparklines. The main VBA object for sparklines is SparklineGroup. To create sparklines, you apply the SparklineGroups.Add method to the target range where you want the sparklines to appear. The Add method has two parameters: Type and SourceData.

The Type parameter can be xlSparkLine for a line, xlSparkColumn for a column, or xlSparkColumn100 for win/loss.

The SourceData parameter must be a string referring to the range containing the values to be charted. The orientation of the SourceData must match the target range. If you apply the Add method to B2:D2 (a three-cell wide range), the source must also be three columns wide, but it can have any number of rows. If the target range is B2:B4 (three rows tall), the source must also be three rows tall but can have any number of columns.

- If the data is on the current worksheet, the argument can be as simple as:

  ```
  SourceData:="D3:F100"
  ```

- If the data is on another worksheet, then include the sheet name in the argument like this:

  ```
  SourceData:="Data!D3:F100" or SourceData:="'My Data'!D3:F100"
  ```

- If you've defined a workbook-level named range, such as SparklineData, use the name as the source data like this:

  ```
  SourceData:="SparklineData"
  ```

- If you're using a list object, you'll have to build the string so it includes the sheet name and range. Assuming your data is in "tblData" on sheet "Data" , do this:

  ```
  SourceData:="Data!" & Worksheets("Data").ListObjects("tblData") & _
      .DataBodyRange.Address
  ```

Level Up!

The SourceData code line for the list object looks a little clunky. This is a case where declaring objects can make the code much cleaner. By assigning the table to Lo and defining sl_Data as the data range, the final code is easier to follow:

```
SourceData:="'" & Lo.Parent.Name & "'!" & sl_Data.Address
```

Refer to Chapter 4, "Laying the groundwork with variables and structures," to learn more about declaring objects.

Figure 17-1 shows a table of stock closing prices for three years. Notice the actual data for the sparklines is in three contiguous columns: D, E, and F. This section and the next will guide you through creating sparklines from this data. We'll start by adding the three default sparklines. Then, we'll scale those three cells to form a single chart spanning three columns.

	A	B	C	D	E	F
1	Date 2023	Date 2024	Date 2025	Close 2023	Close 2024	Close 2025
2	1/2/2023	1/2/2024	1/2/2025	101.12	160.62	217.69
3	1/3/2023	1/3/2024	1/3/2025	97.40	158.62	217.90
4	1/4/2023	1/4/2024	1/6/2025	101.93	159.03	212.25
5	1/5/2023	1/5/2024	1/7/2025	102.06	157.58	218.29
6	1/6/2023	1/8/2024	1/8/2025	102.80	160.09	219.62
7	1/9/2023	1/9/2024	1/9/2025	104.27	162.09	217.49
8	1/10/2023	1/10/2024	1/10/2025	103.60	161.34	214.93

FIGURE 17-1 Arrange the data for the sparklines in a contiguous range.

In this example, the data is in the tblData list object on the Data worksheet, and the sparklines are created on the Dashboard worksheet. The WSD object variable is used for the Data worksheet. WSL is used for the Dashboard worksheet. Lo is used for the list object.

Because we're using only the last three columns in the table, we'll set a range object to hold that data, like this:

```
Set sl_Data = Lo.ListColumns(4).DataBodyRange.Resize(, 3)
```

The sparklines are created in a row of three cells. Since there are 253 data rows, each sparkline cell is showing 253 points. The sparkline grows to the size of the cell, so this code makes each cell fairly wide and tall:

```
'Create headings
With WSL.Range("B1:D1")
    .Value = Array(2023, 2024, 2025 )
    .HorizontalAlignment = xlCenter
    .Style = "Title"
    .ColumnWidth = 39
    .Offset(1, 0).RowHeight = 100
End With
```

The following code creates three default sparklines:

```
Dim SG as SparklineGroup
Set SG = WSL.Range("B2:D2").SparklineGroups.Add(Type:=xlSparkLine, _
    SourceData:="'" & Lo.Parent.Name & "'!" & sl_Data.Address)
```

As shown in Figure 17-2, these sparklines aren't perfect (but the next section shows how to format them). There are a number of problems with the default sparklines. Think about the vertical axis of a chart. Sparklines always default to have the scale automatically selected. Because you never really get to see what the scale is, you cannot tell the range of the chart.

Gaps because vertical scales are different

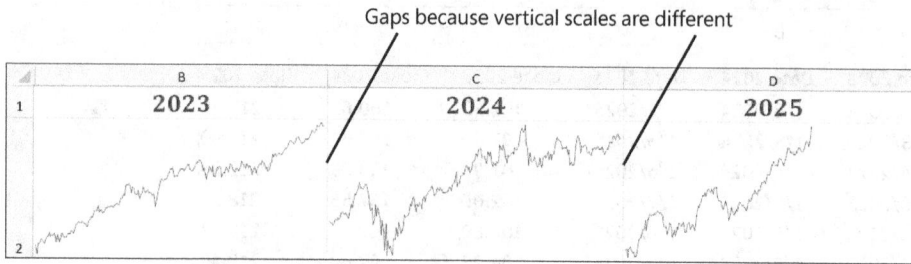

FIGURE 17-2 Three default sparklines are shown here.

Figure 17-3 shows the minimum and maximum for each year. From this data, you can guess that the sparkline for 2023 probably goes from about 95 to 160. The sparkline for 2024 probably goes from 130 to 235. The sparkline for 2025 probably goes from 210 to 310.

	A	B	C	D	E	F
1	Date 2023	Date 2024	Date 2025	Close 2023	Close 2024	Close 2025
250	12/27/2023	12/26/2024	12/29/2025	158.67	222.75	
251	12/28/2023	12/27/2024	12/30/2025	158.96	224.96	
252	12/29/2023	12/30/2024	12/31/2025	157.59	224.15	
253		12/31/2024		157.70	221.68	
254					222.42	
255						
256		Min		97	135	212
257		Max		159	232	305

FIGURE 17-3 Each sparkline assigns the minimum and maximum scales to be just outside these limits.

Scaling sparklines

The default choice for the sparkline vertical axis is that each sparkline has a different minimum and maximum. There are two other choices available.

One choice is to group all the sparklines but continue to allow Excel to choose the minimum and maximum scales. You still won't know exactly what values are chosen for the minimum and maximum.

To force the sparklines to have the same automatic scale, use this code:

```
'Allow automatic axis scale, but all three of them the same
With SG.Axes.Vertical
   .MinScaleType = xlSparkScaleGroup
   .MaxScaleType = xlSparkScaleGroup
End With
```

Note that .Axes belongs to the sparkline group, not to the individual sparklines themselves. In fact, almost all the good properties are applied at the SparklineGroup level. This has some interesting ramifications. If you want one sparkline to have an automatic scale and another sparkline to have a fixed scale, you have to create each of those sparklines separately or at least ungroup them.

Figure 17-4 shows the sparklines when both the minimum and the maximum scales are set to act as a group. All three lines nearly meet now, which is a good sign. You can guess that the scale runs from about 95 up to perhaps 310. Again, though, there is no way to tell. The solution is to use a custom value for both the minimum and the maximum axes.

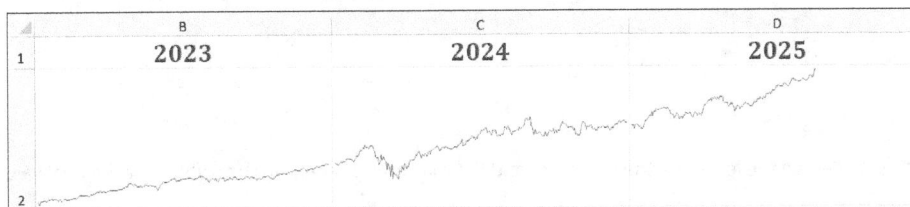

FIGURE 17-4 All three sparklines have the same minimum and maximum scales, but you don't know what it is.

Another choice is to take absolute control and assign a minimum and a maximum for the vertical axis scale. The following code forces the sparklines to run from the minimum found in the data to the maximum found in the data:

```
Set AF = Application.WorksheetFunction
AllMin = AF.Min(sl_Data)
AllMax = AF.Max(sl_Data)
AllMin = Int(AllMin)
'Add 0.9 to max to ensure space from top of cell
AllMax = Int(AllMax + 0.9)
With SG.Axes.Vertical
    .MinScaleType = xlSparkScaleCustom
    .MaxScaleType = xlSparkScaleCustom
    .CustomMinScaleValue = AllMin
    .CustomMaxScaleValue = AllMax
End With
```

Figure 17-5 shows the resulting sparklines. Now, you know the minimum and the maximum, but you need a way to communicate it to the reader.

FIGURE 17-5 You've manually assigned a minimum and a maximum scale, but it does not appear on the chart.

One method is to put the minimum and maximum values in A2. With 8-point bold Calibri, a row height of 113 allows 10 rows of wrapped text in the cell. So, you could enter the maximum value, then vbLf eight times, and then the minimum value. (Using vbLf is the equivalent of pressing Alt+Enter when you are entering values in a cell.)

On the right side, you can put the final point's value and attempt to position it within the cell so that it falls roughly at the same height as the final point. Figure 17-6 shows this option.

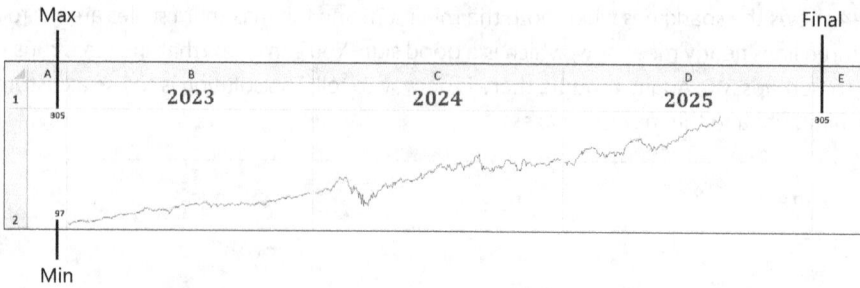

FIGURE 17-6 Labels on the left show the minimum and the maximum. Labels on the right show the final value.

The following code produces the sparklines in Figure 17-6:

```
Sub StockSparklineMacro()
Dim AF as WorksheetFunction
Dim SG As SparklineGroup
Dim SL As Sparkline
Dim WSD As Worksheet 'Data worksheet
Dim WSL As Worksheet 'Dashboard
Dim Lo As ListObject 'Table on Data sheet
Dim sl_Data As Range 'specific range
Dim AllMin As Integer, AllMax As Integer, FinalVal As Integer, Rg As Integer
Dim FromTop As Integer
Dim RgTenth As Double '
Dim RtLabel As String
On Error Resume Next
Application.DisplayAlerts = False
Worksheets("Dashboard").Delete
On Error GoTo 0
Set WSD = Worksheets("Data")
Set WSL = ActiveWorkbook.Worksheets.Add
WSL.Name = "Dashboard"
Set Lo = WSD.ListObjects("tblData")
Set sl_Data = Lo.ListColumns(4).DataBodyRange.Resize(, 3)
'Set up headings
With WSL.Range("B1:D1")
  .Value = Array(2019, 2020, 2021)
  .HorizontalAlignment = xlCenter
  .Style = "Title"
  .ColumnWidth = 39
  .Offset(1, 0).RowHeight = 100
End With
Set SG = WSL.Range("B2:D2").SparklineGroups.Add(Type:=xlSparkLine, _
  SourceData:="'" & Lo.Parent.Name & "'!" & sl_Data.Address)
Set AF = Application.WorksheetFunction
AllMin = AF.Min(sl_Data)
AllMax = AF.Max(sl_Data)
AllMin = Int(AllMin)
AllMax = Int(AllMax + 0.9)
'Allow automatic axis scale, but all three of them the same
With SG.Axes.Vertical
  .MinScaleType = xlSparkScaleCustom
```

```
     .MaxScaleType = xlSparkScaleCustom
     .CustomMinScaleValue = AllMin
     .CustomMaxScaleValue = AllMax
   End With
   'Add two labels to show minimum and maximum
   With WSL.Range("A2")
     .Value = AllMax & vbLf & vbLf & vbLf & vbLf _
       & vbLf & vbLf & vbLf & vbLf & AllMin
     .HorizontalAlignment = xlRight
     .VerticalAlignment = xlTop
     .Font.Size = 8
     .Font.Bold = True
     .WrapText = True
   End With
   'Put the final value on the right
   FinalVal = Round(WSD.Cells(Rows.Count, 6).End(xlUp).Value, 0)
   Rg = AllMax - AllMin
   RgTenth = Rg / 10
   FromTop = AllMax - FinalVal
   FromTop = Round(FromTop / RgTenth, 0) - 1
   If FromTop < 0 Then FromTop = 0
   Select Case FromTop
     Case 0
       RtLabel = FinalVal
     Case Is > 0
       RtLabel = Application.WorksheetFunction. Rept(vbLf, FromTop) & FinalVal
   End Select
   With WSL.Range("E2")
     .Value = RtLabel
     .HorizontalAlignment = xlLeft
     .VerticalAlignment = xlTop
     .Font.Size = 8
     .Font.Bold = True
   End With
   End Sub
```

Formatting sparklines

Most of the formatting available with sparklines involves setting the color of various elements of the sparkline.

There are a few methods for assigning colors in Excel. Before diving into the sparkline properties, you can read about the two methods of assigning colors in Excel VBA.

Using theme colors

A theme is composed of a body font, a headline font, a series of effects, and then a series of colors.

The first four colors are used for text and backgrounds. The next six colors are the accent colors. There are also two colors used for hyperlinks and followed hyperlinks. The 20-plus built-in themes include colors that work well together. For now, let's focus on the accent colors.

Go to Page Layout | Themes, and next to the theme dropdown is a Colors dropdown. Open that dropdown and select Customize Colors from the bottom of the list. Excel shows the Create New Theme Colors dialog (see Figure 17-7). This dialog gives you a good picture of the 12 colors associated with the theme.

Throughout Excel, there are many color chooser dropdowns. As shown in Figure 17-8, a section of each dropdown is called Theme Colors. The top row under Theme Colors displays the four fonts and six accent colors. The exception is the color menu in the Create New Theme Colors dialog, where the top row also includes the hyperlink colors.

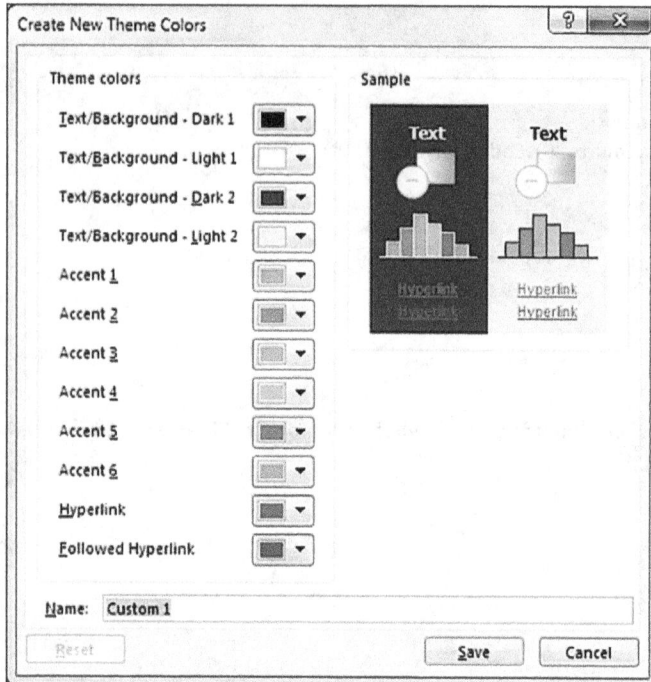

FIGURE 17-7 Twelve categories can be customized with different colors.

If you want to choose the last color in the first row, the VBA is as follows:

```
ActiveCell.Font.ThemeColor = xlThemeColorAccent6
```

Going across that top row of Figure 17-8, these are the 10 colors:

```
xlThemeColorDark1
xlThemeColorLight1
xlThemeColorDark2
xlThemeColorLight2
xlThemeColorAccent1
xlThemeColorAccent2
xlThemeColorAccent3
xlThemeColorAccent4
xlThemeColorAccent5
xlThemeColorAccent6
```

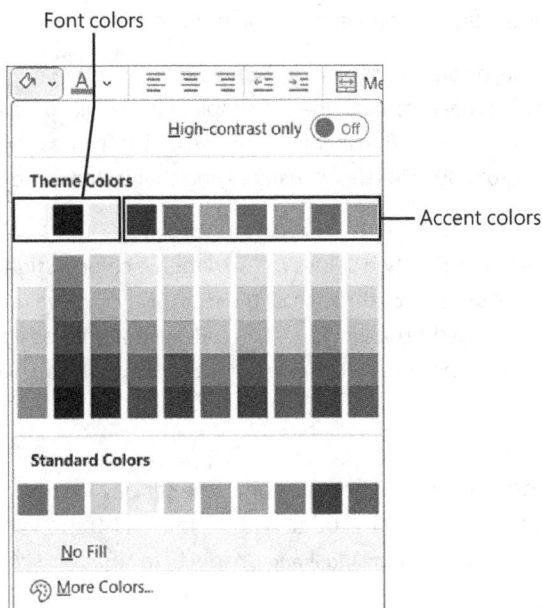

Font colors

Accent colors

FIGURE 17-8 All but the hyperlink colors from the theme appear across the top row.

> **Caution** The first four colors seem to be reversed. `xlThemeColorDark1` is a white color. This is because the VBA constants were written from the point of view of the font color to use when the cell contains a dark or light background. If you have a cell filled with a dark color, you want to display a white font. Hence, `xlThemeColorDark1` is white, and `xlThemeColorLight1` is black.

On your computer, open the Fill Color dropdown menu on the Home tab and look at it in color. If you are using the Office theme, the last column is various shades of green. The top row is the actual color from the theme. Then, five rows go from a light green to a very dark green.

Excel lets you modify the theme color by lightening or darkening it. The values range from –1, which is very dark, to +1, which is very light. For example, the very light green in row 2 of Figure 17-8 has a tint and shade value of 0.8, which is almost completely light. The next row has a tint and shade level of 0.6. The next row has a tint and shade level of 0.4. That gives you three choices that are lighter than the theme color. The next two rows are darker than the theme color. These two darker rows have values of –.25 and –.5.

If you turn on the macro recorder and choose one of these colors, you see a confusing bunch of code:

```
.Pattern = xlSolid
.PatternColorIndex = xlAutomatic
.ThemeColor = xlThemeColorAccent6
.TintAndShade = 0.799981688894314
.PatternTintAndShade = 0
```

If you are using a solid fill, you can leave out the first, second, and fifth lines of code.

The .TintAndShade line looks confusing because computers cannot round decimal tenths very well. Remember that computers store numbers in binary format, where a simple number like 0.1 is a repeating decimal. As the macro recorder tries to convert 0.8 from binary to decimal, it "misses" by a bit and comes up with a very close number: 0.799981688894314. This is really saying that it should be 80 percent lighter than the base number.

If you are writing code by hand, you only have to assign two values to use a theme color. Assign the .ThemeColor property to one of the six x1ThemeColorAccent1 through x1ThemeColorAccent6 values. If you want to use a theme color from the top row of the dropdown, the .TintAndShade should be 0 and can be omitted. If you want to lighten the color, use a positive decimal for .TintAndShade. If you want to darken the color, use a negative decimal.

> **Tip** The five shades in the color palette dropdowns are not the complete set of variations. In VBA, you can assign any two-digit decimal value from –1.00 to +1.00. Figure 17-9 shows 201 variations of one theme color created using the .TintAndShade property in VBA.

	B	C	D	E	F	G	H	I	J	K
1	Darker (Negative Tint & Shade)									
3	-1.00	-0.99	-0.98	-0.97	-0.96	-0.95	-0.94	-0.93	-0.92	-0.91
4	-0.90	-0.89	-0.88	-0.87	-0.86	-0.85	-0.84	-0.83	-0.82	-0.81
5	-0.80	-0.79	-0.78	-0.77	-0.76	-0.75	-0.74	-0.73	-0.72	-0.71
6	-0.70	-0.69	-0.68	-0.67	-0.66	-0.65	-0.64	-0.63	-0.62	-0.61
7	-0.60	-0.59	-0.58	-0.57	-0.56	-0.55	-0.54	-0.53	-0.52	-0.51
8	-0.50	-0.49	-0.48	-0.47	-0.46	-0.45	-0.44	-0.43	-0.42	-0.41
9	-0.40	-0.39	-0.38	-0.37	-0.36	-0.35	-0.34	-0.33	-0.32	-0.31
10	-0.30	-0.29	-0.28	-0.27	-0.26	-0.25	-0.24	-0.23	-0.22	-0.21
11	-0.20	-0.19	-0.18	-0.17	-0.16	-0.15	-0.14	-0.13	-0.12	-0.11
12	-0.10	-0.09	-0.08	-0.07	-0.06	-0.05	-0.04	-0.03	-0.02	-0.01
14	Zero	0								
16	Lighter (Positive Tint & Shade)									
18	+0.01	+0.02	+0.03	+0.04	+0.05	+0.06	+0.07	+0.08	+0.09	+0.10
19	+0.11	+0.12	+0.13	+0.14	+0.15	+0.16	+0.17	+0.18	+0.19	+0.20
20	+0.21	+0.22	+0.23	+0.24	+0.25	+0.26	+0.27	+0.28	+0.29	+0.30
21	+0.31	+0.32	+0.33	+0.34	+0.35	+0.36	+0.37	+0.38	+0.39	+0.40
22	+0.41	+0.42	+0.43	+0.44	+0.45	+0.46	+0.47	+0.48	+0.49	+0.50
23	+0.51	+0.52	+0.53	+0.54	+0.55	+0.56	+0.57	+0.58	+0.59	+0.60
24	+0.61	+0.62	+0.63	+0.64	+0.65	+0.66	+0.67	+0.68	+0.69	+0.70
25	+0.71	+0.72	+0.73	+0.74	+0.75	+0.76	+0.77	+0.78	+0.79	+0.80
26	+0.81	+0.82	+0.83	+0.84	+0.85	+0.86	+0.87	+0.88	+0.89	+0.90
27	+0.91	+0.92	+0.93	+0.94	+0.95	+0.96	+0.97	+0.98	+0.99	+1.00

FIGURE 17-9 These are shades of one theme color.

To recap, if you want to work with theme colors, you generally change two properties: the theme color in order to choose one of the six accent colors and the tint and shade to lighten or darken the base color, like this:

```
.ThemeColor = xlThemeColorAccent6
.TintAndShade = 0.4
```

> **Note** One advantage of using theme colors is that your sparklines change color based on the theme. If you later decide to switch from the Office theme to the Metro theme, the colors change to match the theme.

Using RGB colors

For the past three decades, computers have offered a palette of 16 million colors. These colors derive from adjusting the amount of red, green, and blue light in a cell.

In your elementary school art class, you probably learned that the three primary colors are red, yellow, and blue. You could make green by mixing some yellow and blue paint. You could make purple by mixing some red and blue paint. You could make orange by mixing some yellow and red paint. As other classmates and I soon discovered, you could make black by mixing all the paint colors. Those rules all work with pigments in paint, but they don't work with light.

Those pixels on your computer screen are made up of light. In the light spectrum, the three primary colors are red, green, and blue. You can make the 16 million colors of the RGB color palette by mixing various amounts of red, green, and blue light. Each of the three colors is assigned an intensity from 0 (no light) to 255 (full light).

You will often see a color described using the RGB function. In this function, the first value is the amount of red, the second value is the amount of green, and the third value is the amount of blue:

- To make red, you use =RGB(255,0,0).

- To make green, use =RGB(0,255,0).

- To make blue, use =RGB(0,0,255).

- What happens if you mix 100% of all three colors of light? You get white! To make white, use =RGB(255,255,255).

- What if you shine no light in a pixel? You get black: =RGB(0,0,0).

- To make purple, you use some red, a little green, and some blue: =RGB(139,65,123).

- To make yellow, use full red and green and no blue: =RGB(255,255,0).

- To make orange, use less green than for yellow: =RGB(255,153,0).

In VBA, you can use the RGB function just as it is shown here. The macro recorder is not a big fan of using the RGB function, though. It instead shows the result of the RGB function. Here is how you convert from the three arguments of the RGB function to the color value:

- Take the red value times 1.

- Add the green value times 256.

- Add the blue value times 65,536.

> **Note** Why 65,536? It is 256 raised to the second power.

If you choose a red for your sparkline, you frequently see the macro recorder assign .Color = 255. This is because =RGB(255,0,0) is 255.

When the macro recorder assigns a value of 5287936, what color does this mean? Here are the steps you follow to find out:

1. In Excel, enter =Dec2Hex(5287936). You get the answer 50B000, which is the color that web designers refer to as #50B000.

2. Go to your favorite search engine and search for "color chooser." Choose a utility that allows you to type in the hex color code and see the color. Type 50B000. You see that #50B000 is RGB(80,176,0).

While at the color chooser web page, you're offered additional colors that complement the original color. Click around to find other shades of colors and see the RGB values for those.

To recap, to skip theme colors and use RGB colors, you set the .Color property to the result of an RGB function.

Formatting sparkline elements

Figure 17-10 shows a plain sparkline. The data is created from 12 points that show performance versus a budget but don't show the scale.

If your sparkline includes both positive and negative numbers, it helps to show the horizontal axis so that you can figure out which points are above budget and which points are below budget.

To show the axis, use the following:

```
SG.Axes.Horizontal.Axis.Visible = True
```

Figure 17-11 shows the horizontal axis. This helps to show which months were above or below budget.

1		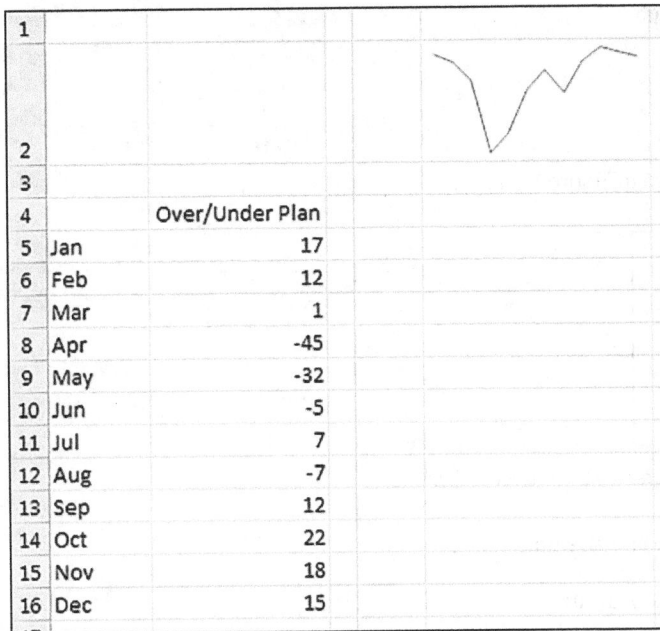
2		
3		
4		Over/Under Plan
5	Jan	17
6	Feb	12
7	Mar	1
8	Apr	-45
9	May	-32
10	Jun	-5
11	Jul	7
12	Aug	-7
13	Sep	12
14	Oct	22
15	Nov	18
16	Dec	15

FIGURE 17-10 This is a default sparkline.

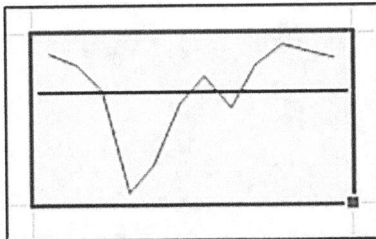

FIGURE 17-11 Add the horizontal axis to show which months were above or below budget.

Using code from the section "Scaling sparklines" earlier in this chapter, you can add high and low labels to the cell to the left of the sparkline:

```
Set AF = Application.WorksheetFunction
MyMax = AF.Max(Range("B5:B16"))
MyMin = AF.Min(Range("B5:B16"))
LabelStr = MyMax & vbLf & vbLf & vbLf & vbLf & MyMin
With SG.Axes.Vertical
    .MinScaleType = xlSparkScaleCustom
    .MaxScaleType = xlSparkScaleCustom
    .CustomMinScaleValue = MyMin
    .CustomMaxScaleValue = MyMax
End With
With Range("D2")
    .WrapText = True
    .Font.Size = 8
```

```
      .HorizontalAlignment = xlRight
      .VerticalAlignment = xlTop
      .Value = LabelStr
      .RowHeight = 56.25
   End With
```

The result of this macro is shown in Figure 17-12.

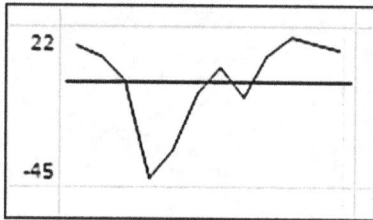

FIGURE 17-12 Use a nonsparkline feature to label the vertical axis.

To change the color of the sparkline, use this:

```
SG.SeriesColor.Color = RGB(255, 191, 0)
```

The Show group of the Sparkline Tools Design tab offers six options. You can further modify those elements by using the Marker Color dropdown menu. You can choose to turn on a marker for every point in the data set, as shown in Figure 17-13.

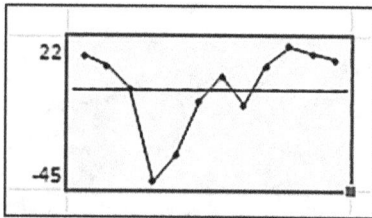

FIGURE 17-13 Show all markers on the sparkline.

This code shows a black marker at every point:

```
With SG.Points
   .Markers.Color.Color = RGB(0, 0, 0) 'black
   .Markers.Visible = True
End With
```

Instead, you can use markers to show only the minimum, maximum, first, and last points. The following code shows the minimum in red, the maximum in green, and the first and last points in blue:

```
With SG.Points
   .Lowpoint.Color.Color = RGB(255, 0, 0) 'red
   .Highpoint.Color.Color = RGB(51, 204, 77) 'green
   .Firstpoint.Color.Color = RGB(0, 0, 255) 'blue
   .Lastpoint.Color.Color = RGB(0, 0, 255) 'blue
```

```
      .Negative.Color.Color = RGB(127, 0, 0) 'pink
      .Markers.Color.Color = RGB(0, 0, 0) 'black
      'Choose Which points to Show
      .Highpoint.Visible = True
      .Lowpoint.Visible = True
      .Firstpoint.Visible = True
      .Lowpoint.Visible = True
      .Negative.Visible = False
      .Markers.Visible = False
   End With
```

When setting the Markers property, the color applies to all points, even if individual points—such as High Point—have a different color assigned. However, what determines visibility is which options are selected. In Figure 17-14, deselecting the Markers and Negative points allows only the high, low, first, and last points to be visible.

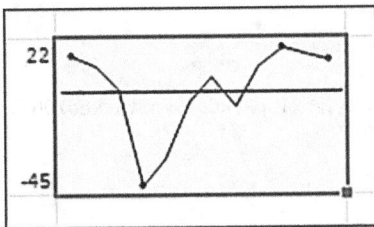

FIGURE 17-14 This sparkline shows only key markers.

> **Note** Negative markers are particularly handy when you are formatting win/loss charts, which are discussed in the next section.

Formatting win/loss charts

Win/loss charts are a special type of sparkline for tracking binary events. A win/loss chart shows an upward-facing marker for a positive value and a downward-facing marker for any negative value. For a zero, no marker is shown.

You can use these charts to track proposal wins versus losses. In Figure 17-15, a win/loss chart shows the last 25 regular-season baseball games of the famed 1951 pennant race between the Brooklyn Dodgers and the New York Giants. This chart shows that the Giants went on a seven-game winning streak to finish the regular season. The Dodgers went 3–4 during this period and ended in a tie with the Giants, forcing a three-game playoff. The Giants won the first game, lost the second, and then advanced to the World Series by winning the third playoff game. The Giants leaped out to a 2–1 lead over the Yankees but then lost three straight.

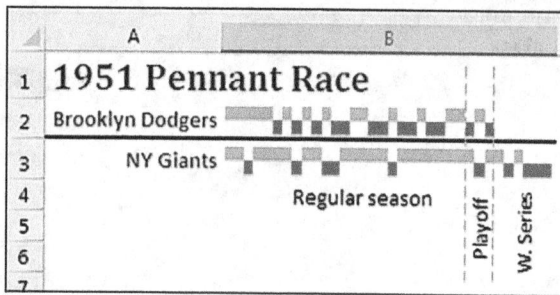

FIGURE 17-15 This win/loss chart documents the most famous pennant race in history.

> 📝 **Note** The words *Regular season*, *Playoff*, and *W. Series*, as well as the two dotted lines, are not part of the sparkline. The lines are drawing objects manually added by choosing Insert | Illustrations | Shapes.

To create the chart, you use `SparklineGroups.Add` with the type `xlSparkColumnStacked100`, like this:

```
Set SG = Range("B2:B3").SparklineGroups.Add( _
    Type:=xlSparkColumnStacked100, SourceData:="C2:AJ3")
```

You generally show the wins and losses using different colors. One obvious color scheme is red for losses and green for wins.

There is no specific way to change only the "up" markers, so change the color of all markers to green:

```
'Show all points as green
SG.SeriesColor.Color = 5287936
```

Then, change the color of the negative markers to red:

```
'Show losses as red
With SG.Points.Negative
   .Visible = True
   .SeriesColor = 255
End With
```

It is easier to create the up/down charts. You don't have to worry about setting the line color, and the vertical axis is always fixed.

Creating a dashboard

Sparklines provide the benefit of communicating a lot of information in a very tiny space. In this section, you'll see how to fit over 130 charts on one page.

Figure 17-16 shows a data set that summarizes a 1.8-million-row data set. I used the Power Pivot add-in for Excel to import the records and then calculated three new measures:

- YTD sales by month by store

- YTD sales by month for the previous year

- Percent increase of YTD sales versus the previous year

A key statistic in retail stores is how you are doing now compared to the same time last year. Also, this analysis has the benefit of being cumulative. The final number for December represents whether the store was up or down compared to the previous year.

	A	B	C	D	E	F	G	H	I	J	K	L	M
1	YTD Sales - % Change from Previous Year												
2													
3	Store	Jan	Feb	Mar	Apr	May	Jun	Jul	Aug	Sep	Oct	Nov	Dec
4	Sherman (	1.9%	-1.3%	-0.8%	-0.2%	-0.1%	-0.1%	0.2%	-0.1%	0.0%	0.7%	0.4%	1.1%
5	Brea Mall	6.3%	-0.5%	-0.2%	0.1%	0.1%	-0.8%	-0.1%	-0.7%	-0.5%	-0.3%	-0.5%	0.1%
6	Park Place	4.4%	-0.8%	-0.4%	-0.5%	-0.4%	-0.4%	-0.3%	-0.8%	-0.9%	-0.6%	-1.1%	-1.5%
7	Galleria at	-0.3%	-3.5%	-3.2%	-1.8%	-1.0%	-0.8%	-0.5%	-0.4%	-0.5%	-0.2%	-0.8%	-1.4%
8	Mission V	7.3%	-0.1%	-1.2%	-0.8%	-0.2%	-0.3%	0.0%	0.0%	-0.2%	-0.3%	0.1%	0.1%
9	Corona De	5.2%	-0.2%	-1.0%	-0.1%	0.4%	0.6%	0.4%	0.1%	0.5%	0.8%	0.4%	0.4%
10	San Franci	0.6%	-1.8%	-2.0%	-0.9%	-0.6%	-0.9%	-0.5%	-1.1%	-0.7%	-0.6%	-0.4%	-0.5%

FIGURE 17-16 This summary of 1.8 million records is a sea of numbers.

Observations about sparklines

After working with sparklines for a while, some observations come to mind:

- Sparklines are transparent. You can see through them to the underlying cell. This means that the fill color of the underlying cell shows through, and the text in the underlying cell shows through.

- If you make the font really small and align the text with the edge of the cell, you can make the text look like a title or a legend.

- If you turn on text wrapping and make the cell tall enough for 5 or 10 lines of text in the cell, you can control the position of the text in the cell by using vbLf characters in VBA.

- Sparklines work best when they are bigger than a typical cell. For all the examples in this chapter, I made the column wider, the height taller, or both.

- Sparklines created together are grouped. Changes made to one sparkline are made to all sparklines.

- Sparklines can be created on a worksheet separate from the data.

- Sparklines look better when there is some white space around the cells. This would be tough to do manually because you would have to create the sparklines one at a time. It is easy to do here because you can leverage VBA.

Creating hundreds of individual sparklines in a dashboard

You address all the issues just listed as you are creating this dashboard. The plan is to create each store's sparkline individually. This way, a blank row and column appear between the sparklines.

After inserting a new worksheet for the dashboard, you can format the cells in Figure 17-17 with this code:

```
'Set up the dashboard as alternating cells for the sparkline and then blank
For c = 1 To 11 Step 2
  WSL.Cells(1, c).ColumnWidth = 15
  WSL.Cells(1, c + 1).ColumnWidth = 0.6
Next c
For r = 1 To 45 Step 2
  WSL.Cells(r, 1).RowHeight = 38
  WSL.Cells(r + 1, 1).RowHeight = 3
Next r
```

Keep track of which cell contains the next sparkline with two variables:

```
NextRow = 1
NextCol = 1
```

Figure out how many rows of data there are in the list object on the Data worksheet. Loop through the object's data body range. For each row, you make a sparkline.

Build a text string that points back to the correct row on the Data sheet, using this code, and use that as the source data argument when defining the sparkline:

```
ThisSource = "Data!B" & Lo.DataBodyRange.Row & ":M" & Lo.DataBodyRange.Row
Set SG = WSL.Cells(NextRow, NextCol).SparklineGroups.Add( _
  Type:=xlSparkColumn, SourceData:=ThisSource)
```

> **Note** Lo.DataBodyRange.Row returns the sheet row number, not the data body range row number. If the data body range starts on row 4, ThisSource is 4, not 1.

In this case, you want to show a horizontal axis at the zero location. The range of values for all stores was –5% to +10%. The maximum scale value here is being set to 0.15 (which is equivalent to 15%) to allow extra room for the "title" in the cell:

```
SG.Axes.Horizontal.Axis.Visible = True
With SG.Axes.Vertical
  .MinScaleType = xlSparkScaleCustom
  .MaxScaleType = xlSparkScaleCustom
  .CustomMinScaleValue = -0.05
  .CustomMaxScaleValue = 0.15
End With
```

As in the previous example with the win/loss chart, you want the positive columns to be green and the negative columns to be red:

```
'All columns green
SG.SeriesColor.Color = RGB(0, 176, 80)
'Negative columns red
SG.Points.Negative.Visible = True
SG.Points.Negative.Color.Color = RGB(255, 0, 0)
```

Remember that the sparkline has a transparent background. Thus, you can write really small text to the cell, and it behaves almost like chart labels.

The following code joins the store name (Cells(i,1).Value) and the final percentage change for the year (FinalValue) into a title for the chart. The program writes this title to the cell but makes it small, centered, and vertically aligned:

```
FinalVal = Lo.DataBodyRange.Cells(i, Lo.ListColumns.Count).Value
ThisStore = Lo.DataBodyRange.Cells(i, 1).Value & " " & _
    Format(FinalVal, "+0.0%;-0.0%;0%")
'Add a label
With WSL.Cells(NextRow, NextCol)
  .Value = ThisStore
  .HorizontalAlignment = xlCenter
  .VerticalAlignment = xlTop
  .Font.Size = 8
  .WrapText = True
End With
```

The final element is to change the background color of the cell based on the final percentage (FinalVal) so that if it is up, the background is light green, and if it is down, the background is light red:

```
'Color the cell light red for negative, light green for positive
With WSL.Cells(NextRow, NextCol).Interior
  If FinalVal <= 0 Then
    .Color = RGB(255, 0, 0)
    .TintAndShade = 0.9
  Else
    .Color = RGB(197, 247, 224)
    .TintAndShade = 0.7
  End If
End With
```

After that sparkline is done, the column or row positions are incremented to prepare for the next chart:

```
NextCol = NextCol + 2
If NextCol > 11 Then
  NextCol = 1
  NextRow = NextRow + 2
End If
```

After this, the loop continues with the next store.

The complete code is shown here:

```
Sub StoreDashboard()
Dim SG As SparklineGroup
Dim WSD As Worksheet 'Data worksheet
Dim WSL As Worksheet 'Dashboard
Dim Lo As ListObject 'Data table
Dim c As Integer, r As Integer, NextCol As Integer
Dim i As Long, NextRow As Long
Dim ThisStore As String, ThisSource As String
Dim FinalVal As Double
On Error Resume Next
Application.DisplayAlerts = False
Worksheets("Dashboard").Delete
On Error GoTo 0
Application.ScreenUpdating = False
Set WSD = Worksheets("Data")
Set WSL = ActiveWorkbook.Worksheets.Add
WSL.Name = "Dashboard"
'Set up the dashboard as alternating cells for the sparkline and then blank
For c = 1 To 11 Step 2
  WSL.Cells(1, c).ColumnWidth = 15
  WSL.Cells(1, c + 1).ColumnWidth = 0.6
Next c
For r = 1 To 45 Step 2
  WSL.Cells(r, 1).RowHeight = 38
  WSL.Cells(r + 1, 1).RowHeight = 3
Next r
NextRow = 1
NextCol = 1
Set Lo = WSD.ListObjects("Table1")
For i = 1 To Lo.DataBodyRange.Rows.Count
  If i > Lo.DataBodyRange.Rows.Count Then Exit For
  FinalVal = Lo.DataBodyRange.Cells(i, Lo.ListColumns.Count).Value
  ThisStore = Lo.DataBodyRange.Cells(i, 1).Value & " " & _
    Format(FinalVal, "+0.0%;-0.0%;0%")
  ThisSource = "Data!B" & Lo.DataBodyRange.Row & ":M" & Lo.DataBodyRange.Row
  Set SG = WSL.Cells(NextRow, NextCol).SparklineGroups.Add( _
    Type:=xlSparkColumn, SourceData:=ThisSource)
  SG.Axes.Horizontal.Axis.Visible = True
  With SG.Axes.Vertical
    .MinScaleType = xlSparkScaleCustom
    .MaxScaleType = xlSparkScaleCustom
    .CustomMinScaleValue = -0.05
    .CustomMaxScaleValue = 0.15
  End With
  'All columns green
  SG.SeriesColor.Color = RGB(0, 176, 80)
  'Negative columns red
  SG.Points.Negative.Visible = True
  SG.Points.Negative.Color.Color = RGB(255, 0, 0)
  'Add a label
```

```
With WSL.Cells(NextRow, NextCol)
  .Value = ThisStore
  .HorizontalAlignment = xlCenter
  .VerticalAlignment = xlTop
  .Font.Size = 8
  .WrapText = True
End With
'Color the cell light red for negative, light green for positive
With WSL.Cells(NextRow, NextCol).Interior
  If FinalVal <= 0 Then
    .Color = RGB(255,0,0)
    .TintAndShade = 0.9
  Else
    .Color = RGB(197, 247, 224)
    .TintAndShade = 0.7
  End If
End With
NextCol = NextCol + 2
 If NextCol > 11 Then
   NextCol = 1
   NextRow = NextRow + 2
 End If
Next i
Application.ScreenUpdating = True
Set SG = Nothing
Set WSD= Nothing : Set WSL = Nothing
Set Lo = Nothing
End Sub
```

Figure 17-17 shows the final dashboard, which prints on a single page and summarizes 1.8 million rows of data.

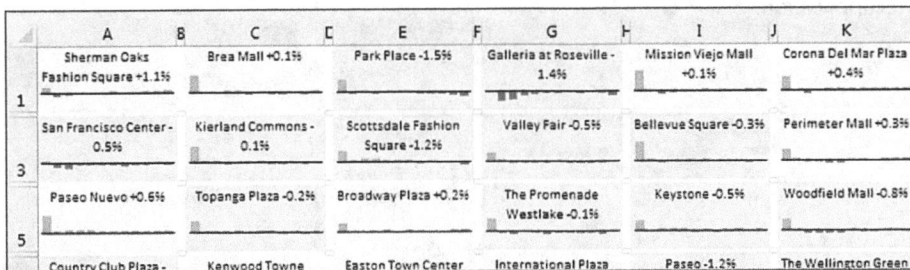

FIGURE 17-17 One page summarizes the sales from more than 100 stores.

If you zoom in, you can see that every cell tells a story. In Figure 17-18, Park Meadows in cell I33 had a great January, managed to stay ahead of last year through the entire year, and finished up 0.8%. Lakeside in cell I35 also had a positive January, but then it had a bad February and a worse March. Lakeside struggled back toward 0% for the rest of the year but ended up down seven-tenths of a percent.

> **Note** The report is addictive. I find myself studying all sorts of trends, but then I have to remind myself that I created the 1.8-million-row data set using `RandBetween` just a few weeks ago! The report is so compelling that I am getting drawn into studying fictional data.

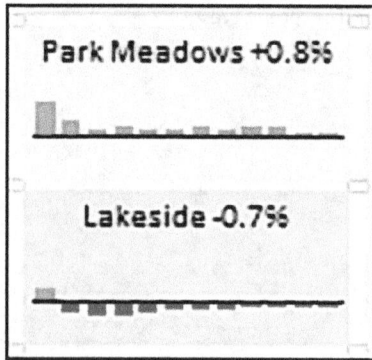

FIGURE 17-18 Note the detail of two sparkline charts.

Next steps

Sparklines let you create miniature column or line charts directly inside cells, making it easy to spot trends at a glance. Excel doesn't offer labels for sparklines, but with a bit of VBA ingenuity, you can add custom chart or axis titles, improving clarity and usability. In Chapter 18, "Reading from the web using M and VBA," you find out how to use Power Query to automatically import data from the Internet to your Excel applications.

Reading from the web using M and VBA

In this chapter, you will:

- Get credentials for accessing a website API

- Build a query in Power Query using the M language to retrieve data from the web for one specific value

- Generalize the queries using VBA

- Use Global Variables and Loops in M

- Use `Application.OnTime` to periodically analyze data

The Internet keeps evolving. For previous editions of this book, you used VBA to automate a web query. All the information needed to get the data was passed as parameters in the URL.

As websites and HTML evolve, the days of wide-open websites with parameters in the URL are numbered. The websites used in previous editions of this book have changed their structure, and the legacy web query approach no longer works.

Microsoft has been focused on improving the Power Query tools to pull data from the web. Power Query has several advantages, including the ability to provide your login and password through Power Query, as well as Power Query's programming language, M, which allows you to make calls to an Application Programming Interface (API) that drives many websites.

In this chapter, you will use Power Query and the M language to build a report that accesses the Spotify music database with the search term "Bruce Springsteen." Once the query is working in Power Query, you can use VBA to change the search term to any artist that you type.

> **Note** Refer to Chapter 23, "The Windows Application Programming Interface (API)," for more information about APIs and how they can expand Excel's capabilities.

Get credentials for accessing an API

In order to access many websites programmatically, you need to create a developer account. These accounts might allow you to initially access a limited number of records each day for free. But if your workbook becomes wildly successful and is used by many people, then you might need to subscribe to the website and pay in order to access their data.

If you don't have a Spotify account, you can set up a free account, which includes a large database of artist, album, and song data. Basic access is free, and the daily limits should be enough for you to experiment with the Power Query technology.

> **Note** The following steps and screenshots reflect the Spotify developer portal at the time of this writing. By the time you're reading this and creating your own account, some screens or navigation paths might be different, though the overall process should remain the same.

1. Go to *https://developer.spotify.com/.*

2. If there's no Sign Up For Spotify link on the page, click Log In and then Sign Up For Spotify to access the Spotify API.

3. Once your account is ready (there may be a delay as Spotify grants you access), click your profile name and select Dashboard from the dropdown.

4. Click the Create app button to create a new app. Fill in the required App Name, App Description, and Redirect URLs fields. In Figure 18-1, a name such as PowerQuery and a description of the API connection for Power Query are used.

5. Select the API you want to use. For our example, the Web API is the only one we need.

6. Accept the Spotify's Developer Terms of Service and Design Guidelines.

7. Click Save.

After clicking the Save button, you're taken to the Spotify for Developers dashboard, as shown in Figure 18-2, where you're provided with a Client ID and a Client Secret code unique to the app. You'll use these values in Power Query to authenticate your session.

Congratulations! That is all you need to do in order to create a Spotify app that you will use to communicate with the Spotify API to retrieve data in Power Query.

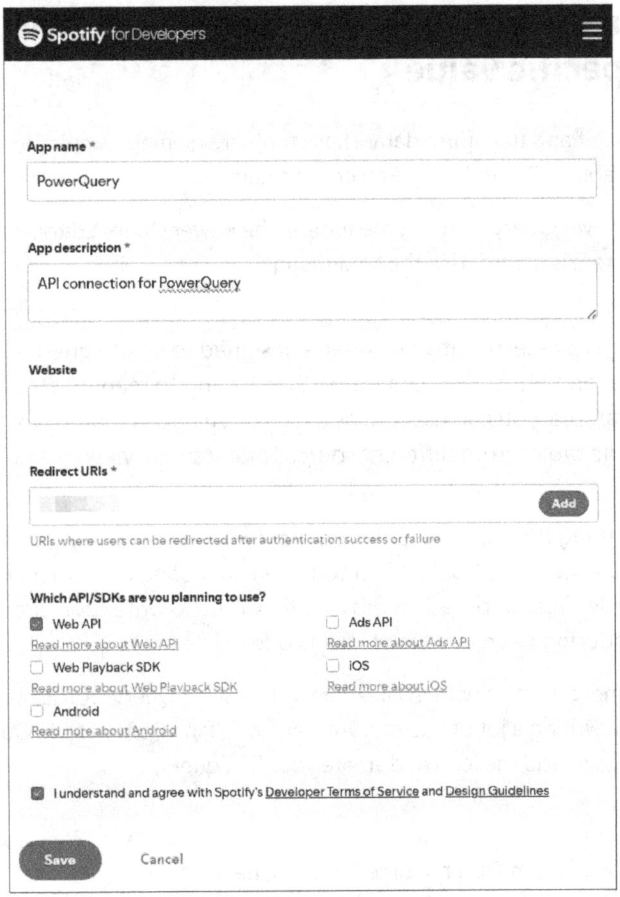

FIGURE 18-1 After signing in to Spotify for Developers, create an app and give it a name.

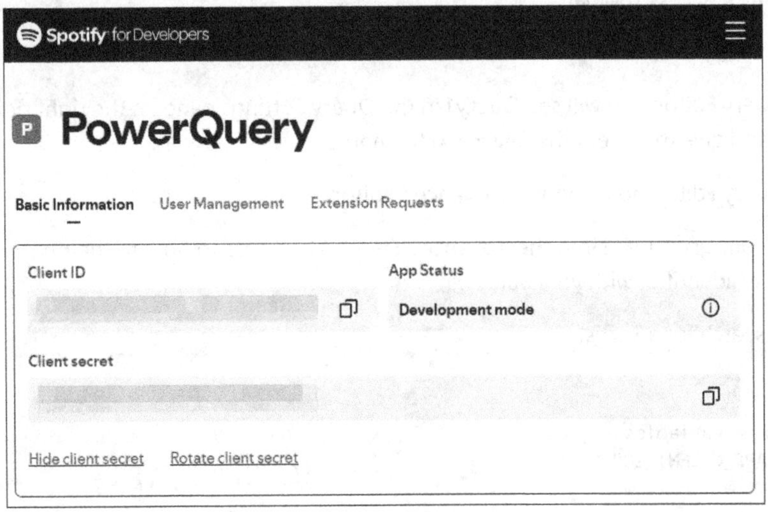

FIGURE 18-2 The Client ID and Client Secret values are the ones you need to authenticate your query in Power Query.

Build a query in Power Query using the M language to retrieve data from the web for a specific value

The Power Query tools were added to get and transform data. These tools are gaining popularity within Microsoft, as they are now available in Power BI and Power Automate.

Generally, you build a program in Power Query by using the tools in the Power Query Editor. As you clean your data using the tools, a program is recorded in the M language.

> **Note** M is short for "Mashup." M is a case-sensitive language designed to create queries that mix data. You use it to process and transform data rather than having to manipulate the original data structure. For example, you can use it to add new calculation columns to imported data or to merge multiple tables from different sources into a single view.

You probably got started with VBA using the macro recorder, but now you've moved beyond the macro recorder, and that is why you purchased this book. When you clean data using the Power Query Editor, it is like using an M macro recorder. Your approach in this chapter will be to write code directly in the Power Query Advanced Editor, producing cleaner, more efficient code.

To get to the Advanced Editor, you need to start with a blank query. The Blank Query icon is buried in the menu structure, so if you plan on writing a lot of M code, you can add Blank Query to the Quick Access Toolbar (QAT). Follow these steps to add the icon and create your first query:

1. Open a new workbook in Excel.

2. On the Data tab, choose Get Data | From Other Sources | Blank Query.

3. Right-click Blank Query and choose Add To Quick Access Toolbar. The Blank Query icon will be added to the Quick Access Toolbar.

4. Click the Blank Query icon.

5. In the Power Query Editor, you will see Query1 in the Query Settings pane on the right side. Click that field and give the query the **SearchArtist** name.

6. In the Power Query Editor, go to Home | Advanced Editor.

7. Type the code from Listing 18-1 into the Advanced Editor. Make sure to update the `clientId` and `clientSecret` identifier with your values.

LISTING 18-1 M code to search for an artist

```
let
  //generate token
  //declare some fixed variables
  clientId = "YOUR_APP_CLIENT_ID",
```

```
        clientSecret = "YOUR_APP_CLIENT_SECRET",
        binaryText = Text.ToBinary(clientId & ":" & clientSecret),
        base64Text = Binary.ToText(binaryText, BinaryEncoding.Base64),
        authCode = "Basic " & base64Text,
        urlAuth = "https://accounts.spotify.com/api/token",
        //define variables using a function call
        Source = Json.Document(
          Web.Contents(
            urlAuth,
            [
              //define a record to use as HTTP header
              Headers = [
                #"Authorization" = authCode,
                #"Content-Type"  = "application/x-www-form-urlencoded",
                #"Cache-Control" = "no-cache, no-store, must-revalidate"
              ],
              Content = Text.ToBinary("grant_type=client_credentials")
            ]
          )
        ),
        Token = "Bearer " & Source[access_token],
        //search for artist
        urlSearch
          = "https://api.spotify.com/v1/search?query=bruce+springsteen&offset=0&" &
            "limit=20&type=artist",
        APIResult = Json.Document(
          Web.Contents(
            urlSearch,
            [Headers = [#"Authorization" = Token, #"Content-Type" = "application/json"]]
          )
        ),
        // Extract items and convert to table
        Artists = APIResult[artists],
        Items = Artists[items],
        ItemsAsTable = Table.FromList(Items, Splitter.SplitByNothing(), null, null,
          ExtraValues.Error),
        Result = Table.ExpandRecordColumn(
          ItemsAsTable,
          "Column1",
          {"id", "name", "popularity"},
          {"ID", "Name", "Popularity"}
        )
    in
      Result
```

> **Note** Refer to the Case Study at the end of this section for an explanation of the let expression.

> **Tip** If your M code is getting long, like the one you just entered, *PowerQueryFormatter.com* can help tidy it up and make it easier to read.

In Listing 18-1, the `Web.Contents` function points to an API endpoint, `urlAuth`, and returns the access token, `Token`, used to authenticate the API in later calls that fetch the actual data.

Access versus Refresh Tokens

APIs like Spotify use access tokens to authorize requests to access their systems. These tokens are temporary and expire after about an hour, so you'll need to generate a new one when that happens. See the "Get credentials for accessing an API" section of this chapter for details on how to do this.

Some APIs support refresh tokens, which let you request a new access token automatically without logging in again. However, that option requires a more advanced setup and isn't used in this chapter. If you're building a more complex integration in the future, check the API's documentation. For Spotify, look under "Refreshing tokens" in Spotify's Tutorials section.

To search for an artist in the Spotify database, consult the Spotify Developer documentation at *https://developer.spotify.com/documentation/web-api/reference/*, and you will find that the Search API is accessed through *https://api.spotify.com/v1/search*.

The Search API requires two parameters named `q` (query) and `type`. The `urlSearch` parameter is used in the code to hold the URL parameter:

```
urlSearch = "https://api.spotify.com/v1/
search?query=bruce+springsteen
&offset=0&limit=20&type=artist",
```

This URL returns data for the `bruce+springsteen` query in `artist` type records from the Spotify database.

The `offset` and `limit` parameters are used to query a set number of records starting from a certain position—in this case, the first 20 records. Web APIs return data as a paginated result to avoid huge data transfers. Instead of fetching all data, it will return results in batches. Currently, the maximum number of records per page is 50, but you should check the API documentation for updates.

The `Headers` record provides the authentication token and specifies the format of the response. In this case, `Token` holds the credentials to authenticate with the API, and `application/json` tells the server to return the data in JSON format.

Near the end of the code, the Spotify API returns a single record. The lines after the `// Extract items` and `convert to table` comment are used to drill down into the record to return fields and then to convert those fields into a table.

Click Done to close the Advanced Editor and see the result.

Power Query nags you about data privacy. Click Continue, and then choose Ignore Privacy Levels and click Save. The data preview window shows the search results for Bruce Springsteen, as shown in Figure 18-3.

Look at the Applied Steps pane in Power Query. Each named step in your M code appears as a line in Applied Steps. Just for fun, click each of the steps for APIResult through ItemsAsTable. Someone who is only using the Power Query interface is going to be super frustrated when they get three-quarters of the way through the process and end up with a single result of "Record," as shown in Figure 18-4. It only takes a few lines of M code to arrive at a useful result, versus many gyrations in the Power Query Editor.

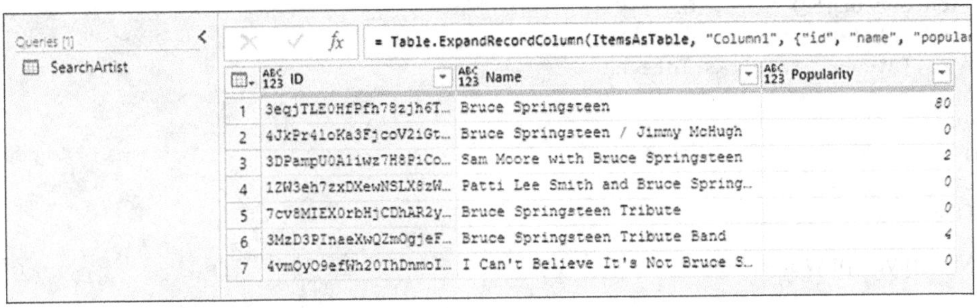

FIGURE 18-3 A query that is hard-coded to search for artists with Bruce Springsteen in the name.

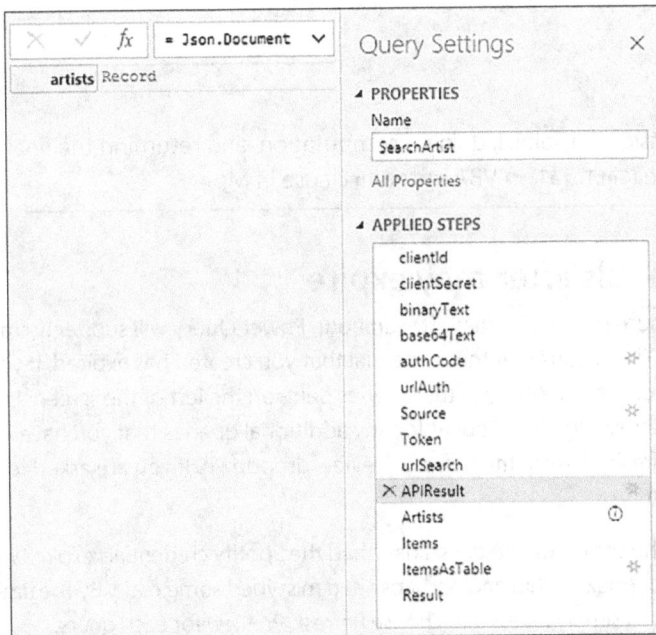

FIGURE 18-4 Even though you wrote your code in the Advanced Editor, you still have a list of Applied Steps and can preview the data at any step along the way by clicking it.

Refreshing the credentials after they expire

Once you have a working query, there is a chance that after an hour, Power Query will suddenly start reporting an authentication error. This means that the credential that you created has expired. If you are in the Power Query Editor, select the first query in the Queries pane on the left of the screen. In the Home tab of the ribbon, choose Refresh Preview. Repeat for any additional queries that you have in the Queries pane, or just select Refresh All from the Refresh Preview dropdown. If you are asked for the type of credentials, choose Anonymous.

While writing this chapter over the course of two days, I have had the Spotify credentials expire twice. The first time this happened, I was perplexed, thinking perhaps I had mistyped some code. By the time it happened again, I was confident that I simply needed to choose Refresh Preview for each query.

Building a custom function in Power Query

In VBA, if you have a bit of code that will be called from multiple procedures, it might be good to put that code in a custom function. The same concept applies to Power Query.

A custom function in VBA might look like this:

```
Function fnSayHello(name)
fnSayHello = "Hello " & name
End Function
```

The similar custom function in M would look like this:

```
(name) as text =>
let
  Result = "Hello " & name
In
  Result
```

There is a bit of code that will be used in both the `SearchArtist` and later in the `ArtistAlbums` and `AlbumTracks` queries. Right now, before you duplicate `SearchArtist` to make the `ArtistAlbums` query, it is time to move the code out to its own function.

> **Tip** Here is an awesome way to start a new query without leaving the Power Query Editor. There is a Queries pane to the left of the data preview. If you only see the vertical word "Queries," then use the > icon at the top of the pane to expand the pane.
>
> Then, right-click the Queries pane (not an actual query) and choose New Query | Other Sources | Blank Query, as shown in Figure 18-5.

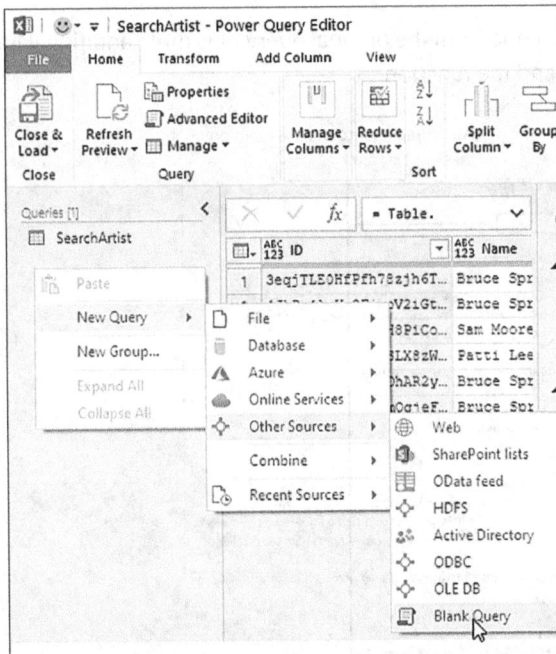

FIGURE 18-5 In VBA, you can start a new macro without leaving the VBA Editor. It is a bit more subtle but possible in the Power Query Editor.

Start a new query and rename it fnGetToken by using the Name box in the Query Settings pane. Open the Advanced Editor and enter the following code into the code pane:

```
() as text =>
  let
    clientId = "YOUR_APP_CLIENT_ID",
    clientSecret = "YOUR_APP_CLIENT_SECRET",
    binaryText = Text.ToBinary(clientId & ":" & clientSecret),
    base64Text = Binary.ToText(binaryText, BinaryEncoding.Base64),
    authCode = "Basic " & base64Text,
    urlAuth = "https://accounts.spotify.com/api/token",
    Source = Json.Document(
      Web.Contents(
        urlAuth,
        [
          Headers = [
            #"Authorization" = authCode,
            #"Content-Type"  = "application/x-www-form-urlencoded",
            #"Cache-Control" = "no-cache, no-store, must-revalidate"
          ],
          Content = Text.ToBinary("grant_type=client_credentials")
        ]
      )
    ),
    Token = "Bearer " & Source[access_token]
  in
    Token
```

To make a function, you use the same code from the original query plus three additional lines. Figure 18-6 compares the original code and the function.

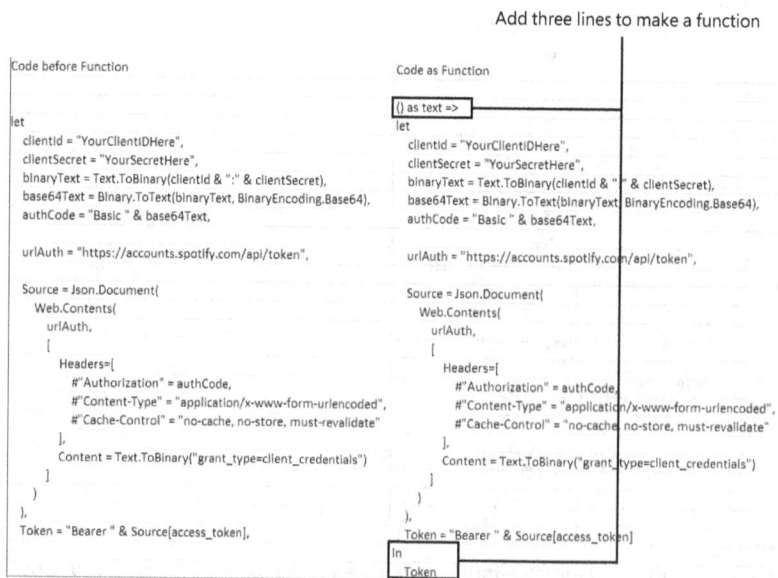

FIGURE 18-6 An extra line at the top and two at the bottom turn this code into a function.

> **Level Up!**
>
> The `fnGetToken` function is called every time you search for an artist, list albums, or get songs. That means you're asking Spotify for a new token every time, even if your current token hasn't expired.
>
> Because access tokens usually last about an hour, this wastes calls—especially during testing. To avoid that, you can set up Power Query to reuse the existing token as long as it's still valid—60 minutes for Spotify.
>
> This chapter will keep the current code for simplicity—it's easier to understand while learning. But if you're ready for the upgrade, refer to the "Reducing API access token requests" section in Chapter 13, "Excel power," for the code and to learn how it works.

Using the new function in your code

Now that we've moved the code for generating a token to its own function, we need to edit the `SearchArtist` query to use it. From the Power Query Editor, right-click the `SearchArtist` query in the Queries pane and choose Advanced Editor.

Delete the code after `let`, down to and including `Token = "Bearer"`.

In the place of the deleted code, add this new line:

```
Token = fnGetToken(),
```

The `SearchArtist` query is significantly shorter now, as shown in Figure 18-7.

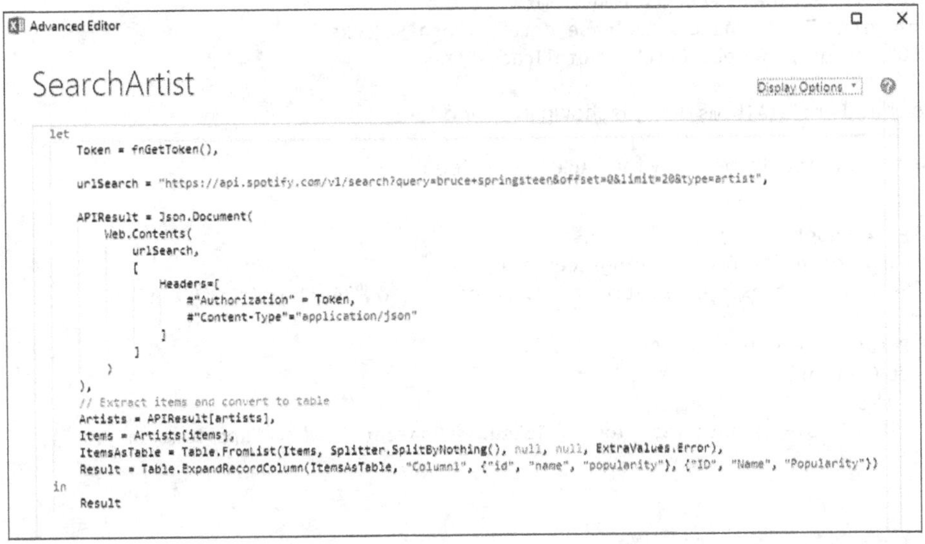

FIGURE 18-7 After moving the credentials to a custom function, the code to retrieve the list of arguments is considerably shorter.

Moving the logic for getting a token out to a function that can be called by both SearchArtist and the soon-to-be-created ArtistAlbums and AlbumTracks queries means that your code is easier to maintain. If you later need to change the Client ID or the Client Secret, there is only one place to change it—in fnGetToken.

Duplicating an existing query to make a new query

Next, it is time to make two new queries to retrieve a list of albums and then a list of songs on the album.

Right-click SearchArtist in the Queries pane and choose Duplicate. Rename the new query as ArtistAlbums. Edit the duplicated query in the Advanced Editor.

The urlSearch line needs to be changed to use the API endpoint to request albums for a given artist ID. Copy the artist ID for Bruce Springsteen from the query preview (see Figure 18-3) and paste it into this line of code. Also note that the URL after v1 now points to artists instead of search:

```
urlSearch = "https://api.spotify.com/v1/artists/3eqjTLEOHfPfh78zjh6TqT/albums",
```

Later in the query, these two lines of code...

```
Artists = APIResult[artists],
Items = Artists[items],
```

...are streamlined into a single line of code:

```
Items = APIResult[items],
```

The list of fields to return changes to this:

```
Result = Table.ExpandRecordColumn(ItemsAsTable,
  "Column1", {"id", "name", "release_date", "total_tracks"},
  {"ID", "Name", "ReleaseDate", "TotalTracks"})
```

The edited ArtistAlbums query is shown in Listing 18-2.

LISTING 18-2 ArtistAlbums query for Bruce Springsteen

```
let
  Token = fnGetToken(),
  // hard-coded for Bruce Springsteen for now
  urlSearch = "https://api.spotify.com/v1/artists/" & "3eqjTLEOHfPfh78zjh6TqT/
albums",
  APIResult = Json.Document(
    Web.Contents(
      urlSearch,
      [Headers = [#"Authorization" = Token, #"Content-Type" = "application/json"]]
    )
  ),
```

```
// Extract items and convert to table
// Remove the Artists = as there is one less level to drill through
Items = APIResult[items],
ItemsAsTable = Table.FromList(Items, Splitter.SplitByNothing(), null, null,
    ExtraValues.Error),
Result = Table.ExpandRecordColumn(
    ItemsAsTable,
    "Column1",
    {"id", "name", "release_date", "total_tracks"},
    {"ID", "Name", "ReleaseDate", "TotalTracks"}
)
in
    Result
```

Figure 18-8 shows the query preview for the ArtistAlbums query.

ABC 123 ID	ABC 123 Name	ABC 123 ReleaseDate	ABC 123 TotalTracks
1 5devPxQnSKVF2Ed0CVwQ…	Letter To You	2020-10-23	12
2 1V2AYh4idtsw2CY1JG2N…	Western Stars - Songs From The Film	2019-10-25	14
3 6BhqFpIgY83rqoZ2L78L…	Western Stars	2019-06-14	13
4 42euss1aYHJvhxttuMbw…	Springsteen on Broadway	2018-12-14	35
5 0zFnhdX1FnfuExL1bVdn…	Chapter and Verse	2016-09-23	18
6 5QbfBwvuHoe2fz1TCCV6…	The Ties That Bind: The River Coll…	2015-12-04	32
7 6QH61tpFEZXObrQHmgpK…	High Hopes	2014-01-14	12
8 75kN1qUWvE10QcnpE6nE…	Wrecking Ball	2012-03-06	13
9 1vHt4VQ8zOxUNmMXR80Y…	Wrecking Ball	2012-03-06	11

FIGURE 18-8 Retrieving a list of albums for Bruce Springsteen.

Querying the list of songs on an album

Duplicate the ArtistAlbums query and name the new query as AlbumTracks. The URLSearch for the
"Letter to You" album is:

```
urlSearch = "https://api.spotify.com/v1/albums/5devPxQnSKVF2Ed0CVwQZh/tracks",
```

The results to return are as follows:

```
Result = Table.ExpandRecordColumn(ItemsAsTable,
    "Column1", {"id", "name", "track_number"},
    {"TrackID", "SongName", "TrkNumber"})
```

Figure 18-9 shows the list of songs and the query code.

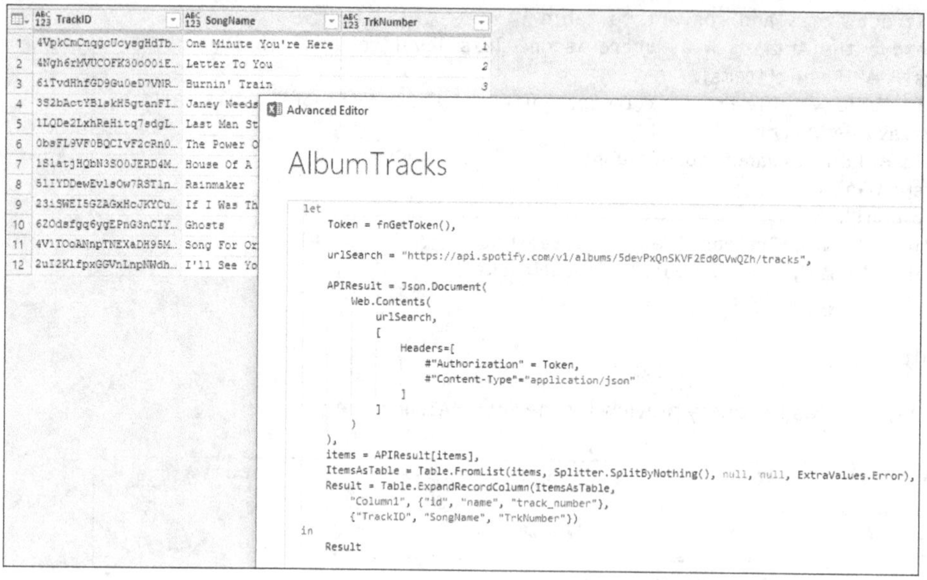

FIGURE 18-9 A list of songs for one album.

Generalizing the queries using VBA

So far, you have three web queries that can only find the track listing for Bruce Springsteen's "Letter to You" album. You might want to search for Mark Knopfler or ELO instead.

> **Note** *Who?* If Springsteen and Knopfler aren't your jam, you'll be able to search for artists such as Queen, Evanescence, Korn, or Pink Floyd instead. Now that's music!

You can use VBA to pass an argument to the query in Power Query.

Simplifying the SearchArtist query to a single line of code

Your goal is to change the SearchArtist, ArtistAlbums, and AlbumTracks queries to a single line of code that can be updated by VBA.

This can be done by moving most of the query logic to three new custom functions. Here are the steps to simplify the SearchArtist query.

Duplicate the SearchArtist query and rename it as fnGetArtists. Edit the code in the Advanced Editor to add a new first line with a parameter. Change the URLSearch line to concatenate the URL with that parameter:

```
(strQuery as text) as table =>
let
```

```
Token = fnGetToken(),
urlSearch = "https://api.spotify.com/v1/search?query=" & strQuery &
    "&offset=0&limit=20&type=artist",
```

Click Done and open the `SearchArtist` query. With all the logic moved out to the `fnGetArtists`, you can simplify the `SearchArtist` query to a single line of code:

```
let Result = fnGetArtists("bruce springsteen") in Result
```

Your strategy will be to use VBA to update that line of code! In VBA, you can change the code in a query by using the `.Formula` property:

```
ThisWorkbook.Queries(id).Formula = "let Result = fnGetArtists(""" & strQuery & _
    """) in Result"
```

You will see this line of VBA in context soon.

But first, you need to simplify the other two functions.

Simplifying the ArtistAlbums query

Duplicate `ArtistAlbums` and rename it as `fnGetAlbums`. Open the Advanced Editor. Add a new first line:

```
(strId as text) as table =>
```

Change the `URLSearch` line to:

```
urlSearch = "https://api.spotify.com/v1/artists/" & strId & "/albums",
```

Close the Advanced Editor. Open the `ArtistAlbums` query in the Advanced Editor, and it becomes a single line of code that calls `fnGetAlbum`, passing in the artist's Spotify ID to retrieve their album list:

```
let Result = fnGetAlbums("3eqjTLE0HfPfh78zjh6TqT") in Result
```

Simplifying the AlbumTracks query

Duplicate the `AlbumTracks` query and rename it as `fnGetTracks`. Open the Advanced Editor. Add a new first line:

```
(strId as text) as table =>
```

Change the `URLSearch` line to:

```
urlSearch = "https://api.spotify.com/v1/albums/" & strId & "/tracks",
```

Close the Advanced Editor. Open the `AlbumTracks` query in the Advanced Editor, and it becomes a single line of code that calls `fnGetTrack`, passing in the album's Spotify ID to retrieve the album's tracks:

```
let Result = fnGetTracks("5devPxQnSKVF2Ed0CVwQZh") in Result
```

Grouping queries to clean up the queries list

You now have seven queries in the Queries pane. It's a good idea to clean up the environment to keep the project organized. Power Query allows grouping objects. To group the four functions, select the first function in the Queries pane. Ctrl+Click the other three function queries to include them in the selection.

Right-click and choose Move to Group | New Group, as shown in Figure 18-10.

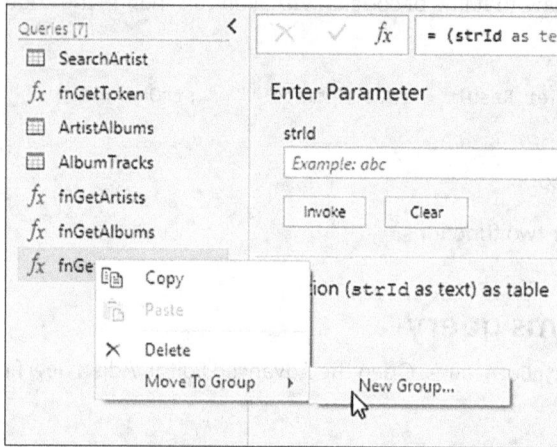

FIGURE 18-10 Choose to group the fn queries.

Power Query asks you for the name for the group. Type **Functions** and click OK. In a few seconds, the Queries pane will be reorganized, with four functions shown in the Functions group and the remaining three functions grouped into Other Queries.

Group the other three functions into a new group called Results.

Each group can be collapsed or expanded using the triangle next to the group name. Figure 18-11 shows the Functions group collapsed and the Results group expanded.

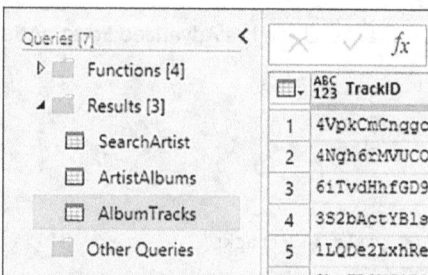

FIGURE 18-11 Group the queries into folders to keep them organized.

Planning the arrangement of query results on your dashboard

So far, none of the queries have been intentionally loaded to an Excel sheet. Depending on your Excel settings (File | Query Options | Default Query Load Settings), Power Query may have automatically added each query to its own worksheet. That's not what we want. Instead, we'll load all three results on a single dashboard worksheet.

Close the Power Query Editor by using the "X" in the top-right corner to return to Excel. Excel will ask if you want to keep or discard the changes. Choose Keep. Excel may insert three new worksheets, one with a table for each query's results. If so, delete those three query sheets. Follow these steps to set up the dashboard worksheet:

1. Find the original worksheet, Sheet1.

2. Rename this sheet Dashboard.

3. In cell A1, type **My Music Dashboard** and apply the Heading1 style.

As shown in Figure 18-12, one arrangement could be to have a button to select the artist in E1:H2. The list of artists could start in A3. The list of albums could start in E4. The list of tracks could start in J5.

The exact location for these queries will have an impact on the VBA that you write, so make a note of where you will be loading the queries.

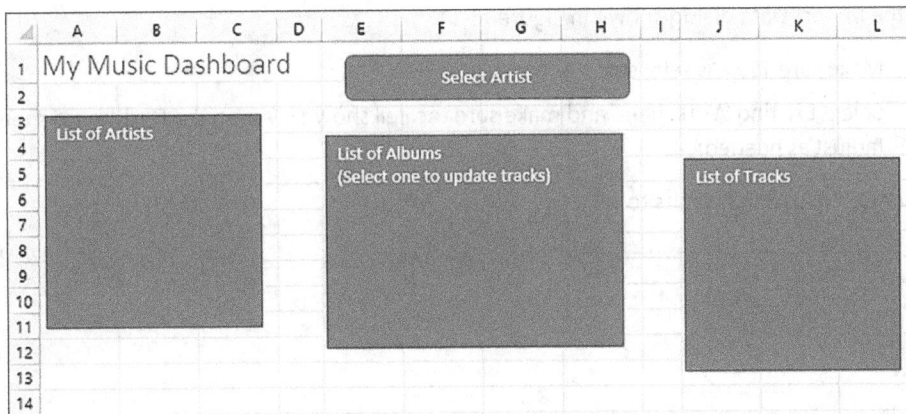

FIGURE 18-12 Choose an arrangement for the query results (boxes are representative of the final design objects).

If you don't see the Queries & Connections task pane along the right edge of Excel, choose Data | Queries & Connections. The groups that you created in the Power Query Editor are used to organize this task pane as well.

4. Select cell A3 in the Dashboard worksheet.

5. Right-click SearchArtists and choose Load To, as shown in Figure 18-13.

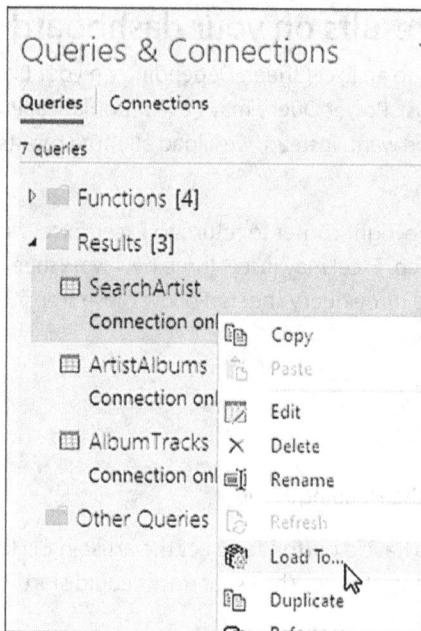

FIGURE 18-13 Choose Load To from the Excel grid.

6. In the Import Data dialog shown in Figure 18-14

    a. Make sure Table is selected.

    b. Select Existing Worksheet, and make sure the cell shown is A3 on the Dashboard sheet (adjust as needed).

7. Click OK to load the results to A3.

FIGURE 18-14 Take control of where the query will load.

Repeat these steps to load the Albums to E4 and the Tracks to J5.

Each query automatically changes the column widths to fit the longest value. At this point, you don't need the Queries & Connections task pane, so use the "X" in the top-right corner to close it.

Add a shape to the top of the spreadsheet that can be used to run a macro. Add a label of **Select Artist**. Right-click the shape and choose Assign Macro. In the Macro dialog, click New to create a new macro on a new module. Use the code from Listing 18-3 as the macro for the button. Note that your sub name may be different, reflecting the name of the shape you drew.

LISTING 18-3 Code to search for an artist

```
Sub RectangleRoundedCorners2_Click()
Dim id As String
Dim qtSearchArtist As QueryTable
Dim strQuery As String
id = "SearchArtist"
Set qtSearchArtist = ThisWorkbook.Worksheets("Dashboard") _
  .ListObjects(id).QueryTable
If Not qtSearchArtist.Refreshing Then
  strQuery = InputBox("Enter artist name.", "Search Artist")
  If Trim(strQuery) = "" Then
    Exit Sub
  End If
  'Update the query to search for the typed artist
  ThisWorkbook.Queries(id).Formula = _
    "let Result = fnGetArtists(""" & strQuery & """) in Result"
  qtSearchArtist.Refresh False
  qtSearchArtist.Parent.Cells(1, 1).Select
End If
End Sub
```

To refresh the `ArtistAlbums` query table, you will use the worksheet's `SelectionChange` event instead of a button. So, when you click an artist ID in columns A:C of the dashboard, it will update the `ArtistAlbums` query and display the result.

Use the following macro from Listing 18-4 in the code pane for the Dashboard worksheet.

LISTING 18-4 Code in the Dashboard's sheet module

```
Private Sub Worksheet_SelectionChange(ByVal Target As Range)
Dim id As String
Dim ThisArtist As String, ThisAlbum As String
Dim qtArtistAlbums As QueryTable, qtAlbumTracks As QueryTable
If Target.Cells.Count = 1 Then   'make sure only one cell is selected
  If Target.Column <= 3 Then
    'an artist's cell was selected
    If Target.Row > 3 Then
      ThisArtist = Cells(Target.Row, 1).Value   'get the artist's id
      If Trim(ThisArtist) <> "" Then
        'if the id isn't blank, build and refresh the album query
        id = "ArtistAlbums"
        Set qtArtistAlbums = ActiveSheet.ListObjects(id).QueryTable
```

```
        If Not qtArtistAlbums.Refreshing Then
          ThisWorkbook.Queries(id).Formula = "let Result =" & _
              "fnGetAlbums(""" & ThisArtist & """) in Result"
          qtArtistAlbums.Refresh False
          Application.Goto Range("E4")
        End If
      End If
    End If
  ElseIf Target.Column >= 4 And Target.Column <= 7 Then
    'an album was selected
    If Target.Row > 4 Then
      ThisAlbum = Cells(Target.Row, 5)  'get the album's id
      If Trim(ThisAlbum) <> "" Then
        'if the id isn't blank, build and refresh the tracks query
        id = "AlbumTracks"
        Set qtAlbumTracks = ActiveSheet.ListObjects(id).QueryTable
        If Not qtAlbumTracks.Refreshing Then
          ThisWorkbook.Queries(id).Formula = "let Result =" & _
              "fnGetTracks(""" & ThisAlbum & """) in Result"
          qtAlbumTracks.Refresh False
          Application.Goto Range("J5")
        End If
      End If
    End If
  End If
End If
Set qtArtistAlbums = Nothing
Set qtAlbumTracks = Nothing
End Sub
```

When you click an artist in columns A:C, the albums list automatically updates. Choose an album in the second query table; the track list automatically updates, as shown in Figure 18-15.

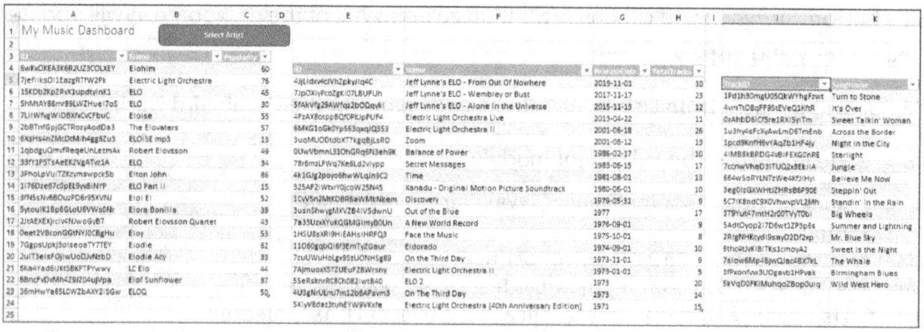

FIGURE 18-15 You've built a dashboard that is pulling data from the Spotify developer API.

This example shows how you can use VBA to manage the queries created in Power Query. It is also an introduction to coding in M, the language of Power Query.

Using global variables and loops in M

The examples so far in this chapter should give you a pretty good introduction to using M in Power Query as a programming language.

If you are going to start developing in M, you will need a few more concepts. For example, the preceding dashboard runs into a problem if an album has more than 20 tracks. You would need to loop through multiple pages to retrieve all the results. I'm including a second workbook, 18-SpotifyPaging.xlsm, with the downloadable files to demonstrate the solution—but I won't be fully explaining it here. However, introducing you to the M equivalents of these VBA concepts will assist you in your journey:

- Storing settings in global variables in VBA or a Settings table in Power Query

- Error handling in M with `try`

- Using If-then logic in M

- Using a loop in VBA or `List.Generate` in M

These concepts will help you as you begin to develop robust applications in M.

Storing global variables in a Settings record in Power Query

If you have variables that will be used in several queries, you can store them in a Settings record that is created via a query. These can be referred to in any other query.

Create a new query called `config` and copy and paste the following M code in the Advanced Editor:

```
let
    Settings = [
        apiBase = "https://api.spotify.com/",
        apiVersion = "v1",
        apiSearch = "/search",
        apiArtists = "/artists/{id}",
        apiAlbums = "/albums/{id}",
        recordsPerPage = 50,
        pagesMax = 5
    ]
in
    Settings
```

Note that the query is called `config`. The "Settings" identifier here is simply for readability, and the word "Settings" is not used again.

Once you have the `config` query, any other query can refer to a field in the `config` query like this: `config[recordsPerPage]`.

Figure 18-16 shows the results of the config query in Power Query.

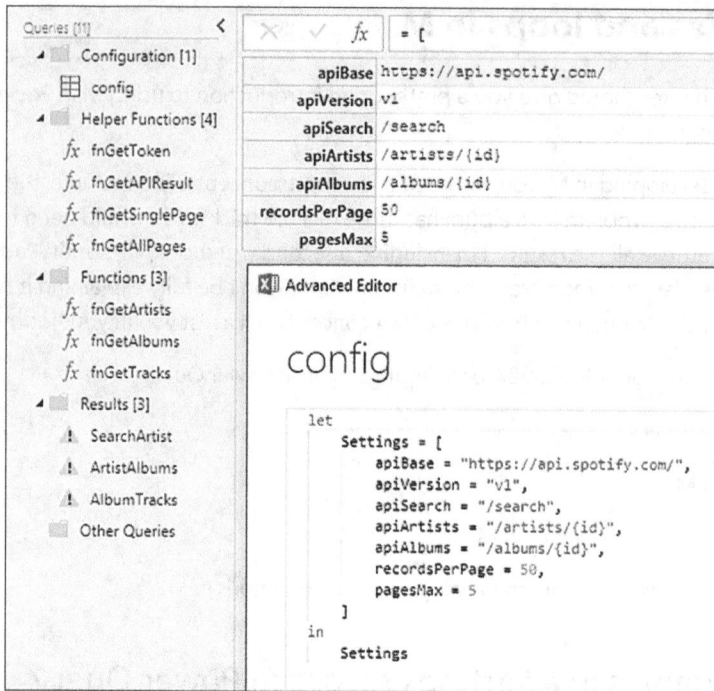

FIGURE 18-16 Store global variables for reuse in a `config` query.

Simple error handling using try with otherwise

Say that you are returning five items at a time from a web page. You are looping through, returning items 0-4, 5-9, and 10-14. It is possible that an album might only have nine tracks, and the final call will fail.

The following code is taken out of context from the `fnGetSinglePage` query. The code is trying to return the parent of a value in the Source record. If you request a page that doesn't exist, you can get an error. To handle possible errors, use the `try ThingThatMightFail otherwise SubstituteValue` syntax. In this case:

- ThingThatMightFail = `Record.Field(Source, parent)`

- SubstituteValue = `null`

So, to allow your query to fail gracefully if the `parent` field doesn't exist, the expression in the code becomes:

```
try Record.Field(Source, parent) otherwise null
```

Using If logic in M

In VBA, you have `If ... ElseIf ... Else ... End If` logic. In the M language, you will be assigning the results of the `If` to a step name. There is no `End If` needed.

Here is the code in VBA:

```
If a = 1 Then
  Data = "one"
ElseIf a = 2 Then
  Data = "two"
ElseIf a = 3 Then
  Data = "three"
Else
  Data = "more than three"
End If
```

Here is the equivalent code in M. Note that data = is only specified at the beginning of the conditional chain, the ElseIf from VBA is two words in M, and all the keywords are lowercase:

```
data = if a = 1 then "one"
  else if a = 2 then "two"
  else if a = 3 then "three"
  else "more than 3"
```

Here is an actual example that combines if, else, and try. This is from the fnGetSinglePage query in the sample workbook.

```
data = if parent is null then
    //If parent is not defined then the column element is already in the root
    //so we set the data as Source
    Source
  else
    //The parent is defined, so the column element will be
    //the sub record of the record called as the value of the parent parameter
    try Record.Field(Source, parent) otherwise null
```

Looping using List.Generate

The final construct is to perform the equivalent of a For ... Next loop from VBA in M. Consider this simple loop in VBA:

```
For i = 1 to 10
  Cells(i, 1).Value = "This is row " & i
Next i
```

Here is the equivalent loop in M:

```
let
    Result = List.Generate(
        () => [i = 1],
        each [i] <= 10,
        each [i = [i] + 1],
        each "This is row " & Text.From([i])
    )
in
    Result
```

The four lines of the List.Generate loop are:

- **Initial function:** () => [i = 1]

  List.Generate starts with an initial function returning a record that contains the iteration variable i, initially set to 1. This function is executed only once to assign the starting values of the iteration variable, which is used throughout the loop. This returned record (the one that holds i) is then used in the scope of List.Generate function.

- **Condition function:** each [i] <= 10

  List.Generate checks the condition at the start of each iteration and only continues if the function returns true. Here, we are using i as the loop counter, and the loop will run as long as i is less than or equal to 10.

- **Next function:** each [i = [i] + 1]

  This function produces the next record by updating the variable defined in the initial function. In this case, it increments i by 1, returning a new record to be used in the next iteration.

- **Selector function:** each "This is row " & Text.From([i])

  Finally, this function defines the output for each item in the list. In our example, it returns a custom string based on the current value of i.

In short, the first two lines define the loop's range (1 to 10), the third defines how to increment it (i + 1), and the last defines what to do with the record. Figure 18-17 shows the result.

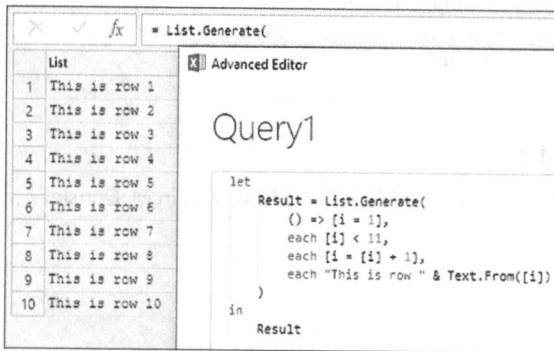

```
fx        = List.Generate(

   List
1  This is row 1        Advanced Editor
2  This is row 2
3  This is row 3        Query1
4  This is row 4
5  This is row 5            let
6  This is row 6                Result = List.Generate(
7  This is row 7                    () => [i = 1],
                                    each [i] < 11,
8  This is row 8                    each [i = [i] + 1],
9  This is row 9                    each "This is row " & Text.From([i])
10 This is row 10               )
                            in
                                Result
```

FIGURE 18-17 List.Generate in M is similar to a For Next loop in VBA.

Caution VBA has no problem doing type conversion on the fly. If you want to join text and a number, that will work in VBA. However, for Power Query, if you are going to join text and a number, you need to convert the number to text first. Hence, the need for Text.From([i]]) in the preceding code.

For a real-life example, this is a fnGetAllPages function. It uses a List.Generate loop to call fnGetSinglePage repeatedly:

```
(url as text, parent as any, column as text) as list =>
//This function fetches multiple pages of data from an API
//url, parent, and column are input parameters
//list is the return type
(url as text, parent as any, column as text) as list =>
  let
    //Use List.Generate to build the paginated list
    AllPagesResult = List.Generate(
      //Initial values: i starts at 0, res is the first page of data
      () => [i = 0, res = fnGetSinglePage(url, 0, parent, column)],
      //Keep looping while we're under total records and page limit
      each [i] * config[recordsPerPage] <= [res][Total] and
        [i] < config[pagesMax],
      //Increment page index, fetch the next page of data
      each [
        i = [i] + 1,
        res = fnGetSinglePage(url, ([i] + 1) * config[recordsPerPage],
          parent, column)
      ],
      //Select the Data field from the result record
      each [res][Data]
    )
  in
    AllPagesResult
```

Notice that in this query, the comments are above the corresponding line. In M, comments must go between expressions, never inside them. If you can't place a comment after the expression ending comma, put it on the line before the related code.

This completes the introduction to the M language. The rest of this chapter switches back to a discussion of using VBA to schedule a macro to run every *x* minutes.

Application.OnTime to periodically analyze data

VBA offers the OnTime method for running any VBA procedure at a specific time of day or after a specific amount of time has passed.

You can write a macro to capture data every hour throughout the day. This macro would have times hard-coded. The following code will, theoretically, capture data from a website every hour from 8 AM to 5 PM:

```
Sub ScheduleTheDay()
Application.OnTime EarliestTime:=TimeValue("8:00 AM"), _
  Procedure:= "CaptureData"
Application.OnTime EarliestTime:=TimeValue("9:00 AM"), _
  Procedure:= "CaptureData"
```

```
Application.OnTime EarliestTime:=TimeValue("10:00 AM"), _
   Procedure:= "CaptureData"
Application.OnTime EarliestTime:=TimeValue("11:00 AM"), _
   Procedure:= "CaptureData"
Application.OnTime EarliestTime:=TimeValue("12:00 PM"), _
   Procedure:= "CaptureData"
Application.OnTime EarliestTime:=TimeValue("1:00 PM"), _
   Procedure:= "CaptureData"
Application.OnTime EarliestTime:=TimeValue("2:00 PM"), _
   Procedure:= "CaptureData"
Application.OnTime EarliestTime:=TimeValue("3:00 PM"), _
   Procedure:= "CaptureData"
Application.OnTime EarliestTime:=TimeValue("4:00 PM"), _
   Procedure:= "CaptureData"
Application.OnTime EarliestTime:=TimeValue("5:00 PM"), _
   Procedure:= "CaptureData"
End Sub

Sub CaptureData()
Dim WSQ As Worksheet
Dim NextRow As Long
Set WSQ = Worksheets("MyQuery")
'Refresh the web query
WSQ.Range("A2").QueryTable.Refresh BackgroundQuery:=False
'Make sure the data is updated by waiting 10 seconds
Application.Wait Now + TimeValue("0:00:10")
'Copy the web query results to a new row
NextRow = WSQ.Cells(Rows.Count, 1).End(xlUp).Row + 1
WSQ.Range("A2:B2").Copy WSQ.Cells(NextRow, 1)
Set WSQ = Nothing
End Sub
```

Using Ready mode for scheduled procedures

The OnTime method runs only when Excel is in Ready, Copy, Cut, or Find mode at the prescribed time. If you start to edit a cell at 7:59:55 AM and keep that cell in Edit mode, Excel cannot run the CaptureData macro at 8:00 AM, as directed.

In the preceding code example, I specified only the start time for the procedure to run. Excel waits anxiously until the spreadsheet is returned to Ready mode and then runs the scheduled program as soon as it can.

The classic example is that you start to edit a cell at 7:59 AM, and then your manager walks in and asks you to attend a surprise staff meeting down the hall. If you leave your spreadsheet in Edit mode and attend the staff meeting until 10:30 AM, the program cannot run the first three scheduled hours of updates. As soon as you return to your desk and press Enter to exit Edit mode, the missed runs are executed one after another; you find that the first three scheduled updates of the program all happen between 10:30 and 10:31 AM.

Specifying a window of time for an update

You can provide Excel with a window of time within which to make an update. The following code tells Excel to run an update at any time between 8:00 AM and 8:05 AM:

```
Application.OnTime EarliestTime:=TimeValue("8:00 AM"), _
   Procedure:= "CaptureData ", _
   LatestTime:=TimeValue("8:05 AM")
```

If the Excel session remains in Edit mode for the entire five minutes, the scheduled task is skipped.

Canceling a previously scheduled macro

It is fairly difficult to cancel a previously scheduled macro. You must know the exact time that the macro is scheduled to run. To cancel a pending operation, call the OnTime method and use the Schedule:=False parameter to unschedule the event. The following code cancels the 11:00 AM run of CaptureData:

```
Sub CancelEleven()
Application.OnTime EarliestTime:=TimeValue("11:00 AM"), _
   Procedure:= "CaptureData", Schedule:=False
End Sub
```

It is interesting to note that the OnTime schedules are remembered by a running instance of Excel. If you keep Excel open but close the workbook with the scheduled procedure, it still runs. Consider this hypothetical series of events:

1. Open Excel at 7:30 AM.

2. Open Schedule.xlsm and run a macro to schedule a procedure at 8:00 AM.

3. Close Schedule.xlsm, but keep Excel open.

4. Open a new workbook and begin entering data.

At 8:00 AM, Excel reopens Schedule.xlsm and runs the scheduled macro. Excel doesn't close Schedule.xlsm. As you can imagine, this is fairly annoying and alarming if you are not expecting it. If you are going to make extensive use of Application.OnTime, you might want to have it running in one instance of Excel while you work in a second instance of Excel.

> **Note** If you are using a macro to schedule a macro a certain amount of time later, you could remember the time in an out-of-the-way cell to be able to cancel the update. See an example in the "Scheduling a macro to run *x* minutes in the future" section of this chapter.

Closing Excel cancels all pending scheduled macros

If you close Excel by choosing File | Exit or by closing all workbooks, all future scheduled macros are automatically canceled. When you have a macro that has scheduled a bunch of macros at indeterminate times, closing Excel is the only way to prevent the macros from running.

Scheduling a macro to run *x* minutes in the future

You can schedule a macro to run at a certain time in the future. The following macro uses the Time function to return the current time and adds 2 minutes and 30 seconds to the time. The following macro runs something 2 minutes and 30 seconds from now:

```
Sub ScheduleAnything()
'This macro can be used to schedule anything
WaitHours = 0
WaitMin = 2
WaitSec = 30
NameOfScheduledProc = "CaptureData"
' --- End of Input Section -------
'Determine the next time this should run
NextTime = Time + TimeSerial(WaitHours, WaitMin, WaitSec)
'Schedule ThisProcedure to run then
Application.OnTime EarliestTime:=NextTime, Procedure:=NameOfScheduledProc
End Sub
```

Later, canceling this scheduled event would be nearly impossible. You won't know the exact time that the macro grabbed the TIME function. You might try to save this value in an out-of-the-way cell:

```
Sub ScheduleWithCancelOption
NameOfScheduledProc = "CaptureData"
'Determine the next time this should run
NextTime = Time + TimeSerial(0,2,30)
Range("ZZ1").Value = NextTime
'Schedule ThisProcedure to run then
Application.OnTime EarliestTime:=NextTime, _
    Procedure:=NameOfScheduledProc
End Sub

Sub CancelLater()
NextTime = Range("ZZ1").value
Application.OnTime EarliestTime:=NextTime, _
    Procedure:=CaptureData, Schedule:=False
End Sub
```

Scheduling a verbal reminder

The text-to-speech tools in Excel can be fun. The following macro sets up a schedule that reminds you when it is time to go to a staff meeting:

```
Sub ScheduleSpeak()
Application.OnTime EarliestTime:=TimeValue("9:14 AM"), _
```

```
    Procedure:="RemindMe"
End Sub

Sub RemindMe()
Application.Speech.Speak _
  Text:="Tracy. It is time for the staff meeting."
End Sub
```

If you want to pull a prank on your manager, you can schedule Excel to automatically turn on the Speak On Enter feature. Follow this scenario:

1. Tell your manager that you are taking them out to lunch to celebrate April 1.

2. At some point in the morning, while your manager is getting coffee, run the ScheduleSpeech macro. Design the macro to run 15 minutes after your lunch starts.

3. Take your manager to lunch.

4. While the manager is away, the scheduled macro runs.

5. When the manager returns and starts typing data in Excel, the computer will repeat the cells as they are entered. This is slightly reminiscent of the computer on *Star Trek* that repeated everything Lieutenant Uhura said.

After this starts happening, you can pretend to be innocent; after all, you have a strong alibi for when the prank began to happen. Here's the code you use to do it:

```
Sub ScheduleSpeech()
Application.OnTime EarliestTime:=TimeValue("12:15 PM"), _
  Procedure:="SetUpSpeech"
End Sub

Sub SetupSpeech()
Application.Speech.SpeakCellOnEnter = True
End Sub
```

> **Note** To turn off Speak On Enter, you can either dig out the button from the QAT customization panel (look in the category called Commands Not On The Ribbon) or, if you can run some VBA, change the SetupSpeech macro to change the True to False.

Scheduling a macro to run every two minutes

Say that you want to ask Excel to run a certain macro every two minutes. However, you realize that if a macro gets delayed because you accidentally left the workbook in Edit mode while going to the staff meeting, you don't want dozens of updates to happen in a matter of seconds.

The easy solution is to have the `ScheduleAnything` procedure recursively schedule itself to run again in two minutes. The following code schedules a run in two minutes and then performs `CaptureData`:

```
Sub ScheduleAnything()
'This macro can be used to schedule anything
'Enter how often you want to run the macro in hours and minutes
WaitHours = 0
WaitMin = 2
WaitSec = 0
NameOfThisProcedure = "ScheduleAnything"
NameOfScheduledProc = "CaptureData"
' --- End of Input Section -------
'Determine the next time this should run
NextTime = Time + TimeSerial(WaitHours, WaitMin, WaitSec)
'Schedule ThisProcedure to run then
Application.OnTime EarliestTime:=NextTime, _
  Procedure:=NameOfThisProcedure
'Get the Data
Application.Run NameOfScheduledProc
End Sub
```

This method has some advantages. It doesn't schedule a million updates in the future. You have only one future update scheduled at any given time. Therefore, if you decide that you are tired of seeing the national debt every 15 seconds, you only need to comment out the `Application.OnTime` line of code and wait 15 seconds for the last update to happen.

Next steps

This chapter showed you how to build a working solution that pulls data from the Spotify API using Power Query, incorporating custom M code, looping logic, and a centralized configuration query. It also showed you how to use VBA's `OnTime` method to automate running procedures at a later time. Chapter 19, "Text file processing," covers importing from a text file and writing to a text file. Being able to write to a text file is useful when you need to write out data for another system to read.

Text file processing

In this chapter, you will:

- Import from text files
- Write text files

VBA simplifies both reading and writing from text files. This chapter covers importing from a text file and writing to a text file. Being able to write to a text file is useful when you need to write out data for another system to read or even when you need to produce HTML files.

Importing from text files

There are two basic scenarios when reading from text files. If a file contains fewer than 1,048,576 records, it is not difficult to import the file using the `Workbooks.OpenText` method. If the file contains more than 1,048,576 records, you have to read the file one record at a time.

> **Level Up!**
>
> The following methods work well for consistent data with minimal processing needs. But, if the data requires field-specific actions, such as running specific actions based on values, consider reading the data directly into memory. Parsing and processing in memory can be more efficient and provide flexibility for complex tasks. For example, the "Converting a fixed-width report to a data set" section in Chapter 13 demonstrates how to use a custom object and collection for this purpose.

Importing text files with fewer than 1,048,576 rows

Text files typically come in one of two formats. In one format, the fields in each record are separated by some delimiter, such as a comma, pipe, or tab. In the second format, each field takes a particular number of character positions. This is called a *fixed-width file*, and this format was very popular in the days of COBOL.

Excel can import either type of file. You can also open both types by using the OpenText method. In both cases, it is best to record the process of opening the file and then use the recorded snippet of code.

Opening a fixed-width file

Figure 19-1 shows a text file in which each field takes up a certain amount of space in the record. Writing the code to open this type of file is slightly arduous because you need to specify the length of each field. In Bill's collection of antiques, he still has a metal ruler used by COBOL programmers to measure the number of characters in a field printed on a green-bar printer. In theory, you could change the font of your file to a monospace font, such as Courier, and use this same method or manually count the number of characters, including spaces in each field. However, using the macro recorder is a slightly more up-to-date method.

```
sales.prn - Notepad                                          —   □   ×
File  Edit  Format  View  Help
Region  Product  Date    Customer   Quantity   Revenue COGS Profit
East    XYZ      7/24/25QRS INC.       1000    228101022012590
Central DEF      7/25/25JKL, CO         100      2257  984 1273
East    ABC      7/25/25JKL, CO         500    10245 4235 6010
Central XYZ      7/26/25WXY, CO         500    11240 5110 6130
East    XYZ      7/27/25FGH, CO         400     9152 4088 5064
Central XYZ      7/27/25WXY, CO         400     9204 4088 5116
East    DEF      7/27/25RST INC.        800    18552 787210680
```

FIGURE 19-1 This file is fixed width. Because you must specify the exact length of each field in the file, opening this file is quite involved.

Turn on the macro recorder by selecting Record Macro from the Developer tab. Use the default macro name. From the File menu, select Open, and browse to the folder where the text file is saved. Change the Files Of Type to All Files and select your text file.

In the Text Import Wizard's step 1, specify that the data is Fixed Width and click Next. Excel looks at your data and attempts to figure out where each field begins and ends. Figure 19-2 shows Excel's guess on this particular file. Because the Date field is too close to the Customer field, Excel missed drawing that line.

To add a new field indicator in step 2 of the wizard, click in the appropriate place in the Data Preview window. If you click in the wrong column, click the line and drag it to the right place. If Excel inadvertently put in an extra field line, double-click the line to remove it. Figure 19-3 shows the Data Preview window after the appropriate changes have been made. Note the little ruler above the data. When you click to add a field marker, Excel is actually handling the tedious work of figuring out that the Customer field starts in position 25 and has a length of 11.

In step 3 of the wizard, Excel assumes that every field is in General format. Change the format of any fields that require special handling. Click the third column and choose the appropriate format from the Column Data Format section of the dialog. Figure 19-4 shows the selections for this file.

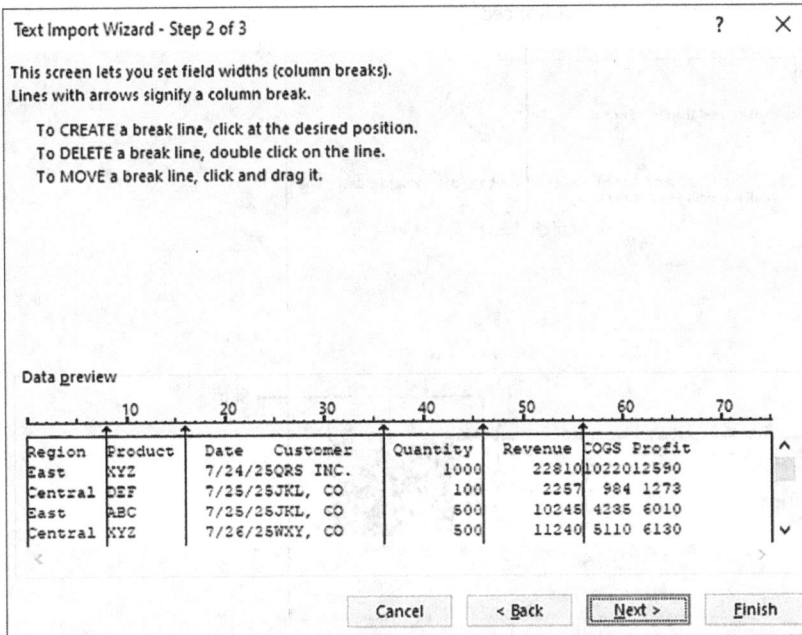

FIGURE 19-2 Excel guesses where each field starts and ends. In this case, it guessed incorrectly for four of the fields.

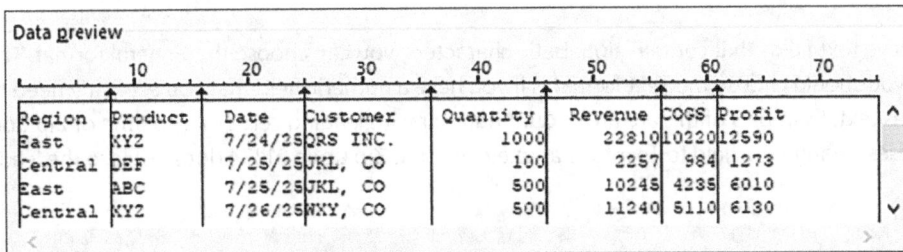

FIGURE 19-3 After you add new field markers and adjust the marker between Customer and Quantity to the right place, Excel can build the code that gives you an idea of the start position and length of each field.

If you have date fields, click the heading above that column and change the column data format to a Date format. If you have a file with dates in year-month-day format or day-month-year format, select the dropdown next to Date and choose the appropriate date sequence.

If you prefer to skip some fields, click those columns and select Do Not Import Column (Skip) from the Column Data Format section. This is useful in a couple of instances. If the file includes sensitive data that you do not want to show to a client, you can leave it out of the import. For example, perhaps this report is for a customer to whom you do not want to show the cost of goods sold or profit. In this case, you can choose to skip these fields in the import. Occasionally, you will encounter a text file that is both fixed-width and delimited by a character such as a pipe—|. Setting the one-character-wide pipe columns as Skip is a great way to get rid of the pipe characters.

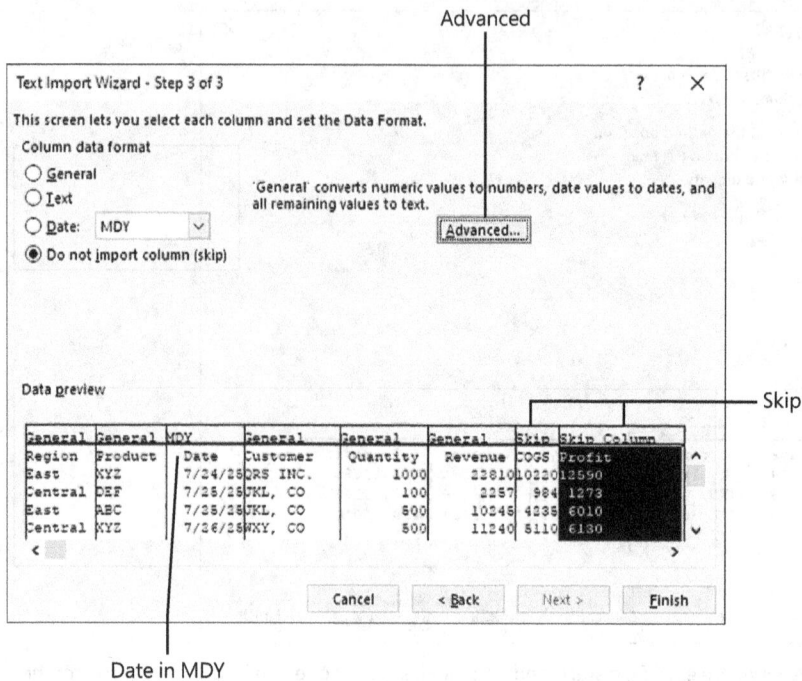

FIGURE 19-4 The third column is a date, and you do not want to import the COGS and Profit columns.

If you have text fields that contain alphabetic characters, you can choose the General format. The only time you should choose the Text format is if you have a numeric field that you explicitly need to be imported as text. Examples of this are an account number with leading zeros or a column of Zip Codes. In these cases, change the field to Text format to ensure that Zip Code 01234 does not lose the leading zero.

> **Note** After you import a text file and specify that one field is text, that field exhibits seemingly bizarre behavior. Try inserting a new row and entering a formula in the middle of a column imported as text. Instead of getting the results of the formula, Excel enters the formula as text. The solution is to delete the formula, format the entire column as General, and then enter the formula again.

After opening the file, turn off the macro recorder and examine the recorded code, which should look like this:

```
Workbooks.OpenText Filename:="C:\sales.prn", Origin:=437, StartRow:=1, _
    DataType:=xlFixedWidth, FieldInfo:=Array(Array(0, 1), Array(8, 1), _
    Array(17, 3), Array(25, 1), Array(36, 1), Array(46, 1), Array(56, 9), _
    Array(61, 9)), TrailingMinusNumbers:=True
```

The most confusing part of this code is the `FieldInfo` parameter. You are supposed to code an array of two-element arrays. Each field in the file gets a two-element array to identify both where the field starts and what type of field it is.

The field start position is zero-based. Because the Region field is in the first character position, its start position is listed as zero.

The field type is a numeric code. If you were coding this by hand, you would use the `xlColumnDataType` constant names. However, for some reason, the macro recorder uses the harder-to-understand numeric equivalents.

By using Table 19-1, you can decode the meaning of the individual arrays in the `FieldInfo` array. `Array(0, 1)` means that this field starts zero characters from the left edge of the file and is a General format. `Array(8, 1)` indicates that the next field starts eight characters from the left edge of the file and is in General format. `Array(17, 3)` indicates that the next field starts 17 characters from the left edge of the file and is a Date format in month-day-year sequence.

TABLE 19-1   XLCOLUMNDATATYPE VALUES

Value	Constant	Used For
1	xlGeneralFormat	General
2	xlTextFormat	Text
3	xlMDYFormat	MDY date
4	xlDMYFormat	DMY date
5	xlYMDFormat	YMD date
6	xlMYDFormat	MYD date
7	xlDYMFormat	DYM date
8	xlYDMFormat	YDM date
9	xlSkipColumn	Skip Column
10	xlEMDFormat	EMD date (for use in Taiwan)

As you can see, the `FieldInfo` parameter for fixed-width files is arduous to code and confusing to look at. This is one situation in which it is easier to record the macro and copy the code snippet.

Opening a delimited file

Figure 19-5 shows a text file in which the fields are comma-separated. The main task in opening such a file is to tell Excel that the delimiter in the file is a comma and then identify any special processing for each field. In this case, you definitely want to identify the third column as being a date in MDY format.

```
Region,Product,Date,Customer,Quantity,Revenue,COGS,Profit
East,XYZ,7/24/2025,QRS INC.,1000,22810,10220,12590
Central,DEF,7/25/2025,"JKL, CO",100,2257,984,1273
East,ABC,7/25/2025,"JKL, CO",500,10245,4235,6010
Central,XYZ,7/26/2025,"WXY, CO",500,11240,5110,6130
East,XYZ,7/27/2025,"FGH, CO",400,9152,4088,5064
```

FIGURE 19-5 This file is comma delimited. Opening this file involves telling Excel to look for a comma as the delimiter and then identifying any special handling, such as treating the third column as a date. This is much easier than handling fixed-width files.

> **Note** If you try to record the process of opening a comma-delimited file whose file name ends in .csv, Excel records the `Workbooks.Open` method rather than `Workbooks.OpenText`. If you need to control the formatting of certain columns, rename the file to have a .txt extension before recording the macro. You can then edit the recorded macro to change the file name back to a .csv extension.

Turn on the macro recorder and record the process of opening the text file. In step 1 of the wizard, specify that the file is delimited.

In step 2 of the Text Import Wizard, the Data Preview window might initially look horrible. This is because Excel defaults to assuming that the fields are separated by tab characters (see Figure 19-6).

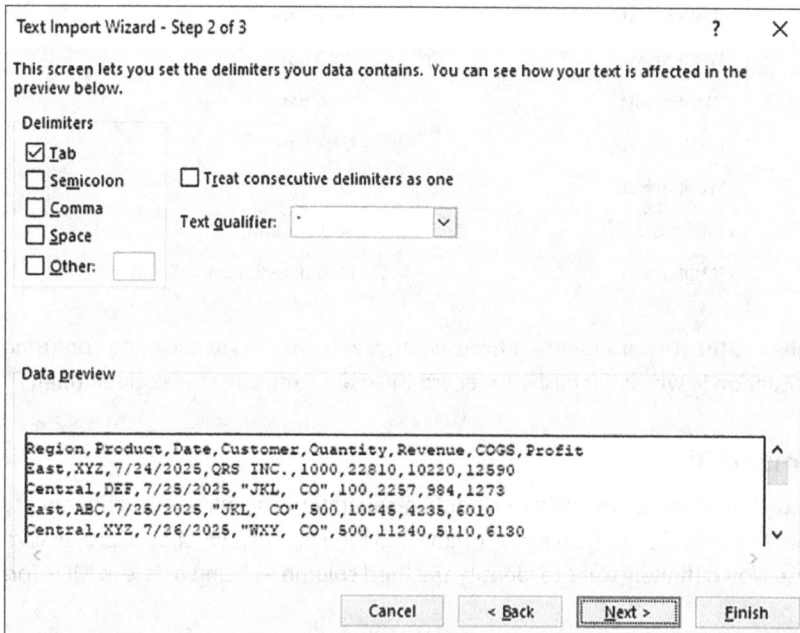

FIGURE 19-6 Before you import a delimited text file, the initial Data Preview window is a confusing mess of data because Excel is looking for tab characters between fields when a comma is actually the delimiter in this file.

After you've cleared the Tab checkbox and selected the proper delimiter choice, which in this case is a comma, the Data Preview window in step 2 looks perfect, as shown in Figure 19-7.

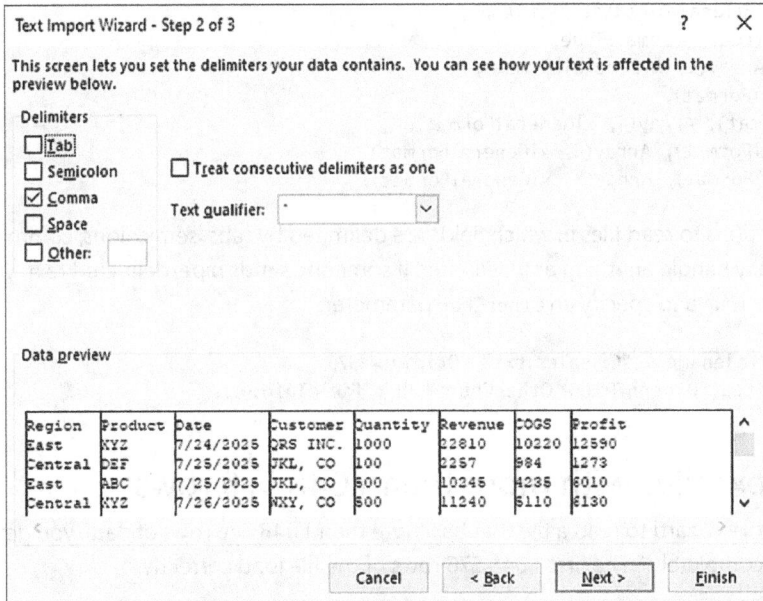

FIGURE 19-7 After the delimiter field has been changed from a tab to a comma, the Data Preview window looks perfect. This is certainly easier than the cumbersome process in step 2 for a fixed-width file. Note that Excel ignores the commas in the Customer field when there are quotation marks around the customer.

Step 3 of the wizard is identical to step 3 for a fixed-width file. In this case, specify that the third column has a date format. Click Finish, and you have this code in the macro recorder:

```
Workbooks.OpenText Filename:="C:\sales.txt", Origin:=437, _
    StartRow:=1, DataType:=xlDelimited, TextQualifier:=xlDoubleQuote, _
    ConsecutiveDelimiter:=False, Tab:=False, Semicolon:=False, _
    Comma:=True, Space:=False, Other:=False, _
    FieldInfo:=Array(Array(1, 1), Array(2, 1), _
    Array(3, 3), Array(4, 1), Array(5, 1), Array(6, 1), _
    Array(7, 1), Array(8, 1)), TrailingMinusNumbers:=True
```

Although this code appears longer than the earlier code, it is actually simpler. In the `FieldInfo` parameter, the two-element arrays consist of a sequence number, starting at 1 for the first field, and then an xlColumnDataType from Table 19-1. In this example, `Array(2, 1)` means, "the second field is of general type." `Array(3, 3)` means, "the third field is a date in MDY format." The code is longer because it explicitly specifies that each possible delimiter is set to `False`. Because `False` is the default for all delimiters, you really need only the one you will use. The following code is equivalent:

```
Workbooks.OpenText Filename:= "C:\sales.txt", _
    DataType:=xlDelimited, Comma:=True, _
    FieldInfo:=Array(Array(1, 1), Array(2, 1), Array(3, 3), _
    Array(4, 1), Array(5, 1), Array(6, 1), _
    Array(7, 1), Array(8, 1))
```

Finally, to make the code more readable, you can use the constant names rather than the code numbers:

```
Workbooks.OpenText Filename:="C:\sales.txt", _
    DataType:=xlDelimited, _Comma:=True, _
    FieldInfo:=Array(Array(1, xlGeneralFormat), _
    Array(2, xlGeneralFormat), _
    Array(3, xlMDYFormat), Array(4, xlGeneralFormat), _
    Array(5, xlGeneralFormat), Array(6, xlGeneralFormat), _
    Array(7, xlGeneralFormat), Array(8, xlGeneralFormat))
```

Excel has built-in options to read files in which fields are delimited by tabs, semicolons, commas, or spaces. Excel can actually handle anything as a delimiter. If someone sends pipe-delimited text, you set the Other parameter to True and specify an OtherChar parameter:

```
Workbooks.OpenText Filename:= "C:\sales.txt", Origin:=437, _
    DataType:=xlDelimited, Other:=True, OtherChar:= "|", FieldInfo:=...
```

Dealing with text files with more than 1,048,576 rows

If you use the Text Import Wizard to read a file that has more than 1,048,576 rows of data, you get this error: "File not loaded completely." The first 1,048,576 rows of the file load correctly.

If you use Workbooks.OpenText to open a file that has more than 1,048,576 rows of data, you are given no indication that the file did not load completely. Excel loads the first 1,048,576 rows and allows macro execution to continue. Your only indication that there is a problem is if someone notices that the reports are not reporting all the sales. If you think that your files will ever get this large, it would be good to check whether cell A1048576 is nonblank after an import. If it is, the odds are that the entire file was not loaded.

Reading text files one row at a time

You might run into a text file that has more than 1,048,576 rows. When this happens, you have to read the text file one row at a time.

You need to open the file for INPUT as #1. You use #1 to indicate that this is the first file you are opening. If you had to open two files, you could open the second file as #2. You can then use the Line Input #1 statement to read a line of the file into a variable. The following code opens sales.txt, reads 10 lines of the file into the first 10 cells of the worksheet, and closes the file:

```
Sub Import10()
ThisFile = "C:\sales.txt"
Open ThisFile For Input As #1
For i = 1 To 10
  Line Input #1, Data
  Cells(i, 1).Value = Data
Next i
Close #1
End Sub
```

Rather than read only 10 records, you want to read until you get to the end of the file. Excel automatically updates a variable called EOF. If you open a file for input as #1, checking EOF(1) tells you whether you have read the last record.

Use a Do While loop to keep reading records until you have reached the end of the file:

```
Sub ImportAll()
 ThisFile = "C:\sales.txt"
 Open ThisFile For Input As #1
 Ctr = 0
 Do While Not EOF(1)
     Line Input #1, Data
     Ctr = Ctr + 1
     Cells(Ctr, 1).Value = Data
 Loop
 Close #1
End Sub
```

After reading records with code such as this, note in Figure 19-8 that the data is not parsed into columns. All the fields are in column A of the file.

Use the TextToColumns method to parse the records into columns. The parameters for TextToColumns are nearly identical to those for the OpenText method:

```
Cells(1, 1).Resize(Ctr, 1).TextToColumns Destination:=Range("A1"), _
    DataType:=xlDelimited, Comma:=True, _
    FieldInfo:=Array(Array(1, xlGeneralFormat), _
    Array(2, xlGeneralFormat), Array(3, xlMDYFormat), _
    Array(4, xlGeneralFormat), Array(5, xlGeneralFormat), _
    Array(6, xlGeneralFormat), Array(7, xlGeneralFormat), _
    Array(8, xlGeneralFormat))
```

Cell A1 contains data for eight columns

	A	B	C	D	E	F	G	H	I	J
						Region Product Date Customer Quantity Revenue COGS Profit				
1	Region	Product	Date	Customer		Quantity		Revenue COGS Profit		
2	East	XYZ	7/24/25	QRS INC.		1000		228101022012590		
3	Central	DEF	7/25/25	JKL, CO		100		2257 984 1273		
4	East	ABC	7/25/25	JKL, CO		500		10245 4235 6010		
5	Central	XYZ	7/26/25	WXY, CO		500		11240 5110 6130		
6	East	XYZ	7/27/25	FGH, CO		400		9152 4088 5064		
7	Central	XYZ	7/27/25	WXY, CO		400		9204 4088 5116		

FIGURE 19-8 When you are reading a text file one row at a time, all the data fields end up in one long entry in column A.

Rather than hard-code that you are using the #1 designator to open the text file, it is safer to use the FreeFile function. This returns an integer representing the next file number available for use by the Open statement. The complete code to read a text file smaller than 1,048,576 rows is as follows:

```
Sub ImportAll()
ThisFile = ThisWorkbook.Path & "\sales.txt"
```

```
    FileNumber = FreeFile
    Open ThisFile For Input As #FileNumber
    Ctr = 0
    Do While Not EOF(FileNumber)
      Line Input #FileNumber, Data
      Ctr = Ctr + 1
      Cells(Ctr, 1).Value = Data
    Loop
    Close #FileNumber
    Cells(1, 1).Resize(Ctr, 1).TextToColumns Destination:=Range("A1"), _
      DataType:=xlDelimited, Comma:=True, _
      FieldInfo:=Array(Array(1, xlGeneralFormat), _
      Array(2, xlGeneralFormat), Array(3, xlMDYFormat), _
      Array(4, xlGeneralFormat), Array(5, xlGeneralFormat), _
      Array(6, xlGeneralFormat), Array(7, xlGeneralFormat), _
      Array(8, xlGeneralFormat))
    End Sub
```

Reading text files with more than 1,048,576 rows

You can use the Line Input method to read a large text file. A good strategy is to read rows into cells A1:A1048575 and then begin reading additional rows into cell AA2. You can start in row 2 on the second set so that the headings can be copied from row 1 of the first data set. If the file is large enough that it fills up column AA, move to BA2, CA2, and so on.

Also, you should stop writing columns when you get to row 1048574 and leave two blank rows at the bottom. This ensures that the code Cells(Rows.Count, 1).End(xlup).Row finds the final row. The following code reads a large text file into several sets of columns:

```
Sub ReadLargeFile()
Dim wksData As Worksheet
ThisFile = ThisWorkbook.Path & "\inventory.txt"
Set wksData = Worksheets("Data")
wksData.Cells.Clear
FileNumber = FreeFile
Open ThisFile For Input As #FileNumber
NextRow = 1
NextCol = 1
Application.ScreenUpdating = False   ' Added for speed
Application.StatusBar = "Reading Dataset 1"
Do While Not EOF(1)
  Line Input #FileNumber, Data
  wksData.Cells(NextRow, NextCol).Value = Data
  NextRow = NextRow + 1
  If NextRow = Rows.Count Then
    'Parse these records
    Application.StatusBar = "Parsing"
    Range(wksData.Cells(1, NextCol), wksData.Cells(Rows.Count, NextCol)). _
        TextToColumns Destination:=Cells(1, NextCol), DataType:=xlDelimited, _
        Comma:=True, FieldInfo:=Array( _
        Array(1, xlGeneralFormat), _
```

```
        Array(2, xlGeneralFormat), _
        Array(3, xlGeneralFormat), _
        Array(4, xlMDYFormat))
    'Copy the headings from section 1
    If NextCol > 1 Then
      wksData.Range("A1:D1").Copy Destination:=Cells(1, NextCol)
    End If
    'Set up the next section
    NextCol = NextCol + 26
    NextRow = 2
    Application.StatusBar = "Reading Next Dataset"
  End If
Loop
Close #FileNumber
'Parse the final Section of records
FinalRow = NextRow - 1
If FinalRow = 1 Then
  'Handle if the file coincidentally had 1084574 rows exactly
  NextCol = NextCol - 26
Else
  Application.StatusBar = "Parsing Final DataSet"
  wksData.Range(Cells(2, NextCol), Cells(FinalRow, NextCol)).TextToColumns _
      Destination:=Cells(2, NextCol), DataType:=xlDelimited, Comma:=True, _
      FieldInfo:=Array( _
      Array(1, xlGeneralFormat), _
      Array(2, xlGeneralFormat), _
      Array(3, xlGeneralFormat), _
      Array(4, xlMDYFormat))
  If NextCol > 1 Then
    wksData.Range("A1:D1").Copy Destination:=wksData.Cells(1, NextCol)
  End If
End If
DataSets = (NextCol - 1) / 26 + 1
Worksheets("Various").Range("E57").Value = DataSets
Application.StatusBar = False
Application.ScreenUpdating = True
End Sub
```

Usually, you should write the DataSets variable to a named cell somewhere in the workbook so that later, you know how many data sets you have in the worksheet.

As you can imagine, using this method, it is possible to read 660,601,620 rows of data into a single worksheet. The code you formerly used to filter and report the data has now become more complex. You might find yourself creating pivot tables from each set of columns to create a data set summary and then summarizing all the summary tables with a final pivot table. At some point, you need to consider whether the application really belongs in Access. You can also consider whether the data should be stored in Access with an Excel front end, which is discussed in Chapter 21, "Using Access as a back end to enhance multiuser access to data."

Using Power Query to load large files to the Data Model

If your goal is to create a pivot table from the text file, you can bypass the worksheet grid and load millions of rows directly into the Data Model. Now that Power Query is built into Excel, the macro recorder will record the process of importing data to the Data Model with Power Query. Use the following steps:

1. On the Data tab, in the Get & Transform Data group, select From Text/CSV.

2. Browse to the text file, select it, and click Import.

3. In the preview window, from the Load dropdown select Load To.

4. In the Import Data dialog, choose Only Create Connection And Add This Data To The Data Model. Click OK. The data is loaded to the Power Pivot engine.

If you use the macro recorder during this process, your recorded code includes the M language statements required to define the query:

```
Sub ImportToDataModel()
'ImportToDataModel Macro
Dim csvPath As String
csvPath = ThisWorkbook.Path & "\sales.csv"
ActiveWorkbook.Queries.Add Name:="sales", Formula:="let" & Chr(13) & _
    Chr(10) & " Source = Csv.Document(File.Contents(""" & csvPath & """), " & _
    "[Delimiter="","",""", Columns=8, Encoding=1252, QuoteStyle=QuoteStyle.None])," & _
    Chr(13) & Chr(10) & " #""Promoted Headers"" = " & _
    "Table.PromoteHeaders(Source, [PromoteAllScalars=true])," & Chr(13) & _
    Chr(10) & " #""Changed Type"" = " & _
    "Table.TransformColumnTypes(#""Promoted Headers"",{{""Region"", type text}," & _
    "{""" & "Product"", type text}, {""Date"", type date}, " & _
    "{""Customer"", type text}, {""Quantity"", Int64.Type}, " & _
    "{""Revenue"", Int64.Type}, {""COGS"", Int64.Type}, " & _
    "{""Profit"", Int64.Type}})" & Chr(13) & Chr(10) & "in" & Chr(13) & _
    Chr(10) & " #""Changed Type"""
ActiveWorkbook.Connections.Add2 "Query - sales", _
    "Connection to the 'sales' query in the workbook.", _
    "OLEDB;Provider=Microsoft.Mashup.OleDb.1;Data Source=$Workbook$;" & _
    "Location=sales;Extended Properties=", """sales""", 6, True, False
End Sub
```

> **Note** Power Query formulas inside VBA require double double-quotes ("") to represent a single quote mark. This can make the syntax look messy fast. For example, ""Region"" becomes "Region" in the final query. Be careful when editing—misplaced or missing quotes are a common cause of syntax errors.

You can now use Insert, From Data Model under the Pivot Table dropdown, as the source for the pivot table.

Writing text files

The code for writing text files is similar to the code for reading text files. You need to open a specific file for output as #1. Then, as you loop through various records, you write them to the file by using the `Print #1` statement.

Before you open a file for output, make sure that any prior examples of the file have been deleted. You can use the `Kill` statement to delete a file. `Kill` returns an error if the file was not there in the first place. In this case, you use `On Error Resume Next` to prevent an error.

The following code writes out a text file for use by another application:

```
Sub WriteFile()
ThisFile = "C:\Results.txt"
'Delete yesterday's copy of the file
On Error Resume Next
Kill ThisFile
On Error GoTo 0
'Open the file
Open ThisFile For Output As #1
FinalRow = Cells(Rows.Count, 1).End(xlUp).Row
'Write out the file
For j = 1 To FinalRow
  Print #1, Cells(j, 1).Value
Next j
End Sub
```

If you need to append data to an existing file, remove the parts that delete the file and use the following to open the file:

```
Open ThisFile For Append As #1
```

This will append data to the bottom of the file.

Next steps

The ability to read text files into Excel is a very useful one, especially if you require a program to import multiple files on a daily basis. You can loop through a user-specified folder, looking for specific files, import the data, format it, update charts and pivot tables, and then update a log file reflecting the success of your program. The next chapter steps outside the world of Excel and talks about how to transfer Excel data into Microsoft Word documents. Chapter 20, "Automating Word," looks at using Excel VBA to automate and control Microsoft Word.

Automating Word

In this chapter, you will:

- Use early and late binding to reference a Word object

- Use the `New` keyword to reference the Word application

- Use the `CreateObject` function to create a new instance of an object

- Use the `GetObject` function to reference an existing instance of Word

- Use constant values

- Be introduced to some of Word's objects

- Control form fields in Word

Word, Excel, PowerPoint, Outlook, and Access all use the same VBA language. The only difference is their object models. For example, Excel has a `Workbooks` object, and Word has `Documents`. In addition to the Microsoft Office applications, many other programs—both from Microsoft and third-party developers—can also be controlled through VBA, as long as those programs support automation. This allows you to interact with and automate a wide variety of software beyond just Office applications.

To access another program's object library, Excel must establish a link to it by using either early binding or late binding. With *early binding*, the reference to the application object is created when the program is compiled. With *late binding*, the reference is created when the program is run.

This chapter provides an introduction to accessing Word from Excel. It does not review Word's entire object model or the object models of other applications. Refer to the VBA Object Browser in the appropriate application to learn about other object models.

> **Note** While this chapter focuses on controlling Word from Excel, the concepts covered here apply to other programs as well.

Using early binding to reference a Word object

Code written with early binding executes faster than code with late binding. A reference is made to Word's object library before the code is written so that Word's objects, properties, and methods are available in the Object Browser. Tips such as a list of members of an object also appear, as shown in Figure 20-1.

The disadvantage of early binding is that the referenced object library must exist on the system. For example, if you write a macro referencing Word 365's object library, it will fail on a system with Word 2010—even if the program is using objects available in both versions—because it cannot locate the Word 365 object library.

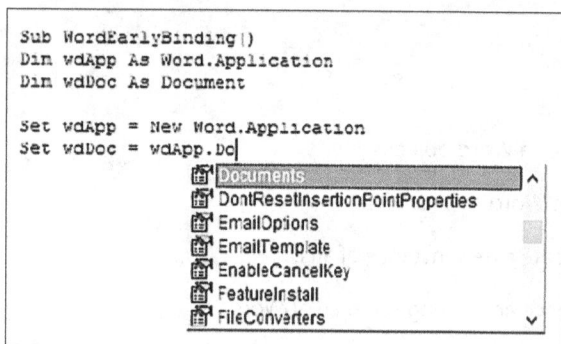

```
Sub WordEarlyBinding()
Dim wdApp As Word.Application
Dim wdDoc As Document

Set wdApp = New Word.Application
Set wdDoc = wdApp.Do
                    Documents
                    DontResetInsertionPointProperties
                    EmailOptions
                    EmailTemplate
                    EnableCancelKey
                    FeatureInstall
                    FileConverters
```

FIGURE 20-1 Early binding allows access to a Word object's syntax.

You add the object library through the VB Editor, as described here:

1. Select Tools | References.

2. Check Microsoft Word 16.0 Object Library in the Available References list (see Figure 20-2). If the object library is not found, Word is not installed. If another version is found in the list, such as 14.0, another version of Word is installed, and you should check that.

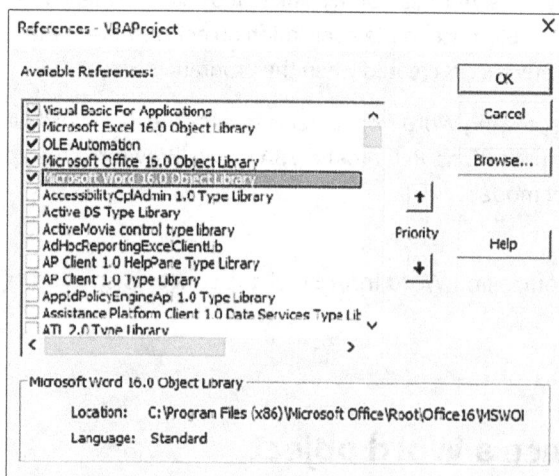

3. Click OK.

```
References - VBAProject                                    X

Available References:                           [   OK   ]
 ☑ Visual Basic For Applications      ^         [ Cancel ]
 ☑ Microsoft Excel 16.0 Object Library
 ☑ OLE Automation
 ☑ Microsoft Office 15.0 Object Library          [ Browse... ]
 ☑ Microsoft Word 16.0 Object Library
 ☐ AccessibilityCplAdmin 1.0 Type Library    +
 ☐ Active DS Type Library
 ☐ ActiveMovie control type library
 ☐ AdHocReportingExceClientLb           Priority
 ☐ AP Client 1.0 HelpPane Type Library           [  Help  ]
 ☐ AP Client 1.0 Type Library            +
 ☐ AppIdPolicyEngineApi 1.0 Type Library
 ☐ Assistance Platform Client 1.0 Data Services Type Lib
 ☐ ATL 2.0 Type library               v
 <                              >

 ┌ Microsoft Word 16.0 Object Library ─────────────────
 │   Location:   C:\Program Files (x86)\Microsoft Office\Root\Office16\MSWORD
 │   Language:   Standard
```

FIGURE 20-2 Select the object library from the Available References list.

After the reference is set, Word variables can be declared with the correct Word variable type, such as `Document`. However, if the object variable is declared As `Object`, this forces the program to use late binding. The following example uses early binding to create a new instance of Word and open an existing Word document:

```
Sub WordEarlyBinding()
Dim wdApp As Word.Application
Dim wdDoc As Document
Set wdApp = New Word.Application
wdApp.Visible = True 'make Word visible
Set wdDoc = wdApp.Documents.Open(ThisWorkbook.Path & _
  "\Automating Word.docx")
Set wdApp = Nothing
Set wdDoc = Nothing
End Sub
```

The declared variables, `wdApp` and `wdDoc`, are Word object types. `wdApp` is used to create a reference to the Word application in the same way the Application object is used in Excel. `New Word.Application` is used to create a new instance of Word. If you are opening a document in a new instance of Word, Word is not visible. If the application needs to be shown, it must be unhidden (`wdApp.Visible = True`). When the program is done, release the connection to Word by setting the object, `wdApp`, to `Nothing`.

> **Tip** Excel searches through the selected libraries to find the reference for the object type. If the type is found in more than one library, the first reference is selected. You can influence which library is chosen by changing the priority of the reference in the list of selected libraries.

When the process is finished, it's a good idea to set the object variables to `Nothing` and release the memory being used by the application, as shown here:

```
Set wdApp = Nothing
Set wdDoc = Nothing
```

If the referenced version of Word does not exist on the system, an error message appears when the code is compiled. View the References list; the missing object is highlighted with the word *MISSING*, as shown in Figure 20-3.

If a previous version of Word is available, you can try running the program with that version referenced. Many objects are the same between versions.

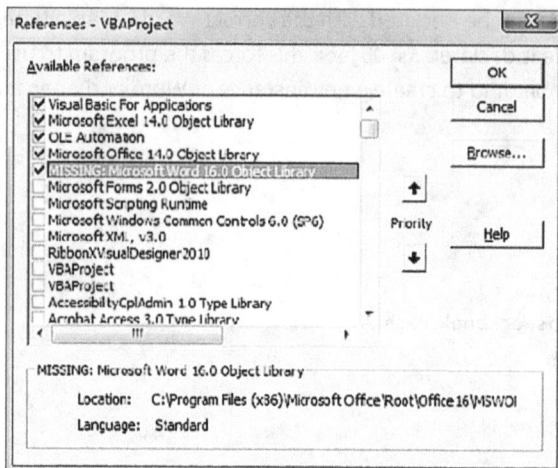

FIGURE 20-3 Excel won't find the expected Word 365 object library if someone opens the workbook on a system with Microsoft Office 2010 installed.

Using late binding to reference a Word object

When using late binding, you create an object that refers to the Word application before linking to the Word library. Because you do not set up a reference beforehand, the only constraint on the Word version is that the objects, properties, and methods must exist. When differences exist between Word versions, the program checks the version and uses the correct object accordingly.

The disadvantage of late binding is that, because Excel does not know what is going on, it does not understand that you are referring to Word. This prevents the tooltips from appearing when referencing Word objects. In addition, built-in constants are not available. This means that when Excel is compiling, it cannot verify that the references to Word are correct. After the program is executed, the links to Word begin to build, and any coding errors are detected at that point.

The following example creates a new instance of Word and then opens and makes visible an existing Word document:

```
Sub WordLateBinding()
Dim wdApp As Object, wdDoc As Object
Set wdApp = CreateObject("Word.Application")
Set wdDoc = wdApp.Documents.Open(ThisWorkbook.Path & _
  "\Automating Word.docx")
wdApp.Visible = True
Set wdApp = Nothing
Set wdDoc = Nothing
End Sub
```

An object variable (`wdApp`) is declared and set to reference the application (`CreateObject("Word.Application")`). Other required variables are then declared (`wdDoc`), and the application object (`wdApp`) is used to refer to these variables in Word's object model. Declaring `wdApp` and `wdDoc` as objects forces the use of late binding. The program cannot create the required links to the Word object model until it executes the `CreateObject` function.

> **Caution** Since late binding doesn't automatically access the application's object library, you cannot rely on the default values of properties. For example, since the default property of the `Range` object in Word is `Text`, you might code this:
>
> ```
> paraText = wdApp.ActiveDocument.Paragraphs(1).Range
> ```
>
> This will work because `Text` is the default property of the `Range` object. But if you're accessing Word with late binding, the above line of code may not work as expected. It's a good habit to explicitly specify the property, like this:
>
> ```
> paraText = wdApp.ActiveDocument.Paragraphs(1).Range.Text
> ```

Using the New keyword to reference the Word application

In the early-binding example, the keyword `New` was used to open a new instance of the Word application (`Set wdApp = New Word.Application`). The `New` keyword can be used only with early binding; it does not work with late binding. `CreateObject` could be used, but `New` simplifies the code when you've already told Excel about the class, like `Word.Application`, by setting a reference (`Dim wdApp as Word.Application`).

> **Note** If an instance of the application is running and you want to use it, use the `GetObject` function instead. See "Using the GetObject function to reference an existing instance of Word" later in this chapter for more information on that function.

> **Caution** If your code to open Word runs smoothly but you don't see an instance of Word (and should because you code it to be `Visible`), open Task Manager and look for the process Microsoft Word. If it exists, from the Immediate window in Excel's VBA Editor, type the following (this requires you to set a reference to the Word object library first):
>
> ```
> Word.Application.Visible = True
> ```
>
> If multiple instances of Microsoft Word are found, you need to make each instance visible and close the extra instance(s) of Microsoft Word.

Using the `CreateObject` function to create a new instance of an object

The previous late-binding example (Set wdApp = CreateObject("Word.Application")) used the `CreateObject` function, which can also be used for early binding. You use it to create a new instance of an object—in this case, the Word application. `CreateObject` has a class parameter, which consists of the `Name` and `Type` of the object to be created (`Name.Type`). For example, the examples in this chapter have used (`Word.Application`), in which `Word` is the `Name` and `Application` is the `Type`.

Using the `GetObject` function to reference an existing instance of Word

The `GetObject` function can either connect to an existing instance of Word or create a new one, depending on how you use its two optional parameters: the full file path and the class name. The first parameter specifies the full path and filename to open, and the second parameter specifies the application program.

The following example uses only the first parameter, leaving off the application, and allows the default program, which is Word, to open the document:

```
Sub UseGetObject()
Dim wdDoc As Object
Set wdDoc = GetObject(ThisWorkbook.Path & "\Automating Word.docx")
wdDoc.Application.Visible = True
'more code interacting with the Word document
Set wdDoc = Nothing
End Sub
```

This example opens a document in an existing instance of Word if there is one; otherwise, it creates one. It ensures that the Word application's `Visible` property is set to `True`. Note that to make the document visible, you have to refer to the application object (`wdDoc.Application.Visible`) because `wdDoc` is referencing a document rather than the application.

> **Note** Although the Word application's `Visible` property is set to `True`, this code does not make the Word application the active application. In most cases, the Word application icon stays in the taskbar, and Excel remains the active application on the screen.

The following example only uses the second parameter, the application. It uses errors to learn whether Word is already open before pasting the selected chart at the end of a document. If Word is not open, it opens Word and creates a new document:

```
Sub IsWordOpen()
Dim wdApp As Word.Application 'early binding
ActiveChart.ChartArea.Copy
```

```
On Error Resume Next
Set wdApp = GetObject(, "Word.Application") 'returns Nothing if Word isn't open
If wdApp Is Nothing Then
  'because Word isn't open, open a new instance
  Set wdApp = GetObject("", "Word.Application")
  With wdApp
    .Documents.Add
    .Visible = True
  End With
End If
On Error GoTo 0
With wdApp.Selection
  .EndKey Unit:=wdStory
  .TypeParagraph
  .PasteSpecial Link:=False, DataType:=wdPasteOLEObject, _
    Placement:=wdInLine, DisplayAsIcon:=False
End With
Set wdApp = Nothing
End Sub
```

Using `On Error Resume Next` forces the program to continue even if it runs into an error. In this case, an error occurs when you attempt to link wdApp to an object that does not exist. wdApp will have no value. The next line, `If wdApp Is Nothing Then`, takes advantage of this and opens an instance of Word, adds an empty document, and makes the application visible. Use `On Error Goto 0` to return to normal VBA error-handling behavior.

> **Tip** Note the use of empty quotes for the first parameter in `GetObject("", "Word.Application")`. This is how you use the `GetObject` function to open a new instance of Word.

Using constant values

The preceding example used constants, such as wdPasteOLEObject and wdInLine, that are specific to Word. When you are programming using early binding, Excel helps by showing these constants in the member list.

With late binding, tooltips don't appear. So what can you do? You might write your program using early binding and then change it to late binding after you compile and test the program. The problem with this method is that the program will not compile because Excel doesn't recognize the Word constants.

The words wdPasteOLEObject and wdInLine are just terms for your convenience as a programmer. Behind each of these text constants is the real value that VBA understands. The solution to this is to retrieve and use these real values with your late-binding program.

Using the Watches window to retrieve the real value of a constant

One way to retrieve the value of a constant is to add a watch for constants. Then, you step through your code and check the value of the constant as it appears in the Watches window, as shown in Figure 20-4.

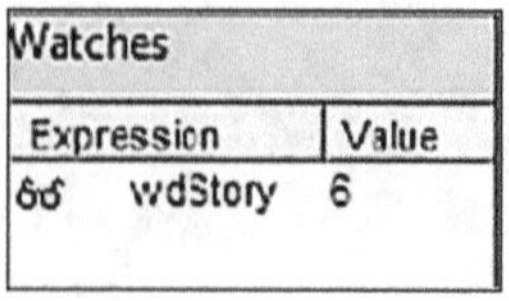

FIGURE 20-4 Use the Watches window to get the real value behind a Word constant.

> **Note** See "Querying by using a Watches window" in Chapter 2, "This sounds like BASIC, so why doesn't it look familiar?" for more information on using the Watches window.

Using the Object Browser to retrieve the real value of a constant

Another way to retrieve the value of a constant is to look up the constant in the Object Browser. However, you need the Word library to be set up as a reference to use this method. Once it is set up, right-click the constant and select Definition. The Object Browser opens to the constant and shows the value in the bottom window (see Figure 20-5).

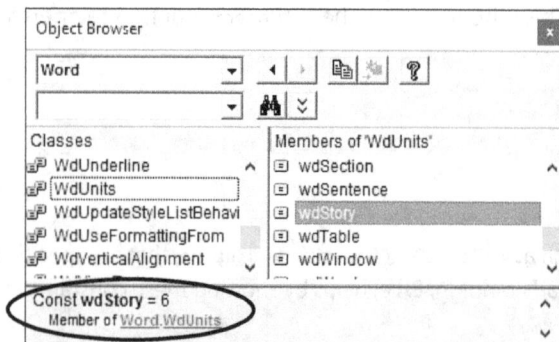

FIGURE 20-5 Use the Object Browser to get the real value of a Word constant.

> **Tip** You can set up the Word reference library to be accessed from the Object Browser. However, you do not have to set up your code with early binding. When you do this, the reference is at your fingertips, but your code is still late binding.

Replacing the constants in the earlier code example with their real values would look like this:

```
With wdApp.Selection
   .EndKey Unit:=6
   .TypeParagraph
   .PasteSpecial Link:=False, DataType:=0, Placement:=0, _
      DisplayAsIcon:=False
End With
```

However, what happens a month from now, when you return to the code and you try to remember what those numbers mean? The solution is up to you. Some programmers add comments to the code, referencing the Word constant. Other programmers create their own variables to hold the real value and use those variables in place of the constants, like this:

```
Dim xwdStory As Integer, xwdPasteOLEObject As Integer
Dim xwdInLine As Integer
xwdStory = 6
xwdPasteOLEObject = 0
xwdInLine = 0
With wdApp.Selection
   .EndKey Unit:=xwdStory
   .TypeParagraph
   .PasteSpecial Link:=False, DataType:=xwdPasteOLEObject, _
      Placement:=xwdInLine, DisplayAsIcon:=False
End With
```

> **Note** If instead of the chart you see {EMBED Excel.SheetMacroEnabled.12}, you have field codes turned on. Press ALT+F9 to toggle them off. The "Show field codes instead of their values" option is also available in Word via the Options | Advanced menu under the Show document content section.

Using early and late binding at the same time

Yes, you can definitely use both early and late binding in the same program. For instance, you might prefer early binding when you're programming because you'll get tooltips. But when you're ready to distribute the program, late binding is often a better option. Even if all your users are on the same version, things can come up where a different version is needed or a reference is missing. This is why using late binding for distribution is a good idea.

Coding for flexible binding

There are two ways to set the type of binding for your code:

- Uncheck the reference, which forces late binding

- Use a constant to explicitly set the binding to early or late binding

The choice is yours. Examples in this book will use a constant in the code. Either way, you use *compiler directives* to have the compiler process only the relevant lines of code. For example, New can only be used with early binding. Normally, if you're using late binding, the compiler will error on a line using New. But when the relevant line is used within a compiler directive for the binding type, the line is ignored, like this:

```
#Const EarlyBinding = False 'at the top of the module
Sub Word_FlexibleBinding()
#If EarlyBinding = True Then
   'the compiler will ignore these lines
   Dim wdApp As Word.Application
   Dim wdDoc As Document
   Set wdApp = New Word.Application
#Else
   'the compiler will compile these lines
   Dim wdApp As Object, wdDoc As Object
   Set wdApp = CreateObject("Word.Application")
#End If
'the rest of the code that doesn't depend on binding type
wdApp.Visible = True 'make Word visible
Set wdDoc = wdApp.Documents.Open _
   (ThisWorkbook.Path & "\Automating Word.docx")
Set wdDoc = Nothing
Set wdApp = Nothing
End Sub
```

> **Note** Refer to "Managing code variations with compiler directives" in Chapter 4, "Laying the groundwork with variables and structures," for more information on compiler directives.

#Const, #If, and #End If are compiler directives that determine how code is compiled. If the # is left off, the lines are treated as standard runtime instructions and are executed when the program runs. Within the #If statement, individual lines do not need the # symbol since they are evaluated (and run) based on the condition.

After the objects are set up within the correct compiler directive, the rest of the code runs normally. The directives only affect how the setup is handled; everything else is standard VBA.

Handling constants with flexible binding

How you want to handle constants in your code is up to you—you have more than one option. Just remember, for late binding, you must use the integer value, no matter what.

One option would be to use compiler directives for the relevant code sections, like this:

```
#If EarlyBinding = True then
   With wdApp.Selection
      .EndKey unit:=wdStory
      .TypeParagraph
```

```
   .PasteSpecial Link:=False, DataType:=wdPasteOLEObject, _
      Placement:=wdInLine, DisplayAsIcon:=False
  End With
#Else
  With wdApp.Selection
    .EndKey Unit:=6
    .TypeParagraph
    .PasteSpecial Link:=False, DataType:=0, Placement:=0, _
      DisplayAsIcon:=False
  End With
#End If
```

But this does duplicate some lines that don't include constants. Another option would be to use the hardcoded values, like you do for late binding, for both binding types, like this:

```
xwdStory = 6
xwdPasteOLEObject = 0
xwdInLine = 0
With wdApp.Selection
  .EndKey unit:=xwdStory
  .TypeParagraph
  .PasteSpecial Link:=False, DataType:=xwdPasteOLEObject, _
    Placement:=xwdInLine, DisplayAsIcon:=False
End With
```

This reduces the duplication of code and any possible lag from late binding.

Level Up!

You might consider using compiler directives to set the value of the variables holding constant values, as you do for late binding. The code would look like this:

```
#If EarlyBinding = True Then
  'use Word constants directly
  xwdStory = wdStory
  xwdPasteOLEObject = wdPasteOLEObject
  xwdInLine = wdInLine
#Else
  'use hardcoded values
  xwdStory = 6 'wdStory
  xwdPasteOLEObject = 0 'wdPasteOLEObject
  xwdInLine = 0 'wdInLine
#End If
```

However, keep in mind that you don't get any help entering constants with early binding and still have to look up the integer value for late binding. Here's what I suggest: code early binding so you get the tooltips, then, as you run into constants, look up the integer value, define a variable to store the value, and then update your code to reference the new variable.

Understanding Word's objects

You can use Word's macro recorder to get a preliminary understanding of the Word object model. However, much as with Excel's macro recorder, the results will be long-winded. Keep this in mind and use the recorder to lead you toward the objects, properties, and methods in Word.

> **Caution** Word's macro recorder is limited in what it allows you to record. While the mouse can be used to move the cursor or select objects, it doesn't record those movements. But there are no limits on what it records from keyboard movements.

This is what the Word macro recorder produces when you add a new, blank document by selecting File, New, Blank Document:

```
Documents.Add Template:="Normal", NewTemplate:=False, DocumentType:=0
```

You can make this more efficient in Word by using this:

```
Documents.Add
```

`Template`, `NewTemplate`, and `DocumentType` are optional properties that the recorder includes but that are not required unless you need to change a default property or ensure that a property is what you require.

To use the same line of code in Excel, a link to the Word object library is required, as you learned earlier. After that link is established, an understanding of Word's objects is all you need. The next section provides a review of some of Word's objects—enough to get you off the ground. For a more detailed listing, refer to the object model in Word's VB Editor.

> **Note** The examples in this section mix early and late binding. The early binding can be seen by the explicit declaration of the `Word.Document` object. Late binding is implemented by using `GetObject` to directly open the desired document, rather than using `CreateObject` to open Word and then calling `Documents.Open` to open the document.

The `Document` object

Word's `Document` object is equivalent to Excel's `Workbook` object. It consists of characters, words, sentences, paragraphs, sections, and headers/footers. It is through the `Document` object that methods and properties affecting the entire document—such as printing, closing, searching, and reviewing—are accomplished.

Creating a new blank document

To create a blank document in an existing instance of Word, use the Add method, as shown here:

```
Sub NewDocument()
Dim wdApp As Word.Application
Set wdApp = GetObject(, "Word.Application")
wdApp.Documents.Add
'any other Word code you need here
Set wdApp = Nothing
End Sub
```

This example opens a new, blank document that uses the default template.

> **Note** You already learned how to create a new document when Word is closed. Refer to GetObject and CreateObject.

To create a new document that uses a specific template, use this:

```
wdApp.Documents.Add Template:="Client Invoice.dotx"
```

This creates a new document that uses the Client Invoice template. Template can be either the name of a template from the default template location or the file path and name.

Opening an existing document

To open an existing document, use the Open method. Several parameters are available, including ReadOnly and AddtoRecentFiles. The following example opens an existing document as ReadOnly and prevents the file from being added to the Recent File List under the File menu:

```
wdApp.Documents.Open _
   Filename:="C:\Excel VBA Book\" & _
   "Chapter 8 - Arrays.docx", ReadOnly:=True, AddtoRecentFiles:=False
```

Saving changes to a document

After you've made changes to a document, most likely, you'll want to save it. To save a document with its existing name, use this:

```
wdApp.Documents.Save
```

If you use the Save command with a new document without a name, nothing happens. To save a document with a new name, you must use the SaveAs2 method:

```
wdApp.ActiveDocument.SaveAs2 _
   "C:\Excel VBA\MemoTest.docx"
```

SaveAs2 requires the use of members of the Document object, such as ActiveDocument.

> **Note** SaveAs still works, but it isn't an option shown in the tooltips. SaveAs2 offers a compatibility mode argument. If you don't need it, you can still use SaveAs.

> **Caution** Cloud-saving is becoming more common, but VBA cannot save to URLs (such as https). You can save to the local cloud folder, like OneDrive, and let it sync the document to the cloud. However, if the workbook you're working in is cloud-based, using ThisWorkbook. Path will return a URL, which you can't use to save the document. Excel doesn't natively support saving directly to web-based locations using VBA. Refer to the "Checking cloud-based file paths" section in Chapter 13, "Excel power," for a function to check your file's location, allowing you to handle what to do if the returned location is in the cloud.

Closing an open document

Use the Close method to close a specified document or all open documents. By default, a Save dialog box appears for any documents that have unsaved changes. You can use the SaveChanges argument to change this. To close all open documents without saving changes, use this code:

```
wdApp.Documents.Close SaveChanges:=wdDoNotSaveChanges
```

To close a specific document, you can close the active document, like this:

```
wdApp.ActiveDocument.Close
```

or you can specify a document name, like this:

```
wdApp.Documents("Chapter 8 - Arrays.docx").Close
```

Printing a document

Use the PrintOut method to print part or all of a document. To print a document with the default print settings, use this:

```
wdApp.ActiveDocument.PrintOut
```

By default, the print range is the entire document, but you can change this by setting the Range and Pages arguments of the PrintOut method. For example, to print only page 2 of the active document, use this:

```
wdApp.ActiveDocument.PrintOut Range:=wdPrintRangeOfPages, Pages:="2"
```

The Selection object

The Selection object represents what is selected in the document, such as a word, a sentence, or the insertion point. It also has a Type property that returns the selected type, such as wdSelectionIP, wdSelectionColumn, or wdSelectionShape.

Navigating with HomeKey and EndKey

The HomeKey and EndKey methods are used to change the selection; they correspond to using the Home and End keys, respectively, on the keyboard. They have two parameters: Unit and Extend. Unit is the range of movement to make to either the beginning (Home) or the end (End) of a line (wdLine), document (wdStory), column (wdColumn), or row (wdRow). Extend is the type of movement: wdMove moves the selection, and wdExtend extends the selection from the original insertion point to the new insertion point.

To move the cursor to the beginning of the document, use this code:

```
wdApp.Selection.HomeKey Unit:=wdStory, Extend:=wdMove
```

To select the document from the insertion point to the end of the document, use this code:

```
wdApp.Selection.EndKey Unit:=wdStory, Extend:=wdExtend
```

Inserting text with TypeText

The TypeText method is used to insert text into a Word document. Settings, such as the ReplaceSelection setting, can affect what happens when text is typed into the document or when text is selected. The following example first makes sure that the setting for overwriting selected text is enabled. Then, it selects the fourth paragraph (using the Range object, described in the next section) and overwrites it:

```
Sub InsertText()
Dim wdApp As Word.Application
Dim wdDoc As Document
Set wdDoc = GetObject(ThisWorkbook.Path & "\Random text.docx")
Set wdApp = wdDoc.Parent
wdApp.Visible = True
wdApp.Options.ReplaceSelection = True
wdDoc.Paragraphs(4).Range.Select
wdApp.Selection.TypeText "Overwriting the selected paragraph."
Set wdApp = Nothing
Set wdDoc = Nothing
End Sub
```

The Range object

The Range object uses the following syntax:

```
Range(StartPosition, EndPosition)
```

The Range object represents a contiguous area or areas in a document. It has a starting character position and an ending character position. The object can be the insertion point, a range of text, or the entire document, including nonprinting characters such as spaces or paragraph marks.

The Range object is similar to the Selection object, but in some ways, it is better. For example, the Range object requires less code to accomplish the same tasks, and it has more capabilities. In addition, it saves time and memory because the Range object does not require Word to move the cursor or highlight objects in the document to manipulate them.

Defining a range

To define a range, enter a starting position and an ending position, as shown in the following code:

```
Sub RangeText()
Dim wdApp As Word.Application
Dim wdDoc As Document
Dim wdRng As Word.Range
Set wdDoc = GetObject(ThisWorkbook.Path & "\Random text.docx")
Set wdApp = wdDoc.Parent
wdApp.Visible = True
'Range(StartPosition,EndPosition)
Set wdRng = wdDoc.Range(0, 50)
wdRng.Select
Set wdApp = Nothing
Set wdDoc = Nothing
Set wdRng = Nothing
End Sub
```

Figure 20-6 shows the results of running this code. The first 50 characters are selected, including nonprinting characters such as paragraph returns.

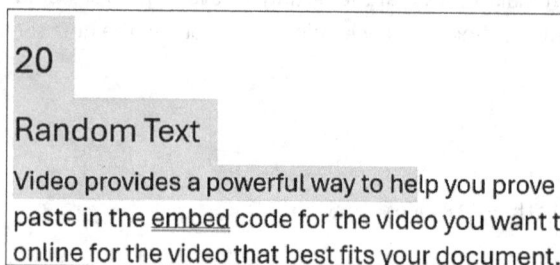

FIGURE 20-6 The Range object selects everything in its path.

> **Note** In Figure 20-6, the range was selected (`wdRng.Select`) for easier viewing. It is not required that the range be selected in order to be manipulated. For example, to delete the range, do this:
>
> `wdRng.Delete`

The first character position in a document is always zero, and the last is equivalent to the number of characters in the document.

The Range object also selects paragraphs. The following example copies the third paragraph in the active document and pastes it into Excel. Depending on how the paste is done, the text can be pasted into a text box (see Figure 20-7) or into a cell:

```
Sub SelectSentence()
Dim wdApp As Word.Application
Dim wdDoc As Word.Document
Dim wdRng As Word.Range
```

```
Set wdDoc = GetObject(ThisWorkbook.Path & "\Random text.docx")
Set wdApp = wdDoc.Parent
wdApp.Visible = True
With wdDoc
  If .Paragraphs.Count >= 3 Then
    Set wdRng = .Paragraphs(3).Range
    wdRng.Copy
  End If
End With
With Worksheets("Sheet2")
  'This line pastes the copied text into a text box
  'because that is the default PasteSpecial method for Word text
  .Range("A5").PasteSpecial
  'This line pastes the copied text into cell A1
  .Paste Destination:=.Range("A1")
End With
Set wdApp = Nothing
Set wdDoc = Nothing
Set wdRng = Nothing
End Sub
```

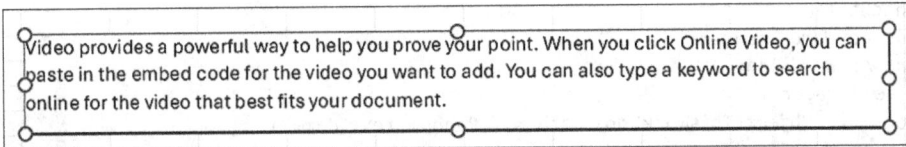

Video provides a powerful way to help you prove your point. When you click Online Video, you can paste in the embed code for the video you want to add. You can also type a keyword to search online for the video that best fits your document.

FIGURE 20-7 Paste Word text into an Excel text box.

Formatting a Range

After a range is selected, you can apply formatting to it (see Figure 20-8). The following program loops through all the paragraphs of the active document and applies bold to the first word of each paragraph:

```
Sub ChangeFormat()
Dim wdDoc as Word.Document
Dim wdRng As Word.Range
Dim cnt As Integer
Set wdDoc = GetObject(ThisWorkbook.Path & "\Random text.docx")
wdDoc.Parent.Visible = True
With wdDoc
  For cnt = 1 To .Paragraphs.Count
    Set wdRng = .Paragraphs(cnt).Range
    With wdRng
      .Words(1).Font.Bold = True
      .Collapse 'deselects the text
    End With
  Next cnt
End With
Set wdDoc = Nothing
Set wdRng = Nothing
End Sub
```

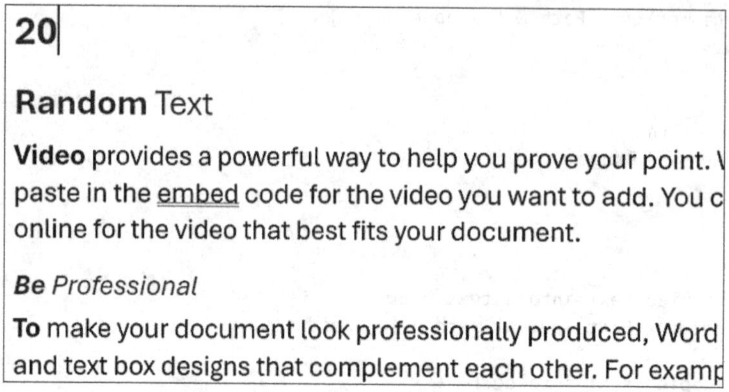

FIGURE 20-8 Format the first word of each paragraph in a document.

A quick way to change the formatting of entire paragraphs is to change the style (see Figures 20-9 and 20-10). The following program finds a paragraph with the Normal style and changes it to the Quote style:

```
Sub ChangeStyle()
Dim wdDoc As Word.Document
Dim wdRng As Word.Range
Dim cnt As Integer
Set wdDoc = GetObject(ThisWorkbook.Path & "\Random text.docx")
wdDoc.Parent.Visible = True
With wdApp.ActiveDocument
  For cnt = 1 To .Paragraphs.Count
    Set wdRng = .Paragraphs(cnt).Range
    With wdRng
      If .Style = "Normal" Then
        .Style = "Quote"
      End If
    End With
  Next cnt
End With
Set wdDoc = Nothing
Set wdRng = Nothing
End Sub
```

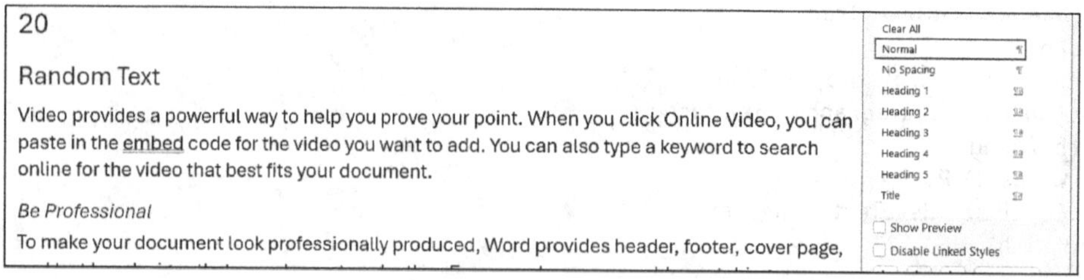

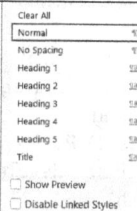

FIGURE 20-9 Before: A paragraph with the Normal style needs to be changed to the Quote style.

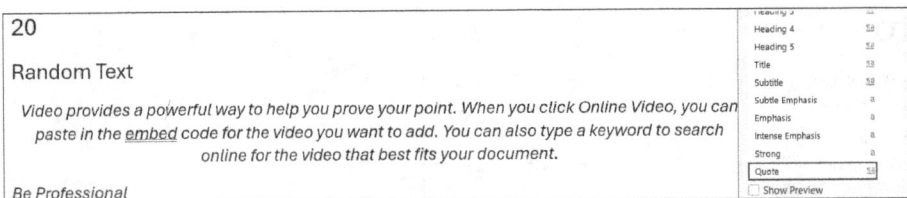

FIGURE 20-10 After: Apply styles with code to change paragraph formatting quickly.

Bookmarks

Bookmarks are members of the `Document`, `Selection`, and `Range` objects. They can make it easier to navigate around Word. Instead of having to choose words, sentences, or paragraphs, use bookmarks to manipulate sections of a document swiftly.

> **Note** You're not limited to using only existing bookmarks. You can create new bookmarks using code.

Bookmarks appear as gray I-bars in Word documents. In Word, go to File | Options | Advanced | Show Document Content and select Show Bookmarks to turn on bookmarks.

After you have set up bookmarks in a document, you can use the bookmarks to move quickly to a range to insert text or other items, such as charts. The following code automatically inserts text and a chart after bookmarks that were previously set up in a document. Figure 20-11 shows the results.

```
Sub FillInMemo()
Dim myArray()
Dim curWeek as Integer
Dim wdDoc As Word.Document
Dim wdRng As Word.Range
myArray = Array("To", "CC", "From", "Subject", "Chart")
curWeek = DatePart("ww", Date, vbMonday, vbFirstFourDays)
Set wdDoc = GetObject(ThisWorkbook.Path & "\Weekly Sales.docx")
wdDoc.Parent.Visible = True
'insert text
Set wdRng = wdApp.ActiveDocument.Bookmarks(myArray(0)).Range
wdRng.InsertBefore ("Warsky Jadelight")
Set wdRng = wdApp.ActiveDocument.Bookmarks(myArray(1)).Range
wdRng.InsertBefore ("Chraz Veralla")
Set wdRng = wdApp.ActiveDocument.Bookmarks(myArray(2)).Range
wdRng.InsertBefore ("Meredia Mayvin")
Set wdRng = wdApp.ActiveDocument.Bookmarks(myArray(3)).Range
wdRng.InsertBefore ("Sales for week " & curWeek)
'insert chart
Set wdRng = wdApp.ActiveDocument.Bookmarks(myArray(4)).Range
Worksheets("Qty Summary").ChartObjects("Chart 1").Copy
wdRng.PasteAndFormat Type:=wdPasteOLEObject
wdDoc.Parent.Activate
Set wdDoc = Nothing
Set wdRng = Nothing
End Sub
```

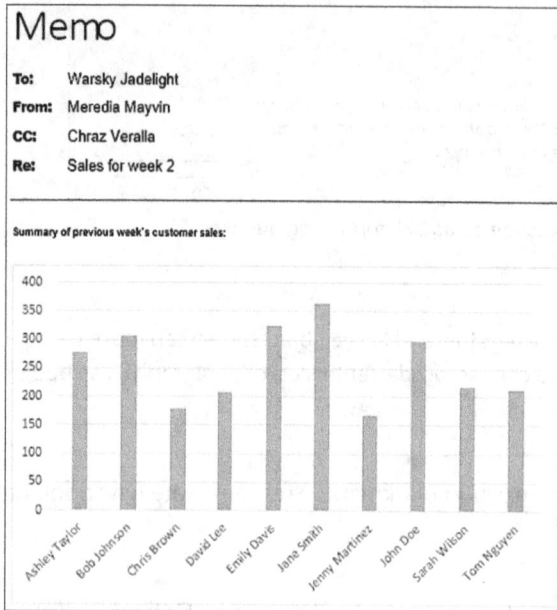

FIGURE 20-11 Use bookmarks to enter text or charts into a Word document.

> **Note** For more information on using arrays, see Chapter 8, "Arrays."

Controlling form fields in Word

You've seen how to modify a document by inserting charts and text, modifying formatting, and deleting text. However, a document might contain other items, such as controls, that you need to modify.

For the following example, a template named New Client.dotx was created, consisting of text and a bookmark. The bookmark is placed after the Name field. Content control checkboxes were also added. The controls are found in the Controls section of the Developer tab in Word, as shown in Figure 20-12.

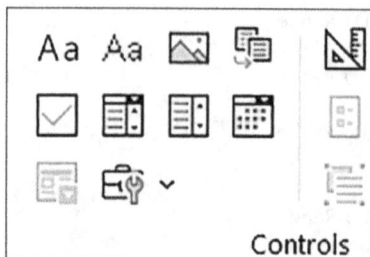

FIGURE 20-12 You can use the Content Control form fields to add checkboxes to a document.

Unlike Legacy Tools, you can't rename the control. Instead, you have to set a unique tag to identify the control. While in Design Mode, select the entire control field, right-click on the selection and select Property from the context menu to open the Content Control Properties window shown in Figure 20-13. Enter a tag to identify the control, such as chkCustYes. To find a specific control, you'll have to loop through all the controls and check the tag value, as shown in the code sample below.

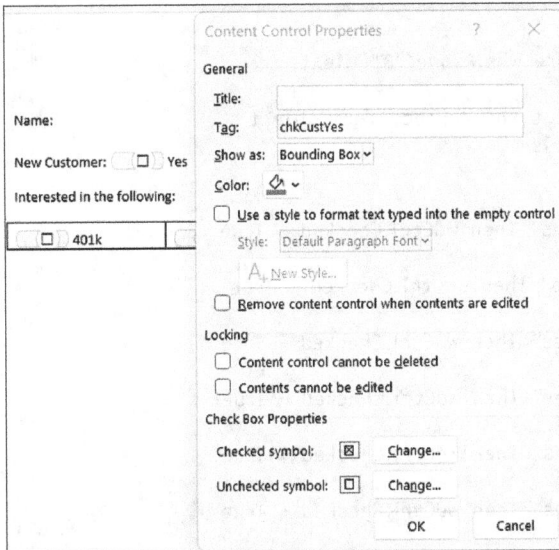

FIGURE 20-13 Set the control's tag in the Content Control Properties window so you can find the control programmatically.

The questionnaire was set up in Excel, and it enables a person to enter free text in B1 and select from data validation in B2 and B4:B7, as shown in Figure 20-14.

FIGURE 20-14 Create an Excel sheet to collect your data.

The following code goes into a standard module:

```
Sub FillOutWordForm()
Dim TemplatePath As String
Dim wks As Worksheet
Dim wdApp As Object
```

```
Dim wdDoc As Object
Dim wdCtrl As Object
'Open the template in a new instance of Word
TemplatePath = ThisWorkbook.Path & "\New Client.dotx"
Set wdApp = CreateObject("Word.Application")
Set wdDoc = wdApp.Documents.Add(Template:=TemplatePath)
Set wks = Worksheets("Form Data")
'Place our text values in document
With wdApp.ActiveDocument
    .Bookmarks("Name").Range.InsertBefore wks.Range("B1").Text
End With
'Loop through all the controls to select the correct form object
For Each wdCtrl In wdDoc.ContentControls
    Select Case UCase(wdCtrl.Tag)
        Case Is = "CHKCUSTYES"
            If wks.Range("B2").Value = "Yes" Then wdCtrl.Checked = True
        Case Is = "CHKCUST20"
            If wks.Range("B2").Value = "No" Then wdCtrl.Checked = True
        Case Is = "CHK401K"
            If wks.Range("B4").Value = "Yes" Then wdCtrl.Checked = True
        Case Is = "CHKROTH"
            If wks.Range("B5").Value = "Yes" Then wdCtrl.Checked = True
        Case Is = "CHKSTOCKS"
            If wks.Range("B6").Value = "Yes" Then wdCtrl.Checked = True
        Case Is = "CHKBONDS"
            If wks.Range("B7").Value = "Yes" Then wdCtrl.Checked = True
    End Select
Next wdCtrl
wdApp.Visible = True
wdApp.Activate
Set wdDoc = Nothing
Set wdApp = Nothing
Set wks = Nothing
End Sub
```

The name goes straight into the document. The checkboxes use logic to verify whether the person selected Yes or No to confirm whether the corresponding checkbox should be checked. Figure 20-15 shows a sample document that has been completed.

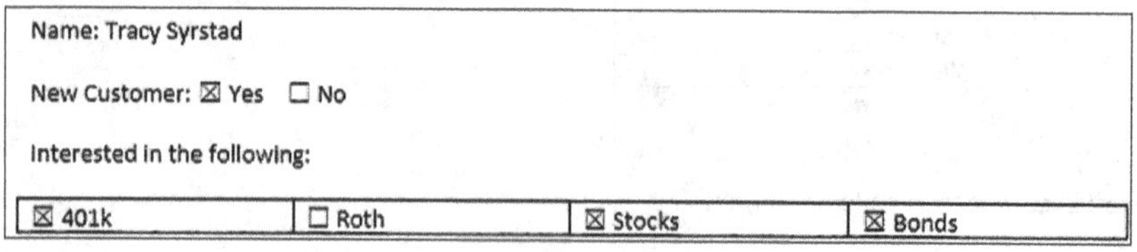

FIGURE 20-15 Excel can control Word's form fields and help automate filling out documents.

> **Level Up!**
>
> If you need to loop through the controls multiple times, consider using a collection. You can loop through all the controls once, add each one to the collection, and use the tag as the key for easy access later. For more on collections, check out Chapter 9, "Creating custom objects and collections."

Next steps

The ability to access object libraries of other applications lets you take advantage of the strengths of these applications, such as creating professional-looking reports in Word. Chapter 19, "Text file processing," showed you how to read from a text file to import data from another system. In this chapter, you learned how to connect to another Office program and access its object module. In Chapter 21, "Using Access as a back end to enhance multiuser access to data," you'll connect to an Access database and learn how to write to ACCDB files. Compared to text files, Access files are faster, indexable, and support multiuser access.

CHAPTER 21

Using Access as a back end to enhance multiuser access to data

In this chapter, you will:

- Understand the difference between ADO and DAO

- Learn how to connect Excel to an Access database

- Add, retrieve, update, and delete records using ADO

- Work with single and multiple-record recordsets

- Modify database structure by adding tables or fields

- Summarize records with ADO

- Connect to SQL Server and run stored procedures

The example near the end of Chapter 19, "Text file processing," proposes a method for storing 660,601,620 records in an Excel worksheet. At some point, you need to admit that even though Excel is the greatest product in the world, there is a time to move to Microsoft Access, at least partially, and take advantage of database files.

Although Excel Online supports collaboration, automation is limited. If you need to support multiple users and still run VBA, using Excel for data entry and storing the data in a database gives you the best of both worlds.

Understanding Access database formats and compatibility

A *database engine* is a software component that reads from and writes to a database file. It's what enables Excel (through ADO or DAO) to send queries to an Access database and retrieve results. The current engine for Access is ACE (Access Connectivity Engine). It supports both .accdb and .mdb files and is available in both 32-bit and 64-bit versions. If you have a current version of Access installed, you already have the ACE engine.

Note The older Jet engine (used with .mdb files) was 32-bit only and is no longer supported in modern systems. All examples in this chapter use ACE, which supports both .mdb and .accdb formats and works with 32- and 64-bit Office.

"Bit" refers to the version of Excel installed—either 32-bit or 64-bit. Table 21-1 outlines the various file formats, compatible engines, and distribution requirements. If users don't have Access installed (needed for an ACE engine), a redistributable can be downloaded from *https://www.microsoft.com/en-us/download/details.aspx?id=54920*.

TABLE 21-1 Which Access format works in your version of Excel?

File format (Excel bit version)	ACCDB (64-bit)	ACCDB (32-bit)	MDB (64-bit)	MDB (32-bit)
Compatible Engine	ACE 64-bit	ACE 32-bit	ACE 64-bit	ACE 32-bit
Requires Redistributable	Yes[1]	Yes[1]	Yes[1]	Yes[1]

[1] unless Access 2007 or newer is installed

Note Excel and Access files aren't bit-dependent—you can create them in 32-bit Office and use them in 64-bit Office without problems.

ADO versus DAO

There are two commonly used libraries for accessing data in external databases from Excel VBA: Data Access Objects (DAO) and ActiveX Data Objects (ADO). While there are other data access technologies, these are the two most relevant for Excel-based solutions. The concepts behind DAO and ADO are similar, especially when working with recordsets. However, when interacting programmatically with the database structure, syntax and capabilities differ significantly. Still, the code is close enough that if you're experienced with one, you can usually follow code written for the other. Table 21-2 lists key factors to consider when deciding which library to use.

TABLE 21-2 Choosing between DAO and ADO

Factor	DAO	ADO
Best suited for	Access databases	Multiple data sources (Access, SQL Server, and the like)
Integration with Access	Tight—supports TableDefs, Indexes, Relationships	Limited—treats Access as a generic data source
Syntax complexity	Slightly more verbose	Generally more concise
Performance with Access	Optimized for local Access databases	Comparable, but slightly less integrated
Flexibility across platforms	Windows only, Access-focused	Windows only, but broader backend support

Factor	DAO	ADO
Excel VBA compatibility	Fully supported, especially for Access integration	Fully supported for general data access
Schema access (tables, fields, and so on)	Strong—designed for direct schema manipulation (TableDefs, Fields, Indexes)	Limited—can query schema via `OpenSchema`, but less integrated

To use any code in this chapter, open the VB Editor. Select Tools | References from the main menu and then select Microsoft ActiveX Data Objects Library (version 2.8 or higher) from the Available References list, as shown in Figure 21-1.

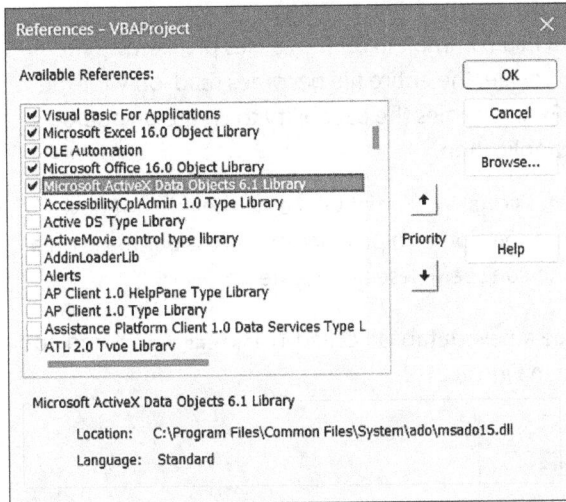

FIGURE 21-1 To read or write from an Access file, add the reference for Microsoft ActiveX Data Objects Library 2.8 or higher. Most examples use version 6.1, but earlier versions, such as 2.8, are still supported.

Level Up!

You could distribute your program with the library selected (early binding), but what if the users have a different version? When programming, it's a very good idea to have the library selected so you can access the tooltips. But for distribution, you should use late binding. Refer to Chapter 20, "Automating Word," for more information on early and late binding.

Tip This chapter uses ADO, but the bonus sample file, ProjectFilesChapter21-DAO Access.xlsm, uses DAO.

Case study: Creating a shared Access database

Linda and Janine are two buyers for a retail chain of stores. Each morning, they import data from the cash registers to get current information on sales and inventory for 2,000 styles. Throughout the day, either buyer may enter transfers of inventory from one store to another. It would be ideal if Linda could see the pending transfers entered by Janine and vice versa.

Each buyer has an Excel application with VBA running on her desktop. They each import the cash register data and have VBA routines that facilitate the creation of pivot table reports to help them make buying decisions.

Attempting to store the transfer data in a common Excel file causes problems. When either buyer attempts to write to the Excel file, the entire file becomes read-only for the other buyer. With a shared workbook, Excel disables the capability to create pivot tables, which is required in Linda and Janine's application.

Neither Linda nor Janine has the professional version of Office, so they do not have Access running on their desktop PCs. The solution is to produce an Access database on a network drive that both Linda and Janine can see. These are the steps:

1. Using Access on another PC, produce a new database called `Transfers.accdb` and add a table called `tblTransfer`, as shown in Figure 21-2.

tblTransfer	
Field Name	**Data Type**
ID	AutoNumber
Style	Short Text
FromStore	Number
ToStore	Number
Qty	Number
TDate	Date/Time
Sent	Yes/No
Receive	Yes/No

FIGURE 21-2 Multiple people using their own Excel workbooks will read and write to this table inside an ACCDB file on a network drive.

2. Move the `Transfers.accdb` file to a network drive. You might find that this common folder uses different drive-letter mappings on each machine. It might be `H:\Common\` on Linda's machine and `I:\Common\` on Janine's machine.

3. On both machines, open the VB Editor and, under Tools | References, add a reference to the Microsoft ActiveX Data Objects Library, as shown in Figure 21-1.

4. In both of their Excel workbooks, find an out-of-the-way cell in which to store the path to `Transfers.accdb`. Name this cell `Tpath`.

The application provides nearly seamless multiuser access to both buyers. Both Linda and Janine can read or write to the table at the same time. The only time a conflict occurs is when both parties attempt to update the same record simultaneously.

Other than the out-of-the-way cell reference to the path to `Transfers.accdb`, neither buyer is aware that her data is being stored in a shared Access table, and neither computer needs to have Access installed.

The remainder of this chapter gives you the code necessary to allow the application included in the preceding case study to read or write data from the `tblTransfer` table.

The tools of ADO

You encounter several terms when using ADO to connect to an external data source:

- **Recordset**—An ADO recordset is a set of records from a table, query, or SQL SELECT statement. You can loop through the recordset, view, edit, add, or delete records directly in memory. Use a recordset when you need to interact with data row by row.

- **Connection**—The connection defines the path to the database and the type of database. In the case of Access databases, you specify that the connection is using the Microsoft ACE Engine.

- **Cursor**—Think of the cursor as a pointer that keeps track of which record you are using in the database. There are several types of cursors and two places for the cursor to be located (described in the following bullets).

- **Cursor type**—A *dynamic* cursor is the most flexible cursor. If you define a recordset and someone else updates a record in the table while a dynamic cursor is active, the dynamic cursor knows about the updated record. Although this is the most flexible cursor, it requires the most overhead. If your database doesn't have a large number of transactions, you can specify a *static* cursor, which returns a snapshot of the data when the cursor is established.

- **Cursor location**—The cursor can be located either on the *client* or on the *server*. With a client cursor, Excel (via ADO) manages the records locally in memory. With a server cursor, the database engine (such as ACE or SQL Server) manages record navigation. Even if the database file is stored on your local drive, configuring a server cursor means the ACE engine is controlling the cursor logic. On a very large external data set, it would be better to allow the server to control the cursor. For small data sets, a client cursor is faster.

- **Lock type**—The point of this chapter is to allow multiple people to access a data set at the same time. The lock type determines how ADO prevents crashes when two people attempt to update a record simultaneously. With an *optimistic* lock type, an individual record is locked only when you attempt to update the record. If your application will be doing 90 percent reads and only occasionally updating, then an optimistic lock is perfect. However, if you know that every time you read a record, you will soon update the record, you should use a *pessimistic* lock type. With pessimistic locks, a record is locked as soon as it is edited. If you know that you will never write back to the database, you can use a *read-only* lock, which enables you to read the records without preventing others from writing to them.

The primary objects needed to access data in an ACCDB file are an ADO connection and an ADO recordset. The ADO connection defines the path to the database and specifies that the connection is using the Microsoft ACE Engine.

After establishing the connection to the database, you typically use it to define a recordset. A recordset can be a table, a subset of records in the table, or a predefined query in the Access database. To open a recordset, you have to specify the connection, and then you can specify values for the CursorType, CursorLocation, LockType, and Options parameters.

Assuming that you have only two users trying to access the table at a time, you should use a dynamic cursor and an optimistic lock type. For large recordsets, the adUseServer value of the CursorLocation property enables the database server to process records without using up RAM on the client machine. If you have a small recordset, it might be faster to use adUseClient for the CursorLocation. When the recordset is opened, all the records are transferred to the client machine's memory, allowing faster navigation from record to record.

Reading data from the Access database is easy, provided that you have fewer than 1,048,576 records—the maximum number of rows in Excel. You can use the CopyFromRecordset method to copy all selected records from the recordset to a blank area of the worksheet.

To add a record to an Access table, use the AddNew method for the recordset. You then specify the value for each field in the table and use the Update method to commit the changes to the database.

To delete a record from the table, move to the record you want to delete and use the Delete method for the recordset. You can then use the Update method to commit the changes to the database. You also have the option of using the Delete method of the connection object, the method used in this chapter.

> **Note** If you ever find yourself frustrated with ADO and think, "If I could just open Access, I could knock out a quick SQL statement to do exactly what I need," you can use the Execute method of the connection object to send that SQL directly to the database. Rather than use ADO to read through the records, the Execute method sends a request to the database to run the SQL statement that your program builds. This effectively enables you to handle any tasks that your database might support but that are not handled by ADO. The types of SQL statements you can execute depend on the database engine you're connected to.

Other tools are available that allow you to verify the existence of a table or a specific field within a table. You can also use VBA to add new fields to a table definition on the fly.

Connecting to a database

Before you can begin interacting with a database, you need to connect to it. This requires a *connection string*. The connection string tells the ADO interface where the database is located, which engine to use (ACE), and how to authenticate.

For connecting Excel to an Access database, the connection string is fairly straightforward. The `Provider` is the ACE engine, and the `Data Source` is the path to our database. If the database is password-protected—which ours is not—use the authentication parameter, `Jet OLEDB:Database Password`, like this:

```
"Provider=Microsoft.ACE.OLEDB.16.0;" & _
"Data Source=C:\YourDB.accdb;" & _
"Jet OLEDB:Database Password=MySecret;"
```

> **Note** Every database provider—Access, SQL Server, Excel, and so on—has its own required format for connection strings. These formats can be inconsistent and version-specific. *ConnectionStrings.com* is a comprehensive reference with examples to help you find the connection string you need.

Because you need to connect to the database before every operation (such as adding and retrieving), it's a good idea to create a function you can call at the start of each operation. The `GetDBConnection` function is called by the other procedures in this chapter, as shown here:

```
Function GetDBConnection() As ADODB.Connection
Dim conn As ADODB.Connection
Dim myConn As String
myConn = "Provider=Microsoft.ACE.OLEDB.16.0;Data Source=" & _
  ThisWorkbook.Path & Application.PathSeparator & "Transfers.accdb"
Set conn = New ADODB.Connection
'Open the connection
conn.Open myConn
Set GetDBConnection = conn
End Function
```

Adding a record to a database

Going back to the case study earlier in the chapter, the application you are creating has a userform where buyers can enter transfers. To make the calls to the Access database as simple as possible, a series of utility modules handle the ADO connection to the database. This way, the userform code can simply call `AddTransfer(Style, FromStore, ToStore, Qty)`.

Here's how you add records after the connection is defined:

1. Open a recordset that points to the table. In the code that follows, see the sections commented as `'Open the Connection`, `'Define the Recordset`, and `'Open the Table`.

2. Use AddNew to add a new record.

3. Assign a value to each field in the new record.

4. Use Update to update the recordset.

5. Close the recordset and then close the connection.

The following code adds a new record to the tblTransfer table:

```
Public Sub AddSingleRecord(ByVal Style As String, ByVal FromStore As Long, _
    ByVal ToStore As Long, ByVal Qty As Long)
Dim conn As ADODB.Connection
Dim rst As ADODB.Recordset
'Open the Connection
Set conn = GetDBConnection
'Define the Recordset
Set rst = New ADODB.Recordset
rst.CursorLocation = adUseServer
'Open the table
rst.Open Source:="tblTransfer", ActiveConnection:=conn, _
    CursorType:=adOpenKeyset, LockType:=adLockOptimistic, Options:=adCmdTable
'Add a record
rst.AddNew
'Set up the values for the fields. The first four fields
'are passed from the calling userform. The date field
'is filled with the current date.
rst("Style") = Style
rst("FromStore") = FromStore
rst("ToStore") = ToStore
rst("Qty") = Qty
rst("tDate") = Date
rst("Sent") = False
rst("Receive") = False
'Write the values to this record
rst.Update
'Close
rst.Close
conn.Close
'Clean up
Set conn = Nothing
Set rst = Nothing
End Sub
```

Retrieving records from a database

Reading records from an Access database is easy. As you define a recordset, you pass a SQL string (a SELECT query) to return the records you are interested in.

> **Tip** A great way to generate the SQL is to design the query in Access that retrieves the records. While viewing the query in Access, select SQL View from the View dropdown on the Query Tools Design tab of the ribbon. Access shows you the SQL statement required to execute that query. You can use that SQL statement as a model for building the SQL string in your VBA code.

After the recordset is defined, use the `CopyFromRecordSet` method to copy all the matching records from Access to a specific area of the worksheet.

The following routine queries the `tblTransfer` table to find all records in which the `Sent` flag is not yet set to True:

```
Sub GetUnsentTransfers()
Dim conn As ADODB.Connection
Dim rst As ADODB.Recordset
Dim myConn As String
Dim sSQL As String
Dim WSTemp As Worksheet
Dim FinalRow As Long
'Build a SQL String to get all fields for unsent transfers
sSQL = "SELECT ID, Style, FromStore, ToStore, Qty, tDate FROM tblTransfer"
sSQL = sSQL & " WHERE Sent=FALSE"
'connect to the database
Set conn = GetDBConnection
Set rst = New ADODB.Recordset
rst.CursorLocation = adUseServer
rst.Open Source:=sSQL, ActiveConnection:=conn, _
  CursorType:=adOpenForwardOnly, LockType:=adLockOptimistic, _
  Options:=adCmdText
'Setup the sheet
Set WSTemp = Worksheets("Retrieving Records")
With WSTemp
  .Range("A1:F1").EntireColumn.Clear
  'Add Headings
  .Range("A1:F1").Value = Array("ID", "Style", "From", "To", "Qty", "Date")
  'Copy from the recordset to row 2
  .Range("A2").CopyFromRecordset rst
End With
'Close the connection
rst.Close
conn.Close
'Format the report
FinalRow = WSTemp.Cells(Rows.Count, 1).End(xlUp).Row
'If there were no records, then stop
If FinalRow = 1 Then
  MsgBox "There are no transfers to confirm"
Else
  'Format column F as a date
  WSTemp.Range("F2:F" & FinalRow).NumberFormat = "m/d/y"
  'Show the userform - used in next section
  frmTransConf.Show
End If
```

```
Set rst = Nothing
Set conn = Nothing
Set WSTemp = Nothing
End Sub
```

The results are placed on a blank worksheet. The final few lines display the results in a userform to illustrate how to update a record in the next section.

The CopyFromRecordSet method copies records that match the SQL query to a range on the worksheet. Note that you receive only the data rows. The headings do not come along automatically. You must use code to write the headings to row 1. Figure 21-3 shows the results.

	A	B	C	D	E	F
1	ID	Style	From	To	Qty	Date
2	2102	B12256	340012	340018	6	5/14/25
3	2103	B15878	340009	340013	10	5/14/25
4	2104	B14135	340001	340020	1	5/14/25
5	2105	B11275	340010	340017	8	5/14/25
6	2106	B10133	340003	340019	4	5/14/25
7	2107	B15422	340010	340018	5	5/14/25
8	2108	B10894	340012	340014	9	5/14/25
9	2109	B10049	340008	340019	3	5/14/25
10	2110	B11764	340002	340010	3	5/14/25
11	2111	B10894	340003	340017	10	5/14/25
12	2112	B12754	340004	340015	6	5/14/25
13	2113	B17935	340010	340014	10	5/14/25

FIGURE 21-3 Range("A2").CopyFromRecordSet brought matching records from the Access database to the worksheet.

Updating an existing record

To update an existing record using ADO, you need to build a recordset with just the one record to update. This requires the user to select a unique key when identifying the records. After you have opened the recordset, use the Fields property to modify the field in question, and then use the Update method to commit the changes to the database.

The earlier example returned a recordset to a blank worksheet and then called the userform frmTransConf. This form uses a simple Userform_Initialize to display the range in a large list box:

```
Private Sub UserForm_Initialize()
Dim wsRecords As Worksheet
Set wsRecords = Worksheets("Retrieving Records")

'Determine how Records we have
FinalRow = wsRecords.Cells(Rows.Count, 1).End(xlUp).Row
If FinalRow > 1 Then
  Me.lbXlt.RowSource = "A2:F" & FinalRow
End If
Set wsRecords = Nothing
End Sub
```

The list box's properties have the `MultiSelect` property set to `True`.

After the `Userform_Initialize` procedure is run, the unconfirmed records are displayed in a list box. The logistics planner can mark all the records that have been sent, as shown in Figure 21-4.

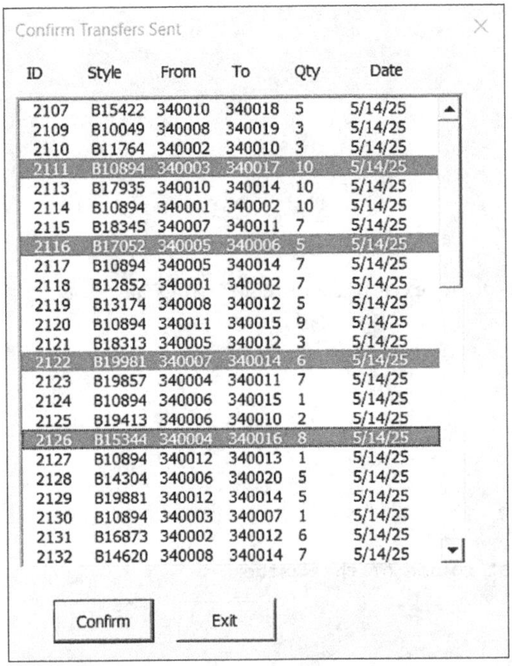

FIGURE 21-4 This userform displays particular records from the Access recordset. When the buyer selects certain records and then clicks the Confirm button, you can use ADO's `Update` method to update the Sent field on the selected records.

What Looks Efficient Isn't Always Practical

I once thought this was the "correct" way to update records in ADO:

```
rst.Update Array("Field1", "Field2"), Array("Value1", "Value2")
```

My project had a lot of fields to update, so I wrote helper functions to build the arrays, clean up the strings, and do everything "right." And still, every time something needed tweaking, I found myself counting variable positions, trying to figure out which value lined up with which field. It was frustrating, hard to debug, and honestly, a waste of time.

That syntax works, but almost no one uses it. The standard approach shown below—setting fields one by one with `rst("Field")` = `value` and then calling `rst.Update`—takes more lines, but it's clear, maintainable, and actually debuggable.

So, learn from me, and don't make the mistake of chasing compact code and the "right way" at the expense of clarity and maintainability.

The code attached to the Confirm button follows:

```vb
Private Sub cbConfirm_Click()
Dim conn As ADODB.Connection
Dim rst As ADODB.Recordset
Dim eaRecord As Long, CountSelect As Long
Dim ThisID As String, sSQL As String
'If nothing is selected, warn them
CountSelect = 0
For eaRecord = 0 To Me.lbXlt.ListCount - 1
  If Me.lbXlt.Selected(eaRecord) Then
     CountSelect = CountSelect + 1
  End If
Next eaRecord
If CountSelect = 0 Then
  MsgBox "There were no transfers selected. To exit without confirming any " & _
     "tranfers, use Exit."
  Exit Sub
End If
'Establish a connection Transfers.accdb
Set conn = GetDBConnection
'Loop through the listbox and if a record is Selected
'Update the database
For eaRecord = 0 To Me.lbXlt.ListCount - 1
  If Me.lbXlt.Selected(eaRecord) Then
     'retrieve the record ID from the first column of the listbox
     ThisID = Me.lbXlt.List(eaRecord, 0)
     'Mark ThisID as complete
     'Build SQL String
     sSQL = "SELECT * FROM tblTransfer Where ID=" & ThisID
     Set rst = New ADODB.Recordset
     With rst
       .Open Source:=sSQL, ActiveConnection:=conn, CursorType:=adOpenKeyset, _
         LockType:=adLockOptimistic
       'Check if the recordset returned a match
       If Not rst.EOF Then
         'Update the field
         .Fields("Sent").Value = True
         .Update
       End If
       .Close
     End With
  End If
Next eaRecord
'Close the connection
conn.Close
Set rst = Nothing
Set conn = Nothing
'Close the userform
Unload Me
End Sub
```

Including the ID field in the fields returned in the prior example is important if you want to narrow down the information to a single record. Also, you may have noticed the EOF property; this stands for

End of File and returns True if you're looping through the recordset and have passed the last row. It also returns True if the recordset is empty, as could be the case here, because no match was found. It's a quick way to confirm at least one record was returned. If the record doesn't exist, trying to update or delete it will fail.

> **Note** This example returns a single record. For multi-record sets, see "Looping through multiple records with MoveNext" later in this chapter.

Level Up!

For better performance, you can use the Execute method inside the loop to run an SQL UPDATE for each selected ID. This approach updates the database directly—there's no recordset retrieval. However, because the change happens immediately when the SQL statement runs, you lose the flexibility to inspect or modify the data beforehand as you could if it were loaded into a recordset first. The following lines of code replace the entire For loop used in the recordset method:

```
'SQL Execute Method used for updating records
'replaces entire previous For loop
For eaRecord = 0 To Me.lbXlt.ListCount - 1
  If Me.lbXlt.Selected(eaRecord) Then
    ThisID = Me.lbXlt.List(eaRecord, 0)
    sSQL = "UPDATE tblTransfer SET Sent = True WHERE ID = " & ThisID
    conn.Execute sSQL
  End If
Next eaRecord
```

Deleting records via ADO

Deleting a record is similar to updating a record: you build a recordset containing just the one record you want to delete and then use the Delete method followed by Update to commit the change to the database. The following lines find a record based on its ID and delete it:

```
Sub DeleteSingleRecord(ByVal RecID As Long)
Dim conn As ADODB.Connection
Dim rst As ADODB.Recordset
Dim sSQL As String
'Open the Connection
Set conn = GetDBConnection
'Build a SELECT statement to isolate the target record
sSQL = "SELECT * FROM tblTransfer WHERE ID = " & RecID
'Open a recordset with one matching record
Set rst = New ADODB.Recordset
rst.Open Source:=sSQL, ActiveConnection:=conn, _
    CursorType:=adOpenKeyset, LockType:=adLockOptimistic
'Check if the recordset actually returned a match
```

```
If Not rst.EOF Then
  'Delete the record and commit the change
  rst.Delete
  rst.Update
Else 'inform the user record wasn't found
  MsgBox "Record " & RecID & " not found"
End If
rst.Close
conn.Close
Set rst = Nothing
Set conn = Nothing
End Sub
```

For example, to delete record 2136, call the sub like this:

```
Sub DeleteOneRecord()
DeleteSingleRecord 2136
End Sub
```

Level Up!

If you don't need to inspect the record first, you can skip the recordset entirely and delete the record directly using a SQL statement with the EXECUTE method:

```
Sub DeleteWithSQL(ByVal RecID As Long)
Dim conn As ADODB.Connection
Dim sSQL As String
Set conn = GetDBConnection
sSQL = "DELETE FROM tblTransfer WHERE ID = " & RecID
conn.Execute sSQL
conn.Close
Set conn = Nothing
End Sub
```

This method is faster and simpler—but as with updates, you're making the change immediately without a chance to preview the data beforehand.

Summarizing records via ADO

One strength of Access is its ability to run summary queries that group data by a particular field. If you build a summary query in Access and examine the SQL view, you'll see that complex queries can be written. Similar SQL can be built in Excel VBA and passed to Access via ADO.

You can use ADO not just to retrieve or update individual records but also to run summary queries directly from Excel. These queries can calculate totals, counts, or other aggregations—grouped by a specific field, just like in Access. Instead of creating and saving a query in Access, you can build the SQL statement in VBA and run it on demand.

The following code builds and runs a summary SQL query that calculates net open transfers by store and filtered by style. It groups incoming and outgoing transfers, combines the results, and places the summarized totals onto the worksheet.

```
Public Sub NetTransfers(ByVal Style As String)
Dim conn As ADODB.Connection
Dim rst As ADODB.Recordset
Dim sSQL As String
Dim ws As Worksheet
'Define the target worksheet
Set ws = Worksheets("Summarizing Records")
ws.Range("A1:C1").EntireColumn.Clear
'Build the SQL summary query
sSQL = "SELECT Store, SUM(Quantity) AS NetQty, MIN(mDate) AS FirstDate FROM (" _
  & "SELECT ToStore AS Store, SUM(Qty) AS Quantity, MIN(TDate) AS mDate " & _
  "FROM tblTransfer WHERE Style = '" & Style & "' AND Receive = FALSE " & _
  "GROUP BY ToStore " & _
  "UNION ALL " & _
  "SELECT FromStore AS Store, SUM(-1 * Qty) AS Quantity, " & _
  "MIN(TDate) AS mDate " & _
  "FROM tblTransfer WHERE Style = '" & Style & "' AND Sent = FALSE " & _
  "GROUP BY FromStore) GROUP BY Store"
'Establish database connection
Set conn = GetDBConnection
'Open the recordset
Set rst = New ADODB.Recordset
rst.CursorLocation = adUseServer
rst.Open sSQL, conn, adOpenForwardOnly, adLockReadOnly, adCmdText
'Write headers
ws.Range("A1:C1").Value = Array("Store", "Qty", "Date")
'Format the date column
ws.Range("C2:C" & ws.Cells(ws.Rows.Count, "C").End(xlUp).Row).NumberFormat = _
  "m/d/yyyy"
'Output results
ws.Range("A2").CopyFromRecordset rst
'Cleanup
rst.Close
conn.Close
Set rst = Nothing
Set conn = Nothing
Set ws = Nothing
End Sub
```

> **Note** If you're not comfortable writing SQL by hand, you're not alone. Summary queries like this can look intimidating, but most of the logic is just SELECT, GROUP BY, and basic math. For reference, sites like *W3Schools.com* offer clear examples of standard SQL syntax. Most of their SQL examples work in Access, although not all features are supported in exactly the same way.

Other utilities via ADO

Consider the application you created for this chapter's case study: The buyers now have an Access database located on their network, but they may not have a copy of Access installed. To keep things running smoothly, it's helpful to make your workbook self-updating. You can use ADO to check whether required tables or fields exist in the database and create them on the fly if needed. This ensures the shared database always has the structure the application expects—regardless of which user opens it first.

> **Note** These checks can run automatically from the `Workbook_Open` event. That way, updates happen silently the first time the application is launched after deployment.

Checking for the existence of tables

If your application needs to create a new table, you don't want to automatically run a `CREATE TABLE` command, especially in a shared database. Only the first person who opens the workbook should add the table; everyone else should skip it. The function below checks whether the table already exists, returning `True` if it does and `False` if it does not. The calling procedure can then decide whether to run the creation code.

The following code uses the `OpenSchema` method to query the database schema:

```
Function TableExists(ByVal WhichTable As String) As Boolean
'Returns True if the specified table exists in the database
Dim conn As ADODB.Connection
Dim rst As ADODB.Recordset
TableExists = False
'establish the database connection
Set conn = GetDBConnection
'open the recordset, returning a list of all tables
Set rst = conn.OpenSchema(adSchemaTables)
'loop through all the tables in the recordset
Do Until rst.EOF
  If LCase(rst!Table_Name) = LCase(WhichTable) Then
    TableExists = True
    Exit Do 'table found, so stop looking and exit the loop
  End If
  rst.MoveNext
Loop
rst.Close
conn.Close
Set rst = Nothing
Set conn = Nothing
End Function
```

When you open a schema recordset using `OpenSchema(adSchemaTables)`, each row represents a table in the database. One of the fields returned is `Table_Name`, which contains the name of that table.

The expression `rst!Table_Name` is shorthand for `rst.Fields("Table_Name").Value`. It returns the name of the table in the current row of the recordset.

Looping through multiple records with MoveNext

The query in the previous example returns a recordset with an unknown number of records. To process each one, we used a `Do Until` that continues until the end of the recordset. To move from one record to the next, we called the `MoveNext` method.

When a recordset contains more than one row, `MoveNext` advances the cursor to the next record. Without it, your code would remain on the first row and never progress, resulting in an infinite loop. This is the standard method for processing all records in a recordset.

For example, you might want to find all transfers that were sent more than seven days ago but haven't been marked as received. A query like that could return several records. To flag each one as overdue, open the recordset and loop through it using the `MoveNext` method.

Checking for the existence of a field

Sometimes, you want to add a new field to an existing table. As with tables, you should check whether the column already exists before adding it. The following code does this with the `OpenSchema` method, but this time, it looks at the columns in the tables:

```
Function ColumnExists(ByVal WhichColumn As String, _
  ByVal WhichTable As String) As Boolean
'Returns True if the specified column exists in the given table
Dim conn As ADODB.Connection
Dim rst As ADODB.Recordset
ColumnExists = False
'establish the database connection
Set conn = GetDBConnection
'open the recordset, returning a list of all columns in all tables
Set rst = conn.OpenSchema(adSchemaColumns)
'loop through all the columns in the recordset
Do Until rst.EOF
  'try to match the column and table
  If LCase(rst!Column_Name) = LCase(WhichColumn) And _
    LCase(rst!Table_Name) = LCase(WhichTable) Then
    ColumnExists = True
    Exit Do
  End If
  rst.MoveNext
Loop
rst.Close
conn.Close
Set rst = Nothing
Set conn = Nothing
End Function
```

Adding a table on the fly

Once you've confirmed that a required table doesn't exist, you can create it by sending a SQL CREATE TABLE command. The syntax for the SQL command is:

```
CREATE TABLE TableName (
   FieldName1 DataType [constraints],
   FieldName2 DataType [constraints],
   ...
)
```

Constraints are optional rules you can apply to a field—such as PRIMARY KEY, NOT NULL, and DEFAULT. However, Access only supports a subset of standard SQL constraints, and not all constraints are allowed for all field types. So, if possible, build the table manually in Access first and then view its SQL definition.

The following procedure uses Execute to pass the SQL statement directly to the Access engine:

```
Sub CreateReplenishTable()
'Creates tblReplenish with five fields:
'Style
'A = Auto replenishment for A
'B = Auto replenishment level for B stores
'C = Auto replenishment level for C stores
'RecActive = Yes/No field
Dim conn As ADODB.Connection
Dim cmd As ADODB.Command
'establish the database connection
Set conn = GetDBConnection
'Create the command object and attach the connection
Set cmd = New ADODB.Command
Set cmd.ActiveConnection = conn
'Define the SQL to create the table
cmd.CommandText = "CREATE TABLE tblReplenish (" & _
   "Style Char(10) PRIMARY KEY, " & _
   "A Int, B Int, C Int, RecActive YesNo)"
'Run the SQL against the database
cmd.Execute , , adCmdText
conn.Close
Set cmd = Nothing
Set conn = Nothing
End Sub
```

The five fields we created in the new table are:

- Style Char(10) PRIMARY KEY—A text field (up to 10 characters) used as the table's primary key

- A Int, B Int, C Int—Three numeric fields representing replenishment levels by store type

- RecActive YesNo—A boolean field that stores either True/False or Yes/No values

Adding a field on the fly

If you determine that a field does not exist, you can add it by sending a SQL ALTER TABLE command to the database. The syntax for the SQL command is:

```
ALTER TABLE TableName ADD COLUMN FieldName DataType [constraints]
```

As with adding a table, constraints are optional rules you can apply to a field—such as PRIMARY KEY, NOT NULL, and DEFAULT. However, Access only supports a subset of standard SQL constraints, and not all constraints are allowed for all field types. This limitation also applies to data types. If possible, add the column manually in Access first and then view its SQL definition to verify compatibility.

```
Sub AddField()
'Adds a field named Grp to the tblReplenish table
Dim conn As ADODB.Connection
Dim cmd As ADODB.Command
'Establish the database connection
Set conn = GetDBConnection
'Create the command object and attach the connection
Set cmd = New ADODB.Command
Set cmd.ActiveConnection = conn
'Define the SQL to add a new column to the table
cmd.CommandText = "ALTER TABLE tblReplenish " & _
    "ADD COLUMN Grp Char(25)"
'Run the SQL against the database
cmd.Execute , , adCmdText
'Clean up
conn.Close
Set cmd = Nothing
Set conn = Nothing
End Sub
```

The column we added to the table has the following characteristics:

- **Name**—Grp

- **Data type: Char(25)**—Stores up to 25 characters

Connecting to SQL Server from Excel

If your data is in an SQL Server database, you can use ADO to connect Excel directly to the database and return results to Excel.

The following SQL Server example is based on Microsoft's AdventureWorks sample database, which can be downloaded from the Microsoft Learn site at *https://learn.microsoft.com/en-us/sql/samples/adventureworks-install-configure*.

You'll need an existing SQL Server instance on which to install it. Once that's set up, you can run the following code to test the stored procedure dbo.usp_GetProductList:

```vba
Sub DataExtract()
'Here is a SQL Server code sample, but it doesn't actually work
'unless you have an SQL server setup and downloaded
Dim cnPubs As ADODB.Connection
Dim rsPubs As ADODB.Recordset
Dim strConn As String
Dim ws As Worksheet
Dim K As Long
Dim myCell As Range, myRng As Range
'clear out all previous data
Set ws = Worksheets("SQL Example")
ws.Cells.Clear
'Define SQL Server connection string
'Data Source = a typical local dev SQL instance
'Initial Catalog = real MS sample DB you can download
'SSPI - Windows Auth (common in dev)
strConn = "Provider=SQLOLEDB;" & _
    "Data Source=MY-SERVER\SQL2019;" & _
    "Initial Catalog=AdventureWorks2019;" & _
    "Integrated Security=SSPI;"
'Open the connection
Set cnPubs = New ADODB.Connection
'Now open the connection.
cnPubs.Open strConn
'Open the recordset
Set rsPubs = New ADODB.Recordset
With rsPubs
    .ActiveConnection = cnPubs
    'run a stored procedure on the server
    'EXEC - SQL keyword for "execute a stored procedure"
    'dbo - the schema (usually dbo for default in SQL Server)
    'usp_GetProductList - the name of the stored procedure
    .Open "EXEC dbo.usp_GetProductList"
    ws.Range("A2").CopyFromRecordset rsPubs
    'Write column headers
    For K = 0 To .Fields.Count - 1
        ws.Cells(1, K + 1).Value = .Fields(K).Name
        ws.Cells(1, K + 1).Font.Bold = True
    Next K
    .Close
End With
cnPubs.Close
'Flatten and align values
Set myRng = ws.UsedRange
For Each myCell In myRng
    myCell.Value = myCell.Value
    myCell.HorizontalAlignment = xlRight
Next myCell
Set myRng = Nothing
Set myCell = Nothing
Set rsPubs = Nothing
Set cnPubs = Nothing
Set ws = Nothing
End Sub
```

Next steps

This chapter showed how to connect Excel to Access databases using ADO, including reading, updating, and modifying records. It also covered key compatibility considerations, dynamic schema changes, and a brief look at connecting to SQL Server. In Chapter 22, "Advanced userform techniques," you'll discover more controls and techniques you can use in building userforms.

Advanced userform techniques

In this chapter, you will:

- Access the UserForm toolbar

- Learn how to use CheckBox, TabStrip, RefEdit, and ToggleButton controls

- Use a collection to control multiple controls

- Select a cell on a sheet while a userform is open

- Use hyperlinks in userforms

- Add controls at runtime

- Add help to a userform

- Set up a multicolumn list box

- Create transparent forms

Chapter 10, "Userforms: An introduction," covered the basics of adding controls to userforms. This chapter continues the topic, looking at more advanced controls and methods for making the most out of userforms.

Using the UserForm toolbar in the design of controls on userforms

In the VB Editor, under View | Toolbars, you'll find a few toolbars that do not appear unless you select them. One of these is the UserForm toolbar, shown in Figure 22-1. It has functionality useful for organizing the controls you add to a userform; for example, you can use it to make all the controls you select the same size.

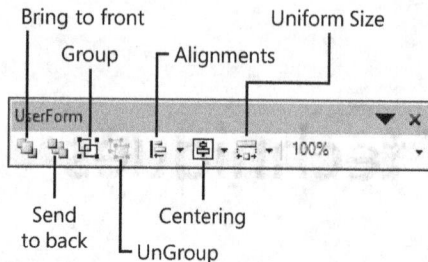

FIGURE 22-1 The UserForm toolbar has tools for organizing the controls on a userform.

More userform controls

The following sections cover more userform controls you can use to help obtain information from people. At the end of each of the following subsections is a table that lists the control's events.

CheckBox controls

Checkboxes allow the user to select one or more options on a userform. Unlike the option buttons discussed in Chapter 10, a person can select one or more checkboxes at a time.

The value of a selected CheckBox is True; the value of an unselected CheckBox is False. If you set the value of a CheckBox to null (CheckBox1.Value = "" or CheckBox1.Value = Null), when the userform runs, the checkbox will have a grayed-out check in it, as shown in Figure 22-2. This can be useful for verifying that users have viewed all options and made a selection.

FIGURE 22-2 Use the null value of the CheckBox to verify that a person has viewed and answered all options.

You can use code like the following to review all the checkboxes in the Languages group of the dialog shown in Figure 22-2. If a value is null, the user is prompted to review the selections:

```
Private Sub btnClose_Click()
Dim Msg As String
Dim Chk As Control
Set Chk = Nothing
'narrow down the search to just the 2nd page's controls
```

```
For Each Chk In frm_Multipage.MultiPage1.Pages(1).Controls
   'only need to verify checkbox controls
  If TypeName(Chk) = "CheckBox" Then
     'and just in case we add more checkbox controls,
     'just check the ones in the group
    If Chk.GroupName = "Languages" Then
       'if the value is null (the property value is empty)
      If IsNull(Chk.Object.Value) Then
         'add the caption to a string
        Msg = Msg & vbNewLine & Chk.Caption
      End If
    End If
  End If
Next Chk
If Msg <> "" Then
  Msg = "The following checkboxes were not verified:" & vbNewLine & Msg
  MsgBox Msg, vbInformation, "Additional Information Required"
Else
  Unload Me
End If
End Sub
```

Table 22-1 lists the events for CheckBox controls.

TABLE 22-1 CheckBox control events

Event	Description
AfterUpdate	Occurs after a checkbox has been selected/cleared.
BeforeDragOver	Occurs while the person drags and drops data onto the checkbox.
BeforeDropOrPaste	Occurs right before the person is about to drop or paste data onto the checkbox.
BeforeUpdate	Occurs before the checkbox is selected/cleared.
Change	Occurs when the value of the checkbox is changed.
Click	Occurs when the person clicks the control with the mouse.
DblClick	Occurs when the person double-clicks the checkbox with the mouse.
Enter	Occurs right before the checkbox receives the focus from another control on the same userform.
Error	Occurs when the checkbox runs into an error and cannot return the error information.
Exit	Occurs right after the checkbox loses focus to another control on the same userform.
KeyDown	Occurs when the person presses a key on the keyboard.
KeyPress	Occurs when the person presses an ANSI key. An ANSI key is a typeable character such as the letter A.
KeyUp	Occurs when the person releases a key on the keyboard.
MouseDown	Occurs when the person presses the mouse button within the borders of the checkbox.
MouseMove	Occurs when the person moves the mouse within the borders of the checkbox.
MouseUp	Occurs when the person releases the mouse button within the borders of the checkbox.

TabStrip controls

⌨ The MultiPage control, discussed in Chapter 10, allows a userform to have several pages. Each page of the form can have its own set of controls independent from the other pages.

In contrast, a TabStrip control also allows a userform to have many tabs, but the controls on each tab are identical; they are drawn only once. Yet when the form is run, the information changes depending on which tab strip is active (see Figure 22-3).

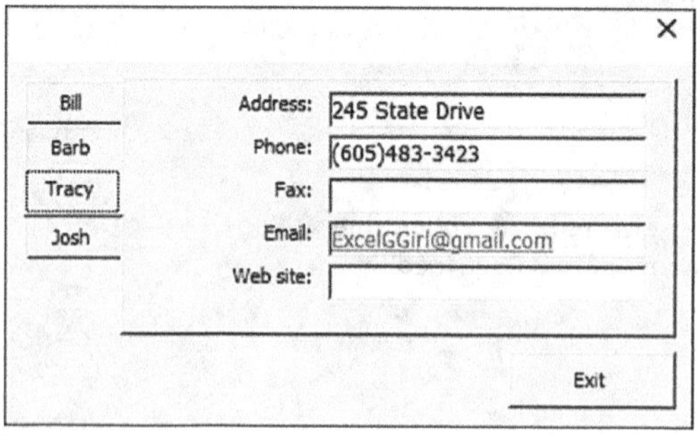

FIGURE 22-3 A tab strip allows a userform with multiple pages to share controls but not information.

By default, a tab strip is thin, with two tabs at the top. Right-clicking a tab enables you to add, remove, rename, or move that tab. Size the tab strip to hold all the controls. Outside the tab strip area, draw a button for closing the form.

You can move the tabs around the strip, as shown in Figure 22-3, by changing the TabOrientation property. The tabs can be at the top, bottom, left, or right side of the userform.

The following lines of code were used to create the tab strip form shown in Figure 22-3. The Initialize sub calls the sub SetValuesToTabStrip, which sets the value for the first tab:

```
Private Sub UserForm_Initialize()
SetValuesToTabStrip 1 'As default
End Sub
```

These lines of code handle what happens when a new tab is selected:

```
Private Sub TabStrip1_Change()
Dim lngRow As Long
lngRow = TabStrip1.Value + 1
SetValuesToTabStrip lngRow
End Sub
```

This sub provides the data shown on each tab. A sheet was set up, with each row corresponding to a tab:

```
Private Sub SetValuesToTabStrip(ByVal lngRow As Long)
With frm_Staff
  .lbl_Address.Caption = Cells(lngRow, 2).Value
  .lbl_Phone.Caption = Cells(lngRow, 3).Value
```

```
        .lbl_Fax.Caption = Cells(lngRow, 4).Value
        .lbl_Email.Caption = Cells(lngRow, 5).Value
        .lbl_Website.Caption = Cells(lngRow, 6).Value
    .Show
    End With
End Sub
```

The tab strip's values are automatically filled in. They correspond to the tab's position in the strip; moving a tab changes its value. The value of the first tab of a tab strip is 0, which is why, in the preceding code, we add 1 to the tab strip value when the form is initialized to get it to correspond with the row on the sheet.

> **Tip** If you want a single tab to have an extra control, the control could be added at runtime, when the tab is activated, and removed when the tab is deactivated.

Table 22-2 lists the events for the TabStrip control.

TABLE 22-2 TabStrip control events

Event	Description
BeforeDragOver	Occurs while the person drags and drops data onto the control.
BeforeDropOrPaste	Occurs right before the person drops or pastes data into the control.
Change	Occurs when the value of the control is changed.
Click	Occurs when the person clicks the control with the mouse.
DblClick	Occurs when the person double-clicks the control with the mouse.
Enter	Occurs right before the control receives the focus from another control on the same userform.
Error	Occurs when the control runs into an error and cannot return the error information.
Exit	Occurs right after the control loses focus to another control on the same userform.
KeyDown	Occurs when the person presses a key on the keyboard.
KeyPress	Occurs when the person presses an ANSI key. An ANSI key is a typeable character, such as the letter A.
KeyUp	Occurs when the person releases a key on the keyboard.
MouseDown	Occurs when the person presses the mouse button within the borders of the control.
MouseMove	Occurs when the person moves the mouse within the borders of the control.
MouseUp	Occurs when the person releases the mouse button within the borders of the control.

RefEdit **controls**

The RefEdit control allows a person to select a range on a sheet; the range is returned as a string value of the control. You can add it to any form. When you click the button on the right side of the field, the userform disappears and is replaced with the range selection form that is used for selecting ranges with Excel's many wizard tools, as shown in Figure 22-4. Click the button on the right of the field to show the userform once again.

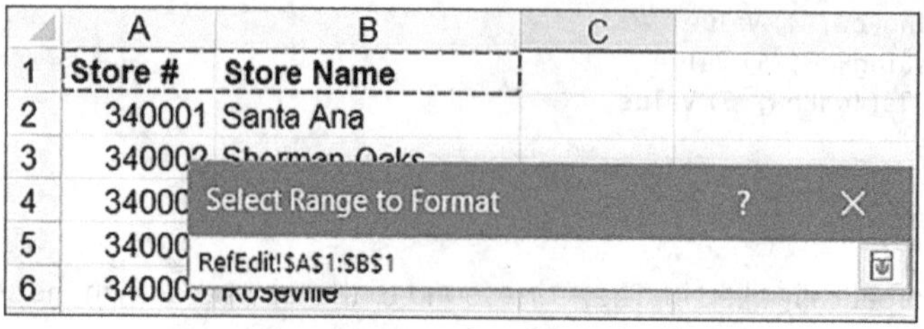

FIGURE 22-4 Use RefEdit to enable a person to select a range on a sheet.

The following code used with a RefEdit control allows a person to select a range, which is then made bold:

```
Private Sub cb1_Click()
Range(RefEdit1.Value).Font.Bold = True
Unload Me
End Sub
```

Table 22-3 lists the events for RefEdit controls.

Caution RefEdit control events are notorious for not working properly. If you run into this problem, use a different control's event to trigger the code.

TABLE 22-3 RefEdit control events

Event	Description
AfterUpdate	Occurs after the control's data has been changed.
BeforeDragOver	Occurs while the person drags and drops data onto the control.
BeforeDropOrPaste	Occurs right before the person drops or pastes data into the control.
BeforeUpdate	Occurs before the data in the control is changed.
Change	Occurs when the value of the control is changed.
Click	Occurs when the person clicks the control with the mouse.
DblClick	Occurs when the person double-clicks the control with the mouse.
DropButtonClick	Occurs when the person clicks the drop button on the right side of the field.
Enter	Occurs right before the control receives the focus from another control on the same userform.
Error	Occurs when the control runs into an error and cannot return the error information.
Exit	Occurs right after the control loses focus to another control on the same userform.
KeyDown	Occurs when the person presses a key on the keyboard.
KeyPress	Occurs when the person presses an ANSI key. An ANSI key is a typeable character, such as the letter A.
KeyUp	Occurs when the person releases a key on the keyboard.

Event	Description
MouseDown	Occurs when the person presses the mouse button within the borders of the control.
MouseMove	Occurs when the person moves the mouse within the borders of the control.
MouseUp	Occurs when the person releases the mouse button within the borders of the control.

ToggleButton **controls**

A toggle button looks like a normal command button, but when it's clicked, it stays pressed until it's clicked again. This allows a True or False value to be returned based on the status of the button. Table 22-4 lists the events for the ToggleButton controls.

TABLE 22-4 ToggleButton control events

Event	Description
AfterUpdate	Occurs after the control's data has been changed.
BeforeDragOver	Occurs while the person drags and drops data onto the control.
BeforeDropOrPaste	Occurs right before the person drops or pastes data into the control.
BeforeUpdate	Occurs before the data in the control is changed.
Change	Occurs when the value of the control is changed.
Click	Occurs when someone clicks the control with the mouse.
DblClick	Occurs when the person double-clicks the control with the mouse.
Enter	Occurs right before the control receives the focus from another control on the same userform.
Error	Occurs when the control runs into an error and cannot return the error information.
Exit	Occurs right after the control loses focus to another control on the same userform.
KeyDown	Occurs when the person presses a key on the keyboard.
KeyPress	Occurs when the person presses an ANSI key. An ANSI key is a typeable character, such as the letter A.
KeyUp	Occurs when the person releases a key on the keyboard.
MouseDown	Occurs when the person presses the mouse button within the borders of the control.
MouseMove	Occurs when the person moves the pointer within the borders of the control.
MouseUp	Occurs when the person releases the mouse button within the borders of the control.

Using a scrollbar as a slider to select values

Chapter 10 discusses using a SpinButton control to enable someone to choose a date. A spin button is useful, but it enables you to adjust up or down by only one unit at a time. An alternative method is to draw a horizontal or vertical scrollbar in the middle of the userform and use it as a slider. People can use arrows on the ends of the scrollbar as they would the spin button arrows, but they can also grab the scrollbar and instantly drag it to a certain value.

The userform shown in Figure 22-5 includes a label named Label1 and a scrollbar called ScrollBar1.

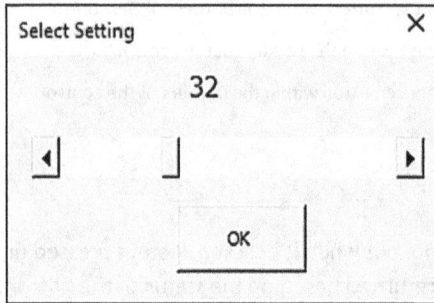

FIGURE 22-5 Using a ScrollBar control allows the person to drag to a particular numeric or data value.

The userform's Initialize code sets up the Min and Max values for the scrollbar. It initializes the scrollbar to a value from cell A1 and updates the Label1.Caption:

```
Private Sub UserForm_Initialize()
Me.ScrollBar1.Min = 0
Me.ScrollBar1.Max = 100
With Worksheets("Scrollbar").Range("A1")
  'ensure the value in A1 is within range, else an error is generated
  If .Value < 0 Or .Value > 100 Then
    .Value = 0
  Else
    Me.ScrollBar1.Value = .Value
  End If
End With
Me.Label1.Caption = Me.ScrollBar1.Value
End Sub
```

Two event handlers are needed for the scrollbar. The Change event triggers when a person clicks the arrows at the ends of the scrollbar. The Scroll event triggers when they drag the slider to a new value:

```
Private Sub ScrollBar1_Change()
'This event triggers when the user touches
'the arrows on the end of the scrollbar
Me.Label1.Caption = Me.ScrollBar1.Value
End Sub

Private Sub ScrollBar1_Scroll()
'This event triggers when the user drags the slider
Me.Label1.Caption = Me.ScrollBar1.Value
End Sub
```

Finally, the event attached to the button writes the scrollbar value out to the worksheet:

```
Private Sub btnClose_Click()
Worksheets("Scrollbar").Range("A1").Value = Me.ScrollBar1.Value
Unload Me
End Sub
```

Table 22-5 lists the events for ScrollBar controls.

TABLE 22-5 ScrollBar control events

Event	Description
AfterUpdate	Occurs after a person has changed the control's data.
BeforeDragOver	Occurs while someone drags and drops data onto the control.
BeforeDropOrPaste	Occurs right before the person drops or pastes data into the control.
BeforeUpdate	Occurs before the data in the control is changed.
Change	Occurs when the value of the control is changed.
Enter	Occurs right before the control receives the focus from another control on the same userform.
Error	Occurs when the control runs into an error and cannot return the error information.
Exit	Occurs right after the control loses focus to another control on the same userform.
KeyDown	Occurs when the person presses a key on the keyboard.
KeyPress	Occurs when the person presses an ANSI key. An ANSI key is a typeable character, such as the letter A.
KeyUp	Occurs when the person releases a key on the keyboard.
Scroll	Occurs when the slider is moved.

Controls and collections

Userform controls can be grouped into collections, which can be managed using class modules. This is an efficient way to apply the same logic or event handling to multiple controls. The following example selects or clears all the checkboxes on the userform, depending on which label someone chooses.

Place the following code in the class module, clsFormCtl. It consists of one property, chb, and two methods, SelectAll and UnselectAll.

The SelectAll method selects a checkbox by setting its value to True:

```
'this 1st line is placed at the top of the module
Public WithEvents chb As MSForms.CheckBox

Public Sub SelectAll()
chb.Value = True
End Sub
```

The UnselectAll method clears the checkbox:

```
Public Sub UnselectAll()
chb.Value = False
End Sub
```

That sets up the class module. Next, the controls need to be placed in a collection. The following code, placed behind the form `frm_Movies`, places the checkboxes into a collection. The checkboxes are part of the frame `frm_Selection`, which makes it easier to create the collection because it narrows the number of controls that need to be checked from the entire userform to just those controls within the frame:

```
'this 1st line is placed at the top of the module
Dim col_Selection As New Collection

Private Sub UserForm_Initialize()
Dim ctl As MSForms.CheckBox
Dim chb_ctl As clsFormCtl
'Go through the members of the frame and add them to the collection
For Each ctl In frm_Selection.Controls
  Set chb_ctl = New clsFormCtl
  Set chb_ctl.chb = ctl
  col_Selection.Add chb_ctl
Next ctl
End Sub
```

When the form is opened, the controls are placed into the collection. All that's left now is to add the code for labels to select and clear the checkboxes:

```
Private Sub lbl_SelectAll_Click()
Dim ctl As clsFormCtl
For Each ctl In col_Selection
  ctl.SelectAll
Next ctl
End Sub
```

The following code clears the checkboxes in the collection:

```
Private Sub lbl_unSelectAll_Click()
Dim ctl As clsFormCtl
For Each ctl In col_Selection
  ctl.Unselectall
Next ctl
End Sub
```

All the checkboxes can be selected and cleared with a single click of the mouse, as shown in Figure 22-6.

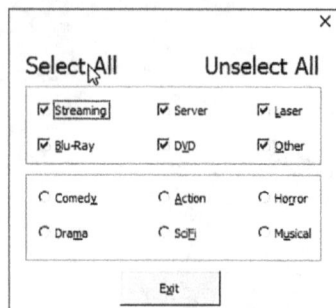

FIGURE 22-6 Use frames, collections, and class modules together to create quick and efficient userforms.

> **Tip** If your controls cannot be placed in a frame, you can use the `Tag` property to create an improvised grouping. `Tag` is a property that holds more information about a control. Its value is of type `String`, so it can hold any type of information. For example, you can use it to create an informal group of controls from different groupings.

Modeless userforms

Have you ever had a userform active but needed to manipulate something on the active sheet or switch to another sheet? Forms can be *modeless*, in which case, they don't have to interfere with the functionality of Excel. A person can type in a cell, switch to another sheet, copy and paste data, and use the ribbon—as if the userform were not there.

By default, a userform is *modal*, which means that there can be no interaction with Excel other than with the form. To make the form modeless, change the `ShowModal` property to `False`. For example, to make Userform1 modeless when it's opened, do this:

```
Userform1.Show False
```

After it is modeless, someone can select a cell on the sheet while the form is active, as shown in Figure 22-7.

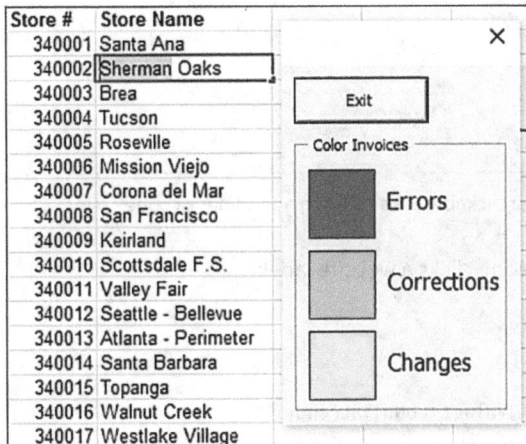

FIGURE 22-7 A modeless form enables a person to enter a cell while the form is still active.

Using hyperlinks in userforms

In the userform example shown in Figure 22-3, there is a field for email and a field for website address. It would be nice to click these and have a blank email message or web page appear automatically. You can do this by using the following program, which creates a new message or opens a web browser when someone clicks the corresponding label:

```
Private Declare PtrSafe Function ShellExecute Lib "shell32.dll" Alias _
    "ShellExecuteA"(ByVal hWnd As Long, ByVal lpOperation As String, _
    ByVal lpFile As String, ByVal lpParameters As String, _
    ByVal lpDirectory As String, ByVal nShowCmd As Long) As LongPtr
Const SWNormal = 1
```

The application programming interface (API) declaration and any other constants go at the very top of the module.

This sub controls what happens when the email label is clicked, as shown in Figure 22-8:

```
Private Sub lbl_Email_Click()
Dim lngRow As Long
lngRow = TabStrip1.Value + 1
ShellExecute 0&, "open", "mailto:" & Cells(lngRow, 5).Value, _
    vbNullString, vbNullString, SWNormal
End Sub
```

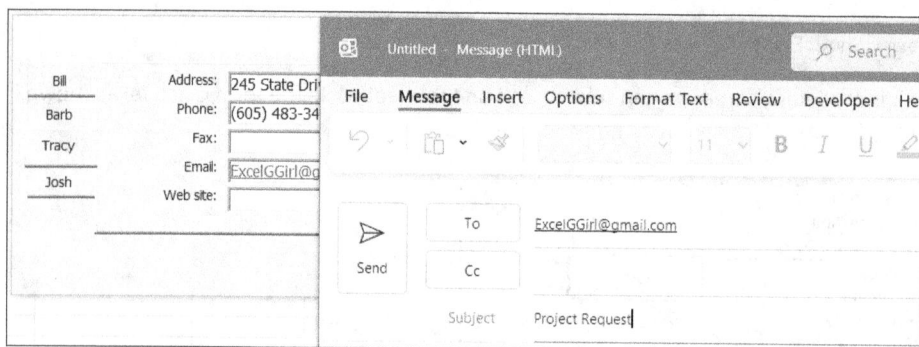

FIGURE 22-8 Turn email addresses and websites into clickable links by using a few lines of code.

This sub controls what happens when someone clicks a website label:

```
Private Sub lbl_Website_Click()
Dim lngRow As Long
lngRow = TabStrip1.Value + 1
ShellExecute 0&, "open", Cells(lngRow, 6).Value, vbNullString, _
    vbNullString, SWNormal
End Sub
```

Adding controls at runtime

It's possible to add controls to a userform at runtime. This is convenient if you're not sure how many items you'll be adding to a form.

Figure 22-9 shows a plain form with only one button. This plain form is used to display any number of pictures from a product catalog. The pictures and accompanying labels appear at runtime as the form is being displayed.

A sales rep making a sales presentation uses this form to display a product catalog. She can select any number of SKUs from an Excel worksheet and press a hotkey to display the form. If she selects six items on the worksheet, the form displays with a small version of each picture, as shown in Figure 22-10.

If the sales rep selects fewer items, the images are displayed larger, as shown in Figure 22-11.

A number of techniques are used to create this userform on the fly. The initial form contains only one button, cbClose. Everything else is added on the fly.

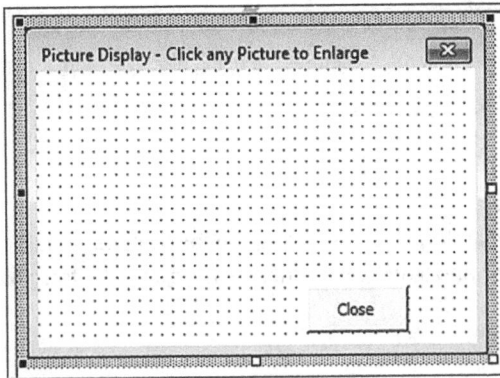

FIGURE 22-9 You can create flexible forms if you add most controls at runtime.

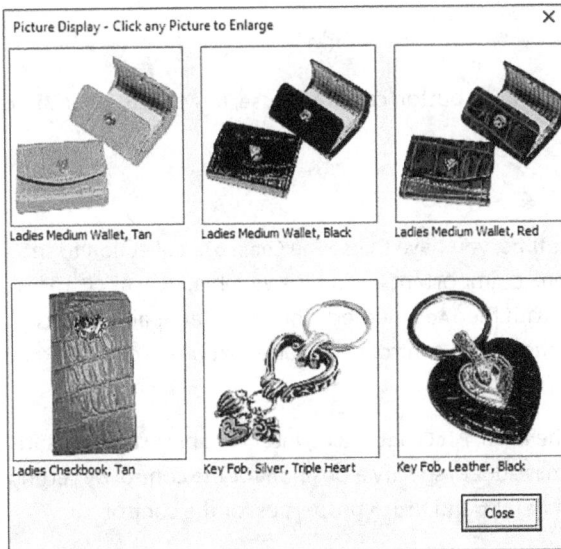

FIGURE 22-10 The sales rep asked to see photos of six SKUs. The UserForm_Initialize procedure adds each picture and label on the fly.

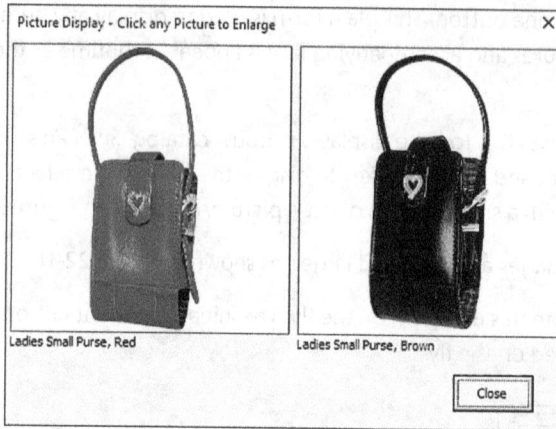

FIGURE 22-11 The logic in `UserForm_Initialize` decides how many pictures are being displayed and adds the appropriately sized image controls.

Resizing the userform on the fly

Giving the best view of the images in the product catalog involves having the form appear as large as possible. The following code uses the form's `Height` and `Width` properties to make sure the form fills almost the entire screen:

```
'resize the form
Me.Height = Int(0.98 * ActiveWindow.Height)
Me.Width = Int(0.98 * ActiveWindow.Width)
```

Adding a control on the fly

For a normal control added at design time, such as a button called `cbClose`, it is easy to refer to the control by using its name:

```
Me.cbClose.Left = 100
```

However, for a control that's added at runtime, you have to use the `Controls` collection to set any properties for the control. For this reason, it's important to set up a variable, such as `LC`, to hold the name of the control. Controls are added with the `.Add` method. The important parameter is `bstrProgId`. This property dictates whether the added control is a label, a text box, a command button, or something else.

The following code adds a new label to the form. `PicCount` is a counter variable used to ensure that each label has a unique name. After the form is added, specify a position for the control by setting the `Top` and `Left` properties. You should also set `Height` and `Width` properties for the control:

```
LC = "LabelA" & PicCount
Me.Controls.Add bstrProgId:="forms.label.1", Name:=LC, Visible:=True
Me.Controls(LC).Top = 25
```

```
Me.Controls(LC).Left = 50
Me.Controls(LC).Height = 18
Me.Controls(LC).Width = 60
Me.Controls(LC).Caption = Cell.Value
```

> **Caution** You lose some of the tooltips with this method. Normally, if you start to type `Me.cbClose.`, the tooltip presents the valid choices for a command button. However, when you use the `Me.Controls(LC)` collection to add controls on the fly, VBA does not know what type of control is referenced. In this case, it is helpful to know you need to set the `Caption` property rather than the `Value` property for a label.

Sizing on the fly

In reality, you need to be able to calculate values for `Top`, `Left`, `Height`, and `Width` on the fly. You do this based on the actual height and width of a form and based on how many controls are needed.

Adding other controls

To add other types of controls, change the `ProgId` used with the `Add` method. Table 22-6 shows the `ProgIds` for various types of controls.

TABLE 22-6 Userform controls and corresponding `ProgIds`

Control	ProgId
CheckBox	Forms.CheckBox.1
ComboBox	Forms.ComboBox.1
CommandButton	Forms.CommandButton.1
Frame	Forms.Frame.1
Image	Forms.Image.1
Label	Forms.Label.1
ListBox	Forms.ListBox.1
MultiPage	Forms.MultiPage.1
OptionButton	Forms.OptionButton.1
ScrollBar	Forms.ScrollBar.1
SpinButton	Forms.SpinButton.1
TabStrip	Forms.TabStrip.1
TextBox	Forms.TextBox.1
ToggleButton	Forms.ToggleButton.1

Adding an image on the fly

There is some unpredictability in adding images to a userform. Any given image might be shaped either landscape or portrait. An image might be small or huge. The strategy you might want to use is to let an image load at full size by setting the `.AutoSize` parameter to `True` before loading it:

```
TC = "Image" & PicCount
Me.Controls.Add bstrProgId:="forms.image.1", Name:=TC, Visible:=True
Me.Controls(TC).Top = LastTop
Me.Controls(TC).Left = LastLeft
Me.Controls(TC).AutoSize = True
On Error Resume Next
Me.Controls(TC).Picture = LoadPicture(fname)
On Error GoTo 0
```

After the image has loaded, you can read the control's `Height` and `Width` properties to determine whether the image is landscape or portrait and whether the image is constrained by available width or available height:

```
'The picture resized the control to full size determine the size of the picture
Wid = Me.Controls(TC).Width
Ht = Me.Controls(TC).Height
'CellWid and CellHt are calculated in the full code sample below
WidRedux = CellWid / Wid
HtRedux = CellHt / Ht
If WidRedux < HtRedux Then
   Redux = WidRedux
Else
   Redux = HtRedux
End If
NewHt = Int(Ht * Redux)
NewWid = Int(Wid * Redux)
```

After you find the proper size for the image so that it draws without distortion, set the `AutoSize` property to `False` and use the correct height and width to have the image not appear distorted:

```
'Now resize the control
Me.Controls(TC).AutoSize = False
Me.Controls(TC).Height = NewHt
Me.Controls(TC).Width = NewWid
Me.Controls(TC).PictureSizeMode = fmPictureSizeModeStretch
```

Putting it all together

This is the complete code for the picture catalog userform:

```
Private Sub UserForm_Initialize()
'Display pictures of each SKU selected on the worksheet
'This may be anywhere from 1 to 36 pictures
PicPath = ThisWorkbook.Path & "\ch22_Images\"
Dim Pics()
'resize the form
```

```vba
Me.Height = Int(0.98 * ActiveWindow.Height)
Me.Width = Int(0.98 * ActiveWindow.Width)
'determine how many cells are selected
'We need one picture and label for each cell
CellCount = Selection.Cells.Count
ReDim Preserve Pics(1 To CellCount)
'Figure out the size of the resized form
TempHt = Me.Height
TempWid = Me.Width
'The number of columns is a roundup of SQRT(CellCount)
'This will ensure 4 rows of 5 pictures for 20, etc.
NumCol = Int(0.99 + Sqr(CellCount))
NumRow = Int(0.99 + CellCount / NumCol)
'Figure out the height and width of each square
'Each column will have 2 points to left & right of pics
CellWid = Application.WorksheetFunction.Max(Int(TempWid / NumCol) - 4, 1)
'each row needs to have 33 points below it for the label
CellHt = Application.WorksheetFunction.Max(Int(TempHt / NumRow) - 33, 1)
PicCount = 0 'Counter variable
LastTop = 2
MaxBottom = 1
'Build each row on the form
For x = 1 To NumRow
  LastLeft = 3
  'Build each column in this row
  For Y = 1 To NumCol
    PicCount = PicCount + 1
    If PicCount > CellCount Then
      'There is not an even number of pictures to fill out the last row
      Me.Height = MaxBottom + 100
      Me.cbClose.Top = MaxBottom + 25
      Me.cbClose.Left = Me.Width - 70
      Repaint 'redraws the form
      Exit Sub
    End If
    ThisStyle = Selection.Cells(PicCount).Value
    ThisDesc = Selection.Cells(PicCount).Offset(0, 1).Value
    fname = PicPath & ThisStyle & ".jpg"
    TC = "Image" & PicCount
    Me.Controls.Add bstrProgId:="forms.image.1", Name:=TC, Visible:=True
    Me.Controls(TC).Top = LastTop
    Me.Controls(TC).Left = LastLeft
    Me.Controls(TC).AutoSize = True
    On Error Resume Next
    Me.Controls(TC).Picture = LoadPicture(fname)
    On Error GoTo 0
    'The picture resized the control to full size
    'determine the size of the picture
    Wid = Me.Controls(TC).Width
    Ht = Me.Controls(TC).Height
    WidRedux = CellWid / Wid
    HtRedux = CellHt / Ht
    If WidRedux < HtRedux Then
      Redux = WidRedux
```

```
        Else
          Redux = HtRedux
        End If
        NewHt = Int(Ht * Redux)
        NewWid = Int(Wid * Redux)
        'Now resize the control
        Me.Controls(TC).AutoSize = False
        Me.Controls(TC).Height = NewHt
        Me.Controls(TC).Width = NewWid
        Me.Controls(TC).PictureSizeMode = fmPictureSizeModeStretch
        Me.Controls(TC).ControlTipText = "Style " & ThisStyle & " " & ThisDesc
        'Keep track of the bottommost & rightmost picture
        ThisRight = Me.Controls(TC).Left + Me.Controls(TC).Width
        ThisBottom = Me.Controls(TC).Top + Me.Controls(TC).Height
        If ThisBottom > MaxBottom Then MaxBottom = ThisBottom
        'Add a label below the picture
        LC = "LabelA" & PicCount
        Me.Controls.Add bstrProgId:="forms.label.1", Name:=LC, Visible:=True
        Me.Controls(LC).Top = ThisBottom + 1
        Me.Controls(LC).Left = LastLeft
        Me.Controls(LC).Height = 18
        Me.Controls(LC).Width = CellWid
        Me.Controls(LC).Caption = ThisDesc
        'Keep track of where the next picture should display
        LastLeft = LastLeft + CellWid + 4
    Next Y      'end of this row
    LastTop = MaxBottom + 21 + 16
  Next x
  Me.Height = MaxBottom + 100
  Me.cbClose.Top = MaxBottom + 25
  Me.cbClose.Left = Me.Width - 70
  Repaint
  End Sub
```

Adding help to a userform

You have already designed a great userform in this chapter, but there is one thing missing: guidance for users. The following sections show four ways you can help people fill out the form properly.

Showing accelerator keys

Built-in forms often have keyboard shortcuts that allow actions to be triggered or fields selected with a few keystrokes. These shortcuts are identified by an underlined letter on a button or label.

You can add this same capability to custom userforms by entering a value in the `Accelerator` property of the control. Pressing Alt + the accelerator key selects the control. For example, in Figure 22-12, Alt+T selects the Streaming checkbox. Repeating the combination clears the box.

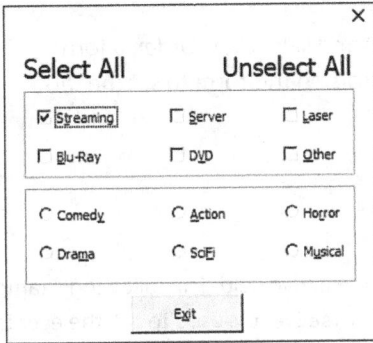

FIGURE 22-12 Use accelerator key combinations, like Alt+T, to select Streaming to give userforms the power of keyboard shortcuts.

Adding control tip text

When a cursor passes over a ribbon control, tip text appears, hinting at what the control does. You can also add tip text to userforms by entering a value in the `ControlTipText` property of a control. In Figure 22-13, tip text has been added to the frame surrounding the various categories.

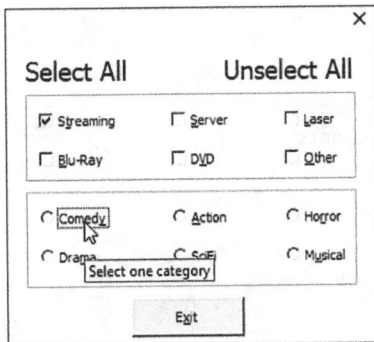

FIGURE 22-13 Add tips to controls to provide help to people.

Creating the tab order

People can tab from one field to another. This is an automatic feature in a form. To control which field the next tab goes to, set the `TabStop` property value for each control.

The first tab stop is 0, and the last tab stop is equal to the number of controls in a group minus one. Remember that you can create a group with a frame. Excel doesn't allow multiple controls within a group to have the same tab stop. After tab stops are set, a person can use the Tab key and spacebar to select or deselect various options.

Coloring the active control

Another method for helping a person fill out a form is to color the active field. The following example changes the color of a text box or combo box when it is active. RaiseEvent is used to call the events declared at the top of the class module. The code for the events is part of the userform.

Place the following code in a class module called clsCtlColor:

```
'the 1st 3 lines go at the very top of the module
Public Event GetFocus()
Public Event LostFocus(ByVal strCtrl As String)
Private strPreCtr As String

Public Sub CheckActiveCtrl(objForm As MSForms.UserForm)
With objForm
  If TypeName(.ActiveControl) = "ComboBox" Or _
    TypeName(.ActiveControl) = "TextBox" Then
    strPreCtr = .ActiveControl.Name
    On Error GoTo Terminate
    Do
      'use DoEvents to allow Excel to process pending events
      DoEvents
      If .ActiveControl.Name <> strPreCtr Then
        If TypeName(.ActiveControl) = "ComboBox" Or _
          TypeName(.ActiveControl) = "TextBox" Then
            RaiseEvent LostFocus(strPreCtr)
            strPreCtr = .ActiveControl.Name
            RaiseEvent GetFocus
        End If
      End If
    Loop
  End If
End With
Terminate:
  Exit Sub
End Sub
```

Place the following code behind the userform:

```
'the 1st line is placed at the top of the module
Private WithEvents objForm As clsCtlColor

Private Sub UserForm_Initialize()
Set objForm = New clsCtlColor
End Sub
```

This sub changes the `BackColor` of the active control when the form is activated:

```
Private Sub UserForm_Activate()
If TypeName(ActiveControl) = "ComboBox" Or _
  TypeName(ActiveControl) = "TextBox" Then
    ActiveControl.BackColor = &HC0E0FF
End If
objForm.CheckActiveCtrl Me
End Sub
```

This sub changes the `BackColor` of the active control when it gets the focus:

```
Private Sub objForm_GetFocus()
ActiveControl.BackColor = &HC0E0FF
End Sub
```

This sub changes the `BackColor` back to white when the control loses the focus:

```
Private Sub objForm_LostFocus(ByVal strCtrl As String)
Me.Controls(strCtrl).BackColor = &HFFFFFF
End Sub
```

This sub clears the `objForm` when the form is closed:

```
Private Sub UserForm_QueryClose(Cancel As Integer, CloseMode As Integer)
Set objForm = Nothing
End Sub
```

Case study: Setting up multicolumn list boxes

You've created several spreadsheets containing store data. The primary key of each set is the store number. Several people use the workbook, but not everyone memorizes stores by store numbers. You need some way of letting people select a store by its name. At the same time, you need to return the store number to be used in the code. You could use XLOOKUP or MATCH, but there is another way.

A list box can have more than one column, but not all the columns need to be visible. In addition, a person can select an item from the visible list, but the list box can return the corresponding value from another column.

Draw a list box and set the ColumnCount property to 2. Set the RowSource to a two-column range called Stores. The first column of the range is the store number; the second column is the store name. At this point, the list box displays both columns of data, as shown in Figure 22-14. To change this, set the ColumnWidths to 0, 100—and the text automatically updates to 0 pt;100 pt. The first column is now hidden. Figure 22-15 shows the list box properties as they need to be.

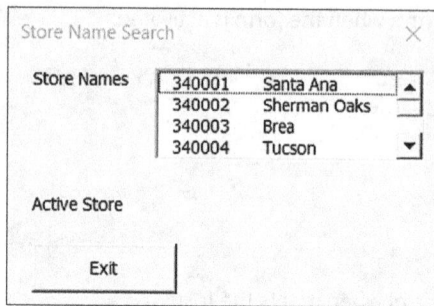

FIGURE 22-14 The store number is included in the list box design and will still be accessible with code.

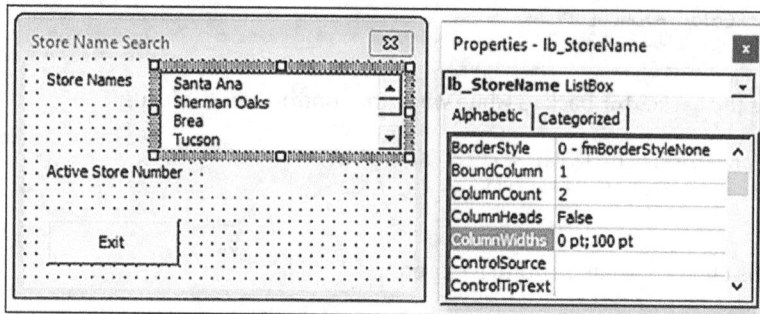

FIGURE 22-15 Setting the list box properties creates a two-column list box that appears to be a single column of data.

The appearance of the list box has now been set. When someone activates the list box, she sees only the store names. To return the value of the first column, set the `BoundColumn` property to 1. You can do this through the Properties window or through code. This example uses code to maintain the flexibility of returning the store number (see Figure 22-16):

```
Private Sub UserForm_Initialize()
lb_StoreName.BoundColumn = 1
End Sub


Private Sub lb_StoreName_Click()
lbl_StoreNum.Caption = lb_StoreName.Value
End Sub
```

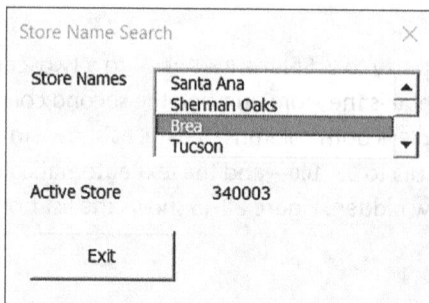

FIGURE 22-16 Use a two-column list box to allow the user to select a store name but return the store number.

Creating transparent forms

Have you ever had a form that you had to keep moving out of the way so you could see the data behind it? The following code sets the userform at a 50 percent transparency (see Figure 22-17) so that you can see the data behind it without moving the form somewhere else on the screen (and blocking more data).

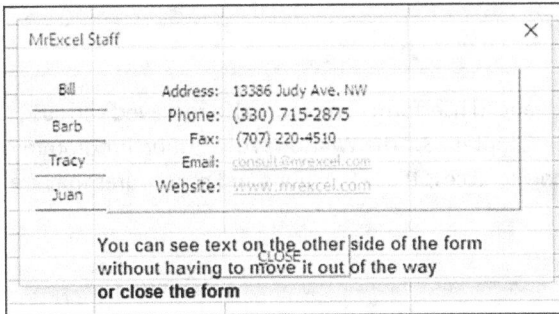

FIGURE 22-17 Create a 50 percent transparent form to view the data on the sheet behind it.

Place the following code in the declarations section at the top of the userform:

```
Private Declare PtrSafe Function GetActiveWindow Lib "USER32" () As LongPtr
Private Declare PtrSafe Function SetWindowLongPtr Lib "USER32" Alias _
  "SetWindowLongA" (ByVal hWnd As LongPtr, ByVal nIndex As Long, _
 ByVal dwNewLong As LongPtr) As LongPtr
Private Declare PtrSafe Function GetWindowLongPtr Lib "USER32" Alias _
  "GetWindowLongA" (ByVal hWnd As LongPtr, ByVal nIndex As Long) As Long
Private Declare PtrSafe Function SetLayeredWindowAttributes Lib "USER32" _
  (ByVal hWnd As LongPtr, ByVal crKey As Integer, _
  ByVal bAlpha As Integer, ByVal dwFlags As LongPtr) As LongPtr
Private Const WS_EX_LAYERED = &H80000
Private Const LWA_COLORKEY = &H1
Private Const LWA_ALPHA = &H2
Private Const GWL_EXSTYLE = &HFFEC
Dim hWnd As Long
```

Place the following code behind a toggle button. When the button is pressed, the transparency is reduced 50 percent. When a person toggles the button back up, the transparency is set to 0:

```
Private Sub ToggleButton1_Click()
If ToggleButton1.Value = True Then
  '127 sets the 50% semitransparent
  SetTransparency 127
Else
  'a value of 255 is opaque and 0 is transparent
  SetTransparency 255
End If
End Sub
```

```
Private Sub SetTransparency(TRate As Integer)
Dim nIndex As Long
hWnd = GetActiveWindow
nIndex = GetWindowLong(hWnd, GWL_EXSTYLE)
SetWindowLong hWnd, GWL_EXSTYLE, nIndex Or WS_EX_LAYERED
SetLayeredWindowAttributes hWnd, 0, TRate, LWA_ALPHA
End Sub
```

Next steps

This chapter showed you how to use more advanced userform controls. It also reviewed various methods to maximize the use of userforms. In Chapter 23, "The Windows Application Programming Interface (API)," you'll discover more about how to access these functions and procedures that are hidden in files on your computer.

The Windows Application Programming Interface (API)

In this chapter, you will:

- Understand the parts of an API declaration

- Learn how to use an API declaration

- Make 32-bit- and 64-bit-compatible API declarations

- Review some API function examples

In Chapter 20, "Automating Word," we learned how reference libraries can be used to connect to other programs and access their objects, properties, and methods. APIs (Application Programming Interfaces), on the other hand, allow you to interact with external systems, such as services and hardware, but in a very different way. Instead of using a reference library, you connect to an API by specifying the function or service you want to access and its location (such as a DLL, URL, or endpoint).

If you look in the Windows System directory \Windows\System32 (Windows NT systems), you'll see many files with the extension .dll. These files, which are Dynamic Link Libraries (DLLs), contain various functions and procedures that other programs, including VBA, can access. They give the user access to functionality used by the Windows operating system and many other programs.

Caution   Keep in mind that Windows API declarations are accessible only on computers running the Microsoft Windows operating system.

This chapter does not teach you how to write API declarations, but it does teach you the basics of interpreting and using them. Several useful examples of Windows API functions are also included. Jan Karel Pieterse of JKP Application Development Services (www.jkp-ads.com) is working on an ever-growing web page that lists the proper syntax for the 64-bit declarations. You can find it at *www.jkp-ads.com/articles/apideclarations.asp*.

Understanding an API declaration

The following is an example of an API function:

```
Private Declare PtrSafe Function GetUserName _
  Lib "advapi32.dll" Alias "GetUserNameA" _
  (ByVal lpBuffer As String, nSize As Long) _
  As LongPtr
```

There are two types of API declarations, which are structured similarly:

- **Functions**—Return information.

- **Procedures**—Do something to the system.

Basically, you can tell the following about this API function:

- It is `Private`; therefore, you can use it only in the module in which it is declared. Declare it `Public` in a standard module if you want to share it among several modules.

> **Caution**   API declarations in standard modules can be public or private. API declarations in class modules must be private.

- It will be referred to as `GetUserName` in a program. This is the variable name assigned in the code.

- The function being used is found in `advapi32.dll`.

- The alias, `GetUserNameA`, is what the function is referred to as in the DLL. This name is case sensitive and cannot be changed; it is specific to the DLL (Dynamic Link Library). There are often two versions of each API function. One version uses the ANSI character set and has aliases that end with the letter *A*. The other version uses the Unicode character set and has aliases that end with the letter *W*. When specifying the alias, you are telling VBA which version of the function to use.

- There are two parameters: `lpBuffer` and `nSize`. These are two arguments that the DLL function accepts.

> **Caution**   The downside of using APIs is that there may be no errors when your code compiles or runs. This means that an incorrectly configured API call can cause your computer to crash or lock up, so it is a good idea to save often.

Using an API declaration

Using an API is no different from calling a function or procedure you created in VBA. The following example uses the GetUserName declaration in a function to return the Windows username to Excel.

```
Public Function UserName() As String
Dim sName As String * 256
Dim cChars As Long
cChars = 256
If GetUserName(sName, cChars) Then
  UserName = Left$(sName, cChars - 1)
End If
End Function

Sub ProgramRights()
Dim NameofUser As String
NameofUser = UserName
Select Case NameofUser
  Case Is = "Administrator"
    MsgBox "You have full rights to this computer"
  Case Else
    MsgBox "You have limited rights to this computer"
End Select
End Sub
```

Run the ProgramRights macro, and you learn whether you are currently signed on as Administrator. The result shown in Figure 23-1 indicates that Administrator is the current username.

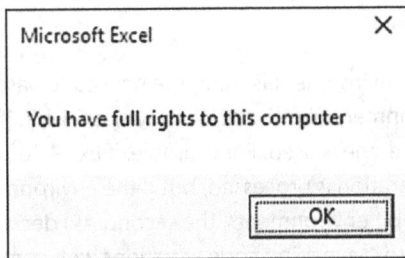

FIGURE 23-1 The GetUserName API function can be used to get a user's Windows login name—which is more difficult to edit than the Excel username. You can then control what rights a user has with your program.

Making 32-bit- and 64-bit-compatible API declarations

With Excel 2010, Microsoft improved the compatibility between 32-bit and 64-bit API calls by allowing 64-bit calls to work on 32-bit systems but not vice versa. This is not the case with Excel 2007, so if you're writing code that might be used in Excel 2007, you need to check the bit version and adjust accordingly.

The examples in this chapter are 64-bit API declarations and might not work in 32-bit Excel 2007 or older without some changes. For example, say that in a 64-bit version, you have this declaration:

```
Private Declare PtrSafe Function GetWindowLongptr Lib "USER32" Alias _
"GetWindowLongA" (ByVal hWnd As LongPtr, ByVal nIndex As Long) As LongPtr
```

It will need to be changed to the following to work in the 32-bit version:

```
Private Declare Function GetWindowLongptr Lib "USER32" Alias _
"GetWindowLongA" (ByVal hWnd As Long, ByVal nIndex As Long) As LongPtr
```

The difference is that PtrSafe needs to be removed from the declaration. You might also notice that there is a new variable type in use: LongPtr. Actually, LongPtr isn't a true data type; it is LongLong for 64-bit environments and Long in 32-bit environments. This does not mean that you should use it throughout your code; it has a specific use, such as in API calls. But you might find yourself using it in your code for API variables. For example, if you return an API variable of LongPtr to another variable in your code, that variable must also be LongPtr.

If you need to distribute a workbook to Excel 2007 32-bit and 64-bit users, you don't need to create two workbooks. You can create a compiler directive If...Then...Else statement in the declarations area and set up the API calls for both versions. So, for the preceding two examples, you could declare them like so:

```
#If VBA7 Or Win64 Then
Private Declare PtrSafe Function GetUserName Lib "advapi32.dll" _
 Alias "GetUserNameA" (ByVal lpBuffer As String, nSize As Long) _
 As LongPtr
#Else
Private Declare Function GetUserName Lib "advapi32.dll" _
 Alias "GetUserNameA" (ByVal lpBuffer As String, nSize As Long) _
 As LongPtr
#End If
```

#If VBA7 Or Win64 checks to see whether the current environment is using the new code base (VBA7, in use only since Office 2010) or whether the environment (Excel, not Windows) is 64-bit. If true, the first API declaration is processed; otherwise, the second one is used. For example, if Excel 2007 64-bit or Excel 2010 or newer is running, the first API declaration is processed, but if the environment is 32-bit Excel 2007, the second one is used. Note that in 64-bit environments, the second API declaration will be colored as an error but will compile just fine. Refer to "Managing code variations with compiler directives" in Chapter 4, "Laying the groundwork with variables and structures," for more information on compiler directives.

API function examples

The following sections provide more examples of helpful API declarations you can use in your Excel programs. Each example starts with a short description of what the function can do, followed by the actual declarations and an example of its use.

Retrieving the computer name

This API function returns the computer name (that is, the name of the computer found under Computer | Computer Name):

```
'place the API declaration(s) at the top of the module
Private Declare PtrSafe Function GetComputerName Lib "kernel32" Alias _
  "GetComputerNameA" (ByVal lpBuffer As String, ByRef nSize As Long) _
  As LongPtr

Private Function ComputerName() As String
Dim stBuff As String * 255, lAPIResult As LongPtr
Dim lBuffLen As Long
lBuffLen = 255
lAPIResult = GetComputerName(stBuff, lBuffLen)
If lBuffLen > 0 Then ComputerName = Left(stBuff, lBuffLen)
End Function

Sub ComputerCheck()
Dim CompName As String
CompName = ComputerName
If CompName <> "BillJelenPC" Then
  MsgBox _
    "This application does not have the right to run on this computer."
  ActiveWorkbook.Close SaveChanges:=False
End If
End Sub
```

The `ComputerCheck` macro uses an API call to get the name of the computer. In this example, the workbook refuses to open on any computer except the hard-coded computer name of the owner.

Checking whether an Excel file is open on a network

You can check whether you have a file open in Excel by trying to set the workbook to an object. If the object is Nothing (empty), you know that the file is not open. However, what if you want to see whether someone else on a network has the file open? The following API function returns that information:

```
'place the API declaration(s) at the top of the module
Private Declare PtrSafe Function lOpen Lib "kernel32" Alias "_lopen" _
  (ByVal lpPathName As String, ByVal iReadWrite As Long) As LongPtr
Private Declare PtrSafe Function lClose Lib "kernel32" _
  Alias "_lclose" (ByVal hFile As LongPtr) As LongPtr
Private Const OF_SHARE_EXCLUSIVE = &H10

Private Function FileIsOpen(strFullPath_FileName As String) As Boolean
Dim hdlFile As LongPtr
Dim lastErr As Long
hdlFile = -1
hdlFile = lOpen(strFullPath_FileName, OF_SHARE_EXCLUSIVE)
If hdlFile = -1 Then
  lastErr = Err.LastDllError
```

```
Else
  lClose (hdlFile)
End If
FileIsOpen = (hdlFile = -1) And (lastErr = 32)
End Function

Sub CheckFileOpen()
If FileIsOpen("C:\XYZ Corp.xlsx") Then
  MsgBox "File is open"
Else
  MsgBox "File is not open"
End If
End Sub
```

You can call the FileIsOpen function with a particular path and file name as the parameter to find out whether someone has the file open.

Retrieving display-resolution information

The following API function retrieves the computer's display size:

```
'place the API declaration(s) at the top of the module
Declare PtrSafe Function DisplaySize Lib "user32" Alias _
  "GetSystemMetrics" (ByVal nIndex As Long) As LongPtr
Public Const SM_CXSCREEN = 0
Public Const SM_CYSCREEN = 1

Function VideoRes() As String
Dim vidWidth as LongPtr, vidHeight as LongPtr
vidWidth = DisplaySize(SM_CXSCREEN)
vidHeight = DisplaySize(SM_CYSCREEN)
Select Case (vidWidth * vidHeight)
  Case 307200
    VideoRes = "640 x 480"
  Case 480000
    VideoRes = "800 x 600"
  Case 786432
    VideoRes = "1024 x 768"
  Case Else
    VideoRes = "Something else"
End Select
End Function

Sub CheckDisplayRes()
Dim VideoInfo As String
Dim Msg1 As String, Msg2 As String, Msg3 As String
VideoInfo = VideoRes
Msg1 = "Current resolution is set at " & VideoInfo & Chr(10)
Msg2 = "Optimal resolution for this application is 1024 x 768" & Chr(10)
Msg3 = "Please adjust resolution"
Select Case VideoInfo
  Case Is = "640 x 480"
    MsgBox Msg1 & Msg2 & Msg3
```

```
      Case Is = "800 x 600"
         MsgBox Msg1 & Msg2
      Case Is = "1024 x 768"
         MsgBox Msg1
      Case Else
         MsgBox Msg2 & Msg3
   End Select
   End Sub
```

The CheckDisplayRes macro warns the client that the display setting is not optimal for the application.

Customizing the About dialog box

If you go to File | Help | About Windows in File Explorer, you get a nice little About dialog box with information about the File Explorer and a few system details. With the following code, you can get that window to pop up in your own program and customize a few items, as shown in Figure 23-2.

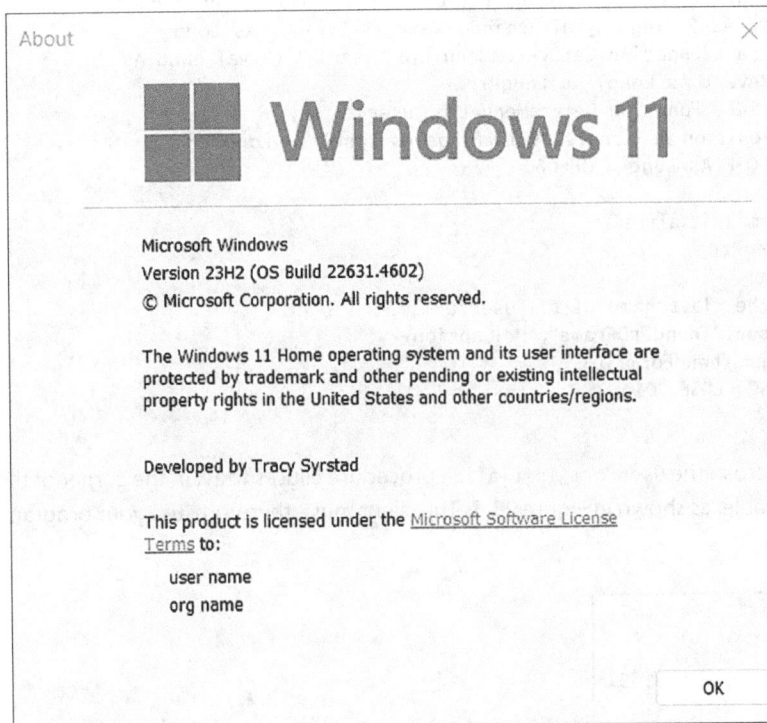

FIGURE 23-2 You can customize the About dialog box used by Windows for your own program.

```
'place the API declaration(s) at the top of the module
Declare PtrSafe Function ShellAbout Lib "shell32.dll" Alias "ShellAboutA" _
   (ByVal hwnd As LongPtr, ByVal szApp As String, ByVal szOtherStuff As _
   String, ByVal hIcon As Long) As LongPtr
Declare PtrSafe Function GetActiveWindow Lib "user32" () As LongPtr
```

```
Sub AboutThisProgram()
Dim hwnd As LongPtr
On Error Resume Next
hwnd = GetActiveWindow()
ShellAbout hwnd, Nm, "Developed by Tracy Syrstad", 0
On Error GoTo 0
End Sub
```

Disabling the X for closing a userform

A person can use the X button located in the upper-right corner of a userform to shut down the form. You can capture the close event with QueryClose, but to prevent the button from being active and working at all, you need an API call. The following API declarations work together to disable the X button and force the person to use the Close button instead. When the form is initialized, the X button is disabled. After the form is closed, the X button is reset to normal:

```
'place the API declaration(s) at the top of the module
Private Declare PtrSafe Function FindWindow Lib "user32" Alias "FindWindowA" _
    (ByVal lpClassName As String, ByVal lpWindowName As String) As Long
Private Declare PtrSafe Function GetSystemMenu Lib "user32" (ByVal hWnd As _
    LongPtr, ByVal bRevert As Long) As LongPtr
Private Declare PtrSafe Function DeleteMenu Lib "user32" (ByVal hMenu As _
    longPtr, ByVal nPosition As Long, ByVal wFlags As Long) As LongPtr
Private Const SC_CLOSE As Long = &HF060

Private Sub UserForm_Initialize()
Dim hWndForm As LongPtr
Dim hMenu As LongPtr
'ThunderDFrame is the class name of all userforms
hWndForm = FindWindow("ThunderDFrame", Me.Caption)
hMenu = GetSystemMenu(hWndForm, 0)
DeleteMenu hMenu, SC_CLOSE, 0&
End Sub
```

The DeleteMenu macro in the UserForm_Initialize procedure causes the X in the corner of the userform to be unavailable, as shown in Figure 23-3. The client must, therefore, use your programmed Close button.

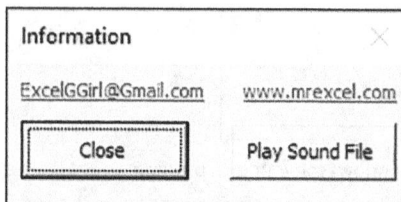

FIGURE 23-3 Disable the X button on a userform to force users to use the Close button to shut down the form properly and prevent them from bypassing any code attached to the Close button.

Creating a running timer

You can use the NOW function to get the time, but what if you need a running timer that displays the time as the seconds tick by? The following API declarations work together to provide this functionality. The timer is placed in cell A10 of Sheet1:

```
'place the API declaration(s) at the top of the module
Public Declare PtrSafe Function SetTimer Lib "user32" (ByVal hWnd As Long, _
  ByVal nIDEvent As Long, ByVal uElapse As Long, ByVal lpTimerFunc As LongPtr) _
  As LongPtr
Public Declare PtrSafe Function KillTimer Lib "user32" (ByVal hWnd As Long, _
  ByVal nIDEvent As LongPtr) As LongPtr
Public Declare PtrSafe Function FindWindow Lib "user32" Alias "FindWindowA" _
  (ByVal lpClassName As String, ByVal lpWindowName As String) As LongPtr
Private lngTimerID As LongPtr
Private datStartingTime As Date

Public Sub StartTimer()
StopTimer 'stop previous timer
datStartingTime = Now
lngTimerID = SetTimer(0, 1, 10, AddressOf RunTimer)
End Sub

Public Sub StopTimer()
Dim lRet As LongPtr, lngTID As LongPtr
If IsEmpty(lngTimerID) Then Exit Sub
lngTID = lngTimerID
lRet = KillTimer(0, lngTID)
lngTimerID = Empty
End Sub

Private Sub RunTimer(ByVal hWnd As Long, ByVal uint1 As Long, _
  ByVal nEventId As Long, ByVal dwParam As Long)
On Error Resume Next
Sheet1.Range("A10").Value = Format(Now - datStartingTime, "hh:mm:ss")
End Sub
```

Run the StartTimer macro to have a running timer update in cell A10.

Playing sounds

Have you ever wanted to play a sound to warn users or congratulate them? To do this, you can add a sound object to a sheet and then call that sound. However, it would be easier to use the following API declaration and specify the proper path to a sound file:

```
'place the API declaration(s) at the top of the module
Public Declare PtrSafe Function PlayWavSound Lib "winmm.dll" Alias _
  "sndPlaySoundA" (ByVal LpszSoundName As String, ByVal uFlags As Long) _
  As LongPtr
```

```
Public Sub PlaySound()
Dim SoundName As String
SoundName = "C:\Windows\Media\Chimes.wav"
PlayWavSound SoundName, 0
End Sub
```

Next steps

Using APIs gives you access to Windows functionality not available within Excel. In Chapter 24, "Handling errors," you find out about error handling. In a perfect world, you want to be able to hand off your applications to a coworker, leave for vacation, and not have to worry about an unhandled error appearing while you are on the beach. Chapter 24 discusses how to handle obvious and not-so-obvious errors.

Handling errors

In this chapter, you will:

- Find out what happens when an error occurs

- Do basic error handling with the `On Error GoTo` syntax

- Get to know generic error handlers

- Use errors to your advantage

- Understand the ills of protecting code

- Find out more about problems with passwords

- Examine errors caused by different versions

Errors are bound to happen. Even when you test and retest your code, something unexpected eventually happens after a report is put into daily production and used for hundreds of days. Your goal should be to avoid obscure errors as you code. For this reason, you should always be thinking of what unexpected things could happen someday that could make your code not work.

What happens when an error occurs?

When VBA encounters an error, and you have no error-checking code in place, the program stops and presents you or your client with an error message, such as the Run-Time Error 1004 message shown in Figure 24-1.

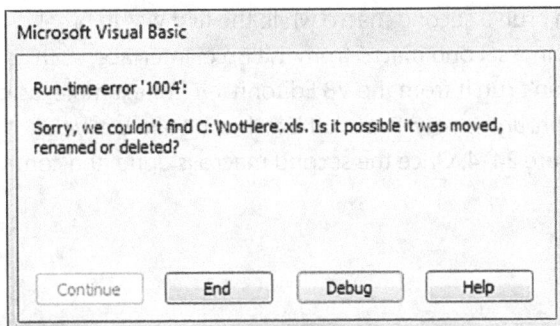

```
Microsoft Visual Basic

  Run-time error '1004':

  Sorry, we couldn't find C:\NotHere.xls. Is it possible it was moved,
  renamed or deleted?


   [ Continue ]   [  End  ]   [ Debug ]   [  Help  ]
```

FIGURE 24-1 With an unhandled error in an unprotected module, you get a choice to end or debug.

When presented with the choice to end or debug, you should click Debug. (If Debug is grayed out, then someone has protected the VBA code, and you will have to call the original developer.) The VB Editor highlights in yellow the line that caused the error. When you hover the cursor over any variable, you see the current value of the variable, which provides information about what could have caused the error (see Figure 24-2).

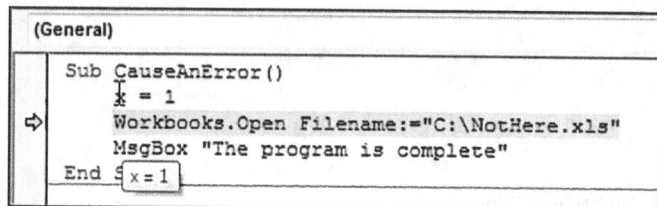

```
(General)

    Sub CauseAnError()
        x = 1
⇨       Workbooks.Open Filename:="C:\NotHere.xls"
        MsgBox "The program is complete"
    End S[ x = 1 ]
```

FIGURE 24-2 After clicking Debug, the macro is in break mode. Hover the cursor over a variable; after a second, the current value of the variable is shown.

Excel has been notorious for returning error messages that are not very meaningful. For example, dozens of situations can cause a 1004 error. Seeing the offending line highlighted in yellow and examining the current value of any variables can help you trace the real cause of an error.

After examining the line in error, click the Reset button to stop the macro's execution. (See the sidebar, "When to avoid the Reset button," for situations where you should avoid resetting your code.) The Reset button is the square button under the Run item in the main menu, as shown in Figure 24-3.

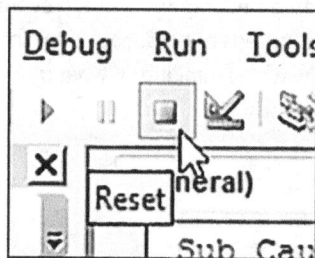

FIGURE 24-3 The Reset button looks like the Stop button in the set of three buttons that resembles a DVD control panel.

> **Caution** It used to be that you couldn't run a second macro while the first was in break mode—those days are gone. You can run a second macro from the Excel interface, such as the ribbon or a button. However, you can't run it from the VB Editor itself (for example, using the Run button or pressing F8 to step through a new macro). If Excel won't allow it, you'll receive the error message shown in Figure 24-4. Once the second macro is done, the control returns to the one still in break mode.

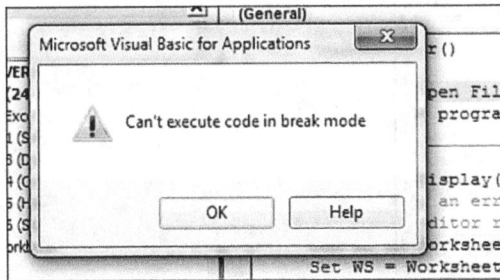

FIGURE 24-4 This message appears if you forget to click Reset to end a debug session and then attempt to run another macro.

When to avoid the Reset button

When you click the Reset button, all code ends immediately—exactly where it is. Any Excel settings that the code modified are not automatically restored. This can have unexpected effects. For example, if your code turns off events (`Application.EnableEvents = False`), events will remain off until either Excel is restarted or you type `Application.EnableEvents = True` in the Immediate pane.

Instead of clicking Reset right away, jump to the part of your code that restores Excel to its previous settings. From there, you can either step through those lines by pressing the F8 key or click Run to continue the code from the new position. For more information on moving around in code, see "Backing up or moving forward in code" in Chapter 2, "This sounds like BASIC, so why doesn't it look familiar?"

A misleading Debug error in userform code

In previous Excel versions, certain errors in userform code could cause the form to unload, the highlighted line to be outside the userform, or Excel to suppress the error entirely. In Excel 365, these issues have largely been resolved. Errors are trapped and highlighted in the VB Editor, making debugging much easier. However, if you encounter a situation that you can't troubleshoot and suspect it may be related to the userform, the following guide will assist you in troubleshooting the issue.

After you click Debug, the line Excel highlights may not always point to the actual error. For example, if your macro displays a userform and an error occurs within the form's code, Excel may highlight the line in your macro that called the form—not the line where the error actually happened. This can be misleading. To find the real error, follow these steps:

1. After the error message box shown in Figure 24-5 is displayed, click the Debug button.

   You can see that the error allegedly occurs on a line that displays a userform, as shown in Figure 24-6. Because you have read this chapter, you know that this is not the line in error.

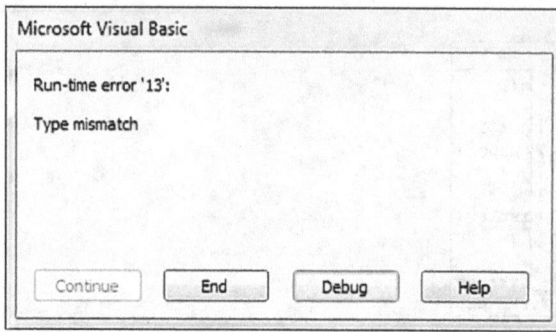

Microsoft Visual Basic

Run-time error '13':

Type mismatch

| Continue | End | Debug | Help |

FIGURE 24-5 Select Debug in response to this error 13.

2. Press F8 to execute the Show method. Instead of getting an error, you are taken into the UserForm_Initialize procedure.

3. Keep pressing F8 until you get the error message again. Stay alert because as soon as you encounter the error, the error message box will be displayed. Click Debug, and you are returned to the frmChoose.Show line. It is particularly difficult to follow the code when the error occurs on the other side of a long loop, as shown in Figure 24-7.

```
Sub PrepareAndDisplay()
    ' sometimes an error happens in a userform
    ' yet the editor reports it as the next line
    Dim WS As Worksheet
    Set WS = Worksheets("Sheet1")

    FinalRow = WS.Cells(Rows.Count, 1).End(xlUp).Row
    WS.Cells(1, 1).Sort _
        Key1:=WS.Cells(1, 1), Order1:=xlAscending, Header:=xlYes

    frmChoose.Show

    MsgBox "Macro complete"

End Sub
```

FIGURE 24-6 The line in error is indicated as the frmChoose.Show line.

Imagine trying to step through the code in Figure 24-7. You carefully press F8 5 times with no problems through the first pass of the loop. Because the problem could be in future iterations through the loop, you continue to press F8. If there are 25 items to add to the list box, 48 additional presses of F8 are required to complete the loop safely. Each time before pressing F8, you should mentally note that you are about to run some specific line.

At the point shown in Figure 24-7, pressing the F8 key again displays the error and returns you to the frmChoose.Show line back in Module1. This is an annoying situation.

At that point, you need to start pressing F8 again. If you can recall the general area where the debug error occurred, click the mouse cursor in a line right before that section and use Ctrl+F8 to run the macro up to the cursor. Alternatively, right-click that line and choose Run to Cursor.

```
UserForm
    Private Sub CommandButton1_Click()
        Unload Me
    End Sub


    Private Sub UserForm_Initialize()
        Dim WS As Worksheet
        Set WS = Worksheets("Sheet1")

        FinalRow = WS.Cells(Rows.Count, 1).End(xlUp).Row
        For i = 2 To FinalRow
            Me.ListBox1.AddItem WS.Cells(i, 1)
        Next i

        ' The next line is actually the line that causes an error
⇨   |   Me.ListBox1(0).Selected = True



    End Sub
```

FIGURE 24-7 With 25 items to add to the list box, you must press F8 53 times to get through this three-line loop.

Sometimes, an error will occur within a loop. Add `Debug.Print i` inside the loop and use the Immediate pane (which you open by pressing Ctrl+G) to locate which time through the loop caused the problem.

Basic error handling with the On Error GoTo syntax

The basic error-handling option is to instruct VBA to direct the code to a specific area of the macro in the event of an error. In this area, you might have special code that alerts users to the problem and enables them to react.

A typical scenario is to add the error-handling routine at the end of the macro. To set up an error handler, follow these steps:

1. After the last code line of the macro, insert the `errHandler:` label. The label can be whatever word you want as long as a colon follows it.

2. To ensure the error handler only runs if an error occurs, you can check for this with `If err.Number <> 0 Then`. If the number is 0, then there are no errors, so the code within the `If` statement won't run. You can even check for specific error numbers.

3. Write the code to handle the error. If you want to return control of the macro to the line after the one that caused the error, use the `Resume Next` statement.

In your macro, just before the line that might likely cause the error, add a line reading `On Error GoTo errHandler`. Note that in this line, you do not include the colon after the label name.

Immediately after the line of code that you suspect will cause the error, add code to turn off the special error handler. Since this is not intuitive, it often confuses people. The code to cancel any special error handling is `On Error GoTo 0`. There is no label named 0. Instead, this line is a fictitious one that instructs Excel to revert to its normal state of displaying the debug error message when an error is encountered. This is why it is important to cancel the error handling.

The following code includes a special error handler to handle the necessary action if the file has been moved or is missing:

```
Sub HandleAnError()
Dim MyFile As Variant
'Set up a special error handler
On Error GoTo FileNotThere
Workbooks.Open Filename:="C:\NotHere.xls"
'If we get here, cancel the special error handler
On Error GoTo 0
MsgBox "The program is complete"
'The macro is done. Use Exit sub, otherwise the macro
'execution WILL continue into the error handler
Exit Sub
'Set up a name for the Error handler
FileNotThere:
MyPrompt = "There was an error opening the file. It is possible the "
MyPrompt = MyPrompt & " file has been moved. Click OK to browse for the "
MyPrompt = MyPrompt & "file, or click Cancel to end the program"
Ans = MsgBox(Prompt:=MyPrompt, Buttons:=vbOKCancel)
If Ans = vbCancel Then Exit Sub
'The client clicked OK. Let him browse for the file
MyFile = Application.GetOpenFilename
If MyFile = False Then Exit Sub
'What if the 2nd file is corrupt? We don't want to recursively throw
'The client back into this error handler. Just stop the program
On Error GoTo 0
Workbooks.Open MyFile
'If we get here, then return the macro execution back to the original
'section of the macro, to the line after the one that caused the error.
Resume Next
End Sub
```

You definitely do not want this error handler invoked for another error later in the macro, such as a divide-by-zero error.

> **Note** It is possible to have more than one error handler at the end of a macro. Make sure that each error handler ends with either `Resume Next` or `Exit Sub` so that macro execution does not accidentally move into the next error handler.

Generic error handlers

Some developers (like me) prefer to direct an error to a generic error handler to utilize the `Err` object. This object has properties for error number and description. If it's an error you're expecting, you can include an English definition to the user, like this:

```
On Error GoTo HandleAny
Sheets(9).Activate
HandleAny:
```

```
If Err.Number <> 0 then 'there was an error
  Msg = "Sheet not found" & chr(10) & Err.Number & ": " & Err.Description
  MsgBox Msg
End if
End Sub
```

Level Up!

My coding style involves using a lot of functions that are called by a main sub. Why? Because I can error-check every step of the process and provide the user with a clear error message similar to the one in the previous sample. Additionally, many of those functions, such as opening a workbook, can be placed in my code library for reuse.

I'm working on a project that opens a workbook and then processes the data. The code for opening the workbook would be its own function that, if successful, returns the open workbook to the main sub. The function code would be like this:

```
Function OpenDataWorkbook(ByRef wkbkData As Workbook, ByRef errMessage As _
  String) As Boolean
Dim WorkbookPath As String
On Error GoTo errHandler
'for the heck of it, let's disable events
Application.EnableEvents = False
'set the workbook path
WorkbookPath = ThisWorkbook.Path & Application.PathSeparator & _
  "DataWorkbook.xlsx"
'open the workbook
Set wkbkData = Workbooks.Open(WorkbookPath)
'now the code checks for success
errHandler:
If Err.Number <> 0 Then 'there was an error
  'chr(10) is a linebreak
  errMessage = "Unable to open workbook" & Chr(10) & WorkbookPath & Chr(10) & _
    "Please ensure the file exists"
  OpenDataWorkbook = False
  Err.Clear 'clear the error
Else
  'there was no error
  OpenDataWorkbook = True
End If
'no matter what, the code gets here
'so we can enable events
Application.EnableEvents = True
'and since it's the end of the function, I don't need to reset error handling
End Function
```

And my main sub that calls the function would be like this:

```
Sub ProcessData()
'the main sub
Dim DataWorkbook As Workbook
Dim ErrorMessage As String
```

```
'call the function to open the data workbook
If Not OpenDataWorkbook(DataWorkbook, ErrorMessage) Then
  'the open failed, so skip to the error handler
  GoTo errHandler
End If
'the open did not fail so let's continue
'Regardless of whether an error occurred, execution jumps to errHandler
'Use an If block to separate true error-handling logic (Err.Number <> 0)
'from the standard cleanup or return tasks that follow.
errHandler:
If Err.Number <> 0 Then
  'in case we already have an error message, let's concatenate them
  ErrorMessage = ErrorMessage & Chr(10) & _
    "Unknown error: " & Err.Number & ": " & Err.Description
    Err.Clear
End If
If Len(ErrorMessage) > 0 Then
  MsgBox ErrorMessage, vbCritical, "Unable to continue"
Else
  MsgBox "Data Processed"
End If
'this will still run ok even if there was an error
Set DataWorkbook = Nothing
End Sub
```

Breaking a project down into functions like this makes it easier to troubleshoot and identify issues. If something goes wrong, you know exactly where to look. It keeps your main sub cleaner, so you don't spend time digging through hundreds of lines of code to find where the error originated.

Handling errors by choosing to ignore them

Some errors can simply be ignored. For example, suppose you want to use VBA to create an index.html file. Your code erases any existing index.html file from a folder before writing out the next file.

The Kill (FileName) statement returns an error if FileName does not exist, though this probably is not something you need to worry about. After all, you are trying to delete the file, so you probably don't care whether someone already deleted it before running the macro. In this case, tell Excel to just skip over the offending line and resume macro execution with the next line. The code to do this is On Error Resume Next:

```
Sub WriteHTML()
MyFile = ThisWorkbook.Path & Application.PathSeparator & "Index.html"
On Error Resume Next
Kill MyFile
On Error GoTo 0
Open MyFile for Output as #1
'etc.
End Sub
```

> **Note** Be careful with `On Error Resume Next`. You can use it selectively in situations where you know the error can be safely ignored. You should immediately return error checking to normal after the line that might cause an error with `On Error GoTo 0`.
>
> If you attempt to have `On Error Resume Next` skip an error that cannot be skipped, the macro immediately steps out of the current macro. If you have a situation in which `MacroA` calls `MacroB`, and `MacroB` encounters a nonskippable error, the program jumps out of `MacroB` and continues with the next line in `MacroA`. This is rarely a good thing. That's one advantage of using a generic error handler—it gives you a chance to control how the code exits or recovers rather than letting it silently fail or skip key steps.

Case study: Overlooking page setup problems

VBA code to handle printer settings runs much faster if you turn off `PrintCommunication` at the beginning of the following code and turn it back on at the end of the code.

When you record a macro and perform page setup, even if you change just one item in the Page Setup dialog, the macro recorder records two dozen settings for you. These settings notoriously differ from printer to printer. For example, if you record the `PageSetup` on a system with a color printer, it might record a setting for `.BlackAndWhite = True`. This setting may be ignored or cause an error on another system where the printer does not offer this choice. Your printer might offer a `.PrintQuality = 600` setting. If the client's printer offers only a 300 resolution setting, this code fails. For this reason, you should surround the `PageSetup` with `On Error Resume Next` to ensure that most settings are applied, while the trivial ones that fail do not cause run-time errors. Here is how to do this:

```
On Error Resume Next
Application.PrintCommunication = False
With ActiveSheet.PageSetup
  .PrintTitleRows = ""
  .PrintTitleColumns = ""
End With
ActiveSheet.PageSetup.PrintArea = "$A$1:$L$27"
With ActiveSheet.PageSetup
  .LeftHeader = ""
  .CenterHeader = ""
  .RightHeader = ""
  .LeftFooter = ""
  .CenterFooter = ""
  .RightFooter = ""
  .LeftMargin = Application.InchesToPoints(0.25)
  .RightMargin = Application.InchesToPoints(0.25)
  .TopMargin = Application.InchesToPoints(0.75)
  .BottomMargin = Application.InchesToPoints(0.5)
  .HeaderMargin = Application.InchesToPoints(0.5)
```

```
        .FooterMargin = Application.InchesToPoints(0.5)
        .PrintHeadings = False
        .PrintGridlines = False
        .PrintComments = xlPrintNoComments
        .PrintQuality = 300
        .CenterHorizontally = False
        .CenterVertically = False
        .Orientation = xlLandscape
        .Draft = False
        .PaperSize = xlPaperLetter
        .FirstPageNumber = xlAutomatic
        .Order = xlDownThenOver
        .BlackAndWhite = False
        .Zoom = False
        .FitToPagesWide = 1
        .FitToPagesTall = False
        .PrintErrors = xlPrintErrorsDisplayed
    End With
    Application.PrintCommunication = True
    On Error GoTo 0
```

Suppressing Excel warnings

Some messages appear even if you have set Excel to ignore errors. For example, try to delete a work-sheet using code, and you still get the message, "Microsoft Excel will permanently delete this sheet. Do you want to continue?" This is annoying. You do not want your clients to have to answer this warning; it gives them a chance to choose not to delete the sheet your macro wants to delete. In fact, this is not an error but an alert. To suppress all alerts and force Excel to take the default action, use `Application.DisplayAlerts = False`, like this:

```
Sub DeleteSheet()
Application.DisplayAlerts = False
Worksheets("Sheet2").Delete
Application.DisplayAlerts = True
End Sub
```

Encountering errors on purpose

Because programmers hate errors, this concept might seem counterintuitive, but errors are not always bad. Sometimes it is faster to simply encounter an error.

Suppose, for example, that you want to determine whether the active workbook contains a work-sheet named `Data`. To find this out without causing an error, you could use the following eight lines of code:

```
DataFound = False
For Each ws in ActiveWorkbook.Worksheets
  If ws.Name = "Data" then
```

```
      DataFound = True
      Exit For
   End if
Next ws
If not DataFound then Sheets.Add.Name = "Data"
```

If your workbook has 128 worksheets, the program loops through 128 times before deciding that the Data worksheet is missing.

An alternative is to try to reference the Data worksheet. If you have error-checking set to Resume Next, the code runs, and the Err object is assigned a number other than 0:

```
On Error Resume Next
X = Worksheets("Data").Name
If Err.Number <> 0 then Sheets.Add.Name = "Data"
On Error GoTo 0
```

This code runs much faster. Errors usually make programmers cringe. However, in this case, as well as in many others, the errors are perfectly acceptable.

Level Up!

As stated earlier, I like creating separate functions so that I can handle errors within the specific function. Below is the function I use in many projects to check if a sheet exists. It's similar to the previous lines of code, but it's a bit more flexible.

TargetBook is the workbook where the sheet can be found; it doesn't always have to be the workbook in which the code is located. The argument is optional, meaning that if it is in the same workbook as the code, it is not necessary to include it.

Len(…) checks the length of the sheet name in the workbook. If it exists, the length will be greater than 0 and, therefore, return True. If the sheet isn't found in the workbook, it will return False.

```
Function WorksheetExists(ByVal SheetName As String, _
   Optional TargetBook As Workbook) As Boolean
'if the TargetBook is not included, then set it to the ActiveWorkbook
If TargetBook Is Nothing Then
   If ActiveWorkbook Is Nothing Then Exit Function
   Set TargetBook = ActiveWorkbook
End If
On Error Resume Next
WorksheetExists = Len(TargetBook.Worksheets(SheetName).Name) <> 0
On Error GoTo 0
End Function
```

Helping others help you (when you're not there)

If you're developing code for someone else—whether it's a client across the world or a coworker running reports while you're on vacation—errors may still happen. A well-written program should handle them gracefully, ideally logging the issue with enough detail for you to diagnose it later.

Still, some errors may slip through or require live troubleshooting. If you're supporting users remotely, ensure they know how to identify and report genuine errors. Many users confuse informational messages (like MsgBox prompts) with actual error dialogs since both may include beeps or unexpected pop-ups.

Make it easy for them: instruct users to take a screenshot or read the error message to you while it's still on the screen. Remote access tools like Zoom or AnyDesk can also help you see what's happening in real time. The more precise the information—such as the error number, message, and what they were doing when it occurred—the faster you'll be able to fix it.

Errors that won't show up in Debug mode

This problem is happening more frequently today. You write a macro that does stuff. When you run the macro, you get an error. But then you click Debug and start stepping through code with F8. The macro runs fine without errors.

Every time you step through the code one line at a time, the macro works. Every time you run the code using the Run button, you get the error. Cue the hair-pulling.

Here's what's happening: At one time, a single line of macro code would run, and Excel would pause until that line was complete. However, it now appears that the command sometimes returns control to the macro before it has actually been completed. Charting guru Jon Peltier reports that this frequently happens when inserting new charts. For example, let's say you have a macro where line 1 inserts a chart, and line 2 does something to the chart. In that case, it could be really bad if line 2 attempted to run before the chart was fully created.

Of course, when you are running code one line at a time, the routine is to see which line is highlighted in yellow, press F8, see that the next line is highlighted in yellow, press F8, and so on. You might be pressing F8 just one second later, but that one second is enough for the chart to finish rendering.

The workaround is to insert a DoEvents line between commands that rely on something finishing in the background, like this:

```
Set myChart = ActiveSheet.Shapes.AddChart2
DoEvents
myChart.Chart.ChartTitle.Text = "Sales by Region"
```

DoEvents instructs Excel to temporarily yield control, allowing Excel and background processes to catch up. It's not an actual pause, though, and may not be enough. In that case, use Application.Wait to pause the macro for a second or two, like this:

```
Application.Wait Now + TimeValue("0:00:01")
```

On rare occasions, you may have to use both—DoEvents followed by `Application.Wait`. The only way to know is by testing.

Errors while developing versus errors months later

When you have just written code that you are running for the first time, you expect errors. In fact, you might decide to step through the code line by line to watch the progress the first time through.

It's another thing to have a program that has been running daily in production suddenly stop working because of an error. That can be perplexing. The code has been working for months, so why did it suddenly stop working today? It's easy to blame a change in the data layout. However, when you get right down to it, it is really the fault of developers for not considering the possibilities.

The following sections describe a couple of common problems that can strike a program months later.

Run-Time Error 9: Subscript out of range

You set up an application for a client, and you provided a Menu worksheet where some settings are stored. Then, one day, this client reports getting the error message shown in Figure 24-8.

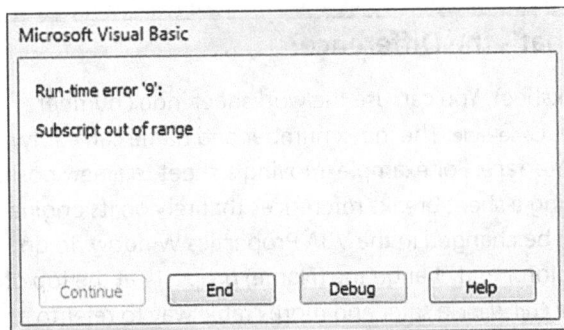

FIGURE 24-8 Run-Time Error 9 often occurs when you expect a worksheet to be there, but it has been deleted or renamed by the client.

Your code expected a worksheet named Menu. For some reason, the client either accidentally deleted the worksheet or renamed it. When the following code tried to select the sheet, the client received an error:

```
Sub GetSettings()
Dim x as Variant
x = ThisWorkbook.Worksheets("Menu").Range("A1").Value
End Sub
```

This is a classic situation where you cannot believe that the client would do something so crazy. After you have been burned by this one a few times, you might go to lengths like implementing this code to prevent an unhandled debug error because of a missing object:

```
Sub GetSettings()
Dim x As Variant
'WorksheetExists is a separate function that checks for the sheet
'see the section "Encountering errors on purpose" in this chapter
If Not WorksheetExists("Menu", ThisWorkbook) Then
  MsgBox "Expected to find a Menu worksheet, but it is missing"
Else
  x = ThisWorkbook.Worksheets("Menu").Range("A1").Value
End If
End Sub
```

> ## Level Up!
>
> Depending on the size and complexity of your project, it may be worthwhile to create a validation procedure that checks for all required objects upfront. By calling it at the start of other procedures, you ensure that nothing important has changed—and you avoid cluttering the rest of your code with repeated existence checks.

CodeNames vs. Sheet Names: What's the Difference?

There are three ways to refer to a worksheet. You can use the worksheet index number, the worksheet name, or the worksheet CodeName. The index number and name can easily change through actions in the Excel interface. For example, moving a sheet to a new position changes its index number, and renaming a sheet breaks references that rely on its original name. However, the CodeName can only be changed in the VBA Properties Window. To do this, select the sheet in the Project Explorer and change the (Name) property at the top of the Properties window. This makes the CodeName a safer and more stable way to refer to a worksheet.

Figure 24-9 shows the VBA Project Explorer workbook, which contains five worksheets. The sheet that shows in the Excel user interface with the name Menu has a CodeName of Sheet6. Even if someone renames the sheet in the interface, the CodeName will remain Sheet6.

While studying the codenames in Project Explorer, it seems that there used to be another worksheet with a CodeName of Sheet2 that has been deleted. While deleting an earlier sheet will change the index number of later worksheets, it does not change the CodeName.

All three of these lines of code will select the Menu worksheet:

```
Worksheets(5).Activate
Worksheets("Menu"). Activate
Sheet6. Activate
```

Codename   Worksheet name

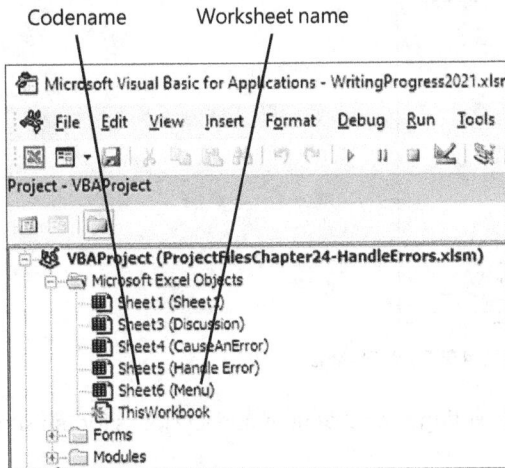

FIGURE 24-9 It can be safer to refer to the worksheet using the CodeName.

Using the codename is a handy option for small projects with just a few worksheets. But in larger projects—especially those where sheets may be copied, deleted, or moved between workbooks—referring to the sheet by name is usually more practical. That's where checking for an object's existence, as discussed earlier, helps make your code more reliable and easier to maintain.

Run-Time Error 1004: Method range of object global failed

You have code that imports a text file each day. You expect the text file to end with a Total row. After importing the text, you want to convert all the detail rows to italics.

The following code has worked fine for months:

```
Sub SetReportInItalics()
TotalRow = Cells(Rows.Count,1).End(xlUp).Row
FinalRow = TotalRow -1
Range("A1:A" & FinalRow).Font.Italic = True
End Sub
```

Then, one day, the client calls with the error message shown in Figure 24-10.

Upon examining the code, you discover that something bizarre went wrong when the text file was transferred via FTP to the client that day. The text file ended up as an empty file. Because the worksheet was empty, TotalRow was determined to be row 1. If you assume that the last detail row was TotalRow−1, the code is set up to attempt to format row 0, which clearly does not exist.

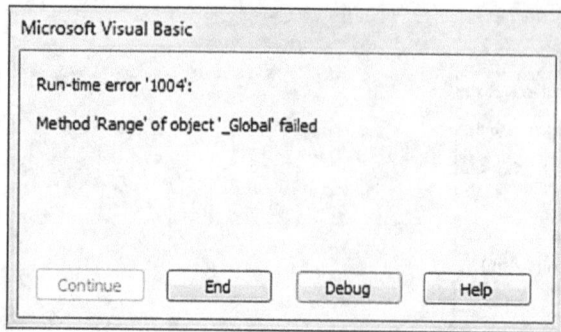

FIGURE 24-10 Run-Time Error 1004 can be caused by a number of things.

After an episode like this, you find yourself writing code that preemptively looks for this situation:

```
Sub SetReportInItalics()
TotalRow = Cells(Rows.Count,1).End(xlUp).Row
FinalRow = TotalRow-1
If FinalRow > 0 Then
  Range("A1:A" & FinalRow).Font.Italic = True
Else
  MsgBox "It appears the file is empty today. Check the FTP process"
End If
End Sub
```

> **Tip** Always check for the standard "unexpecteds"—like missing files, empty data sets, or cells containing error values such as #N/A. These issues can trigger frustrating errors if your code isn't prepared for them. Even after decades of programming, I still encounter client-created situations that I never anticipated. It's frustrating—especially when I thought I'd covered everything—but at least it's rarely something I should have caught.

The ills of protecting code

It is possible to lock a VBA project so that it cannot be viewed. However, doing so is not recommended. When code is protected, and an error is encountered, your user is presented with an error message but no opportunity to debug. The Debug button is there, but it is grayed out and useless in helping you discover the problem.

Also, be aware that Excel's VBA protection is notoriously weak. Several low-cost tools can unlock a protected project in seconds. In short, you need to understand that VBA code is not secure—and then get over it.

If you absolutely need to truly protect your code, invest $100 for a license to Unviewable+ VBA Project from Esoteric Software. This crowd-funded software enables you to create a compiled version of a workbook, preventing most people from viewing the VBA code. For more details, visit *http://mrx.cl/hidevba*.

Case study: Password cracking lesson

A client once handed me a workbook originally developed by someone else, but the VBA project was locked, and the original developer was no longer responding. The client needed urgent changes, but without access to the code, I couldn't help. Ultimately, the client used a third-party tool to unlock the project, which silently replaced the password. While I was able to complete the requested work, the original developer was later locked out of his own file. The lesson? Locking your project may give a false sense of security and can create serious headaches for both you and anyone trying to maintain the workbook in the future.

Excel's built-in VBA password feature is easily bypassed. If protecting your source code is truly necessary, consider investing in a tool like Unviewable+ from Esoteric Software. It creates a compiled version of the workbook with far stronger protections, making it much harder for others to access or modify the code. Just be aware: stronger protection means you'll also need a solid recovery plan—because if you lose access, no one's getting back in.

More problems with passwords

Office 2013 introduced a new SHA-2 class SHA512 algorithm to calculate encryption keys. This algorithm causes noticeable slowdowns in macros that protect or unprotect multiple sheets, especially when used in loops.

The encryption method Excel uses depends not just on the version you're running but also on the file format. If you open and work with a legacy .xls file in Excel 365, Excel preserves the older, faster encryption model. However, as soon as you re-save the file as a .xlsm or other modern format and reapply protection, Excel upgrades the protection to the newer standard—along with all its benefits and trade-offs. Here's how the behavior changes depending on what you do with the file:

If you open an old Excel 97 .xls file in Excel 365 and you know the passwords, you won't have any issues unlocking the sheets, workbook, or VBA project. Excel 365 fully supports the older protection scheme for reading and editing.

If you reapply protection but leave the file in .xls format, Excel continues to use the older, legacy encryption. This means:

- You maintain full compatibility with Excel 97 and other early versions.

- Performance is fast—there's no noticeable slowdown when using Protect or Unprotect in your macros.

- However, the protection remains weak and can still be bypassed with basic tools.

If you instead save the file as a modern format like .xlsm, Excel upgrades the encryption:

- Worksheet and workbook protection now use SHA-512, which is stronger but slower.

- Compatibility with Excel 97 is broken, and you won't be able to remove worksheet or workbook protection in those older versions. Note that this does not affect VBA project protection, which uses a separate—and still weak—protection scheme that hasn't changed in years.

- Macros that apply or remove protection may run more slowly, especially if they loop through many sheets or repeatedly toggle protection on and off.

That said, the slowdown is generally minor for most users. If your macro protects a few sheets once or twice, you probably won't notice a difference. But if you're looping through dozens of sheets with protection toggled each time, the lag becomes more noticeable, especially on lower-end systems.

In short, keep the following in mind:

- For compatibility, use the .xls file type.

- For stronger protection, convert to .xlsm—but be aware that you're trading backward compatibility and possibly some speed.

Errors caused by different versions

Even within Excel 365, not all users run the same build. New features and object model updates roll out gradually, which means code that runs fine on your machine might throw a compile error on someone else's because you used a method or parameter that was added recently.

To reduce the risk:

- When in doubt, you can isolate newer or less-tested code in its own module. When a user runs a macro in a module, Excel compiles the entire module. If the module contains a feature that is not available, the compile will fail. By isolating the version-sensitive code in a separate module, you prevent Excel from compiling the code until it's run. And other modules remain unaffected.

- Use #If conditional compilation to separate platform-specific or version-sensitive code. Refer to "Managing code variations with compiler directives" in Chapter 4, "Laying the groundwork with variables and structures," for more information on compiler directives.

- If your project relies on external libraries (like scripting, XML, or ADO), missing references can also trigger compile errors at startup—double-check those before distributing. Consider using late binding to avoid these errors. Refer to Chapter 20, "Automating Word," for more information on late binding.

Excel for Mac and Windows are mostly aligned but not identical. API calls, file paths, and some UI logic still differ. When in doubt, test on both platforms to ensure compatibility.

Next steps

In this chapter, you've learned how to make your code more bulletproof for your clients. In Chapter 25, "Customizing the ribbon to run macros," you find out how to customize the ribbon to allow your clients to enjoy a professional user interface.

CHAPTER 25

Customizing the ribbon to run macros

In this chapter, you will:

- Learn where to add ribbon code: the customui folder and file

- Add controls to a ribbon

- Understand the RELS file

- Use images on buttons

- Troubleshoot error messages

- Learn other ways to run a macro

Unlike the command bars of old, a ribbon isn't designed via VBA code. Instead, if you want to modify the ribbon and add your own tab, you need to modify the Excel file itself, which isn't as impossible as it sounds. The new Excel file is actually a zipped file containing various files and folders. All you need to do is unzip it, make your changes, and you're done. Okay, it's not *that* simple—a few more steps are involved—but it's not impossible.

Before beginning, go to the File tab, select Options | Advanced | General, and select Show Add-In User Interface Errors. This allows error messages to appear so that you can troubleshoot errors in your custom toolbar.

> **Note** See the "Troubleshooting error messages" section later in this chapter for more details.

> **Caution** Unlike when programming in the VB Editor, you won't have any assistance with automatic correction of letter case—and the XML code, which is what the ribbon code is, is very particular. Note the case of the XML-specific words; for example, for id, using ID will generate an error.

One thing to keep in mind is that with the change to the single-document interface (SDI) that was made to Excel 2013 (and later versions), the custom ribbon tab attached to a workbook is visible only when that workbook is active. When you activate another workbook, the tab will not appear on the ribbon. The exception is with an add-in; its custom ribbon is visible on any workbook open after the add-in is opened.

> **Note** See Chapter 26, "Creating Excel add-ins," for more information on creating an add-in.

> **Note** The original CommandBars object in legacy Excel still works, but the customized menus and toolbars are now all placed on the Add-Ins tab.

Where to add code: The customui folder and file

Create a folder called **customui**. This folder contains the elements of your custom ribbon tab. Within the folder, create a text file and call it **customUI14.xml**, as shown in Figure 25-1. Open the XML file in a text editor; either Notepad or WordPad works.

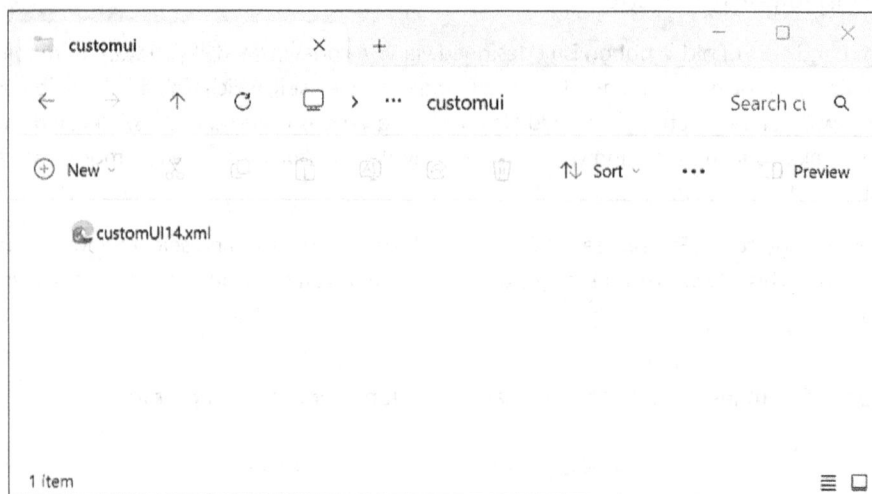

FIGURE 25-1 Create a customuUI14.xml file within a customui folder.

> **Tip** My favorite text editor is Notepad ++ by Don Ho (see *www.notepad-plus-plus.org*). Like the VB Editor, it colors XML-specific syntax after you choose XML as the language you're typing. It also has a lot of other useful tools.

Insert the basic structure for the XML code, shown here, into your XML file. For every opening tag grouping, such as <ribbon>, there must be a closing tag, </ribbon>:

```xml
<customUI xmlns="http://schemas.microsoft.com/office/2009/07/customui">
  <ribbon startFromScratch="false">
    <tabs>
      <!-- your ribbon controls here -->
    </tabs>
  </ribbon>
</customUI>
```

startFromScratch is optional and has a default value of false. You use it to tell the code whether the other tabs in Excel will be shown or not. true means to show only your tab; false means to show your tab and all the other tabs.

> **Caution** Note the case of the letters in startFromScratch—the small s at the beginning followed by the capital F in From and capital S in Scratch. It is crucial that you not deviate from this.

The <!-- your ribbon controls here --> you see in the previous code is commented text. Just enter your comments between <!-- and -->, and the program ignores the line when it runs.

> **Note** If you're creating a ribbon that needs to be Excel 2007 compatible, you need to use the schema found here: *http://schemas.microsoft.com/office/2006/01/customui*. Also, where you see **customUI14** in this chapter, use **customUI**.

Creating a tab and a group

Before you can add a control to a tab, you need to identify the tab and group. A tab can hold many different controls you can group, like the Font group on the Home tab.

Name your tab **My First Ribbon** and add a group called **My Programs** to it, like this (see Figure 25-2 in the next section):

```xml
<customUI xmlns="http://schemas.microsoft.com/office/2009/07/customui">
  <ribbon startFromScratch="false">
    <tabs>
      <tab id="CustomTab" label="My First Ribbon">
        <group id="CustomGroup" label="My Programs">
          <!-- your ribbon controls here -->
        </group>
      </tab>
    </tabs>
  </ribbon>
</customUI>
```

`id` is a unique identifier for the control (in this case, the tab and group). `label` is the text you want to appear on your ribbon for the specified control.

Adding a control to a ribbon

After you've set up the ribbon and group, you can add controls. Depending on the type of control, there are different attributes you can include in your XML code. (Refer to Table 25-1 for more information on various controls and their attributes.)

The following code adds a normal-sized button with the text **Click to Run** to the Reports group and runs the sub `HelloWorld` when the button is clicked (see Figure 25-2):

```
<customUI xmlns="http://schemas.microsoft.com/office/2009/07/customui">
  <ribbon startFromScratch="false">
    <tabs>
      <tab id="CustomTab" label="My First Ribbon">
        <group id="CustomGroup" label="My Programs">
          <button id="button1" label="Click to run"
          onAction="Module1.HelloWorld" size="normal"/>
        </group>
      </tab>
    </tabs>
  </ribbon>
</customUI>
```

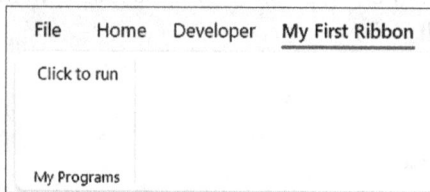

FIGURE 25-2 Run a program with a click of a button on your custom ribbon.

The properties of the button include

- `id`: A unique identifier for the control button

- `label`: Holds the text you want to appear on your button

- `size`: The button's size, which has a default value of `normal`; the other option is `large`.

- `onAction`: The procedure, `HelloWorld`, to call when the button is clicked

The procedure, shown here, goes in a standard module, `Module1`, in the workbook:

```
Sub HelloWorld(control As IRibbonControl)
MsgBox "Hello World"
End Sub
```

Notice the argument `control As IRibbonControl`. This is the standard argument for a procedure, which a button calls via the `onAction` attribute. Table 25-2 lists the required arguments for other attributes and controls.

TABLE 25-1 Ribbon control attributes

Attribute	Type or Value	Description
description	String	Specifies description text displayed in menus when the `itemSize` attribute is set to `Large`.
enabled	true, false	Specifies whether the control is enabled.
getContent	Callback	Retrieves XML content that describes a dynamic menu.
getDescription	Callback	Gets the description of a control.
getEnabled	Callback	Gets the enabled state of a control.
getImage	Callback	Gets the image for a control.
getImageMso	Callback	Gets a built-in control's icon by using the control ID.
getItemCount	Callback	Gets the number of items to be displayed in a combo box, dropdown, or gallery.
getItemID	Callback	Gets the ID for a specific item in a combo box, dropdown, or gallery.
getItemImage	Callback	Gets the image of a combo box, dropdown, or gallery.
getItemLabel	Callback	Gets the label of a combo box, dropdown, or gallery.
getItemScreentip	Callback	Gets the ScreenTip for a combo box, dropdown, or gallery.
getItemSupertip	Callback	Gets the enhanced ScreenTip for a combo box, dropdown, or gallery.
getKeytip	Callback	Gets the KeyTip for a control.
getLabel	Callback	Gets the label for a control.
getPressed	Callback	Gets a value that indicates whether a toggle button is pressed or not pressed. Gets a value that indicates whether a check box is selected or cleared.
getScreentip	Callback	Gets the ScreenTip for a control.
getSelectedItemID	Callback	Gets the ID of the selected item in a dropdown or gallery.
getSelectedItemIndex	Callback	Gets the index of the selected item in a dropdown or gallery.
getShowImage	Callback	Gets a value that specifies whether to display the control image.
getShowLabel	Callback	Gets a value that specifies whether to display the control label.
getSize	Callback	Gets a value that specifies the size of a control (normal or large).
getSupertip	Callback	Gets a value that specifies the enhanced ScreenTip for a control.
getText	Callback	Gets the text to be displayed in the edit portion of a text box or edit box.
getTitle	Callback	Gets the text to be displayed (rather than a horizontal line) for a menu separator.
getVisible	Callback	Gets a value that specifies whether the control is visible.

Attribute	Type or Value	Description
id	String	Acts as a user-defined unique identifier for the control (and is mutually exclusive with idMso and idQ—so specify only one of these values).
idMso	Control id	Acts as a built-in control ID (and is mutually exclusive with id and idQ—so specify only one of these values).
idQ	Qualified id	Acts as a qualified control ID, prefixed with a namespace identifier (and is mutually exclusive with id and idMso—so specify only one of these values).
image	String	Specifies an image for the control.
imageMso	Control id	Specifies an identifier for a built-in image.
insertAfterMso	Control id	Specifies the identifier for the built-in control after which to position this control.
insertAfterQ	Qualified id	Specifies the identifier of a control whose idQ property was specified after which to position this control.
insertBeforeMso	Control id	Specifies the identifier for the built-in control before which to position this control.
insertBeforeQ	Qualified id	Specifies the identifier of a control whose idQ property was specified before which to position this control.
itemSize	large, normal	Specifies the size for the items in a menu.
Keytip	String	Specifies the KeyTip for the control.
label	String	Specifies the label for the control.
onAction	Callback	Called when the user clicks the control.
onChange	Callback	Called when the user enters or selects text in an edit box or combo box.
screentip	String	Specifies the control's ScreenTip.
showImage	true, false	Specifies whether the control's image is shown.
showItemImage	true, false	Specifies whether to show the image in a combo box, dropdown, or gallery.
showItemLabel	true, false	Specifies whether to show the label in a combo box, dropdown, or gallery.
showLabel	true, false	Specifies whether the control's label is shown.
size	large, normal	Specifies the size for the control.
sizeString	String	Indicates the width for the control by specifying a string, such as "xxxxxx."
supertip	String	Specifies the enhanced ScreenTip for the control.
tag	String	Specifies user-defined text.
title	String	Specifies the text to be displayed, rather than a horizontal line, for a menu separator.
visible	true, false	Specifies whether the control is visible.

TABLE 25-2 Required arguments for other attributes and controls

Control	Callback Name	Signature
Various controls	getDescription	Sub GetDescription(control as IRibbonControl, ByRef description)
	getEnabled	Sub GetEnabled(control As IRibbonControl, ByRef enabled)
	getImage	Sub GetImage(control As IRibbonControl, ByRef image)
	getImageMso	Sub GetImageMso(control As IRibbonControl, ByRef imageMso)
	getLabel	Sub GetLabel(control As IRibbonControl, ByRef label)
	getKeytip	Sub GetKeytip(control As IRibbonControl, ByRef label)
	getSize	Sub GetSize(control As IRibbonControl, ByRef size)
	getScreentip	Sub GetScreentip(control As IRibbonControl, ByRef screentip)
	getSupertip	Sub GetSupertip(control As IRibbonControl, ByRef screentip)
	getVisible	Sub GetVisible(control As IRibbonControl, ByRef visible)
button	getShowImage	Sub GetShowImage(control As IRibbonControl, ByRef showImage)
	getShowLabel	Sub GetShowLabel(control As IRibbonControl, ByRef showLabel)
	onAction	Sub OnAction(control As IRibbonControl)
checkBox	getPressed	Sub GetPressed(control As IRibbonControl, ByRef returnValue)
	onAction	Sub OnAction(control As IRibbonControl, pressed As Boolean)
comboBox	getItemCount	Sub GetItemCount(control As IRibbonControl, ByRef count)
	getItemID	Sub GetItemID(control As IRibbonControl, index As Integer, ByRef id)
	getItemImage	Sub GetItemImage(control As IRibbonControl, index As Integer, ByRef image)
	getItemLabel	Sub GetItemLabel(control As IRibbonControl, index As Integer, ByRef label)
	getItemScreenTip	Sub GetItemScreenTip(control As IRibbonControl, index As Integer, ByRef screentip)
	getItemSuperTip	Sub GetItemSuperTip(control As IRibbonControl, index As Integer, ByRef supertip)
	getText	Sub GetText(control As IRibbonControl, ByRef text)
	onChange	Sub OnChange(control As IRibbonControl, text As String)
customUI	loadImage	Sub LoadImage(imageId As string, ByRef image)
	onLoad	Sub OnLoad(ribbon As IRibbonUI)
dropDown	getItemCount	Sub GetItemCount(control As IRibbonControl, ByRef count)
	getItemID	Sub GetItemID(control As IRibbonControl, index As Integer, ByRef id)

Control	Callback Name	Signature
	getItemImage	Sub GetItemImage(control As IRibbonControl, index As Integer, ByRef image)
	getItemLabel	Sub GetItemLabel(control As IRibbonControl, index As Integer, ByRef label)
	getItemScreenTip	Sub GetItemScreenTip(control As IRibbonControl, index As Integer ByRef screenTip)
	getItemSuperTip	Sub GetItemSuperTip(control As IRibbonControl, index As Integer, ByRef superTip)
	getSelectedItemID	Sub GetSelectedItemID(control As IRibbonControl, ByRef index)
	getSelectedItem Index	Sub GetSelectedItemIndex(control As IRibbonControl, ByRef index)
	onAction	Sub OnAction(control As IRibbonControl, selectedId As String, selectedIndex As Integer)
dynamicMenu	getContent	Sub GetContent(control As IRibbonControl, ByRef content)
editBox	getText	Sub GetText(control As IRibbonControl, ByRef text)
	onChange	Sub OnChange(control As IRibbonControl, text As String)
gallery	getItemCount	Sub GetItemCount(control As IRibbonControl, ByRef count)
	getItemHeight	Sub GetItemHeight(control As IRibbonControl, ByRef height)
	getItemID	Sub GetItemID(control As IRibbonControl, index As Integer, ByRef id)
	getItemImage	Sub GetItemImage(control As IRibbonControl, index As Integer, ByRef image)
	getItemLabel	Sub GetItemLabel(control As IRibbonControl, index As Integer, ByRef label)
	getItemScreenTip	Sub GetItemScreenTip(control As IRibbonControl, index as Integer, ByRef screen)
	getItemSuperTip	Sub GetItemSuperTip(control As IRibbonControl, index as Integer, ByRef screen)
	getItemWidth	Sub getItemWidth(control As IRibbonControl, ByRef width)
	getSelectedItemID	Sub GetSelectedItemID(control As IRibbonControl, ByRef index)
	getSelectedItem Index	Sub GetSelectedItemIndex(control As IRibbonControl, ByRef index)
	onAction	Sub OnAction(control As IRibbonControl, selectedId As String, selectedIndex As Integer)
menuSeparator	getTitle	Sub GetTitle(control As IRibbonControl, ByRef title)
toggleButton	getPressed	Sub GetPressed(control As IRibbonControl, ByRef returnValue)
	onAction	Sub OnAction(control As IRibbonControl, pressed As Boolean)

Accessing the file structure

Excel files are actually zipped files that contain various files and folders to create the workbook and worksheets you see when you open the workbook. To view this structure, rename the file, adding a .zip extension to the end of the file name. For example, if your file name is **Chapter 25 - Simple Ribbon.xlsm**, rename it **Chapter 25 - Simple Ribbon.xlsm.zip**. You can then use your zip utility to access the folders and files within.

Copy your customui folder and file into the zip file, as shown in Figure 25-3. After placing them in the .xlsm file, you need to let the rest of the Excel file know that they are there and what their purpose is. To do that, you need to modify the RELS file, as described in the next section.

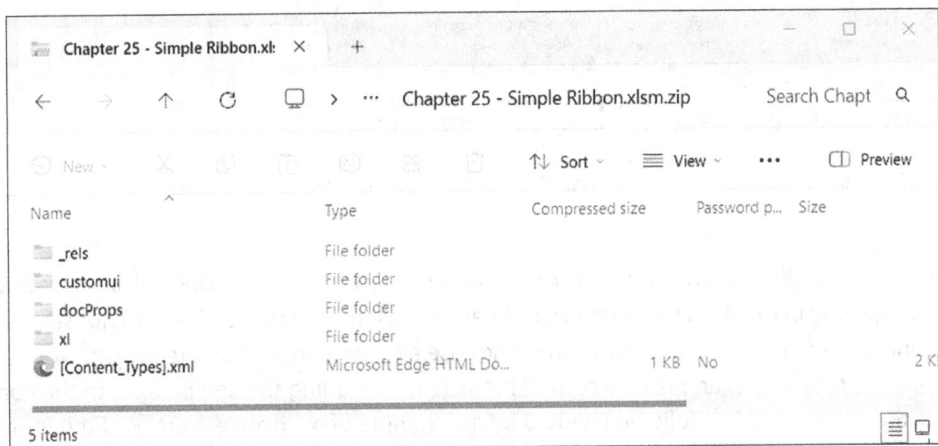

FIGURE 25-3 Using a zip utility, open the .xlsm file and copy over the customui folder and its file.

Understanding the RELS file

The RELS file, found in the _rels folder, contains the various relationships of an Excel file. Extract this file from the zip file and open it using a text editor.

The file already contains existing relationships that you do not want to change. Instead, you need to add one for the customui folder. Scroll all the way to the right of the <Relationships line and place your cursor before the </Relationships> tag, as shown in Figure 25-4. Insert the following code:

```
<Relationship Id="rAB67989"
Type="http://schemas.microsoft.com/office/2007/relationships/ui/_
extensibility"
Target="customui/customUI14.xml"/>
```

Id is any unique string to identify the relationship. If Excel has a problem with the string you enter, it might change the string when you open the file. Target is the customui folder and file. Save your changes and add the RELS file back to the zip file.

> **Note** See the "Found a problem with some content" section later in this chapter for more information.

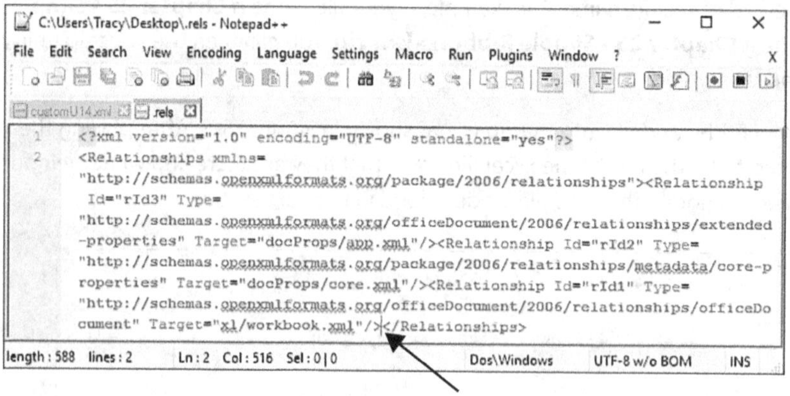

FIGURE 25-4 Place your cursor in the correct spot for entering your custom ribbon relationship.

> **Caution** Even though the previous code appears as four lines in this book, it should appear as a single line in the RELS file. If you want to enter it as three separate lines, do not separate the lines within the quoted strings, and do not use a continuation character as you would in VBA. The preceding examples are correct breaks (not including the line break with the continuation character). The following would be an example of an incorrect break of the fourth line:

```
Target = "customui/
customUI14.xml"
```

Renaming an Excel file and opening a workbook

Rename the Excel file back to its original name by removing the .zip extension. Open your workbook.

> **Note** If any error messages appear when you open the Excel file, see "Troubleshooting error messages" later in this chapter.

It can be a little time-consuming to perform all the steps involved in adding a custom ribbon, especially if you make little mistakes and have to keep renaming your workbook, opening the zip file, extracting your file, modifying, adding it back to the zip, renaming, and testing. To reduce the number of steps and just concentrate on the XML code, check out the Office RibbonX Editor tool, a GitHub open-source project created by Fernando Andreu. Download that program from *https://github.com/fernandreu/office-ribbonx-editor*. This tool updates the RELS file, helps with using custom images, and validates your code.

Using images on buttons

The image that appears on a button can be either an image from the Microsoft Office icon library or a custom image you create and include in the workbook's `customui` folder. With a good icon image, users can tell at a glance what a button is for, especially with a program they use often.

Using Microsoft Office icons on a ribbon

Microsoft has made it fairly easy to reuse Microsoft's button images in custom ribbons. Select File | Options | Customize Ribbon. Place your mouse pointer over any menu command in the list, and a ScreenTip displays, providing more information about the command. Included at the very end, in parentheses, is the image name, as shown in Figure 25-5.

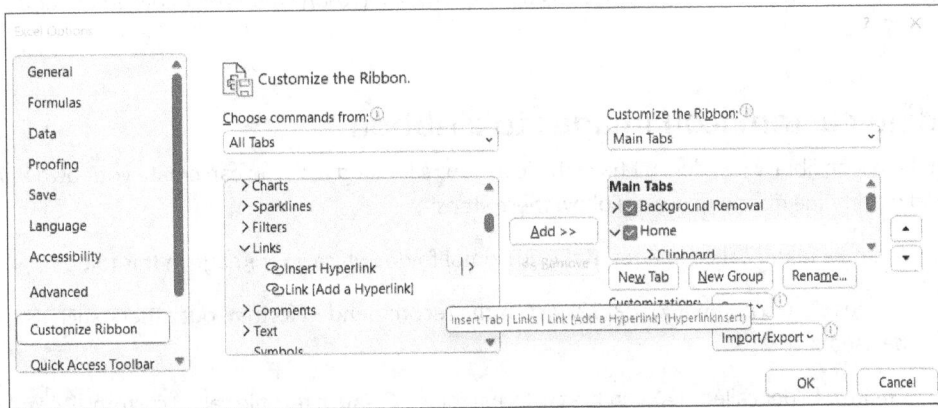

FIGURE 25-5 Placing your pointer over a command, such as Link [Add a Hyperlink], brings up the icon name HyperlinkInsert.

To place an image on your button, you need to go back into the customUI14.xml file and tell Excel what you want. The following code uses the `HyperlinkInsert` icon for the `HelloWorld` button and makes it large, as shown in Figure 25-6. (Note that the icon name is case-sensitive.)

```
<customUI xmlns="http://schemas.microsoft.com/office/2009/07/customui">
  <ribbon startFromScratch="false">
    <tabs>
      <tab id="CustomTab" label="My First Ribbon">
        <group id="CustomGroup" label="My Programs">
          <button id="button1" label="Click to run"
          onAction="Module1.HelloWorld"
          imageMso="HyperlinkInsert" size="large"/>
        </group>
```

```
            </tab>
          </tabs>
        </ribbon>
      </customUI>
```

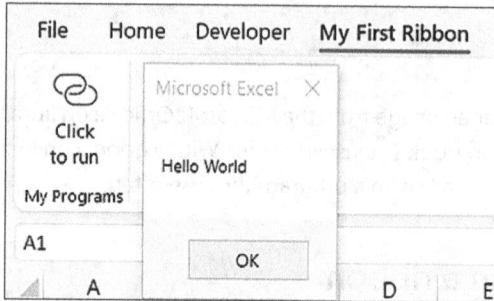

FIGURE 25-6 You can apply the image from any Microsoft Office icon to your custom button.

You aren't limited to just the icons available in Excel. You can use the icon for any installed Microsoft Office application. You can download a Word document from Microsoft with two galleries showing the icons available (and their names) from *http://www.microsoft.com/en-us/download/details.aspx?id=21103*.

Adding custom icon images to a ribbon

What if the icon library just doesn't have the icon you're looking for? You can create your own image file and modify the ribbon to use it. Follow these steps:

1. Create a folder called images in the customui folder. Place your image in this folder.

    Images should be 16x16 or 32x32. PNG is the recommended format, but others, such as JPG, can be used.

2. Create a folder called _rels in the customui folder. Create a text file called customUI14.xml.rels in this new folder, as shown in Figure 25-7. Place the following code in the file (and note that the Id for the image relationship is the name of the image file, helloworld.png):

    ```
    <?xml version="1.0" encoding="UTF-8" standalone="yes"?>
    <Relationships xmlns="http://schemas.openxmlformats.org/package/2006/_
    relationships"><Relationship Id="helloworld"_
    Type="http://schemas.openxmlformats.org/officeDocument/2006/ _
    relationships/image"
    Target="images/helloworld.png"/></Relationships>
    ```

3. Open the customUI14.xml file and add the image attribute to the control, as shown here, before you save and close the file:

    ```
    <customUI xmlns="http://schemas.microsoft.com/office/2009/07/customui">
      <ribbon startFromScratch="false">
        <tabs>
    ```

```xml
<tab id="CustomTab" label="My First Ribbon">
  <group id="CustomGroup" label="My Programs">
    <button id="button1" label="Click to run"
    onAction="Module1.HelloWorld" image="helloworld"
    size="large"/>
  </group>
</tab>
</tabs>
</ribbon>
</customUI>
```

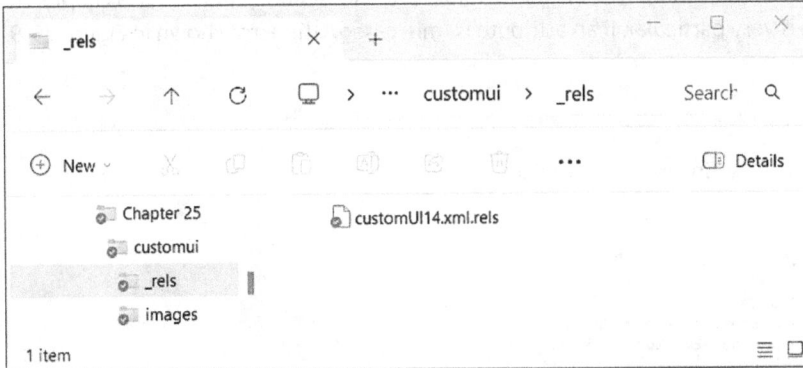

FIGURE 25-7 Create a _rels folder and an images folder within the `customui` folder to hold files relevant to your custom image.

4. Open the [Content_Types].xml file and add the following at the very end of the file but before `</Types>`:

```xml
< Default Extension="png" ContentType="image/.png"/>
```

> **Note** If your image is a JPG, you would use the following:
>
> ```xml
> <Default Extension="jpg" ContentType="application/octet-stream"/>
> ```

5. Save your changes, rename your folder, and open your workbook. The custom image appears on the button, as shown in Figure 25-8.

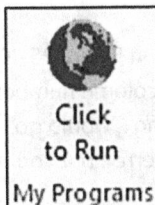

FIGURE 25-8 With a few more changes to your customui folder, you can add a custom image to a button.

Troubleshooting error messages

To be able to see the error messages generated by a custom ribbon, go to File, Options, Advanced, General and select the Show Add-In User Interface Errors option.

The attribute "*Attribute Name*" on the element "customui ribbon" is not defined in the DTD/schema

As noted in the "Where to add code: The customui folder and file" section earlier in this chapter, the case of the attribute is very particular. If an attribute is "mis-cased," the error shown in Figure 25-9 might occur.

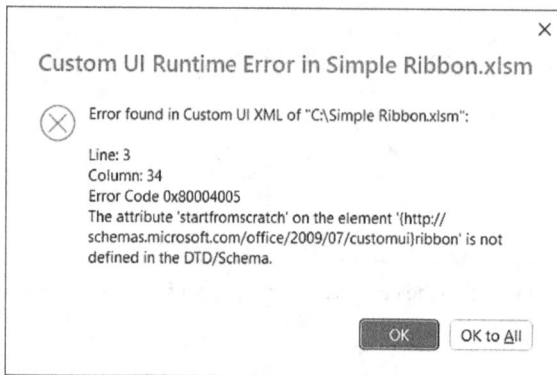

```
                                                              ×
 Custom UI Runtime Error in Simple Ribbon.xlsm

  ⊗    Error found in Custom UI XML of "C:\Simple Ribbon.xlsm":

       Line: 3
       Column: 34
       Error Code 0x80004005
       The attribute 'startfromscratch' on the element '{http://
       schemas.microsoft.com/office/2009/07/customui}ribbon' is not
       defined in the DTD/Schema.



                                  [   OK   ]   [ OK to All ]
```

FIGURE 25-9 Mis-cased attributes can generate errors. Read the error message carefully; it might help you trace the problem.

The code in the customUI14.xml file that generated the error included the following line:

```
<ribbon startfromscratch="false">
```

Instead of `startFromScratch`, the code contained `startfromscratch` (all lowercase letters). The error message even helps you narrow down the problem by naming the attribute with which it has a problem.

Illegal qualified name character

For every opening <, you need a closing >. If you forget a closing >, the error shown in Figure 25-10 might appear. The error message is not specific at all, but it does provide a line and column number to indicate where it's having a problem. Still, it's not the actual spot where the missing > would go. Instead, it's the beginning of the next line. You have to review your code to find the error, but you have an idea of where to start.

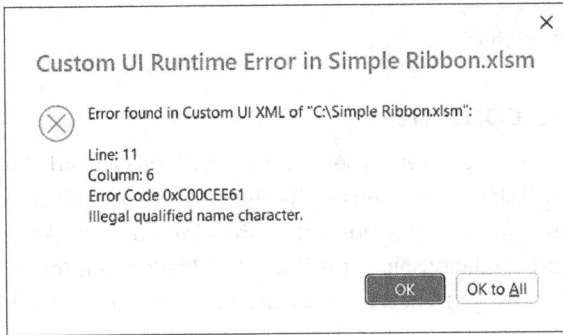

FIGURE 25-10 For every opening <, you need a closing >.

The following code in the customUI14.xml file generated the error:

```
<tab id="CustomTab" label="My First Ribbon">
  <group id="CustomGroup" label="My Programs"
    <button id="button1" label="Click to run"
    onAction="Module1.HelloWorld" image="helloworld_png"
    size="large"/>
```

Note the missing > for the group line (the second line of code). The line should have been this:

```
<group id="CustomGroup" label="My Programs">
```

Element "*customui Tag Name*" is unexpected according to content model of parent element "*customui Tag Name*"

If your structure is in the wrong order, such as the group tag placed before the tab tag, as shown here, a chain of errors appears, beginning with the one shown in Figure 25-11.

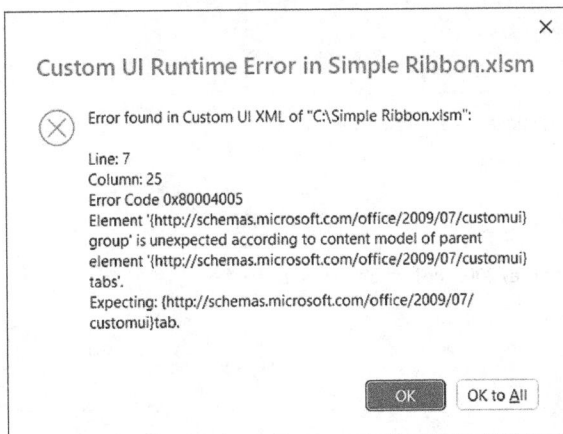

FIGURE 25-11 An error in one line can lead to a string of error messages because the other lines are now considered out of order.

```
<group id="CustomGroup" label="My Programs">
  <tab id="CustomTab" label="My First Ribbon">
```

Found a problem with some content

Figure 25-12 shows a generic catchall message for different types of problems Excel can find. If you click No, the workbook doesn't open. If you click Yes, you then receive the message shown in Figure 25-13. While creating ribbons, though, I found it appearing most often when Excel doesn't like the Relationship ID I have assigned to the customui relationship in the RELS file. What's nice is that if you click Yes in the Found A Problem dialog, Excel assigns a new ID, and when you save and reopen the file, the error should not appear.

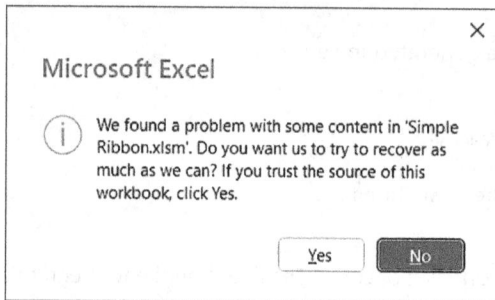

FIGURE 25-12 This rather generic message could appear for many reasons. Click Yes to try to repair the file.

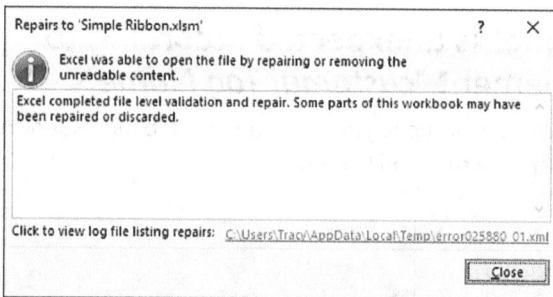

FIGURE 25-13 Excel lets you know whether it has succeeded in repairing the file.

Here's the original relationship:

```
<Relationship Id="rId3"
Type="http://schemas.microsoft.com/office/2007/relationships/ui/ _
extensibility"
Target="customui/customUI14.xml"/>
```

Here's the Excel-modified relationship:

```
<Relationship Id="rE1FA1CF0-6CA9-499E-9217-90BF2D86492F"
Type="http://schemas.microsoft.com/office/2007/relationships/ui/ _
extensibility"
Target="customui/customuUI14.xml"/>
```

In the RELS file, the error also appears if you split the relationship line within a quoted string. You might recall that you were cautioned against this in the "Understanding the RELS file" section earlier in this chapter. In this case, Excel could not fix the file, and you must make the correction yourself.

Wrong number of arguments or invalid property assignment

If there is a problem with the procedure being called by a control, you might see the error message in Figure 25-14 when you try to run code from your ribbon. For example, the `onAction` of a button requires a single `IRibbonControl` argument, such as the following:

```
Sub HelloWorld(control As IRibbonControl)
```

It would be incorrect to leave off the argument, as shown here:

```
Sub HelloWorld()
```

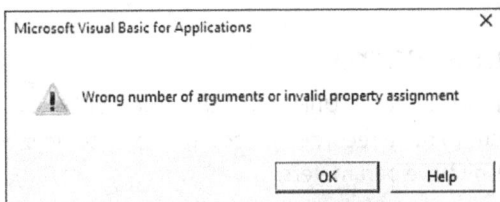

FIGURE 25-14 It's important for the subs being called by your controls to have the proper arguments. Refer to Table 25-2 for the various control arguments.

Invalid file format or file extension

The error message shown in Figure 25-15 looks rather drastic, but it could be deceiving. You could get it if you're missing quotation marks around an attribute's value in the RELS file. For example, look carefully at the following line, and you'll see that the `Type` value is missing its quotation marks:

```
Type=http://schemas.microsoft.com/office/2007/relationships/ui/extensibility
```

The line should have been this:

```
Type="http://schemas.microsoft.com/office/2007/relationships/ui/extensibility"
```

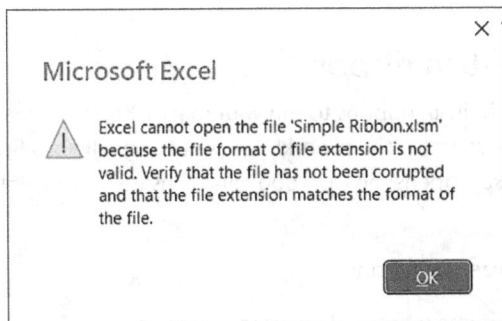

FIGURE 25-15 A missing quotation mark can generate a drastic message, but it's easily fixed.

Nothing happens

If you open your modified workbook and your ribbon doesn't appear—but you don't get an error message—double-check your RELS file. It's possible that you forgot to update it with the required relationship to your customUI14.xml file.

Other ways to run a macro

Using a custom ribbon is the most elegant way to run a macro; however, if you have only a couple of macros to run, it can be a bit of work to modify the file. You could have the client invoke a macro by going to the View tab, selecting Macros, View Macros, and then selecting the macro from the Macros dialog and clicking the Run button, but this is a bit unprofessional—and tedious. Other options are discussed in the following sections.

Using a keyboard shortcut to run a macro

In the section "Filling out the Record Macro dialog" in Chapter 1, "Unleashing the power of Excel with VBA," you learned how to set up a keyboard shortcut to run a recorded macro. You can also do it with a sub you create, as long as it's not Private and doesn't have parameters.

1. Open the Macro dialog by selecting the Developer or View tabs and clicking Macros, or simply by pressing Alt+F8.

2. Select the macro.

3. Click Options and assign a shortcut key to the macro.

4. Click OK, followed by Cancel, to return to the sheet.

> **Caution** When learning how to fill out the Record Macro dialog in Chapter 1, we discussed how many keys are already mapped to important Windows shortcuts. The letters J and M are usually good choices because, as of Excel 365, they had not yet been assigned to Excel's "Ctrl+" shortcut combinations.

Adding a macro button on a built-in ribbon

You can add an icon to a new group on one of the built-in ribbons to run your macro. Keep in mind that icons added to the ribbon are still enabled even when your macro workbook is not open. If you click the icon when the macro workbook is not open, Excel opens the workbook and runs the macro. Follow these steps to add a macro button to the ribbon:

1. Right-click the ribbon and choose Customize The Ribbon.

2. In the list box on the right, choose the tab name where you want to add an icon.

3. Click the New Group button below the list box on the right. Excel adds a new entry called New Group (Custom) to the end of the groups in that ribbon tab.

4. To move the group to the left in the ribbon tab, click the up arrow icon on the right side of the dialog several times.

5. To rename the group, click the Rename button. Type a new name, such as **Report Macros**. Click OK. Excel shows the group in the list box as Report Macros (Custom). Note that the word *Custom* does not appear in the ribbon.

6. Open the upper-left dropdown and choose Macros from the list. The Macros category is fourth in the list. Excel displays a list of available macros in the left list box.

7. Choose a macro from the left list box. Click the Add button in the center of the dialog. Excel moves the macro to the right list box in the selected group. Excel uses a generic VBA icon for all macros.

8. Click the macro in the right list box. Click the Rename button at the bottom of the right list box. Excel displays a list of 180 possible icons. Choose an icon. Alternatively, type a friendly label for the icon, such as Format Report.

9. You can move the Report Macros group to a new location on the ribbon tab. Click Report Macros (Custom) and use the up and down arrow icons on the right of the dialog.

10. Click OK to close the Excel Options dialog. The new button appears on the selected ribbon tab.

Creating a macro button on the Quick Access Toolbar

You can add an icon to the Quick Access Toolbar to run a macro. If a macro is stored in the Personal Macro Workbook, you can have the button permanently displayed in the Quick Access Toolbar. If the macro is stored in the current workbook, you can specify that the icon should appear only when the workbook is open. Follow these steps to add a macro button to the Quick Access Toolbar:

1. Right-click the Quick Access Toolbar and choose Customize Quick Access Toolbar.

2. If your macro should be available only when the current workbook is open, open the upper-right dropdown and change For All Documents (Default) to For *FileName.xlsm*. Any icons associated with the current workbook are displayed at the end of the Quick Access Toolbar.

> **Caution** If the user has already customized their QAT, your icons may be too far to the right to be visible. Consider creating a custom ribbon or using another method to run your macros.

3. Open the upper-left dropdown and select Macros from the list. The Macros category is fourth in the list. Excel displays a list of available macros in the left list box.

4. Choose a macro from the left list box. Click the Add button in the center of the dialog. Excel moves the macro to the right list box. Excel uses a generic VBA icon for all macros.

5. Click the macro in the right list box. Click the Modify button at the bottom of the right list box. Excel displays a list of 180 possible icons (see Figure 25-16). Choose an icon from the list. In the Display Name box, replace the macro name with a short name that appears in the tooltip for the icon.

6. Click OK to close the Modify Button dialog.

7. Click OK to close the Excel Options dialog. The new button appears on the Quick Access Toolbar.

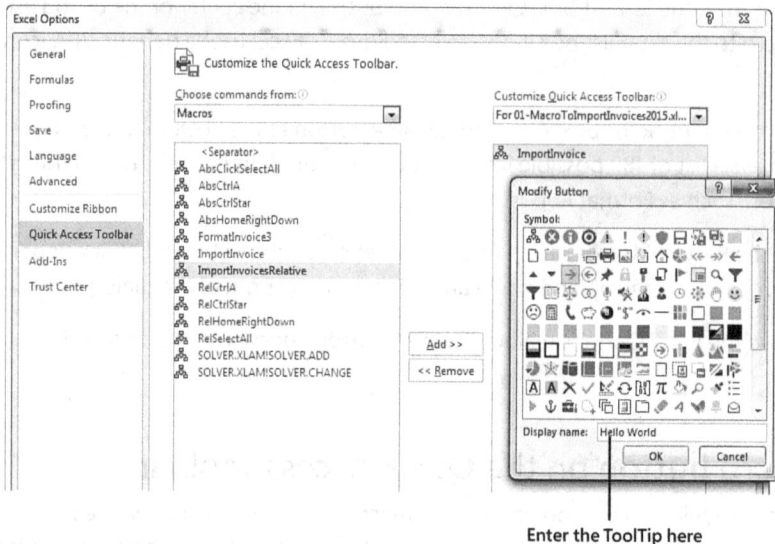

Enter the ToolTip here

FIGURE 25-16 You can attach a macro to a button on the Quick Access Toolbar.

Attaching a macro to a command button

Two types of buttons can be embedded in a sheet: the traditional button shape that you can find in the Form Controls section and an ActiveX command button. You can access both on the Developer tab under the Controls | Insert option.

Attaching a macro to a Form Control button

Form controls are the original worksheet controls and work on both Windows and Mac. They're fairly basic; for example, you can't change their background color. However, if you just need a simple button to trigger a macro, the Form Control button is the way to go. To add a Form Control button with a macro to your sheet, follow these steps:

1. On the Developer tab, click the Insert button and select the button control from the Form Controls section of the dropdown, as shown in Figure 25-17.

Place your cursor in the worksheet where you want to insert the button, and then click and drag to create the shape of the new button. When you release the mouse button, the Assign Macro dialog displays.

2. In the Assign Macro dialog, select a macro to assign to the button and click OK.

3. Highlight the text on the button and type new meaningful text.

4. To change the font, text alignment, and other aspects of the button's appearance, right-click the button and select Format Control from the pop-up menu.

> **Caution** If you only see the Font tab in the Format Control dialog, you were in Text Edit mode when you right-clicked on the button. To exit Text Edit mode, close the dialog, click a cell so you deselect the button, then right-click the button and select Format Control.
>
> A quick way to tell if you're in Text Edit mode is that the Assign Macro option is unavailable in the context menu.

FIGURE 25-17 The Form Controls are found under the Insert icon on the Developer tab.

5. To reassign a new macro to the button, right-click the button and select Assign Macro from the context menu.

Attaching a macro to an ActiveX control

ActiveX controls are newer than Form Controls and slightly more complicated to set up. Instead of simply assigning a macro to a button, you have a Click event where you can either call an existing macro or have the macro code embedded in the event. Follow these steps:

1. On the Developer tab, click the Insert button and select the Command Button icon from the ActiveX Controls section.

2. Place your cursor in the worksheet where you want to insert the button, and then click and drag to create the shape of the new button.

3. To format the button, right-click the button and select Properties or select Controls | Properties from the Developer tab. You can now adjust the button's caption and color in the Properties window, as shown in Figure 25-18. If nothing happens when you right-click the button, enter Design mode by clicking the Design Mode button on the Developer tab.

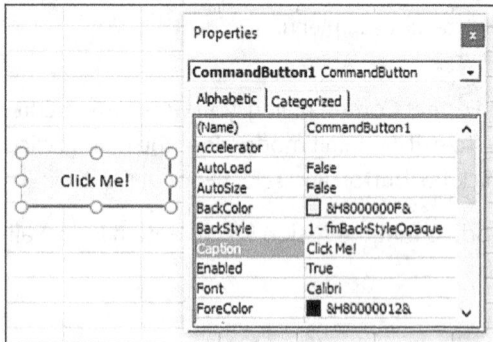

FIGURE 25-18 Use the Properties window to adjust aspects of the ActiveX button.

4. To assign a macro to the button, right-click it and select View Code. This creates the header and footer for the Click event in the code window for the current worksheet. Type the code you want to run or the name of the macro you want to call.

> **Note** There is one annoying aspect of this Properties window: It is huge and covers a large portion of your worksheet. Eventually, if you want to use the worksheet, you're going to have to resize or close this Properties window. When you close the Properties window, it is also hidden in the VB Editor. I prefer to be able to close this Properties window without affecting my VB Editor environment.

Attaching a macro to a shape

The previous methods assigned a macro to an object that looks like a button. You can also assign a macro to any drawing object on the worksheet. To assign a macro to an Autoshape (which you get by selecting Insert | Illustrations | Shapes), right-click the shape and select Assign Macro, as shown in Figure 25-19.

This method is useful because you can easily add a drawing object with code and use the OnAction property to assign another macro to the object. There is one big drawback to this method: If you assign a macro that exists in another workbook, and the other workbook is saved and closed, Excel changes the OnAction for the object to be hard-coded to a specific folder.

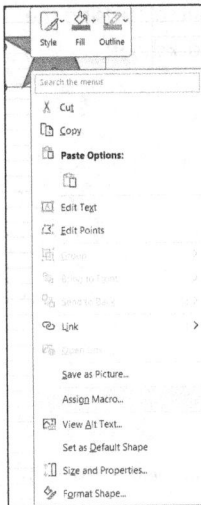

FIGURE 25-19 Macros can be assigned to any drawing object on the worksheet.

Running a macro from a hyperlink

There is a trick you can use to run a macro from a hyperlink. Because many people are used to clicking a hyperlink to perform an action, this method might be the most intuitive for your clients.

The trick is to set up placeholder hyperlinks that simply link back to themselves. Right-click the cell with the text you want to link to, and from the context menu, select Link. In the Insert Hyperlink dialog, click Place In This Document. Figure 25-20 shows a worksheet with four hyperlinks. Each hyperlink points back to its own cell.

> **Note** To open the Insert Hyperlink dialog from the ribbon, go to Insert | Links, and click the Link button (not the dropdown).

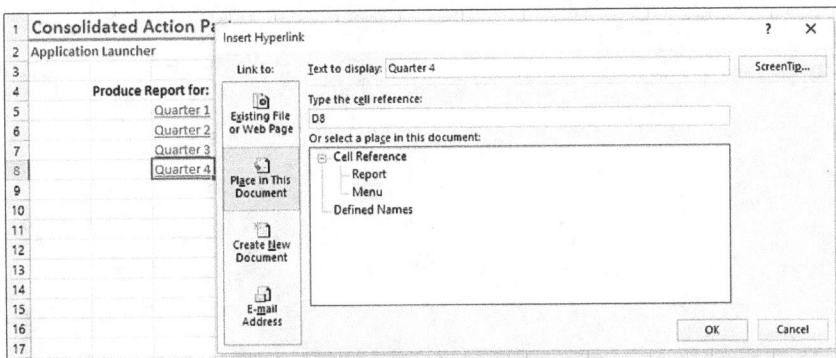

FIGURE 25-20 To run a macro from a hyperlink, you must create placeholder hyperlinks that link back to their cells. Then, using an event handler macro in the worksheet's code module, you can intercept the hyperlink and run any macro.

When a client clicks a hyperlink, you can intercept this action and run any macro by using the FollowHyperlink event. Enter the following code in the code module for the worksheet:

```
Private Sub Worksheet_FollowHyperlink(ByVal Target As Hyperlink)
Select Case Target.TextToDisplay
  Case "Quarter 1"
    RunQuarter1Report
  Case "Quarter 2"
    RunQuarter2Report
  Case "Quarter 3"
    RunQuarter3Report
  Case "Quarter 4"
    RunQuarter4Report
End Select
End Sub
```

The corresponding code will run depending on the text in the hyperlink's cell. So, if the user clicks Quarter 2, then the RunQuarter2Report macro will run.

Next steps

From custom ribbons to simple buttons or hyperlinks, there are plenty of ways to ensure that your clients never need to see the Macro dialog. In Chapter 26, you find out how to package your macros into Excel add-ins that you can easily distribute to others.

Creating Excel add-ins

In this chapter, you will:

- Learn what a standard add-in is

- Learn how to create, install, and uninstall an add-in

- Use a hidden workbook as an alternative to an add-in

You can create standard add-in files for your clients to use by employing VBA. After the client installs your add-in on her PC, the program will be available to Excel and will load automatically every time she opens Excel. This chapter discusses standard add-ins.

> **Note** Office Scripts are not considered add-ins. They're a separate automation feature designed specifically for Excel Online and are only available when a workbook is stored in OneDrive or SharePoint. You won't see the Automate tab unless those conditions are met. For a brief introduction to Office Scripts, see "Introduction to Office Scripts in Excel Online" in Chapter 27.

Be aware that there are two other types of add-ins: COM add-ins and Office add-ins. Neither of these can be created with VBA. You need either Visual Basic .NET or Visual C++ to create COM add-ins. Office add-ins are built using HTML, CSS, and JavaScript with the Office JavaScript API. Chapter 27, "An introduction to creating Office add-ins," familiarizes you with the basics of creating Office add-ins.

Characteristics of standard add-ins

If you are going to distribute an application, you might want to package the application as an add-in. Typically saved with an `.xlam` extension, an add-in offers several advantages:

- Usually, clients can bypass your `Workbook_Open` code by holding down the Shift key while opening the workbook. With an add-in, they cannot bypass the `Workbook_Open` code in this manner.

- After you use the Add-ins dialog to install an add-in (by selecting File | Options | Add-ins | Manage Excel Add-Ins | Go), the add-in will always be loaded and available.

- Programs in an installed add-in can still run even if the macro security level is set to disallow macros.

- Generally, custom functions work only in the workbook in which they are defined. A custom function added to an add-in is available to all open workbooks.

- The add-in does not show up in the list of open files in the Window menu item. The client cannot unhide the workbook by choosing View | Window | Unhide.

> **Caution**   There is one strange rule for which you need to plan. An add-in is a hidden workbook. Because the add-in can never be displayed, your code cannot select or activate any cells in the add-in workbook. You are allowed to save data in your add-in file, but you cannot select any part of the file. Also, if you do write to your add-in file data that you want to be available in the future, your add-in code needs to handle saving the file. Because your clients will not realize that the add-in is there, they will never be reminded or asked to save an unsaved add-in. You might, therefore, add `ThisWorkbook.Save` to the add-in's `Workbook_BeforeClose` event.

Converting an Excel workbook to an add-in

Add-ins are typically managed using the Add-Ins dialog. This dialog presents an add-in name and description, which you control by entering two specific properties for the file before you convert it to an add-in.

> **Note**   If you're modifying an existing add-in, you must make it visible before you can edit the properties. See the section "Using the VB Editor to convert a file to an add-in" later in this chapter.

To change the title and description shown in the Add-Ins dialog, follow these steps:

1. Select File | Info. Excel displays the Document Properties pane on the right side of the window.

2. From the Properties dropdown menu, select Advanced Properties.

3. Enter the name for the add-in in the Title field.

4. Enter a short description of the add-in in the Comments field (see Figure 26-1).

5. Click OK to save your changes.

6. Click the back arrow at the top left of the screen to return to your workbook.

There are two ways to convert a file to an add-in. The first method, using Save As, is easier but has an annoying by-product. The second method uses the VB Editor and requires two steps, but it gives you some extra control. The sections that follow describe the steps for using these methods.

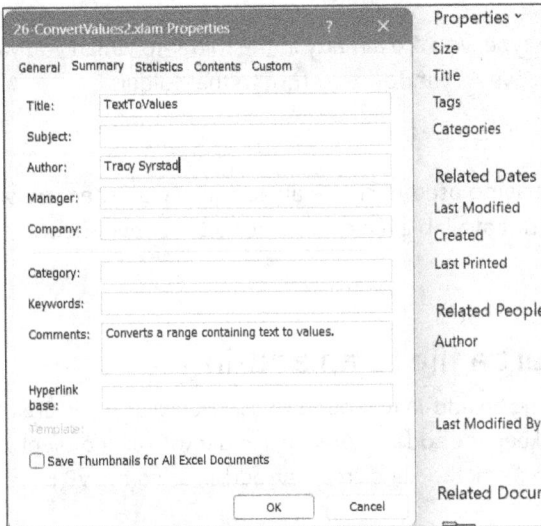

FIGURE 26-1 Fill in the Title and Comments fields before converting a workbook to an add-in.

Using Save As to convert a file to an add-in

Select File | Save As | Browse. In the Save As Type field, scroll through the list and select Excel Add-In (`*.xlam`).

As shown in Figure 26-2, the file name changes from `filename.xlsm` to `filename.xlam`. Also, note that the save location automatically changes to an AddIns folder. The location of this folder varies by operating system, but it will be something along the lines of `C:\Users\username\AppData\Roaming\Microsoft\AddIns`. This is also confusing because after the `.xlsm` file is saved as an `.xlam` type, the unsaved `.xlsm` file remains open. It is not necessary to keep an `.xlsm` version of the file because it is easy to change an `.xlam` back to an `.xlsm` for editing.

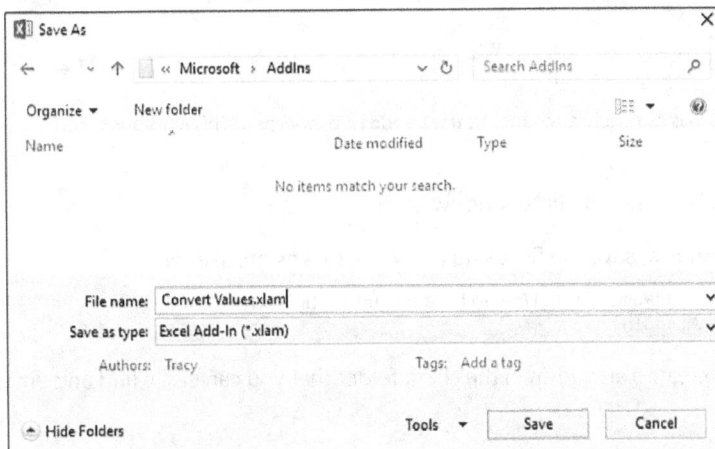

FIGURE 26-2 The Save As method changes the `IsAddin` property, changes the name, and automatically saves the file in your AddIns folder.

> **Tip** If, before selecting the add-in file type, you are already in the folder to which you want to save, just click the back arrow in the Save As window to return to that folder.

> **Caution** When the Save As method is being used to create an add-in, a worksheet must be the active sheet. The add-in file type is not available if a chart sheet is the active sheet.

Using the VB Editor to convert a file to an add-in

The Save As method is great if you are creating an add-in for your own use. However, if you are creating an add-in for a client, you probably want to keep the add-in stored in a folder with all the client's application files. It is fairly easy to bypass the Save As method and create an add-in using the VB Editor:

1. Open the workbook that you want to convert to an add-in.

2. Switch to the VB Editor.

3. In the Project Explorer, click ThisWorkbook.

4. In the Properties window, find the property called IsAddin and change its value to True, as shown in Figure 26-3.

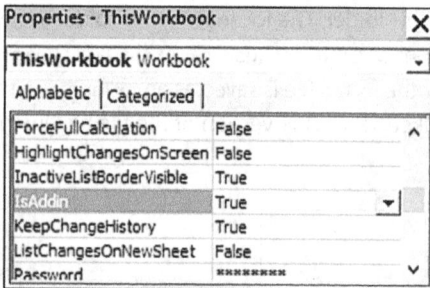

FIGURE 26-3 Creating an add-in is as simple as changing the IsAddin property of ThisWorkbook.

5. Press Ctrl+G to display the Immediate window.

6. In the Immediate window, save the file using an .xlam extension, like this:

```
ThisWorkbook.SaveAs FileName:="C:\ClientFiles\Convert Values.xlam", _
FileFormat:= xlOpenXMLAddIn
```

You've now successfully created an add-in in the client folder that you can easily find and email to your client.

Having a client install an add-in

When you email an add-in to a client, have them save it on their desktop or in another easy-to-find folder. You should tell them to follow these steps:

1. Open Excel and select File | Options. The Excel Options dialog appears.

2. In the left navigation pane, select Add-Ins.

3. At the bottom of the window, select Excel Add-Ins from the Manage dropdown menu (see Figure 26-4).

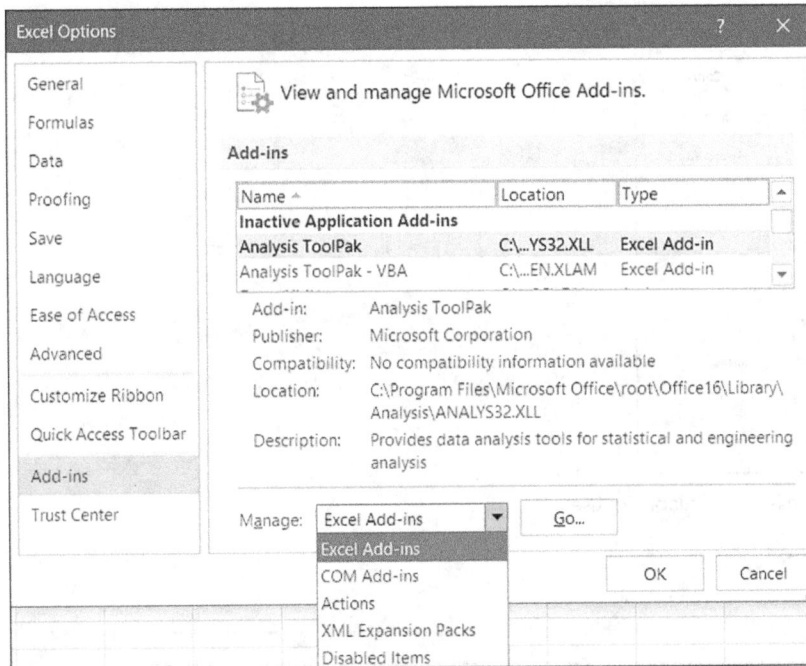

FIGURE 26-4 Make sure to select Excel Add-Ins, not COM Add-Ins, from the dropdown menu.

4. Click Go. Excel displays the familiar Add-Ins dialog shown in Figure 26-5.

5. In the Add-Ins dialog, click the Browse button.

6. Browse to where you saved the file. Highlight the add-in and click OK.

The add-in is now installed. If you allow it, Excel copies the file from where you saved it to the default AddIns folder. In the Add-ins dialog, the title of the add-in and comments, as specified in the File Properties dialog, are displayed (see Figure 26-5).

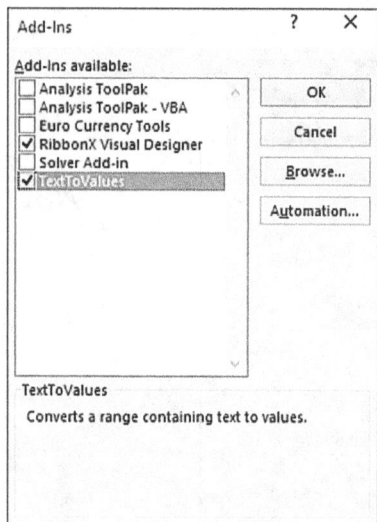

FIGURE 26-5   The add-in is now available for use.

Add-in security

Remember that anyone can go to the VB Editor, select your add-in, and change the IsAddin property to False to unhide the workbook. You can discourage this process by locking the .xlam project for viewing and protecting it in the VB Editor, but be aware that plenty of vendors sell a password-hacking utility for less than $40. To add a password to your add-in, follow these steps:

1.   Go to the VB Editor.

2.   Select Tools | VBAProject Properties.

3. Select the Protection tab.

4. Select the Lock Project for Viewing checkbox.

5. Enter the password twice for verification.

> **Caution** If you protect the code and don't include error handling, people won't be able to click the Debug button if an error message appears. See Chapter 24, "Handling errors," for more information on handling errors in code so that the program ends properly and still provides customers with error information they can pass to you.

Closing add-ins

Add-ins can be closed in three ways:

- Clear the add-in from the Add-Ins dialog. This closes the add-in for this session and ensures that it does not open during future sessions.

- Use the VB Editor to close the add-in. In the VB Editor's Immediate window, type this code to close the add-in:

```
Workbooks("YourAddinName.xlam").Close
```

- Close Excel. All add-ins are closed when Excel is closed.

Removing add-ins

You might want to remove an add-in from the list of available add-ins in the Add-Ins dialog. However, Excel doesn't provide a built-in method to accomplish this. To fully remove it from the list, follow these steps:

1. Close all running instances of Excel.

2. Use Windows Explorer to locate the file. The file might be located in %AppData%\Microsoft\AddIns\.

3. In File Explorer, rename the file or move it to a different folder.

4. Open Excel. You get a message warning you that the add-in could not be found. Click OK to dismiss this warning.

5. Select Excel Add-Ins on the Developer tab. In the Add-Ins dialog, clear the name of the add-in you want to remove. Excel notifies you that the file cannot be found and asks if you want to remove it from the list. Click Yes.

Case study: Maintaining code updates without disrupting user data

Access developers routinely use a separate database to hold macros and forms. They place all forms and programs in one database and all data in a second database. These database files are linked through the Link Tables function in Access.

For large projects in Excel, I recommend using a similar method: provide an Excel Add-in with all the code and forms and a separate Data workbook for the user to interact with.

The advantage of this method is that when it is time to enhance the application, you can mail a new add-in file without affecting the client's data file.

The potential downside is that if the add-in is stored locally, some users may end up running an outdated version. To work around this, you can compare version numbers—checking the version of the running add-in against the latest version stored in a text file.

> **Tip** If the add-in is installed from a Trusted Network Location, IT only has to replace the add-in. The next time the user opens Excel, the updated version will load automatically. But still, you might want to add the following method to ensure the update went smoothly.

In Chapter 19, "Text file processing," you learned how to read from a text file. You can use that method for version control by hard-coding the add-in's version number in the code and storing the most current version number in a text file. Call the sub from the add-in's Workbook_Open event. When Excel (and the add-in) opens, it checks the version number in the text file and compares it to the hard-coded value. The code to do this would look something like this:

```
Sub CheckForUpdateUsingTextFile()
Dim currentVersion As String, latestVersion As String
Dim versionFilePath As String
Dim fso As Object, ts As Object
'Hard-coded current version of the add-in
currentVersion = "1.0.0"
'full path to version text file
versionFilePath = ThisWorkbook.Path & "\Version.txt"
'Create a FileSystemObject to read the file
Set fso = CreateObject("Scripting.FileSystemObject")
'Check if the version file exists
If fso.FileExists(versionFilePath) Then
  'Open the version file for reading (1 = ForReading)
  Set ts = fso.OpenTextFile(versionFilePath, 1)
  If ts.AtEndOfStream = True Then
    'file is empty
```

```
        MsgBox "Version file empty" & Chr(10) & versionFilePath, vbExclamation
    Else
      latestVersion = ts.ReadLine
    End If
    ts.Close
    If latestVersion <> "" Then
      'Compare the current version with the latest version from the text file
      If currentVersion <> latestVersion Then
        MsgBox "A new version (" & latestVersion & _
          ") is available. You are running version " & currentVersion & ".", _
          vbInformation, ThisWorkbook.Name & " - Update Available"
      Else
        MsgBox "You are using the latest version (" & currentVersion & ").", _
          vbInformation, ThisWorkbook.Name & " - Up To Date"
      End If
    End If
  Else
    MsgBox "Version file not found.", vbExclamation, "Error"
  End If
  Set fso = Nothing
  Set ts = Nothing
End Sub
```

> **Note** See Chapter 7, "Event programming," for instructions on setting up the
> `Workbook_Open` event.

This dual-workbook solution works well and allows updates to be seamlessly delivered to the client.

Using a hidden workbook as an alternative to an add-in

One cool feature of an add-in is that the workbook is hidden. This keeps most beginners from poking around and changing formulas. However, it is possible to hide a workbook without creating an add-in.

It's easy to hide a workbook by selecting View | Window | Hide. The trick is to save the workbook when it's hidden. With a file that is hidden, the normal File | Save choice isn't an option. You can save the file from the VB Editor's Immediate window. In the VB Editor, make sure that the workbook is selected in the Project Explorer. Then, in the Immediate window, type the following:

```
ThisWorkbook.Save
```

There is a downside to using a hidden workbook: A custom ribbon tab will not be visible if the workbook it is attached to is hidden.

Next steps

Excel add-ins are a great way to distribute VBA-based tools. However, what if your users aren't allowed to use VBA, or you want to distribute your add-in to a wider audience? Microsoft offers a new way of sharing applications with customers: Office add-ins. These are programs that use JavaScript, HTML, and XML to embed a web page on a sheet. Chapter 27 introduces you to what is involved in creating these apps and deploying them over a network.

An introduction to creating Office Add-ins

In this chapter, you will:

■ Create an Office Add-in

■ Add interactivity to an Office Add-in

■ Learn the basics of HTML and JavaScript

■ Use XML to define an Office Add-in

■ Take a look at Office Scripts in Excel Online

Office Add-ins are applications that provide expanded functionality to a sheet, such as a selectable calendar, or an interface with the web, for example, retrieving information from Wikipedia or Bing. Like Excel add-ins, once Office Add-ins are installed, they're always available. But unlike Excel add-ins, the Office Add-ins have limited interaction with sheets and do not use VBA.

An Office Add-in consists of a web app and a manifest file. The web app can simply be an HTML file that provides the user interface on a task or content pane accompanied by a CSS file to provide styles for the HTML file. Or you can include interactivity by using JavaScript that calls the Office.js API. The manifest is an XML file and is used to register the Office Add-in with Excel. This might sound like a lot of new programming skills, but it's not. I've designed only the most basic web pages, and that was years ago, but I was able to apply my VBA programming skills to JavaScript, which is where the bulk of the programming goes. The language is a little different, but it's not so different that you can't create a simple, useful app.

This chapter introduces you to creating an Office Add-in, followed by the basics of the various programming languages used to create the add-in. It is not meant to provide in-depth instruction, especially for JavaScript.

> **Note** JavaScript custom functions are user-defined functions (UDFs) you create for use with Excel Online. They use the same JavaScript API as Office Add-ins, Office.js. This book doesn't cover creating them. For more information, see *Excel JavaScript UDFs Straight to the Point* by Suat M. Ozgur (ISBN 978-1-61547-247-5).

Tip You don't need a fancy program to write the code for any of the files in an Office Add-in. The Notepad program that comes with Windows does the job. But when you consider the case sensitivity of some programming languages, like JavaScript, using a program that provides some help is a good idea. I spent a couple of hours in frustration over some of the samples in this chapter, wondering why they didn't work when the code was perfect. Except the code wasn't perfect. Again and again, I missed the case sensitivity in JavaScript and XML, and, in one case, I had a curly apostrophe instead of a straight one.

Switching to Notepad++ (*www.notepad-plus-plus.org*) was a quick and easy solution because it highlights keywords and grays out strings (which is how I found the incorrect apostrophe around a string).

Creating your first Office Add-in—Hello World

Hello World is probably the most popular first program for programmers to try out. It's a simple program, just outputting the words "Hello World," but it introduces the basics required by the application. So, with that said, it's time to create a Hello World Office Add-in.

Caution A network-accessible location is required to host the manifest file (XML). You cannot use a local drive or a network drive mapped to a drive letter. If you do not have access to a web server or local development server, you will not be able to test the Office Add-in.

A web server that supports security protocols, such as SSL, is required to host the web app part of the program. The files for the web apps used in this chapter can be found in folders at the following base URL: *https://pub.mrexcel.com/microsoft-365-excel-vba-and-macros/office_add-ins/*. To view a file, include the specific folder and file name to the base URL. For example, to see the CSS code used in the HelloWorld sample, go to *https://pub.mrexcel.com/microsoft-365-excel-vba-and-macros/office_add-ins/interactive-sample/program.css*.

Caution The manifest file and web app files do not have to be in the same location. You can edit your manifest file to point to my hosted app files. However, your manifest file must be stored in a trusted catalog.

> **Note** In the following steps, you enter text into a text editor. Unlike with the VB Editor, there isn't a compiler to point out mistakes before you run the program. You must enter the text exactly as written, including the case of text within quotation marks.
>
> To open a file for editing, such as with Notepad, right-click the file and select Open With. If you see Notepad, select it; otherwise, select Choose Another App. From the dialog that opens, find Notepad. Make sure that Always Use This App To Open *filetype* Files is *not* selected, and then click OK. The next time you need to edit the file, Notepad appears in the quick list of available programs in the Open With option.

Follow these steps to create your Office Add-in:

1. Create a folder and name it **HelloWorld**. This folder can be on your local drive while you are creating the program. All the web app files will be placed in this folder. When you're finished, you'll have to move them to a web server.

2. Create the HTML program by inserting a text file in the folder and naming it **HelloWorld. html**. Then, open the HTML file for editing and enter the following code into it:

```
<!DOCTYPEhtml>
<html>
  <head>
    <meta charset="UTF-8"/>
    <meta http-equiv="X-UA-Compatible" content="IE=Edge"/>
    <link rel="stylesheet" type="text/css" href="program.css"/>
  </head>
  <body>
    <p>Hello World!</p>
  </body>
</html>
```

Save and close the file.

3. Create the CSS file to hold the styles used by the HTML file by inserting a text file into the folder and naming it program.css. Note that this is the same file name used in the HTML file in the `<link rel>` tag. Open the CSS file for editing and enter the following code in it:

```
body
{
  position:relative;
}
li :hover
{
  text-decoration: underline;
  cursor:pointer;
}
h1,h3,h4,p,a,li
{
  font-family: "Segoe UI Light","Segoe UI",Tahoma,sans-serif;
  text-decoration-color:#4ec724;
}
```

Save and close the file.

4. Create the manifest file by creating a text file and naming it **HelloWorld.xml**. Then, open the XML file for editing and enter the following code into it:

> **Caution** The following code sample and others that follow include lines that extend beyond the width of the page, so I needed to add a _ to indicate a line that is continued. Unlike in VBA, in this case, you should not type the underscores. Instead, when you get to an underscore, just ignore it and continue inputting the code after it on the same line.

```xml
<?xml version="1.0" encoding="utf-8"?>
<OfficeApp xmlns="http://schemas.microsoft.com/office/appforoffice/1.1"
  xmlns:xsi = "http://www.w3.org/2001/XMLSchema-instance"
 xsi:type="TaskPaneApp">
 <Id>08afd7fe-1631-42f4-84f1-5ba51e242f98</Id>
 <Version>1.0</Version>
 <ProviderName>Tracy Syrstad</ProviderName>
 <DefaultLocale>EN-US</DefaultLocale>
 <DisplayName DefaultValue="Hello World app"/>
 <Description DefaultValue="My first app."/>
 <IconUrl DefaultValue=
    "https://pub.mrexcel.com/microsoft-365-excel-vba-and-macros/office_add-ins/ _
       HelloWorld/world-icon.png"/>
 <Hosts>
   <Host Name="Workbook"/>
 </Hosts>
 <DefaultSettings>
   <SourceLocation _
      DefaultValue="https://pub.mrexcel.com/microsoft-365-excel-vba-and-macros _
      /office_add-ins/HelloWorld/HelloWorld.html"/>
 </DefaultSettings>
 <Permissions>ReadWriteDocument</Permissions>
</OfficeApp>
```

Do not close the XML file yet.

5. While the XML file is still open, note the ID 08afd7fe-1631-42f4-84f1-5ba51e242f98. This is a globally unique identifier (GUID). If you are testing on a private network and not distributing this file, you can likely use this GUID. But if you're on a business network with other programmers or if you're distributing the file, you must generate your own GUID. See the section "Using XML to define an Office Add-in," later in this chapter, for more information on GUIDs.

6. Move the HelloWorld folder to a web server if it's not already there. Note the path to the folder and to the HTML file because you will be making use of this information. For example, my HelloWorld folder is located at *https://pub.mrexcel.com/microsoft-365-excel-vba-and-macros/office_add-ins/HelloWorld*.

7. Open the XML file for editing and change <SourceLocation> (located near the bottom of the code) to the location of the HTML file on your web server. Save and close the file.

8. Configure your network share as a Trusted Catalog Address by following these steps:

A. Start Excel and go to File | Options | Trust Center and click Trust Center Settings.

B. Select Trusted Add-In Catalogs from the list on the left side of the dialog.

C. Enter your folder path in the Catalog URL field and click Add Catalog. The path is added to the list box.

D. Select the Show In Menu box.

E. Click OK. You should see a prompt indicating that the Office Add-in will be available the next time Excel starts (see Figure 27-1). Click OK twice.

9. Restart Excel.

> **Caution** Only one of each catalog type can be configured to show in the catalog. If you want users to have access to multiple Office Add-ins at once, the XML for the Office Add-ins must be stored in the same network share. Otherwise, users will have to go into their settings and select which catalog to show.

10. Go to Developer, Add-Ins. In the Office Add-Ins dialog, select Shared Folder. If you don't see anything when you've selected the link, click Refresh. The Hello World Office Add-in should be listed, as shown in Figure 27-2.

> **Note** If you still do not see anything after refreshing, there is something incorrect in the files or the setup. Carefully review all the code and steps. If you do not see anything incorrect, try changing the GUID.

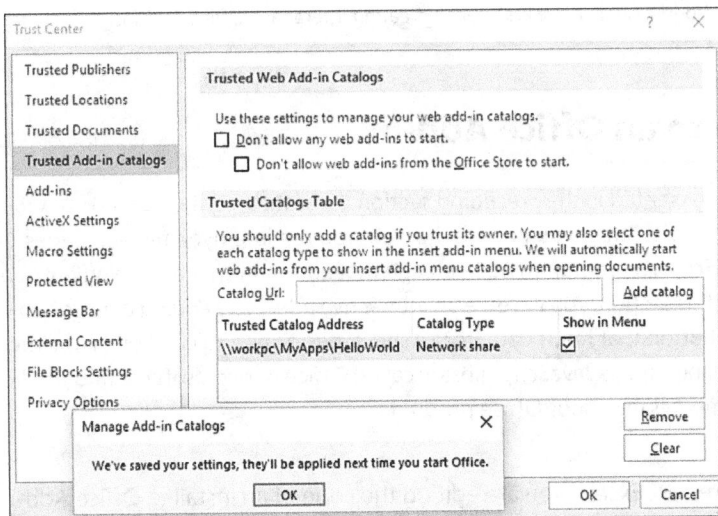

FIGURE 27-1 Configure the location of your Office Add-ins under Trusted Add-in Catalogs.

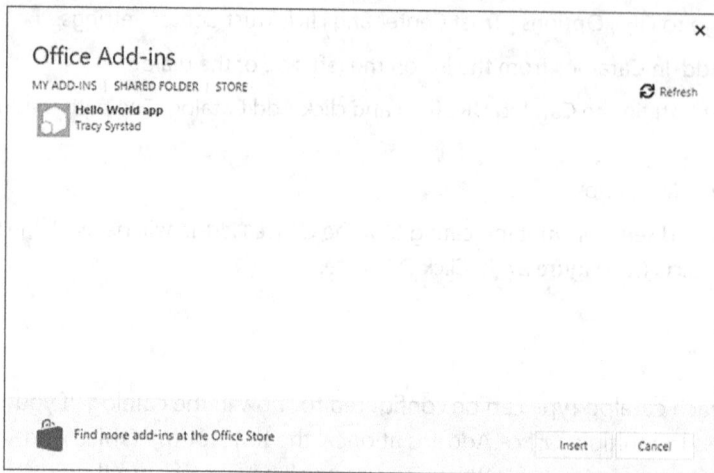

FIGURE 27-2 The Shared Folder lists any Office Add-ins available in the active catalog.

11. Select the Office Add-in and click Insert. A task pane on the right side of the Excel window opens, as shown in Figure 27-3, and displays the words "Hello World!"

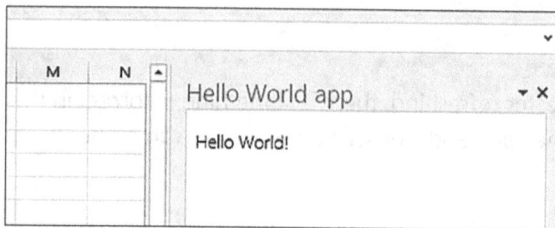

FIGURE 27-3 By creating Hello World, you take the first step in creating interactive Office Add-ins.

Adding interactivity to an Office Add-in

The Hello World Office Add-in created in the preceding section is a static one; it doesn't do anything except show the words in the code. But as you browse the web, you run into dynamic web pages. Some of those web pages use JavaScript, a programming language that adds automation to elements on otherwise static websites. In this section, you'll create an interactive add-in by adding a button to write data to a sheet and another button that reads data from a sheet, performs a calculation, and writes the results to the task pane. We'll be using a JavaScript library called Office.js. Microsoft created this library to provide access to object models in various Office programs.

> **Tip** You don't have to restart Excel if you are editing the code of an installed Office Add-in. Instead, click the Office Add-in's task pane to bring up the right-side pop-out menu arrow, open the menu, and select Refresh.

To create an interactive add-in, follow these steps:

1. Create a folder for the web app and name it interactive-sample.

2. To create the JavaScript file that will provide the interactivity for the two buttons, Write Data To Sheet and Read & Calculate Data From Sheet, first, insert a text file in the interactive-sample folder and name the file **program.js**. Then, open it for editing and enter the following code in it:

```javascript
// Check if the Office.js library is loaded
Office.onReady(function(info) {
  // Initialization code (if needed)
});
//declare and set the values of an array
const myArray = [[234],[56],[1798], [52358]];
//write myArray contents to the active sheet
function writeData() {
  Office.context.document.setSelectedDataAsync(myArray, _
    {coercionType: 'matrix'});
}
/*reads the selected data from the active sheet
so that we have some content to read*/
function ReadData() {
  Office.context.document.getSelectedDataAsync("matrix", _
    function (result) {
    //if the cells are successfully read, print the results in the task pane
    if (result.status === "succeeded"){
      sumData(result.value);
    }
    //if there was an error, print the error in the task pane
    else{
      document.getElementById("results").innerText = _
        result.error.name;
    }
  });
}

/*the function that calculates and shows the result
in the task pane*/
function sumData(data) {
  let printOut = 0;
  //sum together all the values in the selected range
  for (let x = 0 ; x < data.length; x++) {
    for (let y = 0; y < data[x].length; y++) {
        printOut += data[x][y];
    }
  }
//print the results in the task pane
  document.getElementById("results").innerText = printOut;
}
```

3. Save and close the file.

4. Create the HTML program ExcelCalc.html that points to the JavaScript file program.js, and add the two buttons used by the JavaScript code. Remember—do not include the _ as you enter the following HTML code:

```html
<!DOCTYPEhtml>
<html>
    <head>
        <meta charset="UTF-8"/>
        <meta http-equiv="X-UA-Compatible" content="IE=Edge"/>
        <link rel="stylesheet" type="text/css" href="program.css"/>
<!--begin pointer to JavaScript file-->
        <script src = "https://appsforoffice.microsoft.com/lib/1/ _
            hosted/office.js"></script>
        <script src= "program.js"></script>
<!--end pointer to JavaScript file-->
    </head>
    <body>
<!--begin replacement of body-->
        <button onclick="writeData()">Write Data To Sheet</button></br>
        <button onclick="ReadData()">Read & Calculate Data From Sheet _
</button></br>
        <h4>Calculation Results: <div id="results"></div> </h4>
<!--end replacement of body-->
    </body>
</html>
```

In this new code, you've added `<script>` tags and replaced the code between the `<body>` tags. Comment tags, `<!--comments-->`, are included to show where the changes are compared to HelloWorld.html.

5. Save and close the file.

6. Copy the CSS file from HelloWorld.

7. Copy and rename the XML file to **Interactive.xml**. Change the `SourceLocation` to point to the new HTML file, like this:

```
"https://pub.mrexcel.com/microsoft-365-excel-vba-and-macros/office_add-ins/ _
interactive-sample/ExcelCalc.html"/>
```

Since GUIDs must be unique, change the last digit in the GUID from 8 to 7. Give the app a new `DisplayName`, such as `Interactive app`.

8. After ensuring the web app files are on the web server and the manifest file is on the network share, open the Add-ins catalog and go to Shared Folder. If you don't see your new app, click Refresh in the top-right corner.

9. Add the Interactive app and test it by clicking the Write Data To Sheet button. It should write the numbers from myArray onto the sheet.

10. With those cells selected, click Read & Calculate Data From Sheet, and the results of adding the selected numbers together will appear in the Calculation Results line of the task pane, as shown in Figure 27-4.

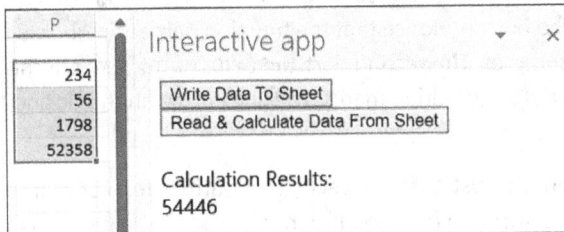

FIGURE 27-4 Use JavaScript to create an Office Add-in that can perform a calculation with data from a sheet.

A basic introduction to HTML

The HTML code in an Office Add-in controls how the task or content pane will look, such as the text and buttons. If you open the HTML file from either add-in, it opens in your default browser and looks as it did in Excel's task pane (though without any functionality). You can design the Office Add-in as you would a web page, including adding images and links. The following sections review a few basics to get you started in designing your own Office Add-in interface.

Using tags

HTML consists of elements, such as images, links, and controls, that are defined by the use of tags enclosed in angle brackets. For example, the starting tag <button> tells the code that what follows, inside and outside the tag's brackets, relates to a button element. For each start tag, you have an end tag, which is usually the same as the opening tag but with a slash—like </button>—but some tags can be empty—like />. A browser does not display tags or anything within a tag's brackets. The text that you want to display needs to be outside the tag's brackets.

Comments have a tag of their own and don't require your typical end tag. As in VBA, commented text doesn't appear on the screen. Add comments to your HTML code like this:

```
<!--This is a comment-->
```

A multiline comment would appear like this:

```
<!--This is a multiline comment.
Notice that nothing special is needed -->
```

Adding buttons

To create the code for a button, you need to label the button and link it to a function in the JavaScript file that will run when the button is clicked. Here's an example:

```
<button onclick="writeData()">Write Data To Sheet</button>
```

The first part, `<button onclick="writeData()">`, identifies the control as a button and assigns the function `writeData` to the click event for the button. Notice that the function name is in quotation marks and includes empty argument parentheses. The second part, `Write Data To Sheet`, is the text of the label on the button. The label name is not in quotation marks. The line ends with the closing tag for the button.

To change other attributes of the button, you just need to specify those attributes. For example, to change the button text to red, add the style attribute for color, like this:

```
<button onclick="writeData()" style="color:Red">Write Data To Sheet</button>
```

To add a tooltip that appears when the mouse is placed over the button, as shown in Figure 27-5, use the `title` attribute, like this:

```
<button onclick="writeData()" style="color:Red"
 title = "Use to quickly add numbers to your sheet">
 Write Data To Sheet</button></br>
```

Use a space to separate multiple attributes. After an attribute name, such as `style`, put an equal sign and then the value in quotation marks. Also, notice that HTML is rather forgiving about where you put your line breaks. Just don't put them within a string, or you might also get a line break on the screen in that position.

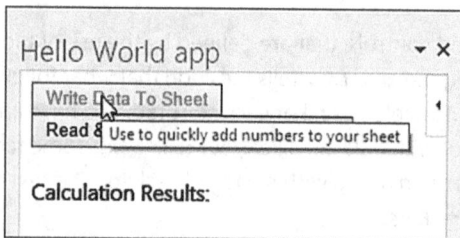

FIGURE 27-5 Add other attributes to your button to change colors or add tooltip text for users.

Using CSS files

CSS stands for Cascading Style Sheets. You create styles in Excel and Word to make it easy to modify how text looks in an entire file without changing every occurrence. You can do the same thing with an Office Add-in by creating a separate style file (CSS) that your HTML code references. In the file, you set up rules for various elements of the HTML file, such as layout, colors, and fonts.

The CSS file provided for the examples can be used for a variety of projects. It includes styles for h1, h3, and h4 headings, hyperlinks (a), paragraph tags (p), and bullets (li).

Using XML to define an Office Add-in

The manifest XML file defines the elements needed to display and run an Office Add-in in Excel, including the GUID, Office Add-in logo, and location of the HTML file. XML also configures how the Office Add-in will appear in the Office Add-ins store and can provide a version number for the program.

> **Caution** XML tags are case-sensitive. When you make changes to the provided samples, be sure you don't change any of the tags but only their values.

Three types of user interfaces are available for an Office Add-in: a task pane, a content pane, or a mail pane. A task pane starts off docked on the right side of the Excel window, but a user can undock it and move it around the window. A content add-in appears as a floating frame within the worksheet. A mail add-in, available in Outlook, appears next to the currently viewed item, such as an email or meeting request. To tell an Office Add-in which type of pane to use, set the `xsi:type` value to either `TaskPaneApp`, `ContentApp`, or `MailApp`.

The GUID is a unique reference number that identifies software. It's usually displayed as 32 alphanumeric digits separated into five groups (8-4-4-4-12) with hyphens. A GUID has so many digits that it's rare for identical ones to be generated. You should always use a unique identifier when creating an Office Add-in. Websites such as *http://www.guidgen.com* generate GUIDs for you.

The store icon should be small, 32×32 pixels for content and task pane apps and 64×64 for mail apps. Update `IconURL` with the full path to the image, like this:

```
<IconUrl DefaultValue="https://pub.mrexcel.com/microsoft-365-excel-vba-and-macros/
office_add-ins/interactive-sample/world-icon.png"/>
```

The `SourceLocation` tag is used to set the full path to the HTML file. If the HTML file cannot be found when the Office Add-in is being installed, an error message appears, stating there was a problem when trying to reach the add-in.

> **Note** If you make changes to XML after you've already configured the location of the catalog or installed the Office Add-in, be sure to click the Refresh link in the Office Add-Ins dialog. For example, if you switch between `TaskPaneApp` and `ContentApp`, the change might not be reflected even if you select to install the Office Add-in again. To be safe, refresh the Office Add-Ins dialog. If that doesn't work, you may have to clear the Add-ins cache by clicking the Clear button in the Trust Center dialog for the catalogs.

Using JavaScript to add interactivity to an Office Add-in

JavaScript provides the wow factor behind an Office Add-in. You can create a very useful reference with just HTML, but to make an interactive Office Add-in, such as a function calculator, you need JavaScript.

The following sections provide a basic introduction to JavaScript. If you are already familiar with JavaScript, you can go ahead to "JavaScript changes for working in an Office Add-in."

> **Note** The `document.getElementById("results").innerText` command used in the following examples is the command for the code to put the returned value in the place reserved by the "results" variable in the HTML file.

> **Note** Microsoft is always making improvements to the JavaScript API, expanding its capabilities to handle Excel's objects. You can keep up with these changes at the API reference site: *https://learn.microsoft.com/en-us/office/dev/add-ins/reference/overview/excel-add-ins-reference-overview*.

The structure of a function

JavaScript code consists of functions called by HTML code and by other JavaScript functions. Just as in VBA, each JavaScript function starts with `Function` followed by the name of the function and any arguments in parentheses. But unlike in VBA, there is no `End Function` at the end; instead, you use curly braces to group the function. See the following subsection, "Curly braces and spaces," for more information.

JavaScript is case-sensitive, including variable and function names. For example, if you create a function called `writeData` but then try to call `WriteData` from another function, the code does not work because, in one case, *write* is in lowercase, and in the other, it has a capital *W*. JavaScript recognizes these as different functions. Create case rules for yourself, such as initial caps for each word in a variable, and stick to them. This helps reduce troubleshooting of JavaScript code issues.

Curly braces and spaces

Curly braces (`{}`) are characters used in JavaScript but not in VBA. You use them to group blocks of code that should be executed together. You can have several sets of braces within a function. For example, you would use them to group all the code in a function; then, within the function, you would use them to group lines of code, such as within an `if` statement.

After you've finished typing a line in VBA and gone to another line, you might notice that the line adjusts itself, adding or removing spaces. In JavaScript, spaces don't usually matter; the exceptions are spaces in strings and spaces between keywords and variables in the code. In the code samples in this section, notice that sometimes I have included spaces (a = 1) and sometimes I have not (a=1); both lines mean the same thing.

Semicolons and line breaks

You've probably noticed the semicolons (;) used in JavaScript code. They might have appeared at the end of every line or maybe only on some lines. Perhaps you've noticed a line without a semicolon or noticed a semicolon in the middle of a line. The reason the use of semicolons appears inconsistent is that, under normal circumstances, semicolons are not required. A semicolon is a statement terminator, similar to the colon (:) in VBA. If you use hard returns in your code, you are already placing line breaks, so the semicolon is not needed. If you combine multiple lines of code onto one line, though, you need a semicolon to let the code know that the next piece of code is not part of the previous code.

> **Tip** Despite semicolons being voluntary, I prefer to use them *just in case*. Code can get complicated, indention gets messed up, and blocks can throw you off. But semicolons add clarity, telling you a line has ended.

Comments

There are two ways to comment out lines in JavaScript. To comment out a single line, place two slashes (//) at the beginning of the line, like this:

```
//comment out a single line in the code like this
```

If you want to comment out multiple lines in VBA, you have to preface each line with an apostrophe or use an underscore (_) at the end of each line, as you would if you were wrapping a line of code. JavaScript has a cleaner method. Place a slash and an asterisk (/*) at the beginning of the first line that you want to comment out. Place an asterisk and a slash (*/) at the end of the last line of the comment. It looks like this:

```
/* Comment out
multiple lines of code
like this */
```

Variables

In VBA, you have the option of declaring variables. If you do declare them, you don't have to declare the variable type, but after a value is assigned to a variable, it's not always easy to change the type. In JavaScript, it's strongly recommended you declare variables. Use the let keyword to declare a variable:

```
let myVar;
```

> **Caution** While var can still be used to declare variables, it is considered outdated and should be avoided. The let keyword offers better control. See "Block scoping," later in this chapter, for more information.

Notice there is no variable type in the declaration. Unlike VBA, JavaScript variables are *dynamically typed*—when a value is assigned to a variable, it becomes that type. If you reference the variable in another way, its type might change.

In the following example, the string "123" is assigned to myVar, but in the next line, a number is subtracted:

```
myVar = "123"; //string
myVar = myVar-2; //number
```

JavaScript just goes with it, allowing you to change the variable from a string to a number. If you run this code, myVar would be 121. Note that myVar+2 would not deliver the same result. See the later subsection, "Strings," for more information.

If you need to ensure that a variable is of a specific type, use one of these functions to do so: Boolean, Number, or String. For example, you have a function that reads in numbers imported onto a sheet. As is common in imports, the numbers could be stored as text. Instead of having to ensure that the user converts the data, use the Number keyword when processing the values like this to force the number to be a number:

```
myVar = Number(importedValue);
```

Constants

Another way to declare a variable is the const keyword. This locks the variable so it cannot be reassigned. The exception is the contents of objects or arrays—the variable cannot be reassigned, but the contents can be modified.

When declaring a constant, you must assign the value at the same time, like this:

```
const x = 5;
const Total = Price * Quantity;
//the following would be incorrect if following the above lines
const x = 6; //you cannot change the value
Total = 77; //you cannot change the value
```

Block scoping

In VBA, when you declare a variable within a procedure, it has procedure-level scope—it can be used anywhere in that procedure after the declaration line. In JavaScript, variables can be declared at the procedure level or within a specific block (such as inside an if statement). Variables declared within a block have *block scope*, meaning they are only accessible inside that block.

The following code won't work because result is declared inside the for loop using let, which means it's block-scoped. The variable only exists within the loop block. Outside the loop, result is undefined and cannot be accessed. To fix this, result should be declared outside the loop.

Note that i is also block-scoped; if you decide to use that variable in another loop, you will have to declare it again.

```
for (let i = 0; i<3; i++) {
let result = "";
result += "Inside loop: " + i + "<br>";
}
document.getElementById("demo").innerHTML = "The result is: " + result;
```

Strings

As in VBA, in JavaScript, you reference strings by using double quotation marks ("string"), but, unlike in VBA, you can also use single quotation marks ('string'). The choice is up to you; just don't start a string with one type of quotation mark and end with another. The capability to use either set can be useful. For example, if you want to show quoted text, you use single quotes around the entire string, like this:

```
document.getElementById("results").innerText = 'She heard him shout, ' +
'"Stay _ away!"';
```

This would be the result in the pane:

```
She heard him shout, "Stay away!"
```

To concatenate two strings, as shown in the previous line, use the plus (+) sign. You also use the plus to add two numbers. So, what happens if you have a variable hold a number as text and add it to a number, as in this example:

```
let myVar = "123";
myVar = myVar+2;
```

You might think that the result would be 125. After all, in the previous example, with -2, the result was 121. In this case, concatenation has priority over addition, and the answer is actually 1232. To ensure that the variable is treated like a number, use the Number function, like this:

```
myVar = Number(myVar) + 2;
```

If the variable it is holding cannot be converted to a number, the function returns NaN for "not a number."

Arrays

Arrays are required for processing multiple cells in JavaScript. Arrays in JavaScript are not very different from arrays in VBA. To declare an unlimited-size array, do this:

```
let myArray = new Array ();
```

> **Note** If you are unfamiliar with using arrays in VBA, see Chapter 8, "Arrays."

The array index always starts at 0. To create an array of limited size, such as 3, do this:

```
let myArray = new Array(2);
```

You can also fill an array at the same time that you declare it. The following creates an array of three elements, two of which are strings and the third of which is a number:

```
let myArray = ['first value', 'second value', 3];
```

To print the second element, second value, of the preceding array, do this:

```
document.getElementById("results").innerText = myArray[1];
```

If you've declared an array with a specific size but need to add another element, you can add the element by specifying the index number or by using the push() function. For example, to add a fourth element, 4, to the previously declared array, myArray, do this (because the count starts at 0, the fourth element has an index of 3):

```
myArray [3] = 4;
```

If you don't know the current size of the array, use the push() function to add a new value to the end of the array. For example, if you don't know the index value for the last value in the preceding array, you can add a new element, fifth value, like this:

```
myArray.push('fifth value');
```

Refer to the section "How to use a For each..next statement in JavaScript" if you need to process the entire array at once. JavaScript has other functions for processing arrays, such as concat(), which can join two arrays, and reverse(), which reverses the order of the array's elements. Because this is just a basic introduction to JavaScript, those functions are not covered here. For a tip on applying a math function to an entire array with a single line of code, see the section "Math functions in JavaScript."

JavaScript for loops

When you added interactivity to the Hello World Office Add-in earlier in this chapter, you used the following code to sum the selected range:

```
for (let x = 0 ; x < data.length; x++) {
  for (let y = 0; y < data[x].length; y++) {
    printOut += data[x][y];
  }
}
```

The two for loops process the array, data, that is passed into the function, with x as the row and y as the column.

A for loop consists of three separate sections separated by semicolons. When the loop is started, the first section, `let x=0`, initializes any variables used in the loop. Commas would separate multiple variables. The second section, `x < data.length`, tests whether the loop should be entered. The third section, x++, changes any variables to continue the loop, in this case, incrementing x by 1 (x++ is short-hand for x=x+1). This section can also have more than one variable, with commas separating them.

> **Tip** To break out of a loop early, use the `break` keyword.

How to do an `if` statement in JavaScript

The basic `if` statement in JavaScript has this syntax:

```
if (expression){
  //do this
}
```

Here, `expression` is a logical function that returns `true` or `false`, just as in VBA. If the expression is `true`, the code continues and runs the lines of code in the `//do this` section. To execute code if the expression is `false`, you need to add an `else` statement, like this:

```
if (expression){
  //do this if true
}
else{
  //do this if false
}
```

How to do a `Select..Case` statement in JavaScript

`Select..Case` statements are very useful in VBA as an alternative to using multiple `If..Else` statements. In JavaScript, similar functionality is in the `switch()` statement. Typically, this is the syntax of a `switch()` statement:

```
switch(expression){
  case firstcomparison : {
    //do this
    break;
  }
  case secondcomparison : {
    //do this
    break;
  }
  default : {
    //no matches, so do this
    break;
  }
}
```

Here, expression is the value you want to compare to the case statements. The break keyword is used to stop the program from comparing to the next statement, after it has run one comparison. That is one difference from a Select statement: Whereas in VBA, after a comparison is successful, the program leaves the Select statement, in JavaScript, without the break keyword, the program continues in the switch statement until it reaches the end. Use default as you would a Case Else in VBA—to cover any comparisons that are not specified.

The preceding syntax works for one-on-one comparisons. If you want to see how an expression fits within a range, the standard syntax won't work. You need to replace the expression with true to force the code into running the switch statement. The case statements are where you use the expression compared to the range. The following code is a little guessing game I wrote. The program picks a random number, and you get one chance to guess what it is. Select the cell with your guess, run the program, and it returns a text description to post to the task pane:

```javascript
//check if the Office.js library is loaded
Office.onReady(function(info) {
//Add any needed initialization.
});
function getNumberToGuess(){
  //get the value of the selected cell
  Office.context.document.getSelectedDataAsync("matrix", function(result){
    let myAnswer;
    //using = will set the status, so use == or ===
    if(result.status=="succeeded"){
      //generate a random number 1-10
      let randomNumber = Math.floor(Math.random()*10 + 1);
      let data = result.value; //get user entry
      let cellValue = data[0][0];
      if (cellValue === "") {
        myAnswer = "No value found in active cell";
      }
      else {
        let userNumber = Number(cellValue);
        switch (true){
          /*use === for comparison
          Using = would assign a value*/
          case ((userNumber <= 0)||(userNumber>10)):
            myAnswer = "Enter a number 1-10 and try again";
            break;
          case (randomNumber == userNumber):
            myAnswer = "You got it! I was thinking of "+ randomNumber;
            break;
          case (randomNumber != userNumber):
            myAnswer = "Nope! I was thinking of " + randomNumber;
            break;
          default:
            myAnswer = "something went wrong";
        } //end switch
      } //end if succeeded
    }
```

```
    else{ //not successful
       myAnswer = "Can't read the sheet";
    } // end getSelectedDataAsync
    document.getElementById("results").innerText = myAnswer;
  }); //end getSelectedDataAsync
}// end getNumberToGuess
```

How to use a For each..next statement in JavaScript

If you have a collection of items to process in VBA, you might use a For each..next statement. One option in JavaScript is the for of loop. For example, if you have an array (myArray) of items, you can use the following code to output the list:

```
//set up a variable to hold the output text
let arrayOutput = "";
/*process the array, one value at a time
  item is a variable to hold the current value.
  from the array during each loop pass*/
for (let item of myArray) {
/*create the output by adding the element
  to the previous value in arrayOutput.
  \n is used to insert a line break */
  arrayOutput += item + '\n'
}
//write the output to the screen
document.getElementById("results").innerText = arrayOutput;
```

You can do whatever you need for each element of the array. In this example, you're building a string by adding each element and a line break so that when it prints to the screen, each element appears on its own line, as shown in Figure 27-6. The myArray variable used in this code was filled in the earlier section, "Arrays."

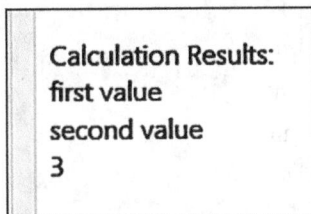

Calculation Results:
first value
second value
3

FIGURE 27-6 JavaScript has its own equivalents to many VBA looping statements, such as the for..of loop, which was used to output each result to its own line.

Mathematical, logical, and assignment operators

JavaScript offers the same basic operators as VBA, plus a few more to shorten your code. Table 27-1 lists the various operators. Assume here that x = 5.

TABLE 27-1 JavaScript operators

Operator	Description	Example	Result
+	Addition	x+5	10
-	Subtraction	x-5	0
/	Division	x/5	1
*	Multiplication	x*5	25
%	Remainder after division	11%x	1
()	Override the usual order of operations	(x+2)*5	35, whereas x+2*5=15
-	Unary minus (for negative numbers)	-x	-5
==	Values are equal	x=='5'	true because JavaScript will coerce the values to the be same type before comparing
===	Values and types are equal	x==='5'	false since the types don't match. x is a number being compared to a string.
>	Greater than	x>10	false
<	Less than	x<10	true
>=	Greater than or equal to	x>=5	true
<=	Less than or equal to	x<=4	false
!=	Values are not equal	x!='5'	false
!==	Values and types are not equal	x!=='5'	true
&&	And	x==5 && 1==1	true
||	Or	x=='5' || 1==2	false
!	Not	!(x==5)	false
++	Increment	++x or x++	6
--	Decrement	--x or x--	4
+=	Equal to with addition	x += 11	16
-=	Equal to with subtraction	x-=22	-17
*=	Equal to with multiplication	x*=2	10
/=	Equal to with division	x/=30	6
%=	Equal to with the remainder	x%=11	1

The increment and decrement operators are two of my favorites; I wish we had them in VBA. Not only do they reduce your code, but they offer flexibility that VBA lacks (post- and pre-increments). You might remember the use of x++ in the interactive sample program earlier in this chapter. You used this in place of x=x+1 to increment the for loop. But it doesn't just increment the value. It uses the value and then increments it. This is called a post-increment. JavaScript also offers a pre-increment, which means the value is incremented and then used. So if you have x=5, both of the following lines of code return 6:

```
//would increment x and then post the value
document.getElementById("results").innerText = ++x; //would return 6
//would post the value of x (now 6 after the previous increment) then increment
document.getElementById("results2").innerText = x++; //would return 6
```

Math functions in JavaScript

JavaScript has several math functions available, as shown in Table 27-2. Using these functions is straightforward. For example, to return the absolute value of the variable myNumber, do this:

```
result = Math.abs(myNumber)
```

TABLE 27-2 JavaScript math functions

Function	Description
Math.abs(a)	Returns the absolute value of a
Math.acos(a)	Returns the arc cosine of a
Math.asin(a)	Returns the arc sine of a
Math.atan(a)	Returns the arc tangent of a
Math.atan2(a,b)	Returns the arc tangent of a/b
Math.ceil(a)	Returns the integer closest to a and not less than a
Math.cos(a)	Returns the cosine of a
Math.exp(a)	Returns the exponent of a (Euler's number to the power a)
Math.floor(a)	Rounds down, and returns the integer closest to a
Math.log(a)	Returns the log of a base e
Math.max(a,b)	Returns the maximum of a and b
Math.min(a,b)	Returns the minimum of a and b
Math.pow(a,b)	Returns a to the power b
Math.random()	Returns a random number between 0 and 1 (but not including 0 or 1)
Math.round(a)	Rounds up or down and returns the integer closest to a
Math.sin(a)	Returns the sine of a
Math.sqrt(a)	Returns the square root of a
Math.tan(a)	Returns the tangent of a

Applying math functions to arrays

If you need to apply a math function to all elements of an array, you can do so by using the map() function and the desired Math function. For example, to ensure that every value in an array is positive, use the Math.abs function. The following example changes each element in an array to its absolute value and then prints the results to the screen, as shown in Figure 27-7:

```
let result = 0;
let arrayOutput = "";
let arrNums = [9, -16, 25, -34, 28.9];
result = arrNums.map(Math.abs);
for (let myValue of result){
  arrayOutput += myValue +'\n';
}
document.getElementById("results").innerText = arrayOutput;
```

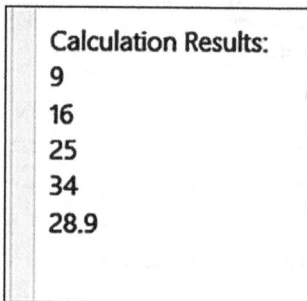

> **Calculation Results:**
> 9
> 16
> 25
> 34
> 28.9

FIGURE 27-7 Using arrays is a common way of storing data in JavaScript, which offers many functions for simplifying working with those arrays.

Writing to the content pane or task pane

After you've processed a user's data, you need to display the results. This can be done on the sheet or in the Office Add-in's pane. Assuming that arrayOutput holds the data you want to write to the pane, do this:

```
document.getElementById("results").innerText = arrayOutput;
```

This code writes data to the Office Add-in's pane, specifically to the HTML element with ID results. To write to the sheet, see "Writing to and reading from a sheet," later in this chapter.

JavaScript changes for working in an Office Add-in

Not all JavaScript code will work in an Office Add-in. For example, you should not use `alert` or `document.write` in Office Add-ins, as they are blocked or can break the page. There are also some new statements for interacting with Excel provided in a JavaScript API that you link to in the HTML file with this line:

```
<script src = "https://appsforoffice.microsoft.com/lib/1/hosted/office.js">
</script>
```

Like the APIs used in VBA, the JavaScript API gives you access to objects, methods, properties, and events that JavaScript can use to interact with Excel. You've now seen some of the most commonly used objects. For more information on these and other available objects, go to *https://learn.microsoft.com/ en-us/office/dev/add-ins/reference/javascript-api-for-office*.

> **Tip** As mentioned previously, `alert` and `document.write` statements won't work. Instead, write directly to the existing HTML element using something like this:
>
> ```
> document.getElementById("results").innerText = "Output goes here.";
> ```

Initializing the Office Add-in

The following event statement must be placed at the top of the JavaScript script:

```
Office.onReady (function (info) {
   //any initialization
});
```

It initializes the Office Add-in to interact with Excel. The `info` parameter returns how the Office Add-in was initialized. If the Office Add-in is inserted for the first time, then `info.reason` will be `inserted`. If the Office Add-in is already part of a workbook that's being opened, then `info.reason` will be `documentOpened`.

Writing to and reading from a sheet

`Office.context.document` represents the object that the Office Add-in is interacting with—the sheet. It has several methods available, most importantly the two that enable you to read selected data and write to a range.

- `setSelectedDataAsync (data, options, callback)`—used to write to a document

- `getSelectedDataAsync (coercionType, options, callback)`—used to read from a document

The following line uses the `setSelectedDataAsync` method to write the values in `myArray` to the selected range on a sheet:

```
Office.context.document.setSelectedDataAsync(myArray, {coercionType: 'matrix'});
```

The first argument, myArray, is the required data. It contains the values to write to the selected range. The second argument, coercionType, is optional; otherwise, it will choose a default depending on the data type. Its value, 'matrix', tells the code that you want the values treated as a two-dimensional array.

> **Note** coercionType is a property within the options object, what we in VBA would call a dictionary. It allows you to specify certain things, such as how you'd like the data, myArray, formatted. The format options are
>
> - 'text'—plain string
> - 'matrix'—2D array
> - 'table'—structured data
> - 'html'—formatted HTML content

The method for reading from a sheet, getSelectedDataAsync, is similar to the write method:

```
Office.context.document.getSelectedDataAsync('matrix', function (result) {
  //code to manipulate the read data, result
});
```

The first argument, 'matrix', is the coercionType and is required. You don't include the coercionType label here because the method is expecting the value of the coercion type—not an object in which you're specifying a property. It tells the method how the selected data should be returned—in this case, in an array. The second argument, options, is unused in this example. The third argument is the optional callback function, with the result being a variable that holds the returned values (result.value) if the call was successful and an error if not.

To find out whether the call was successful, use the status property, result.status. To retrieve the error message, use this:

```
result.error.name
```

Introduction to Office Scripts in Excel Online

While VBA is used in Excel workbooks around the world, Microsoft says it has no plans to support VBA in Excel Online. Microsoft has created a new macro language, Office Scripts, to be used in Excel Online and on the local PC if the account is attached to OneDrive. It's not as complete as VBA, but Microsoft is updating it constantly. This section offers a brief overview of recording, running, and sharing Office Scripts.

Office Scripts is available to Microsoft 365 commercial and educational users, with Home users currently in preview. In addition, you will need your Microsoft 365 administrator to enable them for the company. For the latest rules, open a browser and search for "Introduction to Office Scripts in Excel."

Scripts are accessed locally or online through the Automate tab, not to be mistaken with Power Automate, a separate service. They are stored in your OneDrive account, not in a workbook. This means they're available to all workbooks you open but cannot be shared by simply sending a file.

> **Caution**   Office Scripts and the recording tool are still evolving. Behavior may improve or change over time as Microsoft continues development. Before relying on Office Scripts for critical work, always verify the current capabilities by checking the latest official documentation at *https://learn.microsoft.com/en-us/office/dev/scripts/*.

The Automate ribbon tab

The Automate tab, shown in Figure 27-8, has two buttons you can use to create scripts:

- Record Actions—the script macro recorder

- New Script—an interface to write a script from scratch

The Script Gallery lists available scripts, including some sample Microsoft ones. Clicking on a script will load it into the Code Editor. Click the All Scripts button to have all scripts appear in a task pane.

The Automate Work button connects to Power Automate, Microsoft's cloud-based workflow service. It allows you to trigger an Office Script automatically based on events such as scheduled times, file updates, or button presses. Using Automate Work requires a Power Automate account, and some features may require an additional subscription.

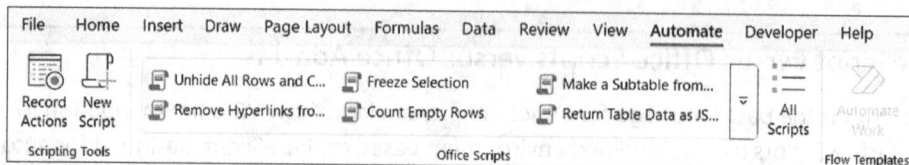

FIGURE 27-8 Record, edit, and run scripts from the Automate tab.

Recording a macro

Recording in Office Scripts is currently limited to basic workbook changes. Confirmed actions that are reliably captured include:

- Editing or entering values into cells

- Applying formatting (such as font changes, fills, number formats, or borders)

- Adding, renaming, moving, or deleting worksheets

- Creating a Table from a data set

- Inserting a pivot table or chart but not modifying elements

By default, the scripts are recorded in absolute mode, but there is an option to enable relative references. The dropdown to switch modes is found on the Record Actions pane, shown in Figure 27-9. This controls how the recorded actions will appear in the code. For example, you start recording in absolute mode, make changes to various cells, then switch to relative mode to make a change to a final cell and stop recording. When you look at the code, everything will be in relative mode because that's the mode you ended your recording with.

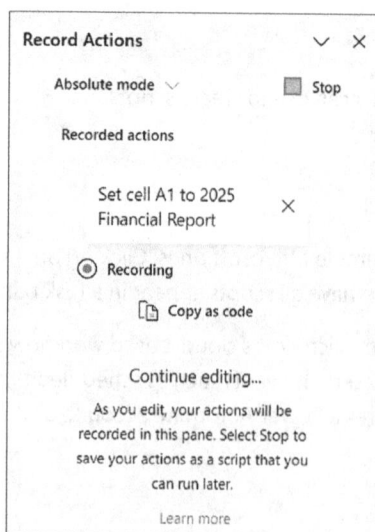

FIGURE 27-9 From the Record Actions pane, you can set absolute or relative mode, see the actions being recorded, and stop the recording.

Currently, steps shown during recording will display absolute addresses, but the script behind the scenes uses relative methods like `.getOffsetRange()` to determine positions based on the starting point. As a result, the script should behave dynamically even though it appears to be hard-coded.

> **Tip** When you start recording, the recording pane becomes the focus, so click in the active cell immediately after starting the recording and use keyboard shortcuts rather than the mouse for navigation. This increases the likelihood that the recorder will generate relative references.

The Stop button is on the right side of the task pane. Click it to stop recording. If you click it early, you can use the Insert Actions button in the bottom right corner to record more actions. See the section "Editing and managing scripts" for more information.

> **Note** The first way I tested Office Scripts was by recreating the steps we recorded in Chapter 1, "Unleashing the power of Excel with VBA." Right away, I realized I couldn't import a file, so I concentrated on the formatting aspects of the macro.
>
> I found that much of the guidance from that chapter, such as starting from a consistent location and limiting unnecessary movement, applies here as well. Office Scripts does not support a direct equivalent of VBA's `Application.Goto`, so cell navigation must be handled through object-based references like `.getRange()` or `.getCell()`.

Editing and managing scripts

After recording, you can view the script in the Code Editor, shown in Figure 27-10. If the Edit Code button is not available, access the editor by opening the menu (below and to the right of the recorded actions) and selecting Advanced Edit. You can do many things in the editor:

- Rename the script by clicking on the Excel supplied name at the top.

- Delete accidental entries.

- Add additional entries. You can do this manually or by using the Insert Action button in the lower right corner of the Code Editor pane.

- Add your own comments to the script by following these rules:

  ```
  // This is a single-line comment
  /*
  This is a block comment
  which can span multiple lines
  */
  ```

  Adding comments is especially useful when reviewing recorded actions, skipping steps, or preparing scripts for others to reuse or extend.

- Hover over a method or object in the editor to display a detailed tooltip that shows a brief description of the method or object and the expected parameters.

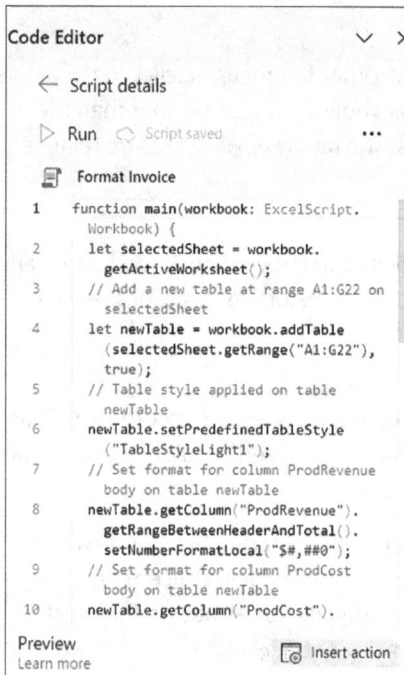

Code Editor ⌄ ✕

← Script details

▷ Run ⟳ Script saved ⋯

▤ Format Invoice

```
1   function main(workbook: ExcelScript.
    Workbook) {
2   let selectedSheet = workbook.
    getActiveWorksheet();
3   // Add a new table at range A1:G22 on
    selectedSheet
4   let newTable = workbook.addTable
    (selectedSheet.getRange("A1:G22"),
    true);
5   // Table style applied on table
    newTable
6   newTable.setPredefinedTableStyle
    ("TableStyleLight1");
7   // Set format for column ProdRevenue
    body on table newTable
8   newTable.getColumn("ProdRevenue").
    getRangeBetweenHeaderAndTotal().
    setNumberFormatLocal("$#,##0");
9   // Set format for column ProdCost
    body on table newTable
10  newTable.getColumn("ProdCost").
```

Preview   ⟲ Insert action
Learn more

FIGURE 27-10 From the Code Editor, you can review, edit, and run the code.

Running and debugging scripts

To run a script, select a script to load it into the Code Editor, then click Run.

Figure 27-11 shows what happens when an error occurs while running a script—the script will stop, and a new frame with three tabs will appear at the bottom of the Code Editor window. The tabs are:

- **Output (#)**—Lists any error messages and shows the exact line number where the error occurred.

- **Problems (#)**—Shows detected issues in the code during editing, such as missing parameters or syntax errors.

- **Help (#)**—Provides links to Microsoft's official documentation for Office Scripts objects, methods, and functions.

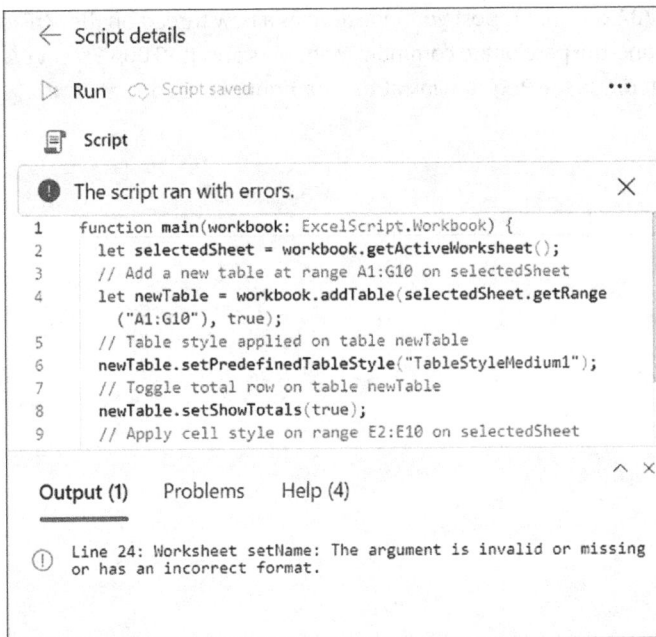

FIGURE 27-11 If the script has errors, Excel will display the error frame at the bottom of the editor.

Next steps

If we, as authors, have done our job correctly, you now have the tools you need to design your own VBA applications in Excel. You understand the shortcomings of the macro recorder yet know how to use it as an aid in learning how to do something. You know how to use Excel's power tools in VBA to produce workhorse routines that can save you hours of time each week. You've also learned how to have your application interact with others so that you can create applications to be used by others in your organization or in other organizations.

If you have found any sections of the book confusing or thought they could have been spelled out better, we welcome your comments and will consider them as we prepare the next edition of this book. Write to us:

ExcelGGirl@gmail.com to contact Tracy

or

Pub@MrExcel.com to contact Bill

Whether your goal is to automate some of your own tasks or to become a paid Excel consultant, we hope that we've helped you on your way. Both are rewarding goals. With 500 million potential customers, we find that being Excel consultants is a friendly business. If you are interested in joining our ranks, you can use this book as your training manual. Master the topics, and you will be qualified to join us.

For assistance with any Excel VBA questions, post your question as a new thread on the MrExcel Message Board. It's free to post, and the passionate community answers about 10,000 Excel VBA questions every year. To get started, use the Register link at the top right of the page at *https://www. mrexcel.com/board*.

Index

Symbols

symbol, 91–92, 482
[_last] entry, 95

Numbers

32-bit Excel, 337, 497, 498, 545
64-bit Excel, 312, 497, 498, 545

A

A1-style formulas
  formula duplication, 119–120
  R1C1 vs,, 48, 117, 120–121
  relative references in, 72
  replaced with R1C1, 123–125
About dialog box, 549–550
above-average records, finding, 224
Absolute mode, 17, 21, 72
absolute references
  mixed with relative, 123
  R1C1 style, 122
ACCDB files, 497, 498
accelerator keys, 536–537
Access
  ACE engine, 497, 502, 503
  adding records to, 502
  connection strings for, 503
  creating shared databases, 500–501
  Excel compatibility and, 497–498
  large file use in, 469
  macros/forms database, 604
  reading/writing from, 499, 502
  self-updating workbooks, 511
  SQL generation, 505
  summarizing records with, 510
  VBA language used by, 473
  when to adopt, 497
  work with, 312
access tokens, 326–327, 434, 439

ACE (Access Connectivity Engine), 497, 502, 503
activating cells, 47
ActiveCell, 43–44
ActiveSheet.Paste, 49
ActiveWorkbook, 70, 71, 180
ActiveX Data Objects (ADO)
  ActiveX control buttons, 592–593
  DAO and, 498
  database connection via, 503, 515
  record deletion with, 509–510
  summarizing records with, 510
  tools, 501–502
  updates to, 511
  updating records with, 506–509
.AddChart2 method, 358–360, 361, 363, 564
AddFields method, 243–244
add-ins, Excel
  alternatives to, 605
  client installation of, 601–602
  client uses of, 597
  closing, 603
  converting workbooks to, 598–599
  installing/uninstalling, 597, 602
  Office Add-ins vs., 597
  removing, 603
  Save As for, 599–600
  security of, 602–603
  standard, 597–598
  UDF sharing via, 334
  updating, 602
  VB Editor to convert files to, 600
  version updates, 604
  visibility of, 598, 601
Add-ins, Office
  adding interactivity to, 612–615, 617–630
  Add-ins group to add, 4
  components of, 607
  CSS for, 616
  editing installed, 612
  Excel add-ins vs., 607

G

M

Q

R

X

Plug into learning at

MicrosoftPressStore.com

The Microsoft Press Store by Pearson offers:

- Free U.S. shipping

- Buy an eBook, get multiple formats – PDF and EPUB – to use on your computer, tablet, and mobile devices

- Print & eBook Best Value Packs

- eBook Deal of the Week – Save up to 60% on featured title

- Newsletter – Be the first to hear about new releases, announcements, special offers, and more

- Register your book – Find companion files, errata, and product updates, plus receive a special coupon* to save on your next purchase

Pearson